China's Deep Reform

China's Deep Reform

Domestic Politics in Transition

Edited by
Lowell Dittmer and Guoli Liu

ROWMAN & LITTLEFIELD PUBLISHERS, INC.
Lanham • Boulder • New York • Toronto • Oxford

ROWMAN & LITTLEFIELD PUBLISHERS, INC.

Published in the United States of America
by Rowman & Littlefield Publishers, Inc.
A wholly owned subsidiary of The Rowman & Littlefield Publishing Group, Inc.
4501 Forbes Boulevard, Suite 200, Lanham, Maryland 20706
www.rowmanlittlefield.com

P.O. Box 317, Oxford OX2 9RU, UK
Copyright © 2006 by Rowman & Littlefield Publishers, Inc.

British Library Cataloguing in Publication Information Available

Library of Congress Cataloging-in-Publication Data

China's deep reform : Domestic politics in transition / Lowell Dittmer and Guoli Liu.
   p. cm.
Includes bibliographical references and index.
ISBN-13: 978-0-7425-3930-3 (cloth : alk. paper)
ISBN-10: 0-7425-3930-X (cloth : alk. paper)
ISBN-13: 978-0-7425-3931-0 (pbk. : alk. paper)
ISBN-10: 0-7425-3931-8 (pbk. : alk. paper)
   1. China—Politics and government—1976–2002. 2. China—Politics and government—2002– . I. Dittmer, Lowell. II. Liu, Guoli, 1961–

DS779.26.C22   2006
951.06—dc22

                                2005033520

Printed in the United States of America

♾ ™ The paper used in this publication meets the minimum requirements of American National Standard for Information Sciences—Permanence of Paper for Printed Library Materials, ANSI/NISO Z39.48-1992.

Contents

Figures

Tables

Acknowledgments

The editors wish to thank the contributors for their strong support, especially their serious efforts at revising and updating their chapters for this book. In working on this project, we received valuable advice and suggestions from many colleagues, including Weixing Chen, Bruce Dickson, Joseph Fewsmith, Sujian Guo, Xiaobo Hu, Scott Kennedy, He Li, Gang Lin, Emerson Niou, Kellen S. Tsai, T. Y. Wang, Brantly Womack, Quansheng Zhao, and several anonymous reviewers. For copyrighted materials, permission from the authors and publishers to reprint is gratefully acknowledged.

Chapter 1 is a revised and updated version of Lowell Dittmer and William Hurst, "Analysis in Limbo: Contemporary Chinese Politics and the Maturation of Reform," *Issues and Studies*, December 2002–March 2003, 11–48.

Chapter 2 is a significantly revised and updated version of Lowell Dittmer and Yu-Shan Wu, "The Modernization of Factionalism in Chinese Politics," *World Politics*, July 1995, 467–494. © The Johns Hopkins University Press.

Chapter 3 is a significantly revised and updated version of Li Cheng and Lynn White, "The Sixteenth Central Committee of the Chinese Communist Party: Hu Gets What?" *Asian Survey* 43, no. 4 (2003): 553–597.

Chapter 4 is a revised and updated version of Bruce J. Dickson, "Cooptation and Corporatism in China: The Logic of Party Adaptation," *Political Science Quarterly* 115, no. 4 (2000): 517–541. Reprinted by permission from *Political Science Quarterly*.

Chapter 5 is a revised and updated version of Baogang Guo, "Political Legitimacy and China's Transition," *Journal of Chinese Political Science* 8, no. 1–2 (2003): 1–25.

Chapter 6, Andrew Nathan, "China's Constitutionalist Option," *Journal of Democracy*, October 1996, 43–57. © National Endowment for Democracy and The Johns Hopkins University Press. Reprinted with permission of The Johns Hopkins University Press.

Chapter 7 is significantly revised, updated, and excerpted from a longer article by Randall Peerenboom, "Globalization, Path Dependency, and the Limits of Law:

Administrative Law Reform and Rule of Law in the People's Republic of China," *Berkeley Journal of International Law* 19, no. 161 (2001): 161–264.

Chapter 8, Yingyi Qian, "The Process of China's Market Transition (1978–98): The Evolutionary, Historical, and Comparative Perspectives," *Journal of Institutional and Theoretical Economics* 156: 1 (2000): 157–171.

Chapter 9, Shaoguang Wang, "Openness and Inequality: The Case of China," *Issues and Studies,* December 2003, 39–80.

Chapter 10 is a revised and updated version of Tony Saich, "Negotiating the State: The Development of Social Organizations in China," *China Quarterly,* March 2000, 124–141. Reprinted with permission of Cambridge University Press.

Chapter 11 is a significantly revised and updated version of Guobin Yang, "The Co-evolution of the Internet and Civil Society in China," *Asian Survey,* May–June 2003, 405–422.

Chapter 12 is a significantly revised and updated version of Joseph Fewsmith, "Historical Echoes and Chinese Politics: Can China Leave the Twentieth Century Behind?" In Tyrene White, ed., *China Briefing, 2000* (Armonk, NY: Sharpe), 11–48.

Chapter 13, Tianjian Shi, "Village Committee Elections in China: Institutionalist Tactics for Democracy," *World Politics*, April 1999, 385–412. © The Johns Hopkins University Press. Reprinted with permission of The Johns University Press.

Chapter 14, Kevin J. O'Brien, "Villagers, Elections, and Citizenship in Contemporary China," *Modern China*, October 2001, 407–435. © Sage Publications. Reprinted with permission.

Chapter 15 is a revised and updated version of Marc J. Blecher, "Hegemony and Worker's Politics in China," *China Quarterly,* June 2002, 283–303.

Chapter 16 is a significantly revised and updated version of Veronica Pearson, "Women and Health in China: Anatomy, Destiny and Politics," *Journal of Social Policy,* October 1996, 529–543. For materials appeared in the earlier article, reprinted with the permission of Cambridge University Press.

Chapter 17 is a significantly revised and updated version of Ting Gong, "Forms and Characteristics of China's Corruption in the 1990s: Change with Continuity," *Communist and Post-Communist Studies* 30, no. 3 (1997): 277–288.

Chapter 18, Edward S. Steinfeld, "Market Visions: The Interplay of Ideas and Institutions in Chinese Financial Restructuring," *Political Studies* 52 (2004): 643–663. Reprinted with permission of Blackwell Publishing.

Introduction: The Dynamics of Deep Reform

GUOLI LIU AND LOWELL DITTMER

China's "deep reform" is the most important political and socioeconomic trend within China today, and no one can understand Chinese domestic and foreign policies without clear knowledge of this process. This anthology collects and updates key essays on the most significant issues of China's post-1989 reform and opening to the outside world, offering a comprehensive resource for students and scholars of contemporary China.

The purpose of this book is to contribute to scholarly understanding of the origin, content, and significance of the latest phase of China's reform and opening to the world that has unfolded since 1989, commonly referred to in the PRC as "deep reform" *(shenhua gaige)*. While Deng Xiaoping was described as the "chief architect" of China's reform and opening to the outside world, Jiang Zemin considered himself a "chief engineer" of deep reform. In his 2005 New Year message, President Hu Jintao called for "continuing to deepen the reform."[1] In his report to the National People's Congress (NPC) in March 2005, Premier Wen Jiabao repeatedly emphasized that the most challenging socioeconomic and political problems in China today can only be resolved through the deepening of reform: "We will press ahead with reform and opening up. We will make reform the driving force behind all aspects of our work, integrate efforts to deepen reform with efforts to implement a scientific outlook on development and to tighten and improve macro regulation, and use reform to solve institutional problems in our development."[2] Our contention in this volume is that China's "deep reform" is in part a continuation but in part also a transformation of the reform movement that Deng Xiaoping began. It is a continuation of the top prioritization of economic modernization, in the shifting of economic initiative from the state to society (in the form of the processes of marketization and privatization), and in the emphasis on international standards of

1

merit over ideological criteria for upward mobility. But it is a transformation in the sense that whereas the first decade of reform could be seen as a simple reversal of the radical extremism of the Maoist era, reform deepening involves a reaction not only against communist radicalism but against some of the excesses of reform itself—thus a reaction against the populist voluntarism the reform leadership (rightly or wrongly) thought characterized the 1989 Tiananmen protest, the runaway investment binges of local political leaders that led to the booms and "hard landings" of the 1980s, or the blind worship of the West the CCP traced to the opening to the outside world. Thus the era of reform deepening, which begins with the silent reassessment that followed the Tiananmen tragedy, has been a far more complex form of reform.

With the successful transition of the leadership of the party, state, and military in 2002–2004, China's deep reform may be entering yet another new stage. This timely and significant volume includes chapters by some of the most penetrating minds in social sciences and China studies, and it should enable students, scholars, policymakers, as well as the educated public to gain new insight about the dynamics of change in one of the world's emerging political economic dynamos. It is necessary to examine the changing nature of China's reform and highlight the core features of deep reform.

THE TRANSFORMING NATURE
OF DEEP REFORM

China's reform since 1989 and especially since 1992 has been quite different from the previous reforms. The most appropriate term to define this recent stage of China's reform is "deep reform." Deep reform has been transforming the nature of Chinese politics, economics, and society. Thus it is important to ask the following questions: What is deep reform? Where does it come from? What is distinctive about reform since 1989? Since 1978, reform has been a key theme of China's economic and political development.[3] After one decade of rapid economic growth, China's reforms encountered serious obstacles. By 1988 Deng Xiaoping himself had realized the urgent need for deeper reform: "China is conducting a deep reform in order to create better conditions for future development. We do not just set our sight on the twentieth century but also think about the new century. The problem is that if we do not move ahead we have to retreat. Only deep and comprehensive reform can guarantee that we can build a well-to-do *(xiaokang)* society by the end the twentieth century and make more progress in the next century."[4] The third plenary session of the Thirteenth CCP Congress in September 1988 first proposed "comprehensive deep reform."

Deep reform has multiple international and domestic causes, preeminently including the need to reconcile the contradictions and conflicts of earlier reforms. The 1989 Tiananmen crisis and the collapse of the Soviet bloc forced Chinese leaders to carefully consider their options. Some conservative officials in Beijing thought the domestic and international crises resulted from too much reform, too soon. But Deng and other reformers drew a totally different conclusion. They saw the collapse of the Soviet Union as a result of not having had effective reforms soon enough. Deng clearly realized that it was a dead end not to reform. Only fundamental and comprehensive reform could save China from a Soviet-type train wreck. After the 1989 crisis in Beijing, Deng strongly urged Jiang Zemin and other Chinese leaders to uphold the policy of reform and opening.

As he became increasingly impatient with the slow and cautious pace of reform pursued by his successors in 1990–1991, Deng made the famous southern tour in 1992 to publicly promote further opening and reform. He emphasized that whoever did not firmly support reform and opening should be removed from power. Jiang Zemin, Li Peng, and the rest of the Politburo leadership promptly and publicly agreed. Since then, deep reform has been the phrase that best catches the spirit and substance of political change and economic development in China. The Fourteenth CCP Congress in September 1992 decided to establish a "socialist market economy with Chinese characteristics." The Fifteenth CCP Congress in 1997 set the goal of building "a state based on the rule of law." Building a market economy and a state based on the rule of law are two fundamental goals of China's deep reform, which includes the following core features.

First, the most fundamental development is to build a complete market economy instead of a halfway economy between plan and market. Marketization has become a clear goal and the growth of mixed ownership has been encouraged. Unlike the earlier stage of experimental reform aptly described as "crossing the river by feeling the stones under feet," since 1992 Chinese reformers have set a clear goal of establishing a socialist market economy. In addition to lifting state control and allowing prices to float, the rapid growth of private economy, joint ventures, solely foreign owned enterprises, and reorganization of state-owned assets have led to a truly "mixed ownership economy." The range of the economic reform has been much broader. Initially, the economic system was reformed incrementally to improve incentives and increase the scope of the market. The new reform has penetrated much more deeply into fiscal, financial, administrative, property rights, and other key aspects of the Chinese economy. Many formerly forbidden rules were broken and many closed areas were opened up. The reformers initiated a financial reform in 1994 in order to increase state capacity. Since then, there has been more centralization of financial power and a shift from central planning to market regulation. State revenue has increased significantly as a result of the nationwide collection of the value added tax. The reformers have aimed at more centrally controlled, managed growth and left behind the boom and bust cycles of the 1980s. State capacity has grown as a result of these financial reforms. Such deep reform has allowed China to sustain high growth rates despite the Asian financial crisis in 1997 (true, it also helped that China's currency is not yet directly exchangeable on world markets). Market reform has both positive and negative consequences. On the one hand, reform has led to greater efficiency and higher productivity. On the negative side, incomplete market reform has resulted in widespread corruption and a growing disparity between the rich and the poor.

Second, the open-door policy has progressed to comprehensive opening in the context of globalization. Having learned the tough lessons of Mao Zedong's self-reliance policy, which went to extremes during the Cultural Revolution (1966–1976), and then tasted the first sweet fruits of Deng's opening policy after 1978, Chinese reformers realized that isolationism was a dead end and that comprehensive opening provided the best opportunity for socioeconomic development. After a temporary retrenchment from opening to the outside world in 1989–1991, China began a bold new phase of opening to all countries in the world in 1992. Such dramatic and decisive opening has led to a sharp rise in both foreign trade and direct foreign investment. The rapidly growing connections between China and the outside world have had a profound impact on all major institutions and aspects of social behavior. The scope and speed of China's opening to the outside world has accelerated since 1992, leading to China's entry into the World Trade Organization (WTO) in 2001. Comprehensive opening is reflected in the growing volume of trade, financial transactions, travel, and other exchanges between China and all major regions of the world. China's total imports and exports have increased from US$135.7 billion in 1991 to more than US$1.1 trillion in 2004. China has become the world's third largest foreign trader behind the United States and Germany. This is truly extraordinary considering the fact that China ranked thirty-second with a small trade volume of $20 billion in 1978. China has also become the largest recipient of direct foreign investment in the world, receiving more than $570 billion. The degree of interdependence between China and the world economy has grown to an unprecedented level. As a consequence, China has gained multiple benefits, chiefly an accelerated economic growth rate. On the other hand, China has also been exposed to the growing pressure and risks of globalization. The 1997 Asian financial crisis and the 2003 SARS epidemic were two examples of the new challenges confronting the Chinese.

Third, "the rule of law" has been transformed from a governing instrument to a fundamental goal of reform. Chinese reformers have taken the legal system more seriously than ever before. They realized that their legitimacy and governance must have a legal and constitutional foundation. Numerous new laws have been enacted and put into practice. But China still has a long way to go before solidly establishing the rule of law. Although the constitution has been amended several times, many parts of the 1982 constitution (written under the context of highly centralized political power and command economy) have become outdated. The next stage of deep reform may require more fundamental constitutional change.

Fourth, meaningful political reforms including political institutionalization and systemic leadership transition have taken place. Tiananmen destroyed forever the myth that China could engage in economic reform without touching the political system. In reaction to that traumatic event, the leadership not only emphasized a certain amount of recentralization and popular control but a renewed focus on political reform and improved governance. Indeed, any significant economic reform would be impossible without some political change of the formerly highly centralized Chinese political system. Deng Xiaoping initiated the first round of political change in 1978–1981, and after temporary setbacks in 1986 Zhao Ziyang unleashed new initiatives at the Thirteenth Party Congress in 1987. In the 1990s, political reform has adjusted its direction, now focusing on (1) relatively smooth leadership transition from the third generation to the fourth generation, (2) institutionalization of political elite selection from the top to the basic levels, (3) further separation of political and administrative functions of the party-state, (4) gradual expansion of the range of political discourse associated with information revolution, (5) village elections and experiment of self-governance in residential communities, and (6) reformulation of official ideology including the emergence of the "three represents." Thus deep reform has led to a new level of ideological pragmatism and relegitimization through development. Productivity and prosperity have become the ultimate criteria for economic and political success. Jiang Zemin formalized this in his contribution to official ideology, the "three represents." This formulation stresses that the CCP's mission is to represent the most advanced productive forces, the most advanced culture, and the fundamental interests of the overwhelming majority of the Chinese people. Though apparently bland and innocuous, this dramatic departure from proletarian revolution and class warfare has allowed the leadership to refocus its tasks on modernization without institutional breakdown. As a result, Chinese politics today is more institutionalized, more predictable, and more performance oriented. In contrast to deep reform in financial and trading sectors, China's political change, though extensive, has been relatively slow. The contradiction between deep economic reform and slow political reform has become a bottleneck for the next stage of China's reform. And there are some indications that the "fourth generation" leadership will make political reform a higher priority. For instance, fighting against corruption is one of the biggest challenges facing the CCP leadership, threatening to undermine the legitimacy of the government and erode the basis of the ruling party. And Hu Jintao said that in order to resolve the corruption issue, the CCP must "deepen reform to create a new system."[5] This would be a further step in the direction of deep reform.

Finally, deep reform is linked to a new grand strategy for the "peaceful rise" *(heping jueqi)* of China. Deng Xiaoping initiated China's "peace and development" line in the 1980s, and since that time China has been one of the biggest beneficiaries of the post–Cold War reduction of interstate violence.[6] On the other hand, China's deep reform and rapid growth have made a growing contribution to regional and world economic vitality. Whereas the rise and fall of nations has often been accompanied by crisis and instability (as in the case of Germany and Japan in the first half of the twentieth century), China's deep reform is based on the premise of a peaceful rise. It remains to be seen whether this paradigm shift will materialize.

Considered separately, many of the elements of deep reform emerged before

1992. Taken together, however, it is clear that the reform since 1992 has reached a qualitatively new level of development. As this process has been taking place, the study of China's political development has also made progress. It is interesting to examine the following questions: How has China's deep reform been understood by social scientists? What contributions has the study of China made to advance the discipline of political science? What are the main obstacles to bridging the gap between political science and China studies? What are the most promising research questions? What are the most serious theoretical challenges and the most promising opportunities? It is of course much easier to raise such questions than to answer them all. But in the interest of at least taking a step in that direction, a theoretical overview may be useful.

Conventional wisdom (as well as comparison with the abortive "big bang" transitions elsewhere in the socialist world) suggests that high growth rates are the result of moving "from stone to stone in crossing the river." Yet this seriously underestimates the vital role of governance. As Dwight H. Perkins points out, "The core problem for China's development was the issue of governance. Modern economic growth requires a government that can provide the needed infrastructure for development, including stable and supportive policy and a stable legal environment for private (or public) investors."[7] China's impressive economic growth is at least partially if not mainly a result of the new political strategy for development. At the same time, socioeconomic development has created new challenges for governance.

In chapter 1, Lowell Dittmer and William Hurst provide a critical survey of the state of China studies. Despite the resurgent vitality of the transformation overtaking China, the precise source and thrust of that dynamism has diversified and become far less obvious. The field of Chinese political analysis has changed and grown as China has changed and grown, becoming increasingly polycentric, ambiguous, and sophisticated. Dittmer and Hurst examine the shifting focuses of the China field, including central politics and elite analysis, local and regional politics, ideology and political culture, state–society relations, and Chinese foreign policy. They also discuss two analytical approaches that have seen considerable progress over the past decade: levels of analysis and methodological techniques.

China scholars in the West have been searching for models for the Chinese political system for a long time. According to Gabriel A. Almond and Laura Roselle, the interaction between political theory and area studies in the last several decades has taken the form of model fitting—crude, clumsy, and sometimes sanguine at the outset, increasingly deft and experimental as time experience accumulated. Of all the area studies, Russian and Chinese political analysis has been perhaps most open to this model-fitting process.[8] An outdated model was the totalitarianism developed largely from studies of Stalinist Russia.[9] When China proclaimed its intention of following the Soviet model in the early 1950s, there was a tendency in the West to assume that China had incorporated the totalitarian mode. However, the totalitarian model was not satisfactory as a framework for the analysis of Chinese politics. Discontent with the totalitarian model led to willingness to experiment with a family of pluralist models—interest group theory, corporatism, and issue network and policy community theories. Contrary to the implications of the totalitarian model, China under reform is extremely diverse. Many central policies are hence discretionary, and those that are general are often adapted to local circumstances in the course of implementation. The vast modernization and development literature has also nourished certain assumptions about Chinese politics and development, for example, that China can be conceived as a country struggling hard to modernize itself. Many China scholars have included in their works many references to other bodies of literature, but they have also commonly assumed, in the area studies tradition, that the system they study is sufficiently distinctive to provide the basis for a separate model.[10] The theory of communist neotraditionalism put forth by Andrew Walder (borrowing from the comparative communist literature) suggests that the Chinese society is characterized by competition and conflict at all levels, and that people have a choice of means through which to pursue their interests.[11]

In the reform era, as China moved toward the establishment of a market economy and away from ideological rigidity, some scholars put forth a pluralist paradigm. Political competition can begin, albeit within a fairly narrowly drawn system of political controls. The atomization of individuals predicted in the totalitarian model is at best a temporary phenomenon: social groups, not necessarily the same as had existed before the communist government came to power, arise and begin to articulate and otherwise pursue their common interests. Those who favor this paradigm cite evidence that a civil society is emerging in China in which citizens feel free to voice their dissatisfactions with party and government leaders.[12] Prior to 1990, quantitative analysis was extremely difficult (and rare) in the China field. Since 1990, it has become more widespread. Dittmer and Hurst maintain that in the interests both of advancing our understanding of China and of promoting the further integration of the study of China into social science disciplines, China scholars must take quantitative work more seriously.

Both China studies and political science can benefit from concerted and systematic efforts to link the two. It is time to move toward the integration of China studies and political science by striving to produce more theoretically oriented and empirically grounded studies. Chinese politics has been and continues to be a politics of transformation. As Tang Tsou stated, "Attention must be focused on significant problems rather than on novel research techniques. For many of our novel techniques would be difficult to apply, while our theoretical insights would enable us to see deep significance in seemingly stereotyped materials and trivial events."[13] Four decades ago, Chalmers Johnson emphasized that "the main tasks of China scholarship in America should be to train more China-oriented political scientists and to think about how to explain political events in China."[14] Johnson's advice remains relevant today. We have now reached a point to take stock and see if we can discern what future paths can best help to integrate the study of Chinese politics and society into the wider disciplines without sacrificing a concern for issues of unique importance to the China case.

As politics has changed, so has the study of Chinese politics. The proliferation of data and multiplication of analytical approaches has however raised the issue of how to coordinate different approaches to the same problem. In Elizabeth Perry's view, this must involve careful comparisons across time and space. If social scientists can do so, the study of China can mature from a "consumer field" (dependent for its analytical insights upon imports from the study of other countries) to a "producer field" (capable of generating original insights of interest to such general comparativists as Barrington Moore and Theda Skocpol).[15] This vision can only be realized if China scholars systematically integrate rich field research with social science (especially political science) theories and methodology. In any event, no single theory has been able adequately to explain the changing nature of Chinese politics, nor is that our intention in this volume. What we need today is a group of middle level theories that can provide penetrating analysis of the dynamics of deep reform.

By focusing on various key elements of China's deep reform, this collection can contribute to both the theoretical and empirical study of China. The volume is divided into six parts: (1) leadership change and elite politics, (2) political and legal reform, (3) political economy in transition, (4) the changing public sphere, (5) village elections and workers' politics, and (6) the shadow side of reform: emerging problems and tough challenges.

LEADERSHIP CHANGE AND ELITE POLITICS

Leadership transition and elite politics occupy a critical position in China studies because elite dynamics so directly affects the nature and direction of Chinese politics. As Lowell Dittmer and Yu-Shan Wu point out in chapter 2, the informal dimension, with factional politics at the core, has always been paramount in Chinese politics. A faction may be defined as a vertically organized structure composed of face-to-face (rather than corporate) clientelist ties between leaders and led. Such ties are cultivated essentially through the constant exchange of goods and favors, resulting in relationships that involve unwritten but nonetheless well-understood rights and obligations among faction members.[16]

Dittmer and Wu argue that a modified factional model is the most useful analytical tool to understand elite politics in the CCP at its present stage of development. They apply this model to factional behavior during the reform era, in an attempt to demonstrate the dynamic interplay of economic variables and factional political maneuvers. During the Cultural Revolution period, people joined factions for survival and security, both political and physical. During the Deng Xiaoping period, physical security became far more secure, allowing policy debate (degree of reform and pace of growth) to become focal, hence the pro-growth versus pro-stability rift. When Jiang took over, a new elite consensus emerged that emphasized reform with stability, so the leadership would brake excessive growth but at the same time continue structural reform (like the one in 1994)—hence the desynchronization of reform and business cycles. The Jiang-Zhu leadership's better handling of the business cycle (soft landing) and pursuit of reform during the down phase of the cycle ushered in an economic and political stability unseen in the 1980s. There was still elite factionalism, but not on ideological grounds (as under Mao), nor on macropolicy ground (as under Deng). Now factionalism was fueled by elites struggling for resources, prestige, and power. Two emerging new bases of elite schism are central institution building, as in the development of the NPC; and regionalism, as in Jiang's Shanghai gang versus the Beijing gang. The political business cycle (PBC) in the new era thus reflects not the policy preferences of pro-growth and the pro-stability groups, but the inherent interest of the incumbents to buy off local officials, ensure stability, and build a positive image for a national audience at the five-year meeting cycle of the NPC and CCP's national congresses.

In chapter 3, Li and White provide a timely and thorough study of the Sixteenth CCP Central Committee, addressing the issue of the political succession from Jiang Zemin to Hu Jintao and beyond, statistically analyzing a comprehensive database to arrive at penetrating insights about elite formation and change. Their database consists of the biographical traits of all 356 Central Committee (CC) members (198 full members and 158 alternates). In their analysis, they pay particular attention to leadership generations, bureaucratic affiliations, regional representations, educations, career paths, and early political socializations. A main reason why the CCP has been able to stay in power for over half a century lies in the adaptability of its elite. At the Sixteenth CC in November 2002, 107 full members (54 percent) and 113 alternate members (72 percent) were new to those posts. The combined number of newcomers in both categories is 61 percent. Only about a tenth of the full CC members have been on the committee for more than a decade. The Sixteenth CCP Congress represents a new level of political institutionalization. The generational power transition from the third to the fourth generation was remarkably smooth. If the new leaders are united, they have an opportunity to consolidate political institutionalization. Li and White skillfully demonstrate how to fruitfully apply social scientific methods to elite studies. They conclude their study of the emerging patterns of power sharing by stating: "Only time will tell whether this process eventually leads to a system in which factional politics become more transparent and legitimated, so that various parts of the public have their interests protected and their voices heard."

Bruce Dickson (chapter 4) considers the political implications of China's economic reforms for the CCP by focusing on the two key elements of organizational adaptation: the cooptation of new members and the creation of new links with outside organizations. He examines both theoretical and practical issues of cooptation in a comparative perspective. As the CCP abandoned class struggle as its "key link" and shifted to economic modernization, the party increasingly recruited those who were "younger, better educated, and more professionally competent." Improvements in the education qualifications of local officials from provincial to the county level were dramatic: in 1981, only 16 percent had a college education; twenty years later in 2001, 88 percent did. Within the CC, the proportion of those with a college degree rose from 55 percent in 1982 to 99 percent in 2002. Dickson carefully reviewed the intense debate over co-opting entrepreneurs. It was not until Jiang Zemin openly advocated the "three represents" policy that the CCP officially welcomed entrepreneurs into the party. Yet in reality, the number of private entrepreneurs has been growing in the party over the years. At the end of 1991, over 200,000 party members are reported to have registered as private entrepreneurs, representing 4 percent of party members and 8 percent of entrepreneurs. A nationwide survey in 1995 found that 17 percent of private entrepreneurs were party members, and by 2004, 30 percent of entrepreneurs were "red capitalists."[17] According to a survey in 2005, one of every three owners of private businesses in China is a CCP member. The survey shows that the proportion of CCP members among private business people has risen dramatically, and among large private companies the percentage is even higher. Many of these "red capitalists" were CCP members who quit their jobs in government or state-owned firms to open their own businesses.[18] Cooptation and new organizational links thus offer alternatives to traditional party building as means to link the party with society. While noting the positive trends of cooptation and corporatism, Dickson warns, we should not lose sight of the negative consequences for the CCP and the implications for the political system as a whole.

POLITICAL AND LEGAL REFORMS

This section highlights several critical issues of China's legal and political reforms. As a result of profound socioeconomic change, the internal and external pressures for more political reforms have intensified in recent years. Multiple factors have contributed to a serious challenge to the legitimacy of the Chinese leadership. For instance, the diversification of the economy has created favorable conditions for a pluralist society. Different voices from many new social classes as well as old ones can now be heard openly. Powerful ideas such as citizenship, human rights, individualism, transparency, political accountability, and the rule of law, are gradually taking form in China's political life. China's deep reform since 1989 has come to a critical point for the prioritization of political reform.[19] Due to the sensitivity of political reform in the post-Tiananmen context, the current leadership tends to speak more in terms of "building a political civilization," which is aimed at promoting political development. Keeping the Chinese situation in mind, a careful review of social science literature suggests that political development involves three dimensions:

> First is the development of state capacity, as ultimately measured in its ability to maintain rapid and reasonably equitable economic growth and redistributive capacity. Secondly, although growth is primary, it can easily run out of control and damage or temporarily derail the developmental process. Thus in addition, institutionalization is

required, giving rise to an oscillation between political development and political decay. Finally, the concept of political culture was introduced to bring mass publics into the political equation, showing on the one hand how they are moulded or socialized by the state, and on the other how their evolving desires contribute to the nation-state's collective identity. This process involves a dialectic between the emancipation of the masses to participate more actively in politics and the restraining of that activity to accord with certain rules of civility, ultimately leading towards some form of "democratization."[20]

Transition toward democratic governance and the rule of law is a central task of China's political reform. Congruence of authority patterns and political institutions is a key variable affecting long-term political stability and sustainable economic development. Since Mao Zedong, it is increasingly difficult for any Chinese leader to resort to "charismatic" authority. Deng Xiaoping did not like the personality cult, he emphasized building strong political institutions. Deng himself nevertheless still relied to a significant degree on his personal authority. In contrast to Deng's informality regarding official titles, Jiang Zemin simultaneously held the positions of general secretary of the CCP, president of the PRC, and chairman of the Central Military Committee. Obviously Jiang's authority was more institutional than personal. Hu Jintao is following Jiang's footsteps in simultaneously holding the top positions of the party, the state, and the military.

Baogang Guo (chapter 5) argues that the Chinese government has shown remarkable adaptability to a changing political environment. Transition toward a market economy has redefined the meanings of legitimacy in the Chinese context, seriously challenging the existing system of legitimization. While the first generation of CCP leaders led by Mao Zedong relied heavily on the revolution as a basis for legitimacy, the second and third generations have shifted emphasis to rationalization and institutionalization in the past two decades. Pragmatism and technocracy have replaced idealism and the personality cult that characterized the first generation. As the fourth generation leaders led by Hu Jintao take over the government, they also face the ongoing challenge of rebuilding the system of legitimization. Since the collapse of the Communist bloc in the early 1990s, the legitimacy of the CCP is increasingly based not only on economic performance but also on nationalism or patriotism. Thus the legitimacy of the CCP could be undermined by continuing high levels of corruption, on the one hand, or by a serious economic downturn, on the other. A sharp downturn in the fortunes of ordinary citizens after a generation of high growth and prosperity is a recipe that is considered politically dangerous. Further reform of the institutions linking state to society will be required within the general parameters of maintaining stability.[21]

After carefully analyzing numerous proposals of Chinese political reform, Andrew Nathan (chapter 6) points out that the heart of most political reform proposals is empowerment of the NPC. Chinese scholars have put forward proposals to invigorate the process by which the NPC is elected. As a result of reform, the Leninist core has developed mechanisms to bargain with, consult, and persuade other actors in an increasingly complex society. But power is neither grounded in popular consent nor limited by laws. As marketization erodes the old techniques of control, the leaders have turned to law to direct lower-level officials and constrain independent economic actors. If the reform proposals reviewed by Nathan were implemented, China would still be a dominant one-party system with weak separation of powers and weak federalism. In Nathan's view, the constitutionalist scenario gains credibility from the improbability of the alternatives. Constitutionalism is one of the most conservative options for change in a situation where stasis seems impossible.

In fact, deep reform has been accompanied by important constitutional changes. In this regard, the widespread misperception that "China underwent economic reform without political change" is an overstatement. For instance, the 1982 Chinese constitution has been revised in 1993, 1997, 1999, and 2004. Each constitutional amendment is significant in its own right. The constitutional changes led to the legitimization of the market economy, the rule of law, private ownership, and human rights. Although such changes have fallen short of the high expectation of radical reformers, they have gone beyond many previous restrictions. The role of the NPC has been transformed from a rubber stamp into an increasingly meaningful power organ.[22]

Randall Peerenboom (chapter 7) provides a penetrating analysis of Chinese administrative law reform and rule of law in the era of globalization. The hallmark of a modern legal system is the rule of law. The essence of rule of law is the ability of law to impose meaningful limits on the state and individual members of the ruling elite. Peerenboom sensibly points out that China appears to be on its way toward implementing a socialist variant that meets the requirements of a "thin rule of law." That is, China seems to be in transition from an instrumental rule by law legal system in which law is a tool to be used as the party-state sees fit to a rule of law system where law does impose meaningful restraints on the party, state, and individual members of the ruling elite. Administrative law reforms have empowered society to some extent by giving citizens the right to challenge state actors through administrative reconsideration, administrative litigation, and administrative supervision. Considerable progress has been made in realizing rule of law generally. Despite the progress, of course, much remains to be done. One obvious next step will be to increase public participation in the rule-making and decision-making processes, requiring the deepening of political reform.

The Fifteenth CCP Congress held in 1997 officially adopted "rule according to law." The congress portrayed rule of law as central to economic development, national stability, and party legitimacy. In 1999, the National People's Congress amended the 1982 constitution. One key constitutional amendment states, "The PRC should implement rule according to law, and build a socialist state based on rule of law." If successfully established and implemented, the rule of law may provide a foundation for China's development of democracy and the market economy. Thus democratization of laws and the legalization of democracy pose a dual challenge for China's political reform. The principle of "replacement of the rule of man by the rule of law" implies that relations between state and party must change and that the CCP must surrender at least some of its authority to law.[23] Equality of all before the law is a principle expressed in China's Constitution and Criminal Procedure Law and much discussed in the Chinese media. Under this principle, party cadres are not above the law and offenders who violate the law must be punished according to the law. Implementing the rule of law will bring about fundamental political change, improve human rights in China, and let China join the world and earn the respect of other countries. Thus one obvious way of meeting the challenge of globalization is to establish institutions compatible with it—democracy and the rule of law—and not try to rely on market forces alone.[24]

There are clear signs that the political system has adapted to the new circumstances and China's political system is becoming increasingly institutionalized. Institutionalization here refers to increased structural differentiation, more regularized decision-making processes, and more state autonomy from society. In the prereform period, instead of establishing a set of laws as the legal foundation of society, leaders frequently remade the rules in response to their changing interests. Chinese reformers have envisioned a rule of law based on judicial independence, procedural regularity, and fairness, and universal adherence. A new system supporting the rule of law is emerging. Chinese citizens are becoming more aware of their rights and how to protect them. A Beijing political scientist argues the most important political development since the reform and opening is incremental democratization. The goal of Chinese political reform includes many elements such as enhancing administrative efficiency, containing corruption, maintaining social stability, and changing the functions of the government. But the top priority must be developing democracy—building a highly democratic political system that allow the people to fully enjoy freedom and equal rights.[25]

POLITICAL ECONOMY IN TRANSITION

Comprehensive transition to the market has been a central task of China's deep reform. Yingyi Qian (chapter 8) analyzes the Chinese economic reform in two broad stages. In the first stage (1979–1992), the system was reformed incrementally to improve incentives and increase the scope of the market. In the second stage (from 1993), new institutions supporting the market are being built before old institutions have been destroyed. One outstanding feature of the reform can be described as "seeking truth from facts." Deng's strategy is to conduct bold experiments in selected regions and enterprises. If the reform measures work, they will be expanded into other regions; if the measures fail, they will be abandoned. Such a trial and error approach worked very well in the first stage of the reform. The market-oriented reform after 1978 represented an approach of piecemeal social engineering. Since 1978, China has transformed itself incrementally from a centrally planned economic system to an emerging market system. Building on this success, China's second stage of reform has evolved smoothly without any political revolution.

The role of the Chinese state is changing in the transition from the command economy to a market economy. Under the command system, the state played a dominant role in all aspects of socioeconomic development. The state was overemphasized and the market was suppressed. The failure of the command economy resulted in serious rethinking of the role of the state. Chinese reformers realized that the role of the state must be transformed in order to build a market economy. The driving forces behind China's growth have been the nonstate sectors including village and township enterprises, joined ventures, and private business. While these sectors enjoyed dramatic growth, the state sector has been declining. For instance, the state-owned enterprises' share in the national industrial output declined from around 80 percent in the early 1980s to less than 50 percent by 1995. Barry Naughton insightfully describes the reform process as "growing out of the plan."[26] The existing state enterprises have declined in importance as a result of the growth of new enterprises, such as joint ventures and village, township, province, and private enterprises.

The first stage of reform succeeded in substantially improving people's living standards, and as a result, reform received solid and popular support. However, by the early 1990s, the economic system as a whole was still a halfway house between a planned and a market economy. Under deep reform, China would need to achieve at least three objectives: first, to set the goal of transition to a market system; second, to establish market-supporting institutions incorporating international best practices; and third, to privatize and restructure state-owned enterprises.

Economic reform and political reform are interdependent. The ultimate success of economic reform depends on comprehensive political reform. One critical issue of political reform in China today is administrative reform. Since the early 1980s, China has launched several projects to reform governmental institutions, in 1982–1985, 1988, and 1992–1995. Achievements were made, but each time, after the fervor for reform had died down, governmental institutions became bloated once again. In 1998 a major reform for streamlining the government bureaucracy took place. The number of ministries in the central government was trimmed from forty-five to twenty-nine, and the number of civil servants was cut by half, from 8 million to 4 million. Bureaucracy has an inherent tendency to expand and become inefficient. Only after fundamental change in the role of the government, administrative reform can be successful.

Privatization of state-owned enterprises (SOEs) and layoffs of state workers began to occur on a large scale in 1995. As many state firms face the problem of overemployment, with surplus staff including both middle range workers and managerial personnel, the resettling of government employees is a tremendous challenge. In fact, millions of workers in the state sector have been laid off *(xiagang)*. The nonstate sector generally has more work for rural migrants or the highly educated than for the laid-off; and the immense challenges of both resource scarcity and administrative incapacity characterize the national-scale social welfare program.[27]

When China joined the World Trade Organization (WTO) in 2001, the Chinese government agreed to abide by all of the WTO rules—from the protection of foreign intellectual property to the elimination of local content requirements that China had imposed on many wholly foreign-owned joint venture manufacturing companies.[28] Entry into the WTO shows the commitment of China's leadership to accelerate domestic economic reform. China's accession to the WTO signifies that it has entered a new stage in its opening-up program. The salient features of the new stage are (1) moving from policy-based opening up to institutionalized opening up, (2) moving from partial opening up to all-round opening up, and (3) moving from opening up in some competitive areas to opening up in all sectors, with emphasis on the service sector.[29] The impact of the WTO is likely to be complex, affecting some sectors negatively and others positively, and varying over time, with the costs likely to be seen in the short term and the benefits more evident over the longer term. China's opening to the outside world has over the course of the past two decades created a variety of economic and political forces in China with an interest in preserving and expanding those relations. China's participation in WTO will have considerable impact on China's political system.[30]

Shaoguang Wang (chapter 9) explores the relationship between openness and inequality. There can be no doubt that the aggregate gains China has derived from its open-door policy have outweighed the aggregate costs. Such gains and costs are, however, not equally distributed. Opening is a process that generates losers as well as winners. Rising income inequality and a pervasive sense of insecurity could spark a political backlash against an open policy in general and free trade in particular. Wang reviews China's actual progress in opening its economy and changing patterns of income distribution over the past twenty years. The fiscal squeeze resulting from openness exacerbated rather than alleviated the inequality of primary income distribution up to the mid-1990s. The degree of openness can be measured by trade and FDI flows. China's foreign trade has increased as a fraction of GDP from barely 10 percent in 1978 to over 70 percent in 2004. Measured by trade/GDP ratio, China is more "open" than the United States and Japan. Foreign direct investment (FDI) flows constitute another indicator of China's external orientation. In 1983, FDI accounted for only 0.3 percent of GDP, but by 2002, the ratio of FDI to GDP reached around 4 percent, a level high even compared to those of the United States, Japan, and Germany. In fact, among all countries in the world, China now stands as the largest recipient of FDI. However, as the Chinese economy has become increasingly integrated with the world economy, the distribution of primary income in the country has worsened. Whatever aggregate gains openness may engender, they are unlikely to be evenly distributed across social strata simply via the operation of the market. Only the government can, through redistribution, correct rising inequality. To maintain social stability, the Chinese government will need to provide social insurance to the most vulnerable in society. This explains why taxes have become more progressive, the level of fiscal revenues and expenditures have risen, and the government has funneled more money into social services and safety-net building. In order to build a "harmonious society," the Chinese leaders must take effective measures to establish institutions to ameliorate the adverse effects of opening.

THE CHANGING PUBLIC SPHERE

As the reform deepens, China's public sphere has been evolving rapidly. This section examines the changing public sphere by focusing on the development of social organizations, the coevolution of the Internet and civil society, and the interaction of diverse intellectual trends in reform China.

One notable feature of the reform program sponsored by the CCP has been the expansion of social organizations. Tony Saich's study (chapter 10) sheds light on the complex interplay between the party-state and society. Structures and regulations exist to bind these organizations to state patronage and control their activities. However, social practice reveals a pattern of negotiation that minimizes state penetration and allows such organizations to reconfigure the relationship with the state in more beneficial terms that can allow for policy input or pursuit of members' interests and organizational goals. By the end of 2002, there were some 133,357 registered social organizations, defined as community entities composed of a certain social group with common intention, desires, and interests. In addition, there are 700,000 civilian nonprofit institutions, which are set up by enterprises, social groups or individuals to provide nonprofit social services. Reforms have reduced the intrusive role of the state and have created far greater social differentiation. Each social organization in China has negotiated with the state its own niche, deriving from a complex interaction of institutional, economic, and individual factors. Saich suggests that it is not mere expediency that causes new social formations or organizations to tie their fortunes to the existing state structures, especially at the local level, but that it is strategically optimal for them. As the government downsizes further, citizens have greater responsibility for their own welfare, more functions will be devolved to national and especially local social organizations, people will look more to the local provider for goods rather than the central party or to state directives and regulations. The notion of negotiating the state tries to do justice to the increasing complexities of social reality in China.

Guobing Yang (chapter 11) studies how the Internet and civil society in China interact in ways that shape the development of both. He argues that civil society and the Internet energize each other in their coevolutionary development, even as both are constrained by other forces. The Internet facilitates civil society activities by offering new possibilities for citizen participation. Civil society facilitates the development of the Internet by providing the necessary social basis—citizens and citizen groups—for communication and interaction. The interactions between the Internet and civil society take multiple forms. These interactions have led to two important types of digital formations—virtual public spheres and web-based organizations. Yang illustrates these interactions and digital formations with empirical examples. He reveals that civil society use of the Internet by far surpasses e-government and e-commerce in China today. There are two broad types of Internet–civil society interactions. The first may be called socially initiated interactions, where action originates in the social world and then is taken to the Internet, yielding interactions. The second type may be referred to as Internet-originated interactions, in which case action originates on the Internet and then reaches beyond.

Joseph Fewsmith (chapter 12) examines continuity and change in Chinese politics, focusing on conflicting intellectual trends. Several key themes have remained important over more than a century in China: China's relationship with the West (politically, economically, and culturally); the simultaneous desire for wealth and power and social fairness; popular political expression and participation; and the relationship of the present to the past. Many historical events themselves contain contradictory elements. People today also have a different interpretation of those events. One of the most important historical events in modern Chinese history was the May Fourth movement of 1919. Fewsmith argues that the May Fourth tradition has always contained contradictory elements: a radical critique of traditional Chinese culture and the demand to learn from the West and to introduce science and democracy were combined with a nationalism that rejected cosmopolitanism in favor of nativism. It is interesting that science, democracy, enlightenment, and nationalism all remain important yet sometimes conflicting goals of China's reformers. According to Fewsmith, nationalism has been the leitmotif of twentieth-century China. Chinese intellectuals were as nationalistic in the 1980s as they were in the 1990s, but in the earlier decade their nationalism took a more cosmopolitan approach, seeing a path to wealth and power through learning from the West. As intellectuals become more critical of reform, they simultaneously become more critical of the neoclassical economics and political liberalism of the West that has been widely adopted as an implicit model for China's reform. There has been a new desire to forge a uniquely Chinese path to reform, and this desire to explore a "native" approach that conforms with Chinese culture and tradition necessarily entails an emphasis on asserting Chinese national identity.[31] Fewsmith concludes this insightful chapter by analyzing the "gradual transition" from Jiang Zemin to Hu Jintao.

VILLAGERS, ELECTIONS, AND WORKERS' POLITICS

There is a saying that all politics is local. Although this could be an overstatement, it is reasonable to say that local politics most directly affects people's lives. In contrast to the numerous studies of Chinese national politics, local politics has been perhaps unduly neglected.[32] In recent years there have been significant changes in

Chinese local politics, among the most important and controversial of which is village elections.

Tianjian Shi (chapter 13) provides an insightful analysis of village elections in China. Chinese electoral reform provides answers to the following important theoretical questions: Who promotes reforms in authoritarian societies? What motivates them to do so? How do relatively weak reformers defeat stronger opponents under authoritarian rule? Shi found political leaders to be a crucial factor in facilitating democratic reform; democratically committed midlevel officials rather than top national leaders played the crucial role in bringing endogenous changes to China. In contrast to other societies, the pressure for reform in China came from peasants rather than the middle class. Once the reform was well under way, peasants were gradually mobilized by the reforms themselves to participate in village elections, and their participation, in turn, advanced the reform process. Shi offers an interesting account of the actors and rules for village democracy in action.

At the grassroots level where the majority of the Chinese live, the government has focused on restructuring rural governance by introducing democracy. In 1987 the NPC adopted the Organic Law of Village Committee (draft). The law stipulated that the chairman, vice chairman, and members of village committees should be directly elected by the residents of the village. Since then, elections have spread beyond experimental villages. Even though the CCP still organizes the elections, elections in rural China did create uncertainty for village rulers. These semicompetitive elections in China have also induced changes in local governance. Shi's study shows that just as institutional settings can be used by conservatives to resist reform, they can also be used by reformers to promote political change. In addition, peasants are important forces driving electoral reform in China—a finding that challenges the widely accepted myth that peasants are the obstacles to democracy.

In order to ensure that the system would spread smoothly, the central government designated many locations as "demonstration sites" for others to follow. For instance, from 1990 to 1995, some 82,266 villages were set up as demonstration sites. Since the central government did not attempt to implement the law nationwide at the same time, provincial regulations were gradually implemented. According to the Ministry of Civil Affairs, as of 1997 more than 80 percent of China's 930,000 villages have conducted at least one round of relatively democratic elections.[33] Village democracy entailed the direct, secret, and competitive election of the village head and the village council as well as establishment of a village assembly or representative assembly. The 1998 law on self-governance demanded that village affairs be public, particularly finances, and that the villagers' committees (VCs) regularly inform villagers of expenditures and allow ordinary villagers to check accounts. Elections led to fairly sizable turnover among village chiefs and the prospect of reelection had a restraining effect on incumbents.[34]

Each round of elections offers an opportunity for educating people in the proper techniques of free elections. The village is a good place to start educating the rural population to the technical elements of a free election, but at the same time, it might be one of the most difficult places to introduce genuine political competition.[35] Direct elections to county and township congresses offer greater opportunities for political participation. Ordinary voters and People's Congress delegates have choices among candidates in elections at the township level, though these choices are normally constrained by CCP's preselection of candidates designated for positions of leadership. The role of voters and congress delegates as electorates is not necessarily trivialized by this role of the party organization as selectorate. Rather, the system is configured so that local party committees want to select candidates who will win, ideally with a margin of victory big enough to legitimate the party choice.[36]

Based on an immersion in local politics, Kevin J. O'Brien (chapter 14) assesses the state of political citizenship in rural China. After discussing the often local and rural origins of citizenship and the meaning of the term itself, he reviews the limited reforms that have taken place in the election of high-ranking state leaders and People's Congress deputies. He then focuses on a more promising avenue of inclusion: the VC elections that began in the late 1980s. As a breeding ground for citizenship rights, VCs have two decisive advantages over people's congresses: they are more autonomous, and they control things people care about. O'Brien suggests that Chinese villagers are best thought of as occupying an intermediate position between subjects and citizens. When they use unenforced citizenship rights as a weapon, they are demanding that the representatives of state power treat them equitably, respect their claims, and deliver on promises made by officials at higher levels. They are exploiting the spread of participatory ideologies and patterns of rule rooted in notions of equality, rights, and rule of law.

Chinese farmers were the initial beneficiaries of Deng's agricultural reform including the household responsibility system. Since the mid-1990s, however, peasant income has lagged behind rapidly rising urban incomes. The rural sector has experienced more hardship under deep reform, as peasant burdens have resulted in increasing rural unrest. Drawing on increasing state revenue and confronted with the growing demand for agricultural development, the Chinese government was finally able to reduce or exempt the agricultural tax for several hundred million peasants in 2004, with plans to exempt all agricultural taxes within four years. This became one of the most popular and widely publicized policy changes at the March 2005 NPC meeting, making it possible that this goal could be achieved even earlier.[37]

As rural elections and rural reform have made meaningful progress, tough issues have emerged in urban areas. Marc Blecher (chapter 15) views Chinese workers as having low potential for collective action, seeing themselves as existing primarily within the market, and as having lost their rights consciousness. What most analysts of the politics of Chinese workers over the past decade seem able to agree upon is that the economic status of workers is declining (at least in relative, if not always in absolute, terms) and that their social and political ties to various organs of the state are weakening far more than they are strengthening. Workers' protests since the 1980s, numerous and widely distributed though they may be, have remained spasmodic, spontaneous, and uncoordinated. Strikes and protests have not yet produced significant national strike waves or protest movements. The vast majority of Chinese workers, including the unemployed, remain politically passive. Why is China's working class not mounting a coordinated challenge in the face of the fundamental transformations that have so profoundly afflicted so many workers and that threaten so many more who have not yet felt the ax? Blecher's chapter begins to explore a unique line of explanation: that workers have become subject to the dual hegemony of the market and of the state. Both the state and the market have done measurable net harm, in relative and sometimes even in absolute terms, to much of the Chinese working class. Yet over the past two decades, many of China's workers have come to accept the core values of the market and of the state as legitimate. It is truly fascinating that both Chinese elites and workers, each with distinctive interests, have accepted the core values of the market and the state as legitimate. Whether such widespread acceptance can be sustained will definitely affect the future of China's reform.

EMERGING PROBLEMS AND
FUTURE CHALLENGES

Many new problems and contradictions have emerged as China deepens its reform. For instance, while the traditional public health system is under reform, the emerging system has not been able to meet the growing demands of the Chinese people. In fact, more and more people have been left out of the social and health safety net. Official corruption has become more serious than ever before. Unfortunately, no effective solutions have been found that can stop corruption. Another serious challenge is environmental degradation. With the overwhelming emphasis on economic growth from top to bottom of the officialdom, the environment has often been a victim of uncontrolled and ill-planned economic adventures. According to one estimate, nine of the ten most polluted cities in the world are in China. Although China has enjoyed a long period of sustained high growth rates, nonperforming loans and other financial troubles have not been resolved but intensified in many cases. This section will focus on three emerging problems: public health issues with an emphasis on women's health, change and continuity in the tough fight against corruption, and the mounting troubles in financial restructuring.

Veronica Pearson (chapter 16) studies women's health in the reform era. She also discusses the population policy and its effect on women's well-being. There are large disparities in health service indices between rural and urban areas. Although the government has always denied that the population control program was coercive, it is clear that the cadres at grassroots levels routinely use forceful and sometimes extreme measures. The one child policy has led to a skewed birthrate and a concomitant shortage of women of marriageable age. The normal sex ratio at birth is 100 girls to approximately 105–106 boys. The 2000 census found the ratio to be 100 girls to

117 boys. This is a severe sex imbalance with serious consequences. The liberation and equality of women was one of the primary planks of the CCP's manifesto when it came to power in 1949. Significant progress was made in the earlier year. However, with the decision of the government to introduce market mechanisms into agriculture and eventually industry and all other aspects of economic life, the structures enforcing women's equality were undermined and women became much more vulnerable to being laid off, or simply not hired. Many managers were reluctant to hire women because of maternity leave and energy split between work and running a home. As more and more authority and decision-making power have devolved to the grassroots, women's improved status has been increasingly challenged. Chinese women, especially those in rural areas, have been asking if the government has broken the compact with them that formed a significant foundation for the PRC.

A serious problem in China today is the potential public health crisis. For instance, the Chinese leadership was caught by surprise by the SARS epidemic in spring 2003. The SARS crisis demonstrated that the government was not well prepared for handling this type of sudden crisis. On the other hand, the remarkably coordinated efforts after April 2003 in the fight against SARS also demonstrated that the Chinese government still controls a significant amount of political and social capital in dealing with a health crisis. When the top leaders are determined and the political machines are mobilized, decisive measures can be taken in a short period of time. In February 2004, Vice Premier Wu Yi emphasized the Chinese government must take decisive measures against the growing AIDS crisis. More openness in mass media in reporting health crisis and social problems will put great pressure on the government to respond to such problems in a more timely and more transparent way.

Recent years have witnessed a spread of corruption into new economic areas as the scope of reform widened in China. Ting Gong (chapter 17) identifies major forms of corruption in China under reform. In her view, whereas deepened marketization has added more momentum to China's economic growth, it has been accompanied by a surge of corruption in various areas. New and different forms of corruption have occurred in recent years despite the gradual shrinking of nonmarket elements in the economy. Gong investigates sophisticated tactics of corruption including illicit transfer of state assets in ownership diversification and land corruption. As China's reform spreads to various new economic areas, corruption is growing in complicity and sophistication. Another alarming trend is that corruption has become increasingly transnational, as many corrupt activities involve collaborative operations of domestic government officials with overseas individuals or organizations. The deepening of the market reform in recent years has not reduced corruption so much as altered its form and characteristics. Without political reform, a market economy alone cannot effectively contain corruption. The continued surge of corruption has had a negative impact on China's marketization and modernization efforts, resulting in an economic loss of some 13–16 percent of GDP every year, conservatively estimated.[38] It also threatens social stability, the very environment China needs for economic development. Rampant corruption has caused not only public cynicism and disillusionment, but also street protests or even riots where people found it unbearable.[39] The Chinese leaders have realized that fighting against corruption is a matter of life or death. If they fail to deal with this serious problem, rampant corruption will undermine regime legitimacy and weaken the economic foundation of China.

Edward S. Steinfeld (chapter 18) critically examines the interplay of ideas and institutions in Chinese financial restructuring. Despite an impressive record of growth, the Chinese economy in recent years has exhibited substantial and persistent problems of capital misallocation. The amount of bad loans shouldered by Chinese banks in 2004 was as high as $500 billion.[40] There has been deepening insolvency of the national banking system, ineffectual financial sector bailouts and continued government effort to support large industrial conglomerates, many of which have been failing commercially. It is quite obvious that deep reform has created more complex problems in the Chinese economy. Unfortunately there is no easy solution to such problems. The deterioration in government finances, the bad loan problem in the state banking system and the losses of SOEs are characteristics of the recent reform period. The three problems are intricately linked. For example, social security payments could be made either by SOEs or through the government budget. If they are made by the SOEs, they reduce SOE profits; if they are financed through the government budget, they increase the budget deficit. SOE wage payments could either reduce SOE profits, or increase state bank (bad) loans. Thus the state sector, that is government, state banks, and SOEs, needs to be considered in total.[41]

China's profound, rapid, and complex political and socioeconomic changes provide fertile ground for pioneering social scientific analysis, but also present daunting theoretical and practical challenges. China's deep reform might present a viable alternative to the failed command system and the traumatic shock therapy experienced by Russia. Indeed, China could provide valuable lessons for other countries in the process of transition from the command economy to a market economy. Due to China's unique cultural and historical background as well as distinctive institutional setting, however, we should not overgeneralize lessons from China. It is very important to differentiate China's specific measures of deep reform from the strategies and policies that could have general applicability. We hope this volume will contribute to understanding China's deep reform and building bridge between China studies and social scientific exploration. The ultimate success of this scholarly endeavor, as of China's reform itself, will require creative and painstaking work of several generations.

NOTES

1. *Remin ribao*, January 1, 2005, 1.

2. In his report on the work of the government delivered at the Third Session of the Tenth National People's Congress on March 5, 2005, Premier Wen Jiabao used the term *shenhua gaige* ("deepen reform") nine times. He also used the term *tuijin gaige* ("advance

reform") many times. It is obvious that the current PRC leadership takes deep reform as a top priority. *Renmin ribao*, March 15, 2005.

3. Lowell Dittmer, *China under Reform* (Boulder, CO: Westview, 1994).

4. Deng Xiaoping, *Deng Xiaoping wenxuan*, vol. 3 [Selected works of Deng Xiaoping], (Beijing: Renmin chubanshe, 1993), 268.

5. *Remin ribao*, January 12, 2005, 1.

6. For various perspectives on this issue, see Guoli Liu, ed., *Chinese Foreign Policy in Transition* (New York: de Gruyter, 2004).

7. Dwight Perkins, "History, Politics, and the Sources of Economic Growth: China and the East Asian Way of Growth," in *China in the Twenty-first Century: Politics, Economics,* and *Society,* ed. Fumio Itoh (Tokyo: United Nations University Press, 1997), 29.

8. Gabriel A. Almond and Laura Roselle, "Model Fitting in Communist Studies," in *Post-Communist Studies and Political Science: Methodology and Empirical Theory in Sovietology,* ed. Frederic J. Fleron Jr. and Erik Hoffmann (Boulder, CO: Westview, 1993), 27.

9. Carl J. Friedrich and Zbigniew K. Brzezinski, *Totalitarian Dictatorship and Autocracy* (New York: Praeger, 1961).

10. James R. Townsend and Brantly Womack, *Politics in China* (London: Scott, Foresman, 1986), 22. Peking University historian Luo Rongqi made a serious effort to apply modernization theory to study China. See Luo Rongqi, *Xiandaihua xinlun: Shijie yu zhonguo de xiandaihua jincheng* [New perspectives on modernization: The world and China's modernization process], (Beijing: Beijing University Press, 1993).

11. Andrew G. Walder, *Communist Neo-Traditionalism: Work and Authority in Chinese Industry* (Berkeley: University of California Press, 1986).

12. See Baogang He, *The Democratic Implications of Civil Society in China* (New York: St. Martin's, 1997); and Yu Keping, *The Emerging Civil Society and Its Significance to Governance in Reform China* (Beijing: Shehui kexue wenxian chubanshe, 2002).

13. Quoted in A. M. Halpern, "Contemporary China as a Problem for Political Science," *World Politics* 15, no. 3 (1963): 374.

14. Chalmers Johnson, "The Role of Social Science in China Scholarship," *World Politics,* January 1965, 271.

15. Elizabeth J. Perry, "Partners at Fifty: American China Studies and the PRC" (paper prepared for conference Trends in China Watching, George Washington University, October 8–9, 1999), www.gwu.edu/~sigur/perry99.htm (accessed November 5, 2003).

16. Andrew Nathan, "A Factional Model for CCP Politics," *China Quarterly,* January and March 1973, 34–66.

17. See Bruce Dickson, *Red Capitalists in China: The Party, Private Entrepreneurs, and Prospects for Political Change* (New York: Cambridge University Press, 2003).

18. Xinhua News Agency, www.chinadaily.com.cn/english/doc/2005-02/11/content_416126.htm (accessed February 11, 2005).

19. For contending perspectives on this critical issue, see Lowell Dittmer, "Three Visions of Chinese Political Reform," *Journal of Asian and African Studies,* December 2003, 347–376.

20. Lowell Dittmer, "Leadership Change and Chinese Political Development," *China Quarterly,* December 2003, 904.

21. For an overview of China's political reform, see John P. Burns, "The People's Republic of China at 50: National Political Reform," *China Quarterly,* September 1999, 580–594.

22. Murray Scot Tanner, *The Politics of Lawmaking in Post-Mao China: Institutions, Processes, and Democratic Prospects* (Oxford: Clarendon Press, 1999).

23. Stanley B. Lubman, *Bird in a Cage: Legal Reform in China after Mao* (Stanford, CA: Stanford University Press, 1999), 4–5.

24. Joseph Fewsmith, *China since Tiananmen: The Politics of Transition* (New York: Cambridge University Press, 2001), 128.

25. Yu Keping, *Zenglian minzhu yu shanzhi: Zhuangbian zhong de zhongguo zhengzhi* [Incremental democracy and good governance: Chinese politics in transition] (Beijing: Shehui Kexue Wenxian Chubanshe, 2003), 155–157.

26. Barry Naughton, *Growing Out of the Plan: Chinese Economic Reform, 1978–1993* (New York: Cambridge University Press, 1996).

27. Dorothy J. Solinger, "Labour Market Reform and the Plight of the Laid-off Proletariat," *China Quarterly*, June 2002, 304–326.

28. Nicholas R. Lardy, *Integrating China into the Global Economy* (Washington, DC: Brookings Institution, 2002), 2.

29. Chi Fulin, *China: The New Stage of Reform* (Beijing: Foreign Languages Press, 2004), 14–19.

30. Joseph Fewsmith, "The Political and Social Implications of China's Accession to the WTO," *China Quarterly*, September 2001, 573–591.

31. For a systematic analysis of China's intellectual debates, see Fewsmith, *China since Tiananmen*. For a study of national identity in contemporary China, see Lowell Dittmer and Samuel S. Kim, eds., *China's Quest for National Identity* (Ithaca, NY: Cornell University Press, 1993).

32. For a recent study of Chinese local politics, see Yang Zhong, *Local Government and Politics in China: Challenges from Below* (Armonk, NY: Sharpe, 2003).

33. Yongnian Zheng, "Political Incrementalism: Political Lessons from China's Twenty Years of Reform," *Third World Quarterly* 20, no. 6 (1999): 1157–1177.

34. Thomas P. Bernstein and Xiaobo Lu, "Taxation without Representation: The Central and Local States in Reform China," *China Quarterly*, September 2000, 724–763.

35. Robert A. Pastor and Qingshan Tan, "The Meaning of Village Elections," *China Quarterly*, June 2000, 490–512.

36. Melanie Manion, "Chinese Democratization in Perspective: Electorates and Selectorates at the Township Level," *China Quarterly*, September 2000, 764–782.

37. In both 2004 and 2005, the first CCP central documents are about agricultural issues. This clearly indicates that the Chinese leaders take the *san nong* (peasants, agriculture, and rural areas) problems very seriously. The 2005 number one central document calls for "deepening agricultural reform." Reducing and exempting agricultural tax is a very important step in this direction. See "What Benefits Will the Number One Document Bring to 900 Million Farmers?" www.xinhuanet.com.cn (accessed January 31, 2005).

38. Hu Angang, "Public Exposure of Economic Losses Resulting from Corruption," www.iwep.org.cn/wec/english/articles/2002_04/2002-4huangang.pdf (accessed November 4, 2004).

39. Feng Chen, "Subsistence Crises, Managerial Corruption, and Labor Protests in China," *China Journal* 163 (2000): 41–63.

40. Fareed Zakaria, "Does the Future Belong to China?" *Newsweek*, May 9, 2005, 32. Although recognizing the daunting challenges facing China today, this *Newsweek* special report is quite optimistic about the future of China.

41. Carsten A. Holz, "Economic Reform and State Sector Bankruptcy in China," *China Quarterly*, June 2001, 342–367.

1

Analysis in Limbo?

Contemporary Chinese Politics amid the Maturation of Reform

Lowell Dittmer and William Hurst

As befits the limbo into which China has slipped over the past two decades—between plan and market, between the consolidation of democratic centralism and first steps toward political reform, between robust extensive growth and either intensive growth or economic stagnation, between the deepening institutionalization of politics at the top and growing signs of political decay in the wake of marketization at the bottom—the study of Chinese politics has, over the same period, slipped into a limbo between substantive concerns, between levels of analysis, and between methodological approaches. In the decade since Deng Xiaoping's famed southern tour, as China has undergone a slough of changes, the China field has seen the rise and fall of several important research paradigms and substantive debates. Our purpose here is to sketch a road map of these developments in the field, flagging approaches, methods, and debates along the way that we believe will become or remain salient over the next decade and beyond. We begin by looking at some of the theses and debates that have dominated the field recently, then proceed to an analysis of methodological advances, which might be deemed by some as noteworthy as the shifts of substantive perspective.

THE SHIFTING SUBSTANTIVE FOCUS OF THE CHINA FIELD

The substantive focus has also shifted in recent years away from analysis of the state—at least the central party-state apparatus. From Schurmann, to Shram, to

Schwartz, to Tsou, a generation of China scholars offered progressively refined interpretations of the ideological lines, organizational forms, factional struggles, and
power dynamics of China's top ruling elite.[1] But since the death of Mao, the central
leadership arena, once the site of nation-transforming drives and dramatic, high-
stakes elite power plays, has become increasingly institutionalized. The reformers'
general summary of experience seems to have been that while the bottom of the
hierarchy had been overinstitutionalized during the Maoist period and needed to
break out of its excessive regimentation in order to become more productive, the
top elites had been underinstitutionalized and needed more discipline to stop lurch-
ing from one extreme to the other. Thus though there has since Tiananmen been a
growing reconcentration of power at the center, arresting the decentralization and
devolution trends of the 1980s, the new leadership, socialized by the discipline of
engineering, has adopted a more conventional, buttoned-down administrative style
and its initiatives have been far more measured. Internal disagreements still occur,
but the losers, though still evicted from the magic circle, are no longer made object
lessons in mass campaigns mobilized for the moral edification of the "masses." That
would be inconsistent with the new elite subculture of civility that has been cultivated since the death of Mao. The emphasis has been on discretion, keeping disagreements contained within the party to such an extent that although factional
differences still seem to manifest themselves (e.g., in the politics of personnel promotion), it has become difficult to identify the various factional groupings with distinctive policy agendas. In the face of this determined blandness, the political analysis
of central elites seems to have fallen into desuetude in the wider field.

To be sure, there are significant exceptions. The contemporary study of high-level
central politics has focused on key political actors—individual biographies, small
groups, or aggregates—implicitly conceding that political structural reform has been
minimal during this period. Indeed, not all of the finest works produced during this
period have focused on current developments. The works of MacFarquhar, Teiwes,
Jing Huang, and Qiu Jin have all taken advantage of new archival, memorial, or
interview data to cast new light on the heyday of elite power politics, the Maoist
period. MacFarquhar completed his magisterial trilogy focused on one crucial decade, the Great Proletarian Cultural Revolution, with a final volume equal in length
(733 pages) to its two antecedents.[2] But whereas MacFarquhar's compilation of data
is demonstrably exhaustive (at this point in time), his interpretation of that data may
not be the last word—indeed, his perspective tends to shift in the course of the
three volumes, from an early acceptance of Mao's paranoid vision, in which the great
helmsman maneuvers to make a comeback from a position of internal exile on the
second "front" (to which he had been banished after the great leap forward), to his
concluding position that though Mao had indeed launched the Cultural Revolution
(CR) to entrap and destroy his opponents, his political supremacy had never really
been at risk. Mao was not surrounded by enemies or "time bombs," but by somewhat bewildered supporters intent upon consolidating the revolution, a project with
which he fundamentally disagreed. The substantive picture that emerges is essen-

tially a "Mao in command" model, in which an aging leader ruthlessly manipulates his dwindling arsenal of political resources to maintain his own hegemony.

The MacFarquhar approach to Chinese leadership analysis, as illustrated in this as in previous works, is to focus not on an individual leader but on a watershed event, flashing back to an elaborate reconstruction of the elite actions and motives leading up to that particular outcome; the implicit assumption is that of a top-down dynamic.[3] This involves the careful consideration of appearance data and other Aesopian indicators, under the assumption that each high-level CCP cadre is not only a decision maker and something of an original theorist but a public performer, whose every public act is carefully gauged to signal certain cues to one's confederates and to attract new supporters (hopefully without antagonizing rivals). Frederick Teiwes, Qiu Jin, and Jing Huang use essentially the same approach, with somewhat greater reliance on interviews. Qiu Jin brings to her study much more "inside dope" *(neibu ziliao)*, by virtue of her close relationship to one of the principals in the Lin Biao affair, which leads her to greater emphasis on the role of family dynamics (e.g., the clash between Ye Qun and Jiang Qing, the strain between Ye and her two children) and to the elite subculture in which these were played out (and Teiwes, relying for the most part on public sources, essentially bears her out).[4] Jing Huang's study is in a sense the most ambitious of this genre, tracing elite factionalism from its alleged origins in the territorial "mountaintops" *(shantou)* that arose due to the physical inaccessibility of isolated base areas during the Sino-Japanese war and the war of national liberation, and which were allegedly maintained all the way through the CR (due to the assignment of whole groups of cadres to particular regions in the postliberation period). Where others see episodic confrontations, Huang sees the historic rise and fall of the "Yanan round table," a hub-and-spokes arrangement of informal patron–client ties among whom lateral communication was forbidden (as "factionalism"), allowing only vertical communication with the chairman.[5] These studies are premised on the common assumption that primary group ties have the tenacity to withstand the shocks of intraelite power dynamics, leading not only to the reliance on patronage to build loyalty groups or factions, but to the increasing reliance on nuclear family members (the wives of Liu Shaoqi, Mao Zedong, Lin Biao, Kang Sheng, Zhou Enlai; the children of Liu Shaoqi and Lin Biao). Only David Bachman diverges from this model of an ambivalent network of informal ties in his innovative interpretation of the factional dynamics of the great leap forward as a clash between a financial clique and a heavy industry/central planning group. Although this interesting notion will require further empirical research, a model of elite interest aggregation based on the functional differentiation of labor under Mao may be ahead of its time. Another puzzle is how to account for such exceptions to primary group loyalty as Mao himself, who repeatedly betrayed (and ultimately destroyed) his factional network in a series of policy reversals, most spectacularly by throwing in his lot (during the CR) with a motley congeries of hot-headed youth. True, Mao also had a conventionally recruited factional network, consisting of relatives, former bodyguards, and secretaries, but no one could take his loyalty for granted, not even his wife.

The leading analysts of contemporary Chinese elite politics, Joseph Fewsmith, Richard Baum, and Cheng Li, have introduced both methodological refinements and new substantive insights to factional analysis. Fewsmith has broadened his purview to include policy intellectuals and ideological discourse in his analysis (though the empirical linkage to policy "lines" calls for further research), taking into account the opening of ideology from caesaro-papist "directives" to intergroup formulation; substantively, he has subjected Tang Tsou's model of an inevitable "struggle to win all or lose all" to empirical test, introducing refinements to take into account the aim-inhibited tension between Deng Xiaoping and Chen Yun over the pace and direction of reform in the 1980s. Richard Baum's thorough study of reform in the 1980s introduces the dynamic of opening and closing (*fang* and *shou*), originally used to characterize the liberalization of media controls, to help us understand the spasmodic pace of reform. Cheng Li has emerged as the outstanding quantitative analyst of elite dynamics, reviving in more systematic and comparative fashion the time-tested criteria for understanding the transformation of the membership of the Central Committee and the National Party Congress: birthplace, age, education, career background, gender, nationality, and work unit.[6] In his most recent work he also revives the concept of elite generations for the first time since it was systematically introduced by William Whitson during the CR.[7] This should be useful so long as it avoids the ecological fallacy, generalizing from generational characteristics to particular leaders. Kevin O'Brien and Murray Scot Tanner have subjected the National People's Congress to renewed scrutiny, demonstrating how limited structural reform has enhanced the political power of the national legislature, once mocked as a mere "rubber stamp."[8] There is general agreement among these scholars that (despite specific glaring exceptions) an elite subculture of civility and discretion has been established, minimizing the public discussion of ideological or policy differences, regularizing the convention and procedures of decision-making forums, giving rise to the appearance of increasing stability and managerial competence. Formidable pitfalls still jeopardize the progress of China's maturing reform, not least of which is the increasing paucity of relatively undistorted, noncorrupt routes of political feedback from the masses to the elite.

In the relative absence of work on the central party-state, there has been growing interest in the local state, stimulated no doubt by the decentralization and devolution of power during the Deng Xiaoping period, as notably analyzed by Susan Shirk. Whereas the focus in the early 1980s had been on the grassroots levels—the village, the township, the county—by the late 1980s the emphasis had shifted to the province, relatively neglected since the CR. A rich analytical harvest ensued, including much monographic literature on the individual provinces, comparative studies of center–province coordination of anti-inflation efforts, fixed asset investment policy, and so forth; even a journal specifically addressed to provincial issues was launched.[9] Although this literature is so rich it is difficult to generalize (indeed, that is one of the central points), we may perhaps infer from it at least three points: (1) Contrary to the image of totalitarian *Gleichschaltung* (consolidation), China is extremely diverse. Many central policies are hence discretionary, and those that are general are often adapted to local circumstances during implementation. The first casualty of this finding was Shirk's conception of "bureaucratic politics," which properly highlights the importance of provincial and local leadership but fails to explain regional differences. (2) The balance of power between center and province is constantly fluctuating, and provincial leaderships have gained economic resources in the reform era via marketization, privatization, and the expropriation of extrabudgetary funds, and by the shift from "two down" to "one down" (i.e., after 1982, the center can appoint only the top tier of provincial cadres, leaving the provincial leadership to appoint their own subordinates). While delegating economic authority, the center continues to exercise political sovereignty by controlling the military and by appointing or rotating the provincial leadership. (Notwithstanding visions of "Chinese-style federalism," provincial representation on the Central Committee has statistically declined from the CR period to the reform era, though this trend may have been arrested at the Sixteenth Party Congress.) The balance of power is not zero-sum, as the provinces are agencies of the center, with whom a modicum of cooperation is mutually advantageous. (3) Since Deng's southern tour, center–province relations have been moving toward institutionalization. Whereas these relations were previously characterized by an ambiguity that both sides sought to preserve as a bargaining cushion in case of future uncertainties, more recent reforms have introduced a clearer delineation of jurisdictional boundaries and an articulation of respective rules (compare the 1994 shift from the highly discretionary fiscal contractual system to tax sharing, which is characterized by uniform requirements and is moving toward legal codification of the delineation of responsibility).

Interest in the role of officially sanctioned ideas, or "ideology," in inspiring and regulating the political system has languished along with the neglect of the central party-state. There are still a number of contributions to the literature premised on the assumption that ideological or theoretical factors have been central to the restructuring of China's political economy, but they tend to have been marginalized in the field, in stark contrast to the reception given the classic of this genre, Franz Schurmann's *Ideology and Organization in Communist China*. For example, Yan Sun offers a carefully wrought account of Chinese discourse over the reform of China's political economy (with relative emphasis on economy), including the ideologically fraught issues of ownership, distribution, socialist transition, and class struggle; her conclusion is that in balance, by retaining continuity within the overarching framework of Marxism-Leninism-Mao Zedong thought (while making drastic pragmatic adjustments of that framework to fit market realities), China has avoided many of the destabilizing consequences of overthrowing that framework completely, as occurred in Eastern Europe and the former Soviet Union.[10]

Feng Chen too, in *Economic Reform and Political Legitimacy*, focuses on the neglected role of ideology in Chinese structural reform, and, like Sun, opines that "a total change of fundamental principles would shake the very foundations of the system" (209). Chen's narrative is more effectively calibrated with the politics of economic reform than that of Sun, who tends to leave her discourses in their intellectual settings and rely on a rhetoric of synchrony *(post hoc ergo propter hoc)* rather than causally linking them to structural reform in the "real" world.[11] Such studies are in our judgment a useful corrective to the recent tendency to assume with Fukuyama that ideology is essentially defunct since the death of Mao and the collapse of the bloc. They point out to the contrary that despite its far more elastic contours and attendant loss of popular credibility, Marxist ideology continues to enforce a certain discipline and a long-term perspective on Chinese political theorizing and encourage agenda setting for the collective future. Ideology is still alive and important, but more for the elite than the mass, ambiguous, and lower in profile, the product of increasingly disparate influences, and no longer monopolized by a caesaro-papist leadership. But both studies are in a bit of a conceptual quandary, tending to fall back on the old hierophantic paradigm in which ideology functions as a "general line" to which society marches in lock step and failing to come to terms with the specific form of ideological secularization now overtaking China,[12] part of a general phenomenon that has preoccupied students of religion in Western society throughout the modern era.[13]

The study of state–society relations has continued to thrive, chiefly in the form of analysis of the state's relationship to what we might call "strategic groups."[14] Such groups as workers, peasants, cadres, and intellectuals have all received a good deal of attention, and recently entrepreneurs have also begun to generate interest. Soldiers and the military, however, have been something of a fifth wheel in this trend. With the exceptions of Murray Scot Tanner[15] and You Ji, no recent attempts have been made by Western scholars to analyze the relationship of the military to the state or the role of soldiers or other members of China's security apparatus in society outside of the foreign policy and national security contexts—which is not to deny the existence of excellent studies of these organs as organizational resources.[16] To the extent that analysis of soldiers, policemen, and other agents of state security in China has been done in the past ten years, the general conclusion has been that both the military and the security apparatus have been brought increasingly under the tight control of the central state-party center. At the same time, it is generally agreed that the economic status of police and soldiers has been falling steadily, certainly since the military was forbidden from running consumer businesses, as police and military salaries have stagnated, benefits have lagged, and the costs of living have increased.[17] Which is to say that as these units' potential volatility as strategic groups has escalated, the center has intensified efforts at hierarchical discipline.

Part of this focus has been on enterprises or business units in various sectors. Banks, state-owned enterprises (SOEs), private enterprises, and foreign-invested firms have all been the object of a range of recent studies. The contours of the debates emerging around these investigations merit more detailed examination.

Recent analyses of Chinese workers or the Chinese working class are generally in agreement as to workers' declining political, social, and economic position, in at least relative terms.[18] They differ, however, in their theoretical frameworks, levels of analyses, and their findings on other aspects of workers' politics. Though there are some quantitative and macrolevel studies, the vast majority of research on workers over the past ten years has been based on interview research and microlevel case studies. The interesting divisions, therefore, has occurred mostly in the realm of substantive findings rather than in method or approach. Specifically, the findings of researchers on workers' politics can be divided along three dimensions: the potential of workers for collective action, the degree to which workers situate themselves in either the market or the state, and the level of "rights consciousness" or "legal consciousness" among workers.[19] If we divide the extant literature, we see that some scholars, Marc Blecher for instance,[20] see Chinese workers as having a low potential for collective action, seeing themselves as existing primarily within the market, and as having lost their rights consciousness (or having been caught up by a new false consciousness of rights).[21] Others, like Ching Kwan Lee, view workers as having a high potential for collective action, as seeing themselves still very much as state rather than market actors, and as having a highly developed rights/legal consciousness.[22] Other researchers, like Mary Gallagher, split between these two extremes. Gallagher, in her studies of formal labor disputes, argues that workers are indeed becoming much more aware of their legal rights as citizens and workers under reform are using these newly discovered rights to take legal action. On the other hand, she also finds that workers have relatively low potential for collective action and are rarely successful when they do engage in any form of dispute with their units. While she does not clearly state whether workers situate themselves within the state or in the market, it can be inferred from her work that they must be at the cusp between the two in a much more acute sense than seems to be the case according to either Lee or Blecher. Still others, such as Feng Chen, William Hurst, and Kevin O'Brien, have conceptualized rights consciousness in a much broader sense and in a manner more closely associated with moral economy arguments.[23] These scholars argue that some workers (retirees and those facing genuine crises of subsistence) are more likely to engage in collective action than others, that workers still see themselves as part of the state rather than the market, and that a certain type of rights consciousness—one rooted firmly in what could be called the socialist social contract—exists among many workers. To the extent that these authors conceptualize rights consciousness more broadly and attempt to disaggregate the sorts of workers who might be more likely to engage in collective action, they operate in a slightly different paradigm of research from that of Blecher, Lee, and Gallagher. Finally, some scholars, such as Dorothy Solinger, have focused largely on questions of how to categorize workers in various types of employment relationships with SOEs and on the manner in which workers leaving the state have tried, without much success, to enter the market. Solinger's recent work in particular draws into sharp focus the dilemmas facing laid-off workers struggling to make ends meet in the informal sectors and the problems involved in even trying to count workers in various categories.[24] What all analysts of the politics of Chinese workers over the past ten years seem able to agree upon, however, is that the economic status of workers is declining (at least in relative if not always absolute terms) and that their social and political ties to various organs of the state are weakening far more than they are strengthening.

Work on rural politics and Chinese peasants has centered around the relationship between rural residents and the local state. The two main thrusts of these analyses can be termed taxation and representation—the state's capacity to extract resources and its agents' extractive behavior, juxtaposed with the role of village elections, the collective action of rural residents, and the new concepts of citizenship for rural migrants. On the taxation side, we find scholars such as Thomas Bernstein and Xiaobo Lu concerned with the study of "peasant burdens."[25] These scholars argue that the agents of the local state—if not always its principals—seek ever higher extractions from increasingly burdened farmers in many regions of China. Despite calls from the center to reduce tax and fee burdens on farmers, village, township, and county governments—especially in central China, where resources are not as abundant as on the coast and central assistance is not as forthcoming as in the western regions—often turn to illegal or semilegal fees and special taxes to fund projects ranging from road building, to school construction, to investments in local township and village enterprises, to simple self-enrichment. On the representation side, the consensus is less clear. Here there are at least two primary strains of research—one that concentrates on elections and other "cooperative" channels of representation, and one that focuses on collective action, lawsuits, and protest. Amid much diversity in both strains, it is generally agreed that peasants have become much more participatory in the local state—whether as voters or as activists—than they were as recently as 1990.

Finally, some—though far too few—scholars have paid a good deal of attention to migrant workers (over 70 million of them, by conservative estimates, as of 1997) who "float" from rural areas to the cities in pursuit of employment. The unquestioned leader in this research is Dorothy Solinger, who argues that rural migrants have become a sort of second-class citizenry in Chinese cities under reform.[26] Despite her general emphasis on their disadvantaged or secondary status, Solinger does admit that even these peasants in the city enjoy some form of citizenship in the Chinese context. One could argue that this is more than peasants in the villages enjoyed prior to reform. Also, the cash brought into rural economies or spent in cities by these migrants has definitely improved the overall economic status of China's rural population relative to where it stood in the 1980s. As this economic benefit has accrued, however, peasants have become increasingly bound to the state, as the state both extracts more from them and affords them more opportunities to exert at least limited influence on local governments and even assume some quasi-official status and rights in the cities.[27]

Research on cadres has focused largely on issues of corruption, but has also produced interesting findings regarding investment and developmental policies. To date, the definitive statement on cadre corruption has come from Xiaobo Lu, who argues that "bureaucratic involution," as one of several optional responses to reform and opening, has not infrequently resulted in corruption among agents of the Chinese party-state (his focus, like that of the leadership, tends to be on the grass roots).[28] As the center loses its grip on local level cadres, corrupt individuals (or whole units) are able to pursue various illicit paths to self-enrichment. A more optimistic picture of cadre behavior is painted by Jean Oi, who argues that in many localities cadres shape local production and industrialization in the manner of an efficient corporation. Though the role of corruption is not in focus in Oi's analysis, it is clear even in her version of the story that local cadres, under decreasingly close supervision from higher levels, have often been quick to avail themselves of opportunities to enrich both their localities and themselves.[29]

The study of intellectuals has followed two divergent trends. On the one hand, resorting essentially to discourse analysis, there has been a focus on new schools of political thought developing since Tiananmen and on their respective influence on the state. Joseph Fewsmith in particular has carefully divided prominent intellectuals into two main groups, liberals and the "new left."[30] The new left is further subdivided between new nationalists, new statists, and postmoderns. Each of these categories of intellectuals, he argues, bears influence among a particular faction of politicians, though no single intellectual or group carries decisive weight in any policy debate. Other contributors to the study of intellectual discourse in China include Frank Dikotter's sweeping and controversial study of the discourse on race (only the epilogue of which is concerned with the post-1949 period), or Michael Sullivan's interesting discussion of the impact of Western thinking on Chinese views of the socialist transition.[31] Geremie Barme, on the other hand, has stressed the anomie felt by intellectuals, students, artists, and others in China's cultural elite under reform.[32] While somewhat less constrained in their pursuit of their creative arts and studies, these people still lack any real expressive freedom and are meanwhile also cut off from the state benefits and influence they had previously enjoyed. Trapped in a consumerist society that cares little for art or scholarship, intellectuals in Barme's vision often look back on the days of ideological struggle as a time when at least their lives had meaning and the state and society cared about what they produced. Thus, in terms of both welfare and coercion, intellectuals have grown apart from the state. At the same time, the development of a market for intellectual and artistic products—from private tutoring, to consulting, to visual and performing arts, to commercial publishing, even (for the top 5 percent or so) links to international cultural markets—has afforded intellectuals opportunities to improve their economic status hitherto never imagined. Though some are falling through the cracks, on the whole, Chinese intellectuals today almost certainly enjoy a rising economic status. The unresolved contradiction of perspective between Barme and his more optimistic colleagues may have to do with different research foci and sampling techniques: whereas Fewsmith, Sullivan, and others focus on established policy intellectuals interested in contributing to what used to be called the "party line" or "general line," conceived as an ideological "leading indicator" of national political–economic development (e.g., Deng Xiaoping's "four cardinal principles," Jiang Zemin's "three represents"), Barme is interested in intellectuals as what we would call a strategic group (both, of course, are right).

The study of the rise of the professionals, such as lawyers, and their potential political role, is still in its infancy. To date, however, most findings have largely paralleled those about intellectuals. Whereas lawyers were until recently conceived as state legal cadres, Ethan Michelson, in his study of Chinese lawyers, has found that attorneys have largely left (or been ejected from) the embrace of the state (thereby losing much of their political influence), while their overall economic status seems to have improved. Much remains to be done if we are to learn about the economic social and political lives of all the relevant groups of Chinese professionals, but so far the evidence points to their improving economic status and weakening ties to the state.

The study of private businessmen and entrepreneurs is still in its infancy in the China field (reflecting in part the relative immaturity of this group in the national economy, despite the fact that the CCP has begun making serious overtures to the private sector (the term "middle class" is not yet ideologically kosher) in the past few years. There are, again, important exceptions—notably Thomas Gold[33] and David Wank—who have, since the 1980s, studied the gradual social and economic rise of the *getihu*.[34] Ken Foster has begun to tell us about business associations—which represent a mix of private firms and SOEs—and their relations to the local state in one locality in Shandong.[35] Such worthy contributions notwithstanding, much needs to be done before anything definitive can be said about private entrepreneurs in China. There does seem to be a consensus to date, however, that not only is the economic status of entrepreneurs rising—sometimes as much because of the class or family backgrounds of the entrepreneurs as because of their business acumen—but that their ties to the state are growing closer, whether because of *guanxi* and informal ties to officials, because of increasing state regulation of private business affairs, or because of CCP overtures to coopt this energetic new class.

With the possible exceptions of the military and security apparatus, studies of the relationship between the state and these various strategic groups have been thriving in the China field. What so far has been lacking, however, is an attempt to relate the trajectories of these groups to one another in any systematic way. This type of analysis holds much promise for future research. As a preliminary schematization, we might roughly classify strategic groups according to two simple indices: change in the nature of their relationship to the state and change in their economic status (see table 1.1). As entrepreneurs and peasants have seen their economic status rise and their ties to the state strengthened, workers have seen their economic status decline while their ties to the state have also weakened. While cadres and intellectuals have managed to raise their economic status while their ties to the state have grown more tenuous, soldiers and members of the security apparatus have seen their

Table 1.1.   Social Groups' Economic Status and Their Relationship to the State

	Relationship to the State Becoming Closer	Relationship to the State Becoming More Distant
Economic status rising	Peasants, entrepreneurs	Cadres, intellectuals, professionals
Economic status declining	Soldiers, security apparatus	Industrial workers

economic status decline, even as the state has tried to exert increasingly tight control over them.

As mentioned earlier, the relationships between various types of enterprise and the state have also drawn a great deal of attention throughout the 1990s, not usually in the form of strategic group analysis but as one aspect of industrial policy. As the intended "commanding heights" of China's industrial future (despite their current fiscal travails), state-owned enterprises (SOEs) have attracted increasing attention. So far the acknowledged standard has been set in this area by the work of Edward Steinfeld. Steinfeld argues that in many cases SOEs falter or are mismanaged not because of a failure to transfer property rights or lagging privatization, but because the very concept of property rights is not well defined in SOEs. Though a great deal of variance was present among the three steel mills Steinfeld studied, each fell victim to many of the same pitfalls resulting from this lack of specification of property rights. Whether this issue still looms as large as it did when the research was originally conducted, whether this is something unique to the steel industry or can be generalized as an equally or even more severe problem in other sectors, are questions that must await future research, for which there is pressing need. The study of the banking sector, particularly strategic as the financial intermediary that pumps capital into the other SOEs, has generated a great deal of interest since Nicholas Lardy warned of its insolvency in his 1998 book. Though Lardy has moderated his tone since then, others have taken up the cry, pointing to a portfolio of nonperforming loans amounting to an estimated 44 percent of the country's GDP to contend that the solvency of China's banking system is the Achilles' heel of China's economic prospects.[36] While more research is needed before we can claim to fully understand the relationship between Chinese banks and the state, it is clear even now that this relationship has been far from stable throughout the reform period. The entry of China into the World Trade Organization promises in many respects to bring this relationship and its contradictions to a head. If China scholars are to comprehend the changes likely to come in the near future, surely we give more attention to China's banking system and its search for financial equilibrium between state and market.

Inasmuch as China has recently overtaken the United States as the world's leading host of foreign direct investment (FDI) with an estimated US$50 billion in 2002, much more attention has been paid to the foreign-invested enterprise (FIE) sector, whose output now comprises nearly 50 percent of China's total export value. In many respects, these firms form the core of impressions of China under reform held by many in the business and policy arenas. Perhaps for this reason, most of the scholarly arguments seem to reflect dominant lines of thinking in these arenas about FIEs in China. Margaret Pearson, for example, maintains that FIEs are channeled into a sort of symbiotic relationship with the Chinese state; one that both serves state purposes and promotes the business interests of firms.[37] From another angle, Anita Chan exposes the depravation and horrors in the lives of workers in many FIEs in the famous Pearl River delta region.[38] Still others have written more general studies of the role of foreign direct investment in China's political–economic development.[39] For all of this progress in our understanding of the foreign-invested sector, the China field still has not produced the sort of comprehensive analysis of the role of FIEs in the development and transition of China's socialist economy.[40]

The analysis of Chinese foreign policy has unfortunately remained the stepchild of the profession, characterized by a glut of relatively brief bilateral analyses but relatively few ambitious or conceptually innovative approaches. This is particularly unfortunate in view of the sudden and dramatic changes of the international political ecology that have accompanied the collapse of the Communist bloc and the end of the Cold War, permitting Beijing to redefine its role in a new world order (or disorder) in which Beijing could no longer enhance its strategic leverage by navigating between the two superpowers, as in the heyday of the "strategic triangle." Dittmer and Kim made at least an introductory sally at the concept of national identity, pointing out that if identity is at least in part a function of identification with certain international categories, China's post–Cold War national identity was in considerable turmoil because of the bankruptcy of one of its former identificands (the Soviet bloc, or "second world") and the increasing incoherence and developmental irrelevance of the other (the third world).[41] Yong Deng has capably pursued this line of analysis, hypothesizing that since the Cold War the international system has broken down into two basic categories: a developed "core" (consisting of some combination of NATO, the OECD, and the Group of Eight) and an underdeveloped "periphery," and that even after two decades of hypergrowth, China's self-conception is that of being stuck in the periphery, whence it is now striving to become a "responsible great power."[42] The will-o'-the wisp of great power status, as conventionally understood, also includes a military–strategic component, to whose construction Beijing has been contributing well over a tenth of its annual budget since the end of the Cold War, which of course begs the question of what Beijing is going to do with its growing arsenal. There have been several thoughtful attempts to shed light on this important but ultimately imponderable question, usually via diachronic comparisons. In one exceedingly ambitious and methodologically demanding historical comparison, Iain Johnston analyzes Ming dynasty military archives, where he finds evidence that contrary to the myth of an irenic Confucianism, what he calls a parabellum strategic culture (roughly analogous to Western realism) has long been dominant—and suggests that it still is.[43] But aside from the dangers of tautology, the central finding of an enduring parabellum strategic culture is frustratingly open-ended. Michael Swaine and Ashley Tellis draw specific policy implications from their equally sweeping historical overview of China's grand strategy, anticipating that since China's historic territorial ambitions will await attainment of sufficient military power to achieve them, China may be expected to make a bid to challenge U.S. "hegemony" in the Asian Pacific region around 2015–2020.[44] There is no question that China has opened itself to its imperial past since the collapse of the bloc in its quest for national identity, but so many relevant variables are not held constant in such sweeping comparisons that Allen Whiting's more chronologically limited historical comparisons—to eight cases of the use of force for deterrence or coercion in the history of the PRC—seems to us more immediately useful. Whiting points out, for example, that in such cases as the Korean War or the Sino-Soviet border clash (not to mention the Chinese revolution), Beijing has been quite willing to attack a superior adversary, striking boldly to teach a (political) lesson even for quite limited territorial gains.[45] The implications for, say, Taiwan are obvious. Also relevant to such discussions is the rise of nationalism, which may have helped motivate some of Mao's radical foreign policy initiatives but was ideologically taboo and never explicit. Since Tiananmen, nationalism has been much more strongly emphasized by a regime increasingly concerned about the loss of its ideological raison d'être, and the mass response has indeed been enthusiastic beyond all expectations. Yet the regime's tendency to define nationalism in opposition to democratization and Westernization bodes for future tension between Chinese nationalism and the economic globalization to which the regime is likewise committed.[46] The policy import of Chinese nationalism of course depends on how it is perceived, and by dint of a series of recent studies we now have a much better idea how Chinese elites perceive a great many foreign policy phenomena.[47]

LEVELS OF ANALYSIS: NO LONGER JUST MACRO VERSUS MICRO

Over the 1990s, the long-standing tension in the China field between macro- and microlevel analysis was heightened by the proliferation of microlevel analyses. As foreign scholars have gained access to ever larger numbers of research locales and as certain Chinese localities have opened more and more of their archives, research institutes and even government bureaus to academic study by foreigners, the lure of intensive analysis of a single locality or small set of localities has also increased. Meanwhile, the release in recent years of increasingly detailed and abundant aggregate statistics and central government documents and reports, as well as the increasing willingness of central officials to be interviewed by foreign scholars on certain topics, have opened up more possibilities for the study of Chinese politics at the macrolevel. There have, of course, been ever larger numbers of scholars eager to take advantages of these new opportunities.

As the China field has slowly moved from a field of data shortage to one of data surplus at both the micro- and macrolevels of analysis (but particularly the former), this data has not, however, become so easy to compile or digest as to afford most scholars the luxury of working at multiple levels of analysis with any realistic prospect of success. Given this situation, most scholars have congregated at the poles—exclusively pursuing either macrolevel studies in pursuit of sweeping generalizations about all of China or single-locality field work-based studies from which they too often generalize without any conception of the regionally specific character of their findings.

The importance of "middle-range theory" was first championed by Robert K. Merton, one of the giants of modern sociology, who pointed out that between grand theory and empirical research there is an often neglected middle range of analysis characterized by carefully linking some of the microlevel data to a framework abstract enough to permit useful comparison and theory construction but not so large-scale as to lose sight of the data in sweeping generalizations.[48] Along these lines, several recent scholars have managed to combine carefully selected case studies for interesting comparisons, based on rigorously compiled data sets they built themselves, just as others have conducted circumspect and theoretically relevant microlevel case studies. Even more encouraging is the work of several scholars—such as Edward Steinfeld and Dorothy Solinger—who have begun to construct careful comparisons of localities rooted in multiple microlevel case studies, selected on the basis of macrolevel analysis of regional and national trends, the combined results of which speak back to larger debates.[49] It is unfortunate that this type of "middle-range" analysis has not progressed further and that even the most outstanding practitioners still have important shortcomings in their work.[50]

METHODOLOGICAL APPROACHES
AND TECHNIQUES

Prior to 1990, quantitative analysis was extremely difficult (and rare) in the China field.[51] Since 1990, it has become more widespread, as in many other subfields of the social sciences. That said, quantitative analysis remains in a minority position in the China field for a variety of reasons ranging from the quality and availability of Chinese quantitative data to the difficulties and restrictions surrounding survey research in China to the sociology of knowledge and training in the field. At this time, most graduate programs still do not emphasize quantitative training for China scholars, journals in the field still place much greater weight on qualitative fieldwork or archival historical research than on quantitative analysis, and inadequate resources are available to researchers for the construction and dissemination of new and better data sets. While the qualitative–quantitative distinction is a crude one, and we do not argue that quantitative analysis ought to be dominant in the China field as some have argued it has become in political science as a whole, we do maintain that, in the interests both of advancing our understanding of China and of promoting the further integration of the study of China into social science disciplines, China scholars must take quantitative work more seriously. That having been said, quantitative research on China has come a long way since the death of Mao.

The earlier work of Shi Tianjian, Melanie Manion, and Yang Dali,[52] which rely mostly on descriptive uses or very basic regressions employing official statistics, has given way to more sophisticated work by these same authors, joined by others such as Tang Wenfang, William Parish, and Pierre Landry.[53] The decreasing reliance of quantitative scholars on spotty and unreliable official statistics and their ability to compile new and more reliable data sets, combined with their increasing levels of technical sophistication, is responsible for these developments, which (political constraints permitting) may be expected to continue. There has also been a growing trend toward quantitative analysis supplemented by a small set of in-depth interviews, one or more case studies, ethnographic or archival work. Several recent dissertations have employed this methodological combination to great effect, including those by Mary Gallagher, Cai Yongshun, and Ethan Michelson, among others.[54] The inverse combination—qualitative research supplemented by quantitative analysis (most likely in the selection of cases)—also holds much promise but has yet to be used widely or to much effect.

Among those who remain entirely on the qualitative side of the fence, the old divide between primarily archival or document-based research and primarily ethnographic or interview-based research has persisted and intensified over the past ten years. Once again, this is due mostly to the proliferation of available sources and the opening up of previously closed access in both these areas. At the same time new archives are opened to foreign scholars, more localities, populations and topics are approved for interview-based study. Interview-based research in particular has gained momentum over the past decade. Prior to 1990, very little interview-based research was conducted in China. Instead, most scholars relied on conduction émigré interviews in Hong Kong or elsewhere, since access to most localities and populations in China was not possible.

With the opening of fieldwork in China came a flood of interview-based research in the late 1980s and 1990s, accompanied by an almost instant end to émigré interviews. This development has had a mixed outcome. Although few would dispute the notion that interviews conducted with actors on the ground in China provide a far more proximate and more accurate picture of events than do émigré interviews, interview-based research in the China field has produced new problems. All too often researchers have conducted their interviews in one site only and then attempted to generalize to other localities and regions. While practitioners of émigré interviews also faced problems of regional specificity, because most of their interviewees came from Guangdong, the better researchers endeavored to sample interviewees from as many regions as possible[55] or focused their sampling on one particular locality in order to provide as complete a picture as possible.[56] For their pains, émigré interview practitioners were rewarded with samples of interviewees that were often far more representative, either across regions or within a single local-ity, of the complete population of interest in China than those typically used by interview-based researchers in the country today. Despite this problem, interview-based research has taken off in China and is improving rapidly. Few researchers would now conduct interviews at only one site and fail to place this in its proper context. There are still many researchers willing to make general arguments on the basis of evidence from only one or a very small set of sites, but this practice, too, is on the wane. Increasingly, interview-based research is the method of choice for many promising scholars, particularly including those now seeking to develop middle-range levels of analysis.

Archival and document-based research has also made great strides. While by the mid-1990s, researchers such as Elizabeth Perry and Li Xun had begun to produce more fine-grained analysis of single periods and localities than were normative in the past, by the end of the decade, some researchers were beginning to move beyond this approach.[57] More and more researchers in this tradition are also seeking to build larger arguments out of small sets of comparative case studies of localities during multiple historical periods. Recent work by such scholars as Mark Frazier and Eliza-beth Remnick demonstrates the power of combining careful archival research with the middle-range level of analysis outlined earlier.[58] Susan Whiting's recent study, based on fieldwork in three east China villages—Songjiang (Shanghai), Wuxi (Jian-gsu), and Yueqing (Wenzhou, Zhejiang)—uses and advances neo-institutional the-ory to show how property rights can either contribute to growth or not, based on the "path dependent" history of institutions in the region; she also brings "corporatist" assumptions into question, pointing to the possible divergence of interest between local cadres and the enterprise bottom line.[59] Whether describing taxation and the sex trade across several cities or the rise of the *danwei* system in some of China's leading industrial centers, the strength of such work shines through.[60]

Both archival and ethnographic types of qualitative research have made great strides since 1990, though of course both have a long way to go. While practitioners of both traditions have begun to conduct small sets of case study comparisons and have raised the bar for both types of data collection and analysis, most researchers have yet to begin choosing their cases as systematically as they could, and few researchers are sufficiently careful to avoid generalizations not well supported by their data.

CONCLUSION

Perhaps because the central leadership overinstitutionalized and overregimented the lower levels while allowing maximum flexibility to the higher levels, the inaugura-tion of reform has pursued the relative emancipation of the lower levels while sub-jecting higher levels to greater discipline and institutionalization. In the light of this shift of the "action," we have seen a shift from the analysis of the party-state toward the study of strategic groups or categories of subordinate governments or firms. If the China field continues this relative prioritization of research efforts, it must address several remaining gaps. First, while the field is beginning to come to some basic consensus about the economic status and political relationship of a number of different strategic groups to the state, we know almost nothing of the relationships among these groups or of the role of "interaction effects" in determining their bilateral ties with the state (e.g., the relationship between workers and factory management, or between basic units and employees). Second, the field has not yet begun to address the relationships between political actors and categories of firms or organizations. Rather, we have so far studied actors and organizations separately, as if the one bore no relationship to the other. Third, all of this empirical scholarship has yet to address any larger political economic questions. We may know, for instance, that workers are losing their economic status and losing their close ties with the state, but we do not know what this means for the future of any putative working class or labor movements, the changing makeup of the CCP, or for the future shape "socialism with Chinese characteristics." We may know that FIEs treat their workers badly and exist in symbiotic relationships with the state, but we have no clear idea what this means for China's continued economic growth or for the institutionalization of its political economy as its reform matures.

The China field is, generally speaking, more mature than it was at the close of the 1980s. We have now, however, reached a point at which we must take stock and see if we can descry what future paths can best help to integrate the study of Chinese politics and society into the wider disciplines of the social sciences, drawing from the insights of these disciplines without sacrificing a concern for issues of genuine substantive importance in China.

We offer, in conclusion, three modest proposals for potentially fruitful paths leading to the China field's further development. First, although promising theoretical contributions at any level are certainly always welcome, we suggest the utility of doing more work at the "middle-range" level of analysis discussed above. Thus we can perhaps avoid the atheoretical, balkanized study of single localities or microphenomena, as well as the often inaccurate or essentialist generalizations about "all of China" to which we have too often succumbed in the past. By examining a series of localities, phenomena, or time periods closely and comparing them with one another, China scholarship has begun to build more reliable and theoretically useful generalization about China within certain ranges.

Second, the China field might usefully begin to take quantitative analysis more seriously, and actively promote combinations of methods that draw on the complementary strengths of one or more additional methods to supplement the weak points of the primary method employed. While no method should dominate the field, no method should be left unexploited. Such a combination of methodological approaches and techniques would also promote the formation of more reliable conclusions about China and help point the way to possible applications of such conclusions to the construction of more general theories of comparative politics.

Finally, we must of course always be conscious of the field's substantive foci, fill in the gaps that exist where important groups or categories of organizations remain unstudied, and call on scholars to more carefully place their objects of study within the context of China as a whole. By thinking more carefully about what we know and do not know empirically we can begin not only to fill in gaps, but also to construct broader arguments that speak to larger theoretical concerns.

NOTES

1. See, for example, Franz Shurmann, *Ideology and Organization in Communist China* (Berkeley: University of California Press, 1968); Benjamin I. Schwartz, *Communism and China: Ideology in Flux* (Cambridge, MA: Harvard University Press, 1968); Stuart R. Schram, *The Thought of Mao Tse-tung* (Cambridge: Cambridge University Press, 1988); and Tang Tsou, *The Cultural Revolution and Post-Mao Reforms* (Chicago: University of Chicago Press, 1986).

2. Roderick MacFarquhar, *The Origins of the Cultural Revolution*. Vol. 3, *The Coming of the Cataclysm, 1961–1966* (New York: Columbia University Press, 1997).

3. See, for example, R. MacFarquhar, *The Hundred Flowers* (London: Stevens, 1960).

4. Jin Qiu, *The Culture of Power: The Lin Biao Incident and the Cultural Revolution* (Stanford, CA: Stanford University Press, 1999); Frederick Teiwes with Warren Sun, *The Tragedy of Lin Biao: Riding the Tiger during the Cultural Revolution, 1966–1971* (Honolulu: University of Hawaii Press, 1996).

5. Jing Huang, *Factionalism in Chinese Communist Politics* (New York: Cambridge University Press, 2000).

6. Cheng Li, *China's Leaders: The New Generation* (Lanham, MD: Rowman & Littlefield, 2001).

7. William Whitson, *The Chinese High Command* (New York: Praeger, 1973).

8. Kevin O'Brien, *Reform without Liberalization: China's National People's Congress and the Politics of Institutional Change* (New York: Cambridge University Press, 1990); Murray Scot Tanner, *The Politics of Lawmaking in Post-Mao China: Institutions, Processes, and Democratic Prospects* (New York: Oxford University Press, 1999).

9. See Hans Hendricksche and Feng Chongyi, eds., *The Political Economy of China's Provinces: Comparative and Competitive Leadership* (London: Routledge, 1999); Peter T. Y. Cheung, Jaeo Ho Chung, and Zhimin Lin, eds., *Provincial Strategies of Economic Reform in Post-Mao China* (Armonk, NY: Sharpe, 1998); Linda Chelan Li, *Centre and Provinces: China 1978–1993, Power as Non-Zero-Sum* (London: Clarendon, 1998); Zhiyue Bo, *Chinese Provincial Leaders: Economic Performance and Political Mobility since 1949* (Armonk, NY: Sharpe, 2002); Yasheng Huang, *Inflation and Investment Controls in China: The Political Economy of Central-Local Relations during the Reform Era* (New York: Cambridge, 1996); John Fitzgerald, ed., *Rethinking China's Provinces* (New York: Routledge, 2002); and Yasheng Huang, *Inflation and Investment Controls in China* (New York: Cambridge University Press, 1996); the journal *Provincial China* has been published by the Institute of International Studies at the University of Sydney since 1997.

10. Yan Sun, *The Chinese Reassessment of Socialism, 1986–1992* (Princeton, NJ: Princeton University Press, 1995).

11. Feng Chen, *Economic Transition and Political Legitimacy in Post-Mao China: Ideology and Reform* (Albany: University of New York Press, 1995).

12. For a recent contribution more alert to this tendency, see Kalpana Misra, *From Post-Maoism to Post-Marxism* (New York: Routledge, 1998).

13. See, for example, Thomas Luckman, *The Invisible Religion: The Problem of Religion in Modern Society* (New York: Macmillan, 1967); Steve Bruce, ed., *Religion and Modernization* (New York: Oxford University Press, 1992).

14. We prefer "strategic groups" to "interest groups," as the latter term is fraught with the premises of interest/pressure group theory as it was first articulated in a pluralistic context—interest groups are assumed to be economically autarkic and politically autonomous. A strategic group is one deemed indispensable to the smooth functioning of the system (hence "strategic") and thus—though hardly autonomous or autarkic—in a position to exert the tacit threat of withholding enthusiastic support for a policy deemed inimical to its economic, political, or professional interests. See Thomas Heberer, *Unternehmer als strategische Gruppen: Zur sozialen und politischen Funktion von Unternehmern in China und Vietnam,* Mitteilungen des Instituts für Asienkunde, no. 331 (Hamburg: Institut für Asienkunde, 2001), 108–125.

15. Murray Scot Tanner, "Ideological Struggle over Police Reform, 1988–1993," in Edwin A. Winkler, ed., *Transition from Communism in China: Institutional and Comparative Analyses* (Boulder, CO: Lynne Rienner, 1999); Murray Scot Tanner, "State Coercion and the Balance of Awe: The 1983–1986 'Stern Blows' Anti-Crime Campaign," *China Journal,* July 2000, 93–125.

16. See You Ji, *The Armed Forces of China* (London: Tauris, 1999).

17. See James C. Mulvenon, *Soldiers of Fortune: The Rise and Fall of the Chinese Military-Business Complex, 1978–1998* (Armonk, NY: Sharpe, 2001).

18. "Workers" and "working class" as used here refer primarily to the socialist proletariat as conceptualized by the CCP prior to the late 1980s—workers in state-owned and urban collective firms.

19. These two terms are not entirely satisfactory, nor is their usage by most scholars in the field. The concept of rights consciousness is less restrictive than that of legal consciousness, and most would likely agree that rights consciousness could easily exist in the absence of any rule of law. Legal consciousness, on the other hand, seems to imply a widespread knowledge of the law, accessibility of courts or other legal forums, and a shared belief in the efficacy and fairness of the legal system. These conditions have not been demonstrated to exist in the case of Chinese workers, and the indiscriminate use of the concepts of rights consciousness and legal consciousness by foreign scholars only obfuscates the empirical findings of their research.

20. Marc J. Blecher, "Hegemony and Workers' Politics in China," *China Quarterly,* June 2002, 283–303.

21. Blecher does not use this precise term, but his conception of hegemony seems to amount to the suppression of rights consciousness for workers.

22. Ching Kwan Lee, "The 'Revenge of History': Collective Memories and Labor Protests in Northeastern China," *Ethnography,* December 2000, 217–237.

23. See Feng Chen, "Subsistence Crises, Managerial Corruption, and Labour Protests in China," *China Journal,* July 2000, 41–63; William Hurst and Kevin J. O'Brien, "China's Contentious Pensioners," *China Quarterly,* June 2002, 345–360.

24. See, for example, Dorothy J. Solinger, "Labour Market Reform and the Plight of the Laid-off Proletariat," *China Quarterly,* June 2002, 304–326; Dorothy J. Solinger, "Why We

Cannot Count the 'Unemployed,'" *China Quarterly,* September 2001, 671–688; Solinger, "The View from Wuhan: China's Uncountable Unemployed," *China Economic Quarterly* 6, no. 4 (2002): 34–39.

25. Thomas Bernstein and Xiaobo Lu, *Taxation without Representation in Rural China* (Cambridge: Cambridge University Press, 2002).

26. Dorothy J. Solinger, *Contesting Citizenship in Urban China: Peasant Migrants, the State, and the Logic of the Market* (Berkeley: University of California Press, 1999).

27. See Li Zhang, *Strangers in the City: Reconfigurations of Space, Power, and Social Networks within China's Floating Population* (Stanford, CA: Stanford University Press, 2001).

28. See Lowell Dittmer and Xiaobo Lu, "Organizational Involution and Socioeconomic Reform in China: An Analysis of the Work Unit," in Lowell Dittmer, Haruhiro Fukui, and Peter Lee, eds., *Informal Politics in East Asia* (New York: Cambridge University Press, 2000); Xiaobo Lu, *Cadres and Corruption: The Organizational Involution of the Chinese Communist Party* (Stanford, CA: Stanford University Press, 2000); Xiaobo Lu, "Booty Socialism, Bureaupreneures, and the State in Transition: Organizational Corruption in China," *Comparative Politics,* April 2000, 273–294.

29. Jean C. Oi, *Rural China Takes Off: Institutional Foundations of Economic Reform* (Berkeley: University of California Press, 1999).

30. Joseph Fewsmith, *China since Tiananmen: The Politics of Transition* (Cambridge: Cambridge University Press, 2001).

31. Frank Dikotter, *The Discourse of Race in Modern China* (Stanford, CA: Stanford University Press, 1992); Michael J. Sullivan, "The Impact of Western Political Thought on Chinese Political Discourse on Transitions from Leninism, 1986–1992," *World Affairs,* Fall 1994, 79–92; see also Neil Renwick and Qing Cao, "China's Political Discourse towards the Twenty-first Century: Victimhood, Identity, and Political Power," *East Asia,* Winter 1999, 111.

32. Geremie R. Barme, *In the Red* (New York: Columbia University Press, 1999); Geremie R. Barme, *Shades of Mao* (Armonk, NY: Sharpe, 1996).

33. Thomas B. Gold, "China's Private Entrepreneurs: Small-Scale Private Business Prospers under Socialism," *China Business Review,* November–December 1985, 46–50; Thomas B. Gold, "Gorilla Interviewing among the *Getihu,*" in Perry Link, Richard Madsen, and Paul G. Pickowicz, eds., *Unofficial China: Popular Culture and Thought in the People's Republic* (Boulder, CO: Westview, 1989), 175–192; Gold, "Urban Private Business in China," *Studies in Comparative Communism,* Summer 1989, 187–202; Gold, "Urban Private Business and Social Change," in Deborah Davis and Ezra Vogel, eds., *Chinese Society on the Eve of Tiananmen: The Impact of Reform* (Cambridge, MA: Council on East Asian Studies, Harvard University, 1990), 157–178; Gold, "Urban Private Business and China's Reforms" in Richard Baum, ed., *Reform and Reaction in Post-Mao China: The Road to Tiananmen* (London: Routledge, 1991), 84–103; Victoria E. Bonnel and Thomas B. Gold, eds., *The New Entrepreneurs of Europe and Asia: Patterns of Business Development in Russia, Eastern Europe, and China* (Armonk, NY: Sharpe, 2001).

34. David L. Wank, *Commodifying Communism* (Cambridge: Cambridge University Press, 1999); Wank, "The Institutional Process of Market Clientelism: *Guanxi* and Private Business in a South China City," *China Quarterly,* September 1996, 820–838.

35. Kenneth Foster, "Embedded within State Agencies: Business Associations in Yantai," *China Journal,* January 2002, 41–66.

36. See Gordon Chang, *The Coming Collapse of China* (New York: Random House, 2001), for a dire interpretation of these implications.

37. Margaret M. Pearson, *Joint Ventures in the People's Republic of China: The Control of Foreign Direct Investment under Socialism* (Princeton, NJ: Princeton University Press, 1991); Margaret M. Pearson, "The Janus Face of Business Associations in China: Socialist Corporatism in Foreign Enterprises," *Australian Journal of Chinese Affairs,* January 1994, 25–46.

38. Anita Chan, *China's Workers under Assault* (Armonk, NY: Sharpe, 1999).

39. See: Yasheng Huang, *Selling China: Foreign Direct Investment during the Reform Era* (Cambridge: Cambridge University Press, 2003).

40. One example of such a work from the study of a different part of the world (and a different era) is Peter Evans, *Dependent Development: The Alliance of Multinational, State, and Local Capital in Brazil* (Princeton, NJ: Princeton University Press, 1979).

41. Lowell Dittmer and Samuel Kim, eds., *China's Quest for National Identity* (Ithaca, NY: Cornell University Press, 1993).

42. Yong Deng, "Escaping the Periphery," in Weixing Hu, Gerald Chan, and Daojiang Zha, eds., *China's International Relations in the Twenty-first Century* (Lanham, MD: University Press of America, 2000), 41–70.

43. Alastair Iain Johnston, *Cultural Realism: Strategic Culture and Grand Strategy in Chinese History* (Princeton, NJ: Princeton University Press, 1995); see also Xuezhi Guo's important book, *The Ideal Chinese Political Leader: A Historical and Cultural Perspective* (Westport, CT: Praeger, 2002), which compares the realist and the Confucian perspectives (but is not limited to foreign policy).

44. Michael Swaine and Ashley Tellis, *Interpreting China's Grand Strategy: Past, Present, and Future* (Santa Monica, CA: RAND Corp., 2000).

45. Allen S. Whiting, "China's Use of Force, 1950–1996, and Taiwan," *International Security,* Fall 2001, 103–132.

46. See Yongnian Zheng, *Discovering Chinese Nationalism in China: Modernization, Identity, and International Relations* (New York: Cambridge University Press, 1999); Baogang He and Yingjie Guo, *Nationalism, National Identity, and Democratization in China* (Aldershot, UK: Ashgate, 2000).

47. See Yufan Hao and Guocang Huan, eds., *China Views the World* (New York: Pantheon, 1989); Allen Whiting, *China Eyes Japan* (Berkeley: University of California Press, 1989); David Shambaugh, *Beautiful Imperialist: China Perceives America, 1972–1990* (Princeton, NJ: Princeton University Press, 1991); Daojiang Zha, "Chinese Understanding of International Political Economy," in Weixin Hu et al., eds., *China's International Relations in the Twenty-first Century,* 117–142.

48. See Robert K. Merton, *Social Theory and Social Structure* (New York: Free Press, 1968); Merton, *On Theoretical Sociology: Five Essays* (New York: Free Press, 1967).

49. Edward S. Steinfeld, *Forging Reform in China: The Fate of State-Owned Industry* (Cambridge: Cambridge University Press, 1998); Dorothy J. Solinger, "Clashes between Reform and Opening: Labor Market Reform in Three Cities," in Bruce Dickson and Chao Chienmin, eds., *Remaking the Chinese State: Strategies, Society, and Security* (London: Routledge, 2001).

50. Steinfeld's work is thin on the ground (in all three of the cases he examines, particularly Ma'An Shan), and he does not do a good job of linking back to any larger issues other than the already confused property rights debate. Solinger's work is based primarily on a sin-

gle-city case study of Wuhan; the other cities are added to better situate the one case she can really tell her readers anything new or subtle about.

51. There are, of course, a few important exceptions to this claim. Much of the work of William Parish, Martin K. Whyte, and a number of economists (e.g., Thomas Rawski) was largely quantitative, even before 1990. However, most of this earlier quantitative work was primarily based on descriptive statistics and the use of either émigré interviews or official statistical data.

52. See Andrew Nathan and Tianjian Shi, "Cultural Requisites for Democracy in China; Findings from a Survey," *Daedelus,* July 1993, 95–123; Tianjian Shi, *Political Participation in Beijing* (Cambridge, MA: Harvard University Press, 1997); Melanie Manion, *Retirement of Revolutionaries in China: Public Policies, Social Norms, Private Interests* (Princeton, NJ: Princeton University Press, 1993); Dali L. Yang, *Calamity and Reform in China: State, Rural Society, and Institutional Change since the Great Leap Famine* (Stanford, CA: Stanford University Press, 1996).

53. See Tianjian Shi, "Cultural Values and Democracy in the People's Republic of China," *China Quarterly,* June 2000, 540–559; Dali L. Yang, *Beyond Beijing: Liberalization and the Regions in China* (London: Routledge, 1997); Melanie Manion, "Chinese Democratization in Perspective: Electorates and Selectorates at the Township Level," *China Quarterly,* September 2000; Wenfang Tang and William Parish, *Chinese Urban Life under Reform: The Changing Social Contract* (Cambridge: Cambridge University Press, 2000); Pierre Landry, "Markets, Performance, and the Political Fate of Chinese Mayors" (paper presented at the 2002 annual meeting of the American Political Science Association, Boston, August 29–September 1, 2002).

54. Mary E. Gallagher, "Contagious Capitalism: Globalization and the Politics of Labor in China" (Ph.D. diss., Princeton University, 2001); Yong-Shun Cai, "The Silence of the Dislocated: Chinese Laid-off Employees in the Reform Period" (Ph.D. diss., Stanford University, 2001); Ethan Michelson, "Email to Ask If Filed Already!" (Ph.D. diss., University of Chicago, 2003).

55. Parish and Whyte.

56. For example, Anita Chan, Richard Madsen, and Jonathan Unger, *Chan Village under Mao and Deng,* rev. and enl. ed. (Berkeley: University of California Press, 1992).

57. See, for example, Elizabeth J. Perry, *Shanghai on Strike: The Politics of Chinese Labor* (Stanford, CA: Stanford University Press, 1993); Elizabeth J. Perry and Li Xun, *Proletarian Power: Shanghai in the Cultural Revolution* (Boulder, CO: Westview, 1997).

58. See Elizabeth Remnick, "The Significance of Variation in Local States: The Case of Twentieth China," *Comparative Politics,* July 2002, 399–418; Mark Frazier, *The Making of the Chinese Industrial Workplace: State, Revolution, and Labor Management* (Cambridge: Cambridge University Press, 2002).

59. Susan Whiting, *Power and Wealth in Rural China: The Political Economy of Institutional Change* (New York: Cambridge University Press, 2001).

60. However, these works still draw larger arguments than their evidence allows. In particular, Frazier's omission of the Northeast from his study of industrial organization in pre- and post-1949 China and Remnick's similar failure to consider inland cities where little or no foreign influence occurred undermine attempts to make claims about processes that supposedly unfolded across the entire country in various periods.

I

LEADERSHIP CHANGE AND ELITE POLITICS

2

Leadership Coalitions and Economic Transformation in Reform China

Revisiting the Political Business Cycle

LOWELL DITTMER AND YU-SHAN WU

The informal dimension has always been of paramount importance in Chinese politics. This was the case when Mao Zedong was in command and, despite all attempts to minimize its impact, it has remained the case since his demise. Yet it may be argued that the nature of informal politics has changed in significant respects in the course of reform. How should we approach this phenomenon? With the People's Republic of China (PRC) moving to a new stage of political development, can we provide an analysis that is valid in both historical periods? These are the questions this chapter attempts to answer.

We argue that just as Chinese politics as a whole has been changing to reflect the economic shift from plan to market and from public to private ownership, elite factionalism has been evolving as well. Whereas a model of hybrid reform is best suited to the current Chinese economy, a *modified factional model* is the most useful analytical tool for us to understand elite politics in the PRC at its present stage of development. Our most basic change in the original model is that Chinese factionalism should be seen to concern itself not only with particularistic group and member interests, but with economic and other policy issues. This introduces the possibility for us to analyze the relationship between macroeconomic issues in the public arena and factional disputes within the leadership core—an analysis we undertake in the second half of this chapter.

This change is a concomitant of the shift in the locus of major policy debate in the post-Mao period. We argue that reform united Cultural Revolution victims after Mao's death, becoming a consensus upon the defeat of Hua Guofeng and the neo-Maoist "small gang of four." But then, following Riker's minimal coalition principle, the reform coalition disintegrated.[1] Within the general reform camp, Deng Xiaoping's pro-growth group began to come into competition with Chen Yun's pro-stability group, pitting those who supported the agricultural sector in a broad sense (including township and village enterprises and collective enterprises) against a coalition of central planners on the State Council and ideological conservatives in the Central Committee's Propaganda Department. Occasionally entering the melee on behalf of the conservatives was a group of retired but influential veteran civilian and military cadres. Factional friction intensified on a schedule set by China's cyclical developmental path, which was a by-product of the synchronization of the business cycles (boom and bust) and the reform policy cycles (launching reform and receding to retrenchment). This synchronization was contingent rather than a priori: reform is not necessarily correlated with economic expansion, nor retrenchment with contraction. Synchronization exacerbated the intensity of the cycle, precipitating popular protest at some phases and subjecting the reformers to periodic criticism by conservative elites for having precipitated inflation, overheating, and other macroimbalances. The latter grouping used the opportunity to rein in reform excesses and purge reformers, temporarily stalling reform momentum. This is what observers witnessed in the 1980s.

After Jiang Zemin succeeded Deng and reined in the 1993–1994 inflation, the pro-growth and pro-stability elite groups narrowed their policy gap. An elite consensus emerged that called for deepened reform amid measured growth. The business and reform cycles thus diverged, as reform measures were taken in a context of macrostability. This then brought down fluctuations of the business cycle, prevented overheating, and thwarted the emergence of nationwide social unrest of the kind witnessed in the 1980s. Factional power struggle persisted in the top echelon, albeit in a different form and over different issues. Economic cycles still find their root in elite politics, not in the duel between pro-growth and pro-stability factions, but in the desire by the incumbent faction to buy off local supporters and boost regime status in public eyes at critical moments of political contestation. This is political business cycles with Chinese characteristics in the "deepened" phase of China's reform era.

Political business cycles (PBCs) are well-known in Western democracies.[2] However, the discovery of such cycles in state socialist countries in general,[3] and in China in particular, was more recent.[4] The case of China is of particular interest, for the basic economic structure of that country has been in the process of shifting from the traditional state socialist model to a market economy, and yet the political structure remains dominated by the Chinese Communist Party (CCP). In Western democracies the PBCs are election driven, as incumbent politicians tend to use fiscal and financial tools in their hands to boost the economy,[5] or to increase transfer payments when the elections draw near,[6] thus impressing the voters and tilting their choices toward the incumbents. What are the mechanisms that bring about PBCs in a reforming socialist economy like China, and will they continue to exist when market reform deepens? For those interested in the political economy of China, this is a question of great importance and interest.

Ten yeas ago we launched a model to explain the PBCs in China in the 1980s. We found the economic fluctuations (the boom–bust cycles) and the reform cycles (reform and retrenchment) are closely correlated and that both cycles are embedded in China's factional competition. When the reformers are in power, they pursue pro-growth reform policies, often at the risk of high price and social unrest. This renders reformers vulnerable and invites criticism from conservatives. When the factional balance tilts toward the conservatives, their retrenchment policies often restore stability but at the cost of sluggish growth and mounting unemployment. One then sees the reformers on the attack. The boom–bust cycles in China are thus synchronized with informal politics and factional competition between the reformers and the conservatives. Here one finds the mechanism of China's PBCs. The reform coalition restored ideological/policy consensus following the purge of the radical reform leadership in 1989, as formalized in the adoption of a "socialist market economy" at the Fourteenth Plenum, and the PBC lost some of its oscillatory choppiness, but the economic cycles have continued, in growing correlation with the cycle of formal party-state meetings. Elite factionalism has also continued, also synchronized with the meeting cycle.

The first section of this chapter provides a preliminary attempt to conceptualize informal politics, due to space limitations foregoing another review and critique of the rich literature on the topic.[7] The second section applies this model to factional behavior during the reform era, in an attempt to demonstrate the dynamic interplay of economic variables and factional political behavior. Our major purpose is to reconceptualize factional politics to understand the evolution of these groupings in a reform environment, making it possible to map out the relations between factional dynamics and PBCs. We are less concerned with providing an exhaustive explanation of the history of elite factionalism or of any particular factional episode than with offering a fresh theoretical perspective to analyze leadership dynamics in China's new political economy.

THE CHANGING NATURE OF
INFORMAL POLITICS

At the core of informal politics is "relationships." There are according to our conceptualization two types of relationship, one of which is value-rational, the other purpose-rational. (Although the terms are Weberian, *caveat lector*: whereas Weber categorizes actions, in the context of which a value-rational act is aimed at the realization of an absolute value, in reference to a relationship it has a different connotation.) A value-rational relationship is one that is valued as an end in itself, rather than being aimed at some other goal. Such relationships are typically built on connections *(guanxi)* of various sorts: shared kinship ties, common geographic origin, old school ties, or some other bonding experience. A purpose-rational relationship, on the other hand, is instrumental to the achievement of other ends. A purpose-rational relationship is typically formed with those colleagues, subordinates, and superiors with whom one has routine occupational contacts. Whereas the aggregation of one's value-rational connections forms an informal power base whereby one can exert informal power, or *shili*, one's occupational or "business" connections together comprise one's formal power base whereby official power *(quanli)* can be exercised. A formal power base is legal and explicit and can be mobilized for a wide range of organizational objectives. However, career officials will be reluctant to rally around a colleague when personal interests are at stake and when the risks of implication are high. They are likely to balance a colleague's requests against career and bureaucratic interests. Thus if the implicated cadre is to find support, this is the time when the informal network must be mobilized. To be sure, though one's web of personal connections are flexible and can be mobilized on a personal basis, it is implicit and illegal and may fail to rise to the task at hand. In any event, informal politics is defined in terms of the realm of *shili* and formal politics in the realm of *quanli*, and the two may interact in various complex ways.

There are two sets of concepts here. Value-rational relationships are to informal political networks and *shili* politics as purpose-rational relationships are to formal power bases and *quanli* politics. In each set, the higher-level concept is defined in terms of specific lower-level concepts: thus informal politics is defined in terms of informal political bases, which in turn is defined by value-rational relationships. However, the relationship between *quanli* and *shili* being rather fluid, there are many empirically marginal cases. *Shili*, an informal political base, may also be built on relatively purpose-rational relationships, as clients enter into reciprocal ties with a patron having personal interests high on their agenda. The other side of the coin is that whereas "old comrades-in-arms" types of *guanxi* may constitute important value-rational relationships for a veteran politician's informal power base, a patron may on occasion dispense with such connections—even in such a highly "informal" political power play as the Cultural Revolution, which saw Mao dump much of the Hunanese "mafia" in favor of a ideologically based coalition of mixed value-rational (e.g., Jiang Qing) and purpose-rational (e.g., Lin Biao) connections. During the reform era, more and more value-rational relationships seem to be transforming into purpose-rational ones, with the old ties built during the preliberation period either dying out or adapting to the new system of needs. Limiting informal politics to the wielding of *shili* is also somewhat problematic. It is usually true that an actor will be inclined to mobilize his formal bureaucratic constituency to fight for shared organizational interests in routine bureaucratic politics and resort to informal base mobilization only in a personal crisis, but politicians can and do occasionally mobilize their bureaucratic constituencies in pursuit of critical self-interests. Mao's purge of Peng

Zhen and the Beijing Municipal Party Committee at the outset of the Cultural Revolution or the sweeping purge of the People's Liberation Army (PLA) following the September 13 Incident or the demotion of the Yang family army in 1992 illustrate the close connection between politicians and their bureaucratic constituencies. Similarly, an informal power base can be used to advance formal, bureaucratic interests, as politicians "pull" personal connections *(la guanxi)* to staff their own bureaucratic machines. The institution of the "expanded conference," apparently unique to China among Communist party-states (at least in its scale and frequency) was devised precisely in order to allow scope for such informal mobilization.

Formal politics usually appears impersonal and policy oriented, while informal politics is more particularistic, often incorporating traditional or charismatic elements. However, empirically there are all sorts of mixed cases. The decision to name Lin Biao as the official successor to Mao Zedong at the Ninth Congress of the CCP in 1969 and to write it into the CCP constitution was a formal legal act, for example, but it was also a decision made by dint of Mao's charismatic authority in the overall context of a quasi-dynastic premortem succession struggle. In a society governed by legal-rational principles, formal politics normally conforms to these rules and appears objectively impersonal, as in the West. But in a political system that is essentially traditional or charismatic, legal-rational aspects tend to be subverted by the informal political environment. The boundaries of informal politics are thus to some extent elastic, not to be predetermined by Weber's ideal types but rather expanding to fit the political culture. Inasmuch as that culture has been evolving along with the surrounding political economy, the already loosely defined informal structure has been undergoing continual transformation.

The chief organizational embodiment of informal politics is the faction. According to Andrew Nathan, a faction is a vertically organized structure composed of face-to-face clientelist ties between leader and led. Chinese politics is said to be inherently factional in nature, notwithstanding Mao's attempt to put it on a more impersonal footing based on radical ideology. We need not be detained here by such issues as whether factional politics is intrinsically balance-of-power or a "game to win all or lose all," our point is that factions are the basic building bloc in the struggle for power, a point on which Nathan, Tsou, Pye, and other scholars concur. As Chinese politics evolved from Mao's radicalism to the pragmatism of the reform era, factionalism has taken new form but hardly disappeared.

The nature of factionalism has changed with the transformation of the political economy and bureaucratic culture in which it is embedded. Depending on ambient political circumstances, factions may have three sets of goals: security, material interests, and policy commitments. These goals constitute a natural hierarchy, with security the top priority, material interests the second, and policy preferences the third. Factional models, in the narrow sense of being exclusively concerned with personal security and career enhancement, were most applicable to the turbulent politics of the Cultural Revolution years. At that time people fell back on personal connections willy-nilly to defend their careers or even their lives.[8] This observation prompted

Lucian Pye to emphasize the paramount role of Chinese culture and psychologically ingrained security drives in bringing about rampant factionalism.[9] From our point of view, the Cultural Revolution made security (both political and physical) a scarce commodity for Chinese Communist elites, so it was only natural for them to orient their factional activities toward a quest to maximize it.[10] Yet policy packages might also be affected by career crashes, and bonds formed in situations of high stress tend to cohere. At those times when security is a less demanding concern, factional politics will not suddenly be replaced by bureaucratic politics or even by opinion groups, but the existing factional groupings will reorient their agendas toward goals that are at a lower level on the elite value hierarchy. Thus in the course of reform and opening to the outside world, Chinese factionalism has come to manifest itself mainly in groups competing for resources and material benefits, contributing greatly to official corruption at the lower levels and at higher levels to the growing inclusion of bureaucratic interests and other policy issues on factional agendas.

This revised model helps us explain the spread of factionalism. Despite a consistently repressive official view of factionalism throughout the Maoist and post-Mao eras, despite the forceful (and to a certain extent successful) efforts of Deng Xiaoping and Jiang Zemin to construct strong institutions and legal systems, we would suggest that the realm of informal politics may have actually expanded during reform, even as its political manifestation has declined in salience. There are several reasons for this. Deng Xiaoping's successful effort to introduce greater civility to CCP elite politics reduced the relevance of personal security as an incentive for the creation of a factional base, allowing diverging bureaucratic interests or policy preferences to play a greater role. Greater civility of course also implies higher tolerance for factional opposition. Second, despite having led periodic crackdowns against ideological deviations, Deng's greatest single contribution to "Marxism-Leninism Mao Zedong thought" was to infuse it with greater pragmatism: white cat, black cat, if it catches rats, it's a good cat; crossing the river by groping for stones; and so forth. Thus Mao's attempt to eliminate factionalism by demanding universal adherence to a common ideology, already rendered dubious by the ideological "line struggles" of the Cultural Revolution, was further attenuated by Deng's dismissal of ideology from relevance to a wide range of policy issues. The lower profile of ideology allows factionalism wider ambit for recruitment and maneuver. Finally, Deng's self-effacing refusal to occupy a formal position corresponding to his informal power base diminished the credibility of the formal structure, as did his mobilization of retired senior cadres in Politburo sessions in May 1989 to override what they all deemed the intolerable weakness and vacillation of the formal leadership in response to the Tiananmen protests. Although there was still a lingering ideological dimension to the arrest and trial of the Gang of Four (in 1976 and 1981 respectively) and perhaps to a lesser extent in the split between Deng and Hua Guofeng, the elimination of the "small gang of four" was followed by a broad ideological consensus in support of reform and opening to the outside world. This consensus however soon broke down into two elite coalitions prioritizing radical reform and rapid growth on the one side and more moderate reform and stability on the other.

The upshot is that factions have adapted to the changing political landscape of economic modernization by broadening their goals and participating in policy debates with increasing self-assurance. Given its base in personal *guanxi*, a faction can renegotiate its stance on policy issues with great tactical flexibility, as Deng demonstrated by his sudden reversals on Democracy Wall in February 1979 or on price reform in the summer of 1988. Yet factional goal displacement is partial and tentative, as survival remains sine qua non, and it is the career interests of the patron rather than the logic of material and ideal group interests per se that may be expected to dictate policy preferences in the crunch. This was illustrated by the fragmentation of the "reform faction" over the diverging personal interests of Deng Xiaoping, Hu Yaobang, and Zhao Ziyang in 1986–1989. In the context of "hybrid reform," in which economic reform continues apace while political reform remains restrained, it is not surprising that factions have undergone only partial transformation to bureaucratic politics.

Recognizing that factions remain the major building blocs of PRC power politics although they have expanded their goals, we can map out the interaction patterns between factional dynamics and shifts in China's political economy. In general terms, we see policy as the result of factional maneuver. The outcome of the policies then feeds back to impact on the resources at each faction's disposal. This causes shifts in the distribution of capabilities among factions and a different balance of power. Factions thus alternate at holding the power center in a continuous feedback process resulting in the alteration of old policies and the initiation of new ones.

In more specific terms, the ruling faction has a natural tendency to defend its record by pointing out the positive results of the economic and political policies it has initiated, while sidelined factions tend to stress the defects of those policies. The political–economic reality, however, strengthens the position of certain factions at the expense of others. If the policy outcome by and large is positive, the ruling faction's position is strengthened. If the outcome is negative, power may migrate to the opposing faction, which will now take a leading position in changing the old policy or initiating new ones. Because this is an ongoing feedback process, it is impossible to determine the ultimate cause of changes in the political economy. We are primarily interested in identifying the interaction patterns between factional politics and changing currents in the political economy. But first we need to capture the essence of the economic and political changes in reformist China. For that purpose, we find three economic and political cycles to be of particular importance.

THE POLITICAL BUSINESS CYCLE

In the Deng Xiaoping period a cyclical dynamic emerged in China's political economy. Three kinds of cycles are of particular interest to us: the business cycle, the reform cycle, and the movement cycle. The business cycle consists of two distinctive phases: boom and bust. The reform cycle likewise has two stages: reform and retrenchment. The movement cycle registers periods of relative social tranquility and bursts of protest. Of particular importance here is the need to differentiate between economic expansion and structural reform: they do not necessarily coincide.[11] For example, as Susan Shirk demonstrates, during the Maoist era economic campaign was accompanied by a crackdown on political dissent and by a contraction of consumption, whereas the economic retrenchment phase of the cycle was accompanied by political and intellectual liberalization (see figure 2.1).[12] Similarly, Hua Guofeng's Ten-Year Plan was a pro-growth strategy unaccompanied by economic reform or intellectual liberalization. The reason is that ideological policy could be used as "symbolic compensation" to various constituencies who might have otherwise opposed the policies being pursued.

In contrast, in the 1980s the synchronization of the business and reform cycles in the 1980s correlates economic expansion with reformist measures, and contraction or slower growth with retrenchment. This renders reformers vulnerable when the economy overheats, and conservatives subject to criticism when growth is sluggish. A policy shift thus ensues at the critical juncture (when the economy is overheated or stalled), and the cycle begins to move in the opposite direction, until it hits a point where another shift is required. The explosions of social unrest are less predictable, but seem most likely to occur when the economy has just suffered from overheating and is now undergoing a painful contraction to slower growth. This timing is bad for the reformers, who must now bear the responsibility of having inflated the economy and precipitated the ensuing contraction, both of which combine to enflame social protest.

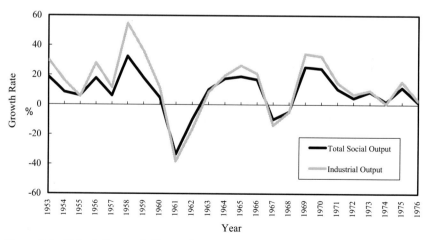

Figure 2.1   China's Economic Fluctuations, 1953–1976

During the 1980s, the PRC's business cycles coincided with its reform cycles. This was not the case at the end of the 1970s, when Deng inherited from Hua an investment-driven, high-growth economy (industrial growth surged to 14.6 percent in 1977 and 13.5 percent in 1978; the accumulation rate went up to 36.5 percent in 1978) and a Soviet-style central planning system, as embodied in Hua's ambitious ten-year plan launched in February 1978. Hua's rather ill-conceived plan for a long-cherished wish list of industrialization projects involved signing contracts with foreign investors worth several hundred million U.S. dollars in 1977–1978, threatening an enormous budget deficit. Deng and his radical reformers then joined forces with moderate reformers under Chen Yun's aegis to remove Hua's legacy. Investments and imports were slashed to bring down trade deficits and a rising inflation rate, while experimental reform measures were tried out (such as the 1983 "tax for profits," or *li gai shui*). Here the business cycle and the reform cycle diverged (contraction with reform). The efforts to cool down the economy were not successful when they were first introduced in 1979, in the name of "readjustment, restructuring, consolidation, and improvement." Hence the high inflation rate of 1980 (6 percent compared with 2 percent in 1979). But in 1981 state enterprise capital investment was actually cut to bring down inflationary pressure and trade deficits, including rescission of about a thousand joint venture contracts (e.g., the huge Baoshan case), and as a result GDP growth crashed to 5 percent that year and imports dropped by 12.4 percent in 1982. This brought about the trade surpluses of 1982–1983, not to be seen again until the end of the 1980s. In 1981 the annual growth rate of the wage bill and average wage were also down by 13.4 percent and 12.8 percent respectively, and industry grew by a mere 4.1 percent, as compared with the previous year's 8.7 percent.

Hua's economic legacy and political influence were effectively eliminated during the early 1980s (as finalized at the Twelfth Party Congress in 1982), as adjustment policies were accompanied by scattered reform measures. At this point, the linkage between reform and high growth, or between planning and contraction/sluggish growth, had not yet been established. The reformers under Deng and the moderates under Chen Yun saw eye to eye in halting Hua's great leap westward *(yang yao jin)* in the cooperative spirit of post–Great Leap Forward readjustment orchestrated by the same Deng and Chen.[13] In short, in this first post-Mao period, a Hua-initiated boom was curtailed by a Deng- and Chen-led bust (see figure 2.2) during which partial reform measures were tried out. The business cycle and the reform cycle were not yet synchronized.[14]

What split the reformers was the new wave of urban–industrial reform launched at the Third Plenum of the Twelfth Central Committee in October 1984 under the leadership of Deng and Zhao, which synchronized systemic reform and expansionary policies for the first time. The crux of the matter was a wage expansion, as the reformers tried to head off labor unrest in anticipation of the effects of price liberalization.[15] As a result, both consumption and investment surged in 1984, accompanied by a loose monetary policy (the state pumped into the economy RMB26.2

billion, more than the total money supply of the past thirty years, as investment surged 15 percent). The economy boomed while reform policies were being implemented. The two curves (the business cycle and the reform cycle) began to converge. Again, this synchronization was by no means inevitable, as clearly shown by the reform experience of Hungary between 1968 and 1972 (the New Economic Mechanism), which deliberately implemented tight wage controls while marketizing the economy.[16] In fact, price reform should occur when demand is slack. But as things stood with industry growing at a rate of 16.3 percent and 21.4 percent respectively, investment by 25 percent and 43 percent, and the wage bill by 20 percent during the same two years, overheating was inevitable. The radical reformers were naturally criticized for mismanaging the economy. Serious policy differences gradually emerged between Deng, who favored growth above all, and Chen, who considered stability the paramount goal. All the ingredients for cyclical development were now in place.

When reform resulted in macroinstability (inflation, trade deficit), the conservatives under Chen demanded retrenchment, a "bird cage economy." Marketization was placed on hold. At the same time, tight monetary and fiscal policies were taken to restore stability in 1986. The business and reform cycles simultaneously moved in a direction opposite to the 1984–1985 one (see figure 2.2). The effects of contractionary policies began to appear in 1986, as imports grew by a mere 1.6 percent (compared with 54.1 percent in 1985), industry by a moderate 8.8 percent (from 18 percent the previous year), and the inflation rate dropped from 8.8 percent to 6.0 percent. The austerity measures this time were less successful than in 1981, as witness the 8.1 percent real-term average wage growth. But clearly the regime had done its best to cool down the economy.

In the second half of 1986, a tight economic situation was accompanied by lively debate on political reform. In the spring both Hu Yaobang and Deng Xiaoping made public statements suggesting that they were offering their reform constituency the prospect of political reform as symbolic compensation for economic retrenchment. The intellectuals responded with imaginative proposals, and the movement cycle began to kick in. University students began to demonstrate for various political and economic causes, utilizing the opportunities presented by various anniversaries and other public rituals to mobilize ("political disturbances" in figure 2.2). At this point the reform grouping split. The lenient attitude taken by Hu in handling these demonstrations cost him his political future, as Deng, his patron, sided with seventeen members of the Central Advisory Committee to remove him from the position of general secretary (and prospective succession to the informal position as "core") at an enlarged politburo meeting in late January 1987 ("reformer unseated" in figure 2.2). Here we see a wave of social unrest happening just as the economy experienced macroinstability and moved from boom to bust. Reform seemed to be bringing about not only an overheated economy but political turbulence. The ensuing period of "antibourgeois liberalization" in the spring and summer of 1987 exhibited conservative trends in both economic and political spheres. In short, both the business

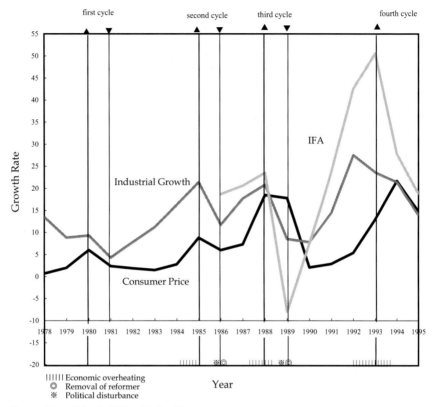

Figure 2.2   China's PBCs: Under Deng

cycle and the reform cycle took a sharp downturn in 1986, which was exacerbated by the political turbulence at the end of that year. Deng adopted his now characteristic posture of economic radical and political reactionary, consigning "bourgeois liberals" to political oblivion.

Since high growth is the paramount consideration of the leading reformist faction under Deng, one would expect expansionary policies to be taken once stability had been achieved. This was the case in 1987–1988, when the radical reformers rallied around Zhao Ziyang, Hu's successor designated by Deng, to pursue ownership reforms in industry, foreign trade, and investment, and finally a major price reform. All economic indicators went up simultaneously. Industry grew by 17.7 percent in 1987, and another 20.7 percent in 1988, while inflation rose by 7.3 percent and 18.5 percent in the same two years (despite an abortive two-tights policy—*shuanqjin zhengce*—in the autumn of 1987 that attempted to halt the trend).

Again, reform was accompanied by expansion and soon overheating. By the fall of 1988 the inflationary situation as touched off by a badly timed price reform got so bad (50 percent per annum) that the reformers were forced to reverse course. As in the last cycle, reform measures were blamed for macroinstabilities, and austerity with retrenchment *(zhili zhengdun)* took command. Both the business cycle and the reform cycle went into a tailspin. In the following year economic hardship and popular discontent over political suppression and official corruption brought about unprecedented social unrest, ignited by Hu's death. This culminated in the confrontation between student demonstrators and the Communist Party, and finally in the bloody suppression near Tiananmen Square on June 4 ("political disturbance" in figure 2.2). Again just as in the past cycle, radical economic reform was blamed for causing first economic instability, then political turbulence. This time Zhao was removed (again, following the pattern of 1987), with his patron abandoning him and siding with the conservatives, using irregular procedures and intervention by the octogenarians at an enlarged Politburo meeting in June 1989 (followed this time by convention of a Central Committee plenum, displaying greater sensitivity to constitutional norms) ("reformer unseated" in figure 2.2). Zhao's fall was accompanied by a sweeping purge of the radical reform bloc, including three full members of the Secretariat: Hu Qili, Rui Xingwen, and Yan Mingfu.

Zhili zhengdun lasted for three years. A protracted period of austerity was needed to combat the worst macroimbalances since reform started in the late 1970s. The inflation rate soared as high as 17.8 percent in 1989 (25.5 percent for the first half of the year). The country's foreign indebtedness reached US$41.3 billion at the end of 1989. Approved foreign direct investment dropped by half from the third quarter of 1989 to the first quarter of 1990, while total investment dropped to near zero for 1990. Foreign exchange reserves dropped to the 1987 level. However, the outward economic strategy initiated by Zhao in 1988 successfully oriented China's coastal economy toward export expansion, and the trade imbalance was redressed as exports surged and control over imports was recentralized and tightened. The PRC was able to achieve a trade surplus of US$8.7 billion in 1990, for the first time since 1983. Foreign exchange reserves jumped from US$17 billion at the end of 1989, to US$28.6 billion at the end of 1990, to US$40 billion in the third quarter of 1991. However, *zhili zhengdun* had its cost, as the economy actually stopped in the first quarter of 1990. Thus economic retrenchment again was paired with a bust. Although from a strictly economic perspective this period would have been ideal for price reform, that was not on the conservative agenda. The reform cycle and the business cycle remained synchronized.[17]

Deng and the reform bloc, severely attenuated at the center but still strong at the provincial level, grew impatient with sluggish growth, though trade performance had been much improved by a successful shift to export expansion, accumulating foreign exchange reserves of nearly US$43 billion by February 1992.[18] In the winter of 1990–1991, Deng formed an alliance with Shanghai party secretary Zhu Rongji and launched a propaganda drive for economic reform in Shanghai (the "Huangfu Ping" articles in *Jiefang Ribao*). Roughly at the same time, industrial growth accelerated significantly in the third quarter of 1990.[19] This attempt to stimulate another boom fizzled out, however, partly because the unsuccessful August Soviet coup attempt followed shortly by the collapse of the Soviet Union excited CCP paranoia and reinforced conservative misgivings about reform. But one year later, Deng's skillfully publicized tour to Wuchang, Shenzhen, Zhuhai, and Shanghai ushered in a new wave of reform measures, again accompanied by a loose monetary and fiscal policy (the narrower monetary index, M1, is estimated to have grown by 40 percent in 1992, M2 by more than 30 percent). The economy grew rapidly in 1992 and 1993 (by 12.8 percent and 13.4 percent respectively, compared to 3.9 percent in 1989, 5 percent in 1990, and 7 percent in 1991), mainly driven by an investment boom, especially in assets such as the real estate and the new stock market, again raising the specter of inflation (officially 3.4 percent in 1991, 6 percent for 1992, 14.5 percent in 1993 but 19.5 percent in the 35 largest cities). For a while it seemed that this time the leadership had contrived a way to avoid the twin deficits, thanks to the shift to export promotion and more rigorous fiscal policies. But by 1993, as in 1979–1980, 1984–1985, and 1987–1988, a surge in merchandise imports (plus the flight of capital through Hong Kong) had precipitated a deficit of more than $12 billion, dropping from a surplus of about 3.5 percent of GDP in 1991 to a deficit of 2 percent in 1993.[20] Meanwhile price reform resumed, dropping the number of state-controlled commodity prices from 737 in 1991 to only 89 by 1992 (20 percent of the total). This all led to a spiraling budget deficit (US$3.45 billion, four times that of 1992), which China's Finance Ministry expected to triple (to $7.7 billion) by 1994.

Clearly China had moved into another boom phase in its business cycle. And, as in the past, this seemed to benefit the reformers in the short term. But the regrouped reform coalition, learning from the 1980s, focused more presciently on bringing inflation under control without the crashes and subsequent layoffs that had precipitated mass protests in 1986 and 1989, in other words, a "soft landing." Zhu Rongji, the "great rectifier" whom Deng brought from Shanghai to serve as vice premier and informal economic czar, sacked the governor of the People's Bank of China in July 1993 and assumed command himself. Zhu then issued a 16-point austerity program designed to control government spending, restore control of the economy to Beijing, and impose a tight monetary policy in several industries, notably real estate. This macromanagement of the economy *(hongguan tiaokong)* lasted three months, though not until the end of the year did the policy impact decisively hit home, as growth of fixed asset investment dropped 75 percent in 1994 from the previous year. Excess demand and asset-price inflation were also curbed. Price inflation was slower to respond (hitting 22 percent in 1994, 15 percent in 1995) but finally declined as well, culminating in 1997–1998 in a deflationary trend. The "soft landing," though less severe than in the 1980s, was accompanied by a greater decline in GDP growth than considered optimal (GDP growth slowed to 11.8 percent in 1994 and 9.5 percent in 1995, hitting a low of 7.8 percent in 1998 according to official statistics, which most China economists however considered an overestimate by several percentage points).[21]

Even during this period of "soft landing," when select sectors of the economy were cooled down, the government did not apply the brakes on reform. Under Zhu Rongji's guidance, the Chinese economy went through a bust in the business cycle, without however simultaneously sliding backward in the reform cycle. The business cycle and the reform cycles were desynchronized. The post–Fourteeth Congress Chinese leadership seemed determined to deepen reform while keeping the growth rate in check. Here one finds the gradual dissolution of the pro-growth versus pro-stability cleavage that characterized elite politics and the Chinese PBCs in the 1980s.

The post-1995 recession, combined with the impact of the Asian financial crisis in 1997–1998, persuaded the government once again to increase investment, now focusing on infrastructure investment (as we explain below). Here the convening of the Fifteenth Congress played a central role. From 1998 to 2000 the government spent $55 billion on infrastructure and other investment projects. The result was that the public sector's share of fixed asset investment (which had been declining) increased again from just over 50 percent in 1998 to nearly 75 percent in 2000. The banks were also encouraged to increase loans to SOEs, which correspondingly added capacity, their output rising well ahead of overall GDP growth.[22] Accompanying the convening of the Sixteenth Congress in 2002, GDP growth accelerated to 9.1 percent in 2003 and 9.5 percent in 2004, though again, many China economists consider this official statistic an underestimate. And again the center, now under the fourth generation leadership of Hu Jintao and Wen Jiabao, responded, initially by imposing sector-specific constraints on key bottleneck areas, eventually moving to more sweeping macroeconomic controls (discussed below).

COMPARING PRE- AND POST-TIANANMEN PBCs

The post-Tiananmen Chinese political business cycle (PBC) still exists, and as in the first reform decade, it still reflects the interplay of underlying political (and economic) forces. The Party Congresses of 1992 (Fourteenth Congress), 1997 (Fifteenth Congress), and 2002 (Sixteenth Congress) all witnessed upsurges in investment in fixed assets (IFA) that in following years fell precipitously. In the period leading to the three congresses there were growing indications of power competition between different factions. Yet the PBCs differ from their counterparts in the 1980s in at least two respects: the new PBCs are milder than the old ones (yet still clearly discernible) and they are synchronized with Party Congresses, indicating a higher degree of institutionalization, in conformity with the foregoing Soviet pattern.[23]

As far as the first aspect is concerned, the PBCs in the 1990s are milder mainly for two reasons.[24] First, because the Chinese elite, learning from their experience, took pains to curb cyclical fluctuations and to brake the economy on the first sign of overheating.[25] Here one found an unmistakable learning process. As mentioned earlier, a consensus had gradually emerged that emphasized stability, but not at the expense of structural reform. Second, the proportion of the Chinese economy under direct state control has been shrinking, thus reducing the impact of the state-owned enterprise (SOE) sector which is particularly prone to cyclical investment hunger. (According to Hu Angang, central government expenditure as a proportion of GDP has shrunk from 31.2 percent in 1978 to about 18.7 percent by 1990, 16.2 percent in 1993, 11.8 percent in 1994; the state budget deficit is relatively small and already heavily impacted.)[26] As a result, the average annual inflation rate was down from 7.3 percent in the 1980s to 6.1 percent in the 1990s. If one compares the three "landings" of 1985–1986, 1988–1989, and 1994–1995, one finds for the two "hard landings" of the 1980s, inflation was brought down only with significant loss in growth. In 1985–1986 inflation was down by 2.8 percent but GDP was down by 4.7 percent. In 1988–1989 the retrenchment *(zhili zhengdun)* brought down inflation by a meager 0.7 percent and yet the growth rate suffered a 7.2 percent contraction. In comparison, the "soft landing" of 1994–1995 reduced inflation by an impressive 6.9 percent at the expense of only 2.1 percent growth cut. Clearly this displays much greater efficacy in controlling inflation at much less cost in growth.[27] During Jiang Zemin's era, China has been able to sustain respectable growth with price stability (see figure 2.3).[28] At the same period of time, China continued deepening its economic structural reform, culminating in the 2001 entry into WTO and the ensuing liberalization policies and pledges to further open up the economy. To pursue reform in the context of macrostability means less danger of overheating and

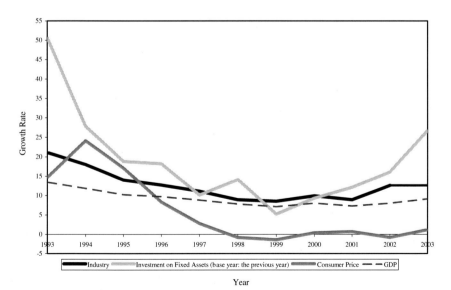

Figure 2.3   Still PBCs in Post-Tiananmen Period?

large-scale social unrest. The Jiang-Zhu leadership was thus immune from the fate of their reform predecessors in the 1980s who were removed from power for the economic and social disturbances caused by the synchronization of reform and expansion. However, we still detect unmistakable efforts to manipulate GDP growth when it is deemed expedient politically. Political manipulation of growth is less perceptible because of reduced state capacity, heightened elite consciousness of cycle damage to the economy, and external economic factors (such as the Asian financial crisis, and a growing proportion of GDP accounted for by foreign-invested enterprises [FIEs] and hence world market vicissitudes).[29] Yet despite these changes, GDP growth surges remain primarily investment-driven, expanding faster than either retail sales consumption or per capita income, and the state sector continues to dominate the country's investment activities, drawing on an exceedingly high rate of domestic savings (38 percent, as of 1985–1992) as funneled through state-owned banks.[30] As will be seen in the following discussion, PBCs are still clearly discernible with proper indicators.

The second aspect of the contrast between the old and new Chinese PBCs is increasing political institutionalization since the beginning of the 1990s. During this period, Party Congresses provide the critical arena for political competition to play out, and informal factions are still the major actors in this game. The three congresses saw Jiang and his Shanghai gang deal with residual old guard resistance from the second generation (the "Yang family army") in 1992, with Jiang's cogeneration rivals (Qiao Shi and Chen Xitong) in 1997, and with fourth generation successors (Hu Jintao and the like) in 2002. The three congresses thus provided arenas for factional battles between Jiang's Shanghai gang on the one hand, and three successive challenges to Jiang's authority on the other. In each case, investment policy was manipulated to elicit political support from the local and provincial forces mobilized to convene and legitimize such periodic adjustments. In sum, the new PBCs differ from the old ones in that they are milder, and that they are synchronized with Party Congresses (whereas the old PBCs were more violent and did not correspond well with Party Congresses), but they are still embedded in the political power game.[31]

Measured by the growth of total investment in fixed assets (IFA), the Chinese economy since the beginning of the 1990s has experienced three cycles that peaked in 1993, 1998, and 2003, as seen in figure 2.4. These are exactly the years of the National People's Congress (NPC) that always follow the Party Congress convened the previous year. The Party Congresses are in turn scheduled to convene one year after the end of each five-year plan (FYP) (e.g., the Eighth FYP ran from 1991 to 1995, the Ninth FYP from 1996 to 2000, the Tenth from 2001 to 2005, and so on), though this is presumably of diminishing importance, as the central plan now accounts for only about 7 percent of GDP (as of 1997). One can convincingly argue that the surges in IFA are directly linked with the convening of the national conferences of the CCP and the NPC.[32] Since the NPCs typically endorse the decisions reached at the preceding Party Congresses, the coincidence of IFA surges and the NPCs can be explained by the time lag between expansionary policies reached in the previous year and their effect on IFA. The factional competition preceding the Party

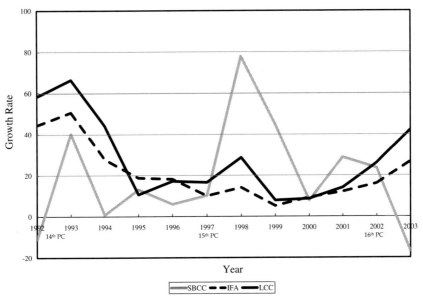

Figure 2.4   The Post-Tiananmen PBCs

Congresses sets the stage for the adoption of expansionary fiscal policies by the elite, who need the support of local officials and the general public at the culminating political moment when the results of elite competition are made public.

Although the IFA fluctuated in sync with political cycles, we find that the 1997–1998 surge was less marked than in 1992–1993 and 2002–2003. If we compare the peak year and the previous year, we find the 1997–1998 surge in IFA was only 4 percent, compared with 6.2 percent in 1992–1993 and 10.6 percent in 2002–2003. If we analyze the sources of IFA, we find the state has played a limited role in the period under consideration. The state budget typically accounted for less than 10 percent of total IFA, while state-directed bank loans accounted for less than 30 percent; the state thus controls a still commanding but minority share of IFA. Foreign and private investment, not under state control, constituted the bulk of total IFA. This means IFA may no longer be an adequate indicator to measure the intention of the state.

The major component of the IFA is capital construction (CC), which we contend is just such an indicator. If we concentrate on state budget as a source of CC, or SBCC, and map the ups and downs of SBCC, then we would have a firmer grasp of the government's fiscal policy (see figure 2.1). We find SBCC oscillated much more sharply than IFA, from − 11.6 percent to 77.8 percent in 1992–1998. The surge of SBCC in 1992–1993 was 51.8 percent, while in 1997–1998 it was 67.6 percent, indicating a tremendous increase in state contribution to capital construction at these two critical points. One puzzle, however, is the trajectory of SBCC in 2002–2003. It took a nosedive from 23.5 percent in 2002 to − 17 percent in 2003. Obviously the state has been braking the economy.

Thus we have a mixed picture. As far as total IFA is concerned, its trajectory coincided with the political cycles of Party Congresses perfectly. However, direct state contribution to total IFA is limited and diminishing. On the other hand, SBCC responded immediately to state manipulation. It fitted the 1992–1993 and 1997–1998 political cycles, but was out of sync with the 2002–2003 cycle. We contend that these two phenomena are in fact connected, that precisely because total IFA had reached the level that the leadership desired, there was no need to accelerate SBCC. On the contrary, being aware of the damage that a wildly fluctuating economy might inflict on society, the leadership began applying the brakes in the latter half of 2002, thus bringing down the SBCC growth rate for that and the following year.

A rational manipulator of the PBCs would concentrate on the economic indicators that are politically relevant at the key moments. For the Chinese leadership it was vital that the nationwide selectorate of elites assembled at Party Congresses witness the economy in good shape—growing and stable. The Chinese economy was not very vigorous in 1998–2001, with inflation down to 0 and below (i.e., deflation) and growth averaging 7.5 percent (a rate on the low side by Chinese standards). Thus when the Sixteenth Congress drew near, the leadership had every reason to accelerate its active fiscal policy *(jiji caizheng)* launched in the aftermath of the Asian financial crisis.[33] That expansionary policy played an important role to sustain China's growth when China's export market was dampened with a strong RMB (in 2001 export was 23 percent of Chinese GDP, five percentage points higher than world average).[34] Now with the Sixteenth Congress in the offing, it was politically imperative to give the economy a further boost. However, the revival of export market, entry into WTO, and large trade surpluses caused rapid accumulation of foreign exchange reserve in the latter half of 2001, which in turn brought about an abrupt increase of money supply, hence the threat of overheating.[35] In 2002 the economy continued to boom, registering an 8 percent growth that was unprecedented since 1997. Total IFA rose from 12.1 percent the previous year to 16.1 percent, surpassing the 1997–1998 level. Even though consumer prices remained low, even a casual observer would expect the economy to heat up rapidly. On the political front, the power transition at the Sixteenth Congress went smoothly, with Jiang and his generation passing political power to Hu Jintao and the fourth-echelon leaders, though Jiang still played mentor and wielded power from behind the scenes as chairman of the party and state military commission.[36] After the power transition, the post–Sixteenth Congress leadership was forced to tackle the imminent overheating problem. Since the economy had regained momentum, and "performed its duty" in the political cycle, the leaders now had to decide whether to apply the brakes.

As it turned out, the SBCC was slashed by 17 percent in 2003, compared with a 23.5 percent increase the previous year, demonstrating the state's determination to cool down the economy. However, total IFA continued to expand, as did industrial output, GDP, and consumer prices. Much had to do with the inability of the central government to rein in local officials, who were obsessed with investment expansion, as statistically indicated by rising local capital construction (LCC). The contrast between the − 17 percent growth of SBCC and the 42.1 percent positive growth of LCC is particularly telling (see figure 2.4), with the former indicating the central government's commitment to stability and the latter demonstrating local officials' preoccupation with rapid growth. The inability of the center to control the localities is evident here. The economy had shifted to high gear, and the Hu-Wen leadership found it imperative to adopt more assertive policies. At the third plenary session of the Sixteenth Central Committee held in October 2003, it was announced that perfecting the macroadjustment system *(wanshan hongguan tiaokong tixi)* is one of the major missions of China's market socialism. In November Premier Wen pronounced ten macroadjustment policies to cool down selective sectors of the economy. By 2004 *hongguan tiaokong* was in high gear, as the leadership was scared by a 9.7 percent GDP growth and a 43 percent IFA increase in the first quarter of the year. The macroadjustment policies included raising the interest rate and reserve rate, temporarily halting transfer of farm to nonfarm use, limiting investment in the steel, aluminum, cement and real-estate industries, and so on.[37] Despite these measures, China's economy continued to steam ahead as it had not done since the soft landing of 1996. The IFA grew by 26.7 percent and the GDP by 9.1 percent in 2003. In the first three quarters of 2004 the IFA grew by 28.9 percent and the GDP by 9.5 percent.

Comparison of the elite factional linkage to the PBC in the 1990s reveals at least three noteworthy differences. First, as it has institutionalized, elite factionalism has been characterized by increasing civility, paralleling developments in the Soviet Union following Khrushchev's secret speech at the Twentieth Congress of the Communist Party of the Soviet Union (CPSU) denouncing Stalin's elite incivility. Faction leaders were no longer publicly humiliated for ideological deviations or incarcerated but usually allowed to retire to a life of relative comfort. True, this trend was already set in motion by Deng Xiaoping, but the Gang of Four were still put on a show trial and given life prison sentences, and Zhao Ziyang remained under house arrest. In contrast, Yang Shangkun and Qiao Shi retired to the influential position of senior officials, sometimes even (discreetly) taking issue with the incumbent leadership. Qiao Shi, for example, gave speeches during the run-up to the Sixteenth Party Congress endorsing age limits (and implicitly derogating any extension of Jiang Zemin's term as general secretary). The result has been a return to the pre–Cultural Revolution norm of "inner-party struggle" (as originally expostulated by Liu Shaoqi) in which an impermeable barrier isolates intraelite discussions from public view, so that factional disagreements manifest themselves only when formally announced on the five-year schedule of the *liang hui*.

Second, as a lasting consequence of the brutal suppression of protesters on June 4, 1989, the movement cycle has not only detached itself from the PBC but completely vanished from the scene as a source of mass input into either policy decisions or elite mobility. Protests continue to occur at a local level concerning local grievances, but there has been no recurrence of contagious national mobilization on national issues; indeed, local protesters often appeal to central intervention against local abuses. Local elections also occur in the rural areas, but these too are exclusively concerned with local concerns. The fact that the nation's public calendar is now completely monopolized by the CCP is no doubt one reason the PBC is intercalated with the *liang hui* meetings. All this political calm has a lot to do with the elite's stability-cum-reform consensus, the desynchronization of the reform and business cycle, the prevention of overheating, and the absence of large-scale social unrest. The transformation of factions in the early 1990s was the focal ingredient in bringing about all the subsequent developments toward greater stability.

Finally, although elite factional conflict continues to exist, more genteelly conducted but still zero-sum in the sense that it culminates in one winning side, one losing side, and the involuntary retirement of the latter, it is no longer functionally related to factional interest in a particular phase of the PBC. During the 1980s, the pro-growth reform faction and the pro-stability moderate faction each had distinct viewpoints and preferences with regard to the PBC. The reformers prioritized rapid growth, marketization and the ideological liberalism (thaw, or *fang*) that typically accompanied marketization, and in building constituencies among those whose interests were positively affected by such developments (local elites, public intellectuals). The moderates continued to support central planning and the state-owned sector and disciplined adherence to ideological orthodoxy, and built constituencies within the planning and heavy industry ministries of the state council and the CC Propaganda Department. Each elite faction would support that phase of the cycle favorable to its bureaucratic and social constituency until that point in the cycle when continuation of that phase appeared obviously untenable, whereupon that faction would retire to the sidelines of policy making and the other faction would assume command and try to eject the rival faction. The most vulnerable faction in the long run proved to be the reformers, as the boom phase of the cycle tended to correlate with an increase in corruption, intellectual liberalism and dissent, ultimately culminating in grassroots-initiated mass protest movements, which an elite heavily populated by Cultural Revolution survivors considered intolerable.

If we examine the three major factional confrontations of the 1990s more closely, it is hard to detect any cleavage based on a functional division of labor. There is abundant evidence of Yang Shangkun's opposition to Jiang Zemin, which seems to have begun with his opposition to the appointment of Jiang to the position of chair of the Central Military Commission, pointing out Jiang's utter lack of military experience. This may have been essentially a fight for turf, but Yang had always been closer to Zhao Ziyang, whom he succeeded as party secretary of Guangdong Province during the Cultural Revolution; even when he opposed Zhao's stance on how to handle the Tiananmen protesters, as he had to do, he tried to induce Zhao to embrace the majority decision. And in the early 1990s, while Jiang formed a close bond with Li Peng and the Party elders in support of a reform hiatus and economic retrenchment (no doubt aware that his strongest backers for promotion had been Chen Yun and Li Xiannian), Yang antedated Jiang in support of Deng's attempts to revive reform momentum. Thus Deng decided during these disappointing years to dump both Jiang and Li at the forthcoming Fourteenth Congress and appoint Zhu Rongji or Li Ruihuan as premier and Qiao Shi as new party core. Yang was delegated to persuade Zhao to make a confession, after which he might be appointed chair of the Chinese People's Political Consultative Conference (CPPCC). The PBC was clearly in play, with Deng, as the swing vote, now shifting to support of the pro-boom reform position. And in his 1992 "voyage to the south" *(nanxun)* Deng did succeed in pushing the cycle to another boom phase. But Jiang, through extraordinarily adroit political maneuvers (and with the help of Zeng Qinghong), managed to reverse course and convincingly embrace reform, then to persuade Deng that Yang was plotting to take over the PLA by promoting over 100 factional constituents to high positions and that if Zhao were rehabilitated he would reverse verdicts on Tiananmen and blame Deng for the bloodbath. Jiang thereby managed to change the terms of the conversation from reform to power politics. Amazingly, this maneuver succeeded brilliantly: Yang Shangkun and Yang Baibing both found themselves sidelined at the Fourteenth Congress, giving Jiang uncontested control of the Central Military Commission. With the Yang family army out of the picture, the economy moved into boom phase now under control of a motley coalition of reformers and converted conservatives, who then proceeded to run the economy based on a hybrid middle-of-the-road policy of ongoing marketization and opening to the outside world plus political centralization and intellectual repression.[38]

Chen Xitong, Jiang's next factional challenger, had been like Yang an ideological conservative and strong supporter of the Tiananmen crackdown but also a staunch and consistent supporter of reform, embracing Deng's 1992 initiatives earlier and more vociferously than Jiang. Moreover, Chen had long been personally close to the Deng family, whose business interests dovetailed with those of his own family, providing him a measure of protection as long as Deng remained politically potent. But he had also been a consistent rival of Jiang Zemin, with his own formidable power base in the capital city. This factional dispute did not according to the available evidence involve the economic cycle at all, but simply power, also putting two major regional factional bases in contention. After some two years of diligent investigation (which he delegated to Zeng), Jiang finally succeeded in unearthing plausible evidence linking Chen's Beijing group to the corrupt activities of some State Security Bureau cadres down in Wuxi, who in turn were also linked to the giant Shougang steel plant in Beijing, and was able to dislodge and finally even imprison him on that basis, although proceedings did not finalize until the Deng family's business interests could be disentangled from the Shougang scandal and Deng himself had passed away. The fact that the legal case against Chen and especially his political associates was a strong one does not of course mean it was pursued on purely legal grounds.[39]

The case of Qiao Shi, who was forced out at the Fifteenth Party Congress as the first victim of the sudden new policy placing an age limit on Politburo membership (except for Jiang Zemin), also lacked visible linkage to any particular phase of the PBC. His career had been predominantly in the public security system, but he reportedly abstained on the decision to impose martial law at Tiananmen and upon his appointment as chair of the NPC at the Fifteenth Party Congress unveiled himself to be an ardent reformer. There he focused on building the legal system, on supervision of government organs by the NPC (and at the local levels by local People's Congresses), and on adherence to constitutional norms. It was in this capacity that Deng at one time considered him a plausible (and more progressive) candidate for core, and Qiao never disavowed interest. Meanwhile Qiao also continued to control the legal-security portfolio within the Politburo Standing Committee. He seemed to be positioning himself as Jiang's rival claimant to leadership of the reform agenda, as for example in 1996, when Jiang was pushing his "talk politics" *(jiang zhengzhi)* campaign, Qiao was concurrently pushing rule of law and the supremacy of the law. In a 1997 interview with *Le Figaro* during a visit to Europe Qiao revived Zhao's goal of separating party from government *(dang zheng fenkai),* shrinking the role of the party to appointments and ideological guidance, and the need for CCP decisions to go through the NPC for legal authorization.[40] Although Qiao had probably been appointed to the NPC chairmanship in order to keep the NPC in line, he seemed to be building the NPC into his own power base, building an independent institutional redoubt of an emerging *Rechtsstaat.* This was a period of some 32 percent of NPC deputies voting against or abstaining on Li Peng's cherished Three Gorges Dam project in 1992, and in 1993 endorsing Li Peng's nomination as premier with the same visible lack of enthusiasm (330 negative or abstaining votes). Whereas the NPC passed only 7 laws between 1966 and 1978, between 1979 and 1994 it passed 251.[41]

We would infer that whereas factional fights are still very much part and parcel of the PBC, which is manipulated by the victors to consecrate their wins, endorse their policy choices and evict their rivals, since Tiananmen the PBC no longer appears to have an intrinsic functional linkage to the policy positions of rival leadership factions. All of them (Jiang's Shanghai gang, Yang Shangkun, Chen Xitong, Qiao Shi, etc.) were pro-reform and pro-stability. In this sense, they inherited both the reformism of the pro-growth reform faction and the preoccupation with stability of the moderate, pro-stability faction of the 1980s. The rival factions of the 1990s were less heterogeneous than their predecessors. Their competition was less about policy agenda than about power, though factional rift was still linked to the PBC. The losing faction is functionally related to the boom phase of the PBC in the sense that this phase is artificially promoted to win popular endorsement of its demotion, but not in the sense that this faction opposed reform or even that particular phase of the cycle. The argument that factions have transmogrified into bureaucratic interest groups or advocates of a particular policy "line" may need to be reconsidered. In retrospect it also seems conceivable that the factional splits of the 1980s were focused not so much on the PBC itself as on how to respond to the mass movements in which it inexorably culminated. After Tiananmen the radical reformers were blamed for the turmoil and suffered downward mobility and a new policy consensus was built around accepting a "socialist market economy," chaperoned by a reinforced proletarian dictatorship. During the Jiang Zemin era, the mainstream faction assumes responsibility for every phase of the much less volatile and hence much less political damaging PBC, leaving rival factions to foment opposition on purely power-political grounds, appearing more opportunistic than their 1980s counter-parts.

To the extent that the institutionalization of factionalism still has an organiza-tional locus, it appears to have taken root in two directions. First, despite elite aware-ness of this tendency and the introduction over the years of numerous administrative countermeasures, there is a long-standing tendency to carve out quasi-autonomous institutional niches in the central apparatus to function as a base, from Lin Biao's reorganization of the PLA in the early 1960s to the "petroleum faction" *(shiyou pai)* in the heavy industrial and planning ministries in the early 1980s. The three most potent current exemplars are: (1) echoing the role of the *genro (yuanlao)* in Japan's Meiji restoration, the retired senior officials continue to function as a bloc in defense of a perceived interest in maintaining ideological values and traditions (though this now includes the age and term limits that forced their own retirements). Though deprived a formal base by the dissolution of the Central Advisory Commission at the Fifteenth Congress, the so-called immortals retain the formal rank last held before their retirement, with "class 1 guard service," access to classified documents and the right to be consulted by still active Politburocrats (or participate in expanded meetings, particularly during the annual summer retreats at Beidaiho).[42] (2) The Youth League group *(tuanpai)*, a younger faction consisting of those who served under Hu Yaobang (as did Hu Jintao) or later under Hu Jintao, share an interest in bureaucratic rejuvenation and generational turnover.[43] (3) the NPC, whose distinct institutional profile first emerged under Peng Zhen in 1983 (Peng stemmed from the factional network of Liu Shaoqi, a distinct pedigree from those of either Deng or Chen Yun) and continued under Qiao Shi, has come to stand for the rule of law. The long-term *telos* of the NPC (and to a lesser degree the CPPCC) has been to become an institutional counterweight to the Party's Central Committee in a more "democratic" central government. The second major emerging factional base has been the geographic base (e.g., the "Shanghai gang"), not as a primordial datum (place of origin, *tongxiang*) or even necessarily as a current power locus, but as a shared experience at a formative phase in one's career. To the extent that regional connections overlap with generalizable economic interests, we may see emerging an east coast grouping committed to rapid and relatively free market economic mod-ernization protecting the interests of the entrepreneurial elite versus a central-western-northeastern grouping committed to a revival of socialist ideals and the redistribution of the material benefits of reform to those left behind. Many other potential bases for factional organization exist, from family (e.g., the "princelings" or *gaogan zidi*) to the old school tie (e.g., the Qinghua clique), but for various reasons, none have been mobilized as operational political vehicles as effectively as have central bureaucratic niches or regional connections. As ever, the political fortunes of any of these groupings may be expected to wax or wane depending on a combination of the assets of the base and the political acumen of its elite representatives.[44]

As to the empirical agents of the PBC, those whose interests are directly affected by the boom and bust phases of the cycle and who lobby for an intensification or prolongation of "their" phase, these seem now to consist of the central economic authorities—primarily the central bank (PBC), the Ministry of Finance, the China Securities Regulatory Commission, the National Development and Reform Commission (former planning commission), and the heavy industrial ministries on the one side, versus the local industries and the local officials who represent their interests on the other. Decentralization and devolution began early in the 1980s under Deng as a way of short-circuiting central resistance to reform, and local industry has remained a consistent advocate of fiscal investment projects and liberalized monetary and credit policies. (To what extent local interests are nationally generalized or regionally differentiated will require further research.) Thus in the most recent boom, the surge in fixed asset investment was driven by local rather than central interests. For example, in the first three quarters of 2003, the central government's share of total government investment in fixed assets (GIFA) was only 11.8 percent, or ¥312.1 billion. That represents a 12 percent decline from the previous year, while local government's share of GIFA represented 88.2 percent of total GIFA (¥233.9.2 billion), a 40.7 percent increase from the previous year.[45] Since Zhao's purge and Deng's *nanxun*, these local interests have been decapitated of a powerful central factional patron, and this may conceivably be responsible for the less choppy PBC, as Zhu Rongji suppressed local interests with considerable vigor in his pursuit of "soft landings." During the five-year meeting cycle of the two congresses, when local interests converge in Beijing, the leadership, however, conceives an interest in a more fiscally magnanimous policy, which local interests eagerly exploit and protract.

CONCLUSION

This chapter argues, first, that Chinese informal politics is best characterized as factional politics. This assertion requires broadening the original definition of factionalism with respect to elite goals, as factions avail themselves of the window of opportunity opened in a more ideologically pragmatic political climate to pursue policies and power that both enhance their particular interests and make a plausible claim to advance the public interest. Yet we retain the main thesis of the approach: that *guanxi*-based, vertically organized, reciprocity-oriented political factions are the building blocs of Chinese informal politics. Factions can be used to promote different sets of elite goals, the most prominent of which are security, material interests, and ideological and policy commitments. At times when intraparty struggle is intense, and the fundamental value of personal security is not reasonably assured, factions are geared to security-maximization, as during the Cultural Revolution years. As politics is more routinized, and economic reform takes command, factions assume different form and serve the elite's desire for preferred policy goals (e.g., pro-growth versus pro-stability; radical reformers aiming at privatization versus moderate reformers aiming at only marketization), or for material benefits and power (see table 2.1). Meanwhile official ideology becomes more pragmatic and open-ended, allowing informal groups to make a plausible case that their policy preferences correspond to the public interest. Chinese informal politics remains factional in the sense that factions are the units of action, but not in the sense that ideology or security politics continues to dominate the political scene.

Second, during the Deng Xiaoping period, Chinese factionalism centered on broad policy issues (while also promoting personal material interests, which unites various factions in their support for Deng's open-door policy and breeds corruption) concerning growth versus stability of the economy under reform. On the one hand, Deng's radical reformers favor rapid growth, even at the expense of stability. On the other hand, the moderate reformers around Chen Yun consider stability the paramount goal *(wending yadao yiqie)*, even overriding considerations of growth. The synchronization of reform and business cycles, plus periodical social unrest occurring when the growth rate slumps, makes reformers and conservatives vulnerable to charges of mismanaging the economy for their respective policy preferences. During the first cycle, a Hua-led boom (the ten-year plan) was followed by a Deng- and Chen-led bust. Here a pro-growth conservative (i.e., neo-Maoist) leadership was blamed for an overheated economy.[46] Reform did not coincide with growth.

This was the last time business and reform cycles would diverge during the Deng period. The 1984 urban industrial reform started the second cycle, in which the lack of wage control and a general loose macroeconomic policy contributed greatly to inflationary pressure in the economy. The business cycle became synchronized with the reform cycle, and the reformers were blamed for the resultant imbalances. As Hua and the petroleum faction had been soundly defeated, Deng's pro-growth group came into increasing conflict with Chen's pro-stability group. The economy then was cooled down as the moderates gained the upper hand. The same scenario was repeated in the third and fourth cycles (1987–1989, 1990–1994), with reform consistently coinciding with a boom and overheating, and the following retrenchment accompanied by sluggish growth or contraction. Put together, the periods of intense reform efforts (from the Third Plenum of the Twelfth Central Committee in October 1984 to the abortive price reform in mid-1985; from the Thirteenth Party Congress in November 1987 to the disastrous price reform in May 1988; and from Deng's southern tour in January–February 1992 to the Fourteenth Congress) preceded hypergrowth and, in the second and third cycle, macroimbalances. Then came a conservative comeback (the austerity measures in 1986 and *zhili zhengdun* in 1988), political turbulence (the student unrest in the winter of 1986–1987 and the pro-democracy demonstrations in the spring of 1989), and the political demise

Table 2.1 Chinese Factionalism and PBCs

	Factional players	Primary factional goal	Distance between factions	Relation between business & reform cycles	PBC fluctuation and resulting social unrest
Cultural Revolution	Mao & cohort vs. the "revisionists"	Security	Great	Inverse	Great/Quelled
Deng Xiaoping	Pro-growth group vs. pro-stability group	Extent of reform and pace of growth	Medium	Synchronized	Great/Eruptive
Jiang Zemin	Shanghai gang vs. factional challengers	Distribution of resources	Short	Desynchronized	Mild/Limited

of a top reformer (Hu Yaobang in January 1987 and Zhao Ziyang in June 1989) (see figure 2.2). The economy was stabilized, but the sluggish growth prompted the reformers to launch an offensive, which initiated the period of intense reform of the next cycle. The expansion and contraction of the economy were attributed to the status of reform, as business cycles came to be considered epiphenomena of reform cycles. This perception acted to perpetuate fluctuations in reform policies, pitting Deng's pro-growth group and Chen's pro-stability group against each other. As long as the synchronization of the business and reform cycles continued, wide policy fluctuations driven by a politics of blame inevitably ensued.

During the Jiang Zemin period, policy making with regard to the maintenance and equilibration of the PBC seems to have been successfully isolated from the factional arena and monopolized by the center (in that sense, Jiang Zemin was, contrary to popular belief, a more powerful "core" than Deng Xiaoping, though he did not provide transformational leadership). This was greatly facilitated by an emergent elite consensus on reform cum stability. Although the PBC continued, as did factional disagreement leading to the ejection of losers from the magic circle, the PBC had little to do with the policy preferences of any factions. It was to a great extent caused by the center to justify its continued rule and to deny rivals any chance to challenge the status quo. As the reform and business cycles desynchronized, thus preventing overheating, one failed to observe social unrest of the 1980s magnitude (see table 2.1). Factionalism thus tended to crystallize around central bureaucratic niches and geographic bases as fought out by their proxies at the center, with the former representing some version of central interests and the latter representing the decentralizing trends that have characterized reform from the outset. To the extent that geographically based factions cohere and become a fount of economic policy reflecting the interests of those bases, we may conceivably witness the formation of coalitions of geographically based factions with complementary interests. Local interests still surge high. There are some indications that this is occurring, but the core and the centrally based factions will try to minimize any such tendency, and there are also strong centripetal forces reinforcing the power of a strong center.

We have argued that factionalism is an omniscient feature of Chinese elite politics, but it is highly flexible over time and circumstance. One crucial factional variable is obviously the PBC: factional rift tends to intensify during the transition from one phase to the other. Here we have two scenarios, one for the 1980s and one for the 1990s. In scenario one we see intensified factionalism during the high tide of a boom phase, when there will be conflict between advocates of continued expansion and critics of overheating; or during the low tide of a bust, when analogous strain may be anticipated between advocates of change versus stability, as we have tried to demonstrate. Scenario two is when the pro-growth versus pro-stability divide has by and large dissipated, replaced by the incumbent faction's manipulation of the PBC to justify its rule and to eject rival factions. But the PBC in these two scenarios is not the only variable. Factionalism covaries inversely with central leadership, which is still personalized in the PRC in the form of the "core." We would expect the power of the core to vary over the course of his term, beginning strong and tapering off as the end approaches (as was true in the case of both Deng Xiaoping and Jiang Zemin). Yet a sudden lapse in the health of the core can at any time trigger a premortem succession crisis. Finally, the cycle of mass participation tends to exacerbate informal politics, as rival factions contend to legitimate their leadership and policy programs before a mass audience. China has a long way to go toward democratic proceduralism, but an aroused mass still retains a potent legitimating power, capable of splitting a hitherto united leadership. During the 1980s, mass movements retained an element of grassroots spontaneity, as a carryover from the Cultural Revolution, usually tending to arise at transition points of the PBC, threatening to reinforce one side or other of the elite balance of power in unpredictable ways. Since Tiananmen, mobilizational entrepreneurism has been quelled, permitting the elite to ritualize mass participation in the five-year cycle of formal meetings of the two great congresses, which has in turn helped to put the PBC on a more regular schedule as well. In sum, factionalism may be more linked with one of the above factors at any given time than with other factors, but it remains the core of Chinese leadership politics.[47]

NOTES

The authors are deeply indebted to the research assistance of Ms Kai-lu Chi and Ms Rou-Lan Chen, and to the Berkeley Center for Chinese Studies for financial support. We wish to thank Rick Baum, Jing Huang, Peter Lee, Cheng Li, Kun-Chin Lin, Andy Nathan, Victor Shih, Dory Solinger, Susan Shirk, Dali Yang, and Suisheng Zhao for their helpful comments on earlier drafts of this chapter.

1. William H. Riker, *The Theory of Political Coalitions* (New Haven, CT: Yale University Press, 1967).

2. William Nordhaus, "The Political Business Cycle," *Review of Economic Studies* 42 (1975): 169–189; Edward R. Tufte, *Political Control of the Economy* (Princeton, NJ: Princeton University Press, 1978).

3. According to Bunce, new Soviet general secretaries tend to pump up public consumption in the period immediately following succession and then move toward less popular policies, once the succession crisis has been resolved. See Valerie Jane Bunce, "Elite Succession, Petrification, and Policy Innovation in Communist Systems: An Empirical Assessment," *Comparative Political Studies* 9 (1976): 3–41; Bunce, "The Succession Connection: Policy Cycles and Political Change in the Soviet Union and Eastern Europe," *American Political Science Review* 74 (1980): 966–977. For a critique, see Philip G. Roeder, "Do New Soviet Leaders Really Make a Difference? Rethinking the 'Succession Connection,'" *American Political Science Review* 79 (1985): 958–976.

4. Hu Angang, "Zhongguo zhengce zhouqi yu jingji zhouqi" [China's policy cycles and business cycles], *Chinese Social Sciences Quarterly* 8 (1994): 85–100; Hu Angang, *Zhongguo jingji bodong baogao* [Report on the fluctuations of China's economy] (Shenyang: Liaoning renmin chubanshe, 1994); Lowell Dittmer and Yu-Shan Wu, "The Modernization of Factionalism in Chinese Politics," *World Politics* 47 (1995): 467–494.

5. For an investigation of the political monetary cycle, see Nathaniel Beck, "Elections and the Fed: Is There a Political Monetary Cycle?" *American Journal of Political Science* 31 (1987): 194–216.

6. For a critique, see Thad A. Brown and Arthur A. Stein, "The Political Economy of National Elections," *Comparative Politics* 14 (1982): 479–497.

7. For comparative perspectives on informal politics, see L. Dittmer, H. Fukui, and Peter N. S. Lee, eds., *Informal Politics in East Asia* (Cambridge: Cambridge University Press, 2000).

8. Joseph W. Esherick and Elizabeth J. Perry, "Leadership Opportunity?" *Studies in Comparative Communism* 16, no. 3 (1983): 171–177.

9. Lucian Pye, *The Dynamics of Chinese Politics* (Cambridge: Oelgeschlager, Gunn & Hain, 1981).

10. This is an ideal type. Empirically speaking, elite power struggles were never entirely detached from policy even during the heyday of classic factionalism. For example, the prolongation of the Great Leap policy followed and resulted from the purge of Peng Dehuai in 1959, and the purge Liu Shaoqi, Deng Xiaoping, and other representatives of the "bourgeois reactionary line" coincided with (and helped facilitate) an across-the-board radicalization of public policy (amid considerable turmoil).

11. Here economic structural reform refers to a major policy effort to transform the economic structure, including Mao's ultraleftist economic campaigns and market reforms under Deng, Jiang, and Hu.

12. Susan Shirk, *The Political Logic of Economic Reform in China* (Berkeley: University of California Press, 1993), chap. 9.

13. Yin I-Ch'ang, "Ts'ung li-shih kuan-tien k'an ching-chi t'iao-cheng" [Economic adjustment viewed from a historical perspective] (paper presented at the Eleventh Sino–American Conference on Mainland China, Institute of International Relations, Taipei, 1982).

14. Chong-Pin Lin, "China: The Coming Changes," *American Enterprise* 2 (1991): 21.

15. Hua, Sheng, Zhang Xuejun, and Luo Xiaopeng, "Zhongguo gaige shinian: Huigu, fansi han qianjing" [Ten years in China's reform: Looking back, reflection and prospect], *Jingji Yanjiu* 9 (1988): 13–37.

16. Yu-Shan Wu, *Comparative Economic Transformations: Mainland China, Hungary, the Soviet Union, and Taiwan* (Stanford, CA: Stanford University Press, 1994), chap. 3.

17. Yu-Shan Wu, "Reforming the Revolution: Industrial Policy in China," *Pacific Review* 3, no. 3 (1990): 243–256.

18. Deng Xiaoping, "Deng Xiaoping tongzhi zai wuchang, shenzhen, zhuhai, shanghai denqdi de tanhua yaodian" [The main points of Comrade Deng Xiaoping's talks in Wuchang, Shenzhen, Zhuhai, and Shanghai], in *Yijiujiuer nian chun: Deng xiaoping yu shenzhen* [The spring of 1992: Deng Xiaoping and Shenzhen], ed. Zhonggong Shenzhen shiwei xuanchuanbu (Shenzhen: Haitian chubanshe, 1992).

19. Fang Xiangdong, "1988–1991 nian zhili zhengdun guigu ji dui weilai jingji yunxing de zhanwang," *Jingji lilun yu jingji guanli* 6 (1991): 1–9.

20. Chrisopher Allsop, "Macroeconomic Control and Reform in China," *Oxford Review of Economic Policy,* Winter 1995, 43–54.

21. See Joe Studwell's editorial in *China Economic Quarterly*, April 20, 2004. Using performance proxies for growth, such as freight, air travel, and power, rather than the socialist expenditure-based methodology, economists have estimated China's actual GDP at no more than 3 percent in 1998.

22. Edward X. Gu, "State Corporatism and Civil Society," in Wang Gungwu and Zheng Yongnian, eds., *Reform, Legitimacy, and Dilemmas: China's Politics and Society* (Singapore: Singapore National University Press, 2000), 71–103.

23. Hu Angang, "Zhongguo zhengce zhouqi yu jingji zhouqi" [China's policy cycles and business cycles], *Chinese Social Sciences Quarterly* 8 (1994): 85–100; Hu Angang, *Zhongguo jingji bodong baogao* [Report on the fluctuations of China's economy] (Shenyang: Liaoning renmin chubanshe, 1994); Valerie Jane Bunce, *Do New Leaders Make a Difference? Executive Succession and Public Policy under Capitalism and Socialism* (Princeton, NJ: Princeton University Press, 1981).

24. Factors other than the two mentioned here include the vicissitudes of the world market, regional financial crisis, and so on. As important as these factors may be in shaping the environment in which the Chinese policy makers found themselves, they are less important than the structural change of the Chinese economy and the elite's consensus on pursuing growth in macrostability.

25. For a discussion of local officials' compliance with the investment-reduction and inflation-control policies of the central government, see Yasheng Huang, *Inflation and Investment Control in China: The Political Economy of Central–Local Relations during the Reform Era* (New York: Cambridge University Press, 1996).

26. As cited in Joseph Y. S. Cheng, introduction to *China in the Post-Deng Era* (Hong Kong: Chinese University Press, 1998), 9–11.

27. Yu-Shan Wu, "Jiang and After: Technocratic Rule, Generational Replacement, and Mentor Politics," in *The New Chinese Leadership and Opportunities after the Sixteenth Party Congress,* China Quarterly Special Issue New Series, no. 4 (London: China, 2004), p. 71.

28. Tao Yifeng, "Shiliuda hou dalu de jingji gaige yu zhengzhi jicheng" [China's economic reform and political succession after the Sixteenth Party Congress], *Mainland China Studies* 46, no. 2 (2004): 27–34.

29. The share of output of foreign-invested enterprises (FIEs) in China's GDP has increased from 0.57 percent in 1980 to about 18 percent in 1996, while the share of SOEs has declined correspondingly. Ko-ho Mok, *Social and Political Development in Post-Reform China* (New York: St. Martin's, 2000), 27ff.

30. The nonstate sectors, except for FIEs, have showed a declining interest in fixed asset investments, defaulting these to the state. Thomas M. H. Chan, "Changes in China's Growth Pattern since the Reform," in Meiru Liu, ed., *Administrative Reform in China and Its Impact on the Policy-Making Process and Economic Development after Mao: Reinventing Chinese Government* (Lewiston, NY: Mellen, 2001), 273–309.

31. We are also shifting our focus from the PBCs as expressed in the boom–bust cycles to the PBCs in investment policy, which is a clearer indicator of the state's intention. In so doing, we no longer use boom–bust fluctuations to detect the underlying factional struggle but see investment cycles as reflective of elite manipulation of the economy for political purposes.

32. Hu Angang, "Bodong baogao" [Report on fluctuation], *Zhongwai guanli daobao* [Zhongwai management report] 2 (1995): 13–17.

33. Lu Jiarui and Xu Shengyin, "Hongguan tiaokong yu wo guo de jingji zhouqi" [Macro-adjustment and economic cycles in China], *Shengchanli yanjiu* (Study of productivity) 6 (2002): 84–86.

34. The active fiscal policy called for issuance of government bonds and expansion of pub-

lic investment as a way to boost the economy. It was taken at the end of 1997 and lasted until the end of 2004. During this period of time, a total of 910 billion RMB government bonds were floated on the market, raising annual growth rate by 2 percent.

35. After seven consecutive years of fall of M2 growth rate (1993–2000), 2001 witnessed an abrupt rise from 12.3 percent to 17.8 percent, closing on the 1997 level.

36. Yu-Shan Wu, "Jiang and After: Technocratic Rule, Generational Replacement, and Mentor Politics," in Yun-han Chu, Chih-cheng Lo, and Ramon H. Myers, eds., *The New Chinese Leadership and Opportunities after the Sixteenth Party Congress* (New York: Cambridge University Press, 2004), 69–89.

37. On October 28, the PBC raised primary interest rate for the first time since 1995, by 0.27 percent.

38. Andrew Nathan and Bruce Gilley, *China's New Rulers: The Secret Files* (New York: New York Review of Books, 2002), 150–154.

39. See Chen Xiaotong, *Chen xitong erzi chen xiaotong zi shu* [The book of Chen Xitong's son Chen Xiaotong] (Hong Kong: Huanqiu shiye gongsi, 1998). Chen Xiaotong maintains that the case against his father was entirely circumstantial, lacking any direct inculpatory evidence, and that the investigation was pursued for ulterior motives, suggesting at one point this merely represented a battle between the Shanghai gang and the Beijing gang.

40. Willy Wo-lap Lam, *The Era of Jiang Zemin* (New York: Prentice-Hall, 1999), 236–288.

41. John Wong, Yongnian Zheng, and Jinshan Li, *China after the Ninth NPC: Meeting Cross-Century Challenges,* East Asian Institute Occasional Paper no. 5 (Singapore: University of Singapore Press, 1998), 56–66.

42. In order of rank, the top senior officials after completion of the succession process at the March 2003 NPC are Jiang Zemin, Li Peng, Wan Li, Qiao Shi, Zhu Rongji, Song Ping, Liu Huaqing, Wei Jianxing, Li Lanqing, Rong Yiren, Bo Yibo, and Song Renqiong. Nathan and Gilley, *China's New Rulers,* 140.

43. This grouping includes Zhou Qiang, 42, secretary of the Central Committee of the CYL; Li Keqiang, 47, governor of Henan Province; Xi Jinping, 48, governor of Fujian Province (and son of party veteran Xi Zhongxun); Zhao Leji, 44, governor of Qinghai Province; Quan Zhezhu, alternate member of the Fifteenth Central Committee and executive vice governor of Jilin Province; and Wu Aiying, alternate member of the Fifteenth Central Committee and deputy secretary of the Shandong Provincial Party Committee. Zhou Qiang is current CYL first secretary and Li Keqiang was his predecessor; both Liu Peng, executive deputy head of the Central Propaganda Department, and Zhao Shi, deputy director of the State Administration of Radio, Film, and Television, were CYL secretaries. Li Keqiang, Liu Peng, and Zhao Shi worked under Hu Jintao when he was CYL first secretary; Zhou Qiang was personally selected by Hu to chair the CYL from his vantage point in the Politburo Standing Committee. Other *tuanpai* members who once worked with Hu include Fujian party secretary Song Defu and Minister of Justice Zhang Fusen. See *Cheng Ming,* July 2002.

44. Lowell Dittmer, "Chinese Factional Politics under Jiang Zemin," *Journal of East Asian Studies* 3 (2003): 97–128.

45. Tung Chenyuan, "Zhongguo jingji qingshi fazhan: Hongguan fazhan yu zhengce" [China's economic outlook: Macroeconomic development and policies] (unpublished manuscript, p. 3), as cited in Yi-Feng Tao, "Rationalization of Political Business Cycle in China" (paper presented at conference the Rise of China Revisited: Perception and Reality, Institute of International Relations, Cheng-Chi National University, Taipei, Taiwan).

46. Yin, "Ts'ung li-shih."

47. It is interesting to see if Chinese factionalism on the top elite echelon can translate into vehicles of political pluralism and act under certain circumstances to bring about changes toward democratization. It is conceivable, based on the Soviet and East European experiences, that schism among Communist ruling elite would create an arena of political contestation and open up policies as some power contenders are in good position to tap popular support. This would create "one-party pluralism" in which multiple candidates endorsed by the party compete for official posts, as seen in the Soviet and Hungarian examples in the late 1980s. In this context, factionalism may function as catalyst for pluralism and democracy at critical political moments.

3

The Sixteenth Central Committee
of the Chinese Communist Party

Emerging Patterns of Power Sharing

CHENG LI AND LYNN WHITE

D id November 2002 begin a new era of Chinese politics? Was the Sixteenth
Congress of the Chinese Communist Party (CCP) the first institutionalized
transfer of power in the People's Republic of China (PRC)? Is it misleading to stress
the importance of political institutionalization in the CCP, which bans any political
party that might challenge its power? On the other hand, in view of the past ebbs
of Leninist authoritarianism in Russia or Eastern Europe, might not evidence of
peaceful succession or factional compromise in China's ruling party be important?
How does the 2002 succession affect CCP legitimacy? What new patterns have
appeared in Chinese elite politics, as gerontocracy seems to decline? What does the
new leadership portend for China's future?

Full answers will take time to emerge. Yet immediately after the Congress, many
analysts made varying assessments, especially about outgoing party chief Jiang
Zemin. Andrew Nathan argued that the Party Congress showed institutional development. Jiang formally retired, some power went to fresh leaders, no military general was paramount, and new Politburo members were partly chosen on their
merits.[1] By contrast, Joseph Fewsmith and others noted that by appointing six of his
protégés to the nine-member Standing Committee of the Politburo, Jiang seemed
to come out of the congress more powerful than ever. Power transition, according
to Fewsmith, was incomplete.[2]

Jiang was able to appoint friends to the new Standing Committee, but some of
his confidants fared poorly in elections at the Congress. Jiang's bodyguard, You

Xigui, received the lowest number of votes for election as an alternate on the Central Committee (CC). Jiang's former personal secretary and the current Shenzhen party secretary, Huang Liman, received the third lowest number of votes.[3] His close ally, former Shanghai deputy party secretary and then minister of education, Chen Zhili, failed to obtain a seat on the Politburo.[4] Congress ballots suggested Jiang's influence was limited.[5]

China watchers have arguably spent too much time speculating about Jiang and his relationship with a handful of top leaders. Rumors and hearsay, rather than data, have become overused sources in Chinese elite studies. Analysts tend to concentrate on just one or several high-placed people, arguably fewer than is optimal for understanding the politics of such a large nation. A habit of tolerating guesswork has become usual. It does not assure critical searches for patterns of power redistribution among types of leaders, for long-term trends in the elite, or for possible links among political factions. Many analysts fixate on gossip about power struggles, without much contemporary evidence and without paying enough attention to the political and regional interests these leaders represent or the apparent constraints faced by them all, including Jiang.

This study addresses the issue of the political succession from Jiang Zemin to Hu Jintao but goes beyond it by exploring many kinds of statistics and other facts about elite formation. We have assembled a database on the biographical traits of all 356 CC members (198 full members and 158 alternates).[6] We have paid particular attention to these leaders' generations, bureaucratic affiliations, regional representations, educations, career paths, and early political socializations. To assess trends, we compare this CC with its predecessors, especially the Fifteenth Central Committee. Analysis of such data should make discourse about China's political elite more firmly based.

Not all CC members are created equal, and compiling information about individuals does not show everything about their networks or the contexts in which they act. We will therefore also try to shed light on the main factions of the late-Jiang/early-Hu era, which are now latent, and especially on their mutual tensions or agreements. Crucial to any review of Chinese elite politics, during this period when succession may be still incomplete, is an understanding of Hu Jintao's power: where it is based, how it differs from Jiang's, what relation is most likely between Hu and Jiang's apparent protégé Zeng Qinghong, and how Hu's leadership may shape China's future.

CHARACTERIZING HU'S LEADERSHIP

Hu's rise in the CCP was heralded by extensive advertisement of him as the "fourth generation" leader and by a stress on the need for "institutionalized succession." Each of these two notions is highly political. Jiang Zemin promoted them at least until the summer of 2002. By identifying Deng Xiaoping as the core of the second generation and himself as the core of the third, Jiang consolidated his own legitimacy in the mid-1990s.[7] By identifying Hu as a leading figure of the fourth generation, Jiang apparently diminished pressure on his own position from other potential leaders in his own age group such as Qiao Shi, Li Peng, Zhu Rongji, and Li Ruihuan.

"Generation," combined with procedures of "term limit" and "retirement age," was one of Jiang's tools for consolidating his power—and these are all now perforce among Hu's mandates and bounds. Hu got the highest number of votes in elections to the Sixteenth Central Committee (all but one of the 2,132 delegates voted for him).[8] Soon after Hu became general secretary of the CCP at the Sixteenth National Party Congress, many in China wished he would take full charge soon, because he personified the country's quest for political institutionalization. Hu often spoke of "political civilization," which in some contexts can be a code phrase justifying political compromise.[9] Jiang's replacement by Hu as chairman of the Central Military Commission (CMC) at the Fourth Plenum of the Sixteenth Central Committee in September 2004 completed the process of top leadership succession, which had begun two years earlier. While this process was short on transparency, it was peaceful, orderly, and institutionalized in form.

In addition to generational differences, Jiang and Hu represent two dissimilar sociopolitical and geographical constituencies. They vary in their personal careers and political associations. Jiang advanced from a base in Shanghai and through an advantageous "princeling" background, but Hu comes from a nonofficial family. Hu's political links have largely been in the Chinese Communist Youth League (CCYL). Hu has spent most of his adult life in poor inland provinces, including fourteen years in Gansu, three years in Guizhou, and four years in Tibet. Also in contrast to Jiang, who reigned over a flow of economic resources to Shanghai and other coastal areas during the past decade, Hu has for years advocated inland needs. The first Politburo meeting that Hu chaired included economic development plans for China's west. Hu has often portrayed himself as concerned about relatively weak social groups such as farmers, migrant workers, and the urban poor. Within two years after he became CCP general secretary, Hu Jintao already steered China's development in line with his perceived mandate. Unlike his predecessor Jiang—who focused on coastal development at the expense of progress in the vast inland region and fixated on gross domestic product (GDP) growth without regard for employment, the environment, or social issues—Hu has publicly stressed the need to achieve balanced regional economic development, social fairness, and government accountability.

In contrast to Jiang, who cultivated a web of patron–client ties largely based on his Shanghai connections, Hu has thus far enjoyed a public image of having avoided an obsession with factional favoritism. Hu has associates, but nobody on the new Politburo is seen as his protégé. Instead, Hu is known for his skills in coalition building and consensus making, which might become a collective characteristic of the fourth generation. Hu Jintao's influence has largely been based on his appealing public image during crises such as the 2003 epidemic of severe acute respiratory syndrome (SARS) and on his political coalition with Wen Jiabao, another widely popular administrator, rather than on political networks. Hu's reputation for refraining from use of his office to build his own client group might aid China's institutional development.

Of course, Hu is skilled at political networking. He has expedited his political career through *guanxi* (political connections), and he has established remarkably broad political linkages. Hu is prominent in the so-called Qinghua University clique. He headed the CCYL in the early 1980s, and he served during the past decade as president of the Central Party School (CPS). Many members of the 2002 CC were associated with at least one of these three institutions.[10] Most of them concurrently hold top provincial leadership posts, especially in China's inland and northeastern provinces.[11] Hu is surrounded by Jiang's protégés on the Politburo Standing Committee, but many of these leaders may be vulnerable due to the political favoritism through which they obtained their seats. Most importantly, with the rise of a more collective leadership, Chinese elite politics have already changed from the zero-sum games of the past to a pattern of power negotiation among competing factions, regions, and social groups. The two political coalitions—one led by party chief Hu and Premier Wen and the other led by former party chief Jiang's protégé Vice President Zeng—serve as checks and balances on each other, thus preventing any single approach from currently dictating the course of China's domestic or foreign policy.

QUANTITATIVE FINDINGS AND DISCUSSION

The Fluidity of Elite Turnover

A reason why the CCP has been able to stay in power for over half a century, especially during the past two decades of change, lies in the adaptability of its elite. Vilfredo Pareto and Gaetano Mosca described the "circulation of elites" as key to the continuance of any ruling group. In Mosca's view, governing leaderships decline when they cease to find an arena for the talents through which they rose to power. They fall if they can no longer render the services they once rendered, or if their strengths become less relevant in a new socioeconomic context.[12] By ceasing to be truly communist, the CCP has adapted for survival. Pareto explains that a revolution (or in his words, a "wholesale circulation of elites") becomes likely when the "piecemeal circulation of elites" is too slow. Channels of enrollment may be clogged by an old elite that prevents "new blood" from entering the power structure.[13] Any enduring regime will try to maintain its internal integrity by defining what types of people can rule, but it will also adapt to its external environment by recruiting fresh talent.

The CCP's institutionalization of technocratic and age criteria for leadership during China's reforms shows a clear effort to find this balance. Under Deng Xiaoping in the early 1980s, the party began to recruit new members from more diverse social and occupational backgrounds. The CCP in its earlier, revolutionary period was largely led by ex-peasants and others whose most important education had been in wars. Now it is led at its highest levels by engineers. This "technocratic turnover" mainly occurred during the 1992 and 1997 Party Congresses.[14] The nine members of the newly formed Standing Committee are all engineers. They have spent most of their careers as party functionaries.

While engineering technocrats overwhelmingly dominate the top leadership of the current CC, other groups such as economists and business administrators are increasingly found just below that level. For the first time in the history of the CCP, the Central Enterprise Work Commission and the Central Financial Work Commission have delegations at the congress.[15] A handful of CEOs from big state-owned enterprises, joint ventures, and banks now serve on the CC as full or alternate members. Jiang Zemin's theory of three legitimizes the recruitment of private entrepreneurs into the party. A majority of these CC entrepreneurs or bankers are from state firms, but a few are from collective or share-holding companies. For the first time, private entrepreneurs (capitalists, by any other name) are also delegates at the Communist Party Congress.

Table 3.1 shows that the portion of fresh faces on each CC, counting full and alternate members together, has stabilized near three-fifths since 1982. On the Sixteenth CC, 107 full members (54 percent) and 113 alternates (72 percent) are new to those posts. The combined number of newcomers in both categories is 61 percent. But if we reduce by the number (40) of new full members who were promoted from alternate status on the previous CC, 180 leaders (including 67 new full members and 113 new alternates) are first-timers on the committee, accounting for 51 percent of the Sixteenth CC. These data suggest that high circulation in the CC has become a norm of the CCP leadership during reforms.

The Politburo (PB) shows a similarly high turnover. The Standing Committee (SC), the most powerful group in China, now has very high circulation. Among the twenty-five full and alternate members of the PB, three-fifths are first-timers. On the SC, except for Hu Jintao, all other eight men are new. Six of the seven previous SC members stepped down from this supreme decision-making body. They were Jiang Zemin (CCP general secretary), Li Peng (NPC head), Zhu Rongji (premier of the State Council), Li Ruihuan (Chinese People's Political Consultative Conference head), Wei Jianxing (secretary of the Central Discipline Inspection Commission), and Li Lanqing (executive vice premier). This was the largest SC turnover ever.[16]

Table 3.2 shows full data on the ages, provincial origins, jobs, vocations, and educations of the twenty-five top party politicians, i.e., the PB members. Fifteen are first-timers in 2002. In fact, all members of the PB except its SC members are newcomers (Wu Yi was promoted from alternate to full member). Among the nine SC members, six entered the PB in 1997. Hu Jintao, Wu Bangguo, and Wen Jiabao have the longest tenures; each has served for about ten years. These three leaders, tapped for future glory long ago, became in March 2003 the PRC president, NPC chair, and premier. Nearly half of the PB members gained CC seats in the 1980s,

Table 3.1   Overview of Elite Turnover on CCP Central Committees and Politburos, 1956–2002

| | | Central Committee (CC) | | | | | | | | | Politburo (PB) | | | | |
| | | Full Member | | | Alternate Member | | | Total Central Committee | | | | | | | (%) of Reelected Who Remain from the Previous PB |
CC	Year Held	No.	New	(%)	No.	New	(%)	No.	New	(%)	No.	New	(%)	Reelected	(%)	
8th	1956	97	32	(33)	73	70	(95)	170	102	(60)	23	13	(43)	10	(57)	(83)
9th	1969	170	122	(71)	109	104	(95)	279	226	(81)	25	15	(60)	10	(40)	(43)
10th	1973	195	55	(28)	124	58	(46)	319	113	(35)	25	9	(36)	16	(64)	(64)
11th	1977	201	71	(35)	132	75	(56)	333	146	(43)	26	11	(46)	15	(54)	(60)
12th	1982	210	96	(45)	138	114	(82)	348	210	(60)	28	14	(50)	14	(50)	(54)
13th	1987	175	114	(65)	110	79	(72)	285	193	(68)	18	12	(66)	6	(34)	(21)
14th	1992	189	84	(44)	130	97	(75)	319	181	(57)	22	15	(68)	7	(32)	(39)
15th	1997	193	109	(57)	151	106	(70)	344	215	(63)	24	8	(33)	16	(67)	(73)
16th	2002	198	107	(54)	158	113	(72)	356	220	(61)	25	15	(60)	10	(40)	(42)

Sources and Notes:

Certain tables in this article update the authors' work on previous party congresses; see Li Cheng and Lynn White, "The Thirteenth Central Committee of the Chinese Communist Party: From Mobilizers to Managers," *Asian Survey*, April 1988, 371–399; Li Cheng and Lynn White, "The Army in the Succession to Deng Xiaoping; Familiar Fealties and Technocratic Trends," *Asian Survey*, August 1993, 757–786; and Li Cheng and Lynn White, "The Fifteenth Central Committee of the Chinese Communist Party: Full-Fledged Technocratic Leadership with Partial Control by Jiang Zemin," *Asian Survey*, March 1998, 231–264. New sources of data, including the information of the Sixteenth CC, are identified in footnote 3. Other tables in the article do not repeat these sources unless data came from elsewhere.

The "new" column under full members counts those promoted from alternate to full membership. The "new" column under alternate members excludes those demoted from full to alternate membership. The "new" column under the total Central Committee includes new full plus new alternate members. The increase in the total number of the new Central Committee members can be reduced by the number promoted from alternate to full membership. On the Sixteenth Central Committee, 40 full members were promoted from alternate status, so the wholly fresh list is 180 (including 67 new full members and 113 new alternate members). This is 50.6 percent of the committee, suggesting the party may have set a goal to make at least half of the CC new.

Table 3.2 Backgrounds of All Members of the Sixteenth Politburo, 2002

Name	Age	Native Province	Current Position	Occupational Title	Educational Background	Year Graduated	Year Joined CCP	Year Entered CC	Year Entered PB
Hu Jintao	59	Anhui	Secretary-General, PRC President	Engineer	Qinghua University	1965	1964	1982 (AM)	1992
Wu Bangguo	60	Anhui	Chair, NPC, PB SC Member	Engineer	Qinghua University	1966	1964	1982 (AM)	1992
Wen Jiabao	59	Tianjin	Premier, PB SC Member	Engineer	Beijing Institute of Geology	1967 (G)	1965	1987	1992 (AM)
Jia Qinglin	61	Hebei	Chair, CPPCC, PB SC Member	Sr. Engineer	Hebei Engineering College	1962	1959	1987	1997
Zeng Qinghong	62	Jiangxi	PRC Vice President, PB SC Member	Engineer	Beijing Institute of Tech.	1963	1960	1997	1997 (AM)
Huang Ju	63	Zhejiang	Exe. Vice Premier, PB SC Member	Engineer	Qinghua University	1963	1966	1987 (AM)	1994
Wu Guanzheng	63	Jiangxi	Secretary of CCDI, PB SC Member	Engineer	Qinghua University	1968 (G)	1962	1982 (AM)	1997
Li Changchun	57	Liaoning	PB SC Member	Engineer	Harbin Institute of Tech.	1966	1965	1982 (AM)	1997
Luo Gan	66	Shandong	PB SC Member	Sr. Engineer	Freiburg Ins. of Metallurgy	1962	1960	1982 (AM)	1997
Wang Lequan	57	Shandong	Party Secretary of Xinjiang		Central Party School	1986 (G)	1966	1992 (AM)	2002
Wang Zhaoguo	60	Hebei	Vice Chair, NPC	Engineer	Harbin Institute of Tech.	1966	1965	1982	2002
Hui Liangyu	57	Jilin	Vice Premier	Economist	Jilin Provincial Party School	1964	1966	1992 (AM)	2002
Liu Qi	59	Jiangsu	Party Secretary of Beijing	Sr. Engineer	Beijing Institute of Iron/Steel	1968 (G)	1975	1992 (AM)	2002
Liu Yunshan	54	Shanxi	Head, CCP Propaganda Dept.		Jining Normal School	1966	1971	1982 (AM)	2002
Wu Yi	63	Hubei	Vice Premier	Sr. Engineer	Beijing Petroleum Institute	1964	1964	1987 (AM)	1997 (AM)
Zhang Lichang	62	Hebei	Party Secretary of Tianjin		Beijing Economics Cor. Uni.	1959	1966	1982 (AM)	2002
Zhang Dejiang	55	Liaoning	Party Secretary of Guangdong		Kim Il Sung University	1968	1971	1992 (AM)	2002
Chen Liangyu	55	Zhejiang	Party Secretary of Shanghai	Engineer	PLA Institute of Engineering	1963	1980	1997 (AM)	2002
Zhou Yongkang	59	Jiangsu	Minister, Ministry of Public Security	Sr. Engineer	Beijing Petroleum Institute	1966	1964	1992 (AM)	2002
Yu Zhengsheng	56	Zhejiang	Party Secretary of Hubei	Engineer	Harbin Mil. Engineering Ins.	1963	1964	1992 (AM)	2002
He Guoqiang	58	Hunan	Head, CCP Organization Dept.	Sr. Engineer	Beijing Ins. Chem. Eng.	1966	1966	1982 (AM)	2002
Guo Boxiong	59	Shaanxi	Vice Chair, CMC		PLA Military Academy	1983	1963	1997	2002
Cao Gangchuan	66	Henan	Vice Chair, CMC	Engineer	Military Eng. School, USSR	1963	1956	1997	2002
Zeng Peiyan	63	Zhejiang	Vice Premier	Sr. Engineer	Qinghua University	1962	1978	1992 (AM)	2002
Wang Gang (AM)	59	Jilin	Director, CCP General Office		Jilin University	1967	1971	1997 (AM)	2002 (AM)

Abbreviations: AM = Alternate Member, CCDI = Central Commission of Discipline Inspection, Chem. = Chemical, CMC = Central Military Commission, Com. = Commission, Cor. = Correspondence, CPPCC = Chinese People's Political Consultative Conference, Dev. = Development, Eng. = Engineering, Exe. = Executive, G = Graduate school, Ins. = Institute, Mil. = Military, PB = Politburo, PRC = People's Republic of China, SC = Standing Committee, SCo = State Council, Sr. = Senior. Standing Committee members' names are in boldface.

when most were just alternates. The other half joined later, in the 1990s. Shanghai party secretary Chen Liangyu and CC general office director Wang Gang first served as CC alternate members as late as 1997. So the turnover of leaders remains high—but so does party elders' self-confidence that they can detect political talent early. The new PB members, like the recent retirees who chose or agreed on them, are overwhelmingly engineers.

As for the whole Sixteenth CC, the longest-tenured member is Ismail Amat, a Uygur and vice chair of the Tenth National People's Congress (NPC) who first served as a full member in 1973. The second longest tenured CC full member is Raidi, a Tibetan and regional deputy party secretary who has advised Hans (including Hu Jintao) on the high plateau and has for years dictated appointments of other Tibetans there. These minority representatives are trusted by Han Chinese leaders because of perceived long-term loyalty in potentially rebellious areas. They keep their CC seats, and younger minority leaders receive promotions more slowly.

Eight senior current leaders first joined the CC as full members at a special meeting in 1985. They are Hu Jintao, Wu Guanzheng, Wang Zhaoguo, Song Defu (executive deputy director of the personnel coordination team under the CC), Jia Chunwang (prosecutor general), Liao Hui (director of the State Council's Hong Kong and Macao Affairs Office), Li Guixian (Chinese People's Political Consultative Conference vice chair), and Yang Zhengwu (Hunan party secretary). Only a tenth of the full CC members have been on the committee for more than a decade. The other 90 percent are fairly new. Most became prominent national leaders in the 1990s. Overall, CC circulation has been rapid. Turnover has been even faster on the more important PB and SC.

Transition to the Fourth Generation

Each generation has characteristics attributable to a major event that affected its members during the most formative time in their maturation as political adults (often when they were between seventeen and twenty-five years old).[17] Generational studies of Chinese leaders can divide cohorts at intervals of about fifteen years.[18] The PRC concept of political generation has often been based on distinctive historical experiences of elites defined by their ages.[19] Four widely recognized cohorts are the "Long March generation," "anti-Japanese war generation," "socialist transformation generation," and "Cultural Revolution generation." Public and official parlance has assigned to each of them a legitimate top leader, respectively Mao Zedong, Deng Xiaoping, Jiang Zemin, and Hu Jintao.

If the CCP will form future elites, by now fifth and sixth generations can also be in view. It is easier to analyze these statistically than to be sure about their top leaders—or the continuance of this kind of succession. Any definition of a political generation must be somewhat arbitrary. Like other social categories—ethnicity, class, income, or ideology—"generation can be imprecise at the boundaries."[20] It is difficult to say exactly "where one generation begins and another ends."[21] Nevertheless, we can try to base generational demarcations on specific years. Writers define the fourth or Cultural Revolution generation as the group born between 1941 and 1956. They were ten to twenty-five years old when the CR began in 1966. So they were forty-six to sixty-one years old by 2002.[22]

Rapid turnover on the CC and PB required retirements by third generation leaders in accord with age limit norms.[23] The CCP Organization Department, when nominating candidates for CC election, has followed three guidelines: (1) with few exceptions, full and alternate members on the old CC nominated for reelection should be less than sixty-four years old; (2) full ministers and provincial chiefs nominated for new memberships should be less than sixty-two; and (3) the nominated vice ministers and deputy province chiefs should be less than fifty-seven.[24]

The 2002 CC is mainly fourth generation. This cohort covers 72 percent (129) of the 179 full members, and 87 percent (111) of the 129 alternate members, insofar as ages can be identified. The oldest full members are Luo Gan, Cao Gangchun (Central Military Commission vice chair), and Ismail Amat, who were all born in 1935. The youngest full CC member is Zhang Qingwei (China Aerospace Science and Technology Corporation vice president), born in 1961. The youngest alternate members are Liu Shiquan (Sanjiang Space Group deputy director) and Su Shulin (China National Petroleum Corporation vice president), both born in 1963.

Table 3.3 shows the average ages of those elected to all the CCs from 1956 to 2002. The new CC has the second youngest average age (55.4 years), only a couple of months older than on the Thirteenth CC of 1987. Seventy-two full and alternate members of the new 2002 CC are less than fifty years old, compared with fifty-one under that age on the previous 1997 CC.[25] Those younger than forty-five, however, have decreased from twenty-one on the previous CC to fifteen on the new one.[26] The narrowing of age cohorts at top levels of the party shows an attempt to normalize legitimacy for rulers chosen from successive, officially defined generations. These are periodic elections, albeit not open or liberal ones, held under norms that partially constrain groups of leaders as well as individual leaders.

Table 3.3.   Average Age of Election to the Central Committee

CC	Year Held	Average Age	DA/DY*
8th	1956	56.4	
9th	1969	59	+0.20
10th	1973	62	+0.75
11th	1977	64.6	+0.65
12th	1982	62	−0.52
13th	1987	55.2	−1.36
14th	1992	56.3	+0.22
15th	1997	55.9	−0.08
16th	2002	55.4	−0.10

*DA = Difference of age; DY = difference of year. A positive ratio indicates an aging leadership, relative to the previous CC; the negative shows a shift to younger leaders. Ratio numbers suggest the extent of such change.

Above the CC are the Secretariat, PB, and SC. Table 3.4 shows average age changes at those levels since 1982. These core leaderships are progressively younger in most transitions. They also now show a rational "echelon structure": age 62 on the SC, 60.4 on the PB, and 59.4 on the Secretariat. This differs from the previous CC, when the Politburo and Secretariat had the same average age.

Another way of estimating cohorts is to look not at birth years, but at the dates on which current leaders first joined the party. Table 3.5 shows these for the most recent two CCs. None of the members of the new CC joined the party before 1949, but on the previous CC, twenty-one members (11 percent) joined during the anti-Japanese/Civil War era. Revolutionary veterans are now almost completely off the political stage. Thirteen full CC members joined as recently as the 1980s. They are in very important posts, including Chen Liangyu (Politburo member and Shanghai party secretary), Huang Zhengdong (Chongqing party secretary), Bo Xilai (trade minister), Wang Qishan (Beijing mayor), Li Rongrong (State Assets Regulatory and Management Commission chair), Xu Guanhua (science and technology minister), Xiang Huaicheng (former finance minister), Wang Guangtao (construction minister), and Li Tielin (CCP Organization Department executive deputy head). Zhou Xiaochun, the new governor of the People's Bank, joined the party as late as 1986.

The fifth generation, however, does not yet occupy many high posts. Their representatives account for just 2 percent of the full members and 8 percent of the alternates by age among civilian CC members. The fifth generation (born after 1957) experienced Deng's economic reforms in their crucible years of political life, and they may be called the reform generation—but no rising star has yet been chosen from this group to serve on the Politburo or Secretariat. The youngest PB member is fifty-five-year-old Liu Yunshan (CCP Propaganda Department director). The age span between the oldest and the youngest on the PB is twelve years. The span between General Secretary Hu Jintao and his youngest colleague on the Politburo is just five years.

The term "fifth generation" is not used in official Chinese media. After the summer of 2002, the phrase "fourth generation of leaders" is also no longer used in government publications. Hu Jintao and his colleagues may be more concerned about how to fulfill their mandate than how to choose their successors. The CCP's norm that leaders are promoted in batches, according to rather narrow age limits,

Table 3.4. Average Ages of CC Core Leadership Groups, 1982–2002

CC	Year Held	PB Standing Committee	Politburo (PB)	Secretariat
12th	1982	73.8	71.8	63.7
13th	1987	63.6	64	56.2
14th	1992	63.4	61.9	59.3
15th	1997	65.1	62.9	62.9
16th	2002	62	60.4	59.4

Table 3.5. Periods When Full Members of the Fifteenth and Sixteenth CCs Joined the Party

Year and Generation Name	15th CC (1997)		16th CC (2002)	
	Members	%	Members	%
1930–1939 Long March/First G.	1	**0.5**	0	0
1940–1949 Anti-Japanese War/Second G.	20	**10.4**	0	0
1950–1959 Socialist Transformation/Third G.	52	**26.9**	7	**3.5**
1960–1969 Cultural Revolution/Fourth G.	56	**29.0**	94	**47.5**
1970–1979 Reform/Fifth G.	31	**16.1**	56	**28.3**
1980–1989—/Sixth G.	5	**2.6**	13	**6.6**
Unknown	28	14.5	28	14.1
Total	193	100.0	198	100.0

nonetheless may have allowed power transition without political crisis—but this practice still allows much play for patron–client ties to affect promotions. It provides no institutional rule for finding which leader in a generation rises to the top. It suggests collective compromise and restraint by the old guard when choosing new elites, but it no longer specifies who should succeed. (This is a far cry from the 1969 CCP constitution, which did not beat around the bush by setting a mere procedure to choose Mao's successor. Its first chapter simply named the next man: Lin Biao.)

The current stress on narrow age cohorts is highly political, and CCP cadres define them in different ways that lead to different results. Joseph Fewsmith makes an interesting argument that the so-called Cultural Revolution (CR) generation may include two quite different subgroups—those who graduated from college when the Cultural Revolution began (e.g., Hu Jintao or Li Changchun) and those who lost the opportunity to get an education because they were sent down to rural areas working as farmers (e.g., Li Keqiang or Xi Jinping).[27] On the new CC, twenty-four members went to "May 7 cadre schools" (labor camps for intellectuals and bureaucrats). Another twenty-six younger members were "sent-down youths," who lost the chance to complete their middle school education and worked as peasants for years. The younger CR group was mostly in college by the time Deng's reform began, often majoring in economics and management rather than engineering. It is debatable whether these two groups should be considered parts of the same generation. Yet their collective memories of the Cultural Revolution are so strong that they may be called the CR generation.

Subgroups in the fourth generation suggest this cohort might stay in power long enough to have a transition of power from the older subgroup to the younger one. Many in the slightly younger cohorts have now emerged as ministers, provincial party secretaries, or governors. This junior half of the fourth generation experienced the Cultural Revolution, but their educational and occupational backgrounds are more like those of the putative fifth generation than like the older fourth generation subgroup. A sharp boundary between the fourth and fifth generations is hard to find, in comparison with the differences between earlier CCP cohorts.

Will the CCP continue its absorption of new kinds of leaders, taking in more entrepreneurs, lawyers, bankers, and other functional experts as it has done over the past quarter century? If that happens, a generational transition of power may become less important than an accommodating distribution of power among political factions, interest groups, social forces, and regions.

The Rise of Top Elites Who Have Backgrounds Administering Provincial Economies

Province leadership has become, during the past decade, the most important stepping-stone to high national posts. China's province-level administrations have enjoyed more autonomy than ever before, during the past half century, to advance their local economic interests. They often do so with support from representatives among top national leaders.[28] Shanghai's rapid development during the past decade, for example, has been closely linked to the enormous power of Jiang Zemin and the "Shanghai gang," who rose to lead China in part because they taxed the city so effectively through the 1980s—but then became the foremost promoters of its halcyon growth in the 1990s.

Inland leaders understandably rue the growing economic gap between the coast and their poorer provinces. They can see the overrepresentation of easterners in the central government. Party Congress deputies from inland often use their votes to block the election of nominees favored by top leaders, especially princelings or officials who have advanced their careers from Shanghai.[29] Table 3.6 compares the fraction of current Politburo members who have been provincial leaders (deputy party secretaries and vice governors or above) with the two previous PBs. This provincial portion began high and rose sharply over the decade: 55 percent in 1992, 68 percent in 1997, and 83 percent by 2002. The percentage of PB members who were province chiefs (party secretaries and governors) increased from 50 percent in 1992 to 59 percent in 1997, and again to 67 percent by 2002.

Table 3.6.   Provincial Leadership Experience of Full Members of the 1992, 1997, and 2002 Politburos

	As High Provincial Leaders*		As Top Provincial Chiefs**	
	No.	%	No.	%
14th Politburo (20 Members)	11	**55.0**	10	**50.0**
15th Politburo (22 Members)	15	**68.2**	13	**59.1**
16th Politburo (24 Members)	20	**83.3**	16	**66.7**

* High province-level leaders are the deputy party secretaries, vice governors, or above.
** Top provincial chiefs refer to the party secretaries and governors only.

All four provincial party secretaries who were earlier on the 1997 PB were promoted to serve on the nine-member SC in 2002. They now hold very high posts in the capital. Wu Bangguo heads the NPC, and Jia Qinglin chairs the Chinese People's Political Consultative Conference. Huang Ju is executive vice premier of the State Council. Wu Guanzheng serves as secretary of the CCP Central Discipline Inspection Commission. In addition, He Guoqiang (former Chongqing party secretary), Liu Yunshan (former Inner Mongolia deputy party secretary), and Zhou Yongkang (former Sichuan party secretary) not only received seats on the new Politburo, they also took charge of the CCP Organization Department, the CCP Propaganda Department, and the Public Security Ministry, respectively. All three also serve on the Secretariat, which handles the daily affairs of the Politburo. Never before in PRC history have so many provincial leaders been so quickly promoted to posts at the top.

The rise of province chiefs and central party chiefs has come largely at the expense of leaders in the central government. Only five from China's outgoing State Council (vice premiers Wen Jiabao and Wu Bangguo, councilors Luo Gan and Wu Yi, and Minister Zeng Peiyan) got seats on the 2002 Politburo. This contrasts with the two previous PBs, to which ten and eleven members respectively were elected from the State Council. In the current State Council, seven have seats in the Politburo and three were recently promoted from provincial party headships (Huang Ju, Hui Liangyu, and Zhou Yongkang). China's rulers have been trying to consolidate what they have called the function of the "ruling party." So the Secretariat, departments under the CC, and provincial party chiefs are more fully represented.

Military representation in the top party leadership has remained constant and small. The 2002 Politburo has an all-time low portion of military officers (8 percent), down from 40 percent in 1969, 31 percent in 1977, 11 percent in 1987, and 8.3 percent in 1997.[30] No military officer serves on the current or previous SC. No marshal or general (like strongmen of yore Lin Biao, Xu Shiyou, Ye Jianying, Yang Baibing, or Zhang Zhen) is among the politicians the party now ranks highest.

Maritime province leaders (not just leaders in *any* organization who happen to have been born near the coast) are very strongly represented in the Politburo. Nine PB members have advanced their careers exclusively from coastal provinces, in comparison to four from inland provinces. Thirteen members (65 percent of the Politburo) concurrently hold or recently held coastal province leadership posts. Seven (35 percent) did so inland. Dominance of the coast in the PB is even more evident when one considers that of all China's thirty-one provinces, only eleven are by the sea.[31]

The regional distribution of members on the whole CC, however, shows an equality norm instead of the dominance of leaders from the coast. Table 3.7 counts province leaders who have full and alternate status on the latest two CCs. In practically all cases, each province administration holds two full seats. This strong institutional norm was first implemented in 1997, and it has now been reinforced by repetition. Although coastal regions are overrepresented on the PB, full memberships on the CC are evenly distributed with almost absolute strictness across all prov-

Table 3.7. Provincial Leaders Holding Full and Alternate Memberships on the Fifteenth and Sixteenth CCs

	15th CC (1997)			16th CC (2002)		
	FM	AM	Total	**FM**	AM	Total
Beijing	2	3	5	2	3	5
Tianjin	2	3	5	2	3	5
Hebei	2	3	5	2	2	4
Shanxi	2	3	5	2	3	5
Neimenggu	2	3	5	2	3	5
Liaoning	2	1	3	2	3	5
Jilin	2	3	5	2	2	4
Heilongjiang	2	3	5	2	3	5
Shanghai	2	2	4	2	2	4
Jiangsu	2	3	5	2	2	4
Shandong	2	4	6	2	5	7
Zhejiang	2	3	5	2	3	5
Anhui	2	2	4	2	3	5
Fujian	2	2	4	2	3	5
Henan	2	3	5	2	2	4
Hubei	2	2	4	2	2	4
Hunan	2	3	5	2	2	4
Jiangxi	2	2	4	2	3	5
Guangdong	2	5	7	2	6	8
Guangxi	2	3	5	2	4	6
Hainan	2	2	4	2	2	4
Sichuan	2	3	5	2	3	5
Chongqing	2	2	4	2	2	4
Guizhou	2	3	5	2	3	5
Yunnan	1	4	5	2	3	5
Xizang (Tibet)	2	2	4	3	2	5
Shaanxi	2	3	5	2	3	5
Gansu	2	2	4	2	3	5
Qinghai	2	2	4	2	2	4
Ningxia	2	2	4	2	2	4
Xinjiang	2	3	5	4	3	7
Total	61	84	145	65	87	152

Abbreviations: FM = Full member, AM = Alternate member.

ince leaderships. Each American state gets two senators, and each Chinese province administration gets two CC full members (albeit the roles of these bodies are dissimilar). The CC members are usually the governor/mayor and the party secretary.

Jia Qinling and Huang Ju were transferred to Beijing a few weeks before the Sixteenth Party Congress. With their departures, the executive vice mayor of Beijing, Meng Xuenong (a protégé of Hu), and the executive vice mayor of Shanghai, Han

Zhen (a Shanghai gang member), could get full CC seats. Otherwise, Meng and Han would probably not have been elected to full memberships due to the "one province administration, two full seats" quota. This has become a norm in CC elections. Central personnel authorities apparently monitor it, as they do the high provincial appointments to which it relates. But it is also a rule that can constrain central leaders and assure that the CC has members familiar with each province. Yunnan in 1997 and Xinjiang and Tibet in 2002 are the only exceptions to test this rule. The Xinjiang and Tibet aberrations probably arise from affirmative action by the CCP Organization Department. It is less clear how nominees for CC alternate status are chosen prior to Party Congress approval. Some provinces, notably Shandong and Guangdong, have more alternates than others.

After CC elections, the equal distribution among province governments of full CC members does not remain static. Top province leaders are often reshuffled among regions or promoted to the central administration. Almost immediately after the November 2002 Congress, Wu Guanzheng (Shandong party secretary), Li Changchun (Guangdong party secretary), Zhang Dejiang (Zhejiang party secretary), Zhou Yongkang (Sichuan party secretary), Hui Liangyu (Jiangsu party secretary), Ji Yunshi (Jiangsu governor), and Bai Keming (Hainan party secretary) were transferred to Beijing or other provinces. This allowed top leaders such as Hu Jintao and Zeng Qinghong to appoint their protégés to important provincial posts, apparently to prepare them for further promotions in the future. For example, Hu's confidant Zhang Xuezhong now is Sichuan party secretary; and Li Yuanchao, an alternate CC member who has ties with both the CCYL and the Shanghai gang, now serves as Jiangsu party secretary. As chiefs in two of China's most important provinces, Zhang and Li are well placed to be leading contenders for seats on the next Politburo.

Despite these shifts after balloting for CCs, the even distribution of full memberships among province managements at the times of elections is nonetheless an institutional development. Top leaders can manipulate outcomes just before or after the elections, but they now also have rules to follow. Leaders from wealthy coastal provinces dominate the PB and especially the powerful SC, but representatives from inland provinces have a majority on the CC—and they might win any issue for which they can make it vote.

After Hu Jintao consolidated his power at the Fourth Plenum of the Sixteenth Central Committee in September 2004, China's provincial leadership underwent a major reshuffling. Most of the newly appointed provincial chiefs had CCYL backgrounds and now serve in either inland or northeastern provinces. This geographic distribution reaffirms that China's less developed inland region is Hu's power base. The new provincial chiefs can gain, over the next two or three years, administrative and political credentials to help their later careers. Hu's associates have been appointed as provincial chiefs earlier than their counterparts in the coastal region, and this may bode that leaders from inland provinces will occupy more seats on the next Politburo.

New Trends in Educational and Occupational Backgrounds

Three developments can be found in recent data about the schooling and professionalism of China's leaders, although the 1980s saw even larger changes on these dimensions. First, the fraction of leaders with college educations has now reached an all-time high. The main news is that some now have postgraduate degrees. Second, although the nine members of the SC are all engineers (see table 3.2), the overall percentage of engineering technocrats in the CC has started to decline. Economists and lawyers, and a few who were trained in humanities or social sciences, are present on the CC. Third, more of the leaders have studied abroad, either as degree candidates or visiting scholars.

Education

Table 3.8 shows that 99 percent of the full and alternate members of the Sixteenth CC went to universities. In the whole Congress, the portion of delegates with junior college degrees or better also rose: 71 percent in 1992, to 84 percent in 1997, 92 percent in 2002.[32] This was the trend throughout the party too, because among all 66.3 million CCP members by the Sixteenth CC, 15.4 million had obtained at least junior college degrees. This is 23 percent of the whole party.[33] Two decades earlier, in 1982, the college-educated portion of CCP members was only 4 percent.

Higher Degrees

PB members' educational levels since 1956 are shown on table 3.9. In 2002 for the first time in PRC history, the whole Politburo has gone to college. PB members with advanced postgraduate degrees have risen: one (5 percent) in 1992, two (8 percent) in 1997, and now four (16 percent). They are Wen Jiabao, Wu Guanzheng, Liu Qi, and Wang Lequan (see table 3.2). Many on the CC have also pursued advanced studies. Among the 321 full and alternate members whose educational backgrounds

Table 3.8. Percentage of College-Educated CC Members, 1956–2002

CC	Year of CC	Percentage
8th	1956	44.3
9th	1969	23.8
10th	1973	NA
11th	1977	25.7
12th	1982	55.4
13th	1987	73.3
14th	1992	83.7
15th	1997	92.4
16th	2002	98.6

Table 3.9 Change in Educational Level of the Politburo, 1956–2002

Educational Level	8th (1956)		9th (1969)		10th (1973)		11th (1977)		12th (1982)		13th (1987)		14th (1992)		15th (1997)		16th (2002)		Ratio of % in 16th PB to Average in Earlier PBs	Ratio of % on PBs since 1987 to the Pre-1987 PBs
	No.	%	No.	%	No.	%	No.	%	No.	%	No.	%	No.	%	No.	%	No.	%		
No schooling	1	4.4	5	20.0	4	16.0	4	15.4	3	10.7	0	0	0	0	0	0	0	0	0	0
Primary school	3	13.0	3	12.0	4	16.0	5	19.2	10	35.7	0	0	0	0	0	0	0	0	0	0
Middle school	3	13.0	8	32.0	9	36.0	6	23.0	3	10.7	5	27.7	3	13.6	2	8.3	0	0	0	0
Military school	4	17.4	2	8.0	1	4.0	5	19.2	3	10.7	1	5.6	1	4.5	2	8.3	2	8.0	0.82	0.25
University	12	52.2	7	28.0	7	28.0	6	23.0	9	32.1	12	66.6	17	77.2	18	75.0	19	76.0	1.59	2.25
Postgraduate	0	0	0	0	0	0	0	0	0	0	0	0	1	4.5	2	8.3	4	16.0	—	—
Total	23	100	25	100	25	100.0	26	99.8	28	99.9	18	100.0	22	99.8	24	99.9	25	100	—	—

Note: Percentages do not add to 100 because of rounding.

can be identified, ninety-one (28 percent) hold postgraduate degrees, and fourteen have doctorates—a small portion, but they are in important posts. Ph.D.s on the CC include Li Keqiang (Liaoning party secretary), Xi Jinping (Zhejiang party secretary), Li Yuanchao (Jiangsu party secretary), Liu Yandong (CCP United Front Department director), Zhou Xiaochuan (People's Bank governor), Wang Jiarui (CCP International Liaison Department director), Bai Chunli (Chinese Academy of Sciences vice president), and Yuan Chunqing (Shaanxi deputy party secretary). Li Yuanchao got his Ph.D. in law from the CPS in 1998. Li Keqiang and Xi Jinping took Ph.D. programs in economics and law on a part-time basis from Beijing University and Qinghua University, respectively.

Many promoted leaders have attended midcareer courses at the CPS. Wang Lequan, a new PB member, attended the CPS to study party affairs and economic management from 1983 to 1986. Between 1997 and 2002, nearly 3,000 provincial and ministerial level leaders attended training programs at the CPS, the State Administration Institute, or the National Defense University.[34] In Guangxi Province, for example, among the top fifteen current local leaders (party secretary, governor, and deputies), all but one attended the CPS.[35] Based on incomplete data, at least fifty-two (15 percent) of the full and alternate CC members have attended the CPS for degree programs or yearlong training.

It would be inaccurate, however, to conclude that most leaders with college experience have gone only to party schools. Most have also studied at China's elite universities. As table 3.2 shows, five of the twenty-four full PB members attended Qinghua University (sometimes called China's MIT) before the Cultural Revolution. Three studied at the Harbin Institute of Technology and Harbin Military Engineering Institute, and six attended other elite universities in Beijing. Most of the Ph.D. holders received their degrees from prestigious universities in China or abroad.

Diversified Academic Fields, Including Law

Table 3.10 shows the academic majors of the college-educated full members in the past two CCs.[36] Although engineers turned politicians dominate the new PB and its Standing Committee (by 75 percent and 100 percent respectively), engineers on the whole CC have actually declined. The percentage of CC members who majored in technology dropped from 43 percent in 1997 to 34 percent now. The portion of those who studied either engineering or natural science dropped by 10 percent. The variability of these technocrats' representation in different leadership posts over the past two decades is shown on table 3.11. Technocrats (engineers or natural scientists who become politicians) increased dramatically from 1982 to 1997. Thereafter, they have significantly declined in all major leadership categories: ministers, province party secretaries, governors, and full CC members.

Leaders trained in social sciences, including law, have now increased on the CC. This is striking because, in the history of the PRC, social scientists have been some-

Table 3.10.   Academic Majors of Full Members of the Fifteenth and Sixteenth CCs Who Have College Degrees

Majors	15th CC (N = 180) No.	15th CC (N = 180) %	16th CC (N = 195) No.	16th CC (N = 195) %
Engineering and Science				
Engineering	78	**43.3**	67	**34.4**
Geology	3	**1.7**	1	**0.5**
Meteorology	1	**0.6**	0	**0**
Agronomy	5	**2.8**	4	**2.1**
Biology	3	**1.7**	0	**0**
Physics	7	**3.9**	9	**4.6**
Chemistry	2	**1.1**	2	**1.0**
Mathematics	0	**0**	2	**1.0**
Architecture	0	**0**	3	**1.5**
Medical science	1	**0.6**	1	**0.5**
Subtotal	*100*	***55.6***	*89*	***45.6***
Economics and Management				
Economics and finance	7	**3.9**	10	**5.1**
Management	3	**1.7**	1	**0.5**
Accounting and statistics	0	**0**	2	**1.0**
Foreign trade	1	**0.6**	0	**0**
Subtotal	*10*	***5.6***	*13*	***6.7***
Social Sciences and Law				
Politics	2	**1.1**	6	**3.1**
Sociology	1	**0.6**	0	**0**
Party history and party affairs	4	**2.2**	7	**3.6**
Journalism	0	**0**	2	**1.0**
Law	3	**1.7**	8	**4.1**
Subtotal	*10*	***5.6***	*23*	***11.8***
Humanities				
History	1	**0.6**	4	**2.1**
Philosophy	2	**1.1**	4	**2.1**
Education	1	**0.6**	3	**1.5**
Chinese language and literature	5	**2.8**	6	**3.1**
Foreign language	7	**3.9**	6	**3.1**
Subtotal	*16*	***8.9***	*23*	***11.8***
Military Education, Military Engineering	*31*	***17.2***	*38*	***19.5***
Unknown	*12*	*6.7*	*9*	*4.6*
Total	180	100.4	195	100.0

Source and Note: Information on the Fifteenth Central Committee is based on Shen Xueming and others, comp., *Zhonggong di shiwujie zhongyang weiyuanhui zhongyang jilü jiancha weiyuanhui weiyuan minglu* [Who's who among the members of the Fifteenth Central Committee of the Chinese Communist Party and the Fifteenth Central Commission for Discipline Inspection] (Beijing: Zhonggong wenxian chubanshe, 1999). Calculated by Cheng Li. Percentages do not add to 100 because of rounding.

Table 3.11.   Technocrats' Representation in High Leadership, 1982–2002

Year	Ministers		Provincial Party Secretaries		Governors		Full CC Members	
	No.	%	No.	%	No.	%	No.	%
1982	1	**2**	0	**0**	0	**0**	4	**2**
1987	17	**45**	7	**25**	8	**33**	34	**26**
1997	28	**70**	23	**74**	24	**77**	100	**52**
2002	15	**52**	13	**42**	16	**52**	89	**46**

Sources: Hong Yung Lee, *From Revolutionary Cadres to Party Technocrats: The Changing Cadre System in Socialist China* (Berkeley: University of California Press, 1991), 268; Kenneth Lieberthal, *Governing China: From Revolution through Reform* (New York: Norton, 1995), 236; Li and White, "The Fifteenth Central Committee of the Chinese Communist Party," 251; and www.xinhuanet.com (accessed December 31, 2002).

times despised and are usually marginal. Jiang Zemin's well-publicized 2002 visit to the People's University, famous for philosophy, economics, and social sciences, suggested that experts in social subjects could play a greater role in government. During his visit to this school, Jiang said that in the future, "Chinese social scientists should be valued as highly as natural scientists."[37]

The number of lawyers in China has risen rapidly. Top politicians now speak often of the need to strengthen the country's legal system. In the early 1980s, there were only 3,000 lawyers to serve China's billion people. China now has roughly 150,000 lawyers. This is presumed to be progress. The number of applicants for master's degrees in law increased from about 18,000 in 2001 to about 27,000 in 2002.[38] Receiving a law degree has become a valuable credential for party leadership. On the Sixteenth CC, several new full and alternate members hold law diplomas. The number of full members with law degrees rose from three (2 percent) to eight (4 percent) between the last two CCs. Most were born in the 1950s and are seen as rising stars in the Chinese leadership. They include Xi Jinping, Li Keqiang, Li Yuanchao, Yuan Chunqing, Cao Jianming (Supreme Court vice president), Zhan Xuan (Higher People's Court president), and Yin Yicui (Shanghai deputy party secretary). Some did undergraduate work in engineering or science but studied law at the graduate level. Xi Jinping, for example, majored in engineering at Qinghua University in 1979 but more recently received a Ph.D. there in law. Xie Zhenhua (State Environmental Protection Administration director) studied physics at Qinghua in 1977, and he got a graduate degree in environmental law at Wuhan University in 1993.

Jiang's work report to the 2002 Party Congress specified that the nation should establish a new Chinese-style legal system by 2010. More recently, Hu Jintao has made widely publicized speeches in which he stresses the rule of law. This suggests that lawyers may become an important elite group in the near future. Wry Americans may conclude that China's prospects are therefore dim, but this analysis might be wrong.

Entrepreneurs

The upward social mobility of businesspeople in reform China is a major historical change. Traditional Chinese society, dominated by gentry-scholar rentiers, devalued merchants (who are now called entrepreneurs). Traders in Mao's time were also strictly restrained, and industrialists became state cadres then. The 4 million private firms and stores that existed in China before 1949 disappeared by the mid-1950s.[39] But by 2004, China had about 3.34 million fully private enterprises, hiring at least 47 million employees. About 25 million other people ran their own small businesses without hiring anybody.[40] These numbers rise so quickly that academic publications do not keep up with them. More than 100 million people now work in private firms—far more than in state-owned enterprises, whose labor force shrank from 72 million in 1992 to 39 million in 2001.[41]

At the 2002 Party Congress, for the first time in history, private businesspeople attended as a distinct group. Seventeen such "entrepreneurs" became members of the presidium of the Congress, and a few were voted onto the CC.[42] State and non-state entrepreneurs who serve on the new CC include Li Yizhong (China Petroleum & Chemical Group chair), Zhang Qingwei (China Aerospace S&T Corporation deputy president), Liu Shiquan (Sanjiang Space Group deputy director), Zhu Yanfeng (China First Auto Corporation president), Xi Guohua (China Netcom chair), Zhang Ruimin (Haier Group chair), Tao Jianxing (Chunlan Group general manager), Wang Mingquan (Everbright Holding Company president), and Lin Zuoming (Shenyang Liming Company CEO). These are alternates on the current CC. Most head state enterprises, but others lead collectives, joint ventures, and/or stockholding companies.

Many of these party-legitimated entrepreneurs received their education in engineering, and some majored in economics. This raises the issue of how to distinguish engineers-turned-entrepreneurs in the political leadership from technocrats. Entrepreneurs are characteristically engaged in risk-taking on markets, while technocrats are primarily defined by three criteria: technical education, professional experience, and leadership position.[43] Because an increasing number of engineers now work as CEOs in businesses, and because some of these "technical entrepreneurs" hold leadership posts, the distinction between businesspeople and technocrats has become blurred. An example is Jiang Mianheng, who is Jiang Zemin's son and a delegate to the 2002 Party Congress. He earned a Ph.D. in natural science in America and is now a vice president of the Chinese Academy of Sciences. He has also served as CEO of Shanghai Alliance Investment, Ltd., a major business partner of a large Taiwanese firm. Jiang Mianheng can be seen as both a technocrat and an entrepreneur (as well as a princeling).

The percentage of entrepreneurs, especially private ones, in the Chinese leadership is still very small. They will likely increase their number on future CCs, however, especially at higher levels. A recent official study by the United Front Department of the CCP Central Committee found that 34 percent of owners of private enterprises in 2004 were members of the Chinese Communist Party.[44] This study also shows that the percentage of CCP members among private entrepreneurs increased significantly during the last decade—from 13 percent in 1993, to 17 percent in 1995, 17 percent in 1997, 20 percent in 1999, and 29.9 percent in 2002. This 2004 study shows that more than half (52 percent) of the private entrepreneurs with the CCP memberships have at least junior college educations. Their growing wealth and influence in Chinese society, and their complicated relations with other elite groups such as older kinds of technocrats, will rightly receive more study in the future.

Returned Students

Another important trend in the educational backgrounds of CC members is the emergence of the returnees from study abroad. By the end of 2003, Chinese who had gone overseas as degree candidates or visiting scholars numbered 700,200.[45] Among them, approximately 172,800 had returned to China.[46] Because of attractive policies, a booming economy, and other factors, the return rate has gone up and keeps rising. Although many in this emerging elite group only recently returned to China, some already have important leadership posts.

Among the 356 full and alternate members of the latest CC, 32 had study or work experiences abroad lasting a year or more. Several served in Chinese embassies. For example, Zeng Peiyan, a new PB member, was in China's Washington embassy from 1982 to 1984. Xiong Guangkai, a PLA General Staff Headquarters deputy chief and CC alternate member, worked in Chinese embassies in Germany for more than two decades. Some studied in communist countries. SC member Luo Gan and PB members Cao Gangchuan and Zhang Dejiang studied in East Germany, Russia, and North Korea, respectively. On the previous Politburo, seven (29 percent) studied in the Soviet Union or other East European countries; and other members of the third generation also had Soviet experience. Among the 11,000 Chinese who studied abroad between 1949 and early 1960, an overwhelming majority went to the Soviet Union.[47] Now many have retired.

By 2002, those in high posts who had studied in communist countries outside China were fewer, and returnees from the West or Japan increased. Table 3.12 lists the latter group on the current CC. Six received advanced degrees, and fourteen studied or worked as visiting scholars. Although the number of returnees rose in the 2002 CC as compared with 1997, their overall presence remains small, 6 percent of all CC members. Most (75 percent) serve as leaders in education, academic research, finance, or foreign affairs. Very few have advanced their careers through province leadership, which has been the surest launch pad to really high posts. A majority (80 percent) was born in east China, and more than half were born in Shanghai or the adjacent provinces of Zhejiang and Jiangsu. Except for Yang Jiechi and Liu Jie, most of these leaders studied abroad after Deng's groundbreaking decision in 1978 to send students to the West, especially to the United States. Finally, these returnees

Table 3.12 Full and Alternate Members in the Sixteenth CC Who Had Educational Experiences in the West and Japan

Name	Born	Native Province	Current Position	Country	Foreign School/Firm	Years	Degree/Visiting Scholar (VS)	Academic Field
Chen Liangyu	1946	Zhejiang	Party Secretary of Shanghai	England	Birmingham University	1992	VS	Public Administration
Chen Zhili	1942	Fujian	State Councilor	USA	Penn State University	1980–82	VS	Material Science
Xu Guanhua	1941	Shanghai	Minister of Science and Technology	Sweden	Stockholm University	1979–81	VS	Information Technology
Lu Fuyuan	1945	Heilongjiang	Minister of Commerce	Canada	Montréal Univ.	1981–83	VS	Engineering
Zhou Xiaochuan	1948	Jiangsu	Governor, People's Bank	USA	Univ. of California at Santa Cruz	1987–88	VS	Finance and Economics
Xu Kuangdi	1937	Zhejiang	President, Chinese Academy of Engineering	Sweden	Industrial firm	1984–85	VS	Metallurgy Research
Lu Yongxiang	1942	Zhejiang	President of Chinese Academy of Sciences	Germany	Aachen Industrial University	1978–81	PhD	Engineering
Liu Mingkang	1945	Fujian	Governor, Bank of China	England	London University	1984–87	MBA	Finance
Zhai Huqu	1950	Jiangsu	President, China Academy of Agriculture	England	Birmingham University	1984–87	PhD	Biology
Yang Jiechi	1950	Shanghai	Ambassador to the U.S.	England	Bath Univ., London School of Eco. and Pol. Sciences	1973–75	VS	International Affairs
Cao Jianming	1955	Shanghai	Vice President, Supreme People's Court	USA and Belgium	San Francisco State Univ. / Belgium	1990–91 / 1988–89	VS	Law

(continued)

Table 3.12 Continued

Name	Born	Native Province	Current Position	Country	Foreign School/Firm	Years	Degree/Visiting Scholar (VS)	Academic Field
Liu Jie	1943	Anhui	President, Anshan Iron and Steel Group Corp.	Japan	Toshiba Co.	1974–76	VS	Engineering
Huang Jiefu	1946	Jiangxi	President of Zhongshan Medical School	Australia	Sydney University	1984–87	VS	Medicine
Wu Qidi	1947	Zhejiang	President of Tongji Univ.	Switzerl'd	Sulies Institute of Technology	1981–85	PhD	Engineering
Bai Chunli	1953	Liaoning	Vice President, Chinese Academy of Science	USA and Japan	Cal Tech, Northeastern University	1985–87 1991–92	Post-Doctoral Fellow, Visiting Professor	Chemistry
Wang Huning	1955	Shanghai	Dep. Director, Central Policy Research Center	USA	Iowa University, Univ. of Michigan	1988–89	VS	Political Science
Min Weifang	1950	Beijing	Party Secretary and VP of Beijing Univ.	USA	Stanford University Texas Univ. Austin	1982–86, 1986–88	PhD Post-Doctoral Fellow	Education Administration
Lin Mingyue	1947	Taiwan	VP, All China Federation of Taiwan Compatriots	USA	Unknown	1980s	MA	Engineering
Pan Yunhe	1946	Zhejiang	President, Zhejiang Univ.	USA	Carnegie Melon Univ.	1986–88	VS	Computer Science
Li Hongzhong	1956	Shandong	Vice Governor, Guangdong	USA	Harvard University (Kennedy School)	1996–97	VS	Public Administration

are unlike the 1950s Chinese students who went to the USSR for engineering or natural sciences only. The academic fields of returnees from the West are more diversified.

These patterns might eventually bode new tensions in Chinese elite politics, if the technocratic criterion for legitimate rule becomes weaker or if returnees are distrusted by locally educated leaders (a problem that has sometimes emerged in Taiwan's politics, for instance). The returnees have more than their distinct educational backgrounds; they may also differ from PRC-educated leaders in other ways. Returnees can generally advance their careers through sectors that are important for education and economics, and they may also have strong regional constituencies. The returnees are a talented group, but the highest other current leaders have usually moved up by slower advancements, in a step-by-step manner through county, city, and province levels of administration. The present top leaders are not "helicopters." It remains to be seen whether the returnees will significantly increase their numbers in future Chinese leaderships, whether China-educated elites and foreign-trained elites will cooperate well, and whether the differences of speed in their career paths will affect the norms of future Chinese successions.

Diverging Career Paths, and Complex Interdependences of Factions

Analysis of the careers of the new Chinese leaders reveals a paradox. Formal channels for career development have affected elite selection, but so have nepotistic and informal political networks (e.g., school ties, blood ties, regional affiliations, and patron–client ties). Institutional mechanisms are increasingly effective (e.g., age criteria for retirement, term limits, intraparty elections, and norms about generations and regional representation). The new heavyweights in Chinese elite politics have all nonetheless expedited their political careers through personal *guanxi* connections. This is true of Hu Jintao, Wen Jiabao, Zeng Qinghong, and Wu Bangguo. Yet they also give evidence of being more interested than their predecessors in seeking legitimacy through institutional norms. Even informally, politicians help their careers most when they make links with more than one actual or latent faction, rather than just a single group. The new leaders have often spanned different geographic and bureaucratic units. Their ties, when most successful, have crossed more than one power network. This particular kind of "bargaining" rather than "bandwagoning" makes factions interdependent. It creates incentives to build coalitions.

Occupations

Table 3.13 categorizes the primary career paths for civilian members of the 2002 CC: industrial enterprises, rural administrations, party organs, *mishu*, secretaries of top leaders, the CCYL, schools and research institutions, financial institutions, the foreign service, and others. The table omits military leaders who deserve a separate

Table 3.13. Primary Career Experiences of Civilian Full and Alternate Members, Sixteenth CC

Primary Career Experience	Full Members		Alternate Members		Total	
	No.	%	No.	%	No.	%
Party functionary organs	34	**21.8**	17	**12.6**	51	**17.5**
Industrial enterprises	29	**18.6**	22	**16.3**	51	**17.5**
Chinese Communist Youth League (CCYL)	15	**9.6**	20	**14.8**	35	**12.0**
Mishu (*Mishuzhang* and office director)	15	**9.6**	8	**5.9**	23	**7.9**
Rural administration	4	**2.6**	13	**9.6**	17	**5.8**
Education and research institutes	6	**3.8**	9	**6.7**	15	**5.2**
Financial and banking institutions	3	**1.9**	6	**4.4**	9	**3.1**
Foreign service	4	**2.6**	1	**0.7**	5	**1.7**
Other (legal affairs, women's federation, sports)	4	**2.6**	8	**5.9**	12	**4.1**
Mixed	42	**26.9**	16	**11.9**	58	**19.9**
Unknown	0	0	15	11.1	15	5.2
Total	156	100.0	135	99.9	291	99.9

Note: Percentages do not add to 100 because of rounding.

study; and it does not show career moves such as the dramatic reshuffling of province administrators. Among the sixty-five full members of the CC who serve as province leaders, thirty-four (52 percent) had previous leadership experiences in other provinces, and twenty (31 percent) previously worked in the national government. This topic is also important enough for a separate study.

The nine occupations listed on the table are somewhat arbitrary, but the longest period a leader has spent in one sector can show the main career. In some cases, a leader's past work experiences have been in two or more sectors; so the table includes a category "mixed career paths." Fifty-eight members (20 percent) of the current CC, including forty-two full members, have mixed occupational experiences.

Economic work managing an urban industry is now a normal path for career advancement (18 percent of the CC). The portion of such occupations among full members is higher than among alternates, especially when those with "mixed" backgrounds are counted. Most have advanced their political careers by serving (often step by step) as director of a factory, head of an industrial bureau, and mayor of a city or minister of the State Council. For example, new SC member Wu Bangguo, after graduating from Qinghua University in 1967, began his career as a technician, and served successively as deputy chief and then chief of the technical section, then deputy director and director of Shanghai no. 3 Electric Tube Factory. From 1978 to 1991 he rose gradually to be deputy manager of Shanghai Electronics, and later deputy secretary of the CCP Shanghai Municipal Committee, where his job was to develop industrial enterprises. By the early 1990s, he was Shanghai party chief. Then he became vice premier in charge of all China's urban industries, trying to guide the reform of state-owned enterprises.

By contrast, seventeen members (6 percent) had careers primarily in rural areas. Hui Liangyu, a new PB member, for example, began his career as an official with the Agricultural Bureau of Yushu County in Jilin, after graduating from the provincial school of agronomy in 1964. He worked his way up as party secretary of a people's commune, party secretary of a county, deputy head of his province's bureau of agriculture, and then vice governor in charge of agriculture, all in Jilin Province from the 1970s through the late 1980s. By 1990, he was deputy director of the Policy Research Office of the CCP Central Committee, focusing on agricultural reform throughout China. During the past decade, he has served successively as party secretary of three provinces. He now serves as the vice premier of the State Council in charge of agriculture.

Table 3.13 shows that 18 percent of civilian CC members have advanced their careers as party cadres in fields such as administration or personnel. New SC member Wu Guanzheng is an example. After graduating from Qinghua in 1968, he worked as a technician and party official in a Wuhan factory for most of the Cultural Revolution. During the past two decades, Wu has been municipal party secretary and mayor in Wuhan, and then party secretary in three different provinces. Such party functionaries are heavily involved in administration and economic development. Few now exclusively do personnel or propaganda work. Seweryn Bialer, studying the Soviet Union of the late Brezhnev period, found similar patterns: leaders increasingly advanced their careers in regions other than Moscow, and in management rather than mobilization.[48] Bialer's suggestions about the Soviet future proved later to be more accurate than those of other Russianists at that time.

During the past two decades, the posts of *mishu* (personal secretary) and *mishuzhang* (chief of staff) have also become important springboards into leadership. While some have worked as *mishu* only at certain career stages, others have been *mishu* for most of their political lives.[49] A study of the fourth generation leaders who served on the 1997 CC and the Central Discipline Inspection Commission shows that approximately 41 percent have worked as *mishu*, *mishuzhang*, or office directors.[50] On the 2002 CC, eighty-eight full members (44 percent) have done this kind of staff work. In the twenty-five-member Politburo, fourteen (56 percent) previously have been *mishu* or *mishuzhang* at various levels. They include no fewer than seven of the nine SC members. Zeng Qinghong served as a *mishu* during several periods, and each such post led to other important appointments for him. Table 3.13 shows that twenty-three members (8 percent) of the CC have advanced their careers primarily through *mishu* work, and the portion at higher levels is greater. Li Jianguo, now Shaanxi party secretary, has spent most of his adult life (twenty-three years) as a *mishu* or *mishuzhang* in Tianjin, including many years as secretary to Li Ruihuan, a third generation heavyweight.

Table 3.13 also shows that some members could move to CC membership exclusively through work in any of three other sectors: educational administration, finance/banking, or foreign service. For example, Bai Chunli (Chinese Academy of Science vice president), Zhou Xiaochuan (new People's Bank governor), and Yang Jiechi (ambassador to the United States) have always served in their current fields. Representation from each of these three sectors is small, but together they are about 10 percent of the CC. They show some occupational diversity in China's elites below the very top level.

Leaders who attained high office through the Youth League also are an important group in the whole CC (12 percent, or more if the mixed careers are included). CCYL cadres have long been seen as natural successors to party leadership. Many have specific previous political associations with Hu Jintao. These are the so-called *tuanpai* leaders, who readily see Hu as their role model. Most now serve as inland province elites. *Tuanpai* members are probably one of the most solid informal political networks on the CC. If infighting were to break out among the top leaders, they would likely become Hu's political allies.

Factions

Table 3.14 shows the distribution between *tuanpai* leaders and the Shanghai gang on the 1997 and 2002 CCs and PBs.[51] Identification of the *tuanpai* leaders is based on three criteria: they are members of the CC who served as CCYL officials at the province level or above; their tenures as provincial CCYL bureaucrats occurred at least partly in the era when Hu Jintao served on the Youth League Secretariat (1982–1985); former CCYL leaders who are also members of the Shanghai gang are excluded (e.g., new Shanghai mayor Han Zhen and new Jiangsu party secretary Li Yuanchao). It is difficult to trace each leader's exact past association with Hu Jintao, but it is reasonable to assume that Hu and these leaders have known each other through CCYL work for a couple of decades or so. Many *tuanpai* officials used to serve on the Youth League national committee. Some, such as Wang Lequan (PB

Table 3.14.   Power Distribution between the *Tuanpai* and the Shanghai Gang

	CCYL Officials (Tuanpai)	Shanghai Gang
15th Central Committee (CC)		
PB Members (total $N = 24$)	1	4
CC Members ($N = 344$)	29	11
16th Central Committee (CC)		
PB Members ($N = 25$)	4	5
CC Members ($N = 356$)	47	20

member and Xinjiang party secretary) and Liu Yandong (new head of CCP United Front Department), are probably Hu's close friends.

Identification of the members of the Shanghai gang can also be based on three criteria: they advanced their careers through political association with Jiang or Zeng in Shanghai; a majority, but not all, were born in Shanghai, Jiangsu, or Zhejiang; and those who are apparently closer to Zhu Rongji than to Jiang and Zeng are excluded (e.g., former Shanghai mayor Xu Kuandi and former People's Bank governor Dai Xianglong). During the 1990s, most provincial leaders have been regularly (in some cases, frequently) reshuffled. The CCP Organization Department's regulations on cadre exchange include the old law of avoidance, decreeing that local leaders should not serve in their home regions.[52] But in Shanghai between 1989 when Jiang became general secretary and 2002, almost no high-ranking officers (full or deputy party secretaries and full or vice mayors) were transferred from other regions to that city's party committee or government.[53] Jiang and Zeng have firmly controlled the choices of Shanghai leaders and have continuously promoted members of this Shanghai gang into the central government.

The Shanghai gang occupied more seats on the 1997 PB than the *tuanpai* did, but the *tuanpai* held more seats on the 1997 CC. This pattern continues on the 2002 Politburo and CC, as table 3.14 shows. Between these years, the number of *tuanpai* leaders increased on both the PB (from 1 to 4) and the CC (from 29 to 47). Neither the *tuanpai* nor the Shanghai gang can wholly control the CC or the Politburo, however. In case of votes, either would have to bargain with additional groups—or each other.

Table 3.15 details the most likely factional links of all members of the 2002 Politburo. Major political networks such as the presumed "Shanghai gang," "*tuanpai* officials," "princelings' party," "Qinghua clique," "petroleum faction," and others are represented on the new PB. These groups have all generated scions for many years. Leaders of the petroleum industry, for example, played an influential role in elite recruitment during the 1970s and early 1980s.[54] Now three PB members, including Zeng Qinghong, new Organization Department head He Guoqiang, and new public security minister Zhou Yongkang, come from China's oil patch. Four other PB members were at the First Ministry of Machine Building and Electronic Industries, overlapping with Jiang, who worked in that ministry for almost two decades.

Two current PB members have princeling backgrounds. The number of these CCP aristocrats on the previous PB was four (Jiang, Li Peng, Li Tieying, and Zeng). The princeling number on the whole CC is now eighteen, and the same number was on the 1997 CC.[55] As new leaders move to the highest levels of authority, however, princeling or patron–client ties that previously enabled them to succeed may become a liability. Delegates to the Congress, as the ballot tallies show, have increasingly prevented princelings and others very close to top leaders from receiving many votes.

Table 3.15 Factional Affiliations of the Members of the Sixteenth Politburo

Name	Shanghai Municipal Leadership	CCYL Central or Provincial Leadership	Qinghua University Network	Ministry Petroleum Industry	Ministries of 1st Machine Building & Electronics	Long-term Association with Inland Region*	Long-term Association with Coastal Region*	Princeling Background	Total No. of Affiliations
Hu Jintao		1982–1985	1959–1968			1985–1992			3
Wu Bangguo	1983–1992		1960–1967				1985–1992		3
Wei Jiabao						1981–1982			1
Qia Qinglin					1962–1978		1985–2002		2
Zeng Qinghong	1984–1989			1981–1984			1986–1989	X	4
Huang Ju	1983–2002					1986–1997	1985–2002		3
Wu Guanzheng			1956–1963			1990–1998	1997–2002		3
Li Changchun			1959–1968				1985–1990, 1998–2002		2
Luo Gan					1962–1980	1981–1983			2
Wang Lequan		1982–1986				1991–	1989–1991		3
Wang Zhaoguo		1982–1984					1987–1990		2
Hui Liangyu						1987–1999	1999–2003		2
Liu Qi							1998–		1
Liu Yunshan		1982–1984				1992–1993			2
Wu Yi				1965–1988			1988–1991		2
Zhang Lichang							1985–		1
Zhang Dejiang						1990–1998	1998–		2
Chen Liangyu	1985–2002						1992–		2
Zhou Yongkang				1970–1998		1999–2003			2
Yu Zhengsheng					1982–1984	1901–	1992–1994	X	4
He Guoqiang				1980–1986		1999–2002	1996–1999		3
Guo Boxiong (M)									0
Cao Gangchun (M)									0
Zeng Peiyan			1956–1962		1962–1982, 1984–1992				2
Wang Gang						1977–1981			1
Total Number	4	4	5	4	4	13	16	2	1

Note: *These columns record years of tenure as a provincial/municipal leader. M = Military. SC members names are boldfaced.

Interdependence

The coexistence of varied political networks suggests some dispersion of influence and balance of power. The increase of regional and professional channels through which new leaders advance their careers creates important kinds of diversification. Political networks also have overlapping memberships. For example, prominent members of the Qinghua clique also belong to either the Shanghai gang or the *tuanpai*. This interdependence among factions means that political compromise can and must occur more frequently. More PB members are affiliated with Jiang and Zeng than with Hu, but the power distribution may not be as disparate as it seems, because princeling backgrounds and the Shanghai gang are unpopular among many other Chinese leaders.

In each of the five most important leadership bodies in the PRC today, the top two positions are filled by one leader from each of the two most obvious coalitions. In the state presidency, we find President Hu Jintao versus Vice President Zeng Qinghong; on the Central Military Commission, Chairman Hu Jintao versus First Vice Chairman Guo Boxiong (who is Jiang's protégé); on the Politburo Standing Committee, Secretary General Hu Jintao versus the second highest ranking member Wu Bangguo (a member of the Shanghai gang); on the State Council, Premier Wen Jiabao versus Executive Vice Premier Huang Ju (another member of the Shanghai Gang); in the National People's Congress, Chairman Wu Bangguo versus First Vice Chairman Wang Zhaoguo (a longtime colleague of Hu Jintao in the Youth League).

This interesting arrangement is by no means coincidental, and it creates checks on leaders. It reflects the desire within the Chinese political establishment to maintain a balance of power between opposing interests. Also, the two senior leaders who lost their jobs as a result of the SARS crisis in the spring of 2003 were each from a different coalition. Former health minister Zhang Wenkang was a member of the Shanghai gang, and former mayor of Beijing Meng Xuenong was a longtime associate of Hu Jintao in the Youth League. Yet while the Youth League faction and the Shanghai gang are arguably the two most powerful elite factions in present-day China, the number of seats they occupy in the Politburo and on the Central Committee is limited. They must actively engage in coalition building to expand their influence.

No individual, no faction, no institution, and no region can currently dominate China. Everyone has to negotiate, and those who are skillful in finding allies are most likely to have success. This explains why all three new top leaders (Hu, Zeng, and Wen) are capable political tacticians, why the *mishu* career that breeds both personal and administrative skills has become an important ladder to high office, and why the Party Congress evinced power sharing rather than vicious factional fighting.

HU-ZENG DYNAMICS AND THE FUTURE TRAJECTORY OF THE CHINESE ELITE

Although CCP politicians have often tried to change succession rules to their own advantage, during the past decade more precepts have been normalized. These include term limits, retirement ages, and now somewhat more balanced regional representation. This has prompted Hu and Zeng to expand their power bases beyond the "*tuanpai* officials" and the "Shanghai gang," respectively. Their spheres of influence may still be geographical: Hu is more popular in inland provinces, and Zeng can present himself as a leader for the interests of rich coastal provinces. Competition between Hu and Zeng need not therefore be zero-sum. Their differences in personal experiences, career backgrounds, political associations, leadership styles, and regional loyalties could breed distrust; but Hu and Zeng may also cooperate in consolidating the rule of their CCP and sharing the benefits of power.

Chinese political institutionalization depends in the medium term on the relationship between these two most powerful figures of the post-Jiang era.[56] As Jiang Zemin's chief strategist for over fifteen years, Zeng is second only to Jiang in the so-called Shanghai gang, and he will likely inherit this powerful network after Jiang's full retirement. Like Jiang, Zeng comes from a princeling family. Also like him, Zeng is known for skills of political favoritism. From 1999 to 2002, Zeng took advantage of his post as the head of the CCP Organization Department to expand his power base by building a broad coalition of all coastal provinces, from Liaoning in the north to Hainan in the south.

Zeng is well placed to form alliances with two elite groups: his fellow princelings and the "returnees from study overseas" (*haiguipai*).[57] A majority of princelings work in coastal provinces. Leaders with princeling backgrounds can expedite their careers by working in coastal cities. Bo Xilai (former Liaoning governor and now trade minister), Xi Jinping (Zhejiang party secretary), and Li Yuanchao (Jiangsu party secretary) previously served as municipal chiefs of Dalian, Fuzhou, and Nanjing. Economic achievements can be scored with relative ease in the rich coastal places where these men have been chiefs. Most returnees from study overseas, also, were born or have worked in coastal areas, usually Shanghai or Beijing.[58] According to a recently released report by the Shanghai municipal government, by the autumn of 2002 Shanghai had over 30,000 returnees, of whom 90 percent held master's or doctoral degrees.[59] Returnees who settled in Shanghai were one-fifth of all China's returnees in 2002.[60]

Differences between inland Hu and coastal Zeng are obvious, but they may not lead to a fierce power struggle. In the past few years, Hu and Zeng have formed a good working relationship. This is especially evident in their joint effort to promote political reform programs at the Central Party School (CPS). Zeng's relationship to his mentor Jiang is also subject to change. It may not be in Zeng's interest to allow Jiang to play a behind-the-curtain role, and this could contribute to the full retirement of the outgoing party chief. If Zeng lacks a willingness to share power and resources with inland interests, however, the potential backlash against him, against the Shanghai gang, and against the rich coast would be strong. It is revealing that, while Hu lost only one vote in the first election at the 2002 Party Congress, Zeng lost eighty-five votes.[61]

Evidence suggests that Zeng has been frankly concerned about growing resentment against himself and the Shanghai gang. He has made recent efforts to change his negative public image. In the fall of 2002, for example, Zeng attended a widely publicized ceremonial meeting to praise the so-called service team of Ph.D.s sent to the western region. The CCP Organization Department selected 114 Ph.D. holders from the coast and shipped them off to serve a year in China's ten western provinces (and Jiangxi).[62] Shanghai and other coastal places have supported development under the go west strategy, which also provides new business opportunities for coastal manufacturers.

Hu's challenge is to maintain his popular image as a leader who relies on institutional power rather than factional networking. At the same time, he would lose too much if he alienated himself from his own longtime associates. Soon after the Congress, several of Hu's close allies were promoted to important national and provincial posts. These include Liu Yandong (new head of the CCP United Front Work Department), Zhang Xuezhong (new Sichuan party secretary), Li Zhilun (new minister of supervision), Li Keqiang (new Liaoning party secretary), Huang Huahua (new Guangdong governor), Zhang Baoshun (new Shanxi governor), Song Xiuyan (new Qinghai governor), and Shen Yueyue (new deputy head of the CCP Organization Department). They all sit on the CC. Because of their relatively young ages, these people are in line for seats on the Politburo at the next Party Congress five years hence, presuming the current succession norms continue.

Hu and Zeng may have to share power in order to maintain sufficiently diverse talents in the CCP. Hu's *tuanpai* leaders, especially those who work in inland provinces, generally have less expertise in foreign trade, finance, technology, and urban construction than their counterparts from the coast, especially those from Beijing, Shanghai, Jiangsu, and Guangdong. On the other hand, Zeng and his associates can see that coastal success in the future depends largely on the inland China market. The power of the Shanghai gang has been restrained by more equal regional representation. The votes of inland province leaders in the CC, on both personnel and policies, are potentially decisive.

Hu and Zeng have clearly cooperated in CPS reforms. During the past decade under Hu's presidency, the CPS has broadened its midcareer training programs and has become a leading think tank for the study of both domestic and international policies. Zeng has been heavily involved in these developments; so it is no surprise that Zeng now succeeds Hu as president of the school. The CPS has become not just a place for theoretical brainstorming about China's political reform, but also a place for Hu and Zeng to experiment with political compromise. Hu and Zeng personally granted diplomas to over 800 graduates of the Class of 2002 in a highly publicized CPS commencement ceremony. In another recent televised meeting of heads of provincial party organization departments, Hu constantly referred to Jiang's theory of the "three represents." Zeng returned the compliment by repeatedly quoting Hu's remarks.[63] Hu and Zeng have formed a relationship that is probably both competitive and cooperative.

Conflict scenarios could occur. Cleavages within the new leadership, especially on social and economic policies, are potentially so fundamental that compromise might become difficult or impossible. China's top leaders must deal with a long list of daunting sociopolitical challenges: economic disparities, the negative impact (especially on Chinese farmers) of entry to the WTO, urban unemployment, rampant official corruption, ethnic tensions, industrial accidents, major health crises, and environmental scandals. On the international front, while the September 11 terrorist attack reduced tensions in U.S.–Chinese relations, an unpredictable external environment surrounds China in Central Asia, Indonesia, and Korea. The issue of Taiwan and other problems in U.S.–Chinese relations, though not imminently dangerous, remain unsolved.

As China faces these daunting challenges at home and abroad, the new leaders may well unite rather than divide. Fear of chaos or regime collapse, as experienced by many authoritarian parties in other countries during the past decade, can be a critical factor that pressures political rivals to parley. Hu and Zeng may be willing to cooperate not because either is motivated by liberal ideals, but because they recognize their own limitations in their quickly changing country. They may see a need to share power. Only time will tell whether this process eventually leads to a system in which factional politics becomes more transparent and legitimated, so that various parts of the public have their interests protected and their voices heard.

NOTES

Cheng Li is professor, Department of Government, Hamilton College, New York, cli@hamilton.edu. Lynn White is professor, Woodrow Wilson School of Public and International Affairs, Princeton University, New Jersey, lynn@princeton.edu. This chapter is the revision of the authors' article that first appeared in *Asian Survey*; see Li Cheng and Lynn White, "The Sixteenth Central Committee of the Chinese Communist Party: Hu Gets What?" *Asian Survey*, July–August 2003, 553–597. The authors thank the publisher of *Asian Survey* for granting permission for this revised and updated essay to appear in this book. For generous support, Li Cheng is grateful for the Woodrow Wilson International Center for Scholars, the United States Institute of Peace, and the Chiang Ching-kuo Foundation. Lynn White thanks Hong Kong University's Centre of Asian Studies, the Chiang Ching-kuo Foundation, and Princeton University.

1. Andrew J. Nathan, "Authoritarian Resilience," *Journal of Democracy,* January 2003. Also see his remarks at the conference entitled the Sixteenth Party Congress and China's Future, www.Chinesenewsnet.com (accessed January 8, 2003).

2. Joseph Fewsmith, "The Sixteenth Party Congress: Implications for Understanding Chinese Politics," *China Leadership Monitor,* Winter 2003.

3. As a standard practice, alternate members of the Central Committee are listed in the order of the number of votes they received. See www.china.org.cn/english/features/48817.htm.

4. Chen was later elected as state councilor at the Tenth NPC, but she received the lowest number of the votes of confirmation in the State Council (240 no votes and 118 abstentions

from 2,935 delegates). The results of the election were open to journalists who covered the Tenth NPC in March 2003. See www.chinesenewsnet.com (accessed March 17, 2003).

5. Jiang perhaps used foreign visits, especially a Texas summit with George W. Bush just before the congress, to enhance his bargaining power in personnel decisions back home. It may or may not be a coincidence that the announcement of promotions for Jia Qinglin and Huang Ju, party chiefs of Beijing and Shanghai, came while Jiang was visiting the United States.

6. The sources are Liao Gailong and Fan Yuan, comps., *Zhongguo renming da cidian: Xiandai dangzhengjun lingdao renwu juan* [Who's who in China: Current party, government, and military leaders] (Beijing: Foreign Languages Press, 1994); Shen Xueming et al., comps., *Zhonggong di shiwujie zhongyang weiyuanhui zhongyang jilü jiancha weiyuanhui weiyuan minglu* [Who's who among the members of the Fifteenth Central Committee of the Chinese Communist Party and the Fifteenth Central Discipline Inspection Commission] (Beijing: Zhonggong wenxian chubanshe, 1999); Ho Szu-yin, comp., *Zhonggong renmin lu* [Who's who in communist China] (Taipei: Institute of International Relations, National Chengchi University, 1999); and *China Directory* (Tokyo: Rapiopress, various years from 1985 to 2002). In addition, we have collected biographic information, often through search engines, from online websites such as www.xinhuanet.com, www.China.com, www.Chinesenewsnet .com, www.sina.com, www.yahoo.com, and www.sohu.com. Two sources that appeared after the data collection are www.16congress.org.cn, and CCP Organization Department and the Research Institute of the CCP History under the Central Committee of the Chinese Communist Party, comp., *Zhongguo gongchandang lijie zhongyang weiyuan dacidian* [Who's who in the Central Committees of the Chinese Communist Party, 1921–2003] (Beijing: CCP Archive Press, 2004).

7. Most China scholars have attributed these two concepts to Deng Xiaoping. While this is valid, Jiang also enthusiastically promoted these ideas at least until the summer of 2002. For more, see Cheng Li, *China's Leaders: The New Generation* (Lanham, MD: Rowman & Littlefield, 2001), 6–10; Cheng Li, "Jiang's Game and Hu's Advantages," *Foreign Policy in Focus*, www.fpif.org (accessed November 21, 2002).

8. *Shijie ribao* [World Journal], November 15, 2002, A3.

9. Joseph Kahn, "A Chinese Write-in Candidate Tests the Official Winds," *International Herald Tribune*, March 3, 2003, 4.

10. On Hu's association with these three political networks, see Cheng Li, "Hu's Followers: Provincial Leaders with Backgrounds in the Communist Youth League," *China Leadership Monitor,* Summer 2002.

11. Cheng Li, "A Landslide Victory for Provincial Leaders," *China Leadership Monitor,* Winter 2003.

12. Gaetano Mosca, *The Ruling Class* (New York: McGraw-Hill, 1936).

13. Vilfredo Pareto, *The Rise and Fall of Elites: An Application of Theoretical Sociology* (Totowa, NJ: Bedminster, 1968).

14. On "technocratic turnover" in the 1992 and 1997 Party Congresses, see Li Cheng and Lynn White, "The Army in the Succession to Deng Xiaoping: Familiar Fealties and Technocratic Trends," *Asian Survey,* August 1993, 757–786; and Li Cheng and Lynn White, "The Fifteenth Central Committee of the Chinese Communist Party: Full-Fledged Technocratic Leadership with Partial Control by Jiang Zemin," *Asian Survey,* March 1998, 245–247.

15. The Sixteenth Congress included thirty-eight delegations. In addition to the two new

delegations from enterprises and financial firms, there were thirty-one provincial and municipal delegations, one from the PLA, one from the central party, one from the central government, one from Hong Kong and Macao, and one representing Taiwan.

16. The second largest turnover occurred at the 1987 Party Congress when, out of the
previous six-man Standing Committee, only Zhao Ziyang remained.

17. William Strauss and Neil Howe, *Generations: The History of America's Future, 1582–
2069* (New York: Morrow, 1992), 60–61. For a theoretical discussion of the concept of polit-
ical generation, see Karl Mannheim, "Consciousness of Class and Consciousness of
Generation," in *Essays on the Sociology of Knowledge* (London: RKP, 1952). Many scholars
define the formative years of personal growth as between seventeen and twenty-five. See
Michael Yahuda, "Political Generations in China," *China Quarterly*, December 1979, 795;
Marvin Rintala, "Generations: Political Generations" in *The International Encyclopedia of the
Social Sciences* (New York: Macmillan/Free Press, 1968); Rodolfo Garza and David Vaughan,
"The Political Socialization of Chicano Elites: A Generational Approach," *Social Science
Quarterly*, June 1984, 290–307. The importance of early adulthood may also be explored
psychologically, as in Erik H. Erickson, *Young Man Luther: A Study in Psychoanalysis and
History* (New York: Norton, 1958).

18. Carol Lee Hamrin, "Perspectives on Generational Change in China" (scope paper for
the workshop organized by the Paul H. Nitze School of Advanced International Studies,
Johns Hopkins University, June 1993), 1.

19. Earlier studies based on generational analysis include Michael Yahuda, "Political Generations in China," 795, and W. William Whitson, "The Concept of Military Generation,"
Asian Survey, November 1968.

20. Strauss and Howe, *Generations*, 59.

21. Ruth Cherrington, "A Case Study of the 1980s Generation of Young Intellectuals,"
British Journal of Sociology, June 1997, 304.

22. David M. Finkelstein and Maryanne Kivlehan, eds., *Chinese Leadership in the Twenty-
first Century: The Rise of the Fourth Generation* (Armonk, NY: Sharpe, 2002); Li, *China's
Leaders*.

23. For a detailed discussion of age limits for high-level leaders, see H. Lyman Miller,
"The Sixteenth Party Congress and China's Political Processes," in Gang Lin and Susan
Shirk, eds., *The Sixteenth CCP Congress and Leadership Transition in China*, Asia Program
Special Report, Woodrow Wilson International Center for Scholars, September 2002, 10–14.

24. *Wenhui bao* [Wenhui Daily], Hong Kong, November 15, 2002.

25. Li Feng, *Shiwuda zhonggong gaoceng xin dangan* [New profiles of the leadership of the
Fifteenth Central Committee of the CCP] (Hong Kong: Wenhua chuanbo, 1997), 158.

26. Li Feng, *Shiwuda*.

27. Joseph Fewsmith, "Generational Transition in China," *Washington Quarterly*, Autumn
2002, 23.

28. For more, see Cheng Li, "After Hu, Who? China's Provincial Leaders Await Promotion," *China Leadership Monitor*, Winter 2002.

29. Li and White, "Fifteenth Central Committee," 247; Li, *China's Leaders*, 164–168.

30. Li and White, "Fifteenth Central Committee," 256.

31. The term "province" includes directly ruled municipalities and autonomous regions.
The eleven coastal units at this level are Liaoning, Beijing, Tianjin, Hebei, Shandong, Jiangsu,
Shanghai, Zhejiang, Fujian, Guangdong, and Hainan. See Wang Shaoguang and Hu Angang,

The Political Economy of Uneven Development: The Case of China (Armonk, NY: Sharpe, 1999), 48.

32. www.China.com.cn (accessed November 6, 2002).

33. www.xinhuanet.com (accessed September 11, 2002).

34. www.chinesenewsnet.com (accessed September 24, 2002).

35. http://gxi.gov.cn (accessed December 7, 2001).

36. If a leader's undergraduate major differs from the major in post-graduate education, this study counts the latter only.

37. http://sina.com (accessed April 24, 2002).

38. *Shijie ribao*, January 13, 2002, A8.

39. *China News Analysis*, January 1, 1994, 2.

40. *Dongfang ribao* [Oriental Daily], November 6, 2002, 1; *Xingdao ribao* [Singapore Island Daily] December 13, 2004, 1.

41. Barry Naughton, "The Chinese Economy: WTO, Trade, and U.S.-China Relations" (paper, November 2002).

42. *Shijie ribao*, November 12, 2002, A3.

43. For more on the definition of entrepreneurs and the contrast with technocrats, see Joseph A. Schumpeter, *Capitalism, Socialism, and Democracy*, (New York: Harper Torchbooks, 1975), 132; Cheng Li, "'Credentialism' versus 'Entrepreneurism': The Interplay and Tensions between Technocrats and Entrepreneurs in the Reform Era," in Chan Kwok Bun, ed., *Chinese Business Networks: State, Economy, and Culture* (New York: Prentice Hall, 1999), 86–111.

44. *Xingdao ribao*, December 13, 2004, 1.

45. This number is based on the statistics released by China's Ministry of Education in February 2004, http://news.xinhuanet.com (accessed February 16, 2004).

46. Among those 527,400 who have remained abroad, 356,600 are still studying; http://news.xinhuanet.com (accessed February 16, 2004).

47. Li, *China's Leaders*, 17–18.

48. Seweryn Bialer, *Stalin's Successors* (New York: Cambridge University Press, 1980).

49. On the prevalence of *mishu* among Chinese leaders, see Cheng Li, "The *Mishu* Phenomenon: Patron–Client Ties and Coalition-Building Tactics," *China Leadership Monitor*, Fall 2002.

50. Li, *China's Leaders*, 150–151.

51. For a complete list of these *tuanpai* leaders and the members of the Shanghai gang, see Li, "*Zhonggong di shiliujie zhongyang weiyuanhui renshi goucheng jiqi quanli junheng*," 16–52.

52. *Liaowang* [Outlook], June 7, 1999, 15–16; Li, "After Hu, Who?"

53. The only exception is Yang Xiaodu, newly appointed vice mayor of Shanghai, but even Yang has substantial experience in the city. Yang was born there in 1953 and was "sent down" to Anhui in 1970. By 1973, he returned to his birthplace to study at the Shanghai Traditional Medical School. He later went to Tibet, where he became vice governor.

54. David M. Lampton, *Paths to Power: Elite Mobility in Contemporary China* (Ann Arbor: Center for Chinese Studies, University of Michigan, 1986).

55. The princelings on the Sixteenth CC are Zeng Qinghong (PB), Yu Zhengsheng (PB), Dai Bingguo, Liu Yandong, Liao Hui, Zhou Xiaochuan, Hong Hu, Bo Xilai, Xi Jinping, Ma Kai, Li Yuanchao, Wang Qishan, Tian Chengping, Bai Keming, Deng Pufang, Chen Yuan, Wang Ruolin, and Li Tielin. For a list of the princelings on the 1997 CC, see Li and White, "The Fifteenth Central Committee of the Chinese Communist Party," 259.

56. For more about the relationship between Hu and Zeng, see Cheng Li, *Emerging Patterns of Power Sharing: Inland Hu vs. Coastal Zeng?* Asia Program Special Report, Woodrow Wilson International Center for Scholars, September 2002, 28–34.

57. For a detailed discussion, see Cheng Li, "The 'Shanghai Gang': Force for Stability or Cause for Conflict?" *China Leadership Monitor,* Winter 2002.

58. For more about overseas study returnees and their regional distribution, see Cheng Li, "*Zhonggong di shiliujie zhongyang weiyuanhui renshi goucheng jiqi quanli junheng*" [The Sixteenth Central Committee of the Chinese Communist Party: Paths to membership and balance of power], in Ding Shufan, ed., *Hu jintao shidai de tiaozhan* [Challenges for the Hu Jintao era] (Taipei: Xinxinwen Publishing House, 2002), 16–52.

59. *Shijie ribao,* October 31, 2002, A7.

60. According to Shu Huiguo (vice minister of personnel of the PRC from 1978 to the end of 2002), China sent 450,000 students to study abroad as degree candidates or visiting scholars. Among these, 150,000 returned to China. *Shijie ribao,* January 6, 2003, A7.

61. The total number of votes is 2,132. *Shijie ribao,* November 15, 2002, A3.

62. www2.chinesenewsnet.com (accessed September 27, 2002).

63. www6.chinesenewsnet.com (accessed August 8, 2002).

4

Cooptation and Corporatism in China

The Logic of Party Adaptation

BRUCE J. DICKSON

The political implications of China's economic reforms center on the adaptability of the Chinese Communist Party (CCP). Can it successfully adapt to the new economic and social environment its reforms are creating? Or is its ability to cope being undermined by these changes? In the midst of rapid economic change, scholars have identified trends that may be evidence of potential political transformation. On the one hand, entrepreneurs and skilled expertise are being recruited into the party. Cooptation facilitates adaptation by bringing into the party new elites who may invigorate it with new ideas and new goals. In addition, local party and government officials are developing corporatist arrangements to promote economic change. These trends give hope to some that economic reform will eventually lead to gradual political change, allowing China's transition from communism to be more like Hungary or Poland (or even Taiwan) and thereby avoid the turmoil that accompanied political change in the rest of Eastern Europe and the former Soviet Union. Along with these promising signs of rejuvenation are contrary signs of disintegration. Large numbers of party members are abandoning their party responsibilities to pursue economic opportunities. The nonstate sector of the economy is growing so fast that most enterprises do not have party organizations within them and few new members are being recruited from their workforce. In some rural areas, party organizations are paralyzed, recruitment of new members is difficult, and lineage-based clans are competing with the party for influence. These are warning signs of disintegration, of a party unable to manage its members, to have direct institutional links with the most dynamic sectors of the economy, or to control its society.

Although we cannot predict the ultimate fate of the CCP, comparing the experiences of other Leninist parties can at least clarify the kinds of questions we need to be asking. The challenges faced by the CCP—how to liberalize its economy without destabilizing the political system, how to change its organization and attract new members in order to carry out new tasks, how to balance the need to adapt with the need to uphold party traditions—are not unique. Nor are the strategies it has adopted to meet these challenges. Whether it will be successful, however, will depend largely on the peculiarities of the Chinese context: the legacies of the Maoist era, past decisions by party leaders regarding the scope and pace of economic and political reform, the continued influence of orthodox voices at the apex of the political system, and the evolving relationship between state and society.

Much of the recent scholarship on China has focused on the political system as a whole, and in particular the extent of central state power relative to local governments and society.[1] The impact of economic reform on the CCP itself, as opposed to the state as a whole, has received less extensive attention.[2] This chapter will consider the implications of ongoing economic reforms for the CCP by focusing on the two key elements of organizational adaptation: the cooptation of new members and the creation of new links with outside organizations. It will compare the kinds of elites being coopted into the CCP with those coopted into the ruling parties of Hungary and Taiwan, the best examples of successful transformation of Leninist parties, and therefore consider whether a similar transformation is possible in China. It will then consider the utility of the growing literature on corporatism in China for understanding its changing political economy and its consequent impact on the political system. Both cooptation and corporatism are having positive impacts on China's economy and the CCP, but as I will argue, neither is likely to lead to the transformation of China's political system. The evolutionary forces now at work are likely to be incompatible with the Leninist political system in China and will serve to undermine the foundations of that system, rather than prop it up. The expectation of incremental change, while reassuring in its depiction of political change without turmoil and instability, may therefore be misplaced.

THE ONSET OF ADAPTATION AND
THE LOGIC OF INCLUSION

The CCP's decision at the Third Plenum in December 1978 to abandon class struggle and to pursue economic modernization announced the beginning of the post-Mao reform era and the onset of the CCP's adaptation. These reforms led to profound changes in China's economy and society and consequently its politics. But it also set up a debate within the CCP between those who sought to protect party traditions and preserve their own positions on the one hand, and those who sought the party's adaptation to facilitate economic change, on the other.

Organizations have two main strategies for coping with environmental change: cooptation of new personnel and creation of new links with other organizations. These strategies allow the organization to be better integrated with its environment and better informed of changes occurring therein. Cooptation allows the organization to add new skills, experiences, and resources (such as political support) that may enhance its performance and increase its chance of survival. But cooptation can also threaten the organization if these coopted actors do not share its goals. The organization may receive needed support but as a consequence be diverted from its original mission.[3] Therefore, the cooptation decision may be contested within the organization. Other organizational goals, such as self-preservation and self-replication, can become paramount, limiting the organization's ability to adapt successfully to new challenges. Opponents of adaptation may point to party traditions and established norms as more legitimate grounds for resisting change than sheer self-interest.[4]

The experience of authoritarian parties, and Leninist parties in particular, is consistent with this dilemma posed by cooptation. As they abandon class struggle for the sake of economic modernization, these parties typically switch from an exclusionary to an inclusionary, or cooptive, recruitment policy.[5] Organizations coopt those they depend on, who possess resources they require, or who pose a threat to the organization. In the post-Mao period, the switch from class struggle to economic modernization as the key task of the party has made the party dependent on the technocrats and entrepreneurs who make the economy grow. Former class enemies and counterrevolutionaries are now brought into the party because they have the skills desired by party leaders to accomplish their new policy agenda. This may lead to the rejuvenation of the party, but may also lead to long-term degradation if the interests of these new members conflict with party traditions. As the party tries to adapt by coopting new members, supporters of party traditions resist "assimilating new actors whose loyalty to the organization (as opposed to its ostensible goals) is in doubt."[6] This is precisely the dilemma posed by admitting technocrats and entrepreneurs into the CCP: they are committed to economic growth, but more orthodox leaders question their support of communism and loyalty to the CCP. Those who are more concerned with self-preservation than adaptation resist the arrival of former enemies into their midst.

But the concerns of defenders of party traditions about the potential threat posed by entrepreneurs are not totally self-interested. The main threat to an authoritarian regime is the "diversification of the elite resulting from the rise of new groups controlling autonomous sources of economic power, that is, from the development of an independently wealthy business and industrial middle class."[7] The creation of autonomous sources of wealth weakens one of the key institutional pillars of a communist system: state control over the economy, resulting in organized dependence—the dependence of society on the state for economic security (jobs, housing, food, etc.) as well as political protection.[8] As economic reform creates alternative paths toward career mobility and acquisition of wealth (through education and entrepreneurship), dependence on the state is reduced, and the power of the state and its ruling party is similarly diminished. Thus the fears of party conservatives are not totally self-serving or illusory.

The second key strategy for an organization to cope with environmental change is to create links with other organizations in its environment. These links with other organizations allow information (and potentially influence) to flow between the organizations, elicit support for the organization, and may enhance its legitimacy.[9] Similarly, as a Leninist party enters the period of adaptation (or what Ken Jowitt calls inclusion), it substitutes the manipulation of symbols with the manipulation of organizations.[10] In other words, the party relies less on coercion and propaganda to control society and develops links with other organizations, either new ones that it sanctions or old ones it revives, such as united front organizations, labor unions, or professional associations. These corporate groups allow the party to organize interests emerging in the course of reform. Links between the party and the organizations allow both the articulation of those interests and the preservation of the party's role as the arbiter of competing interests.[11] In China, the state has created a dense web of economic and social organizations in order to channel interest articulation, regularize the flow of information between the state and key groups in society, replace direct state controls over the economy and society with at least partial social regulation, and screen out unwanted groups. Thus official recognition of social organizations serves the dual purpose of incorporating interests and viewpoints the state finds acceptable and repressing those it finds unacceptable or threatening.[12]

As with cooptation, however, the manipulation of organizations carries potential risks. An organization that previously enjoyed extreme autonomy (as is the case for most Leninist parties prior to inclusion) may be "unable to cope with a world in which it does not have arbitrary control."[13] Creating links with other organizations may strengthen those organizations at the expense of the party. These organizations may develop an identity separate from the party and eventually seek to represent the interests of their members and resist acting as agents of the party. What begins with the party's manipulation of organizations may lead to those organizations' manipulation of the party. Such an arrangement is incompatible with a Leninist political system. Cooptation and organizational links with nonparty organizations are key elements of inclusion, but they both come with risks attached. While they are necessary for the party's adaptation, they are not guarantors of the party's survival and may in fact contribute to its demise.

For one-party authoritarian regimes and complex organizations, the period of adaptation may be open-ended as the regime or organization makes repeated adjustments to its ever-changing environment. For Leninist parties, however, there is a tension between policies of inclusion and the party's mobilizational needs. Jowitt's original model of inclusion for Leninist parties implied it was a long-term and presumably open-ended strategy of survival, but later suggested it was simply the phase preceding the "Leninist extinction" because the liberalization that accompanied inclusion weakened the foundations of Leninist parties in Eastern Europe and the Soviet Union.[14] China's leaders have been wary of making a similar mistake and have tried to limit the extent of inclusion in order to achieve "reform without liberalization," but have had a difficult time balancing the two elements of this dichotomy.[15] As the CCP adopted economic modernization as its key task, it confronted precisely the same mobilizational challenges that are inherent to the period of inclusion for Leninist parties identified by Jowitt: increased social heterogeneity as the working classes developed a clearer identity independent of the state;[16] increased occupational and geographic mobility, which challenged the party's ability to monitor and control society;[17] the displacement of the traditional "revolutionary" classes by new elites with professional and technical skills;[18] the cynicism of youth, in particular the changing attitudes toward the party.[19] But the biggest challenge concerns the party's own identity. How can it reconcile its cooptation of wealthy businessmen and the promotion of entrepreneurial skills with its traditional status as a vanguard party representing the interests of workers, peasants, and soldiers? How can the party balance its desire to integrate with society to promote economic modernization with its desire to maintain its monopoly on legitimate political organization and its ability to mobilize society on behalf of political and social goals? To examine these key questions, the following sections will focus on the two key dimensions of inclusion: cooptation of new personnel and creation of new organizational links.

COOPTATION

Since its arrival as the ruling party of China in 1949, a key and divisive issue confronting the CCP has been the appropriate skills and political backgrounds of potential party members. As the party alternated between periods of radicalist upsurges designed to transform the economy and society and periods of restoration designed to resume economic production and social order, criteria for recruitment also changed.[20] During periods of radicalism, when the party pursued utopian goals in its economic and social policies and promoted class struggle in its relations with society, the party rewarded political reliability and ideological fervor, while downgrading—and in some cases persecuting—technical expertise and intellectual freedom. In contrast, when the party emphasized economic development during periods of recovery from radical policies, the party targeted for advancement those with the experience and skills needed to manage the economy and impose order.

Rather than evolving in a linear fashion, therefore, the CCP remained stuck in recurring cycles of transformation and consolidation largely because Mao resisted the institutionalization of the party required by consolidation. As a result, the debate over the proper qualities of party members and cadres was never decisively resolved in favor of either "redness" or expertise. The alleged presence of class enemies and the consequent ongoing need for class struggle meant that some people were excluded from the political system and from the CCP in particular. This is the essence of an exclusionary recruitment policy, appropriate for both the periods of transformation and consolidation.

The transition to economic modernization in the post-Mao period necessitated changes in the definition of the party's work and also in the state–society relationship. Victims of previous political campaigns were released from prison and exonerated; former "class enemies" had their political labels removed and were welcomed into the definition of the "people." In China as in Hungary, reconciliation policies included the end of persecution of alleged class enemies, the release of political enemies from prison camps, expanded exposure to foreign media, greater travel and education opportunities, and enhanced artistic creativity and labor mobility.[21] The party also changed its recruitment policies. It first targeted the people with the types of technical skills needed for economic modernization and then began to coopt new social and economic elites in recognition of their prestige and accomplishments. The cooptation of experts and entrepreneurs prompted a debate within the CCP between those who argued the party had to adapt to survive and those who felt this particular form of adaptation undermined party traditions and thereby reduced its long-term survivability rather than enhanced it.

The Renewed Emphasis on Expertise

As the CCP abandoned class struggle as its core task and shifted to economic modernization, it first weeded out those whose radical tendencies made them unlikely supporters of reform and also rehabilitated the victims of past political campaigns, especially the antirightist movement of 1956–1957 and the Cultural Revolution of 1966–1976. These victims were generally too old and poorly educated to guarantee the success of reform, so the CCP also recruited those who were "more revolutionary, younger, better educated, and more professionally competent." The emphasis on education was particularly apparent. Whereas less than 13 percent of party members had a high school or better education in the late 1970s, by the time of the Sixteenth Party Congress in November 2002 the figure had risen to 53 percent. Improvements in the education qualifications of local officials from the provincial to the county level were even more dramatic: in 1981, only 16 percent had a college education; twenty years later in 2001, 88 percent did. Within the Central Committee (CC), the proportion of those with a college degree rose from 55 percent in 1982 to 99 percent in 2002. The current fourth generation of leaders is characterized by its technocratic credentials (i.e., education and professional experience in science, engineering, or management). All nine members of the Standing Committee of the Politburo and eight of the ten members of the State Council are technocrats. Below this top level, however, the predominance of technocrats has begun to wane. Research by Li Cheng reveals that the percentage of technocrats on the CC fell from 52 percent in 1997 to 46 percent in 2002. At the provincial level, the percentage of technocrats fell even farther, from 75 percent in 1997 to only 42 percent in 2003, and none of the provincial leaders appointed after March 2003 are engineers.

Instead, the new provincial leadership, the likely source of central leaders in the fifth generation, are notable for their backgrounds in the social sciences, the humanities, and the law.[22]

In contrast to the improving educational qualifications, the CCP was less successful recruiting youth and therefore in the mid-1980s adopted the standard that two-thirds of new recruits had to be less than thirty-five years old. During 1997–2002, over 75 percent of new recruits were under the age of thirty-five. However, the party as a whole continued to age and the percentage of all party members under thirty-five actually fell from 27.3 percent in 1987 to 23.3 percent in 2002.[23]

Renewed efforts to recruit frontline workers revealed the tension between inclusion and mobilization. By the late 1980s, more orthodox leaders began to argue that the exclusive reliance on expertise had pushed aside political reliability as a criterion for recruitment and promotion.[24] From their perspective, the proletariat was being squeezed out by economic and technical elites: "progressive" forces (i.e., workers and peasants) were declining in numbers and influence, while those who until recently had been persecuted as "reactionary" forces (intellectuals and entrepreneurs) were on the rise. Although these latter groups had contributed immeasurably to the success of the post-Mao economic reforms, they also threatened the traditional base of the party. The emphasis on workers did not replace the need for expertise, but simply restored the proletariat to its previous position of status in the party.

Concerns about emphasizing expertise over political reliability became especially prominent after the Tiananmen demonstrations of 1989, in which large numbers of party members and cadres openly participated, demonstrating that the party was losing not only its external support but more importantly its internal cohesion. In a December 1989 speech at the Central Party School, CCP general secretary Jiang Zemin said, "We must make sure that the leading authority of all party and state organs is in the hands *of loyal Marxists.*"[25] A commentator's article in *People's Daily,* the CCP's official paper, criticized two errors in recruiting cadres: first, focusing on education and professional competence at the expense of being more revolutionary and, second, giving exclusive priority to intellectuals and ignoring workers, peasants, and others at the grassroots level.[26]

After the imposition of martial law in June 1989, the CCP changed its recruitment policies to match its orthodox rhetoric. The CCP paid new interest to recruiting "workers at the forefront of production." Age and education remained key criteria for new recruits, but now the party also sought out those directly involved in agricultural and industrial production and deemphasized those engaged in administrative or intellectual pursuits. For instance, although 69.2 percent of the 1.87 million new party members recruited in 1994 reportedly were under thirty-five and 70.8 percent had a senior high school education or better, 854,000 (45.7 percent) were "forefront" farmers and workers, and only 328,000 (17.6 percent) were technical experts.[27] The emphasis on recruiting from among frontline workers was meant to reduce the influence of "nonproductive" trades, especially intellectuals and teachers, who were blamed for contributing to the 1989 demonstrations. This did not

end the CCP's efforts to coopt expertise, but reflected its desire to mobilize its traditional supporters to balance the new elites in the organization. In fact, beginning in
the mid-1990s, as the pace of economic reform began to accelerate again, the CCP
reemphasized the value of entrepreneurial skills, especially for cadres. This strategy
of relying on technical and economic elites had a dramatic impact on the composition of the CCP's membership: between 1994 and 2003, the share of workers and
farmers in the CCP dropped from 63 to 44 percent.

The Debate over Coopting Entrepreneurs

Beginning in the mid-1980s, entrepreneurs were coopted into the party in large
numbers. The State Industrial and Commercial Administrative and Management
Bureau reported that 15 percent of owners of private firms were party members.[28] A
1989 survey of private *(siying)* entrepreneurs in Wenzhou found that 31.7 percent
were party members, of whom two-thirds had at least a senior high school education
and 17 percent were former state cadres. In addition, one-quarter of members in
Wenzhou's people-run business associations *(minying gonghui)* were party members.[29] At the end of 1991, over 200,000 party members reportedly registered as
private entrepreneurs, representing 4 percent of party members and 8 percent of
entrepreneurs.[30] A nationwide survey in 1995 found that 17.1 percent of private
entrepreneurs were party members, and by 2004, 30 percent of entrepreneurs were
"red capitalists."[31]

The presence of newly wealthy entrepreneurs in the party irritated some party
veterans, who felt their contributions to the revolution were being betrayed by the
party's new commitment to economic growth. Fearing that bourgeois influences
were spreading into the party, the CCP banned the new recruitment of private
entrepreneurs into the party after the imposition of martial law in 1989; entrepreneurs already in the party could no longer hold official positions.[32] In September
1995, the organization department repeated that the party would not admit private
entrepreneurs "because they are capitalists bent on exploiting the labor force."[33]

Criticism of this trend was especially prominent in the journals representing the
party's orthodox positions, such as *Zhenli de zhuiqiu* (The pursuit of truth). These
journals published exposé-style articles that criticized the practice of recruiting entrepreneurs into the party and appointing them to official positions (which violated
official party policy) and the policy of encouraging party members to take the lead
in getting rich *(daitou zhifu)*. These articles argued that the presence of wealthy people in the CCP contradicted the allegedly proletarian nature of the party, creating
confusion regarding the party's identity and policies.[34] From this perspective, the
trend of coopting entrepreneurs undermined the party and threatened its survival.

Despite the consistency of central policy on this issue in the 1990s, local party
committees circumvented these restrictions. Some local party committees classified
private enterprises as collective or joint stock enterprises, thereby allowing them to
recruit their leaders while remaining in technical compliance with the central ban.[35]

The head of the organization department in an unspecified city in Shandong defended the practice of recruiting entrepreneurs, who had proven their innovativeness, administrative skills, and ability to produce wealth, which he claimed were the main criteria for party membership. "While maintaining party member standards, active recruitment into the party of outstanding people from among the owners of private enterprises can highlight the timeliness of the socialist market economy, and can make full use of the role of party members as vanguards and models in leading the masses along the path of common prosperity."[36] These trends were repeatedly criticized by the center. Orthodox leaders contended that the ability to innovate, manage, and create wealth could not substitute for the political standards also required of party members. In September 1995, Yu Yunyao, deputy director of the CCP's organization department, said even debating the advantages and disadvantages of recruiting entrepreneurs was irresponsible.[37]

Finally, CCP general secretary Jiang Zemin recommended lifting the ban on recruiting entrepreneurs and other new elites into the party in his Party Day speech of July 1, 2001. This recommendation was contained within his advocacy of the "three represents" policy, in which the CCP no longer simply represented the proletarian vanguard but also represented the advanced productive forces, advanced culture, and the general interests of the vast majority of the Chinese people.[38] This was a dramatic shift in the party ideological orientation and its relations with society, but was more importantly an effort to make party policy fit with China's new reality by welcoming into the party the new urban elites ("advanced productive forces") who were most responsible for China's economic and social development.

Why was the ban on private entrepreneurs so ineffective while it was still in place? For one thing, there was little indication it was seriously enforced. More importantly, recruiting entrepreneurs into the party was advantageous for both local officials and entrepreneurs. For officials, it allowed them to coopt potential opposition, to establish links with the private sector and promote growth, and to create personal ties to wealthy and successful entrepreneurs. Why did entrepreneurs want to get into the CCP? Party membership gave them easier access to loans, official discretion, and protection from competition and unfair policy implementation. Moreover, the desire to be "within the system" is stronger than the desire for autonomy in China, where autonomy from the state has major disadvantages. As elsewhere in Asia, entrepreneurs are partners with the state, not adversaries of it. Finally, there is a strong belief that CCP members have advantages in business. The result is a symbiotic relationship that benefits both sides. Local and individual interests outweighed the negligible risk of punishment for violating the formal ban. In fact, the state constitution was revised in spring 1999 to protect the rights of the private sector, and again in 2003 to better protect private property.

Despite the party's steady embrace of the private sector and the lifting of the ban on recruiting private entrepreneurs, the practice of coopting entrepreneurs into the party has virtually stopped, although the reasons are not clear. The growth in the number of "red capitalists" from less than 20 percent before Jiang's July 1 speech to

30 percent in 2004 came not from new recruitment but from the ongoing privatization of state-owned enterprises. Former SOE managers, almost all of whom were party members, instantly became red capitalists once they became owners and managers of newly privatized firms. But other private entrepreneurs did not seek admission into the party. Some felt local party officials were still not sufficiently supportive of the private sector, despite central policy; others felt that party membership would constrain or expose their business practices to closer scrutiny and limit their flexibility; others complained about the rampant corruption within the party. Oddly enough, the cooptation of entrepreneurs into the party was more common when the practice was officially banned than after it became formal party policy.

The Political Implications of Cooptation

What are the political consequences of these policies of cooptation? Will they lead to rejuvenation of the party by drawing in new elites, or will they undermine the foundations of the Leninist system in China? Scholars have generally seen the inclusion of new elites into the party as a positive development. According to Hong Yung Lee, the presence of technocrats in the party and government bureaucracies better balances "the political needs of the Leninist party and the structural prerequisites of economic development."[39] Similarly, Kristen Parris sees entrepreneurs as a "force for change within the party rank and file."[40] While cooptive parties tend to be more adaptable than those with exclusive recruitment policies, *who* is being coopted has important implications for *how* the party adapts. To show why this is so, it is best to distinguish different types of elites.

Yanqi Tong makes a useful distinction between a civil society organized to regulate the supply of goods and services (a "noncritical realm" that does not pose a direct challenge to the regime, and may even be welcomed by it) and a political society designed to "influence state decisions or to obtain a share of state power" (a "critical realm" that does threaten the regime's monopoly on power and therefore becomes the target of repression). The success of the critical realm depends on the existence and support of the noncritical realm. They are complementary, though not equal, and "the development of non-critical and critical realms often represent different stages in the emergence of an autonomous civil society and, in the process, of political change."[41]

In a Leninist system, the presence of this noncritical realm is the result of political liberalization, not its cause. Party leaders, who need allies in their inner party battles and social organizations to take over social and economic self-regulatory functions as the state liberalizes its control over society, support the emergence of this realm of civil society. The rise of a critical realm, in contrast, is the product of its own leaders and is rarely welcomed by the regime, even by party reformers. The noncritical realm of civil society reinforces the regime's decision to liberalize (reduced state interference in the economy and the daily lives of the citizenry), but it is the critical realm of political society that pressures the regime to democratize (public involvement in the selection of state leaders and accountability over their actions).

The implications of this distinction between critical and noncritical realms are best seen by comparing the experience of Leninist parties in Hungary, Taiwan, and China.

In Hungary, the policy of cooptation focused on the critical intelligentsia. Leaders of the Hungarian Socialist Workers Party decided in the early 1960s to coopt nonmanual workers into the party, including not only clerical and managerial staff but also young intelligentsia. Other Eastern European communist parties responded to demands for political reform by purging party ranks of intellectuals and thereby created an external social opposition. The Hungarian party instead eliminated the potential threat of external dissent by drawing critical intelligentsia into the party. In so doing, "the party [in Hungary] both perpetuated its rule and created the means of its eventual downfall."[42] At the central level, intellectuals were channeled into government positions, leaving party loyalists in control of all key party posts. In rural areas, however, conservative party secretaries with extensive patronage networks shut intellectuals out of influential positions.

Frustrated by the lack of upward mobility and by their exclusion from decision-making arenas, local intellectuals organized informal networks which in the 1980s became the basis for the "party reform circles." These party reform circles took shape as political circles outside the party were growing and as the reformist coalition in the party elite, which had forced hard-liner Janos Kadar's resignation as party chief in 1988, was itself splitting, creating more space for political activity.[43] In May 1989, the party reform circles held their first national conference, attended by 440 delegates representing over 10,000 members of 110 reform circles.[44] In alliance with central party reformers, the reform circles achieved the dissolution of the Socialist Workers Party and its reformation as the Hungarian Socialist Party in October 1989. Originally formed as an antiestablishment movement against the official party structure, the circles refused to institutionalize themselves and quickly lost the initiative to older party leaders. The circles broke up shortly after the creation of the Socialist Party. Although they contributed immeasurably to the transformation of the Hungarian party and the democratization of the Hungarian political system, reform circle members were unable to benefit from the changes they brought about.

Cooptation was also a major factor of the transformation of the Kuomintang (KMT), the ruling party in Taiwan.[45] In the early 1970s, the central leaders of the KMT, principally Chiang Ching-kuo and Li Huan, sponsored the Taiwanization policy, which brought large numbers of youth with political ambitions into the party. The policy had two main goals. First, Taiwanization was designed to change the reputation of the KMT. Before Taiwanization, all key positions were held by émigrés from the mainland; beginning in the early 1970s, the KMT gradually shed its mainlander reputation and came to represent a broader spectrum of Taiwan's society. Second, Taiwanization was intended to improve the effectiveness of the ruling party by attracting young people with talent rather than simply political connections. Most new members were recruited when they were still in college, and some were given scholarships for foreign graduate study, mostly in the United States, where they were exposed to the workings of a democratic political system. The KMT coopted these educated youth in order to channel their political ambitions into the KMT and preempt their joining the opposition. The KMT also used the promise of elected office to attract these young elites. With opposition parties banned, an official nomination by the KMT virtually guaranteed electoral victory. At the same time that it coopted some youth, it continued to repress the political opposition that was excluded from the party and made it difficult for them to compete in elections.

The centrally sponsored policy of cooptation known as Taiwanization led to the adaptation of the political system in several ways. First, many of those who played key roles in the transformation of the KMT and the gradual democratization of Taiwan's political system during the 1980s were recruited under the Taiwanization program of the 1970s. Young elites with political ambitions created pressure within the KMT for democratization. They sought more open, competitive elections to advance their careers. Second, their experience in the United States and other foreign countries exposed them to more liberal political systems, further fueling their desire for democratization. These internal pressures in combination with the growing support for democratization outside the party eventually led to the democratic breakthrough of 1986–1987. Third, Taiwanization also led to a basic change in the key task of the KMT: from achieving reunification with the mainland to the economic and political development of Taiwan itself.[46]

In Hungary and Taiwan, the ruling parties reduced the potential threat of external dissent by coopting critical intelligentsia and politically ambitious youth (i.e., those from the critical realm of political society) into the party. In contrast, the CCP continues to exclude critical intelligentsia from the political system in general and the party in particular. Instead, it targets experts and entrepreneurs from the noncritical realm of civil society, but even the entrepreneurs are excluded from holding official posts. The ultimate consequences of the CCP policy of inclusion is not yet clear; indeed, in Hungary and Taiwan there were lengthy gaps between the initial cooptation and the subsequent political effects. But there is little reason to assume that technocrats and entrepreneurs will make similar demands on the CCP that critical intelligentsia did in Hungary and Taiwan. Technocrats and entrepreneurs may indeed prove to be a force for change within the CCP, but more time—and more research—is needed to determine what types of change they will promote.

As members of the noncritical sphere, technocrats and entrepreneurs could play a supporting role in the course of political change. Some have argued that technocrats are more likely to favor democratization than the revolutionaries they replaced; others have argued that technocracy will only lead to a more efficient form of authoritarianism.[47] For my purposes, the key point is that technocrats belong to the noncritical realm. They are primarily concerned with promoting economic growth and to that end limiting the influence of ideology in policy making. But technocrats may also be essential allies of democrats. A key element of Hungary's democratization was the informal alliance of technocrats who desired less party interference in the economy, party reformers who wanted to be rid of conservatives, and democrats outside the party.[48] But in China, "bureaucratic technocrats are not enthusiastic about political democratization."[49] Moreover, most technocrats were trained in China, the former Soviet Union, or Eastern Europe. Unlike KMT elites, many of whom received college degrees in the United States and other Western countries, CCP technocrats lack exposure to alternative political values and institutional arrangements.[50] Although younger technocrats have been acquiring more exposure to the West and in the future may be more open to adaptation, it will be many years before they are the decisive force within the party. Moreover, as noted above, the prevalence of technocrats among central committee members and provincial leaders is already declining in favor of those educated in the social sciences, law, and humanities.

Could entrepreneurs be allies of democrats in China? The evidence so far has been mixed. Margaret Pearson argues that they are not likely to initiate demands for systemic change but could be "available to lend support if others take the lead in pressuring for economic and political change."[51] During the 1989 demonstrations, the Beijing Stone Group provided ample and visible support for student demonstrators, but elsewhere in China entrepreneurs withheld their support. In Xiamen, one of the special economic zones in southern China, entrepreneurs disapproved of students' demands for rapid reform, preferring state-sponsored reform to bottom-up pressures that could result in instability.[52] Entrepreneurs may favor liberalization in order to promote economic growth, but there is little evidence that these same people favor democratization. The growing alignment between local political and economic elites may in fact reinforce the status quo because both sets of actors benefit from its preservation. The party retains its monopoly over political participation and takes credit for the economic growth created by the entrepreneurs. Entrepreneurs may be unwilling to risk the certain benefits of the existing system, despite its many irrationalities, for the uncertainties of an alternative arrangement. Indeed, Jonathan Unger and Anita Chan note that entrepreneurs and even intellectuals who belong to the Chinese People's Political Consultative Congress "support further economic and political reforms—but they are usually *not* pro-democracy."[53]

The reforms in Hungary and Taiwan also had an element of indigenization that is wholly lacking in China. In Hungary, the Communist Party was seen as the creation of the Soviet Union, especially after the repression of the 1956 uprising, and therefore lacked domestic legitimacy. The party used its policy of cooptation and tolerance of pluralism within the party to soften its image as an alien force and to legitimize its rule.[54] In Taiwan, the policy of cooptation was motivated by a desire to change the KMT's image as an unwanted occupying force. The very name of the program, Taiwanization (in Chinese, *bentuhua*, literally indigenization) announces its goal. In so doing, the KMT tried to sink roots in local society, not just to control it, but also to appear more responsive to it. The CCP lacks these motivations for adaptation. One of its primary bases of legitimacy is its victory in the Chinese civil war. It is not motivated by the search for domestic sources of legitimacy nor by the type of ethnic conflict that prompted Taiwanization.

Technocrats and entrepreneurs have had an important impact on the progress of reform and the performance of the CCP. They have been strong supporters of liberalization and have contributed to the rapid pace of economic growth. But their overt support for liberalization must be distinguished from their muted support for democratization. As the comparison with Hungary and Taiwan show, cooptation enhances the adaptability of Leninist parties, but not all coopted elites favor the same types of adaptation. China's technocrats and entrepreneurs, drawn from the noncritical realm of civil society, are unlikely to initiate democratizing reforms, although they may prove to be indispensable allies of those who do favor such reforms.

ORGANIZATIONAL LINKS BETWEEN THE CCP AND SOCIETY: A CORPORATIST SOLUTION?

The second element of party adaptation concerns organizational arrangements. The party may rejuvenate united front groups or create new organizations to incorporate new groups into the political system. Recent scholarship on China has found extensive evidence of this type of inclusion and has defined it as corporatism.[55] The concept of corporatism is a familiar one in comparative politics, and describes a system of representation in which interests are vertically organized into peak associations to limit and institutionalize the participation of key groups in the policy process.[56] Corporatist arrangements may be dominated by the state in an authoritarian political system, a variant known as state corporatism, or they may provide greater autonomy and influence for the groups themselves in a more democratic setting, a variant known as societal corporatism.

The emerging corporatist elements in China's political system provide a rationale for the more harmonious relations between state and society characteristic of inclusion. The corporatist model points out that the state and society relationship is based on achieving consensus and common goals, not a zero-sum struggle for power. As Douglas Chalmers notes, "Corporatism has much in common with socialism's understanding of society after the end of class conflict." A harmony of interests is possible without the total transformation of society.[57] Similarly, Alfred Stepan identified the universal appeal of corporatism to elites facing "a perceived threat of fragmentation" and who reject both the liberal ideals of individualism and checks and balances and the Marxist ideals of class conflict "because they are seen as legitimizing conflict."[58]

Corporatist structures are consequently emerging in China as a substitute for coercion, propaganda, and central planning to maintain party hegemony. As Unger and Chan argue, corporatism is "a mechanism through which the state's grip could be lessened" but not released altogether. "The more the economy decentralizes, the more corporatist associations get established as substitute control mechanisms."[59] This is a perfect illustration of the logic of inclusion: because the CCP is no longer able to manipulate the nation with symbols and propaganda, it therefore tries to manipulate the organizations through which society interacts with the state.

While drawing attention to the evolving corporatist structures, some scholars also allude to another consequence of economic reform. For instance, Unger and Chan assert that "yet at the very same time that these new corporatist structures get erected and firmed up by the Chinese state, forces are simultaneously at work that undermine and weaken the central state's power over them."[60] They believe that at least some of China's groups operating in the current state corporatist mold are "shifting gradually but perceptibly in a 'societal-corporatist' direction," in which organized groups will assert the interests of the people they nominally represent.[61] Gordon White, Jude Howell, and Shang Xiaoyuan also repeatedly allude to the potential of civic associations evolving from a corporatist logic to constitute a civil society, with a dense mix of organizations largely autonomous from constraints imposed by local officials, but still embedded in the state.[62]

This points to a more provocative question, Are corporatist arrangements compatible with a Leninist system? Or will the emergence and evolution of corporatism lead to the decay of Leninist institutions? To answer these questions, it is necessary to explore the implications of the corporatist model.

How useful is corporatism for understanding Chinese politics? In his critique of the interest group model of Soviet politics, William Odom listed three criteria for evaluating a model: it must capture the core elements of the political system; it must be comparative in nature; and it must account for change.[63] According to Odom, the interest group model failed on two accounts: first, it focused most of its attention on peripheral elements of the system (institutional pluralism) and second, it therefore misinterpreted signs of political decay for political development. The advocates of the corporatist model in China are not so ambitious in their claims for political change, but generally limit themselves to analysis of the evolving institutional arrangements that govern China's political economy. Still, they do include allusions of political transformation that deserve greater scrutiny. Like the proponents of the Soviet interest group model, advocates of Chinese corporatism may be misleading us in terms of the expected future course of Chinese politics.

Is China a corporatist system? Most scholars do not argue that China has a full-blown corporatist system, only that there are corporatist elements emerging in the course of economic reform. Corporatism is an ideal type; it does not define a political system, but corporatist elements are present in a variety of contexts. Democratic countries such as Britain and the Netherlands, bureaucratic authoritarian countries such as Brazil and Argentina, military regimes such as Peru and South Korea, one-party regimes such as Mexico and Taiwan, and communist countries such as Poland, the Soviet Union, and most recently China have been described as corporatist. The corporatist model does capture core elements of the China's political system, especially concerning its political economy. The state has created or licensed associations for independent entrepreneurs, owners of private enterprises, enterprises with foreign investment, organized labor, Catholic and Protestant churches, writers, scientists, and other functional interests. These associations are noncompetitive and when two or more exist the state forces them to merge or one or more to disband. Membership is compulsory, and members in business associations are often enrolled when they receive their business license. The leaders of these associations are often officials from the party or government offices responsible for regulating or managing them, and association offices are often in government compounds.[64]

These corporatist elements have very much in common with the key aspects of a Leninist system. A Leninist system is based on the ruling party's monopoly on legitimate political organization. The state may create mass organizations to link state and society, and these organizations are typically staffed and budgeted in large part by the state. A Leninist party also prevents the spontaneous formation of new organizations, especially where an official one already exists, and the presence of organizations outside of its control is a challenge to its authority. During periods of transformation and consolidation, the state uses these organizations as "transmission belts" to send authoritative decisions to lower levels of the organizations. The state grants leaders of these organizations a degree of leeway to manage their organizations and the people they nominally represent, but prevents interests and preferences from working their way back up through the organization to influence state policy. During the period of inclusion, these same organizations become channels for interest representation so that these interests can be incorporated into the state. As the party loses its ability to monitor the activities of these organizations and sanction the behavior of its members, and society more generally, one of the institutional pillars of a Leninist system is weakened.[65] This points out the contradictions in the competing goals of inclusion and mobilization for a Leninist party.

To portray the potential evolution of corporatism, advocates of the corporatist model in China highlight examples of leaders who change from being agents of the state to become advocates for their associations. But the corporatist model considers the state as a "'naturally' divided entity" with different interests derived from its relations with economic and professional groups. According to Chalmers, "One cannot talk of state interests as opposed to those of society when the state is in fact made up of ties with interests in society."[66] Interest representation is not the defining difference between state and societal corporatism. Rather, the power relationship between the state and corporate groups distinguishes the two subtypes, and that relationship is dependent on whether the political system is authoritarian or democratic in nature. Unger found that the federation for large-scale business "is still too tightly bound to the party-state in its structure and staffing" to be described as societal corporatist although it was "gravitating" in that direction due to "a growing desire even on the part of some of its minders for it to play such a societal corporatist role."[67] The desire for increased autonomy for organized interests undoubtedly continues to exist in China, but those wishes are not compatible with the CCP's desire to preserve its power.

Despite its policies of inclusion, the central fact of China's political system remains that it is ruled by a Leninist party. The party enjoys and protects its monopoly on political organization. In his case study of Xiaoshan city, Gordon White found that only the most politically inconsequential of social organizations (sports, arts and culture, retired teachers, and female factory managers) were autonomous, in that there was no overlapping of personnel with the sponsoring government bureau and no financial subsidies.[68] At the same time, bottom-up demands for new and autonomous social organizations (for labor, entrepreneurs, students, etc.) were rejected and repressed. Unger and Chan argue that some of the key demands during the 1989 protests involved gaining state approval for autonomous unions for students and workers in Beijing. "To the extent that they were demanding a *structural* change in the political system, it was to effect a shift to a societal corporatism in which they could choose their own leadership and set their own agendas."[69] But the CCP's rejection of this demand and its violent repression of protestors shows that Leninism, not corporatism, still defines China's political system. Beginning in 1998, the CCP severely and successfully suppressed efforts to create China's first opposition party, the China Democracy Party, showing that a Leninist logic still prevails in China.[70] If the party's monopoly is undermined, we will witness not simply an incremental and gradual evolution from state to societal corporatism, but increased political decay of the communist system itself.

Corporatist trends are nevertheless affecting several key factors of China's political system. An important variation on corporatism as practiced in China is that corporatist groups are usually sanctioned and controlled by local party and government authorities and not always vertically organized into peak associations whose primary interaction is with the central state. This has exacerbated the decentralization of political and economic authority. Just as corporate associations no longer act as transmission belts, local governments no longer act as loyal agents of the center.[71] This is a potential sign of disintegration, not just for the CCP but the political system as a whole. Relatedly, as a result of these newly created institutional links, the party's traditional concern with party building as a means of linking state and society and monitoring compliance with party policy has atrophied.

The creation of a market economy has created new opportunities for pursuing personal goals that do not require joining the party. Indeed, party membership is now seen by many as detrimental to fulfilling individual interests. The new collectively and privately owned and foreign funded enterprises are being created so fast that the party cannot create party organizations within most of them, and many do not even have party members. Party organizations in the countryside have weakened, and recruiting new members has become increasingly difficult. Moreover, many party members in rural areas have become migrant workers seeking jobs in coastal cities, further reducing the party's presence in the countryside. In more prosperous areas, up to 10 percent of migrant workers are party members. Most of them are young and middle-aged and either business oriented or "backbone workers," precisely the kinds of people the party would like to utilize. Once they join the migrant population, these party members lose touch with their original party unit and do not register with the party committee in their new location. Consequently, they no longer fulfill their responsibilities to the party or fulfill their "vanguard role."[72]

The second criterion for a model is that it allows comparisons to be drawn with other countries, and the corporatist model is clearly comparative in nature. But because corporatism is present in so many contexts, it is important to clearly identify the subtypes of the concept so that comparisons are drawn with the right countries. Both state and societal corporatism are monopolistic forms of group politics and therefore are structurally similar. Yet their origins and dynamics are fundamentally different. State corporatism is generally associated with authoritarian regimes, whereas societal corporatism is "more an evolution—perhaps a corruption—of liberalism."[73] Societal corporatism is not compatible with a Leninist system because the former requires the types of autonomous and politically active groups that the latter refuses to tolerate. The notion of state corporatism is less threatening to the regime: instead of autonomy, corporate groups are embedded in the state, where they can be manipulated, their leaders replaced, and their finances controlled. Leninist parties seek to prevent autonomous groups, and for good reason. The Eastern European experience shows that the rise of civil society has a significant—and in some cases decisive—impact on the collapse of communism.[74]

The third criterion of a model's utility is its ability to account for change, and this is where the corporatist model as applied to China most falls short. The depiction of a gradual and incremental evolution from state to societal corporatism is not consistent with the wider literature. According to Philippe Schmitter, state corporatism is unlikely to transform itself continuously toward societal corporatism; instead, it must "degenerate into openly conflictual, multifaceted, uncontrolled interest politics—pluralism in other words."[75] This is exactly what Leninism is designed to prevent. We should not expect that the transition from state to societal corporatism will occur amid regime continuity.

The incremental transformation depicted by the advocates of the corporatist model is based not only on faulty logic but also problematic analogies. Unger and Chan suggest that Japan, South Korea, and Taiwan all made smooth transitions from state to societal corporatism and conclude that a similar transformation in China is possible. But in all three cases the transition from state to societal corporatism was epiphenomenal to changes taking place in the larger political system. In each case, societal corporatism was the consequence of democratization, but the modes of democratization were fundamentally different in each country. Despite the near ubiquity of corporatism in all sorts of political systems, we should be wary of drawing comparisons across different types of political systems. Unger and Chan further suggest that as political liberalization continues in China, "it is far more likely to involve such incremental shifts into societal corporatism rather than the introduction of any form of political democracy." But societal corporatism and democracy are not independent of one another. The emergence of societal corporatism was the consequence of democratization elsewhere in East Asia, not an alterna-

[margin note: Societal vs. state corporatism]

tive to it. In other countries, societal corporatism developed in an already pluralist setting. The combination of societal corporatism and rule by a Leninist party would therefore not likely be a stable one.

Corporatism may survive the transition from communism in China, but communism is unlikely to survive the transition to corporatism. Chan cites the relegalization of Solidarity in spring 1989 as a possible model for increased autonomy of China's labor organizations.[76] But within a few months of this step, the communist government in Poland negotiated its way out of existence. This example of "socialist societal corporatism" existed only for the short period of time between the relegalization of Solidarity in April 1989 and the appointment of the first noncommunist prime minister, Solidarity adviser Tadeusz Mazowiecki, in September 1989.[77] This is a poor precedent, either for theory building or for party policy.

A more promising approach may be to apply Stepan's typology of exclusionary and inclusionary poles within state corporatism.[78] A regime can shift between exclusionary and inclusionary policies over time, and even practice them simultaneously. For instance, the CCP has allowed the All-China Federation of Trade Unions in recent years to advocate strongly the interest of labor in the policy and legislative process, but also imprisoned those who advocate the formation of independent trade unions. Stepan's typology may account for trends that scholars are finding without stretching the concept of societal corporatism beyond recognition.

Corporatist features are clearly emerging in China as a substitute for the CCP's totalitarian impulse to control state and society in the Maoist years. But the ultimate political implications of this trend are still uncertain. Whereas some scholars see the promise of societal corporatism coming into view, others see signs of disintegration. The creation of corporatist organizations to link state and society was part of the CCP's strategy of inclusion and it remains dedicated to preventing the rise of autonomous organizations. Before societal corporatism replaces Leninism as the defining feature of China's political system, the party would have to abandon its monopoly on political organization. This is a fundamental change that the CCP has steadfastly opposed. If the party's control over key organizations erodes to such an extent that state corporatism begins to transform into societal corporatism, the real story will not be about the rise of corporatism but more fundamental political change in China.

CONCLUSION

The logic of inclusion offers a useful framework for analyzing the CCP's policies of coopting new elites and forging links with nonparty organizations, as well as understanding the problems that have arisen as a consequence. Although inclusion seems to be a natural phase in the evolution of Leninist parties, the tension between inclusion and mobilization also indicates why adaptation is so difficult, and why the transformation of Leninist parties is so rare. While cooptation and the creation of organizational links seem necessary to promote economic modernization, neither is sufficient to guarantee the party's survival. Instead of leading to rejuvenation, inclusion may contribute to a Leninist party's disintegration.

The cooptation of new elites is a classic strategy of adaptation for Leninist parties and for organizations in general, but it is a risky strategy. As the case of the CCP shows, coopted elites may not support or even sympathize with party traditions—indeed, the technocrats and entrepreneurs who are now being courted were previously targeted as class enemies. Even though the newly coopted technocrats and entrepreneurs are unlikely to initiate pressures for democratizing reforms, they may be powerful allies if others inside and outside the party do so. The attention given to coopting new elites and promoting economic reforms has also led to deterioration of traditional party building, leaving the party less able to mobilize and control society and its own members at a time of increasing political, economic, and social change.

Proponents of corporatism in China may be doing us a disservice. They are uncovering important changes in China's political economy that may have profound implications for its political system. But in their quest for a comparative concept to analyze changes in China, they have latched onto a concept that does not give sufficient emphasis to the central fact of China's political system—the continued rule of a Leninist party. The corporatist approach also does not give adequate attention to the experience of other Leninist parties for whom political change was tumultuous, not gradual. Hungary and Taiwan are exceptions to this general rule, but as noted above the CCP lacks the key features that prompted their transformation, and corporatism was not a key factor in their democratization. By implying a possible path of incremental political change that is not consistent with either the general literature or the political experience of other countries, advocates of the corporatist approach may mislead us.

The CCP is pursuing policies of inclusion, both by coopting new elites and creating links with nonparty organizations, while at the same time lamenting the loss of its mobilizational capacity. Some local party officials, and many scholars, argue that the solution to this dilemma is to deemphasize mobilizational goals for the sake of greater economic growth. From this perspective, party organs should not be present in the nonstate sectors of the economy specifically because they tend to retard growth and frighten off potential investors. Cooptation and new organizational links offer alternatives to traditional party building as means to link the party with society. From the perspective of the party, however, its organizational interests are being challenged by these policies of inclusion. As its capacity to monitor compliance with its policies, enforce norms of behavior, and mobilize society on behalf of regime goals deteriorates, the Leninist attributes of the CCP and its viability as the ruling party are also undermined. As Samuel Huntington noted, the strength of an authoritarian regime depends in large part on the strength of its party; as the party weakens, so too does the regime it governs.[79] While noting the positive trends of cooptation and corporatism, we should not lose sight of the negative consequences for the CCP and the implications for the political system as a whole.

NOTES

I would like to acknowledge the financial support of the Smith Richardson Foundation and the U.S. Institute of Peace, and the comments and suggestions of Scott Kennedy, Jason Kindopp, Kevin O'Brien, Maria Rost Rublee, Traci Swanson, Martin King Whyte, Yang Zhong, and several anonymous reviewers.

1. See, for instance, Joseph Fewsmith, *China since Tiananmen: The Politics of Transition* (New York: Cambridge University Press, 2001); Murray Scot Tanner, *The Politics of Law Making in Post-Mao China: Institutions, Processes, and Democratic Prospects* (Oxford: Oxford University Press, 1998); Andrew G. Walder, ed., *The Waning of the Communist State: Economic Origins of Political Decline in China and Hungary* (Berkeley: University of California Press, 1995); Susan Shirk, *The Political Logic of Reform in China* (Berkeley: University of California Press, 1993).

2. Some scholars have looked at different facets of this issue: Minxin Pei, *China's Trapped Transition: The Limits of Developmental Autocracy* (Cambridge, MA: Harvard University Press, 2006); Kjeld Erik Brodsgaard and Zheng Yongnian, eds., *Bringing the Party Back In: How China Is Governed* (Singapore: Eastern Universities Press, 2004); Yanqi Tong, *Transitions from State Socialism: Economic and Political Change in Hungary and China* (Lanham, MD: Rowman & Littlefield, 1997).

3. Philip P. Selznick, *TVA and the Grass Roots* (Berkeley: University of California Press, 1949); Jeffrey Pfeffer and Gerald B. Salancik, *The External Control of Organizations: A Resource Dependence Perspective* (New York: Harper & Row, 1978), 164–165.

4. Michael T. Hannan and John Freeman, *Organizational Ecology* (Cambridge, MA: Harvard University Press, 1991), 67–68; Pfeffer and Salancik, *External Control*, 82.

5. Samuel P. Huntington, "Social and Institutional Dynamics of One-Party Systems," in Samuel P. Huntington and Clement H. Moore, eds., *Authoritarian Politics in Modern Society: The Dynamics of Established One-Party Systems* (New York: Basic, 1970); Ken Jowitt, "Inclusion," in *New World Disorder* (Berkeley: University of California Press, 1992).

6. Patrick H. O'Neil, "Revolution from Within: Institutional Analysis, Transitions from Authoritarianism, and the Case of Hungary," *World Politics*, July 1996, 579–603, quote from 585.

7. Huntington, "Social and Institutional Dynamics," 20.

8. Andrew G. Walder, "The Quiet Revolution from Within: Economic Reform as a Source of Political Decline," in Walder, ed., *Waning of the Communist State*.

9. Pfeffer and Salancik, *External Control of Organizations*, 143–147.

10. Jowitt, "Inclusion," 101–102.

11. Huntington, "Social and Institutional Dynamics," 34–36.

12. See Gordon White, Jude Howell, and Shang Xiaoyuan, *In Search of Civil Society: Market Reform and Social Change in Contemporary China* (Oxford: Oxford University Press, 1996).

13. James G. March and Johan P. Olsen, *Rediscovering Institutions: The Organizational Basis for Politics* (New York: Free Press, 1989), 47.

14. Jowitt, "The Leninist Extinction," in *New World Disorder*.

15. Kevin O'Brien, *Reform without Liberalization: China's National People's Congress and the Politics of Institutional Change* (New York: Cambridge University Press, 1990), esp. 6–8; 174–178.

16. Andrew G. Walder, "Industrial Workers: Some Observations on the 1980s," in Arthur Lewis Rosenbaum, ed., *State and Society in China: The Consequences of Reform* (Boulder, CO: Westview, 1992); Ching Kwan Lee, "Pathways of Labor Insurgency," in Elizabeth J. Perry and Mark Selden, eds., *Chinese Society: Change, Conflict, and Resistance*, 2nd ed. (London: Routledge, 2003), 71–92.

17. Dorothy Solinger, "China's Urban Transients in the Transition from Socialism and the Collapse of the Communist 'Urban Public Goods Regime,'" *Comparative Politics*, January 1995, 127–146.

18. Li Cheng and Lynn White, "Elite Transformation and Modern Change in Mainland China and Taiwan: Empirical Data and the Theory of Technocracy," *China Quarterly*, March 1990, 1–35; Hans Hendrischke, "Expertocracy and Professionalism," in David S. G. Goodman and Beverly Hooper, eds., *China's Quiet Revolution: New Interactions between State and Society* (New York: St. Martin's, 1994).

19. Stanley Rosen, "The Victory of Materialism: Aspirations to Join China's Urban Moneyed Classes and the Commercialization of Education," *China Journal*, January 2004, 27–52.

20. Zhao Shenghui, ed., *Zhongguo gongchandang zuzhi shi gangyao* [History of CCP organization] (Anhui: Anhui renmin chubanshe, 1987), chaps. 5–7; Chen Zhili, ed., *Zhongguo gongchandang jianshe shi* [History of CCP party building] (Shanghai: Shanghai renmin chubanshe, 1991), chaps. 5–7. Variations in criteria for party recruitment fit the general pattern of policy cycles described in G. William Skinner and Edwin A. Winckler, "Compliance Succession in Rural China: A Cyclical Theory," in Amitai Etzioni, ed., *A Sociological Reader on Complex Organizations* (New York: Holt, Rinehart & Winston, 1969).

21. Yanqi Tong, "State, Society, and Political Change in China and Hungary," *Comparative Politics*, April 1994, 333–353.

22. Li Cheng, "Hu's New Deal and the New Provincial Chiefs," *China Leadership Monitor*, Spring 2004.

23. *Xinhua*, June 22, 1988, in Foreign Broadcast Information Service: Daily Report—China (hereafter FBIS), June 24, 1988, 19; *Xinhua*, October 6, 1992, in FBIS, October 6, 1992, 29; *Xinhua*, July 7, 1997, in FBIS (online service), July 7, 1997; *Xinhua*, September 1, 2002, in FBIS, September 1, 2002.

24. For instance, see Li Yanxi, "Shelun dangyuan duiwu de shuliang kongzhi" [Limit the number of CCP members], *Xuexi yu shixian* [Wuchang], January 1989, 49–51, in *Fuyin baokan ziliao, D2: Zhongguo gongchandang* [hereafter FBZ], February 1989, 136–138; Zhou Peng, "Shinian lai fazhan dangyuan gongzuo de huigu" [Review of the past ten years of party recruitment], *Dangzheng wenhui*, January 1989, 12, in FBZ, March 1989, 133; Dong Wanmin, "Yange anzhao biaozhun fazhang dangyuan" [Recruit party members strictly according to standards], *Henan ribao*, January 7, 1991, in FBZ, January 1991, 127–128.

25. *Xinhua*, December 29, 1989, in FBIS, January 10, 1990, 17–19 (emphasis added).

26. *Renmin ribao*, March 11, 1990, 1, in FBIS, April 5, 1990, 29.

27. *Xinhua*, June 29, 1995, in FBIS, June 30, 1995, 12–13.

28. Reported in *Jingji cankao*, November 4, 1988, in FBIS, December 7, 1988, 36.

29. Kristen Parris, "Local Initiative and National Reform: The Wenzhou Model of Development," *China Quarterly*, June 1993, 259, 261.

30. From a *Xinwen wenzhai* report cited in *Ming Pao*, August 4, 1992, in FBIS, August 14, 1992, 20.

31. *Zhongguo siying jingji nianjian, 1996* [China's private economy yearbook, 1996] (Beijing: Zhongguo gongshang lianhe chubanshe, 1996), 162.

32. This was first reported in *South China Morning Post*, August 29, 1989, in FBIS, August 29, 1989, and later confirmed in *Zhenli de zhuiqiu*, November 11, 1994, in FBIS, January 12, 1995.

33. Press Digest of the central organization department, as reported in *China News Digest*, September 17, 1995.

34. See, for instance, "Lun dangyuan daitou zhifu yu dailing qunzhong gongtong zhifu," *Zhenli de zhuiqiu*, July 1998, 13–20.

35. Interviews in Zhejiang, summer 1997. Classifying private enterprises as collectives (known as red-hat enterprises) is not done solely, or even primarily, to allow party recruitment; rather it is done for the mutual benefit of entrepreneurs and local officials. See Kristen Parris, "Private Entrepreneurs as Citizens: From Leninism to Corporatism," *China Information*, Winter 1995–Spring 1996, 1–28.

36. Quoted in *Zhenli de zhuiqiu*, November 11, 1994, in FBIS, January 12, 1995, 24–25; the article went on to criticize this viewpoint.

37. *Zhongguo xinwenshe*, September 6, 1995, in FBIS, September 8, 1995, 16.

38. For an elaboration of the rationale and implications of the "three represents" policy, see Bruce Dickson, "Dilemmas of Party Adaptation: The CCP's Strategies for Survival," in Peter Hays Gries and Stanley Rosen, eds., *State and Society in Twenty-first Century China: Crisis, Contention, and Legitimation* (New York: Routledge, 2004).

39. Hong Yung Lee, *From Revolutionary Cadres to Party Technocrats in Socialist China* (Berkeley: University of California Press, 1991), 2. Lee believes that markets and Leninism are incompatible, leading eventually to an authoritarian development state in China.

40. Parris, "Local Initiative and National Reform," 261.

41. Tong, "State, Society, and Political Change," 334. Gordon White and his collaborators make a similar point regarding the separate but potentially reinforcing market and political dynamics of China's emerging civil society; see White, Howell, and Shang, *In Search of Civil Society*, especially 7–10.

42. O'Neil, "Revolution from Within," 587.

43. Tong, "State, Society, and Political Change," 346–347.

44. O'Neil, "Revolution from Within," 594.

45. Bruce J. Dickson, *Democratization in China and Taiwan: The Adaptability of Leninist Parties* (Oxford: Oxford University Press, 1997), 122–130.

46. Dickson, *Democratization*, 204–216.

47. Li and White, "Elite Transformation and Modern Change in Mainland China and Taiwan"; Hendrischke, "Expertocracy and Professionalism."

48. Tong, "State, Society, and Political Change," 347.

49. Hong Yung Lee, "China's New Bureaucracy," in Rosenbaum, ed., *State and Society in China*, 71.

50. Dickson, *Democratization in China and Taiwan*, 134–135.

51. Margaret M. Pearson, "The Janus Face of Business Associations in China: Socialist Corporatism in Foreign Enterprises," *Australian Journal of Chinese Affairs*, January 1994, 25–46; "China's Emerging Business Class: Democracy's Harbinger?" *Current History*, September 1998, 268–272.

52. David L. Wank, "Private Business, Bureaucracy, and Political Alliance in a Chinese City," *Australian Journal of Chinese Affairs*, January 1995, 63–65.

53. Jonathan Unger and Anita Chan, "Corporatism in China: A Developmental State in an East Asian Context," in Barrett L. McCormick and Jonathan Unger, eds., *China after Socialism: In the Footsteps of Eastern Europe or East Asia?* (Armonk, NY: Sharpe, 1995), 111; emphasis in original.

54. John Ishiyama, "Communist Parties in Transition: Structures, Leaders, and Processes of Democratization in Eastern Europe," *Comparative Politics,* January 1995, 158–159.

55. Pearson, "Janus Face of Business Associations"; Unger and Chan, "Corporatism in China"; Chan, "Revolution or Corporatism?"; White et al., *In Search of Civil Society*; Jonathan Unger, " 'Bridges': Private Business, the Chinese Government and the Rise of New Associations," *China Quarterly*, September 1996, 795–819; Christopher Earle Nevitt, "Private Business Associations in China: Evidence of Civil Society or Local State Power," *China Journal,* July 1997, 25–43.

56. Philippe C. Schmitter, "Still the Century of Corporatism?" in Schmitter and Gerhard Lehmbruch, eds., *Trends towards Corporatist Intermediation* (Beverly Hills, CA: Sage, 1979).

57. Douglas A. Chalmers, "Corporatism and Comparative Politics," in Howard J. Wiarda, ed., *New Directions in Comparative Politics* (Boulder, CO: Westview, 1985), 62.

58. Alfred C. Stepan, *The State and Society: Peru in Comparative Perspective* (Princeton, NJ: Princeton University Press, 1978), 58.

59. Unger and Chan, "Corporatism in China," 105, 107.

60. Unger and Chan, "Corporatism in China," 107.

61. Unger and Chan, "Corporatism in China," 129. Unger and Chan make the same point in their separate writings; see, for instance, Unger, " 'Bridges': Private Business, the Chinese Government and the Rise of New Associations"; Chan, "Revolution or Corporatism? Workers in Search of a Solution," in Goodman and Hooper, eds., *China's Quiet Revolution*. Not all advocates of corporatism are so optimistic. Pearson notes "the absence of a compulsion to resolve the tension between autonomy and state dominance"; see "Janus Face of Business Associations," 446.

62. White et al., *In Search of Civil Society*. This is the mirror image of Peter Evans's notion of embedded autonomy: here it is the civil associations that seek connections with the state in order to be effective.

63. William G. Odom, "Soviet Politics and After: Old and New Concepts," *World Politics,* October 1992, 66–98. Odom borrowed these criteria from Huntington's "Paradigms of American Politics: Beyond the One, the Two, and the Many," *Political Science Quarterly,* March 1974, 7.

64. Recent research by Scott Kennedy has found even less corporatist influence in China's business associations. Instead, business has begun to lobby the government on a variety of issues, such as setting industrial standards. This type of collective action by China's private entrepreneurs is more indicative of growing competition and pluralism, at least in the industrial and commercial sectors. See Kennedy, *The Business of Lobbying in China* (Cambridge, MA: Harvard University Press, 2005).

65. Walder makes a similar point in "Quiet Revolution from Within."

66. Chalmers, "Corporatism and Comparative Politics," 67–68.

67. Unger, " 'Bridges,' " 818.

68. White, "Prospects for Civil Society."

69. Unger and Chan, "Corporatism in China," 112.

70. Teresa Wright, "The China Democracy Party and the Politics of Protest in the 1980s–1990s," *China Quarterly*, December 2002, 906–926.

71. See Wang Shaoguang, "The Rise of the Regions: Fiscal Reform and the Decline of Central State Capacity in China," in Walder, ed., *Waning of the Communist State*; and Jia Hao and Lin Zhimin, eds., *Changing Central-Local Relations in China* (Boulder, CO: Westview, 1994); for a contrary view, see Huang Yasheng, *Inflation and Investment Controls in China: The Political Economy of Central-Local Relations during the Reform Era* (New York: Cambridge University Press, 1996).

72. Liang Yanjia and Li Kaisheng, "Jiguan qishiye danwei dangyuan liudong de diaocha he sikao" [Investigation and reflection on floating party members in administrative and enterprise units], *Lingnan xuekan* (Guangzhou), January 1994, 3–56, in FBZ, February 1994, 144–147; *Hong Kong Standard*, December 29, 1994, in FBIS, December 29, 1994, 33–34; *Ming Pao* (Hong Kong), February 3, 1995, in FBIS, February 6, 1995, 24.

73. Chalmers, "Corporatism and Comparative Politics," 60; see also Schmitter, "Still the Century of Corporatism?" 22–25.

74. Marcia A. Wiegle and Jim Butterfield, "Civil Society in Reforming Communist Regimes: The Logic of Emergence," *Comparative Politics*, October 1992, 1–24; Vladimir Tismaneanu, *Reinventing Politics: Eastern Europe from Stalin to Havel* (New York: Free Press, 1992).

75. Schmitter, "Still the Century of Corporatism?" 41.

76. Chan, "Revolution or Corporatism?" 83.

77. Tismaneanu, *Reinventing Politics*, 192–194.

78. Stepan, *State and Society*, 73–81.

79. Huntington, "Social and Institutional Dynamics," 9.

II

POLITICAL AND
LEGAL REFORMS

5

Political Legitimacy
in China's Transition

Toward a Market Economy

Baogang Guo

After more than two decades of rapid changes, China's economic system has been transformed beyond recognition. In contrast, the essential elements of China's political system have remained largely unaffected. This lopsided development has created the so-called China paradoxes. Although the basic framework for a market economy has been put into place, China is still an authoritarian party-state. While economic freedom has become an engine of economic growth, the government retains tight control over the media and political organizations. And even though China has maintained a sustained and stable economic growth, its ruling elite has kept watchful eyes over the increasing signs of social unrests and political instability.[1]

The internal and external pressures for more political reforms have indeed intensified in recent years. A number of factors may have contributed to this. The diversification of the economy, for instance, has created favorable social and economic conditions for a pluralistic society. The emergence of a new middle class, for instance, is not only turning China into one of the world's largest consumer markets but also creating stronger social support for political liberalism.[2] Many believe that, once this class gets stronger and more sophisticated, democratization will be only a matter of time.[3]

Cracks in the current political system can be seen in many areas. The once all-powerful Leninist and Maoist ideologies have been marginalized and weakened. Western ideas, such as human rights, individualism, political accountability, and

147

transparency, are gradually taking root in China's political life. Moreover, the ongoing telecommunications revolution has reduced people's reliance on government-run media. The Internet has increasingly made control over the flow of information by the government more and more difficult.

All of these factors have led to the erosion of the legitimacy of the party-state. This potential crisis of legitimacy is one of the top concerns of the political leaders in Beijing.[4] The newly proposed theory of "three represents" is the latest effort made by the Chinese Communist Party (CCP) to address this concern.[5]

The legitimacy issue has puzzled many political observers in the West. After the 1989 Tiananmen crisis, some Western observers anticipated a speedy downfall of the Chinese communist regime. This did not happen. Now a decade later, we hear again the similar predictions of a "coming collapse of China."[6] These predictions, in my view, may be proven wrong for the same reason: they underestimate the ability of the regime to stay in power, and the aptitude of the CCP for adapting to the changing political environment.[7] In addition, the oversimplification of political legitimacy also contributes to the repeated failure of forecasting China's political future. Many Western scholars who were indoctrinated by liberal legitimacy theories have trouble comprehending the communist system of legitimation in the context of Chinese political culture and history. As Feng Chen points out, "The theory of imminent collapse was flawed because it treated China as if it were a Western democracy where legitimacy directly determines the continuation of political rule."[8] Furthermore, many studies pay little attention to the multifaceted nature of regime legitimacy. Some have mistakenly believed that only a democratic government can be legitimate.[9]

This chapter will take an in-depth look at the issue of political legitimacy. The first section focuses on Chinese traditional theories of political legitimacy and the practices of political legitimation. The second section analyzes the elements of political legitimacy that the CCP's party-state is able to cultivate in different eras. The third section takes a closer look at various challenges to the legitimate bases of the post-Jiang government and analyzes opportunities Beijing may use to strengthen its political legitimacy. The central argument developed in this chapter is that the government in Beijing has managed to legitimize itself through cultivating traditional moral and utilitarian supports. Contrary to many prevailing beliefs, the regime has demonstrated a remarkable level of adaptability to the changing political environment. However, the transition toward a market economy has redefined the meanings of the century-old cognitive model of political legitimacy. Consequently, the existing system of legitimation is being challenged. The regime may face a new crisis of legitimacy if it fails to deal with this new challenge.

POLITICAL LEGITIMACY IN THE
CHINESE CONTEXT

Governments everywhere and throughout history have always sought answers to a fundamental question: Who deserves to have authority and why is a ruler legitimate?

Efforts to define legitimacy have proved to be elusive, to say the least. Nonetheless, there is no shortage of research on this subject either due to the practical nature of the issue. In general, scholars tend to agree that the concept of legitimacy means more than lawfulness. Seymour Martin Lipset, for example, defines legitimacy as "the capacity of the system to engender and maintain the belief that the existing political institutions are the most appropriate ones for the society."[10] David Beetham defines the concept as "a power relationship justified in terms of people's beliefs."[11] Scholars tend to disagree on what constitutes the basis of political legitimacy. Their analyses are more likely to focus on the following two issues: What makes people believe in the ruler's right to govern? In what ways can a ruler maintain such a belief? The first question deals with a normative issue, and the second, an empirical one. David Easton defines the former as "diffuse support" and the latter as "specific support."[12]

In this chapter, I redefine the two dimensions by introducing two slightly different concepts: original justification and utilitarian justification. Original justification refers to the origin of the ruling authority, and the utilitarian justification defines the rulers' staying power or capacity to maintain people's belief in their ruling authority.[13] Original justification may derive from a divine being, a leader of moral character, a unique quality, or simply the will of the people. It deals with the right to govern and provides the moral capital for those who govern. The utilitarian justification derives from the capacity of the rulers to meet people's needs, such as material well-being or physical security. Greek philosophers referred to it as the *eudemonic* legitimacy.[14] I prefer the term "utility" because it can be defined more broadly as the interest of the people rather than being merely the pursuit of happiness in the hedonic sense. The utility justification deals with both the process and outcome of achieving happiness or satisfaction.[15] This concept is closely related to the original justification. A regime with proper original justification can still suffer a legitimacy crisis if the regime cannot effectively satisfy people's needs. A democratic regime, which has the expressed consent of the people, may not be the most effective government if its economic institutions are not compatible with the political institutions; therefore, it can suffer from chronic governing crises as well. An authoritarian developmental state may prove to be highly efficient in balancing the need for rapid economic growth on the one hand and the need for full employment and low inflation on the other. It thus may turn out to be stable and popular.

For most governments, it is always an uphill battle to maintain a delicate balance between the original and utilitarian justifications. Sometimes, there may even be some kind of trade-off involved. Weakness in one area will force the political leaders to rely on strength in the other area. However, a government with a solid basis in legitimacy tends to possess both strong original and utilitarian justifications. In the following discussion, I will conceptualize these assumptions and hypotheses through a reexamination of China's traditional political thoughts. The inquiry will help develop more specific operational variables that can be further tested by empirical analyses. It paves the way for a new analytical framework which is clearly needed in light of the apparent weaknesses found in some of the existing studies.

China is known for her sophistication in maintaining a long-lasting government. There were 25 dynasties, and more than 400 kings or emperors. During the past two and a half millenniums, Chinese philosophers and political thinkers developed complicated theories of political legitimacy. Confucianism has exerted lasting impact on the Chinese political system and thus deserves special attention. Ironically, Chinese translation of the word legitimacy is *he fa xing*, which means literally lawful. But, in its application, the rule by law is less important than the rule by virtue to most Chinese rulers. Confucianism and other political theories have generated a distinctive cognitive model of political behavior. This patterned way of political thinking and behavior make up the basis of political legitimacy of Chinese government.

Original Justification

As I mentioned earlier, the original justification is the moral capital of a political regime.[16] The idea of original justification is not new. On the one hand, Max Weber's analysis of three sources of legitimacy—supernatural, charismatic, and legal-rational—is a synthesis of Western thought on the issue. Traditional authority is based on the claim of godly origin. Charismatic authority is based on the leader's personal charisma, heroism, and other extraordinary individual qualities, such as virtue or popularity. Rational-legal authority is based on popular beliefs in the validity of legal statutes and functional competence based on rationally created rules and procedures.[17] Weber's framework stopped short of linking democratic legitimacy with the will of the people.[18]

Chinese traditional understanding of the original justification, on the other hand, has a strong emphasis on the will of the people, but is inherently weak on the legalist ground due the strong influence of Confucianism. The original justification of political legitimacy can be articulated by using four Chinese concepts: mandate of heaven *(tian ming)*, rule by virtue *(ren zhi)*, popular consent *(min ben)*, and legality *(he fa)*.

Mandate of Heaven

Historically, legitimation of authority involved the use of abstract and religious ideas. The notion that a ruler's right to govern derives from a supernatural force is as old as human civilization. Beginning in the West Zhou dynasty, ancient Chinese emperors always legitimized their political power by *tian* or heaven. The "mandate of heaven" is based on the following principles: heaven grants a ruler's right to rule; there is only one heaven; the emperor is the son of heaven, and therefore his rule is divine rule.

Similar ideas can be found in other civilizations. Augustine, for example, wrote *The City of God*, in which he set out a theoretical framework for the institution of a Christian monarch.[19] French orator Jacques-Benigne Bossuet reinforced medieval notions of kingship in his theory of the "Divine Right of Kings." He argued that certain kings ruled because God chose them and that these kings were accountable to no one except God.[20]

Virtue

For centuries, the term "legitimacy" concerns not only the theocratic basis but the ethical one as well. The moral teaching of Confucius had profound influence on Chinese rulers. Confucius believed that the ruler's virtue and the contentment of the people, rather than power, should be the true measures of a ruler's political success.[21] In the Confucian paradise of the Great Harmony *(da tong)*, there was a system of moral hierarchy in which an emperor is supposed to be the most virtuous man on earth. Since virtue can be nurtured through education, all government officials should be recruited from "gentlemen" *(jun zi)*, or learned scholars. Mencius pushed this virtue-based political idealism even further. He believed that government was primarily an exercise of ethics. The rule of a truly moral king, according to him, was characterized by his benevolence toward his people.

In comparison, ancient Egyptians also based their faith on a teenage goddess or Ma'at of the universe who benevolently ruled all aspects—human, material, and divine—of the universe. She was a symbol of justice and ultimate truth. In ancient Greece, Plato's classic account of the subject is centered on the concept of justice. Justice, according to Plato, is the recognition of each individual's unique role in society. Justice requires that everyone perform duties that he or she is by nature best fit to do. A state becomes just only when philosophers are given the authority to govern because reason and knowledge constitute the basis for claims to political legitimacy, and only philosophers are capable of discovering and understanding divine value—an eternal form of the heaven. In Plato's world, justice is the highest goal of political life; the ability of the wise ruler to offer a just order is the foundation of the government.[22] Both Platonic and Confucian theories of legitimacy are based on the belief that there is an absolute truth. The source of the truth lies in either natural law or divine law.

Popular Consent

Although legitimate rulers demand people's voluntary submission to their authorities, the Chinese understanding of the relationship between the ruler and the people suggests that rulers must constantly seek popular approval, not by way of expressed public opinions, but through winning the hearts and minds of the people. This understanding is reflected in Mencius's *min ben* ideas. *Min ben* can be translated as "regarding the people as the roots of the state." This concept resembles the concept of popular consent without its legalist tone. It focuses primarily on the need to look after the interest of the people.[23] Considering the following quotation from Mencius:

Here is the way to win the empire: win the people and you win the empire. Here is the way to win the people: win their hearts and you win the people. Here is the way to win their hearts: give them and share with them what they like, and do not do to them what they do not like. The people turn to humane ruler as water flows downward and beasts take to wilderness.[24]

Min ben has two meanings: First, people's interests are of utmost importance. Second, rulers must follow the will of the people; show respect for people's needs; let people be the principal decision makers of their own life. After all, according to Mencius, people's interests are above the rulers' interests. Most significantly, *min ben* gives the traditional concept of "mandate of heaven" a new meaning, namely, the acceptance of a ruler by the people shall be a true test of the will of heaven. Mencius even suggested that people had a right to overthrow a ruler who forfeited his mandate.[25]

Legality

Although morality is the central theme of Chinese traditional political theories, governing by established laws and regulations is also an important part of China's political tradition. Legality in the Chinese context, however, is more often based on family rules, clan norms, community customs, and social traditions. Even emperors must observe rules set up by their ancestors. Violation of these rules may violate, weaken, or even destroy an emperor's right to be in power. The right of primogeniture, for example, normally determines the succession order of the emperorship. A breach of this norm may be considered to be usurpation of the throne and can provoke a rebellion against the usurper. Beginning in the Qin dynasty, Chinese legalists began to emphasize the rule by law, mutual obligation, and responsibilities. But the use of law was only considered to be a means to strengthen a ruler's power. Therefore rule by law significantly differs from a modern notion of the rule of law in which the ruler is also restrained by law.

Utilitarian Justification

How to maintain people's belief that the political system is legitimate is equally important to the belief of who should govern. The modern rationalist school of thought believes that people will be happy and supportive of the government only if their needs are satisfied. According to Jeremy Bentham, a British philosopher of the late eighteenth century, the principle of utility dictates an individual's approval or disapproval of a government's legitimacy. The legitimacy of a government, in this view, lies in its ability to maximize individual happiness and minimize pain.[26]

The Chinese Confucianist and the legalist agree that common people are motivated primarily by profit and self-interest. To strengthen the mandate of heaven, the Confucianist believes that rulers must make decisions on behalf of the people *(wei min zuo zhu),* and that those decisions must not harm the well-being of the people. This belief in the government's role as a provider of benefits has enabled rulers in China to play a more active role in managing the economy.[27] When dealing with utilitarian justification, the concepts of benefiting the people *(li min)* and equality of wealth *(jun fu)* are the predominant theme throughout Chinese history.

Benefiting the People

The concept of *li min* can be found in many Chinese classics. According to the book *Han fei zi*, "Profit is his [the ruler's] means of winning over people."[28] *Li min* means asking rulers to give primary consideration to the welfare of the people. It is closely related to the concept of people's livelihood *(min sheng)*. A good ruler should not be preoccupied with benefiting himself and indulging in his personal luxury and comfort. Instead, he should be concerned with the welfare of his subjects first. Among the good deeds mentioned in the classics, rulers should not tax people heavily, should make sure people have enough food, shelter, and clothing, and should control floods and relieve poverty, and so on.

Modern political utility theory also emphasizes the importance of achievement and effectiveness of the government as a way of legitimatizing the government. In his study of social conditions for democracy, Seymour Martin Lipset considers the effectiveness and legitimacy of the political system to be of crucial importance.[29] Samuel Huntington also has discussed the importance of achievement in maintaining legitimacy.[30]

Equality

The idea of equality is deeply imbedded in Chinese political thought. China was known to be one of the most populated countries on earth for the past two millenniums. Scarcity of material resources such as arable land and food caused persistent problems of famines. Concentration of landownership becomes a chronicle social problem. Peasants always dreamed of landownership and equal economic distribution. Justice was always understood as a fare distribution of economic wealth to all. Mencius understands this fairly well. He points our people are not afraid of scarcity of wealth but instead the unequal distribution of it. To ensure equal land distribution, he strongly recommended the well-field system—a communal land system supposedly used during the Zhou dynasty (1046–256 b.c.)—as a way of ensuring equal distribution of land. Xu Xing, one of the agriculturists in the period of Warring States (403–221 b.c.), went even further by advocating social equality. He imagined a society with no distinction between those who worked with their minds and those who worked with their hands as well as between the rulers and the ruled.[31] Over the course of history, various schemes of equal landownership were experimented and implemented. During the Tang dynasty (a.d. 618–907) "the equal-field system" assigned every adult, including women, a fixed amount of land.

Another example was the Taiping Rebellion (A.D. 1850–1864). Hong Xiuquan combined traditional Chinese agrarianism with Christianity and tried to create a Chinese utopia, the Heavenly Kingdom of Eternal Peace *(Tai ping tian guo)*, in southern China. He too proposed a communal land system to ensure equal land-distribution.[32]

The Chinese cognitive pattern of political legitimacy can be described as follows: a ruler, who has the mandate of heaven, possesses the quality of virtue, shows respect to his subjects, follows the rules of the ancestors, and tries to win the hearts and minds of the people, will be considered a just and legitimate one. A just ruler will strengthen his legitimacy by promoting policies that will benefit the people, not himself, by ensuring relatively equal distribution of these benefits, and by allowing the people to do what they do the best. This unique cognitive model has influenced every Chinese government and its rulers throughout history. By carefully observing these norms, a ruler, feudal or modern, can be assured of public support and accepted as legitimate.

HOW HAS THE PARTY-STATE LEGITIMATIZED ITSELF?

Being a regime established through a prolonged armed struggle, the CCP is supposed to have some difficulties to justify its political power. Yet, in reality, the CCP and the new regime in Beijing were very popular and appeared to have acquired the mandate of the people easily. The support that the CCP received from workers, peasants, and intellectuals in the early days appeared to be genuine. There are a number of explanations for this. Communism appeals to many Chinese because it resembles the ideal society Chinese themselves are always longing for, namely the *da tong* (great harmony) society. The communal land system the Communists established helps peasants realize their economic dream of landownership. The removal of old landowner class promotes social equality. However, this moral capital did not last forever. In the absence of a divine justification, a constitutional order, and democratic elections, how the Communists have sustained their political legitimacy over an extended period of time is the main focus of discussion in this section.

The Era of Mao Zedong and Revolutionary Legitimacy

Many Western scholars have characterized the Maoist era as brutal and totalitarian. If so, how could the regime stay in power if it had no political legitimacy? The truth of the matter is that the majority of the people did regard the new government as a legitimate one. For a long time, the CCP relied primarily on revolution itself as a ground for political legitimation.

As a revolutionary party, the CCP cannot and does not seek approval from all social classes; it only claims to be the party of the workers and peasants. It uses a

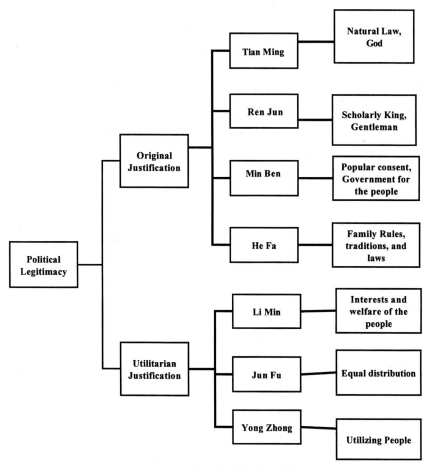

Figure 5.1   The Chinese Cognitive Model of Political Legitimacy

system of majority dictatorship as a basis of legitimacy. Marxist ideology provides the necessary original justification. Mao's personality cult is used as a basis of charismatic legitimacy. People are enshrined as "masters" of the society and their livelihood is taken care of through the state and the rural collectives. Overall, these efforts at support building fit very well with the Chinese traditional system of legitimation and help secure both original and utilitarian justifications for the party and the state.

After the 1949 communist revolution, communist ideology was carefully used to replace the traditional idea of "mandate of heaven." The official ideology was crucial to the institutionalization of CCP's legitimacy. "Without the ideology," writes Peter Moody, "the Party would have no claim to legitimacy."[33] The theories of historical materialism, class struggle, and scientific socialism provided necessary moral justification for the new party-state. Communists believe that they have a historical mission to overthrow capitalism. They are destined to transform the existing society of injustice into an entirely new one. "The socialist system," wrote Mao, "will eventually replace the capitalist system; this is an objective law independent of man's will."[34] According to the theory of scientific socialism, the industrial working class, organized and conscious, is certain to overthrow capitalism and to create a society of abundance with universal brotherhood and true freedom.[35] The Russian leader Lenin insisted that an elite-based communist party must be established to serve as a vanguard of the industrial working class, which, in itself, was also a pivotal social force of a historical transformation. Once in power, according to Lenin, the communists would not share power with anybody and would establish a one-party rule on behalf of the proletariat.[36]

Based on the Leninist party theory, the CCP established a "unified leadership" *(yi yuan hua),* and a party-state after taking power in 1949. According to a decision made in 1949 by the CCP Central Committee, the party committees, instead of government agencies, were the highest decision-making bodies in all work units, and decisions made by these committees had to be obeyed and carried out unconditionally by all government agencies, military units, and mass organizations. This arrangement was meant to be a temporary measure to facilitate the command of the revolutionary forces. However, after taking over power, the unified leadership was imposed on all aspects of society and was strengthened under the influence of party radicals. Party committees were established in every governmental organization. Party secretaries held ultimate power.[37]

In addition to the appeal of the ideology, the CCP also relied heavily on charismatic figures to enhance its public appeal. The Chinese Communist revolution took place in an economically backward peasant society. Good emperors were the peasants' only hope. Personality cult was a mutual choice between the peasant mass and the party. All of the founding Communist leaders became new godlike figures. Mao was enshrined as the sun and godly savior of the Chinese people. During the Cultural Revolution, the worship of Mao reached its peak. Mao's writing became another source of legitimacy. His words became the ultimate truth. People would march in the streets fanatically to celebrate Mao's latest directives. When Mao died in 1976, his successor, Hua Guofeng, had no choice but to rely on a Mao's personal note of approval as a basis of his legitimacy.

Mao was a strong believer of the traditional *min ben* idea. He became a master of the "mass line," a term used by Mao meaning that all decisions must be "from the mass and to the mass." "To link oneself with the masses," Mao wrote, "one must act in accordance with the needs and wishes of the masses. All work done for the masses must start from their needs and not from the desire of any individual, however well-intentioned."[38] His most famous quote, "The people, and the people alone, are the motive force in the making of world history," inspired millions of Chinese people to participate in his massive economic and political campaigns.[39] Mao, however, did not like spontaneous popular actions. He believed that people must be organized and controlled. For that reason, the Chinese Communists embraced state corporatism to put all mass organizations under the umbrella of the CCP and the party-state. Mao justified the party's control by saying that "without the efforts of the CCP, without the Chinese Communists as the mainstay of the Chinese people, China can never achieve independence and liberation, or industrialization and the modernization of her agriculture."[40] Workers, women, and youth were organized into monopolistic organizations and became a part of the extended network of social and political control. All political and social organizations had to accept the CCP's leadership.

On utilitarian grounds, the Maoist era was heavily dependent on the following justifications: national independence, liberation, modernity, social economic equality, and fraternity.[41] Nationalist pride was especially important to the CCP's claim to power. China was unified for the first time since the collapse of the Qing dynasty. No Chinese political force had been able to achieve this objective since China's humiliating defeat in the Opium Wars (1839–1842). Later on, Mao's tough stand against the United States, the Soviet Union, and India reinforced China's national pride and made Mao himself a true national hero.

The persuasive power of national liberation was also applied in domestic politics. The Communists promised a new beginning, a government of the people—a government that would really care for the interests of the common people. Mao wrote,

> We should pay close attention to the well-being of the masses, from the problems of land and labor to those of fuel, rice, cooking oil and salt. . . . All such problems concerning the well-being of the masses should be placed on our agenda. We should discuss them, adopt and carry out decisions and check up on the results. We should help the masses to realize that we represent their interests and that our lives are intimately bound up with theirs. We should help them to proceed from these things to an understanding of the higher tasks which we have put forward, the tasks of the revolutionary war, so that they will support the revolution and spread it throughout the country, respond to our political appeals and fight to the end for victory in the revolution.[42]

He promised that people would truly become the master of the society, enjoying a wide range of democratic rights never seen before in Chinese history. The feeling of being "liberated" experienced by workers and peasants translated into enormous support for the regime.[43] The gratitude and affection people showed toward their new leaders provided moral capital for the new government.

Mao understood that the only way communism can appeal to most people is to bring a better life to them.[44] In a number of areas, the progress made was evident. Women, for instance, were now treated as "one half of the sky" and were promised equal pay for equal work. Women's participation in the workforce reached 49 percent, much higher than the world average of 34.5 percent. Chinese women made about 80 percent of men's income, while at the same time in the United States, women only made about 60–70 percent of what men made in spite of the passage of the Equal Pay Act in 1963.[45]

Through land distribution and land reform, the CCP solved one of the major sources of inequality in China, landownership. Land reform fulfilled the dream of millions of peasants. From 1950 to 1952, over 60 million acres of farmland were confiscated from landlords and redistributed for free to over 300 million poor peasants.[46] However, the privatization of lands did not last long. The collectivization of agricultural lands soon followed. The establishment of people's communes created a communal land system similar to those used during the early period of the Tang dynasty. The collective farms were inefficient but guaranteed economic equality among peasants and provided a degree of economic and social security for poor villagers. Nonetheless, even during the Maoist era, inequality persisted. According to a document written during the Cultural Revolution, many former capitalists, intellectuals, artists, and state and party leaders received much higher salaries than did the common people. Some artists received a monthly salary as high as RMB2,000 (US$240) a month, an astonishing figure if it were compared with the monthly wages of RMB30–50 (US$4–6) that a worker usually received.[47] By the end of the Cultural Revolution, much of the income gap was eliminated, and the pursuit of economic equality turned into extreme egalitarianism.

With a goal to emulate the Soviet style of state socialism, China took only a few short years to eliminate all privately owned enterprises, commerce, transportation, and craft-making industries as well as completing the initial stage of socialist transformation. Many state-owned factories were built during the first and second five-year plans. Millions of farmers joined industrial labor forces. In 1949 there were only 8 million workers in the state-owned enterprises. By 1981, this number jumped to 83.7 million.[48] The wage labor system was abolished. Workers were allowed to participate in the factories' decision-making process. Workers loved their newly acquired job security and political equality. They were by and large complacent about their improved economic status and showed strong support to the communist regime.[49]

The magnitude of the radical social, political, and economic changes the new government engineered was truly unprecedented in Chinese history. Between 1952 and 1974 China's industrial output increased ten times, and agricultural output increased three times. China quickly became a major military power with a strategic nuclear force.[50] Even without a Western-style democratic election, a free market economy, and the rule of law, the CCP could still govern without serious internal challenges. It survived even the most difficult years, such as in the aftermath of the Great Leap Forward and the Cultural Revolution.

However, the rigid command economy and the endless political-style economic campaigns caused economic stagnation by the end of 1970s. The widespread shortage of consumer goods forced the government to set up a strict rationing system. Evidence from an analysis of the changes in the Engel Index (a ratio of expenditure on food against the whole expenditure reflects the changes of people's consumption patterns) showed very little improvement in people's standard of living between 1957 and 1981.[51] Revolution-based legitimacy was running out of steam. The communist political legitimacy suffered the first major crisis in 1976 when people were not even allowed to mourn the death of Zhou Enlai, a highly respected premier, a moderate leader, and a proponent of China's continued modernization and economic development. Legitimation in the Mao era is illustrated in figure 5.2.

The Era of Deng Xiaoping and Jiang Zemin and Rational Legitimacy

After the death of Mao, Deng Xiaoping quickly emerged as China's paramount leader. Deng realized the political chaos and the failure to provide significant improvements in the living standard of the people had weakened the party's legitimacy: "some people had disappointed feelings towards the Party and toward social-

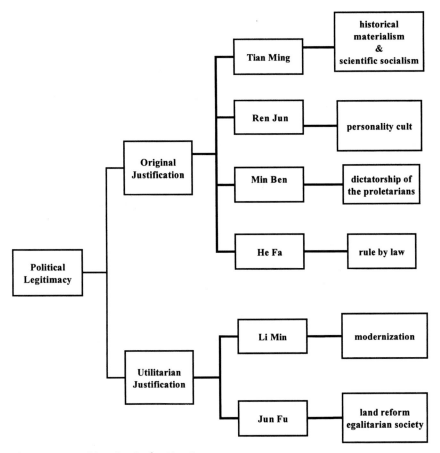

Figure 5.2   Legitimation in the Mao Era

ism."[52] And "in a country as big and as poor as ours, if we don't try to increase production, how can we survive? How is socialism superior, when our people have so many difficulties in their lives?"[53] Faced with a stagnated economy and eroded public confidence, Deng decided to put an end to the pursuit of class struggle and the mass movement. He redirected the people's energy to business and economic development. In the next decade, he successfully put into practice the policy of economic reform and the opening-up to the outside. At the center of this new policy initiative was a determination to modernize China and to increase China's total GDP as fast as that could be done. The government came up with an ambitious goal of quadrupling the gross annual value of industrial and agricultural output in twenty years (1981–2000), and to have the per capita income reach about US$800. The overall standard of living of the people would enter the era of "small comfort" *(xiao kang)*. In the rural area, the reforms began with the abolition of the people's communes and the establishment of the household responsibility system. The reform successfully stimulated the peasants' enthusiasm for increasing agricultural production. Millions of peasants were soon out of poverty and raised themselves above the subsistence level of standard of living. In the urban areas, a free market economic system based on economic freedom and market competition was gradually introduced. Labor contract systems gradually replaced the lifetime employment systems in urban areas, and state-run business were made accountable for their own profits and losses. The stock market was reopened. Private businesses began to grow rapidly. Foreign investment poured in China to take advantage of China's inexpensive labor force.

The utilitarian approach is an affirmative action that effectively curtailed Mao's legacy of class struggle and politics-first mentality. It depoliticizes the society, helps heal deep-rooted factionalism, and restores the economic vitality of China. While the profound market reform might strengthen the party-state's utilitarian justification, it further weakened the CCP's moral capital. Soon after the reform began, intellectuals started demanding more political freedom. Deng quickly denounced the movement as "bourgeoisie liberalization" and came up with the "four cardinal principles" to set limits on political change.[54] To maintain political and social stability, he moved away from Mao's totalitarianism and established a rational, authoritarian order. In this new order, the intellectuals enjoyed a limited freedom as long as it was confined in the big cage of four cardinal principles.

The legal system was also restored. The lawlessness of the Mao era and the experience of the Cultural Revolution helped foster a consensus that a socialist legal system must be established. The constitution of 1982 was a major legal breakthrough for the PRC. It recognized the principle of popular sovereignty, reestablished the principle of the supremacy of law, and restored a system of limited separation of powers and checks and balances.[55] A large number of statutory and administrative laws were enacted during this period. The system of administrative supervision was established to monitor state agencies and personnel. A law passed in 1989 allowed citizens to sue administrative agencies and to hold public officials accountable for their actions.

Although these efforts have not truly established a society based on the rule of law, progress has been made in many areas. The supremacy of law is being gradually established, and the protection for individual freedom has been strengthened. Moreover, according to Pitman Potter, "by relying on the socialist legal system as a source of legitimacy, the regime also strengthens its ability to justify specific actions by reference to law."[56] Nonetheless, as one scholar points out, the legal reform is also a double-edged sword. On the one hand, it does put legal restraint on the power holders, but on the other hand, it gives legitimate tools for the government to use legalized oppression.[57] In the end, a "consultative rule of law regime" is established, which, according to Wei Pan, "is a rule of law regime supplemented by democracy rather than a democracy supplemented by rule of law."[58]

After all, Deng is still part of the old guard, an enlightened one, nevertheless. He devoted his entire life to the cause of communism. For that reason, he had no intention to abandon Marxism, or even Maoism entirely. What he wanted was to rationalize these theories through reforms, and make necessary revisions to them. According to him, China "shall adhere to Marxism and keep to the socialist road. But by Marxism we mean Marxism that is integrated with Chinese conditions, and by socialism we mean a socialism that is tailored to Chinese conditions and has a specifically Chinese character."[59]

The first attempt to revise the theory of socialism was made in the early 1980s. The party formally proposed the theory of primitive socialism, which held that China was still in the primitive stage of socialism. It did not have the strong economic foundation of a full-fledged socialist society. Therefore private ownership must be accepted, protected, and promoted to advance China's economic development. While still holding on to the fundamental core of Leninism and Maoism, the new theory adjusts its instrumental principles to reinterpret the nature of the current task. The discrepancy between the two was blamed for the weakening role of the orthodox ideology as a basis of legitimacy.[60]

However, even with these moderate revisions of an outdated ideology, the problems the CCP faced during the painful transitional period were not easy to resolve. By 1989 the popular discontent over rampant corruption and lack of political freedom escalated into the Tiananmen crisis, the most serious crisis of legitimacy the Communist regime ever faced. Had the old guards decided not to use the military force to put down the student demonstration, the party's unified leadership could have been ended. The willingness to use coercion cooled down the hope for an overnight change to the country's political system, and gave the regime some time to make corrections to address public criticism. Nevertheless, the horrifying experience cast a shadow on the regime's impressive economic accomplishment and undermined its legitimacy even further. Deng soon retired and passed away a few years later. He will most likely be remembered as the last strongman of the authoritarian regime since no one else has replaced him with the same level of prestige and charisma.[61] His programmatic reinterpretation of Marxism was later enshrined as "Deng Xiaoping theory."

When Jiang Zemin stepped in as the new leader amid the 1989 crisis, he represented the coming of a new era, the era of technocracy. Without charismatic personality, strong revolutionary credentials, or an impressive record of personal achievements, he did not enjoy the same level of respect and unquestionable authority. He must now earn people's respect through his own efforts. With Deng still behind the curtain in his first term, Jiang took a hard line toward political reforms. But he further liberalized the economy. Under him, a full-scale urban reform program was launched, and some major breakthroughs were made. Most small and medium-size enterprises were sold, merged, or bankrupted. Stock ownership was used to diversify business property rights. The state's share of the overall economy declined quickly. Private and foreign-owned companies mushroomed. Total foreign direct investment exceeded US$400 billion. The average growth rate was kept at 8–9 percent for a decade. China successfully avoided the financial crisis of East Asia in the late 1990s.

The sustained economic growth brought significant improvement to people's living standard. China's population in poverty went down from 20 percent in 1981 to about 5 percent in 1997, and average per capita GDP in the same period increased from US$200 to US$750. The Engel Index in the urban areas dropped from 57.5 percent to 37.9 percent between 1978 and 2001, and in the rural areas, the index also dropped from 67.7 to 47.8.[62]

The return of Hong Kong and Macao as well as being awarded the right to host the 2008 Olympic Game by the International Olympic Committee (IOC) also increased public confidence and national pride. These successes seemed to strengthen the regime's legitimacy. According to a survey of Beijing residents conducted by Chen Jie and colleagues in 1995, the regime enjoyed a moderately high level of affective support (citizen's evaluation of governmental legitimacy), and this provided a reservoir of diffused support that the system could draw on in the future.[63] Another survey of Beijing residents in 1995 also found no apparent public pressure for democracy.[64]

Nevertheless, the economic success had its cost. Among many other things, the growing economic inequality was the most troubling one. According to Chinese official statistics, China's Gini coefficient, an internationally accepted measurement of the degree of inequality in the distribution of income in a given society, rose from a low level of 0.33 in 1980, to 0.40 in 1994, and 0.46 in 2000. Although the number is skewed somewhat by the differences derived from the historical separation of urban and rural areas, China has joined the countries which have the worst records of unequal distribution of wealth.[65] After a decade of agricultural recovery, thanks mainly to the household responsibility system, peasants have been once again left behind. Over 90 million rural peasants have become migrant workers floating between cities seeking jobs. To reduce the employment pressure, the government has called for the acceleration of the urbanization process and the reform of the household registration system.

Efforts were also made to establish safety nets to help people victimized by the market reform. Reforms of the existing social security system, the health insurance system, the poverty relief program, unemployment and the insurance system were launched in 1992. The new social security network is quite extensive, yet it still covers primarily urban employees or 10 percent of the total population. Peasants, who make up 60 percent of the population, have little protection from aging, sickness, poverty, and unemployment. According to the official statistics, by the end of 2002, there were 147 million workers and retirees enrolled in the Old-age Insurance Program, 94 million enrolled in the basic medical insurance program, 101 million enrolled in the unemployment insurance program, 44 million enrolled in the industrial injuries insurance program, and 34 million enrolled in the childbirth insurance program.[66] China still has a long way to go to perfect its social security system and to eliminate poverty. But as China's economic strength continues to rise, the government will have plenty of opportunities to strengthen its legitimacy in this area.

During the Jiang era, the CCP's original justification for political legitimacy continued to erode. Jiang Zemin attempted to build up his personal image as a charismatic leader but had little success. Official corruption worsened. The exposure of corruption cases involving high-ranking officials, such as Cheng Kejie, the former vice chairman of the Standing Committee of the NPC, and Li Jiating, the former governor of Yunnan, did little to repair the damages that had already been done to the image of the party.

The relationship between the CCP and the industrial workers has also been strained. The foundation of the Communist regime is based on an unwritten social contract between the party-state and the working class. The party gets the social support it needs to stay in power, and the working class is protected by the socialist welfare system. At the end of Jiang's tenure this contract was forgotten or simply ignored. The equal relationship between enterprise cadres and workers was gone; the wage labor system was restored. Over 50 millions workers of state-owned factories were either being laid off or were forced to accept early retirement.[67] According to Feng Tongqing, the relationship between workers and enterprise management "is now based primarily on an exchange of economic interests rather than on cooperative comradeship or collectivity."[68] In private enterprises, violation of workers' rights is a serious problem. In some worst cases, intimidation, physical violence, corporal punishment, and restriction of workers' freedom were reported.[69] The number of labor disputes increased from 28,000 in 1992 to 181,000 in 2002.[70] The government agencies at the local levels are weak in enforcing labor standards but are harsh on labor activists who dare to organize strikes or independent unions.[71]

Jiang realized that in order for the CCP to survive in this environment of growing social antagonism and tension, the party must accelerate the process of transforming itself from a revolutionary party to a ruling party. The theory of "three represents" that he proposed before his semiretirement in 2002 is part of the ideological reconstruction of the CCP. The theory is aimed at broadening the party's social support and boosting the party's image as a party of the people. With his strong lobbying effort, the Sixteenth Party Congress officially adopted the new theory as a part of the party's new mission statement in 2002. However, what has been most discussed about this new theory is the acceptance of private entrepreneurs to become party members. The theory helps justify the fact that one-third of the 2 million private business are actually owned by CCP members. These "red capitalists" employ over 7 million workers and control an estimated RMB600 billion in capital assets.[72] But their overall number is still very small. It is unclear to what extent their presence in the party will make any difference.

In sum, the basis for the party-state's legitimacy during the Deng-Jiang era significantly differs from the Maoist era. While at the Maoist era, the CCP relied on the revolution as a basis for legitimation, it relied primarily on rationalization as a basis for legitimation during the post-Mao era. Legitimation during this era can be illustrated in figure 5.3.

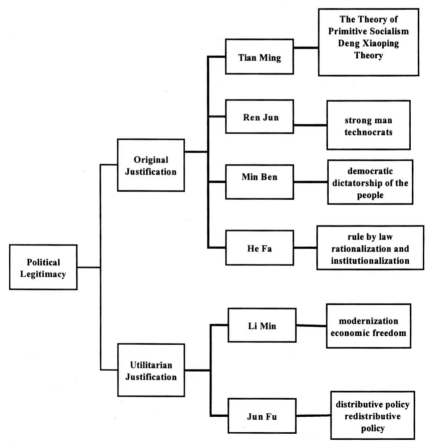

Figure 5.3   Legitimation in the Deng-Jiang Era

THE ERA OF HU JINTAO:
CHALLENGES AND OPPORTUNITIES

The Sixteenth CCP Party Congress, held in November 2002, and the Tenth National People's Congress (NPC), held in March 2003, began the power transfer from the so-called third generation to the fourth one. The retirement of Jiang Zemin from his military post in 2004 marked the completion of the first peaceful power transfer in CCP's history, and a true beginning of the era of Hu Jintao. The new leaders have pledged to continue the work of reforms begun two decades ago. Wen Jiabao, the newly elected premier, vowed to focus more on the sustainable and comparatively rapid development of the national economy. He put the issues of reducing unemployment, improving the social security system, increasing fiscal revenue, cutting public spending, and correcting and standardizing the economic order as his top priorities. It is apparent that the new administration is determined to push for a new reform that will deal with the problems in economic equality and social justice.

The new leaders are all technocrats.[73] All of them joined the CCP after 1949, and they are therefore lacking in revolutionary credentials. But they have accepted Marxist ideology and will not easily abandon that outlook. They all experienced the turbulent years of the Cultural Revolution and have had many years of grassroots working experience. They are all college educated and are proven problem solvers and practical bureaucrats. However, very few of them attended schools or worked in Western countries, and had little reorganization by leadership circle among nations, and some may even share the xenophobic feeling that exists among many Chinese toward foreign powers. Their ascendance to power also owes a lot to the patron–client relationship they have cultivated with the old guard and will continue to work under the shadow of their patrons for years to come. The lack of independent sources of legitimacy is therefore one of their principal weaknesses.[74] Their backgrounds indicate, although not totally, at least three things. First, they are not going to "rock the boat."[75] Instead, they will most likely continue the process of rationalization by focusing on developing rules, norms, procedures, and institutions to codify the policy breakthroughs catalyzed by their predecessors. Second, they are vulnerable and can be victimized by any unforeseeable event, scandal, unrest, or inner party power struggles. Last, they desire to establish their own leadership style and make their own mark on the reform process. In order to consolidate their power, they will need to boost their popular image and utilitarian-based achievements.

It is still too early to assess the policies of the new administration. The outbreak of the SARS epidemic in the first half of the 2003 disrupted the work of the new government. However, the crisis did provide an opportunity for the new leaders to demonstrate their ability to handle a major national crisis and, more importantly, their ability to restore public confidence. Since the outbreak of the SARS epidemic, the government did not share information with the public initially. Its credibility suffered enormously as a result. After hearing the open criticism from the World

Health Organization (WHO), newly elected government officials acted swiftly. The minister of health and the mayor of Beijing were fired. Emergency quarantines were implemented, and SARS treatment centers and hospitals were established. After three months of intensive effort, the SARS outbreak was eventually contained. The SARS scenario not only showed the crisis management skills of this new administration but also demonstrated the ability of the government to utilize the vast amount of national resources and organizational networks it still controls to combat a major epidemic outbreak.

Modernization and economic development will continue to be the primary focus of the new administration. The Sixteenth Party Congress has recommended quadrupling China GDP again in the next two decades. If China achieves this goal, it will have a US$10 trillion economy. This will most likely put China's economy on top of the world, second only to the United States. The sustained economic development will continue to boost the regime's legitimacy, but it may weaken it as well.[76] If rising expectations consistently exceed what economic growth can provide, the level of frustration will rise and a crisis can occur even in a seemly good economic time. Growing unemployment, the widening gap between rich and poor, troubled financial sectors, continuing labor disputes and peasant protests, official corruption, the persistence of separatist movements, and the issue of Taiwan are serious challenges the new leaders will have to face.[77]

After becoming the party's new general secretary, Hu Jintao has delivered several major speeches. His governing philosophy has been gradually revealed. Like his predecessors, Hu holds strong *min ben* and *li min* ideas. Hu reinterprets the essence of Jiang's "three represents" as "three peoples," namely, "use my power for the people, link my feelings to the people, and focus my heart on the pursuit of public welfare."[78] In addition, the importance of the constitution, rule of law, and the supremacy of laws are reemphasized. In a speech to a meeting celebrating the twentieth anniversary of the 1982 Constitution, Hu made it clear that all parties must live within the confines of the constitution and respect the authority of the constitution. He acknowledged that the existing constitution has not been observed adequately, and that the constitution is in need of amendment.[79] In March 2004, the NPC amended the constitution to make it a state policy to protect the lawful rights and interests of private sectors, including the private property rights of citizens. More significantly, after years of quarreling with Western countries on the issue of human rights, the protection of human rights was officially incorporated into the constitution.

Under Hu's leadership, the new administration promised new styles and new thinking to win over people's hearts and minds. For example, the official ceremony for leaders' foreign visitation has been simplified and the size of the delegations reduced.[80] The annual informal meeting and gathering in the Beidaihe Resort was canceled this year. New efforts were made to humanize public policies. The exposure of the Sun Zhigang case by the media, for example, caused public outrage over how people were treated under the system of urban detention of homeless people.[81] The

State Council acted quickly to issue a new decree to abolish the system of detention for people who are homeless or without identification and replaced it with a new system of homeless assistance. All former detention centers now have been converted to public assistance stations to render assistance to people in need on a voluntary basis. I took a sample of news items in the official media on August 8, 2003, when I wrote this chapter, and the following items were among that day's headlines:

1. The government-run official union issued a circular calling for unionization of migrant workers so they will be able to better protect their economic rights. The same circular also calls for the governments at all levels to force employers to purchase industrial accident insurance for these workers.[82]
2. The Ministry of Public Safety just announced thirty measures to simplify the procedures for people who apply for household registration documents, passport, driver's license, and traveling abroad. Citizens in 100 major cities are no longer required to get their work unit's permission prior to applying for travel documents for overseas travel.[83] Similar requirements will soon be removed for marriage and divorce as well.[84]
3. The infamous population control policy has been relaxed in Beijing to allow more people to have a second child.[85] Many other provinces or cities have already implemented such new policies.

These types of day-to-day changes have far-reaching significance. They show that individual freedom is expanding, and citizens' rights are better protected. This helps create a positive image of a kinder and gentler government. If this process continues, the government's popularity and social support will likely be strengthened.

Hu's philosophy of "governing for the people" has been very popular among people. But it may also have its limits. For example, Hu has consistently emphasized the need to strengthen the party's leadership instead of putting restrictions on it. He continues to stress the need for a government "for the people" instead of "by the people." One wonders what's new in this line of thinking. Is this the same old rhetoric of father–son benevolence advocated by Confucianism 2,000 years ago? Chinese traditional political philosophers all recognize the fundamental importance of the people. However, they insist that the ruler is like a parent and should rule as such.

The persistent influence of paternalism, a vestige of feudalism, stands as a major barrier to the realization of modern democracy.[86] The justification that a benevolent government is sufficient enough to maintain regime legitimacy is shortsighted. The idea of democracy is based on political equality and popular sovereignty, not on "happy slaves."[87] Democracy assumes that people know their own interests better, and they can make better decisions on their own without being patronized. The idea of a party-state, however, is based on the assumption that a small elite, the so-called proletarian vanguard, knows best what is good for the people, and people cannot be trusted to choose among themselves if they want to be led by the same elite or not.

This is by far the weakest link in the party-state's moral justification. It is becoming increasingly irrational and less convincing to more and more people accustomed to their new economic freedom. A free market system is inherently incompatible with a noncompetitive political system, since people cannot have true economic freedom without political freedom.[88] If China is determined to have a free market economy, political liberalization must come with it sooner or later. That is why the liberal theory of political legitimacy is so popular among some scholars in China. Western concepts of rule of law, procedure-centered democracy, free competition, and popular political participation are what China needs in reshaping its traditional cognitive model of political legitimacy.

The process to institutionalize a rational-legal legitimacy will probably take many years to accomplish. There are many plausible reasons for that. First, without internal changes in the CCP's guiding theory and structure, substantial political changes are not going to happen anytime soon. The theory of "three represents" is just a beginning, not an end, of such a theoretical reconstruction. There are discussions about the possibility of developing an intraparty democracy. The CCP is experimenting with strengthening the function of party committees within the party, empowering Party Congresses to expand the base of power, and increasing intraparty competition.[89]

Second, even if the party decides to endorse democratization, the legitimacy of the newly installed free market institutions may actually be undermined since the traditional Chinese culture put so much emphasis on social harmony, group cooperation, state intervention, and social equality.[90] Indeed, some have argued that the reason why the CCP is unwilling to speed up political reform is that China's economic success has delayed political reform.[91] The government is afraid that political reform will disrupt economic reform and let out the accumulated strong anticapitalist sentiments such as those manifested by the laborers and peasants in recent years. It is suggested that political reform should be used as a way to break the bottleneck of the economic reform.[92]

Third, the transition from a revolutionary party to a governing party will face serious theoretical challenges. Can the legitimacy of the CCP be based on the will of the majority of the people? Can the CCP be transformed from the party of one class to a party of all people? Can Jiang's theory of "three represents" be materialized? Pan Yue, a known advocate of political reform within the CCP, points out that asking the CCP to represent all people may cause a problem of overrepresentation, and this practice may actually violate the basic political principle of a party system. But he insists that this is not a theoretical issue. It is simply rectifying the fact.[93] Cao Siyuan, another well-known liberal scholar, suggests that the party needs to change its name to "socialist party," to allow open competition inside the party and reform the party's finance.[94]

Last, to institute the rule of law and a system of democratic elections among a population of 1.3 billion is a daunting task. The current village-level elections have been in place for two decades. It is very likely the system will be moved to a higher level. But Deng Xiaoping personally predicted that popular elections of state leaders would not be carried out for another fifty years.

This fourth generation of leaders will not bring China into a fully functional democracy, but will pave the road for its coming. Hu and other Politburo members have too much at stake in the existing system. Although limited political reform programs will be carried out, the most likely scenario in this decade will be continued political liberalization without democratization. Incremental reform will likely to be the main pattern of political reform in China in the next couple of decades. The following diagram illustrates the possible course of action the current political leaders may take to move toward a new rational-legal legitimacy in China in the years to come. The changes that are anticipated during the Hu's era are illustrated in figure 5.4.

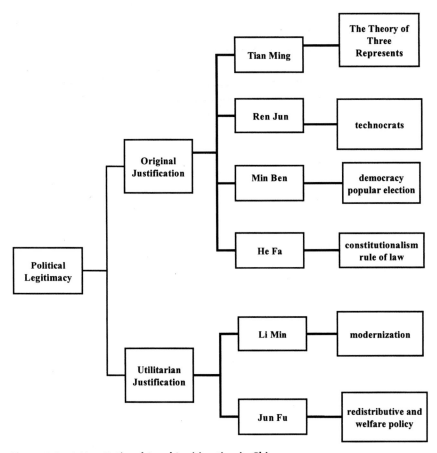

Figure 5.4   A New Rational-Legal Legitimation in China

CONCLUSION

As a society in transition, Chinese Communist leaders have faced constant challenges to their political power. Like their predecessors, they have had to make frequent changes to strengthen their moral and utilitarian justifications, the two key components of political legitimacy. While the first generation of CCP leaders led by Mao relied heavily on using the revolution as a basis for legitimacy, the second and third generations had relied primarily on rationalization and institutionalization in the past two decades. Programatism and technocracy replaced idealism and personality cult that characterized the first generation. Economic development, instead of class struggle, became the top priority of the nation. As the fourth generation leaders take over the government, they, too, face the challenge of rebuilding the system of legitimation.

What we have learned from the history of the People's Republic of China is that the CCP is quite capable of making necessary adaptations to the constantly changing political environment and thus strengthen the CCP's political legitimacy by reinventing itself. The new leaders are likely to continue to make evolutionary adjustment to redefine the CCP's legitimacy base. However, there is no guarantee that the evolutionary change will continue to be successful. In order to make its legitimacy stronger, for example, Beijing has to legitimize political participation from different social groups both inside and outside of the CCP. So far there has been no sign of such a change. But there has been some discussion of broadening inner party democracy. Many believe that China's coming transformation will "likely include measures to legitimize independent social organizations, give citizen groups increased input in policy making (in exchange for some limits on their activities), and develop greater intra-party democracy."[95]

The Chinese perception of legitimacy is rooted in its historical and political traditions. However, this understanding also has its universal underpinning. The analytical framework developed in this chapter synthesizes the findings of many existing studies. It provides theoretical reference points that can be used in the study of regime change and political transition in China, and, more importantly, it is constructed in a larger framework of comparative politics and political legitimacy theory. It therefore could be used as a theoretical framework of a broader scope in the comparative study of political legitimacy across nations and regions around the globe. Although this theoretical framework is developed and used in the Chinese context, some of the concepts used in this study can be further refined, amended, or adapted in other cultural contexts. This analytical framework can be applied to the study of political legitimacy elsewhere and can be tested and enriched by more empirical studies in different cultural setting.

NOTES

The author wishes to thank the following for their helpful comments made on earlier drafts of this chapter: Yang Zhong, A. Jack Waskey, He Li, Jim Stevenson, John Hebestreet, Tang Wei, and anonymous reviewers.

1. Francois Mengin and Jean-Louis Rocca, *Politics in China: Moving Frontiers* (New York: Palgrave Macmillan, 2002).

2. Tzy C. Peng, "The Middle Class in China," *Chinese American Forum* 17, no. 2 (2001): 19–23.

3. Zhao Suisheng, ed., *China and Democracy: Reconsidering the Prospect for a Democratic China* (New York: Routledge, 2001); Jim Frederick, "Thriving in the Middle Kingdom: China Burgeoning Middle Class Holds the Key to the Future of the Country," *Time,* www .time.com/time/asia/features/china_cul_rev/middle_class.html (accessed July 27, 2003).

4. Zheng Min, "Hu Jingtao Acknowledged the Crisis of Governance," *Boxun News,* www.boxun.com (accessed August 9, 2003).

5. The "three represents" mean that the CCP must represent (1) the development trends of advanced productive forces, (2) the orientations of an advanced culture, and (3) the fundamental interests of the overwhelming majority of the people of China. It is first proposed by the former CCP party chief Jiang Zeming.

6. Gordon Chang, *Coming Collapse of China* (New York: Random House, 2001); Ross Terrill, *New Chinese Empire: And What It Means for the United States* (New York: Basic, 2003); Joe Studwell, *The China Dream: The Quest for the Last Great Untapped Market on Earth* (New York: Atlantic Monthly Press, 2002).

7. For example, political scientist Bruce J. Dickson believes that the CCP couldn't be transformed into a democratic party because it lacks adaptability; see *Democratization in China and Taiwan: The Adaptability of Leninist Parties* (Oxford: Clarendon, 1997).

8. Feng Chen, "The Dilemma of Eudemonic Legitimacy in Post Mao China," *Polity,* Spring 1997, 422.

9. Allan Buchanan, "Political Legitimacy and Democracy," *Ethics* 112, no. 4 (2002): 689–770.

10. Seymour Martin Lipset, *Political Man*, exp. ed. (Baltimore, MD: Johns Hopkins University Press, 1981).

11. David Beetham, *The Legitimation of Power* (Atlantic Highlands, NJ: Humanities, 1991), 11.

12. David Easton, "An Approach to the Analysis of Political Systems," *World Politics,* April 1957, 383–400.

13. Roy Macridis and Steven Burg use the concepts of affective support and instrumental support, which are similar to the concepts used here. See Roy C. Macridis and Steven Burg, *Introduction to Comparative Politics: Regimes and Changes* (New York: HarperCollins, 1991), 8–12.

14. Feng Chen, "Dilemma," 423.

15. Aristotle considers the *eudemonia* to be a process instead of a state of happiness. See Aristotle *Nicomachean Ethics* 10, trans. Terence Irwin (Indianapolis: Hackett, 1985).

16. John Kane, *The Politics of Moral Capital* (Cambridge: Cambridge University Press, 2001).

17. Max Weber, *From Max Weber: Essays in Sociology,* ed. H. H. Gerth and C. Wright Mills (New York: Oxford University Press, 1946).

18. Rodney Barjer, *Political Legitimacy and the State* (Oxford: Clarendon, 1990), 52.

19. Augustine, *The City of God against the Pagans/Books XII–XV,* Loeb Classical Library no. 414.

20. Jacques Benigne Bossuet, *Political Treatise,* in J. H. Robinson, ed. *Readings in European History* (Boston: Ginn, 1906), 2:273–277.

21. Confucius, *Analects,* trans. D. C. Lau (New York: Penguin, 1979).

22. Plato, *The Republic of Plato,* ed. Allen Bloom (New York: Basic, 1991).

23. Li Cunshan, "Rujia de renben yu renquan" [Renben and human rights in Confucianism], *Yuandao* 7, no. 18 (2003), www.yuandao.com/zazhi/7ji/rjdmbyrq.html (accessed August 14, 2003).

24. Mencius 4.A.9 , cited in *Sources of Chinese Tradition,* ed. W. M. Theodore de Bary et al. (New York: Columbia University Press, 1960), 1:93.

25. Mencius, trans. D. C. Lau (Harmondsworth, UK: Penguin, 1970).

26. Jeremy Bentham, *An Introduction to the Principles of Morals and Legislation* (1789; New York: Hafner, 1948), 1.

27. Lucian W. Pye, *The Mandarin and the Cadre* (Ann Arbor: University of Michigan Press, 1988), 165.

28. Roger T. Ames, *The Art of Rulership: A Study of Ancient Chinese Political Thought* (Albany: State University of New York Press, 1994), 156.

29. Lipset, *Political Man.*

30. Samuel Huntington: *Third Wave: Democratization in the Twentieth Century* (Norman: University of Oklahoma University Press, 1991).

31. Mencius 3a.4, cited in Schrecker, *Chinese Revolution,* 23.

32. Baogang Guo, "Old Paradigms, New Paradigms, and Democratic Changes in China," in *China in the Post-Deng Era,* ed. Xiaobo Hu and Gang Lin (Singapore: University of Singapore Press, 2001), chap. 4; Jonathan Spence, *God's Chinese Son: The Taiping Heavenly Kingdom of Hong Xiuquan* (New York: Norton, 1997).

33. Peter R. Moody, *Tradition and Modernization in China and Japan* (Belmont, CA: Wadsworth, 1995), 172.

34. Mao Tse-tung, "Speech at the Meeting of the Supreme Soviet of the USSR in Celebration of the Fortieth Anniversary of the Great October Socialist Revolution" (November 6, 1957), in *Selected Works of Mao Tse-tung,* vol. 3.

35. Karl Marx and Friedrich Engels, *The Communist Manifesto* (New York: International, 1948); Ian Shapiro, *The Moral Foundation of Power* (New Haven, CT: Yale University Press, 2003), chap. 4; George Brunner, "Legitimacy Doctrine and Legitimation Procedures in Eastern European Systems," in T. H. Rigby and Ferenc Feher, eds., *Political Legitimacy in Communist States* (New York: St. Martin's, 1982).

36. *Complete Works of Lenin,* 29:489–490, cited in Xie Qingkui et al., *Zhongguo zhengfu tizhi fenxi* [Study of the Chinese system of government] (Beijing: China Radio and Television Press, 1995), 16–17.

37. Xie Qingqui et al., "Study of the Chinese System of Government," 222–225.

38. Mao Tse-tung, "The United Front in Cultural Work" (October 30, 1944), in *Selected Works,* 3:236–237.

39. Mao Tse-tung, "On Coalition Government" (April 24, 1945), in *Selected Works,* 3:257.

40. Mao Tse-tung, "On Coalition Government."

41. Zhong Yang, "Legitimacy Crisis and Legitimation in China," *Journal of Contemporary Asia* 1, no. 1 (1996): 205.

42. Mao Tse-tung, "Be Concerned with the Well-Being of the Masses, Pay Attention to Methods of Work" (January 27, 1934), in *Selected Works,* 1:149.

43. Ralph E. Thaxton, *China Turned Right Side Up: Revolutionary Legitimacy in the Peasant World* (New Haven, CT: Yale University Press, 1999).

44. Mao Tse-tung, "Speech at the Supreme State Conference" (January 25, 1956), in *Selected Works*, vol. 3.

45. Hao Tiechuan, "Quanli shixian de chaxu geju" (Variations in the realization of citizen rights), *China Social Sciences* 5 (1999): 121.

46. Immanuel C. Y. Hsü, *The Rise of Modern China,* 5th ed. (Oxford: Oxford University, 1995), 653.

47. Chinese Online Military Forum, "Document Revealed the Problem of Social and Economic Inequality," www.cmilitary.com/forums/general/messages/276256.html (accessed August 12, 3003).

48. CCP Secretariat and ACFL, *The Condition of the Working Class in China* (Beijing: Central Party School Publishing House, 1983), *International Journal Political Economy,* Spring 1995.

49. Baogang Guo, "From Master to Wage Labor: Chinese Workers at the Turn of the New Millennium," *American Reviews of China Studies* 1, no. 1 (2000): 111–128.

50. Yue Dongxiao, "Riben de qinlue yu lueduo shi zhongguo pinqong de zhijie yuanyin" [The invasion and exploitation by Japan is a direct cause of China's poverty], *Muzi Shumu,* http://shuwu.com/ar/chinese/112730.shtml (accessed September 14, 2003).

51. Yue Dongxiao, "Riben de qinlue yu lueduo shi zhongguo pinqong de zhijie yuanyin."

52. Deng Xiaoping, "The Present Situation and Tasks before Us," January 16, 1980, in *Selected Works of Deng Xiaoping (1982–1992),* 2:248.

53. Deng Xiaoping, "We Shall Concentrate on Economic Development" (September 18, 1982), in *Selected Works,* vol. 3.

54. The four cardinal principles include Marxism-Leninism, socialism, party leadership, and people's democratic dictatorship. Deng Xiaoping, "Uphold the Four Cardinal Principles" (March 30, 1979), in *Selected Works,* vol. 3; David Wen-Wei Chang, *China under Deng Xiaoping: Political and Economic Reform* (London: Macmillan, 1988), 45–50.

55. Xie Qingqui et al., Study of the Chinese system of government, 40–44.

56. Pitman B. Potter, "Riding the Tiger: Legitimacy and Legal Structure in Post-Mao China," *China Quarterly,* June 1994, 325.

57. William P. Alford, "Double-edged Swords Cut Both Ways: Law and Legality in the People's Republic of China," *Daedalus,* Spring 1993, 45–70.

58. Wei Pan, "Toward a Consultative Rule of Law Regime in China," *Journal of Contemporary China,* February 2003, 3–43; for a criticism of the paper, see Suisheng Zhao, "Political Liberalization without Democratization: Pan Wei's Proposal for Political Reform," *Journal of Contemporary China,* May 2003, 333–355.

59. Deng Xiaoping, "Building a Socialism with a Specifically Chinese Character" (June 30, 1984), in *Selected Works.*

60. Feng Chen, *Economic Transition and Political Legitimacy in Post-Mao China* (Uppsala, NY: State University of New York Press, 1995), 10–11.

61. Howard Chua-Eoan and James Walsh, "The Last Emperor," *Time,* March 3, 1997, 60–66.

62. Kong Lingzhi, "Food Consumption and Health Status of Chinese People," presentation to the International Five a Day Symposium in Berlin, January 15, 2003. The author is an official from Department of Disease Control, Ministry of Health, P.R.C., www.5aday .com/berlin/powerpoint/food_consumption/800/index.html (accessed September 14, 2003).

63. Chen Jie, Yang Zhong, Jan Hillard, and John Scheb, "Assessing Political Support in

China: Citizen's Evaluation of Governmental Effectiveness and Legitimacy," *Journal of Contemporary China,* November 1997, 551–566. See also Chen Jie, *Popular Political Support in Urban China* (Stanford, CA: Stanford University Press, 2004).

64. Daniel V. Dowd, Allan Carson, and Shen Mingming, "The Prospects for Democratization in China: Evidence from 1995 Beijing Area Study," *Journal of Contemporary China* 8, no. 22 (1999): 365–380.

65. Gene H. Chang, "Cause and Cure of China's Widening Income Disparity," *China Economic Review* 13 (2002): 335–340.

66. Information Office of the State Council, the People's Republic of China, *Labor and Social Security in China* (Beijing, 2002); Ministry of Labor and Social Security and Bureau of Statistics, the People's Republic of China, *Statistical Survey of Development in Labor and Social Security (2002),* April 30, 2003

67. Baogang Guo, "From Master to Wage Labor," 116.

68. Baogang Guo, "From Master to Wage Labor," 7.

69. Anita Chan, *China's Workers under Assault: The Exploration of Labor in a Globalizing Economy* (Armonk, NY: Sharpe, 2001); see also Anita Chan, "Labor Standards and Human Rights: The Case of Chinese Workers under Market Socialism," *Human Rights Quarterly* 20, no. 4 (1998): 886–904; Baogang Guo, "From Master to Wage Labor."

70. Ministry of Labor and Social Security, P.R.C., *China Annual Labor and Social Security Statistics Summary Reports* (1992, 2002), www.molss.gov.cn (accessed August 13, 2003).

71. Report of the Committee on Freedom of Association, International Labor Organization (ILO), *Violations of the Right to Organize and Trade Unionists' Basic Civil Liberties, Detention of Trade Unionists, and Harassment of Family Members,* Report no. 316, case no. 1930, vol. 81, 1998, series B, no. 2, 1998.

72. According the official survey, 10 percent of private business owners also indicated a desire to apply for party membership. See United Front Department of the CCP et al., *The Fifth National Survey of China's Private Businesses (2002),* www.china.com.cn/chinese/zhu-anti/282715.htm (accessed August 14, 2003).

73. Robert Marquand, "Boomers Assuming Leadership," *Christian Science Monitor* 93, no. 197 (2001): 1.

74. Zong Hairen, *China's New Leaders: The Fourth Generation* (Hong Kong: Mirror Books, 2002); Gao Xin, *China's Top Leaders Bios of China's Politburo Members* (Hong Kong: Mirror Books, 2003).

75. "The Survivors Take Over," *Economist,* March 22, 2003, 37–38.

76. Wen He, "Interest Groups, Path of Reform, and Crisis of Political Legitimacy," *Modern China Studies* 4 (2001): 65–78.

77. David Shambaugh, ed., *Is China Unstable? Assessing the Factors* (Armonk, NY: Sharpe, 2000).

78. Hu Jintao, "Speech at the Graduation Ceremony of the Seminar on the Theory of the Three Represents," *People's Daily,* February 18, 2003.

79. Hu Jintao, "Speech at the Meeting Celebrating the 20th Anniversaries of the 1982 Constitution," *People's Daily,* December 4, 2002.

80. *People's Daily,* March 29, 2003.

81. Sun had been working for the Daqi Garment Company in Guangzhou and held both residency and identification documents, but he did not have the documents on him when he was arrested. He was put into the detention center and later was beaten to death in a police

clinic. See Xinhua News Agency, "Court Reaches Final Decision on Sun Zhigang Case," June 27, 2003, www.china.org.cn (accessed August 8, 2003).

82. The All-China Federation of Trade Unions (ACFTU), "Circular on Strengthening the Work of Protecting the Legal Rights of Migrant Workers," *People's Daily*, August 8, 2003.

83. CCTV, channel 4, August 7, 2003.

84. *Duoweinews*, www.chinesenewsnet.com (accessed August 7, 2003).

85. "The Revised Regulation of Population and Family Planning of Beijing," *People's Daily*, August 8, 2003.

86. Lei Guang, "Elusive Democracy: Conceptual Change and the Chinese Democracy Movement, 1978–1989," *Modern China,* October–December 1996.

87. Don Herzog, *Happy Slaves: A Critique of Consent Theory* (Chicago: University of Chicago Press, 1989).

88. Milton Friedman, *Capitalism and Freedom*, 2nd ed. (Chicago: University of Chicago Press, edition, 1982).

89. Gang Lin, "Ideology and Political Institutions for a New Era," in Gang Lin and Xiaobo Hu, eds., *China after Deng* (Washington, DC: Woodrow Wilson Center Press, 2003), 39–68.

90. Robert Pastor et al., "After the End of History," *New Perspective Quarterly* 17, no. 5 (2000): 80–81.

91. Mary E. Gallagher, "'Reform and Openness': Why China's Economic Reforms Have Delayed Democracy, *World Politics,* April 2002, 339–372.

92. *Jinji Cankao Bao* [Economic Reference News], December 22, 2004.

93. Pan Yue, "Dui gemingdang xiang zhizhengdang zhuanbian de sikao" [An inquiry on the transition from a revolutionary party and a ruling party], http://bbs.chinesenewsnet.com (accessed July 24, 2001).

94. Cao Siyuan, "Zhongguo zhengzhi gaige de mubiao, fangfa, and cuoshi" [The goals, methods, and policies of China' political reform], *Perspectives,* September 2001, www.oycf.org/Perspectives (accessed August 5, 2003).

95. George Gilbly and Eric Heginbotham, "China's Coming Transformation," *Foreign Affairs*, July–August 2001, 26–37.

6

China's Constitutionalist Option

Andrew J. Nathan

O f the plausible scenarios for China's future, the possibility of a new constitutionalism has been taken seriously by only a few Western specialists.[1] Yet the
constitutionalist scenario gains credibility from the improbability of the alternatives.
Civil disorder is the worst fear of most Chinese, and few stand to gain from it. Local
separatism would do more economic harm than good to the southeastern coastal
provinces that are viewed as the most likely to secede, and would be opposed by the
Chinese army. Some in Tibet and Xinjiang would like independence, but they lack
the military power to seize it. Coup plotters would need broad support that would
be difficult to marshal in the vast civil–military command apparatus. No one in the
new generation of leaders seems to have strongman potential. And a factional stale-
mate would be only an interim stage in the search for a solution to the problem of
political authority. So the worst one can say against the constitutionalist scenario is
that it seems too sensible to be a genuine option.

Recent writings by Chinese scholars in China and abroad suggest what the constitutionalist option might look like if it came to pass.[2] Since Deng Xiaoping's reforms
began, the authorities have licensed three waves of discussion of constitutional
issues. The first occurred during the drafting of the new constitution that was promulgated in 1982.[3] The second took place during preparation for Zhao Ziyang's
political report to the Thirteenth Party Congress in 1987. The third has consisted
of a series of studies and conferences in academia and within the staff of the National
People's Congress (NPC) since 1990, paralleled by work among members of the
Chinese democracy movement now in exile.

The discussions are interesting as much for their diagnoses of what is wrong with
the current system as for their proposals for reform. The diagnoses often carry implications too bold to be stated explicitly under today's political constraints. This chapter details four sets of diagnoses and proposals on which the debate has focused, and

which seem likely to be high on the agenda of post-Deng reformers, whether the Chinese Communist Party (CCP) remains in power or not. The debates provide a script for reform efforts that are likely to be made in the coming years no matter who comes to power. For those interested in comparative constitutional design, the debates suggest how people living under a Soviet-style constitution see its possibilities for evolutionary reform.

EMPOWERING THE NATIONAL
PEOPLE'S CONGRESS

The heart of most political-reform proposals is empowerment of the NPC.[4] Under the present constitution the NPC is sovereign. There is no division of powers. The judicial and administrative branches report to the NPC. Either directly or through its Standing Committee, the NPC legislates; elects and recalls the top leaders of the other organs of state; supervises those officials' work, including the state budget and development plans; and interprets the constitution and laws.

But the constitution also acknowledges that the organs of the state operate under CCP leadership. In the NPC this leadership is exercised in a number of formal and informal ways. Party members make up from one-half to over three-fourths of the membership of the NPC, including the top layer of NPC officials and the majority of its Standing Committee, Secretariat, committee heads, and Presidium, as well as the bulk of its staff. Party cells guide the work of all these organs and staff. The central party organs instruct the NPC whom to elect to such posts as head of state, chair of the Military Affairs Commission, president of the Supreme People's Court, and procurator-general. The party center controls the NPC budget, sets its long-term work plan, determines the agenda of its meetings, drafts much of the legislation that the NPC considers (although some drafting work is assigned by the party center to government agencies or NPC staff), and helps guide bills through committees to the final stage of passage by the NPC plenum.

The NPC structure limits its ability to develop an autonomous ethos. It normally meets only once a year, usually in March, for twelve to twenty days; the Standing Committee (consisting of about 150 members) meets every two months for approximately one week. During NPC sessions, the huge membership of about 3,000 convenes in full to vote. Debate and discussion are limited to caucuses of provincial delegations.

Nonetheless, the legislature has shown a growing measure of assertiveness. In 1986, the Standing Committee refused to clear a draft of the bankruptcy law for presentation to the NPC plenum; it had to be returned to the relevant government agency for redrafting. In 1989, a substantial number of delegates opposed a bill drafted by the State Council relating to the delegation of certain legislative powers to the Shenzhen special economic zone, so the bill was postponed and later replaced by one that answered the members' objections. In 1992, only two-thirds of the deputies voted in favor of a proposal to build a huge dam on the Yangtze River at the Three Gorges; approval was postponed. In 1994, 337 votes were cast against the Budget Law, with another 274 abstentions and invalid ballots. In 1995, NPC delegates cast a total of 1,006 abstentions, spoiled ballots, and votes against the nomination of Jiang Chunyun as vice premier, and many withheld support from the draft Central Bank and education laws and from the work reports (reports of work performed over the past year and plans for future work) of the Supreme Procuratorate and the Supreme People's Court. In 1996, hundreds of delegates voted against or abstained from voting on the work reports of the procurator-general and the chief judge of the Supreme People's Court.

These events indicate that NPC members are taking their roles more seriously. The Congress passed 175 laws from 1982 to 1994 and is in the middle of a CCP-assigned five-year legislative plan to promulgate by the end of the century 152 additional laws deemed essential to China's economic and administrative modernization. NPC delegates and staffers have gained a greater sense of responsibility as their duties have expanded.

Freeing the NPC further from CCP control lies at the heart of the proposals for NPC reform, even though the proposals do not mention the problem explicitly. Proposals include the following:

1. Reducing the size of the NPC. Scholars argue that the large size of the NPC makes it unable to discuss proposals in plenary meetings, while discussion in small groups provides no efficient means of communication among members. Since the delegates' groups are divided mostly by territorial administrative unit, the discussion is dominated by high-ranking officials from the localities. To increase the ability to communicate and the efficiency of proceedings, scholars have proposed reducing the membership to between 700 and 2,000.

2. Lengthening sessions. Longer sessions would allow delegates to discuss proposed legislation more adequately.

3. Strengthening the committee and staff systems. The 1982 constitution established a system of six committees for the NPC; two more were set up in 1988. The committees are supposed to help the Standing Committee with the study, review, and drafting of legislation and the supervision of other agencies of government. Scholars have proposed that the system be strengthened, though without suggesting specific methods of doing so. A related proposal is to establish (or strengthen, in the few cases where they exist) professional staff offices to help legislators at the national and provincial levels discharge their duties. The staff would consist of legal specialists working as full-time professionals.

4. Improving the qualifications of NPC members. Scholars have proposed that fewer officials and model workers be chosen for the NPC and that more professional politicians, legal specialists, and social activists be selected. Another proposal has been to establish a training school for NPC members.

5. Clarifying or improving the legislative process. Proposals include allowing NPC delegates to introduce legislation (they can do so in principle but never do in practice), ending CCP prereview of legislation, allowing more time for NPC debate over legislative proposals, opening NPC sessions to the public and the press, and making a practice of voting on each part of a bill separately rather than on the bill as a whole. The idea behind these proposals is to center legislative action within rather than outside the NPC.

6. *Increasing the NPC's role in rule making.* Scholars argue that the boundary between the legislative process and the process of framing administrative regulations is currently misplaced. Because the NPC meets so seldom, fewer rules are put through the legislative process than in most countries. Wide latitude is left for administrative agencies (the State Council, ministries and commissions, and others) to enact regulations that have the character of laws. This phenomenon is referred to as "administrative legislation" *(xingzheng lifa).* For example, the NPC has left the rule-making process pertaining to military affairs almost entirely to the Military Affairs Commission (nominally a state agency but in actuality a party organ). Scholars have proposed a clarification of the division of rule-making powers between NPC and administrative organs in such a way as to give a larger role to the legislature.

7. *Introducing two chambers.* Some scholars argue that the NPC already has certain features of a two-chamber system and that these should be strengthened. Members of the Standing Committee are usually leaders of lower-level People's Congresses or retired senior party, government, or military officials. Currently the Standing Committee exercises more power than the NPC because it meets more often and has more influential members. One proposal is to elect an upper chamber with three members from each province or provincial-level unit, with a lower chamber elected in proportion to population. The division of powers between the two houses is not generally specified.

8. *Introducing the no-confidence vote.* Scholars have proposed that if the work report of the government, Supreme People's Court, or Supreme Procuratorate is not approved by the NPC either initially or after one round of revision, the relevant official (premier, Supreme People's Court president, or procurator-general) should resign.

The common theme of these proposals is to increase the autonomy of the NPC and reduce the CCP's authority over it.

INVIGORATING ELECTIONS

Scholars have also put forward proposals to invigorate the process by which the NPC is elected. If implemented, they would also help make the legislature more autonomous.[5]

Of the four levels of People's Congresses—national, provincial, county, and local—the two higher levels are indirectly elected, with NPC deputies elected by provincial congresses and provincial-congress deputies elected by county congresses. Local (village) People's Congresses have been directly elected since the first elections in 1954. The Electoral Law of 1979 provided for direct election at the county level, as well as for multicandidate elections. With scattered exceptions in 1979–1980, the county-level elections have not turned into competitive campaigns owing to tight party control through the local election committees.

The term "election" is a misnomer for the delegate selection process, which is sometimes referred to more forthrightly as "production" *(chansheng)*. At each level of People's Congresses, the Standing Committee organizes the selection process for the level directly below. The Standing Committee supplies lists of persons who must be chosen in order to meet quotas of females, national minorities, "democratic personages," and other categories and to ensure that top party officials are included. It also supplies lists of other candidates from whom the remaining delegates must be selected. Few of the candidates are well known to the electors.

Reformers propose to free the elections from CCP control in several ways:

1. *Improving the nomination process.* Although ten citizens can join to nominate a candidate, this seldom happens. Even when it does, the final list of nominees is produced through a CCP-controlled consultative process. Rarely are there candidates not approved by the party. (These details pertain to county-level People's Congress elections, but the same types of procedures are used in elections at all levels, including the indirect elections to the NPC Standing Committee.) Reformers propose changes not in the rules but in their implementation, to allow genuine nominations from below with less party control over the process.

2. *Reducing malapportionment.* The Chinese system intentionally gives urban districts four times as many delegates per voter as rural districts in the county-level congresses; the imbalance is even worse at higher levels. This practice is justified by the Marxist theory that the urban proletariat is more progressive than rural peasants. Many reformers are nervous about granting too much power to rural people, whom they view as backward and pro-authoritarian. Political leaders fear that a farmer-dominated legislature would not support long-standing CCP policies unfavorable to rural residents. At least one scholar, however, has proposed reducing the rural-urban disparity to 2 to 1. I am not aware of any proposal to move to a "one person, one vote" system.

3. *Shifting to single-seat districts.* At the county level, each district elects from one to three representatives to the People's Congress. (Taiwan also has a multiseat-district system for its Legislative Yuan, but I have been unable to discover whether these two Chinese systems have a common historical origin.) Some writers have suggested moving to a single-seat system as a way of tightening representatives' links with their constituencies. This reform would force the CCP to work harder to ensure representation of its own cadres and protected categories such as women and national minorities. I do not know whether Chinese scholars have begun to look seriously at other institutional choices in the design of an electoral system, such as balloting rules, which could ultimately affect the party system and the stability of governments.

4. *Direct elections.* Scholars have refuted the idea that China is too backward or too large for direct elections to the NPC. They argue that the idea of direct elections

is found in the Marxist classics, and that Chinese citizens who have been educated in advanced socialist ideas for more than forty years must have as strong a democratic consciousness as did the citizens of capitalist systems when the direct election of parliaments began. As for constituency size as an obstacle to direct elections, they point out that each of the current NPC delegates represents a population of 360,000, fewer than the 510,000 represented by each U.S. congressman.

5. *Competitive campaigns.* Direct election would not be meaningful without reform of campaign procedures. The direct elections for local People's Congresses feature an often perfunctory process of official "introductions" of candidates to voters, either on paper or at meetings. Reformers have suggested that the job be done better, that those who nominate candidates be allowed to speak for them, and that more time be spent on the process. The new procedures could build on the experience of competitive village committee elections that have been going on since 1987, an experiment that some senior leaders see as a first step in training rural residents for a more democratic system.

6. *Multipartyism.* Scholars have also proposed new legislation on parties that would allow multiparty competition, arguing that a party claiming to represent the people's interests should submit to the test of competitive elections. The CCP has advantages over other parties and could benefit from such elections, they contend. They argue that competition is a natural law and a dynamic of social development, not a monopoly of the bourgeoisie. Multiparty elections would keep the CCP on the right track and prevent the emergence of another Cultural Revolution.

Against the concern that electoral competition would create an out-of-control NPC, reformers argue that a more strenuous election process would be good for the CCP. Because the party faces no real competition and has most of the best potential candidates in its ranks, electoral reform would facilitate the advancement of the best CCP members as candidates. If campaigns are competitive, the CCP members closest to the people will win.

CONSTITUTIONAL SUPERVISION

The constitution gives the NPC the power to "supervise the enforcement of the Constitution" (art. 62) and empowers the NPC Standing Committee "to interpret the Constitution and supervise its enforcement" and "to interpret statutes" (art. 67).[6] These powers of supervision and interpretation are not equivalent to constitutional review in a system of divided powers. Since the NPC makes the laws, it could not very well declare one unconstitutional. Rather, "supervising enforcement" *(jiandu shishi)* means supervising the implementation or carrying out of the constitution. Nominally, the NPC does this by hearing work reports from the other organs of government. It has seldom exercised its supervisory power in a more concrete way. A supervision law *(jiandu fa),* which would detail the means by which the NPC can exercise its supervisory power, exists in draft form, but its contents are not public.

Nor does the NPC Standing Committee often exercise its power of constitutional interpretation. It has responded occasionally to requests for interpretation from lower-level People's Congresses. It has also issued a small number of "internal interpretations" *(neibu jieshi)* in response to requests from other government agencies. Such clarifications have the character of ad hoc problem solving, rather than formal constitutional interpretations.

Other agencies often substitute for the NPC Standing Committee in interpreting statutes. For example, the Supreme People's Court issued a brochure on how to understand the concept of marital breakdown under the 1980 Marriage Law. The court has done similar work for the Civil Procedure Law of 1991, the Inheritance Law of 1985, and other laws. These activities seem to go beyond the constitutional authority of the Supreme People's Court to "supervise the administration of justice by the local people's courts" (art. 127); rather, the court got involved because the NPC Standing Committee abdicated authority owing to a lack of time or expertise. The understaffed courts themselves often yield authority to administrative agencies, which have yet more personnel and expertise.

By making these diagnoses, scholars imply that the NPC's constitutional-supervision function should be strengthened. To this end, some have recommended the establishment of a specialized organ to exercise the powers of constitutional interpretation and supervision. Three proposals have been floated. The first is to establish a subsidiary committee under the Standing Committee to advise it in interpreting the constitution.[7] The second is to establish a separate constitutional-supervision committee within the NPC, equal in rank to the Standing Committee and able to supervise all organs of state including the Standing Committee itself. The third is to establish a constitutional court with authority to reverse the actions even of the NPC, in effect creating a separation of powers and broadening the constitutional-supervision function to include constitutional review. Only the first of these proposals could be implemented without a constitutional amendment.

The discussion draws attention to the absence of a locus within the state apparatus where problems of jurisdiction and other intrastate issues can be solved. It also implicitly identifies the problem of CCP dominance as an obstacle to the lawlike functioning of the state. In addressing this issue, scholars have debated whether the CCP could be subjected to constitutional supervision. On the one hand, the party might be considered not subject to the constitution, since CCP leadership is listed as a principle of state power in the constitution's preamble. On the other hand, the academic consensus is that the party is in principle subject to the constitution, both because the constitution lists political parties among the entities that it governs, and by virtue of the party's charter, which calls for it to obey the constitution. But scholars recognize that it is impractical to exercise constitutional supervision over the party now. They envision a transitional stage during which the NPC might review selected CCP documents and notify the party of any contradictions with the constitution so that the party can rectify them itself.

JUDICIAL INDEPENDENCE

The Chinese constitution states that people's courts "shall . . . exercise judicial power independently and are not subject to interference by administrative organs, public organizations or individuals" (Article 126).[8] This is not a provision for what those in the West understand by the term "judicial independence," the protection of each individual judge from interference in the lawful exercise of judicial authority. Literally, it holds that the courts should "independently carry out the judging power" *(duli xingshi shenpanquan)*, meaning (as Chinese scholars interpret it) that the court as an organization should do its job exclusively, rather than having other organs share in the function, as occurred, for example, during the Cultural Revolution.

There is debate about the scope of the term "public organizations" *(shehui tuanti,* literally, "social groups") that appears in Article 126. The question is whether the CCP is included among these entities that constitutionally cannot interfere with the work of the courts. The dominant interpretation is that the category does not include the party. Scholars note that the 1982 phrasing is different from that of 1954, which stated, "People's courts independently carry out judgment, following only the law" (Article 76). In listing the entities that are prohibited from interfering in judicial processes, the 1982 constitution seems to make room for groups that are not listed (i.e., the CCP and the NPC) to get involved. In light of this reasoning and the fact that the constitution mentions the principle of "party leadership" in its preamble, involvement of the CCP in the work of the courts is not deemed interference but rather constitutionally sanctioned leadership.

Party leadership takes three forms. One is collective decision making. Under the "report and approval system," authority for court judgments is vested in a judicial committee of each court *(shenpan weiyuanhui)* that is led by the court president and vice president, who are invariably officials of that court's party group or cell. Thus judicial independence in China is not the independence of individual judges, but the independence of any given court as an organ. As one sitting judge told me, "If the [court] leaders want to change my decision, I have no power to interfere *[gan-she]*." In the Chinese judicial system, then, it is a judge's sticking to his own decision, rather than court authorities' changing it, that constitutes interference.

The second form of CCP leadership is the "asking for instruction" system, by which lower courts are expected to bring important or complicated cases to higher courts to obtain instructions before handing down a judgment. Ostensibly aimed at avoiding the reversal of judgments, the process provides the opportunity for the party organs located in higher-level courts to decide the outcome of cases in lower courts.

Third, local CCP authorities (who are also administrative authorities) often issue directives to local courts on how to decide individual cases. The practice is of questionable constitutionality but is built into the system of party leadership. At each level of the administrative hierarchy (say, in a city), the local party committee has a subsidiary organ known as a political-legal committee *(zhengfa weiyuanhui)*, which brings together the heads of the police, procuratorate, court, department of justice, state-security department, and civil-affairs department so that they can coordinate their work. As part of such coordination, the courts are required to seek the committee's guidance in deciding important or difficult cases *(zhongda fuza anjian)*. If opinions are divided or the case is especially crucial, the political-legal committee may refer the issue to the full party committee at that level of the hierarchy.

The courts not only are led by the CCP but are constitutionally subordinate to the legislative branch. The constitution says the courts are "responsible to" their respective People's Congresses (Article 128). A People's Congress cannot constitutionally interfere in a specific case, but it can require a report on a case, organize an investigation into the suspected mishandling of a case, or cashier and order the indictment of judicial officials who criminally mishandle a case. The frequency with which this happens is uncertain, but improper interference in court cases by People's Congresses was sufficiently problematic that the NPC Standing Committee in 1989 issued a decision stressing the limits on such interference, presumably as a reminder to lower-level People's Congresses.[9] Since local People's Congresses are controlled by local CCP authorities, this seems to be a second channel for party control of the courts.

Judges and scholars have drawn attention to ways in which subordination to the CCP disrupts the courts' ability to perform their functions. Local courts often fail to enforce judgments in favor of out-of-town Chinese (or foreign) plaintiffs. Judges are reluctant to rule against local administrators in suits lodged by individual citizens under the Administrative Litigation Law of 1989 and the Compensation Law of 1994.

Proposals for improving the functioning of the courts are modest. Most involve improving the professional quality of judges and establishing better remuneration and more secure tenure. Judges in China, as in other civil law jurisdictions, are civil servants. Their ranks are equivalent to those of various other bureaucrats across the system. Their incomes tend to be less than those of factory workers, educators, doctors, and government officials in many fields because of the lack of outside opportunities, bonuses, and supplements.

In 1995, the NPC adopted new legislation concerning judges.[10] The Judges Law mandates minimum qualifications for judges and specifies circumstances under which they can be removed from office. In these small ways it increases their independence. It states further that anyone who interferes with judges' exercise of their duties will be prosecuted according to law. But there is no law under which to prosecute such people, nor does the Judges Law define interference. The law does not solve the problem of inadequate remuneration, does not create a standard of judicial conduct, and supplies too many and too broadly stated causes for which judges can be dismissed. Some judicial reformers nonetheless see the Judges Law as the start of a trend toward independent individual judges who have job security, professional prestige, and adequate remuneration.

Other proposals relating to the judiciary include shifting more of the burden of evidence collection from judges to litigants, thus putting judges in a more neutral position; ending the system whereby judges get approval for their rulings from their administrative superiors; and reducing the practice of lower courts' seeking directives on specific cases from higher courts. A proposal has also been made to do away with the police power to sentence people under the "administrative punishment" system of labor reeducation. Moving many acts now deemed noncriminal into the criminal category would increase the number of cases that would have to be taken to court for judgment.

The central point of these reforms would be to strengthen the autonomy of individual judges in trying cases. More boldly, some Chinese legal workers view the arrangement by which People's Congresses can intrude into judicial affairs as invasive and have argued that the NPC's power over courts should be limited to reviewing annual reports. This approaches advocacy of separation of powers.

OTHER PROPOSALS

Aside from the proposals described so far, the constitutionalist debate has raised a number of other significant issues.[11]

1. The legal force of the preamble to the constitution. The debate over the legal force of the preamble is in effect a debate over whether Deng Xiaoping's "four basic principles" (socialism, people's democratic dictatorship, Marxism-Leninism-Mao Zedong thought, and Communist Party leadership), which are contained therein, are legally binding. Some scholars hold that the preamble has legal force. A second view is that while the preamble as a whole does not have legal power since parts of it are simply assertions of historical facts or goals, some stipulations in it have legal authority, including the four principles. A third view holds that the preamble does not have legal authority because it is not written as a formal article. Rather, it is a statement of purposes and values, compliance with which is optional for law-abiding citizens who are not CCP members. Peking University professor Gong Xiangrui has gone so far as to argue that "the Constitution is, after all, not the Party's constitution. The spirit of the Preamble is in conflict with the principles of constitutionalism."[12]

2. Citizens' rights versus human rights.[13] Many scholars argue that the constitutional notion of citizens' rights should be changed to a notion of human rights as a way of symbolizing the importance of individual rights. Legal specialists have argued for years that certain laws—including the Public Demonstrations Law and the State Secrets Law, both passed in 1989—should be revised to protect such rights. The difficulty of finding the right balance between protecting and limiting rights has delayed the adoption of a press law that has been undergoing drafting on and off for more than a decade. A revision of the Criminal Procedure Law in March 1996 increased the impartiality of judges, improved defense lawyers' access to clients and evidence, limited detention without charge to one month, and improved other procedural safeguards for defendants, at least on paper. Proposals have also been made to expunge crimes of counterrevolution from the criminal code and to eliminate the power of the police to imprison people for up to three years without trial (administrative detention).

3. *Separation of powers.* Since the top leadership has ruled this subject out of bounds, it is seldom discussed explicitly. But some scholars privately favor greater separation of powers. They view the Paris Commune model of single-branch government (the historic root of the current system) as an immature one that was adopted under conditions of civil war in a single city and lasted only a few weeks. When implemented in a large country over an extended period of time, it confuses the division of labor between the legislative and executive branches, allows an unhealthy growth of executive powers, and undermines the ability of the legislature to supervise the executive. Some scholars see a germ of separation of powers in the provision in the current NPC Organic Law that states that members of the NPC Standing Committee cannot hold full-time offices in state administrative organs. A similar provision governs members of Standing Committees of local People's Congresses.

4. *Subjecting the Military Affairs Commission to the authority of the NPC.* The Military Affairs Commission is a CCP organ, although it has a second, nominal, identity in the constitution as a state organ. It promulgates its own laws and regulations without the involvement of the NPC. Some scholars argue that this exercise of legislative power violates the constitution; some have suggested amending the constitution to state more strongly that the Military Affairs Commission is subordinate to the NPC.[14] This would be a move toward shifting the military from party to state control, a process referred to in Chinese as "statization" *(guojiahua)* of the military. However, civilian control of the military through the Military Affairs Commission is already weak, and some scholars worry that it would be even weaker under the NPC unless the NPC were much more vigorous than it is now.

5. *Federalism.* China is a unitary state but has some quasi-federalist traditions. The constitution and the Regional Autonomy Law for Minority Nationalities (1984) provide for the nominal autonomy of minority-inhabited areas. Deng Xiaoping's idea of "one country, two systems" for Hong Kong and Taiwan is reflected in the inclusion in the 1982 constitution of Article 31, which provides for the establishment of special administrative regions. Under the reforms, provinces have developed substantial economic, fiscal, and policy-making powers. Some Chinese scholars think that making the system more explicitly federal would help clarify Han–minority relations and center–province relations. Abroad, Yan Jiaqi has argued this position most strongly.[15] Within China, scholars tend to avoid the term "federalism." Nevertheless, several have argued for new, clearer definitions of central and

local powers, or for a financial apportionment committee under the State Council or the NPC Standing Committee to resolve issues of central–local revenue sharing and interprovincial financial transfers. Since the NPC is made up of local CCP elites, strengthening the role of the NPC would likely lead to increased articulation of provincial interests. In contrast to a national breakup, which would be inimical to constitutionalism, the lawful institutionalization of power sharing between the center and the regions would be a move in the direction of a more constitutionalist regime.

LENINISM AND THE RULE OF LAW

Although individually modest, the proposals reviewed here array themselves around the issue of the role of the CCP. The diagnoses of problems and proposals for change are cautious and technical, but they make clear that the authors see the Leninist one-party system as the main obstacle to the rule of law. In fifteen years of legal reform, the Leninist core has developed mechanisms to bargain with, consult, and persuade other actors in an increasingly complex society. But power is neither grounded in popular consent nor limited by laws. As Carol Hamrin and Suisheng Zhao argue, China under Deng is a form of "bureaucratic authoritarianism."[16]

Legal scholars are not a powerful constituency. Yet they possess expertise that the leaders need in order to fix problems in the system. As marketization erodes the old techniques of control, the leaders have turned to law to direct lower-level officials and constrain independent economic actors. Lawyers, judges, law professors, and NPC staff are pointing out that legal institutions cannot perform the tasks they are charged with unless they are given more autonomy. As one Chinese scholar put it, "When conditions are ripe, we should move from conceiving of [our government] as a 'people's democratic dictatorship' and start calling it a 'people's democratic constitutionalism' or a 'socialist constitutionalism.'"[17] Reliable and predictable processes of rule making, adjudication, and enforcement will constrain the party leaders as well as other actors.

There are also more directly political reasons why some CCP leaders have promoted the discussion of constitutionalism. Politicians associated with the NPC (formerly Peng Zhen and Wan Li, now Qiao Shi) want to enlarge the NPC's power in order to increase their own influence. The regime is also influenced by foreign pressure and example with respect to investment law, tax law, contract law, court procedures, intellectual property rights, human rights law, and so on.

Constitutionalism also has opponents. If one faction would benefit from an increase in the NPC's strength, others would benefit from a continuation of the status quo. While law in some ways improves the functioning of the economy, many entrepreneurs and local communities have learned to profit through law evasion and personal connections. The experience of postcommunist Russia is often cited as evidence that China cannot afford to democratize. In its transition "from utopia to development," to use Richard Lowenthal's phrase, the regime has not found a way to replace revolutionary legitimacy with legal-democratic legitimacy. Constitutionalization would serve the CCP's interests in legitimation and stability. If the reform proposals reviewed in this chapter were implemented, China would still be a dominant one-party system with weak separation of powers and weak federalism. To be sure, the process of transition to constitutionalism has been turbulent almost everywhere, and China's earlier history of failed experiments is not encouraging. But constitutionalism—which is not necessarily democracy American-style or Russian-style—is one of the most conservative options for change in a situation where stasis seems impossible.

NOTES

1. See Arthur Waldron, "China's Coming Constitutional Challenges," *Orbis,* Winter 1995, 26. A longer and more fully referenced version of the present chapter appears in *Consolidating the Third Wave Democracies,* edited by Larry Diamond, Marc F. Plattner, Yun-han Chu, and Hung-mao Tien (Baltimore, MD: Johns Hopkins University Press, 1997).

2. Much of the information presented here was gleaned from seminar meetings and papers from the China and constitutionalism study project conducted at Columbia University from 1992 to 1995. The project was supported by the Henry Luce Foundation, the National Endowment for Democracy, and the United Daily News Foundation. Several papers from the project have been published in the *Journal of Asian Law* (formerly *Journal of Chinese Law*), starting with the Spring 1995 issue.

3. Official English translation published in *Beijing Review*, December 27, 1982, 10–29.

4. This section draws chiefly on Cai Dingjian, *Zhongguo renda zhidu* [The Chinese people's congress system] (Beijing: Shehui kexue wenxian chubanshe, 1992); Cang Lin, "Zhongguo lifa gaige de jige wenti" [Several issues in the reform of China's legislation], working paper, China and Constitutionalism project, Columbia University, Spring 1995; Cao Siyuan, *Siyuan wenxuan* [Selected works of (Cao) Siyuan] (Beijing: Jingji ribao chubanshe, 1995); Kevin J. O'Brien, *Reform without Liberalization: China's National People's Congress and the Politics of Institutional Change* (New York: Cambridge University Press, 1990), chap. 7.

5. This section is based chiefly on Li Lin, "Zhongguo xianfa yanjiu de xianzhuang yu zhanwang" [The situation and prospects of constitutional research in China], working paper, China and Constitutionalism project, Columbia University, April 1994, 12–16; Cang Lin, "Zhongguo lifa gaige," 21ff.; and Wang Liqun, "Zhongguo xuanju zhidu de juxian jiqi wanshan" [The limitations of China's electoral system and its improvement], *Renda yanjiu* [NPC Studies] 11 (1992): 8–12.

6. This section draws chiefly on Tao Ren, "Zhongguo de xianfa jiandu he xianfa jieshi" [Constitutional supervision and interpretation in China], working paper, China and Constitutionalism project, Columbia University, Spring 1994. See also Susan Finder, "The Supreme People's Court of the People's Republic of China," *Journal of Chinese Law,* Fall 1993, 164–190; and Anthony R. Dicks, "Compartmentalized Law and Judicial Restraint: An Inductive View of Some Jurisdictional Barriers to Reform," *China Quarterly,* March 1995, 82–109.

7. In 1989, some NPC deputies submitted a proposal to establish such a committee to

help the Standing Committee review constitutional issues; it was never listed on the agenda of the session. *Renmin ribao* [People's Daily], overseas edition, October 30, 1989, 1.

8. This section is based chiefly on Qiang Zhou, "Judicial Independence in China," working paper, China and Constitutionalism project, Columbia University, Spring 1995. See also Shao-chuan Leng and Hungdah Chiu, *Criminal Justice in Post-Mao China: Analysis and Documents* (Albany: State University of New York Press, 1985); Donald C. Clarke, "The Execution of Civil Judgments in China," *China Quarterly*, March 1995, 65–81; and Finder, "Supreme People's Court," 145–224.

9. Peng Chong, report on behalf of the NPC Standing Committee to the full NPC, March 28, 1989, in *Zhonghua renmin gongheguo quanguo renmin daibiao dahui changwu weiyuanhui gongbao* [Gazette of the Standing Committee of the PRC National People's Congress], May 5, 1989, 108.

10. "The PRC Law on Judges," Foreign Broadcast Information Service (FBIS), *Daily Report: China*, March 21, 1995, 32–37.

11. This section draws on interviews with participants in the China and Constitutionalism project and on Li Lin, "Zhongguo xianfa yanjiu."

12. Gong Xiangrui, "Zhongguo xuyao shenme yang de xianfa lilun" [What kind of constitutional theory does China need?], *Faxue* [Law science monthly], April 10, 1989, 6.

13. Albert H. Y. Chen, "Developing Theories of Rights and Human Rights in China," in Raymond Wacks, ed., *Hong Kong, China, and 1997: Essays in Legal Theory* (Hong Kong: Hong Kong University Press, 1993), 123–149.

14. See Jeremy T. Paltiel, "Civil–Military Relations in China: An Obstacle to Constitutionalism?" *Journal of Chinese Law*, Spring 1995, 35–65.

15. Yan Jiaqi, *Lianbang zhongguo gouxiang* [A conception for a federal China] (Hong Kong: Mingbao chuban she, 1992).

16. Carol Lee Hamrin and Suisheng Zhao, eds., *Decision-Making in Deng's China: Perspectives from Insiders* (Armonk, NY: Sharpe, 1995), xxix–lviii.

17. Du Gangjian, "Cong zhuanzheng dao xianzheng" [From dictatorship to constitutionalism], *Zhejiang xuekan* (Zhejiang Journal) 3 (1992): 39.

7

Globalization, Path Dependency, and the Limits of Law

Administrative Law Reform and Rule of Law in the People's Republic of China

RANDALL PEERENBOOM

The People's Republic of China (PRC) has spent the past twenty years rebuilding its legal system and creating a modern administrative law regime as part of its efforts to adapt to the needs of a market economy and a political system that is moving away from its totalitarian past toward a new form of polity. To what extent has the process been a response to or shaped by the forces of globalization, including China's increasing integration into the global economy? Is China's administrative law system converging on the best practices of administrative systems elsewhere, or will the path-dependent nature of reforms push China in a new direction? China is a single-party socialist state saddled with a transition economy, an immature legal system, and a historical legacy of more than two millennia in which the subordinate role of law as a means of achieving social order stunted the growth of a culture of legality. Can institutions, rules, and practices that play a central role in modern Western liberal democracies with mature market economies be transplanted to China or adapted to fit China's circumstances?[1]

In the first part of this chapter, I provide an overview of the impact of globalization on the economic, political, and legal sectors and the implications for administrative law reforms. I suggest that reforms have been, and will continue to be, driven mainly by domestic concerns. Moreover, while there has been and will continue to be convergence, there has been and also will continue to be divergence. Markets, democracy, human rights, and rule of law are broad standards, and each is capable of significant variation in theory and practice. Accordingly, whether one finds convergence, and hence signs of globalization, or divergence, depends to a large extent on the particular indicators that one chooses, the time frame and the degree of abstraction or focus.

In the second part of the chapter, I illustrate how legal reforms in administrative law are affected by contingent local circumstances—path dependencies. In the third part, I set forth a reform agenda for the future and note the limits of legal reforms and law in resolving pressing social and political issues.

GLOBALIZATION

The effects of globalization are most noticeable in the economic realm, where China has embarked on reforms that have increased the role of markets and resulted in China's economy becoming increasingly integrated in global and regional economies. In contrast, political reforms have been slower, as China has resisted the trend toward democracy and challenged the universality of human rights.[2] Legal reforms fall in the middle. China is marching toward a socialist version of rule of law with Chinese (some would argue Asian) characteristics.[3] However, the road ahead remains a long and winding one with many bumps and most likely the occasional detour.[4]

The Economy: A Case for Convergence?

Globalization of the economy has received the most popular and scholarly attention, with the debates centering around three issues: (1) the extent to which globalization is in fact occurring; (2) whether countries are converging on particular economic institutions as opposed to distinct varieties of capitalism; and (3) whether globalization is a good thing.[5]

In the past twenty years, China has moved steadily toward a more market-oriented economy. It has opened its borders to foreign direct investment, overhauled its antiquated foreign trade system in the process of becoming a major trading power, restructured the banking and financial system, engaged in state-owned enterprise (SOE) reform, established stock markets, and become further integrated into the international economic order through its accession to the WTO. In 1993, China became the second most favored destination for foreign capital after the United States and the most favored destination in 2003. Trade has grown dramatically and China is now the third largest trading nation in the world. Although the transition to a market economy is far from complete, the point of no return has passed. To the extent that the sine qua non of globalization is marketization and increased participation in an international economic order, China's economy shows unmistakable signs of globalization.

At the same time, China is often used as a counterexample to convergence theories and, in particular, to contest the notion that there is a single path to economic growth. While many economists touted the advantages of the big bang approach for socialist regimes seeking to modernize their economies, China pursued a more incremental approach. Similarly, advocates of rule of law and Western economists alike have argued that sustainable economic development requires rule of law and, more specifically, clear and enforceable property rights. But China seems to have had tremendous economic growth without either, leaving economists and legal scholars to puzzle over the success of the economy despite market and legal imperfections.[6] China's phenomenal growth rate has been attributed to cultural factors,[7] a distinct form of Chinese capitalism,[8] a *guanxi*[9]-based rule of relationships,[10] clientelism,[11] and corporatism.[12]

The belief in a single path to economic growth has been challenged by the success of China and other East Asian states, and by the repeated failures of economists and international funding agencies over the past fifty years to predict and promote economic development. Nonetheless, the jury is still out as to whether China represents a unique form of capitalism and can continue to sustain high rates of growth without deeper institutional changes and without a more robust rule of law. Economists have noted that China's official growth rates are overstated and that China's growth has resulted in large part from productivity improvements mainly from reallocation of labor from low to high productivity sectors, in particular from agriculture to manufacturing and services.[13] However, long-term growth requires an increase in productivity within individual sectors. According to World Bank studies, only one-fourth of China's growth resulted from improvements in each sector.[14] Thus China's years of easy growth may be coming to an end. A weak legal system, including problems in enforcing property rights, may become even bigger constraints on continued growth in the future.

Assuming that national economies are becoming more integrated, whether such globalization is a positive development or an ominous threat to national identities and local ways of life is contested in China and abroad. Debates continue over whether globalization will promote faster economic growth and equality among nations, whether it will foster or undermine macroeconomic stability, and whether it will create new jobs or increase unemployment among low-skilled workers.[15] The Asian financial crisis caused some reformers to wonder whether reliance on FDI and foreign capital would undermine national security and leave China vulnerable to foreign interests. Plans for making capital accounts freely convertible were subsequently put on hold. Many domestic critics of China's accession to the WTO continue to worry that domestic companies and financial institutions will be crushed by foreign competitors and that a sharp rise in agricultural imports will lead to massive rural unemployment, while SOEs simultaneously shed urban employees in an effort to become more competitive. The result could be heightened social tensions and perhaps chaos as disgruntled urban workers and displaced farmers from the countryside take to the streets to demand jobs. Should the two groups unite, the government might struggle to maintain order. Fortunately, the feared consequences of accession to WTO have yet to appear. Although the number of demonstrations has increased dramatically year by year, few can be linked to WTO accession, at least so far.

Whatever the long-term implications for economic growth and social stability, China's decision to embark on economic reforms and become more integrated into the world economy has significant implications for legal reform generally and administrative reforms in particular. The transition to a market economy required a new form of government and style of regulation. Government officials used to the patterns and practices of a centrally planned economy have had to change their ways. The process has not always been a smooth one. Getting entrenched bureaucrats to abide by the law—when in the past they were the law—has not been easy.

Given China's transition state, arguments about the use of administrative regulation to overcome market failures are given a new twist. In many cases, there is either no market or only an imperfectly functioning one. Many industries are still state monopolies or are dominated by state-owned entities. In such a system, the administration will have a greater role as regulator. Inadequate information resulting from market imperfections also suggests a larger role for the administration than in a well-functioning market. Similarly, agencies are needed to deal with a variety of externalities that are not found in more market-oriented economies, such as the problems caused by the dual-pricing system. For the moment then, as in other East Asian development states during their period of rapid economic growth and restructuring, a strong government and administration with considerable discretion is necessary to respond to the needs of reform.

At the same time, the administration is itself often a cause of market failure. Administrative agencies still are often both regulators and interested parties with affiliated entities that compete with other enterprises regulated by the agency.[16] Moreover, in the absence of a well-functioning legal system and mature markets, companies have found it advantageous to establish close relationships with the government officials who control access to valuable inputs such as technology, capital, and raw materials and can assist in resolving disputes with third parties. Thus the unfinished transition to a market economy has fostered the growth of clientelism and corporatism. As a result, local government officials frequently interfere in the operation of businesses and in the process of judicial review of administrative decisions in an effort to protect local companies in which they have a direct or indirect interest.

Economic reforms have created new incentives for officials and exposed them to new pressures. The combination of more economic activity and weak control mechanisms provides agency officials ample opportunities for corruption and rent seeking.[17] This is particularly problematic because agencies now face additional financial pressure. Cut off from state subsidies, agencies fund salaries and bonuses of employees in part from revenues collected by the agency, which provides a strong incentive to impose random and arbitrary fees.

In light of the costs of corporatism and clientelism, as well as the sharp rise in administrative corruption and rent seeking, the role of administrative agencies is currently being redefined. In keeping with the policy of separation of government and business, agencies are to become regulators rather than market players. Corporatist and clientelist ties between government agencies and businesses are being severed and the nature of the relationship between government and private businesses is becoming more limited, voluntary, and symmetrical. In the future, companies that prefer to forego government assistance in exchange for greater autonomy will find it easier to go their own way without incurring the wrath of government officials or being subjected to discrimination and harassment. Over time, the withdrawal of the administration from business will result in fewer conflicts of interest. Administrative agencies will be regulators but not competitors; and, as the market develops, the role of administrative agencies may diminish, as there will be less need for regulation. The number of approvals required to do business will decrease and become more a matter of formal, rather than substantive, review by administrative agencies. In recent years the State Council has embarked on an ambitious program to overhaul the administrative review system for foreign and domestic companies alike in an effort to enhance efficiency and reduce corruption. The new approach confirms a change in policy toward greater deregulation and reliance on market forces. The recently enacted Administrative Licensing Law has provided further impetus and legal guidelines for a more streamlined approval and registration system.

Even in the long run, the PRC government may be more interventionist than governments such as Hong Kong's, and administrative officials may enjoy a higher degree of discretion and rely to a greater extent on administrative guidance and informal ties to businesses than in other systems. But such differences, while significant, are a matter of degree and consistent with a more fundamental convergence that is likely to occur as the role of administrative agencies in the PRC comes increasingly to approximate that of agencies in countries with mature economies and developed legal systems.

Political Reforms: Continued Divergence

If free markets are the baseline for measuring globalization in the economic area, democracy and human rights are the pole stars for mapping globalization in the political sphere. Judged by those standards, globalization has had less impact on the political order of China than on economic reforms. Although advocates of the big bang approach may take issue with the slow pace and incremental nature of China's economic transition, economic reforms have been rapid and far-reaching in comparison to the glacial pace and cramped nature of political reforms. Nevertheless, proponents of political convergence, perhaps indulging in wishful thinking, still see China as heading toward liberal democracy. There is little evidence that this is the case, at least in the short term, with respect to democracy and, even in the long term, with respect to a liberal view of human rights.[18]

That China is not likely to become a liberal rights–based democracy anytime soon has important consequences for administrative law. The lack of genuine elections above the village level diminishes whatever pressure government officials feel to keep the administration in line. There is no sense of urgency that the ruling party will be voted out of office if the government performs poorly. Moreover, the absence of a strong civil society means that state leaders have largely—but by no means exclusively—determined the direction and pace of administrative reforms. Needless to say, the interests and concerns of state leaders and the public will not always be identical.

Tight restrictions on civil society undermine the effectiveness of postmodern approaches to regulations that rely on greater interest group participation in the rulemaking and monitoring processes. Elite government and administrative officials are able to take advantage of their authority to pass and interpret laws and regulations for their own ends. Reliance on the media and the public to supervise administrative agencies is less promising in a socialist state where the government controls the press and imposes limits on freedom of speech. Although there are *60 Minutes*–like muckraking television shows such as *Jiaodian fangtan* (Focus) and newspapers that publicize criticism of agency actions, venues for speech are still limited and controlled. The reports of dissidents being packed off to reeducation through labor that one regularly sees in Hong Kong papers are not seen in PRC papers. Nor is there a national freedom of information law, although more than twenty provincial and municipal governments have passed open government information regulations, and the State Council and National People's Congress (NPC) are now considering national freedom of information legislation.[19]

That China is not a liberal rights–based democracy goes to the very purpose of administrative law. The view that the purpose of administrative law is to facilitate efficient administration has given way to the belief that administrative law must strike a balance between protecting the rights of individuals and promoting government efficiency.[20] The tension between the two goals is evident in every system. But how China balances the two goals will differ from other systems both in respect to outcomes and justifications. The amount of procedural protections afforded individuals may also differ as a result. There may be a tendency to limit judicial review or to expect greater deference toward administrative decisions on the part of courts. Therefore, some of the grounds for quashing specific acts may be interpreted more narrowly. Courts may be less likely to interpret the notion of abuse of authority to include a concept of fundamental rights or proportionality, as in other countries.[21] Moreover, because the ruling regime in China, like the ruling regimes in other Asian countries, rejects the liberal notion of a neutral state, courts may be more inclined to decide cases in light of a substantive normative agenda for society, as determined by the ruling elite—whether that agenda be economic development, some vaguely defined version of socialism, or a communitarian emphasis on harmony and stability that privileges the interests of the community over the interests of individuals.[22]

To be sure, there may be other reasons, besides the rejection of liberalism, contributing to these divergent practices and outcomes. There are, for example, institutional reasons why courts are deferential to agencies and thus are unlikely to rely on a broad interpretation of abuse of authority to rein in administrative officials. Nevertheless, even in the long term there will likely be divergence in the operations of seemingly similar institutions, in the application of seemingly similar rules, and therefore in the outcome in particular cases due to enduring differences in profound beliefs about the nature of the individual, the purpose of government, and individual rights.

Legal Reforms: Convergence and Divergence

The hallmark of a modern legal system is rule of law. The essence of rule of law is the ability of law to impose meaningful limits on the state and individual members of the ruling elite. Historically, law in China has been conceived of instrumentally as a tool to ensure that the will of the rulers or the policies of the Chinese Communist Party (CCP) are carried out. The function of law has not been to impose meaningful constraints on the ruling elite or to protect individual rights and freedoms against arbitrary infringement by the government. In the mid-1990s, however, Jiang Zemin and the CCP endorsed the establishment of a socialist rule of law state *(shehui zhuyi fazhiguo)* in which the party and government must act in accordance with law. In 1999, the constitution was amended to incorporate expressly the principle of rule of law.

Whether China is indeed moving toward some credible version of rule of law is hotly contested. In my view it is, although that depends on what is meant by rule of law. Generally, rule of law theories can be divided into two types: thin and thick.

A thin theory of rule of law emphasizes the formal or instrumental aspects of rule of law—those features that any legal system allegedly must possess to function effectively as a system of laws, regardless of whether the legal system is part of a democratic or nondemocratic, capitalist or socialist, liberal or theocratic society. These features typically include the following: there must be procedural rules for lawmaking such that only laws made by an entity with the authority to make laws in accordance with such rules are valid; the system must be transparent and laws made public and readily accessible; laws must be prospective, relatively clear, consistent, and stable; laws must be enforced fairly and impartially, with only a narrow gap between the laws on the books and laws as implemented in practice; and laws must be reasonably acceptable to a majority of the populace or the people affected (or at least the key groups affected) by the laws.

Various institutions are also required. The promulgation of laws assumes the existence of a legislature and the government machinery necessary to make the laws publicly available; it also assumes rules for making laws. Congruence of laws on the books and actual practice assumes institutions for implementing and enforcing laws. The fair application of laws implies normative and practical limits on the decision makers who interpret and apply the laws and principles of due process such as access to impartial tribunals, a chance to present evidence, and rules of evidence.

In contrast to thin theories, thick theories incorporate into rule of law elements of political morality, such as particular economic arrangements (free market capitalism, central planning, etc.), forms of government (democratic, single-party socialism, etc.), or conceptions of human rights (liberal, communitarian, etc.). Thick theories of rule of law can be further subdivided according to the particular substantive elements that are favored.

Thus one could distinguish between a liberal democratic, a statist socialist, a neo-authoritarian, and a communitarian rule of law.[23] Liberal democrats would incorporate free market capitalism (subject to qualifications that would allow various degrees of "legitimate" government regulation of the market), multiparty democracy in which citizens choose their representatives at all levels of government, and a liberal interpretation of human rights that gives priority to civil and political rights over economic, social, cultural, and collective or group rights.

The statist socialist rule of law favored by party leaders incorporates a socialist form of economy, which is an increasingly market-based economy but one in which public ownership still plays a larger role than in other such economies; a nondemocratic political system in which the party plays a leading role; and an interpretation of rights that emphasizes stability, collective rights over individual rights with subsistence as the basic right, in contrast to the greater emphasis on civil and political rights in liberal democracies.

Another version of a nonliberal thick theory of rule of law might be called the Asian communitarian version built on market capitalism, perhaps with a greater degree of government intervention than in the liberal version; some genuine form of multiparty democracy in which citizens choose their representatives at all levels of government; plus a communitarian interpretation of rights that gives relatively greater weight to the interests of the majority and collective rights over individual civil and political rights.

Still another variant is a neo-authoritarian or soft authoritarian form of rule of law that, like the communitarian version, rejects a liberal interpretation of rights, but unlike its communitarian cousin, also rejects democracy. Whereas communitarians adopt a genuine multiparty democracy in which citizens choose their representatives at all levels of government, neo-authoritarians permit democracy only at lower levels of government or not at all. For instance, Pan Wei, a prominent Beijing University political scientist, has advocated a "consultative rule of law" that eschews democracy in favor of single-party rule, albeit with a redefined role for the party, and more extensive, yet still limited, freedoms of speech, press, assembly, and association.[24]

Although China may not be moving toward a liberal democratic version of rule of law, it appears to be on its way toward implementing a socialist variant that meets the requirements of a thin rule of law. China currently appears to be in transition from an instrumental rule by law legal system, in which law is a tool to be used as the party-state sees fit, to a rule of law system where law does impose meaningful restraints on the party, state, and individual members of the ruling elite. China ranked in the fifty-first percentile on the World Bank's rule of law index in 2002, up from the thirty-seventh percentile in 1996.[25] Moreover, rule of law and other indicators of good governance and human rights are highly correlated with wealth.[26] Accordingly, comparing a low middle-income country to a high-income country such as the United States, Japan, or Singapore makes about as much sense as comparing a piano to a duck. Comparisons to other countries at its income level are a better indicator of China's performance relative to what can reasonably be expected of a country at its level of economic development. China beats the average for lower-middle-income countries in political stability, government effectiveness, rule of law, and control of corruption. It is about average for regulatory quality, which is biased toward neo-liberal economic principles, and scores poorly on voice and accountability, which measures civil and political rights.

Administrative Law

Administrative law is one area in which there is tremendous variety among legal systems around world. Simply put, there is no single correct way to deal with common administrative problems.[27] While all states rely on generally applicable laws to one degree or another to limit abuses of discretion and provide predictability and certainty, they may differ on how much administrative discretion is desirable. East Asian development states tend to favor a larger, more flexible role for the executive in managing the economy than do Western liberal states. In light of the diversity among administrative law regimes, the lack of a single blueprint for success, and the presence of a distinctive set of institutional, cultural, economic, and political constraints, the development of China's administrative law regime inevitably will be determined primarily by its own contingent, context-specific conditions; legal reformers will choose from the various items on the administrative law reform menu the ones that most suit China's particular circumstances, perhaps including some homegrown options.[28]

Although the menu of options with respect to goals, institutions, mechanisms for controlling administrative discretion, and legal doctrines is expansive and potentially unlimited, modern states with well-developed legal systems and functioning administrative law regimes have tended to converge on a range of favored choices.[29] Not surprisingly, as administrative law reforms have progressed in China, there are signs of increasing convergence. Whereas in the past the purpose of administrative law was considered to be how to facilitate efficient government and ensure that government officials and citizens alike obey central policies, administrative law is now understood to entail balancing government efficiency with the need to protect individual rights and interests. China has also established similar institutions and mechanisms for reining in the bureaucracy, including legislative oversight committees, supervision committees that are the functional equivalent of ombudsmen, internal administration reconsideration procedures, and judicial review. At the level of legal doctrine, China has passed a number of laws modeled on laws from other jurisdic-

tions. Even in the area of outcomes there are signs of convergence, albeit more limited convergence.[30]

Despite convergence with respect to goals, institutions, mechanisms for checking
administrative discretion and legal doctrines, China's administrative law regime produces comparatively suboptimal results due to a variety of context-specific factors,
many of which have little to do with the administrative law system as such.[31]

The most common explanation for China's administrative law troubles places the
brunt of the blame on socialist ideology and the attitudes of China's ruling elite,
particularly senior party leaders. Analyses of China's failures to create an effective
administrative law regime and to strengthen rule of law more generally therefore
typically begin, and all too often end, by noting that China remains a single-party
socialist state.[32] Critics argue that single-party socialism is simply incompatible with
rule of law and a limited government because the leading role of the party cannot
be reconciled with the supremacy of the law and a system in which law limits party
power.

Setting aside the theoretical issue of the compatibility of single-party socialism
and rule of law, hard-nosed realists claim that as a practical matter there is no rule
of law in China, at least to a considerable extent, because senior party leaders and
other interested parties just do not want it. After all, rule of law implies some degree
of separation between law and politics and limits on the party and government
authority.[33] While party leaders are happy to use law as a tool to ensure more efficient implementation of CCP policies, the last thing they want is meaningful
restraints on their own power.[34] To the extent that one can speak of rule of law in
China at all, rather than merely rule by law, it is a statist version of rule of law in
which law is just a better tool to rationalize state power and to control local governments and private actors alike. Law continues to serve as a handmaiden to party
policy and to serve the interests of the state rather than to protect individual rights
and interests.

In contrast, I suggest that single-party socialism in which the party plays a leading
role is in theory compatible with rule of law and with an administrative law system
that requires government actors to act in accordance with the law. Party members
and government officials are required to comply with the law, and their behavior is
increasingly constrained by law, especially when compared to twenty years ago.
Although party organs often fail to abide by the circumscribed role set forth in the
state and party constitutions, on a day-to-day level, direct interference by party
organs in administrative rulemaking or specific agency decisions is not common.
Rather, the party's main relevance to administrative law lies in its ability to promote
or obstruct further political and legal reforms that would strengthen the legal system,
but could also lead to the demise of the party or to a drastic reduction in its power.

Ultimately, the key to the future realization of rule of law in China is power. How
is power controlled and allocated in a single-party socialist state? To the extent that
law limits the party-state, how does the legal system obtain sufficient authority to
control a party that has been above the law? In a democracy, the final check on

government power is the ability of people to throw the government out and elect a new one. In the absence of multiparty democracy, an authoritarian government must either voluntarily relinquish some of its power or else have it taken away by force. Naturally, party leaders will resist giving up power so readily. They may therefore be disinclined to support reforms that would strengthen rule of law but would also allow institutions to become so powerful that they could then provide the basis for challenging party rule. The result may be that, at least on those issues that threaten the survivability of the party, the needs of the party continue to trump rule of law concerns for some time. There are numerous ways in which the legal system can be improved and strengthened that do not rise to the level of a threat to the party. But some reforms, such as those aimed at promoting a more independent judiciary or robust civil society or unfettered political speech and organization, could put the party at risk.

Nevertheless, there are several reasons to support the view that the issue of power can be resolved in favor of rule of law and that law will come to impose meaningful restraints on party and government leaders. First, although the views of senior leaders have been vital to legal reforms in China and will continue to influence the future development of the legal system, whether opposition on the part of certain leaders will be sufficient to block further reforms is doubtful. It is likely that different leaders hold different views, that many of them have not thought through their positions in a systematic way, and that their views are therefore likely to be inconsistent in some respects, and, at least for some of them, soft and subject to change. There also appear to be generational differences, with younger people, particularly those trained in law or exposed to the West, tending to see law as more autonomous and less instrumental.[35] Differences among party elite both in the substance of their views and the firmness with which they hold such views make it difficult to predict how their views will be translated into action. Reform factions within the party may push for deeper legal and political reforms, perhaps even someday genuine democracy. As Jiang Jingguo's deathbed support for greater democracy in Taiwan and the experience of Korea and the Soviet Union show, authoritarian leaders are capable of relinquishing power given the right circumstances. The party's endorsement of rule of law and its subsequent incorporation into the constitution suggest that the party is willing to accept limitations on its power.

Although party leaders may be wary about rule of law, they appreciate its advantages. The Fifteenth Party Congress portrayed rule of law as central to economic development, national stability, and party legitimacy. Party leaders have paid homage to the virtues of rule of law as a way of reining in increasingly unruly local governments. Facing reduced central government support, local government officials have been forced to fend for themselves. In their pursuit of economic growth, local officials have thumbed their noses at Beijing, regularly circumventing or just plain ignoring central laws and policies. Since lower-level officials are more likely than party leaders to feel the bite of rule of law on a daily basis, perhaps their resistance is to be expected. But the interest of local officials in avoiding the law does not further the policy interests of CCP leaders and the central government. Central leaders advocate rule of law in no small measure because they believe it will strengthen the hand of the central authorities in controlling wayward local officials and help rationalize governance.

But for the party to achieve its goals of stability, implementation of central policies, economic development and legitimacy, further legal reforms, including a stronger administrative law regime and a more independent judiciary, are necessary. Currently, widespread discontent over judicial corruption, bias, and incompetence is deterring investors, undermining the legitimacy and effectiveness of the legal system, and ultimately hurting the party. The CCP's only interest in the outcome of most commercial or administrative cases is that the general populace perceives the result as fair. By far the most prevalent source of external interference in the judicial process is not the CCP but local government officials. Only rarely does the CCP interfere in the handling of specific cases. When it does interfere, at least in commercial cases, the CCP often does so to ensure that the result accords with law.[36] On the other hand, because of the institutional arrangements whereby the local People's Congresses appoint and remove judges and local governments fund the courts, government officials are able to pressure judges to find in favor of the administrative agency in administrative litigation cases or local companies in commercial disputes.

From the party's perspective, a stronger legal system with a more independent judiciary has both advantages and disadvantages. While the party for years has acknowledged that local protectionism is undermining the independence of the judiciary, it has refused to address the institutional causes of the problem, presumably because it fears that an authoritative and independent judiciary able to decide commercial and administrative cases on their merits would also be able to decide politically sensitive cases on their merits. Thus the dilemma facing the party is how to strengthen the judiciary without allowing it to become too strong. In deciding whether to support further reforms, the party must determine whether the benefits outweigh the costs. However, that calculus is influenced by factors beyond the party's control.

The need to sustain economic growth will continue to put pressure on China's leaders to carry out reforms, even if this results in further erosion of the party's power. China's leaders realized early on that a market economy required a legal system capable of providing the necessary certainty and predictability demanded by investors. The slogan that a market economy is a rule of law economy has been repeatedly invoked in mantralike fashion. Economic reforms have resulted, however, in a devolution of authority to lower-level governments and to some degree shifted the base of power from the party and state to society. Although the extent to which reforms have weakened the party and diminished central control is much debated, clearly the party and central authorities are much less dominant than in the past. As reforms continue, the balance of power will continue to shift.

Moreover, rule of law is a function of institution building and the creation of a culture of legality. Progress has been made and continues to be made on both fronts.

Legal reformers and members of the judiciary will continue to push for more independent and authoritative courts, if for no other reason than institutional self-interest. Political and legal reforms tend to take on a life of their own, with institutions bursting out of the cages meant to confine them. In Taiwan, for example, the Council of Grand Justices assumed a much greater role in curbing administrative discretion and limiting government as legal and political reforms progressed, thereby contributing to further reforms.[37] In Indonesia, the Suharto government's desire to obtain legitimacy abroad and to deal with corruption and patrimonial practices that were adversely affecting business confidence led to the establishment of administrative courts. But then the courts turned on Suharto, pursuing key allies on corruption charges and defiantly striking down the government's decision to ban a popular weekly news magazine. In response to a groundswell of public support, the judiciary became increasingly aggressive in challenging the government.[38]

Further, although much of the impetus for legal reforms in China has come from the center, the demand for rule of law has increasingly come from citizens, domestic businesses, academics, members of the judiciary, legal reformers in state organs such as the NPC, and even local governments.[39] As economic reforms progressed, private citizens and domestic businesses have accumulated more property and business interests to protect, and they have been increasingly willing to take to the courts to protect them.[40] Local governments have also begun to appreciate the advantages of a law-based order. Notwithstanding Guangdong Province's reputation for flexibility and propensity to circumvent the rules, Guangdong officials were among the first to jump on the rule of law bandwagon because they felt that a flexible approach left them vulnerable to a predatory central government and that implementing rule of law would help Guangdong maintain its competitive edge over other provinces.[41]

In short, legal reforms will continue to be driven to a considerable extent by objective forces, including the needs of a market economy; the demands of foreign investors and domestic businesses; international pressure as evidenced in the amendment of the Criminal Law and Criminal Procedure Law and accession to various human rights treaties; GATT requirements now that China has become a member of the WTO; and the ruling regime's desire for legitimacy, both at home and abroad. China's legal system, therefore, will most likely continue to converge toward a system that meets the standards of a thin rule of law, but the pace and the path of reforms will be determined primarily by domestic factors, with the thick conception of rule of law reflecting the political, economic, and social systems in which the legal system is embedded.

LEGAL REFORMS IN LIGHT
OF PATH DEPENDENCIES

Even assuming China's leaders are wholeheartedly committed to establishing rule of law and an administrative law regime in which the law imposed meaningful constraints on state actors, it could only be imperfectly realized at this point, as indicated by the mediocre results of the many attempts to rein in government officials thus far. China's administrative law system is beset by a number of pressing problems. As a result of more than a decade of feverish legislating, the legal framework is mostly in place. Although some gaps in the framework and loopholes in the existing laws remain, tinkering with doctrine or passing more laws and regulations alone will have little impact. The biggest obstacles to a law-based administrative system in China are institutional and systemic in nature: a legislative system in disarray; a weak judiciary; poorly trained judges and lawyers; the absence of a robust civil society populated by interest groups; a low level of legal consciousness; the persistent influence of paternalistic traditions and a culture of deference to government authority; rampant corruption; and the fallout from the unfinished transition from a centrally planned economy to a market economy, which has exacerbated central–local tensions and resulted in fragmentation of authority.

Moreover, the various mechanisms for reining in government officials, including legislative supervision, administrative supervision, party discipline, letters and petitions, the media, administrative reconsideration and judicial review—are weak. These mechanisms are also hampered by the institutional and systemic problems just mentioned and reflect the limits of the current legal and political environment.[42]

This section illustrates how contingent local factors shape and limit the possibilities of legal reform more generally and administrative law reform in particular by discussing three problems: legislative inconsistency; the attempt to use the Administrative Licensing Law to limit administrative discretion; and proposals to move directly to deregulation, private contracting, and a postmodern regulatory approach.

Legislative Inconsistency

One of the biggest obstacles to administrative rule of law is the lack of clear lawmaking authority and the shockingly high degree of inconsistency between lower-level and higher-level legislation. The main proposals for dealing with these problems have been to (1) limit delegation and require the delegating body to state more specifically the purpose of delegation and standards for compliance; (2) eliminate or limit the inherent authority of agencies and local governments to pass regulations; (3) pass an administrative procedure law that would impose procedural requirements on administrative rulemaking; (4) improve the current mechanisms for handling inconsistency, including establishing a constitutional review body and special review bodies under the NPC, State Council, and People's Congresses and governments; and (5) expand the scope of judicial review to include abstract acts and allow the courts to annul lower-level legislation that is inconsistent with superior legislation. While all of these suggestions may be pursued simultaneously, inconsistency will remain a problem unless the courts are given the power to review at least some abstract acts.

The recently enacted Law on Legislation limits the authority of the NPC to delegate power to the State Council and executive agencies, and to People's Congresses and governments by prohibiting delegation with respect to, among other issues, criminal law matters and issues that affect the basic rights of citizens. It also stipulates that the delegating act must indicate the scope and purpose of delegation, and that the authorized entity must act in accordance with the purpose and scope of delegation and may not subdelegate the matter to another entity. But attempting to rein in administrative discretion by limiting delegation or imposing specificity requirements has not proven effective in other countries where broad delegations of authority to administrative agencies have become the norm. There is little reason to expect that limitations on delegation will be any more effective in China.

While other countries also provide the executive inherent rulemaking authority, in China too many entities have been given expansive and vaguely defined rulemaking authority. Although the Law on Legislation clarifies the lines of authority to some extent, it does not deprive the various lawmaking entities of their inherent authority to pass legislation. People's Congresses and governments may still issue regulations to implement superior legislation in accordance with local legislation, and ministries and commissions may still issue implementing regulations.[43]

An administrative procedure law would impose some limits on administrative rulemaking. It would also allow for more public participation and monitoring. However, the benefits of rules providing for more participation are limited. First, agencies in many legal systems are given a great deal of leeway in setting their own rulemaking procedures. This is inevitable given the diversity of agencies and the wide range of rulemaking from formal rules of very general applicability to informal rules affecting only a narrow range of interests of a small number of people. In fact, many countries do not have a general procedure law that applies to rulemaking. When they do, the requirements are fairly minimal. In the United States, for example, most federal agency rulemaking is characterized as informal and is only subject to notice and comment requirements. Second, even more formal procedural requirements can restrain administrative rulemaking outcomes only to a degree, and only then with the assistance of external—usually judicial—review. Thus far, courts in China have been unwilling to hold agencies to even the existing procedural requirements.

The Law on Legislation strengthened the existing system of review by clarifying the procedures for challenging lower-level legislation that is inconsistent with the constitution or national-level laws. But by itself the Law on Legislation will not be able to fully address the problem of inconsistent legislation.

The process established in the Law on Legislation is itself flawed. The law creates a two-tier track. Complaints from the State Council, Central Military Committee, Supreme People's Court and Procuracy, NPC subcommittees and Standing Committees (SC) of provincial, major city, and autonomous zone People's Congresses must be reviewed by the relevant NPC subcommittee. In contrast, complaints from individuals, social groups, and enterprises are first screened by the work unit (*gong-*

zuo jigou) of the NPCSC. The work unit will pass on to the specialized subcommittees for review only those petitions that it believes pass muster.

Moreover, the Law on Legislation fails to set time limits for several crucial steps in the process. How long the work unit has to forward a complaint to the relevant subcommittee is not stipulated. Nor is there a stipulated deadline for the subcommittee to make a decision once it receives the petition, for the subcommittee to turn the matter over to the Chairman's Committee if the entity that passed the legislation refuses to abide by the subcommittee's decision, for the Chairman's Committee to forward the matter to the NPCSC, or for the NPCSC to annul the legislation.

Equally, if not more worrisome, interested parties are allowed to submit written petitions but they are not given an opportunity to make their case at the subcommittee's hearing or to the Chairman's Committee. The legislature is, in effect, performing a judicial or tribunal function without affording affected parties the procedural rights they would enjoy in a judicial proceeding.[44]

Given these and other shortcomings, there are obvious advantages to assigning primary responsibility for invalidating inconsistent legislation to the courts. Courts deal with particular cases and therefore could rely on the parties to point out inconsistencies. Moreover, courts do not have the conflict of interest that administrative agencies have. Further, the current system is complicated. Different entities have different powers and jurisdiction, and no single entity is responsible for invalidating all types of inconsistent legislation. Allowing the courts to invalidate all inconsistent legislation would simplify matters as the courts have the authority to issue judgments that cut across bureaucratic and territorial lines. Judicial review may also be faster than the current methods. Finally, increasing the power of the courts would be beneficial to the larger project of realization of rule of law in China. Providing PRC courts greater authority would show that the government is committed to rule of law.

To be sure, there are certain disadvantages and problems associated with assigning the task of review to the courts. Some are generic to judicial review everywhere. Judges are not necessarily qualified to decide policy or technical issues. Courts typically lack the resources to research all of these issues, and even if they had the resources, it would be a waste to duplicate the agency's work. Moreover, courts must proceed on a case-by-case basis and are not in a position to monitor the effect of their decisions, which may not be the ideal way to make policy.[45] But these criticisms are less apposite with respect to judicial review of the consistency of administrative regulations. Although the court will need to address some technical issues and cannot escape policy issues entirely, the question of the consistency of an administrative regulation is often a narrower issue.

A more significant obstacle is that empowering the courts to invalidate abstract acts would require a change in the constitution and a fundamental realignment of power. Simply amending the constitution to provide for judicial review would not produce the desired result unless the lack of independence and weak stature of the courts were addressed simultaneously. This would require structural reforms. Specifically, the current system, where courts are funded by the same level government and judges appointed and removed by the same level People's Congresses, would need to be changed to ensure greater independence and autonomy. Funding responsibility should be shifted to the provincial or central level. Personnel decisions could be handled in a number of ways. The decision-making authority could be shifted to the provincial level People's Congress. Alternatively, responsibility could be turned over to or shared with a committee of judges, perhaps under the Ministry of Justice but preferably under the bar association.

Even if courts were given the authority to invalidate administrative regulations, they would need time to build their stature. A newly empowered court could force a constitutional crisis were it to challenge directly an NPC law or State Council administrative regulation.[46] Indeed, for the courts to have sufficient authority to challenge central level ministries would represent a major realignment of power. It may not be politically feasible at this point. Thus one possibility would be to limit the ability of the courts to invalidate abstract acts to all normative documents, the lowest level of regulation.[47] Most of the problems are with these lower-level regulations anyway. Moreover, the courts could expect support from the central authorities because conflicts between these lower-level regulations and central laws or regulations do not benefit the nation. Over time, as the courts gained in confidence and stature, their scope of review could be expanded to include higher-level legislation by provincial People's Congresses, central ministries, and the State Council.[48]

Administrative Discretion and the Licensing Law

One of the most frequent complaints about China's legal system is that administrative officials possess too much discretion. China, however, is hardly alone in struggling to reconcile the requirements of rule of law with the wide-ranging authority afforded government agencies in modern bureaucratic states. As long as one accepts that some degree of bounded discretion is desirable, one will need to address a number of important issues. How much discretion is desirable? Too much discretion will undermine many of the most important virtues of rule of law: predictability, certainty, equal treatment of similarly situated people, and the ability of law to guide behavior and make planning possible. But too little discretion will unduly restrict agencies from governing effectively and achieving just results in particular cases. Under what circumstances will agencies be given the discretion to make new laws or interpret existing ones or to deviate from the letter of the law at the point of application? Do we want administrative agencies to have the final authority? Or should the job of doing equity and interpreting laws be left to the courts? And perhaps most important, what kinds of constraints will there be on the agency's discretion? If the decision is subject to judicial review, how rigorous will the review be?

Although these questions can be debated in the abstract, different situations require different responses. In China today, several factors weigh in favor of affording administrative officials considerable discretion at the point of application. In comparison to their counterparts in more stable economies, administrative officials in China need more discretionary authority to deviate from existing rules to meet the demands of a rapidly changing economy. Many laws, written with a centrally planned economy in mind, are at odds with today's more market-oriented economy. Further, in a country as large and diverse as China, general regulations that may make sense for most of the country may not make sense in a particular area. The lack of experience and low level of legal training of many of the drafters often result in poorly drafted or impractical laws and regulations, and inadequate publication of many rules that may catch the regulated unaware. Hence, officials may be justified in not applying the regulation in a particular case to avoid an unjust result.

Similarly, a number of factors support giving administrative officials in China greater discretion with respect to rulemaking than in other countries. In any system, administrative agencies are given the authority to make and interpret regulations and to set standards due to the technical nature of the subject matter. Issues of competence may be even more pressing in China and support more rulemaking by the administration as opposed to the legislature because of the technical subject matter of much regulation and the low level of professionalism of the legislature relative to the administration. Moreover, People's Congresses tend to be big and unwieldy. The NPC has nearly 3,000 members and meets once a year. There is no way the legislature can meet all of the demand for regulations created by economic reforms. Administrative agencies need to share rulemaking responsibility. In many instances, administrative agencies have been forced to issue rules because the NPC has not been able to pass legislation in the area. The only available rules are administrative rules. Further, although the legislatures are often responsible for interpreting legislation, they are ill-equipped and too overburdened to do so. Thus, much of the burden for interpretation has fallen to administrative agencies that are faced with the need to resolve concrete problems arising in practice.

China's legal reformers face a dilemma. They can either provide administrative officials sufficient discretion to meet the demands of a fluid economic environment and accommodate widespread variations in local conditions, in which case they must accept certain abuses of discretion that are bound to occur in the absence of more effective means of limiting administrative discretion. Or they can pass laws that give administrative officials less discretion than is optimal. The latter approach will produce suboptimal results in some cases where officials follow the law. It will also force, or at least encourage, officials to disregard the law where circumstances are compelling, thus exacerbating the gap between law and practice and contributing to an atmosphere in which law is not taken seriously.

The dilemma was evident in the debates surrounding the scope of authority of local governments and administrative agencies to create licensing requirements. Fearing that local governments and administrative agencies would abuse any discretion given them, drafters of the Administrative Licensing Law sought to rein in local entities by imposing severe constraints on their authority to create licensing requirements. However, there are a number of circumstances where licensing by local governments and agencies is not only appropriate but necessary. The drafters were forced to choose between passing a law that unduly restricts local governments and agencies, which would produce suboptimal results, or passing a law that when considered by itself, would be a more reasonable law, but when considered in the overall context of China's current legal system would provide local governments and officials too much discretion.

Although the long-term solution is clearly to improve the various mechanisms for checking administrative discretion, in the meantime tough choices must be made.

In sum, the common complaint that administrative officials have too much discretion in China fails to address the crucial issue of how much and what kind of discretion officials should have. Although reasonable people may disagree on the details, it is unrealistic to expect that all discretion could be eliminated and simplistic to think that it should be. On the other hand, at times the complaint is the very different one that agency officials are exceeding or abusing their discretion. This complaint goes to the failure of the various means for checking agency discretion to impose meaningful restraints on administrative officials.

Walk before You Run: Postmodern Administrative Law Reforms in the Absence of the Basic Infrastructure of a Modern Legal System and Liberal Democracy

A third example of path dependency involves China's ability to benefit from recent trends in administrative law. An expansive regulatory state has been one of the defining features of modernity along with a market economy, democracy, human rights, and rule of law. Overwhelmed by a growing number of technical, scientific, and economic issues, legislatures delegated much of their rulemaking responsibility to specialist agencies. Recently, however, disenchantment with the regulatory state has led to proposals for new postmodern approaches to regulating.[49] The initial view of administrative agencies as neutral problem solvers who serve the public interest proved too naive and idealistic. Agencies are subject to capture and tend to advance their own institutional interests. The traditional hierarchical, top-down, centralized command and control mode of regulation has been attacked for being undemocratic and failing to allow for sufficient public participation. Furthermore, the process often produces poor results. Critics argue that top-down solutions assume that one size fits all.[50] In reality, the particular circumstances of different localities require more nuanced solutions. Top-down solutions tend to be either over- or underinclusive and fail to respond to local needs. This happens, in part, because they fail to tap into local knowledge. Moreover, the rulemaking process is often exceedingly slow. Meanwhile, technology and initial conditions are changing rapidly. As a result, proposed solutions are already out of date by the time they are ready to be implemented.

One of the proposed cures for the ills of the modern regulatory state has been deregulation. A second response to the agency-centered, top-down approach is to increase the role of private actors in rulemaking, service provision, policy design and implementation.[51] If agencies are subject to capture, then let private actors take on some of their functions. Presumably, private actors on the ground are better positioned to understand the problems and to identify possible solutions. Moreover, greater private actor involvement reduces the democracy deficit by inviting more public participation, thus holding out the possibility of shared governance or perhaps even self-governance.

An even more radical approach would replace the hierarchical, agency-centered command and control system with a directly deliberative polyarchy based on democratic experimentalism.[52] This approach, derived from Japanese industrial management techniques, relies on a fundamentally different method of problem solving. The first step is benchmarking, which entails surveying current or promising ways of solving problems that are superior to those currently used, yet within the existing (local) system's capacity to emulate and eventually surpass. Next comes simultaneous engineering, where interested parties propose changes to the provisional design or solution based on their own experiences and needs. The final component is error correction and learning by monitoring. Participants and independent actors monitor progress by pooling information from their own experiments with information from other localities about the results of their approach to similar problems.

This mode of regulating is direct because much of the input about goals, standards for assessment, and program design comes from below. Citizens define the problems, determine standards, weigh options, and choose solutions. It is deliberative because decisions are based on reasoned discussion rather than just voting.[53] It is a polyarchy in that the performance of each jurisdiction is taken into consideration in the deliberations of other similar jurisdictions. Furthermore, it is democratic in that citizens hold government officials accountable through elections. With its emphasis on political participation, local governance, and individuals taking the lead in identifying and solving local problems, the system is rooted in civic republicanism and a pragmatic, Dewey-inspired participatory democracy.

Each of the branches in this system has a somewhat different role than they currently do in the United States. The legislature authorizes and finances experimental reforms, in exchange for a commitment by the funding recipients to pool information. Government officials campaign and are elected on the basis of their proposals for solving problems that take into account current best practices, local conditions and benchmarking for new solutions. Administrative agencies coordinate information and assist local, provincial, and national governments in benchmarking, simultaneous engineering, and error correction, and serve as a link between the national government and local governments. When agencies issue rules, they do so based on rolling best practices. The judiciary ensures that the experiments fall within the scope authorized by the legislature and that the solutions do not violate individual rights. Courts also verify that the decision makers engaged in a deliberative process, and review the records that set forth the agency's reasons for its decision. Plaintiffs who wish to challenge an agency's rule or decision do so by arguing that the decision maker failed to engage in a deliberative process or adopted practices that were inferior to the best practices in other jurisdictions. The agency would then have to explain its reason for adopting the practice and why other practices would not work as well in light of the particular circumstances. Judges would become active problem solvers rather than just passive referees.

To what extent are these alternatives suitable to China? As we have seen, deregulation is generally not a viable option in China, given the relatively undeveloped state of its markets. But what about privatization and experimental democracy? Both appear to offer certain advantages.

China has yet to rely much on private actors. Greater reliance on private actors, however, is consistent with the recent move to downsize the administration and the government's efforts to separate government and enterprises and turn various government functions over to nonstate actors. For instance, local governments have begun to contract out for mediation services. Private schools and universities are popping up, and private hospitals are providing medical care to those who can afford it.

The experimental, pragmatic nature of a directly deliberative polyarchy is consistent with a deep streak of pragmatism running through Chinese political philosophy,[54] Socialism's commitment to uniting theory with practice and modern leaders' emphasis on results are captured in Deng's famous quip that the color of the cat does not matter as long as it catches mice. Indeed, one of the defining features of PRC governance is the heavy reliance on experiments. The central government regularly approves experiments on a regional basis or passes provisional regulations. Similarly, the emphasis on local solutions to local problems responds to the tremendous regional variation in China and is consistent with the spirit of current practices. China has developed various ways of dealing with local variation, including the establishment of separate regulatory regimes for different areas (as with special economic zones) or drafting very general laws and then giving local governments the discretion to interpret or implement the laws in light of local circumstances. Finally, the more bottom-up, incremental approach is appropriate for China's current state of transition. All too often, China's legislatures and administrative agencies have been unable to keep up with the rapid pace of change. As a result, local governments have forged ahead with experimental reforms in response to market demands without any legal basis. Because laws and regulations are frequently outdated by the time they are issued, they are routinely ignored.

On the other hand, there are many reasons to question the feasibility of greater reliance on private actors and democratic experimentalism given China's current circumstances. A bottom-up, experimental approach is consistent with some aspects of socialist ideology but at odds with other aspects. Democratic centralism assumes that once the center has accumulated information from the various localities, the center will make the final decision. Furthermore, the pragmatic aspect of the process of uniting theory and practice coexists uneasily with the more dogmatic aspect of socialism that insists on a single scientifically correct solution and unification of thought around the party line.

Perhaps more importantly than such ideological and philosophical considerations, the new approaches assume organized interest groups and a vibrant civil society. Neither exists in China. The Hu and Wen government has begun to explore the possibility of less restrictive controls on the civil sector. However, the civil sector remains limited, particularly in its capacity to organize politically and participate actively in the rulemaking process.[55]

Even if these new approaches were politically feasible, their effectiveness would be compromised by many of the factors that undermine the current administrative law regime. The fierce turf struggles that have resulted from the recent downsizing of the government suggest that administrative agencies, for their part, are likely to resist giving up control to private actors. Meanwhile, central agencies are likely to object to the enhanced role played by local governments and agencies. In addition, the experimental approach's heavy reliance on agencies sharing information across department lines runs counter to the vertically organized bureaucratic system *(xitong)* and the agencies' institutional interests in survival during this period of transition.[56]

Local government and administrative officials play a key role in the more decentralized experimental approach. China today, however, suffers from excessive decentralization and fragmentation. Economic reforms have produced increasingly independent local governments intent on achieving economic growth. Thus, even when the central government identifies rolling best practices, there is no guarantee that local governments will follow them. As we have seen, in their pursuit of growth, local governments regularly pass local regulations that are inconsistent with national laws and fail to implement central laws.

Although some local variation is desirable, there are times when national standards are needed. The experimental approach assumes that central authorities will be able to pool information from various localities facing similar problems, coordinate and disseminate information, and establish rolling best practices. But local governments that routinely engage in local protectionism, erect barriers to interregional trade, and pressure courts to find in favor of local companies are unlikely to pool information. This is all the more true when the local governments have gone ahead with experiments without proper authorization and wound up with poor results. Not all local experiments are success stories.

While greater reliance on private actors and bottom-up experiments are partly a response to the problem of holding agency officials accountable, they create their own accountability problems. Under China's current laws, private actors are relatively insulated from legislative, executive, and judicial oversight. In most cases, they could not be challenged under the Administrative Reconsideration Law or Administrative Litigation Law, as is the case under comparable laws in other countries.[57] Moreover, private actors have their own incentives, which may not coincide with the interests of the broader public. They are generally driven by profit. They may be part of an interest group with a particular narrow agenda. They may lack norms of professionalism or public service, especially given the moral vacuum that exists nowadays.

In a corrupt environment where much depends on closely knit clientelist and corporatist relationships, outside monitoring is not likely to be effective and those on the inside are not likely to share their results with others. Without the flow of information, learning by monitoring and error correction do not work. Moreover, democratic experimentalism also assumes an open, tolerant environment in which to engage in reasoned deliberation. But newly emerging groups are often neither liberal nor tolerant. They frequently are more interested in guarding jealously their privileged access to power than expanding the circle to include others in a deliberative process.[58] More generally, monitoring by the public assumes a variety of organized public interest groups and freedom of information, press, and association.

An alternative would be to rely on agencies to oversee private actors or monitor the experimental process. However, that approach presupposes agencies that are basically competent and disinterested, whereas agencies in China frequently seek to protect their own interests and are susceptible to corruption. In theory, democratic elections could provide a means of monitoring. But without elections, government and agency officials cannot be thrown out of office. Legislative oversight, ombudsmen or internal administrative review have not been effective means of monitoring Chinese administrative agencies to date.

Ultimately, then, the courts would have to remain the final backstop. They would have to ensure that agencies are not captured by special interests and that relevant interest groups are not excluded from the process due to clientelist or corporatist relationships. They would also have to hold private actors to their contractual obligations when the government contracted out for services.[59] In addition, they would have to be capable of assessing the relative technical merits of various alternative solutions. Unfortunately, PRC judges are not up to the job at present. Beholden to the local government, they are unlikely to challenge the local government's choice of one method over another. PRC judges also lack the authority and training to become active problem solvers. To date, judges have been given very little power even to interpret laws, and legal education in the PRC emphasizes black-letter law rather than creative thinking and problem-solving skills.

In short, the solutions of greater reliance on private actors and bottom-up experimentalism rely on the infrastructure of a modern state, including a legal system that meets the basic requirements of rule of law, democratic elections, and an active civil society. That infrastructure is not yet in place in China. Although a new age may be dawning in the United States and in other modern democratic states with developed legal systems, China is only now establishing the basic building blocks of a modern legal system. China will not be able to leapfrog over the modernist stage of legal system development directly to the postmodern stage in the way it has bypassed VCRs and gone directly to DVDs. Noting that these postmodern approaches assume, and are more effective given the existence of the infrastructure of a modern state does not preclude the possibility that they could be adapted to the Chinese context and useful in certain circumstances. Obviously there are advantages to involving those affected by a problem in the process of finding a solution, and pooling information and relying on benchmarking are only common sense. Similarly, there may be instances where contracting out government functions to private actors is a viable alternative. Moreover, in the future, China may become democratic and develop a more robust civil society, particularly if communitarians prevail over statist socialists and neo-authoritarians. In the meantime, however, the postmodern approaches should be viewed as complements rather than alternatives to a more traditional administrative law regime and should not detract from efforts to establish the foundations of a modern regulatory state.

CONCLUSION: ADMINISTRATIVE REFORM AND THE LIMITS OF LAW

Although the wide diversity among administrative law systems around the world complicates the task of measuring convergence, China's administrative law regime shows clear signs of convergence with respect to a common set of goals, institutions, and rules shared by other well-developed legal systems. There is even evidence of convergence with respect to outcomes. Given that China is in the midst of creating a modern legal system, greater convergence in the future is likely, regardless of which particular thick conception of rule of law prevails.

Nevertheless, the ways in which the PRC legal system continues to diverge from other systems are perhaps as important as the ways it converges. Even where China has established similar institutions or adopted similar rules, outcomes often differ because the institutions do not work as designed and rules are not followed due to a host of context-specific factors.

The nature, pace, and impact of administrative reforms have been, and will continue to be, shaped mainly by China's particular circumstances. Legal reforms have proceeded in an incremental fashion, much like economic reforms. Senior party leaders have been wary about major institutional changes that could threaten the party. As a result, they have moved slowly on political reforms and in so doing impeded the development of the administrative law system. The refusal to permit elections above the village level, for instance, prevents citizens from throwing corrupt officials out of office. Apart from elections, public participation in the legislative lawmaking and administrative rulemaking and decision-making processes remains limited. The courts are weak, beholden institutionally to local governments and limited under the constitution in their powers to strike down or interpret administrative regulations.

Looking into the future, ideological struggles over the proper conception of rule of law will be one factor shaping administrative law reforms. At first, the legal system may resemble most closely a statist socialism version, although it will undoubtedly contain elements of other forms as well. Perhaps over time the legal system will pass through a more neo-authoritarian phase. In the end, however, it may very well end up approximating most closely a communitarian rule of law. If so, Chinese citizens would enjoy democracy and rule of law but forego the extremes of liberalism in favor of a more balanced form of rule of law in which law both strengthens and limits the state, and the rights of individuals are weighed against the interests of others in the community and in society as a whole.

On a concrete level, administrative law reformers in China face a number of challenges, whatever form of rule of law is adopted. Many of the political, economic, cultural, historical, and institutional factors that have influenced reforms to date will continue to interact in sometimes expected, sometimes unexpected ways to determine the path of development of China's administrative law regime. Because China's administrative law woes are due in large part to general institutional or systemic problems, addressing them will require far-reaching changes that will alter the nature of Chinese society and the current balance of power between state and society, party and government, the central government and local governments, and among the three branches of government.

Market reforms have already shifted the balance of power away from the state toward society to some extent. The balance will continue to shift with the further separation of government and enterprises, the elimination of administrative monopolies, and the creation of a professional civil service in which government officials serve the public as regulators rather than extracting rents or competing with private companies in the marketplace. At present, the government continues to subject most economic and social activities to licensing requirements. The decision as to what needs to be regulated is ultimately a political one. Statist socialists and neo-authoritarians would impose tighter restrictions on a wider range of economic and social activities than communitarians or liberal democrats, though all would tolerate more private activity, particularly in the economic area, than in the past. Laws such as the Administrative Licensing Law are helping to delineate the boundaries of individual autonomy and freedom. Holding government officials to clearly defined substantive and procedural standards allows citizens to take full advantage of whatever freedoms they are granted.

Administrative law reforms have empowered society to some extent by giving citizens the right to challenge state actors through administrative reconsideration, administrative litigation, and administrative supervision. The next step is to increase public participation in the rulemaking and decision-making processes. The Law on Legislation opens the door slightly for greater public participation in the making of national laws. Local congresses are now actively experimenting with hearings. The Administrative Procedure Law may go even farther in providing the public access to administrative rulemaking and decision making.

A more robust civil society, a freer media, and greater reliance on private actors would all benefit the cause of administrative law reform but would require a further shift in power toward society. A more robust civil society would provide the interest groups that play such a central role in bottom-up alternatives to command and control regulation. Along with a more independent media, interest groups could shoulder more of the responsibility for monitoring administrative behavior. As noted, there are signs that the government is relaxing controls on some forms of civil society.

The balance of power among the branches of government, especially the judiciary and executive, must also change if administrative reforms are to be effective. The courts are simply too weak. The independence of the courts needs to be increased by changing the way they are funded and judges are appointed, and their authority must be enhanced in various ways, including by giving judges the right to overturn certain abstract acts.

The balance of power between the central government and local governments remains in flux. While it may be possible to alter the allocation of resources to some extent or to permit areas facing especially dire straits certain privileges, tensions are likely to continue as long as some regions remain poor and local governments are forced to bear much of the cost of economic reform. In the long run, effective administration will require some mix of command and control and bottom-up modes of regulation. The immediate task facing the central government, however, is to find some way to rein in local authorities and ensure that central policies are implemented while still allowing local government and administrative officials sufficient flexibility to respond to local circumstances. The obvious solution—to strengthen the various mechanisms for limiting administration discretion—requires time.

One possibility might be to explore ways to change the incentive structure for local officials. Currently, local officials are evaluated in accordance with a cadre responsibility system that emphasizes quantifiable targets over qualitative factors. Officials who meet their targets are rewarded financially with bonuses and larger allocations of discretionary funds and in other ways such as promotions or honorary awards. Perhaps a quantifiable rule of law index could be created. Officials would be evaluated based on indices such as the percentage of local regulations that are inconsistent with superior legislation, court judgments, and arbitral awards that are unenforced at year's end, administrative cases in which the administrative agency decision is reversed in whole or in part, local court judgments that are reversed on appeal, local judges subject to discipline for corruption, and other factors relevant to rule of law.[60]

As for the more traditional means of controlling administrative behavior, legislative oversight, for instance, could be enhanced by creating more oversight committees staffed by full-time employees with the proper legal and technical background. Committees to examine corruption in the administration or the effectiveness of particular agencies could play a positive role. Giving People's Congresses greater powers to supervise administrative budgets and expenditures might help to some extent.

Administrative supervision would be improved by increasing the independence and authority of administrative supervision organs. This could be achieved by making them answerable only to the legislature and not the local governments and funding them at the provincial level. Separating supervision organs from CCP discipline committees might reduce their authority in the short term but would have long-term rule of law benefits. Supervision by the public and media could also be improved. First, people need to be made aware of their rights. The misperception on the part of some that suing officials is fruitless should be corrected through greater publicity of the many cases in which citizens prevail. Tough rules against retaliation by government officials combined with their strict implementation would help alleviate the fears of many citizens. The draft national freedom of information law could be passed. Realistically, however, it is unlikely that the public or media will emerge as a strong force for reining in the administration anytime soon.

Citizens would be more likely to resort to administrative reconsideration if the review bodies were more independent. China might consider tough rules against ex parte communication and a system where reconsideration personnel are not members of the agency of whose actions they are reviewing. Unfortunately, drafters of the revised Administrative Reconsideration Law failed to take advantage of the opportunity presented by the upgrading of the Administrative Reconsideration Regulations to a law to improve the reconsideration process in any significant way. Accordingly, the popularity of administrative reconsideration will most likely continue to wane. To be sure, administrative reconsideration by its nature is subject to inherent limitations due to the lack of, or at least the appearance of the lack of, independence. Nevertheless, it is disappointing that the legislators did not do more to give the reconsideration process teeth.

Administrative litigation could be strengthened in a variety of ways. In addition to allowing courts to review abstract acts and enhancing the independence of the courts, the scope of review could be expanded to include rights other than personal or property rights, such as political rights. While China need not adopt a private attorney general theory of standing, a clearer and more liberal interpretation of standing would be useful. Enhancing the stature of the judiciary will help the courts overcome their reluctance to take full advantage of the Administrative Litigation Law's rather broad review standards. For example, they may take a broader view of what counts as inconsistent and use the abuse of power standard to examine purpose, relevance, reasonableness, proportionality, and so on. A more expansive interpretation and aggressive application of the current standards would go a long way toward achieving a review of the appropriateness of agency decision making without substituting the judgment of the court for that of the agency.

However, to allow the courts to review the appropriateness of agency decisions at present, untethered by the need to find agency abuse of discretion, would be unwise. During a period of transition, agencies will need more discretion than in more settled periods. Agencies are grappling with a number of novel issues, many of them technical in nature. The current level of legal education and technical training of most judges and the lack of judicial resources to examine many of the technical and policy issues argue against giving the courts expansive authority to second guess agencies. Further, court challenges of the appropriateness of agency decisions is likely to meet with much greater hostility and resistance than a decision that a regulation is inconsistent with higher-level legislation. The courts should marshal their political resources and choose their battles judiciously.

Although China is likely to continue to converge on many of the best practices of other administrative law systems, such convergence need not preclude the possibility of China developing its own unique institutions. For instance, it is possible that China could develop a censorate system along the lines proposed by Sun Yat-sen or create an independent anticorruption agency as in Hong Kong. Of course, China currently has ombudsmen-like administrative supervision bodies and a system of letters and visits. As we have seen, supervision bodies are very weak, in part because they are subordinate to the State Council. But perhaps a stronger, more independent entity could be created. While it is unlikely that the censorate would be created as a constitutional equal to the NPC given the current constitutional structure, perhaps it could be established under the NPC. Nevertheless, the effectiveness of any such entity would still depend on various context-specific factors, including the lack of a culture of legality.

Although various external checks can reduce administrative abuse of discretion, there are limits to what the law can achieve. In the end, no legal system can rely primarily on compulsory enforcement to ensure compliance. The core of any administrative law regime is government officials who respect the law. Citizens and officials alike must internalize norms of respect for law that render compulsory enforcement unnecessary in most cases. It is therefore essential that efforts to establish rule of law and internal norms of legality continue. The party will need to promote rule of law. Party leaders must make good on their promise to separate the party from government and on their own commitment to act in accordance with law. Party organizations must make known their displeasure with interference in court affairs by party members or government officials, take corruption seriously, and subject party members to the courts. And they must encourage government officials to change their attitudes, provide them more legal training, and subject them to stricter discipline.

Unfortunately, however, senior party leaders and legal reformers cannot simply legislate a culture of legality. It will take time to overcome the lingering influence of culture and tradition, weak institutions, and the challenges presented by the still incomplete economic transition. Ultimately party leaders will need to sign off on deeper institutional reforms that could in the end come back to haunt the party. While the party may be forced to risk such reforms to stay in power, whether it will do so is a matter of realpolitik and power and exceeds the limited reach of the law. If the party does decide to continue to retreat from day-to-day governance and to turn over certain functions to other state actors, these other actors can be expected to contest for power. Retreat of the party and the central state does not create a power vacuum. Rather, the result is a semistructured space in which the existing institutions seek to gain additional power. The State Council and administrative agencies have shown themselves to be effective gladiators in the struggle for power among the other branches. Although a stronger court would be less of an immediate threat to the legislative branch, People's Congresses would also lose some power vis-à-vis the courts.

Considerable progress has been made in realizing rule of law generally. Despite the progress, much remains to be done. The creation of a modern legal system is a slow process. Although China can draw on the experiences of other countries, it will need to solve its problems in light of its own particular circumstances.

NOTES

This chapter is excerpted from a longer article of the same title, which appeared in *Berkeley Journal of International Law* 19 (2001): 161–264. I have omitted discussion of the details of administrative law reforms and of the mechanisms of review, additional examples of the path dependencies of reform including a discussion of WTO compliance issues, and most footnotes. I have also revised and updated the text where appropriate and added citations for recent developments and publications.

1. See Randall Peerenboom, *What Have We Learned about Law and Development? Describing, Predicting, and Assessing Legal Reforms in the People's Republic of China* (forthcoming). This volume discusses shortcomings in descriptive metaphors such as legal transplant and selective adaptation, our limited knowledge of the predictive factors that explain the path and outcomes of reforms, and the difficulties of assessing the success of reforms given short time frames and contested standards for what counts as a successful reform.

2. For a recent summary of the rights situation in China, see Randall Peerenboom, "Assessing Human Rights in China: Why the Double Standard?" *Cornell International Law Journal* 38, no. 1 (2005); Peerenboom, "Show Me the Money: The Dominance of Wealth in Determining Rights Performance in Asia," *Duke International Law Journal* 15, no. 1 (2005), placing China in the context of other Asian countries.

3. See Kanishka Jayasuriya, "Corporatism and Judicial Independence within Statist Legal Institutions in East Asia," in *Law, Capitalism, and Power in Asia*, ed. Kanishka Jayasuriya (London: Routledge, 1999), 177–181. Jayasuriya contrasts "East Asian statist" rule of law with Western liberal rule of law; whereas the latter is defined in terms of liberal markets, an autonomous civil society reflecting pluralistic social arrangements and legal institutions with the role of resolving conflicts between various interests in civil society, the former consists of a managed form of capitalism, a regulated civil society characterized by an organic conception of the state, and legal institutions that serve to implement the policy objectives and interests of the state. The tremendous variation among east states makes it difficult to argue for a single East Asian model. For instance, although a development state that takes an active and interventionist role in the economy is one of the pillars of what some have referred to as East Asian statist rule of law, Hong Kong's laissez-faire policies have been the antithesis to interventionism. For a discussion of variety of legal systems and conceptions and rule of law within Asia, see Randall Peerenboom, ed., *Asian Discourses of Rule of Law: Theories and Implementation of Rule of Law in Twelve Asian Countries, France, and the US* (London: Routledge-Curzon, 2004).

4. See Randall Peerenboom, *China's Long March toward Rule of Law* (Cambridge: Cam-

bridge University Press, 2002). For more skeptical views, see Stanley B. Lubman, *Bird in a Cage: Legal Reform in China after Mao* (Stanford, CA: Stanford University Press, 1999), xvi, professing cautious pessimism about the future of legality in China; William Alford, "A Second Great Wall? China's Post Cultural Revolution Project of Law Construction," *Cultural Dynamics* 11, no. 2 (1999): 193–214.

5. See my original article (cited above) for a more detailed discussion of these issues.

6. See Donald C. Clarke, "Regulation and Its Discontents: Understanding Economic Law in China," *Stanford Journal of International Law* 28 (1992): 283–322; Gary H. Jefferson and Thomas G. Rawski, "How Industrial Reform Worked in China: The Role of Innovation, Competition, and Property Rights," in *Proceedings of the World Bank Annual Conference on Development Economics 1994*, ed. Michael Bruno and Boris Pleskovic (Washington, DC: World Bank, 1995), 129; see also David Li, "A Theory of Ambiguous Property Rights in Transition Economies: The Case of the Chinese Non-State Sector," *Journal of Comparative Economics* 23, no. 1 (1996): 13–16.

7. See Martin Weitzman and Xu Chenggang, "Chinese Township and Village Enterprises as Vaguely Defined Cooperatives," *Journal of Comparative Economics* 18, no. 2 (1994): 121–145.

8. Chinese capitalism is characterized by a preference for family businesses, a tendency to resolve disputes through informal mechanisms rather than the courts, a common cultural heritage, adherence to Confucian values, and an emphasis on relationships. See Gordon Redding, *The Spirit of Chinese Capitalism* (Berlin: de Gruyter, 1990).

9. *Guanxi* refers to personal, social, and business connections and networks of relationships.

10. Carol Jones, "Capitalism, Globalization, and Rule of Law: An Alternative Trajectory of Legal Change in China," *Social and Legal Studies* 3 (1994): 212–213.

11. See David L. Wank, *Commodifying Communism* (Cambridge: Cambridge University Press, 1999).

12. Corporatism has been put to three main uses in China. Some have used it as it has been used elsewhere—as a way of looking at state–society relations and as a measure of civil society. See Jonathan Unger and Anita Chan, "China, Corporatism, and the East Asian Model," *Australian Journal of Chinese Affairs* 33 (1995): 29–53. Others have used it as a way of understanding East Asian statist models of economic development. See Margaret M. Pearson, *China's New Business Elite: The Political Consequences of Economic Reform* (Berkeley: University of California Press, 1997). Still others have used it to explain local forms of government–business relations. Jean Oi, for instance, uses corporatism to capture the way in which local governments have treated the local economy as a single corporate entity. Jean C. Oi, *Rural China Takes Off: Institutional Foundations of Economic Reform* (Berkeley: University of California Press, 1999), 11; see also Andrew G. Walder, "The County Government as an Industrial Corporation," in *Zouping in Transition* (Cambridge, MA: Harvard University Press, 1998), 62.

13. Nicholas R. Lardy, *China's Unfinished Economic Revolution* (Washington, DC: Brookings Institution, 1998), 10.

14. Lardy, *China's Unfinished*, 10.

15. Using various methodologies to measure inequality, seven of eight studies found that global income inequality has increased. Joel R. Paul, "Do International Trade Institutions Contribute to Economic Growth and Development?" *Virginia Journal of International Law*

44 (2003): 310. Moreover, rapid growth in China and India account for much of the growth in developing states.

16. See Shen Bin, "Price Fixing Condemned for Hampering Reform," *China Daily*, November 9, 1998, 1, who notes that ministries have encouraged industries to form price cartels for at least eight commodities. See also Chang Weimin, "Criticism Assails Industry Cartels," *China Daily*, November 9, 1998, 1, who criticizes administrative monopolies that set price floors. Shao Honghua, "MOFTEC Researcher on Competition Policy," available in FBIS-CHI-98-913, November 9, 1998, attacks administrative monopolies where government and its affiliated organizations abuse their administrative power to restrict competition.

17. Robert B. Seidman, "Drafting for the Rule of Law: Maintaining Legality in Developing Countries," *Yale Journal of International Law* 12 (1987): 89, observes that during a transition period, laws will necessarily be more vague and give more discretion to decision makers because legislators do not know the answers to novel problems and will need to leave room for experimentation; however, this leads to "goal substitution" in the form of corruption and abuse of discretion.

18. See Larry Diamond and Raymond H. Myers, "Introduction: Elections and Democracy in Greater China," *China Quarterly* 162 (2000): 365–386, who discuss obstacles to democracy in China; see also Peerenboom, *China's Long March*, 516–536, who discusses obstacles to democracy and liberalism and summarizes survey data that shows little support for liberal democracy in China.

19. Jamie Horslee, "Shanghai Advances the Cause of Open Government Information in China, freedominfo.org, posted April 20, 2004, www.freedominfo.org/news/shanghai/index .htm. Of course, many democratic states do not have freedom of information laws.

20. Luo Haocai, ed., *Xiandai xingzhengfa de pingheng lun* [The balance theory of modern administrative law] (Beijing: Beijing University Press, 1997), 1–7.

21. Compare P. P. Craig, *Administrative Law*, 3rd ed. (London: Sweet & Maxwell, 1994), 17–18 (claiming that the standard of ultra vires is being reinterpreted along lines consistent with respect for fundamental rights in the United Kingdom), with Pei Minxin, "Citizens v. Mandarins: Administrative Litigation in China," *China Quarterly* 152 (1997), 856, table 12, noting that abuse of authority was invoked in only 16 of 219 cases where courts quashed illegal acts of agencies compared to sixty times for exceeding legal authority, forty-eight times for insufficient principal evidence, forty times for incorrect application of law, and thirty-two times for violation of legal procedures.

22. Jayasuriya, "Corporatism and Judicial Independence," 19, argues that judicial independence in East Asia is influenced by a statist ideology that rejects the liberal notion of a neutral state in favor of a paternalist state that grounds its legitimacy in a superior ability to fathom what constitutes "the good" for society; therefore, courts are more likely to serve as instruments for the implementation of the policy objectives of the state and ruling elite. On the communitarian interpretation of courts in Singapore, see Eugene K. B. Tan, 'WE' v. 'I': Communitarian Legalism in Singapore," *Australia Journal of Asian Law* 4, no. 1 (2002): 1–29; Thio Li-ann, "An 'i' for an 'I'? Singapore's Communitarian Model of Constitutional Adjudication," *Hong Kong Law Journal* 27, no. 2 (1997): 185.

23. Elsewhere I develop the contrast between these models of rule of law by analyzing each variant's position with respect to the economy, democracy, human rights, legal institutions, rules, practices, and outcomes. One could, of course, create an ever expanding taxonomy by making finer specifications of any of the variables—economy, government, interpretation of rights—or by introducing new ones. See Peerenboom, *China's Long March*, chap. 3.

24. Pan Wei, "Toward a Consultative Rule of Law Regime," *Journal of Contemporary China* 12, no. 34 (2003): 3–43.

25. Daniel Kaufmann, Aart Kraay, and Massimo Mastruzzi, *Governance Matters III: Governance Indicators from 1996–2002* (2003), http://info.worldbank.org/governance/kkz2002.

26. See Peerenboom, "Show Me the Money."

27. Critics of China's administrative law regime often overlook the diversity among administrative law systems everywhere and the common challenges and failures of such systems. Many of the features that draw heaviest criticism are by no means unique to China and in some cases are common to most administrative law systems. Examples include the unitary structure of government, the courts' lack of authority to strike down abstract acts that are inconsistent with superior legislation, the limiting of judicial review to the legality rather than the appropriateness of administrative acts, the preclusion of certain administrative decisions from judicial review and the requirement in some cases that parties first exhaust their internal administrative remedies before seeking judicial review.

28. See Edward Rubin, "Administrative Law and the Complexity of Culture," in *Legislative Drafting for Market Reform: Some Lessons from China,* ed. Ann Seidman, Robert B. Seidman, and Janice Payne (New York: St. Martin's, 1997), 88, who observes that administrative law is difficult to transfer from one system to another because it is highly political in character. It primarily governs the state's relationships to its own citizens and depends heavily on the nation's underlying culture for its effectiveness.

29. See Jayasuriya, "Corporatism and Judicial Independence," 174, who observes that even in East Asian countries with a statist ideology, the development of a market economy has led to greater rationalization within the state, a stronger and more independent judiciary, and a more symmetrical relationship between the judiciary and executive. Both Korea and Japan have recently introduced reforms to limit administrative guidance and discretion.

30. See Pei, "Citizens v. Mandarins," 832–862, who discusses outcomes of administrative law cases.

31. For critical accounts, see generally Peter Corne, *Foreign Investment in China: The Administrative Legal System* (Hong Kong: Hong Kong University Press, 1997); Jiang Mingan, ed., *Zhongguo xingzheng fazhi fazhan jincheng diaocha baogao* [Survey report on the development and progress of China's administrative rule of law] (1998), who reports progress and problems of implementing administrative law reform in various regions of China.

32. See Leslie Palmier, *State and Law in Eastern Asia* (Aldershot, UK: Dartmouth, 1996), 141. "It is certainly not possible to speak of the rule of law, and not even of the rule by law. It is clear . . . that the country's rulers, namely the Communist Party, regard such rules as simply Western 'bourgeois' conventions which limit their freedom of action; arbitrary government, which recognizes no restraint, is usual."

33. The line between politics and law is not always a clear one. Nevertheless, as Alice Erh-Soon Tay notes, "The difference between law and decree, between government proclamation and administrative power on the one hand and the genuine rule of law on the other, is perfectly well understood in all those countries where the rule of law is seriously threatened or has been abolished." Alice Erh-Soon Tay, "Communist Visions, Communist Realities, and the Role of Law," *Journal of Law and Society* 17 (1990): 156.

34. China's legal system is often characterized as rule *by* law rather than rule *of* law because of the instrumental nature of law. Of course, law is used instrumentally in every legal system. Thus a distinction must be made between pernicious instrumentalism and acceptable instru-

mentalism. Legal systems in which the law is *only or primarily* a tool of the state are best described as rule by law, whereas legal systems in which the law imposes meaningful limits on state actors merit the label rule of law.

35. Li Cheng, "Jiang Zemin's Successors: The Rise of the Fourth Generation of Leaders in the PRC," *China Quarterly* 161, no. 3 (2000), who notes that there are more lawyers among the next generation of PRC leaders than the present generation and that the next generation of leaders are more diverse in terms of their formative experiences, political solidarity, ideological conviction, career paths, and occupational backgrounds.

36. According to a survey of 280 judges published in 1993, almost 70 percent of the judges claimed that as a rule they were subject to outside interference, citing the following sources: CCP, 8 percent; government organs, 26 percent; social networks, 29 percent; other, 4 percent. See Gong Xiangrui, ed., *Fazhi de lixiang yu xianshi* [The ideal and reality of rule of law] (Beijing: Zhongguo Zhengfa Daxue Chubanshe, 1993). Another survey of one hundred intermediate and basic level court judges in Chongqing were asked, When you handle compulsory enforcement, what kind of interference do you regularly experience? Forty-five percent responded no interference; 12 percent, CCP interference; 32 percent, government department interference; 15 percent, interference from the People's Congress; 12 percent, interference from within the court; 11 percent, outside interference from nonparties and 6 percent other interference. See Jiang, *Administrative Rule of Law*, 63. In a survey of arbitral award enforcement in China, I found that while interference from local government officials was common, CCP interference was rare and usually only occurred when there was a personal connection between a party member and the respondent against which enforcement was being sought. See Randall Peerenboom, "Seek Truth from Facts: An Empirical Study of Enforcement of Arbitral Awards in the People's Republic of China," *American Journal of Comparative Law* 49 (2001): 285–286.

37. See Sean Cooney, "A Community Changes: Taiwan's Council of Grand Justices and Liberal Democratic Reform," in *Law, Capitalism*, 253; see also Kun Yang, "Judicial Review and Social Change in the Korean Democratizing Process," *American Journal of Comparative Law* 41 (1993): 1–8, noting the more aggressive approach of Korean courts as reforms continued.

38. See David Bourchier, "Magic Memos, Collusion, and Judges with Attitude," in *Law, Capitalism*, 233.

39. See Peerenboom, *China's Long March*; see also Michael Dowdle, "Preserving Indigenous Paradigms in an Age of Globalization: Pragmatic Strategies for the Development of Clinical Legal Aid in China," *Fordham International Law Journal* 24 (2000): 56–82; Dowdle, "The NPC as Catalyst for New Norms of Public Political Participation in China," in *Changing Meanings of Citizenship in Modern China*, ed. Merle Goldman and Elizabeth Perry (Cambridge, MA: Harvard University Press, 2001).

40. See Liu Junning, "Chanquan Baohu yu Youxian Zhengfu" [Protection of property and limited government], in *Zhengzhi zhonguo* [Political China], ed. Dong Yuyu and Shi Binhai (Beijing: Jinri Zhongguo Chubanshe), 40, who argues that while rule of law and limited government are necessary to protect people's property interests that have grown as a result of economic reforms, there still is not a large enough middle class demanding protection of political rights to support political reforms and democracy.

41. See Linda Chelan Li, "The 'Rule of Law' Policy in Guangdong: Continuity or Departure? Meaning, Significance and Processes," *China Quarterly* 161 (2000): 208–214.

42. See my original article, cited above, for a detailed discussion of the various mechanisms for review, including efforts at, and obstacles, to reform.

43. For other shortcomings, see my original article.

44. For other shortcomings, see my original article.

45. For a negative view of judicial review of administrating rulemaking in the United States, see Frank B. Cross, "Shattering the Fragile Case for Judicial Review of Rulemaking," *Virginia Law Review* 85 (1999): 1243–1334.

46. In Malaysia, for instance, the Mahathir government reacted to a string of judicial decisions against it in 1986 and 1987 by impeaching the Supreme Court judges who dared defy the government. See Khoo Boo Teik, "Between Law and Politics," in *Law, Capitalism*, 219–221.

47. This is essentially the approach taken in the Administrative Reconsideration Law.

48. I set aside, for the time being, discussion of a constitutional review entity. A constitutional court could take a variety of forms. Given the low competence and stature of PRC courts, it is unlikely that China would adopt the U.S. model, in which all courts are empowered to hear constitutional claims. More likely is a special entity, probably under the NPC, that would have exclusive jurisdiction over constitutional claims. However, at present there are no plans to establish such an entity.

49. These approaches are postmodern in that they are a reaction to the modern regulatory state. In addition, they challenge the kind of top-down, one-size-fits-all reasoning that typified modernism's quest for metanarratives and grand solutions to problems based on a belief in a single rational order. They are also postmodern in that they build on and take as their starting point the main pillars of modernity: a market economy, liberal democracy, a robust civil society, and rule of law.

50. See Michael Dorf and Charles Sabel, "A Constitution of Democratic Experimentalism," *Columbia Law Review* 98 (1998): 267–371.

51. See generally Jody Freeman, "The Private Role in Public Governance," *New York University Law Review* 75 (2000): 543–675.

52. See Dorf and Sabel, "Constitution," 287–288.

53. When consensus is not possible, voting is used to break the deadlock. See Dorf and Sabel, "Constitution," 320.

54. See David L. Hall and Roger T. Ames, *The Democracy of the Dead: Dewey, Confucius, and the Hope for Democracy in China* (Chicago: Open Court, 1998), 175–189, who suggest that a postsocialist China is more likely to resemble a Deweyean version of Confucian communitarianism than a liberal rights-based democracy.

55. See Tony Saich, "Negotiating the State: The Development of Social Organizations in China," *China Quarterly* 161 (2000): 125–127, who notes that the Leninist tendency to thwart organizational plurality is compounded by a fear of social unrest resulting from economic reforms but also observes that the state's capacity to exert formal control is increasingly limited.

56. Government entities are organized along vertical *(tiao)* and horizontal *(kuai)* lines. Vertically, lower-level entities are responsible to higher-level entities; horizontally, each entity is responsible to the local level People's Congress and ultimately to the party committee.

57. Of course the scope of jurisdiction could be expanded.

58. Compare Peter Evans, "Development as Institutional Change: The Pitfalls of Mono-cropping and the Potentials of Deliberation," *Studies in Comparative International Develop-*

ment 38, no. 4 (2004): 30–52, who argues that legal reforms based on the top-down imposition of foreign models has failed and calls for more democratic participation in setting and implementing the reform agenda. However, the material and social conditions required to realize Habermasian ideals of deliberative democracy are not even achievable in economically advanced liberal democratic societies. Elitist corporatism and clientelism is an obstacle to rule of law: legal reforms have been resisted in Latin America, Africa, and India by elites, who see reforms as challenging their clientelist ties. However, deliberative democracy may not be the solution or even possible. The relative success of Asian states in establishing rule of law, compared to the dismal failure in Latin America and Africa, has not resulted from bottom-up participation, although social pressure has influenced the political calculus of state leaders. Rather, the key has been state leaders who do not run the country solely or predominantly for their own benefit or the profit of a few close family members and friends. Technocrat state leaders, including civil servants and actors with the legal system, have pushed through a steady series of reforms to improve the system and curb corruption.

59. Contracting out to private actors assumes the participation of agencies that can draft contracts, lawyers who can make legal arguments, citizens who will bring suit and courts that provide competent judicial review.

60. The system would have to be structured to avoid creating perverse incentives for local government officials to pressure courts to cover up mistakes in order to obtain a high score, for example, by refusing to hold administrative agencies liable in administrative litigation cases or to overturn on appeal incorrect decisions of the lower courts. Thus officials would receive points for voluntarily addressing certain issues. In addition, outside monitors could be used for audit purposes. If the monitors discovered that local governments were covering up problems to avoid losing points, they would be penalized by a loss of several times the amount of points at stake.

III

POLITICAL ECONOMY
IN TRANSITION

8

~

The Process of China's Market Transition, 1978–1998

The Evolutionary, Historical, and Comparative Perspectives

Yingyi Qian

ALTERNATIVE PATHS OF TRANSITION FROM A PLANNED TO A MARKET SYSTEM

The twentieth century has witnessed two great transformations of economic systems around the world. The first was the transition from a capitalist market system to a socialist centrally planned system. The experiment of socialist central planning has been a failure. The second is a transition in a reverse direction, from a centrally planned system to a market system. This transition, started a decade ago, is still in the making.

There are several different paths of transition. In Eastern Europe and the former Soviet Union, democratization preceded economic liberalization, which was followed by privatization. But even there, the paths of transition were not identical, and the results were also different. For example, while the Czech Republic and Russia implemented voucher mass privatization, Hungary and Poland did not.

Perhaps the biggest difference in transition paths is to be found in China, where economic reform and transition to markets occurred without democratization, liberalization proceeded incrementally, and privatization was delayed until recently. The Chinese transition has so far been a remarkable success, and in the past two decades, China's per capita income has nearly quadrupled. The case of China can hardly be

dismissed because China is a significant country in the group of transition economies. By 1998, China accounted for about three-quarters of the population and
more than half of the total GDP of all transition economies. China will become
even more important in the future: by Maddison's (1998) calculation, its per capita
GDP (in purchasing power parity) is likely to surpass that of the fifteen former
Soviet Union countries in about ten years.

This chapter tells the story of China's two-decade transition to markets.[1] In the
second section, I account for the reform in the first stage (between 1979 and 1993).
This stage is further divided into three periods of five years each: initiation of reform,
high waves of reform, and retreat and revival of reform. Through experiments and
innovations, a variety of transitional institutions emerged and many of them took
unconventional forms. They were the second-best arrangements but quite effective
in providing incentives. As a result, China's reform in this stage was much deeper,
more comprehensive, and more consistent than that in Eastern Europe prior to
1990, which helps explain why reform was a success in China but not in Eastern
Europe.

In the third section, I consider the second stage since 1994. By the end of 1993,
the landscape of China's economy had changed drastically compared to 1978. People's living standards had significantly improved on a broad basis, the state sector
was no longer the dominant part of the economy, and most old revolutionaries were
gone from the political scene. All of these changes facilitated a strategic shift in
the official ideology toward the complete abandonment of central planning and
the embracing of a market system with private ownership. Since 1994, market-
supporting institutions based on the rule of law and incorporating international best
practices are being established. But this process is again different from some Eastern
European countries in that the new institutions are built before the old ones have
been destroyed.

Having examined China's process of market transition, I go on to answer deeper
questions of why China has followed a different path of transition compared to Eastern Europe. Transition is better understood as a path-dependent evolutionary process. Reform strategy matters, but it depends on history. In the fourth section, I
trace the roots of the process to the prereform economic system, by examining the
evolution of the Chinese centrally planned system from 1958 to 1978. Two major
waves of administrative decentralization of 1958 and 1970 had major impacts on
the institutional structure of the Chinese prereform system. Specifically, the Chinese
planning system was decentralized along regional lines, and local governments
played an important role in economic decision making and resource allocation.
Relatedly, central planning was usually crude, aggregated, and not comprehensive,
and moreover, it was not "tight," meaning that plan fulfillment was often not a
binding constraint. These prominent features represented a significant departure
from the textbook model of the Soviet system. The Chinese decentralization not
only led to the rise of many small-scale state-owned enterprises (SOEs) financed
from local government revenues, but also stimulated the emergence of collective

enterprises (such as commune and brigade enterprises in rural areas, predecessors of township-village enterprises) outside the state plan before the advent of reform. This made room for informal outside-the-plan allocation mechanisms to appear within the state sector and even more so between the state and collective sectors. It planted seeds for markets to emerge later in an incremental and decentralized way.

THE FIRST STAGE OF CHINA'S
TRANSITION, 1979–1993

Starting from a planned system characterized by enormous distortions, reform started in an attempt to introduce simple incentives, align prices to the underlying supply and demand, and open up the economy to the outside world. The first stage of transition can be conveniently divided into three phases, each of which ran for about five years.

Initialization of Reform, 1979–1983

The Third Plenum of the Eleventh Chinese Communist Party Congress held in December 1978 is widely regarded as the beginning of the reform era. The main achievement of the meeting was the shift of the party's focus from class struggle to economic development. Preceding this meeting was an intensive ideological debate in mid-1978 between Mao's orthodox version of Marxism-Leninism and pragmatism. Hua Guofeng, Mao Zedong's chosen successor, insisted that "whatever decisions Chairman Mao has made, we all support, and whatever instructions Chairman Mao has given, we all follow." Deng Xiaoping countered this dogmatism with the slogan "practice is the sole judge of truth," echoing his thoughts as early as in 1962: "It doesn't matter whether a cat is white or black so long as it catches mice." In the end, pragmatism prevailed, and the event was known in China as the first wave of emancipation of the mind.   *↗ change of legitimacy, too*

This allowed a shift of ideology within the Communist Party, and it paved the way for the initiation of reform. The accepted ideology during the first phase of reform was the idea of planning as a principal part and market as a supplementary part. This was a big change from Mao's ideology of abolishing markets. But it was by no means an accident; it reflected the deep feelings of politicians and the people over the terrible failure of the economy after the ten year Cultural Revolution, and the striking contrast between China's economic disaster and the outstanding economic performance of the four Asian Tigers nearby. As Deng remarked later, "Without the lessons from the Cultural Revolution, there would have been no new policies [since 1979]. . . . The Cultural Revolution has become our wealth" (September 5, 1988; Bureau 1994, 270). Between 1979 and 1983, five major reforms were pursued: agricultural reform, opening up the economy, fiscal decentralization,

the reform of state-owned enterprises, and support for commune–brigade enterprises.

Agricultural Reform

Agriculture was collectivized in 1955–1956, and the people's communes were established in 1958. Under the commune system and from 1962 onward, the production
team, which consisted of about fifty households, was the basic unit for production
and distribution, and the commune had the authority for allocating quotas for, say,
the acreage for growing rice or cotton.

The major change was the introduction of the household responsibility system,
which emerged spontaneously in poor areas among peasants. The first recorded
practice of this kind took place in December 1978 in the Xiaogang production brigade of Fengyang County in Anhui Province, where twenty peasants representing
twenty households put their fingerprints on a contract to divide the commune's land
among the households. In doing so, they also promised to fulfill the procurement
quota of grain to the state. Essentially, households became residual claimants and
obtained almost all control rights over production, except for the right to dispose of
land. This practice soon spread to other parts of the province and received strong
support from the provincial governor, Wan Li, at a time when no official endorsement was given by the central government. In fact, the 1978 party meeting, which
initiated reform, actually explicitly prohibited such a practice. It was not until late
1980 that the Communist Party for the first time officially allowed the household
responsibility system to exist, but only in poor areas (Party document 75, 1980).
The party started to actively promote the household responsibility system only in
early 1982. By the end of 1982, 80 percent of households had adopted the household responsibility system nationwide, and by 1984, almost all of them had done
so. By that date, the contracts of the household responsibility system had all been
extended to a period of fifteen years.

Agricultural reform is recognized as the first successful reform in China. Bureaucratic interests in the agricultural sector at central and provincial governments were
weak compared to the industrial sector, and the vested interests of local officials at
the commune and the brigade levels were not well organized. Once some areas
(often poor areas) made a breakthrough, other areas followed suit.

Opening Up the Economy

Since 1949 the Chinese economy had been closed to Western countries. When the
conflict with the Soviet bloc broke out in the early 1960s, the Chinese economy was
also closed to the east bloc, and by 1978, it was one of the most closed economies
in the world. In 1979 the government decided to expand foreign trade and welcome
foreign investment. Two provinces, Guangdong and Fujian, were in the forefront of
the opening-up process because of their geographic location. In July 1979, the cen-

tral government decided that the two provinces should pursue reform one step ahead of other regions in the country, allowing them to adopt special policies *(teshu zhengce)* and to implement flexible measures *(linghuo cuoshi)*. For example, the two provinces were allowed to retain all foreign exchange income after remitting to the center 30 percent from the increased amount of exports (Zhou 1984).

In 1980 China established four special economic zones: Shenzhen, Zhuhai, and Shantou adjacent to Hong Kong in Guangdong Province, and Xiamen in Fujian Province across the Taiwan Straits. Not only did these areas enjoy lower tax rates, but more importantly, they enjoyed a special institutional and policy environment and gained more authority over their economic development. For example, they were granted the authority to approve foreign investment projects up to $30 million, while the authority of other regions remained much lower. While the rest of China was still dominated by central planning and public ownership, special economic zones were allowed to become market economies dominated by private ownership. Special economic zones were initially controversial and there was ideological opposition to them. But there were not many vested interests against them, because these zones were set up outside the scope of central planning and did not disrupt planned production and allocation.

Fiscal Decentralization

Although some fiscal decentralization was implemented even before the reform, the fiscal system as a whole was quite centralized in the sense that the Planning Commission at the center had the authority to determine local revenue and expenditure plans on an annual basis. This system was known as the principle of unified revenue and unified expenditure *(tongshou tongzhi)*, meaning that all government revenue and expenditures had to go through the central government. In 1980, a major fiscal reform concerning the central and provincial relationship was initiated, known as the fiscal contracting system under the nickname of "eating from separate kitchens" *(fenzao chifan)*. Under the fiscal contracting system, budgetary revenue income was first divided between central fixed revenue, all of which was remitted to the center, and local revenue, which was shared. The contractual sharing rates varied from province to province. For example, Guangdong was to pay a fixed amount, ¥1 billion, to the central government and keep the rest, and Fujian would receive a fixed amount of subsidies from the central government. That is to say, the revenue sharing schemes made these two provinces residual claimants because they retained 100 percent at the margin. This particular type of contract became the dominant form after 1988.

The new fiscal system was designed to increase incentives to the local governments in revenue collection and local economic development. The fiscal contracting system greatly strengthened the link between local revenue and expenditures, and it gave local governments at all levels the authority and incentives to develop their local economies, because the revenue they were able to retain was closely linked to local economic prosperity. Fiscal decentralization has created multiple power centers, and it has had a lasting economic and political effect on other reforms.

State-Owned Enterprise Reform

The experiment of state-owned enterprise (SOE) reform began even earlier than agricultural reform. In October 1978, under provincial party secretary Zhao Ziyang, Sichuan Province selected six enterprises to undertake an experiment with the theme of expanding enterprise autonomy and introducing profit retention. In the following year, about 100 industrial enterprises in Sichuan joined the experiment. The enterprises had expanded autonomy, including the right to produce and sell products to the market after fulfilling the plan quotas, and authority to promote middle-level managers without approval from the government. The enterprises also had profit retention schemes which allowed them to retain some profits after fulfilling the planned quotas.

In July 1979, the central government issued five documents to promote Sichuan's experience nationwide, but still on an experimental basis. By 1980, about 60 percent of SOEs (in terms of output value) joined the experiments and obtained some limited autonomy. The enterprises were required to put retained profits into three separate funds: welfare (e.g., housing), bonuses, and production development. Enterprises had control over the use of the funds within each category.

Support for Commune and Brigade Enterprises

Although commune and brigade enterprises in rural areas had emerged long before 1979, they did not begin to obtain the freedom to seek profits in industries other than those related to agriculture until after the reform. In July 1979, the State Council issued the Regulation on Some Questions Concerning the Development of Enterprises Run by People's Communes and Production Brigades, which allowed provinces to grant tax holidays of two to three years to new commune and brigade enterprises. They were no longer restricted to the industries that served agriculture, such as producing chemical fertilizer and farm tools, but were allowed to enter into most industries unrelated to agriculture to which only state enterprises had previously had access. They also no longer used only local resources and could sell beyond local markets. Among the fastest growing industries were food processing, textiles, garments, building materials, and coal mining (Wong 1988).

The High Wave of Reform, 1984–1988

By 1984 the success of agricultural reform became apparent and extraordinary. Between 1978 and 1984 per capita grain production increased from about 319 kilograms to about 400 kilograms, and production of other agricultural products increased even more because they were more profitable than grain. Correspondingly, per capita rural real income increased by more than 50 percent in the six-year period. This is in sharp contrast with the stagnation of agriculture over the previous two decades.

Encouraged by the extraordinary success of the agricultural reform, in October 1994, the Third Plenum of the Twelfth Party Congress adopted a decision on reform of the economic system which was aimed at the urban area. This document made a significant ideological shift, "from plan as a principal part and market as supplementary part to planned commodity economy," which put plan and market on equal footing, if not actually placing more weight on the market. Zhao Ziyang, backed by Deng, became the main figure in the party in engineering the reform, and he made dual-track market liberalization and contract responsibility system in SOEs his two primary reform programs in this period.

The Dual-Track Approach to Market Liberalization

In May 1984, the government officially permitted the market track alongside with the planned track for industrial goods, but with a restriction of price ranges of the market track to be within 20 percent of the planned price. In February 1985, such a restriction was removed, and the dual track was formally put in place. Under this system, the planned prices were maintained as before, together with the planned quotas for delivery. However, the above quota quantities produced by SOEs were allowed to be sold on the market and the prices were freely determined by market supply and demand. In this way, any good legally carried two prices—a planned price as before, and a true market price which was not regulated by the government. Because the planned quota was frozen, the market part was able to grow out of the plan (Naughton 1995).

State-Owned Enterprise Reform through Contract Responsibility System

The effort toward SOE reform by the government continued along the lines of expanding enterprise autonomy and increasing profit incentives. In May 1984, the State Council issued a document entitled "On Regulations of Further Expanding Autonomy of State-Owned Enterprises" to expand SOE autonomy in ten areas (known as ten articles for expanding rights, *kuoquan shitiao*). But the autonomy was rather limited and profit retention was negotiated on an annual basis. To address the financial incentive problem, starting in January 1987 the government promoted the contract responsibility system *(chengbao zhi)*. Under this system, contracts lasted for at least three years to avoid annual bargaining. Compared with the previous rounds of enterprise reform, the contract responsibility system delegated more control rights to managers. But its main focus was the increase in profits retained by enterprises and an adoption of various ways for dividing up cash flow between the enterprises and the government. By the end of 1987, about 80 percent of large and medium-size SOEs had adopted the contract responsibility system, and by 1989, almost all SOEs had done so, which continued through 1993.

Financial Reform   PBOC → 4 highly specialized banks

Before the reform there was only one bank, the People's Bank of China (PBOC), which served both as the central bank and the commercial bank. In 1983, the State Council granted the PBOC the authority of a central bank and subsequently transferred commercial operations to four specialized banks: the Agricultural Bank of China (ABC) for the rural sector; the Industrial and Commercial Bank of China (ICBC) for the industrial sector, the People's Construction Bank of China (PCBC) for long-term investment, and the Bank of China (BOC) for foreign exchange business. Since 1984, the four specialized banks have been allowed to compete for deposits and loans in each other's previously monopolized markets, and enterprises are allowed to open accounts with more than one bank. For example, the ABC is able to set up branches in cities and the ICBC is allowed to undertake foreign exchange business. However, all four banks have remained highly specialized in their operations.

Further Opening Up

The success of Guangdong and Fujian provinces and the four special economic zones led the central government in 1984 to declare an additional fourteen coastal cities as "coastal open cities," which gave them new authority similar to that of the special economic zones. Two coastal open cities, Shanghai and Tianjin, obtained authority to approve foreign investment up to $30 million; Dalian up to $10 million; and the remaining eleven cities up to $5 million. Each of these open cities also has the authority to set up development zones inside their regions to implement more liberal policies for attracting foreign capital and technology. In 1988, Hainan was added as the largest special economic zone when it became a separate province.

Entry and Expansion of Non–State Owned Enterprises

However, the most significant achievement in this period was the rapid entry and expansion of urban and rural nonstate enterprises. In China, they are referred to as both private and "collective" (i.e., local government) firms outside the state plan. These firms were under harder budget constraints and had better internal incentive structures. They also indirectly benefited from the various reforms aimed at the state sector, such as fiscal decentralization, financial reform, the dual-price system, and the expansion of the SOE autonomy. For example, fiscal decentralization provides incentives for local governments to develop nonstate enterprises because taxes thus generated were not subject to sharing. The dual-track price reform also made all the previous black markets legal, which greatly helped the growth of nonstate enterprises.

The most significant consequence was observed in the rural areas. In the Central Committee Circular on Agricultural Work of January 1, 1984, the government "encourages peasants to invest in or buy shares of all types of enterprises and encourages collectives and peasants to pool their funds and jointly set up various kinds of enterprises by following the principle of voluntary participation and mutual benefits." In March 1984, the former commune and brigade enterprises were renamed township and village enterprises (TVEs), and the whole rural enterprise sector was extended to include group household and individual enterprises (i.e., private enterprises), in addition to TVEs. Rural enterprises finally obtained legitimacy. True liberalization was applied to rural enterprises, and previous administrative restrictions against rural enterprise entry and expansion were removed from almost all industries. After the abolition of the commune system, township and village governments enthusiastically supported rural industrialization because they relied heavily on the development of rural industry as the way to generate their revenue. Between 1983 and 1988, total rural enterprise output increased by more than fivefold, while in comparison, between 1978 and 1983, it had merely doubled. No wonder that Deng said in 1987: "The greatest achievement that was totally unexpected is that rural enterprises [both TVEs and private enterprises] have developed" (June 12, 1987; Bureau 1994, 236).

The Retreat and Revival of Reform, 1989–1993

The economic woes of inflation and corruption in 1988 and the political backlash following the Tiananmen Square incident in 1989 put economic reform on hold. An austerity program was implemented in 1989 and 1990 to cool down the overheated economy. During that period, the conservatives gained political, ideological, and military power for a possible reversal of reform. In 1990, they discussed the possibility of recollectivization of agriculture and tried to recentralize investment and financial powers from the provinces.

However, all of these efforts failed. The governor of Guangdong Province and the mayor of Shanghai city refused to hand over more revenue to the central government and many other governors followed their lead. On the other hand, the central government's political deadlock did not halt all reform progress. Because of the previous decentralizations, some reforms actually accelerated, but in a decentralized way. In fact, reforms in many southern regions went ahead despite action (or inaction) from the central government.

Unhappy with the economic slowdown (the GDP growth rates of 1989 and 1990 were, respectively, 4.4 percent and 3.9 percent) and the standstill within the central government, Deng Xiaoping made his famous southern tour in January and February 1992. Among his stops were several special economic zones. Using regional support for further reforms, Deng's visit tipped the political balance within the central government. Nationwide reform reached a new high level in 1992.

Phasing Out the Planned Prices

Because of the tight monetary policy, market price levels in 1990 declined, and the difference between the planned and market price was also reduced. As a result, price liberalization moved fast after the Tiananmen Square incident. Guangdong Province took a lead in price liberalization (such as grain), and other provinces followed suit. By 1993, dual prices had almost ended for most industrial products.

Further Opening Up

In 1992, most cities along the Yangtze River and the borders of the country were also granted special privileges as coastal cities, and in addition, Shanghai was granted even greater autonomy. As a result, numerous development zones were established to attract foreign and domestic investment, which also gave rise to a real estate boom. For example, many inland cities which did not qualify as either special economic zones or coastal open cities established numerous development zones inside their regions to enjoy some of the tax benefits and autonomy, and in many cases, without approval from the central government. Foreign direct investment (FDI) increased from US$4.4 billion in 1991, to US$11 billion in 1992, and further to US$28 billion in 1993, when China became the second largest country, next to the United States, in attracting FDI.

State-Owned Enterprise Reforms

The contract responsibility system in SOEs was not interrupted by the Tiananmen Square incident. In fact, the system was enhanced by the Regulations on Transforming the Management Mechanism of State-Owned Industrial Enterprises issued in July 1992 to grant enterprise managers the fourteen rights of control, covering foreign trade, investment, labor, wages, and so on.

Rural Enterprises as an Engine of Economic Recovery

Some rural enterprises suffered greatly during the 1989–1990 austerity program when they experienced substantial credit cuts. About 3 million rural enterprises went bankrupt or were taken over by other enterprises in 1989 (*People's Daily*, March 23, 1990). Total employment in township and village enterprises fell from 48.9 million in 1988 to 47.2 million in 1989 and to 45.9 in 1990, reversing the trend of expansion of more than ten years. However, because rural enterprises were market oriented and were under hard budget constraints, they adjusted themselves quickly. Rural enterprise employment increased by 10 percent and 17 percent in 1992 and

1993 respectively, and the industrial output increased even more, leading the economic recovery.

THE SECOND STAGE OF CHINA'S
TRANSITION: SINCE 1994

The most profound structural change came from the entry and expansion of the nonstate sector, despite the fact that major reform efforts had been concentrated in the state sector. It was the dynamism of the nonstate sector that drove reform to the next stage. In 1984, state industry was still central to the Chinese economy. By the end of 1993, due to the growth of the nonstate sector and even without closing down any SOEs, the state sector was no longer the major part of the economy. In industry, the state's share of output accounted for 43 percent of the national total in 1993, down from 78 percent in 1978, and the share of SOE employment of total nonfarm employment was also down from 60 percent to about 30 percent.

The first fifteen years of reform succeeded in substantially improving people's living standards, and as a result, reform received solid and popular support. However, by the end of 1993, the economic system as a whole was still a halfway house between a planned and a market economy. In the next stage, China would need to achieve at least three objectives: first, to set the goal of transition to a market system; second, to establish market-supporting institutions incorporating international best practices; and third, to privatize and restructure state-owned enterprises.

The Strategic Move: Setting the Goal for a Market System

Establishing the goal of a market system was an evolutionary process in China as shown below by four consecutive milestone events in September 1992, November 1993, September 1997, and March 1999.

The Fourteenth Party Congress, September 1992

During his southern trip in the spring of 1992, Deng made the point that both plans and markets are economic means. He also criticized the debate on whether a reform was socialistic or capitalistic, and indicated that they should discontinue the debate. "Carry out a reform so long as it is beneficial to the increase of social productivity, the country's overall strength, and the peoples' living standards" (Bureau 1994, 240). Following his remarks, the big ideological breakthrough occurred at the Fourteenth Party Congress in September 1992 when the party for the first time endorsed the socialist market economy as China's reform goal. This was known as the second wave of emancipation of the mind.

The Decision of November 1993

In 1993, the Communist Party's Economics and Finance Leading Group, headed by party secretary general Jiang Zemin, worked together with economists to prepare a grand strategy for transition to a market system. Several research teams were formed to study various aspects of transition, ranging from taxation, the fiscal system, the financial system, and enterprises, to foreign trade. The final output was the "Decision on Issues Concerning the Establishment of a Socialist Market Economic Structure" adopted by the Third Plenum of the Fourteenth Party Congress in November 1993.[2] With the objective of a market system in mind, this landmark document made major advances in the areas of reform strategy, a rule-based system, building market-supporting institutions, and property rights and ownership respectively. It was the turning point on China's road to markets.

The Fifteenth Party Congress, September 1997

In the decision of November 1993, state ownership was still regarded as a principal component of the economy while private ownership was a supplementary component of the economy. The Fifteenth Party Congress held in September 1997 made a major breakthrough on ownership issues: State ownership was downgraded to a "pillar" of the economy and private ownership was elevated to an "important component" of the economy. At this time, the official ideology toward private ownership finally became friendly. This is known as the third wave of emancipation of the mind.

The Constitutional Amendments of March 1999

Private ownership and the rule of law were incorporated into the Chinese constitution in March 1999. An amendment to Article 11 of the Constitution places private businesses on an equal footing with the public sector by changing the original clause "the private economy is a supplement to public ownership" to "the nonpublic sector, including individual and private businesses, is an important component of the socialist market economy" (*China Daily,* March 16, 1999). Furthermore, Article 5 of the constitution was amended to include the principle of "governing the country according to law" (*China Daily,* March 16, 1999). These constitutional amendments demonstrated China's commitment to a full market system based on the rule of law.

Major Accomplishments in the First Five Years, 1994–1998

Following the decision of November 1993, a series of radical reforms were launched starting in January 1994.

Foreign Exchange Reform

Before 1994, liberalization of foreign exchange markets followed a dual-track approach and there existed an official rate and a swap rate (i.e., the market rate). Because of the dramatic growth of the market track, by 1993 the share of the plan allocated foreign exchange had fallen to less than 20 percent of the total. On January 1, 1994, plan allocation of foreign exchange was completely abolished, and the two tracks were merged into a single market track. In December 1996, China went one step further to announce current account convertibility of its currency. However, it did not move to capital account convertibility but still maintained capital control. This is one important reason that China weathered the Asian financial crisis rather well. Between 1994 and 1998, the exchange rate remained stable and even appreciated slightly from ¥8.7 per US$1 to ¥8.3 per US$1. Both exports and foreign direct investment increased dramatically, and the country's foreign reserves increased from US$21 billion to US$145 billion.

Tax and Fiscal System Reform

On January 1, 1994, China introduced major tax and fiscal reforms more in line with international practices. This reform introduced a clear distinction between national and local taxes and established a national tax bureau and local tax bureaus, each responsible for its own tax collections. Under the new system, the value added tax (VAT) became the major indirect tax shared by the national and local governments at a fixed ratio of 75 to 25.

In 1995, the new Budget Law took effect. It prohibited the central government from borrowing from the central bank and from deficit financing its current expenditures, but the central government could run a deficit financing in its capital expenditures although it had to finance the deficit with government bonds. It also imposed more stringent restrictions on local governments. Local governments at all levels were required to have their budgets balanced (as before), and furthermore, the law strictly controlled their bond issuance and restricted their borrowing in the financial market (a change from the past).

Monetary Reform

In 1993, the central bank centralized its operations after Vice Premier Zhu Rongji became its governor. Since then, its local branches have been supervised only by the headquarters of the central bank, not as before by the local government of the region in which they are located. In 1995, China passed the Central Bank Law to give the central bank the mandate for monetary policy independent of the local government. These reforms substantially reduced local governments' influence on monetary policy and credit allocation decisions. In 1998, the central bank further replaced its thirty provincial branches with nine cross-province regional branches as in the U.S.

Federal Reserve System. This reform minimized local governments' influence on monetary policies.

Financial System Reform

The Asian financial crisis demonstrated the importance of prudential regulation. China has followed a U.S. model of banking regulations along the lines of the Glass-Steagall Act; not only is commercial banking separated from investment banking but commercial banks cannot hold shares in companies. Three different government agencies now separately regulate commercial banks, security firms, and insurance companies. Before 1998, the state always bailed out troubled financial institutions, but for the first time in 1998, several high-profile banks and investment companies, such as Hainan Development Bank and Guangdong International Trust Investment Company, closed down or went bankrupt. This signaled an important change on the part of the government: it was determined to discipline state financial institutions. Although the government may have incurred some short-run costs in doing that, it gained credibility, which is important in the long run.

Government Reform

Despite many early reforms, the basic government bureaucratic structure in China was still kept intact from the planning era, with, for instance, many industrial ministries remaining for supervising SOEs. In early 1998 a major reform for streamlining the government bureaucracy took place. Most industrial ministries, such as the textile and machinery industries, were abolished and replaced by much smaller corresponding bureaus, which were then absorbed into the State Economic and Trade Commission. The number of ministries in the central government was trimmed from forty-five to twenty-nine (a similar action was taken at the local level in 1999), and the number of civil servants was cut by half, from 8 million to 4 million. To compensate for the losses, displaced civil servants were sold apartments at discount prices according to their seniority and were given an option to study for undergraduate and graduate degrees with tuition fees and stipends paid by the government for three years.

Privatization and Restructuring State-Owned Enterprises

Privatization of SOEs and layoffs of state workers began to occur on a large scale in 1995.[3] Privatization of SOEs was begun initially by local governments as experiments in a few provinces, such as Shandong, Guangdong, and Sichuan. Later, the central government promoted it with the slogan of "grasping the large and releasing the small" *(zhuada fangxiao)*. Privatization of small SOEs was very significant for China, because, in contrast to Eastern Europe and the Soviet Union, China's industrial SOEs were dominated by small- and medium-size enterprises. In 1993, they accounted for 95 percent in number, 57 percent in employment, and 43 percent in output of the state industrial sector. Most of these enterprises were under the supervision of county and city governments. By the end of 1996, up to 70 percent of small SOEs had been privatized in pioneering provinces and about half in many other provinces. In addition, about 10 million workers from SOEs and urban collectives were laid off by the end of 1996, and an additional 11.5 million workers in 1997.

TRACING THE ROOTS: THE EVOLUTION OF THE CHINESE PLANNING SYSTEM FROM 1958 TO 1978

To answer deeper questions of why China and Eastern Europe have followed different paths of transition, I will trace the historical roots in the evolution of the planned system in China in the two decades before the market-oriented reform.[4] Like all other socialist countries, China had political and economic systems that were characterized by the undivided power of the Marxist-Leninist Party, the dominant position of state ownership, and a preponderance of bureaucratic coordination through central planning (Kornai 1992). But the Chinese planning system evolved into quite a different form of central planning from the standard Soviet model, which had important implications for its later transition to a market system.

The Official Critiques of Overcentralization, 1957

In 1953 China began to implement the first five-year plan (1953–1957), which was formulated with the help of the Soviet experts. The plan centered around 694 large projects, in which 156 key projects were designed by the Soviets. By the end of 1956, the basic framework of the Chinese central planning system was established. The number of enterprises subordinated to the central government increased from 2,800 in 1953 to 9,300 in 1957, and their output accounted for 50 percent in state industry. The number of material items allocated by the Planning Commission of the central government increased from 55 in 1952 to 231 in 1957, and from 227 in 1953 to 532 in 1957, if ministries of central government were included. As a result, the main emphasis in planning was by industrial branch (i.e., *tiaotiao*), rather than by region (i.e., *kuaikuai*). During the first five-year period, the central government's budget accounted for 75 percent and local government 25 percent. The role of local governments was very limited, and so was enterprise autonomy.

In the mid-1950s, criticisms of overcentralization grew in all centrally planned economies, including the Soviet Union and Eastern Europe. Mao's criticism focused on incentives rather than allocative efficiency. Mao believed in people's initiatives and incentives, although it was primarily political, not profits or material, incentives in which he put his trust. Mao's two formulas were: decentralization of government authority from central to local levels, and mobilization of people's consciousness through political campaigns and mass movements. In his 1956 speech, "On Ten Important Relationships," Mao (1977) argued:

> Our territory is so vast, our population is so large and the conditions are so complex that it is far better to have the initiatives come from both the central and the local authorities than from one source alone. We must not follow the example of the Soviet Union in concentrating everything in the hands of the central authorities, shackling the local authorities and denying them the right to independent action.
>
> The central authorities should take care to give scope to the initiative of provinces and municipalities, and the latter in their turn should do the same for the prefectures, counties, districts and townships; in neither case should the lower levels be put in a strait-jacket.

The Chinese way of criticizing overcentralization has deep historical roots from its long experience during the war. Because the revolutionary bases of the communists were in rural areas which were divided and surrounded by enemies, mobilization of incentives for production in each base and assurance of self-sufficiency became the main considerations. Based on the experience in these bases before liberalization, China always used local governments, not the central government, to plan agriculture (Zhou 1984, 218).

The First Wave of Administrative Decentralization, 1958

In 1958, the Great Leap Forward called for a high growth rate to overtake Great Britain and catch up with the United States in fifteen years. In this setting, two main institutional changes took place: ownership changes in rural areas, the establishment of the People's Commune; and decentralization within the planning system to alter the relationship between the central and local governments.

Mao was enthusiastic about the People's Commune because it combined "industry, agriculture, military, learning, and commerce" together into one entity, which fitted well with his dream of a new world of communism. Under Mao's initiatives, within two or three months, 99 percent of the peasants were organized into 24,000 People's Communes, with an average size of about 5,000 households.

In the urban areas in 1958, after only one year of the central planning system's full establishment, China began to restructure it. The government proposed dividing the country into seven "cooperative regions" *(xiezuoqu),* requiring each of them to have a complete industrial structure to achieve fast industrialization. The so-called administrative decentralization had several major features. First, most SOEs were delegated to local governments. The number of enterprises subordinated to the central government was reduced from 9,300 in 1957 to 1,200 in 1958. The share of industrial output from SOEs under the central government's supervision shrunk from 40 percent to 14 percent of the national total. Second, central planning was changed from a national to a regional basis. Third, most decisions over fixed investments were made by local governments, and for large projects, the local government were only required to submit a brief planning report to the central government. Fourth, local expenditures were determined by revenue and it was supposed to be fixed for five years (but was later changed to one year). As a result, the share of central revenue decreased from 75 percent to about 50 percent of total revenue. Furthermore, extrabudgetary revenue increased from 8.5 percent of within-budget revenue to 20.6 percent in 1960.

Initially, local responses to both the communes and decentralization were enthusiastic. For example, local small industries boomed for the first time (steel mills were in every backyard). In 1958, the People's Commune established a large number of commune and brigade enterprises, the predecessors of the later TVEs. By the end of 1958, these enterprises employed 18 million people and yielded a total output of ¥6 billion, which increased to ¥10 billion in 1959 (Byrd and Lin 1990). However, both rapidly turned out to be disasters. The institution of communes and their public dining halls, together with bad weather, led to the biggest famine in human history, causing about 20–30 million deaths. Between 1958 and 1962, the value of agricultural net output value declined by 5.9 percent and light industry by 2 percent annually, and national income also declined by 3.1 percent annually.

The economic disaster forced the government to reverse the 1958 policy. In January 1961, a new policy of "readjustment, consolidation, replenishment, and upgrading standards" was adopted. In response to the chaos, two measures were adopted. One was a more liberal policy in rural areas. Production teams, with an average size of about forty to fifty households, became the basic production and accounting units. The government also allowed peasants to cultivate small private plots, run sideline productions, and open rural free markets. In some places, contracting production to households occurred, which was the predecessor of the later household responsibility system.

Another measure was recentralization of planning. Some recentralization had already taken place in 1959: airlines, coal mines, and petroleum prospecting teams had already been put back under the supervision of the central government. Beginning in 1961, all large and medium-size industrial enterprises were again subordinated to the central government, including the defense industry, railroads, and major harbors. By 1965, industrial output from central government enterprises increased to 42.2 percent of the national total, and the number of planning indicators was restored to the 1957 level. The central government also took back authority to approve all large fixed investments.

The Second Wave of Administrative Decentralization, 1970

In 1962, Mao was forced to make a self-criticism of his 1958 policy, which he regarded as a big humiliation. He hated recentralization, as well as small free markets. In 1966 he initiated the Cultural Revolution to create a "new world," a system relying on political campaigns and mass movement rather than bureaucracy and markets.

In 1969, the political issues were settled and the economy recovered from the negative growth of 1967 and 1968. In 1970, the second wave of administrative decentralization began. There were two immediate reasons for this round of decentralization. First, the fourth five-year plan (1971–1975) discussed in early 1970 set a goal of high growth; for example, steel production was required to double in five years. To achieve this goal, the government believed that it must mobilize local initiative through decentralization. Second, Mao assessed that a Soviet invasion and the beginning of World War III was imminent and thus he made preparation for war as the key link. To that end, in February 1970 the government proposed dividing the country into ten cooperative regions *(xiezuoqu),* making each a relatively complete and self-sufficient industrial system to deal with the war. The planning system was changed to one mainly along regional lines *(kuaikuai weizhu).* As Mao put it, "Planning must rely on local governments, mainly by provinces" (Zhou 1984, 233).

The 1970 decentralization shared many features of the 1958 decentralization but went much further. Most large-scale SOEs were again delegated to provincial and municipal governments. The central government only supervised 142 SOEs in 1970, down from 10,533 in 1965, and the share of industrial output produced by SOEs under the central government's control dropped from about 50 percent in 1965 to only 8 percent in 1970. Local governments were made responsible for material allocation and they gained more authority over fixed investment. During this period, 52 percent of investment in the steel and iron industries came from local governments (Wong 1985).

But again administrative decentralization created some chaos and some recentralization began in 1973 under the name of "consolidation" *(zhengdun).* But in comparison with 1958, the extent of the 1970 decentralization was greater and the recentralization afterward was much weaker.

The Initial Conditions for Reform: Differences between China and Eastern Europe

It is interesting to compare China with the Soviet Union. Amid criticisms of over-centralization, in 1957 Khrushchev established 105 Regional Economic Councils to replace the ministries of the central government. This reform failed because of "localism." In 1965 the government replaced Regional Economic Councils with the previous central government ministries. Recentralization entailed a complete reversal, and from then on, the number of planned products continued to grow along with the size of the economy. In comparison, in China, recentralization in the early 1960s only restored it to the 1957 level, and before long the Cultural Revolution erupted and then came the even greater decentralization of 1970.

Granick (1990), an expert on the Soviet and Eastern European economies, recognized that China's planned economy before the reform had special features which were prominent enough to represent a radical departure from the standard Eastern European model. He noted that these peculiarities could not be attributed solely to China's state of economic underdevelopment. It was the planning system after administrative decentralization which produced the systematic difference. Decentralization within the Chinese state sector took the form of regional governments constraining central decision making via their recognized property rights, rather than having it occur through the center granting power to lower bodies so as to best achieve the center's own goals. None of these features existed in the Eastern European model.

Planning

Consider the number of commodities subject to the central government's planned allocation. For the Soviet Union, beginning in 1928, the number of planned commodities increased from none to over 500 by the early 1940s. For China, beginning in 1953, the number increased from none to about 500 or more by 1957. However, for the Soviet Union from 1941, the number of planned commodities continued to increase to 1,600 in 1951, reaching as many as 60,000 in the 1970s. In comparison, for China, because of the two waves of administrative decentralization in 1958 and 1970 and despite the subsequent recentralization effort, the number of planned commodities in 1978 was only slightly higher than the 1957 level, even though the economy had become much larger in two decades (Naughton 1995, 41). As a result, at the time of decentralization in 1957 in the Soviet Union, the number of planned products was more than 2,000, compared to just over 500 in China in the same year.

Industrial Structure

Decentralization had a long-lasting effect on China's industrial structure. The first effect was the expansion of local state-owned small industries. For example, in the early 1970s, more than 300 counties or municipalities set up small steel mills and about 90 percent of counties set up repair factories for agricultural machinery, and by 1978, the proportions of total output under local allocation included 46 percent of coal, 20 percent of steel, 64 percent of cement, 65 percent of machine tools, and 25 percent of trucks (Wong 1985). Among the fifty-eight enterprises making automobiles, most were controlled by local governments (Qian and Xu 1993). In Eastern Europe and the Soviet Union, by contrast, almost all enterprises making automobiles were directly controlled by the central government. The second effect of decentralization was the parallel development of small industries by communes and brigades in the rural areas. The total value of output from commune and brigade enterprises tripled from ¥9.25 billion in 1970 to ¥27.2 billion in 1976. In 1978 there were more than 1.52 million such enterprises, and their output value reached ¥49.3 billion (Byrd and Lin 1990).

An unintended consequence of local industrialization was the fact that, rather than too few small enterprises as in Eastern Europe and the former Soviet Union, China had too many small scale enterprises scattered around the country. Although they were inefficient in terms of scale economies, they formed a potentially competitive industrial structure which eliminated some major problems faced by eastern European countries, such as industrial concentration and lack of competition.

Spontaneous Horizontal Transactions

This administrative decentralization, together with local industrialization, created many local economic centers which were officially sanctioned and encouraged under the slogan of self-reliance. These multiple economic centers eroded central planning and the center's power to control regional economies, but naturally induced horizontal nonplanning channels for resource allocation purposes. Such horizontal transactions occurred both among state enterprises supervised by different local governments and between state and collective enterprises. The economic relations between different regions outside the planning system were called "cooperation relations," and the goods purchased in this fashion were known as "cooperation materials" (Wu and Zhao 1987). Because of their small scale, these enterprises also often had to sell their products at higher prices (than the planned prices) in order to cover their costs. Therefore, for the survival of these enterprises, the central government tolerated the higher prices they charged. The dual plan and market prices had already emerged before the reform.

CHINA'S GREAT TRANSFORMATION:
A CHALLENGE TO WHAT?

Both China and Eastern European countries have experienced a two-stage process in moving from a centrally planned system to a market system. In Eastern Europe, reforms started as early as 1968 in Hungary, 1980 in Poland, and 1985 in the Soviet Union, but their reforms prior to 1990 were a failure (Kornai 1986, 1992). This failure eventually led to a political revolution that jump-started the transition to a market system. To some extent, the big bang transformation in Eastern Europe after 1990 was an alternative to its early unsuccessful piecemeal social engineering.

In contrast, China had two big bang transformations of its own prior to 1978: one was the Great Leap Forward in 1958, and the other was the ten-year Cultural Revolution from 1966 to 1976. The market-oriented reform after 1978 represented an alternative approach to social transformation, and this time it followed the approach of piecemeal social engineering. In the two decades between 1978 and 1998, China has transformed itself incrementally from a centrally planned economic system to an emerging market economic system. China differed from Eastern Europe in that its first stage of reform was a remarkable success. Building on this success, China's second stage of reform—its transition to markets—evolved smoothly without any political revolution.

The Chinese path of transition fits well with Popper's notion of piecemeal social engineering.[5] However, it poses a challenge to the conventional wisdom of transition based on the Eastern European experience. First, in the conventional view, reforming a socialist system in a piecemeal manner cannot be successful. The Chinese experience has shown that this claim is not always true. Second, the conventional view holds that a political system under the rule of the Communist Party is unable to change its dogmatic ideology and thus a political revolution of democratization is necessary for pushing the reform into the transition stage. The Chinese experience has demonstrated that this expectation is not necessarily valid either.

China's transition to markets is better viewed as a path-dependent evolutionary process. As early as 1958, Mao criticized the rigid Soviet model of central planning and recognized the disadvantage of overcentralization. In response, Mao initiated his "third road" model of administrative decentralization together with political campaigns and mass movements to arouse the local governments' and people's enthusiasm. Although administrative decentralization largely failed, it had a big impact on later reforms.

While differing from the transition in Eastern Europe, the process of China's transition to a market system seems to share some common elements with the Industrial Revolution in eighteenth-century England and the general historical pattern of institutional development in the West. The Industrial Revolution is not just a phenomenon of economic development but also a process of fundamental institutional changes. The transition to modern capitalism was a bottom-up process that began in Manchester and Birmingham in northern England, not in the traditional commercial centers of the south. Northern England had weak government regulation, which was conducive to institutional innovation and change. Similarly, China's reform did not start in the existing industrial centers such as Shanghai or northeast China, where the state had strong control, but in the south, in Guangdong Province and other areas where state regulation was weak. Furthermore, China's path of transition appears to fit the historical institutional development pattern in the West: markets developed first, and the rule of law and democracy followed afterward. Therefore, from a longer historical perspective of development, the Chinese path of transition is not unusual.

NOTES

I benefited greatly from many discussions with Jinglian Wu on the evolution of the Chinese economic system.

1. For an analysis of the institutional foundations of China's market transition, see Qian 1999.

2. For the full text of the decision, see *China Daily,* supplement, November 17, 1993, 1.

3. The Chinese do not use the term "privatization," relying on several other terms, such as "transformation of ownership" *(zhuanzhi)* or "restructuring of ownership" *(suoyouzhi gaizao).* Similarly, the Chinese use "nonpublic ownership" as a substitute for "private ownership."

4. Information in this section is from Zhou 1984 or otherwise noted.

5. Murrell (1992) explicitly relates the "conservative political philosophy" of Burke, Popper, and Oakeshott to the discussion of the strategy of economic transition from plan to market. He compares characteristics of two general approaches to social change—piecemeal versus utopian social engineering—and illustrates them with the example of privatization: piecemeal privatization versus mass privatization.

REFERENCES

Bureau for the Compilation and Translation of Works of Marx, Engels, Lenin, and Stalin under the Central Committee of the CCP, trans. 1994. *Selected Works of Deng Xiaoping 1982–1992,* Vol. 3. Beijing: Foreign Language Press.

Byrd, W., and Q. Lin, eds. 1990. *China's Rural Industry: Structure, Development, and Reform.* Oxford: Oxford University Press.

Granick, D. 1990. *Chinese State Enterprises: Regional Property Rights Analysis.* Chicago: University of Chicago Press.

Kornai, J. 1986. "The Hungarian Reform Process: Visions, Hope, and Reality." *Journal of Economic Literature* 24, no. 4: 687–1737.

———. 1992. *The Socialist System.* Oxford: Oxford University Press.

Maddison, A. 1998. *Chinese Economic Performance in the Long Run.* Paris: OECD Development Centre.

Mao, Z. 1977. *Selected Works of Mao Zedong.* Vol. 5. Beijing: People's Press.

Murrell, P. 1992. "Conservative Political Philosophy and the Strategy of Economic Transition." *Eastern European Politics and Societies* 6, no. 1: 3–16.

Naughton, B. 1995. *Growing Out of the Plan.* Cambridge: Cambridge University Press.

Qian, Y. 1999. "The Institutional Foundations of China's Market Transition." Paper prepared for the Annual World Bank Conference on Development Economics. Washington, D.C., April 28–30.

Qian, Y., and C. Xu. 1993. "Why China's Economic Reforms Differ: The M-Form Hierarchy and Entry/Expansion of the Non-State Sector." *Economics of Transition* 1, no. 2: 135–170.

Wong, Chr. W. P. 1985. "Material Allocation and Decentralization: Impact of the Local Sector on Industrial Reform." In E. Perry and Chr. Wong, eds., *The Political Economy of Reform in Post-Mao China.* Cambridge, MA: Harvard University Press.

———. 1988. "Interpreting Rural Industrial Growth in the Post-Mao Period." *Modern China* 14, no. 1: 3–30.

Wu, J., and R. Zhao. 1987. "The Dual Pricing System in China's Industry." *Journal of Comparative Economics* 11, no. 3: 309–318.

Zhou, T., ed. 1984. *Dangdai zhongguo de jingji tizhi gaige* [Economic System Reform in Contemporary China]. Beijing: China Social Science Press.

9

Openness and Inequality

The Case of China

SHAOGUANG WANG

From the very beginning, outward-looking, export-led strategy has been an integral part of China's reform program. In the past twenty years, China has transformed itself from a nearly autarkic economy into an open one. In 2002, China became the sixth largest trading nation and the largest recipient of foreign direct investment (FDI) in the world.[1] There is no doubt that China has derived a great deal of benefits from its open-door strategy. The prevailing opinion among Chinese economists favors greater openness; they show little concern about the resulting social impacts on employment, poverty, and income distribution. In their view, openness is not only a way to promote economic growth but also a vehicle to further collective well-being. The belief is that economic growth by itself is capable of reducing poverty and advancing human development.

This chapter does not question the rationale of China's open policy. Nor does it challenge the premise that, all in all, the aggregate gains from openness outweigh the aggregate costs. However, this analysis assumes that the gains and costs generated by openness will not automatically be evenly distributed. If increased integration with the world economy does result in growing inequality, then its implications for distribution deserve more attention than they have drawn from Chinese economists.

My main concern in conducting this research is with the impact of openness on income distribution in China. In looking at outcomes of distribution, it is necessary to make a clear distinction between the impact on primary vs. secondary incomes. Primary incomes refer to those earned directly from work and investment (e.g., wages or dividends), while secondary incomes consist of deductions from, and additions to, individuals' primary income through taxation and government expenditure.[2] Greater openness may affect the distribution of primary as well as secondary incomes. This chapter seeks to identify who wins and who loses in terms of both primary and secondary distributions, with a focus on whether the government is capable of compensating the losers through taxing the winners.

Before looking at the Chinese experience with economic openness, I present a brief theoretical discussion on the changes in the distribution of primary and secondary incomes that one would expect to result from greater openness. Next I review China's actual progress in opening its economy and changing patterns of income distribution over the past twenty years. After that I look for associations between openness on the one hand and employment and the distribution of primary incomes on the other. Even if openness creates a growing polarity in primary incomes, the overall pattern of income distribution will not necessarily worsen as long as there is an effective mechanism for the government to transfer incomes from the winners to the losers. Then I turn to China's public finance system, examining the extent to which openness affects China's structures of taxes and expenditures. The main finding here is that the fiscal squeeze resulting from openness exacerbated rather than alleviated the inequality of primary income distribution up to the mid-1990s. Finally I discuss the reorientation of government policy since then and conclude that China should be able to compensate the losers of its open-door policy—if the government chooses to do so.

OPENNESS AND INEQUALITY

The term "openness" refers to a country's receptivity to free movement of goods, services, capital, labor, technologies, and information across national borders. One must bear in mind, however, that, even if a country were willing to integrate its economy fully with world markets, the degree of international mobility would still vary greatly among the factors of production. In general, capital is more mobile than labor. Financial capital (portfolio investment) has perhaps the highest mobility. With the help of modern communications, financial investors now operate twenty-four hours a day and can move money around the globe almost instantaneously. Foreign direct physical investment is less mobile but has become increasingly foot-loose of late. Labor used to be very mobile; prior to the nineteenth century, international borders were only approximately known and rarely policed. As late as the early twentieth century, passports were often unnecessary and people could travel freely from one country to another. However, the era of free immigration has long gone.[3] Today, unskilled labor is largely immobile, while professional and technical human resources are more mobile, yet subject to the regulation of the receiving country. Though perhaps unfair, this international economic order is a reality all individual countries have to face.

Characterized by such stratified mobility, globalization in its present form increases both the elasticity of supply for mobile factors such as capital and skilled labor, and the elasticity of demand for immobile factors such as land and unskilled labor. In political terms, globalization enhances the power of those who own capital and human capital, while undercutting the power of those who do not. What are the implications of these effects for income distribution? More specifically, what are the channels through which openness and inequality may be linked? Two channels appear to be crucial: the employment channel and the fiscal channel; the former affects the distribution of primary incomes, whereas the latter affects the distribution of secondary incomes.[4]

The Employment Channel

Let us look at the employment channel first. The impact of trade on the levels and structure of employment and wages is the direct route by which openness can influence distributional outcomes. According to the standard Heckscher-Ohlin-Samuelson model of trade (which can be adapted to capital mobility), openness should help reduce inequality within developing countries because, given full employment, free trade is supposed to increase incomes for the abundant factors and reduce incomes for the scarce factors.[5] In developing countries, capital and skilled labor are scarce, while less skilled labor is abundant. As those countries specialize and shift from capital-intensive toward unskilled labor–intensive production, unskilled wages will rise relative to skilled wages and returns on property. Has this common understanding been accurate?

There are several reasons why this is not necessarily so. First, it is possible that what is labor-intensive in the product mix of the world turns out to be capital- or skill-intensive in the product mix of a developing country. The less developed a country, the more likely this discrepancy holds true. Wherever this occurs, openness may increase rather than decrease wage inequality.[6] Second, if openness is predated by a period in which the state either restricted labor mobility or created underemployment, removal of such restrictions will enable managers, professionals, and skilled labor to enter international markets, and turn hidden underemployment into open unemployment; these two effects tend to worsen income differentials. Third, in former socialist countries, preopenness restrictions generally depressed returns to the well-off (managers, professionals, and skilled labor) and raised rewards to unskilled labor. Removal of the restrictions would make income distribution more unequal. Fourth, in large developing countries, export sectors tend to be concentrated in relatively industrialized regions. The opening of trade will increase profits for producers of exported goods. With poor infrastructure and a low level of personnel development, however, less developed regions may lack the capabilities to benefit from openness. What is worse, import-competing sectors tend to be concentrated in those regions, a situation which makes them extremely vulnerable to the costs of globalization without being able to benefit much from it. Consequently, the existing regional income gaps may widen. Fifth, in large developing countries with a diversified economic structure, the internal mobility of skilled labor may still be higher than that of unskilled labor. Differences in the elasticity of supply and demand will privilege the skilled and the mobile at the expense of the unskilled. Finally, openness is likely to lead to shrinking, capital-intensive formal sectors and expanding, labor-intensive informal sectors. The informalization of the labor force has potentially serious consequences for wages, job security, and the distribution of income because it undermines labor's collective power vis-à-vis capital.[7]

The above discussion suggests that openness is most likely to worsen the distribution of income in three types of countries: least-developed countries, transition countries, and large developing countries. Recent assessment of the connection between globalization and inequality in developing countries seems to have confirmed this hypothesis. While observing no general pattern, those studies did find that openness has been associated with rising inequality in the world's poorest nations,[8] giant countries (such as China, India, Indonesia, and Russia),[9] and countries in market transition.[10]

The Fiscal Channel

The fiscal channel is also important for distributional outcome because both taxes and public expenditures can be devised to remedy income inequality. On the revenue side, progressive taxes can reduce inequality by imposing a heavier tax burden on those who have larger primary incomes. On the expenditure side, public spending can reduce inequality by providing the poor with health, education, housing, social services, subsidies for daily necessities, safety nets, other transfer incomes, and even job opportunities. If a government is able to use both types of methods, income distribution in the country is expected to improve. The question is what are the fiscal consequences we would expect from the reduction in barriers to international factor mobility.

The Structural Power of Capital: Threat of Exit

The dominant economic view emphasizes the structural power of capital—the ability of capital owners to move production and money around the world in search of higher rates of return. Whenever necessary, capital will not hesitate to move to nations with relatively low taxes. The threat of such an exit is believed to have severely limited the state's room to maneuver. If a government chooses to alter the distribution of primary income in favor of the poor through tax policies and transfers, this move may potentially undercut the confidence of business in a profitable rate of return on investment and, by doing so, reduce growth. In order to prevent capital from exercising the exit options offered by openness, governments are likely to engage in tax competition—bidding with one another to lower tax burdens on business progressively to a lowest common denominator. As it becomes more difficult to tax capital and people with high human capital, tax burdens are likely to be shifted to immobile labor. Such a move will not only decrease the progressiveness of the tax system but also reduce the total share of taxation in GDP. When tax revenues decline, public spending will eventually follow. Cumulatively, greater openness may undermine the ability of governments to provide both public services (e.g., health and education) and social insurance expenditures, thus rolling back the state's redistributive functions. In summary, this view holds that openness constrains the freedom of governments to act autonomously and makes inevitable the reduction of taxation and expenditures, a result which is expected to worsen the distribution of secondary incomes and exacerbate overall inequality.[11]

Though correct in pointing out the restraining effects of the global economy on domestic political choices, structural power theory is too deterministic, leaving little room for states to adapt.[12] Recent empirical studies reveal that not all states respond similarly to the same structural pressures from the global market economy. Rather than "race to the bottom," the governments of some open economies have actually strengthened their extractive capacities.[13] If economic logic alone cannot explain the different national reactions to openness, there must exist countervailing pressures that can modify the structural impact of capital mobility and offset the ensuing inegalitarian tendencies. Where do such pressures come from?

The Political Power of the People: The Threat of Voice

Facing not only the threat of the exit of mobile assets, governments also have to deal with market dislocations generated by openness.[14] Opening is a process that generates losers as well as winners. As the scope of the market increases in a country, some social groups may find their income falling relative to that of others, and their future less secure. Rising income inequality and a pervasive sense of insecurity could spark a political backlash against an open policy in general and free trade in particular. If the losers of the open policy happen to be powerful political forces, they may wage fervent battle against the government that imposes the agenda of openness. In order to secure domestic political support for continued openness to the global economy and to maintain social cohesion, the government—as the socializer of risk of last resort—may be forced to compensate the losers and ensure that the fruits of openness are broadly distributed.[15]

The key assumption of this political power argument is that constituencies in favor of openness must continuously and consciously be built.[16] Unless the potential losers are adequately compensated, they may threaten to block or disrupt policies that are on aggregate socially beneficial. Compensation means transferring income from those who flourish in an open economy to those who have been adversely affected under market competition. To generate sufficient tax revenue for redistribution, the top brackets would have to be taxed at a significantly greater proportion than the bottom brackets.

Of course, governments may or may not choose to change tax rates, because richer taxpayers may have the economic and political power to prevent reforms that would affect them negatively. Economically, these privileged groups possess mobile assets

such as capital and skills that enable them to "vote with their feet"; politically, they
have resources and access—be it direct or indirect—to influence policy making.
However, the rich have one vital disadvantage: they are small in number. If increasing trade and capital mobility are accompanied by rising inequality, greater openness
may prompt protests from dispossessed social groups, protests which in turn may
ultimately compel the government to cushion market dislocations with redistributive policies. This possibility exists not only in electoral democracies but also in other
political systems. Here, of course, the type of regime matters. Competitive elections
may force politicians to take the threat of social dislocation more seriously; the presence of democracy may help channel discontent into the political process rather than
into the streets. However, even an undemocratic government may have incentives
to ameliorate economic insecurities and social dislocations; this is because, by fueling
social strife, growing inequality and unemployment are likely to become a cause of
political instability.[17] Although the dispossessed living under a nondemocratic
regime may not be able to register their dissatisfaction at polling booths, they can
resort to other forms of individual and collective actions—such as noncompliance,
criminal activities, strikes, protests, and the like. If the government chooses to turn
a blind eye to their suffering, deep social divisions may eventually put a brake on
economic growth in the country.[18]

In summary, openness sets in motion two types of threats on the part of national
governments: the *exit threat* from the owners of mobile assets and the *voice threat*
from all others. Neither threat can dictate government behavior. In that sense, there
is, and will continue to be, considerable "room for maneuver" for governments.
Numerous studies reveal that up to now the voice threat has outweighed the exit
threat, although there are exceptions.[19] Apparently, governments in many economies
exposed to a significant amount of external risk have tried to mitigate such risk by
taking command of a larger share of the economy's resources and by institutionalizing social security, welfare spending, income-transfer schemes, and other types of
compensatory programs.

OPENNESS AND INEQUALITY IN CHINA, 1980–2002

In this and the following sections I look for broad associations between openness on
the one hand and inequality on the other. My intent is to examine trends following
the openness rather than to explore causality in any rigorous sense.[20]

Increased Openness

From the very beginning, outward-looking, export-led strategy has been an integral
part of China's reform program. Characterized by self-reliance, the Chinese economy during the Mao era was basically one of autarky. Beginning in 1978, various
reform policies have been implemented to promote external transactions. Those

measures included gradual reduction in import tariffs, the removal of nontariff restrictions on imports of capital and intermediate goods, the broadening and simplification of export incentives, the elimination of state trading monopolies, and active encouragement of foreign investment and technology imports. Consequently, China has emerged in recent years as a fairly open economy with significant exposure to international competition.

The degree of openness can be measured by trade and FDI flows.[21] China's foreign trade has increased substantially in the postreform period. Foreign trade as a fraction of GDP grew from barely 10 percent in 1978 to over 40 percent in 1993–1994. Although the ratio declined somewhat in the following years, it rebounded after 1998 and reached a level of 50 percent in 2002 (see the left axis of figure 9.1). Comparative studies show that large country size and low income level normally make for lower trade and export ratios.[22] Taking that relationship into consideration, one may conclude that China's trade dependence is unusually high. In terms of growth, the dollar value of China's foreign trade increased by 30.1 times between 1978 and 2002, while its GDP grew only by 8.58 times in constant prices. Measured by trade/GDP ratio, China is more open than the United States and Japan, not to mention large low-income countries.[23]

FDI flows constitute another indicator of China's external orientation. China had little inflow of foreign investment prior to the early 1980s. In 1983, FDI accounted for only 0.3 percent of GDP, an almost negligible amount. The FDI/GDP ratio peaked at 6.2 percent in 1993, dropping somewhat afterward.[24] By 2002, however,

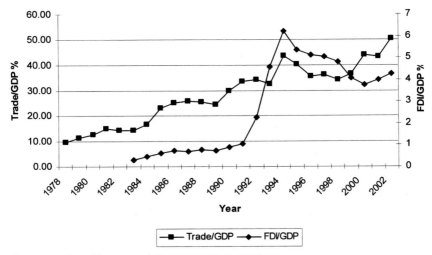

Figure 9.1   Two Measures of Openness, 1978–2002

Source: State Statistical Bureau, *China Statistical Abstract 2003* (Beijing: China Statistical Press, 2003), 156, 168.

the ratio of FDI to GDP remained around 4 percent, a level high even compared to those of large Organization for Economic Cooperation and Development (OECD) countries such as the United States, Japan, Germany, France, and Italy (see the right axis of figure 9.1). In fact, among all countries in the world, China now stands as the largest recipient of FDI.

China has no doubt derived a great deal of benefit from openness. The principal advantages of openness are threefold: (1) by trading with foreign nations, China as a whole can specialize according to its comparative advantage, thus improving its overall allocative efficiency; (2) by interacting with foreign counterparts and attracting FDI, Chinese industries can gain from knowledge spillover, thus helping to overcome production bottlenecks and to improve their technical efficiency; and (3) by competing with foreign firms, Chinese firms are forced to upgrade their product quality and adopt new management methods, thus improving their productive efficiency.

Growing Inequality

In retrospect, it can be said that China's reform and openness have benefited everyone. There are hardly any households whose welfare has not improved since 1978. A careful review of the recent history, however, reveals that Chinese reform has actually gone through two distinct phases. The first phase began in 1978 and ended around 1993. During this period, the game of reform was truly win-win in nature given that all social groups gained. The only difference was that some social groups might have gained relatively more than others.[25] Beginning from around 1994, however, the Chinese reform entered the second phase characterized by worsening unemployment and growing inequality. To be sure, there are still social groups that have profited from the latest round of reforms. For the first time, however, some segments of society have become net losers—losers not only in a relative sense, but also in absolute terms. To the extent that some have gained at the expense of others, the new game of reform has become a zero-sum one. It is revealing that the second phase has happened to be a period in which the degree of openness has been soaring, especially in terms of FDI (see figure 9.1).

The overall inequality in China can be usefully classified into four types: inequality within the rural sector, within the urban sector, between rural and urban sectors, and between regions.

First of all, the gaps between low- and high-income groups within rural China have been widening since the early 1980s.[26] The trend was already unmistakable before 1990, but has become more pronounced since then. In 1990, the average income of the top quintile was only 6.3 times higher than that of the bottom quintile in rural China. By 2000, the ratio had jumped to 1:9.5. While all five quintiles had seen their per capita income more than double between 1990 and 1995, only the top quintile enjoyed a relatively large increase of income between 1995 and 2000. For the bottom quintile, average income remained virtually unchanged in the late half of the 1990s. The second and third quintiles did not fare much better either (see figure

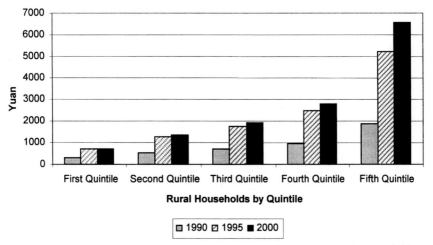

Figure 9.2 Per Capita Income in Rural China by Quintile, 1990–2000 (in *Renminbi*)

Source: Guo Jianjun, "Xianjieduan woguo nongmin shouru zengzhang tezheng, mianlin maodun he duice" [Characteristics, problems, and policies with regard to farmers' income in our country], *Jingji yanjiu cankao* [Materials for Economic Research] 43 (2001): 6.

9.2). It is therefore conceivable that some rural residents within those low and middle quintiles might have suffered real decline in their income. This conjecture is confirmed by the case of Suzhou, one of the most prosperous regions in China, where about one-third of the rural households reported decreases in income in those five years.[27] The situation for poor farmers living in central and western parts of China whose livelihood relied mainly on grain production could be even worse.[28]

Similarly, there had been a significant increase of inequality in urban China prior to 1990.[29] Afterward, due to unemployment and other factors, the situation has become even worse. In 1985, the average per capita income of the top 10 percent of urban households was only 2.87 times higher than that of the bottom 10 percent. By 2002, the ratio had jumped to 5.74 times—an unambiguous sign of polarization (see figure 9.3). Indeed, the richest 10 percent of households have been the biggest winners of recent reform, whose per capita income more than doubled from 1995 to 2002. Although the per capita income of the bottom 5 percent of households also registered a 38.5 percent increase for the same period, this group nevertheless experienced declines in income for two out of the seven years (1996–1997 and 1999–2000).[30] In fact, for a variety of reasons, the data on income presented in figure 9.3 may have failed accurately to reflect the hardship endured by those living at the bottom of urban society.[31] For example, figure 9.3 implies various degrees of increase in income for all social strata in 1996, but a nationwide survey found that about 40 percent of urban households suffered a decline instead.[32] The next year was even worse: those with reduced incomes constituted 45 percent of total urban households, even though figure 9.3 suggests that only the bottom 5 percent of urban households faced such a misfortune.[33]

Like other Third World countries, China has a dual economy. When China launched its reform initiative in 1978, the urban-rural divide was already rather deep: the per capita income of the urban resident was 2.6 times higher than that of their rural counterparts (see figure 9.4). In the early years of reform, the urban-rural gap shrank, but beginning from 1984, the gap began to widen again. Nevertheless, before 1992, the gap was still somewhat smaller than in 1978. The second phase of reform was characterized by the polarization of growth between China's modern and traditional sectors. Thanks to price increases of state procurement of grains, the polarization was temporarily arrested in 1996 and 1997. Given that China's grain prices were already higher than those in international markets, however, the government could not realistically support the agricultural sector by handing out subsidies on a regular basis. Therefore, after 1998 the urban-rural gap began to widen once again, reaching a peak in 2002. All the gains of the earlier reform years had been lost.

Neoclassic economists predict that, coupled with economic growth, the operation of the market by itself tends to bring convergence of regional income. China's experience over the past two decades shows, however, that convergence is by no means automatic. Indeed, the Chinese economy converged in the early years of reform, but the trend was reversed in the 1990s when the economy became more market-oriented and open. Figure 9.5 displays two sets of coefficients of variation (CV) of provincial per capita GDP in constant prices, with one including Beijing, Tianjin, and Shanghai and the other excluding the three metropolises. Both serve as measures of relative inequality between regions. The two curves show U-shaped time paths, with inequality declining in the early years of reform and then reversing course.[34]

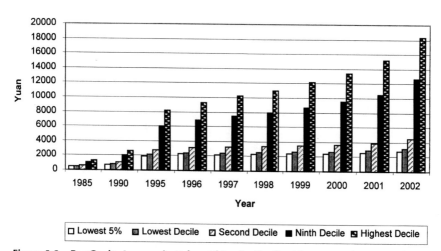

Figure 9.3   Per Capita Income in Urban China by Decile, 1985–2002 (in *Renminbi*)

Source: State Statistical Bureau, *China Statistical Abstract 2003* (Beijing: China Statistical Press, 2003), 104.

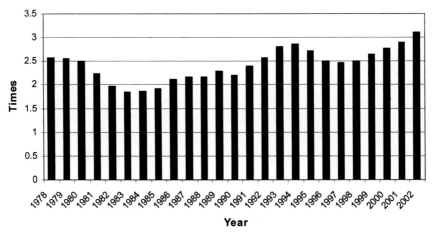

Figure 9.4   Gaps in Per Capita Income between Urban and Rural Residents, 1978–2002

Source: State Statistical Bureau, *China Statistical Yearbook 2003*, CD-Rom (Beijing: China Statistical Press, 2003).

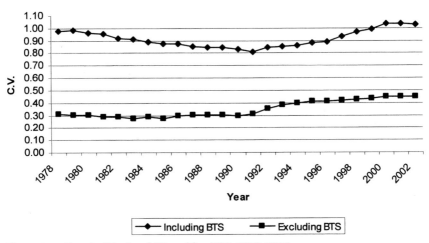

Figure 9.5   Trend of Regional Disparities (CV), 1978–2002

Source: State Statistical Bureau, *China Statistical Yearbook 2003*, CD-Rom (Beijing: China Statistical Press, 2003).

The above discussion clearly shows that the second phase of reforms has widened the gaps in income between regions, between urban and rural populations, and between rich and poor households in both urban and rural China. These inequalities are overlapping and interrelated. Together, the growing interregional, interpersonal, and rural–urban income differentials make China's overall income distribution much more unequal today than ever before in the history of the People's Republic (see figure 9.6). Looking ahead, unless the trend of increasing polarization can be somehow halted or reversed, the glaring inequalities prevailing in Latin America and sub-Saharan Africa are likely to emerge in China soon.

CAUSES OF GROWING INEQUALITY OF PRIMARY INCOMES

According to a World Bank study, China's export structure has moved in the direction of greater labor intensity.[35] Apparently, openness has helped China to restructure its economy in line with its comparative advantages. The question is why such a shift has resulted in increasing rather than decreasing inequality.

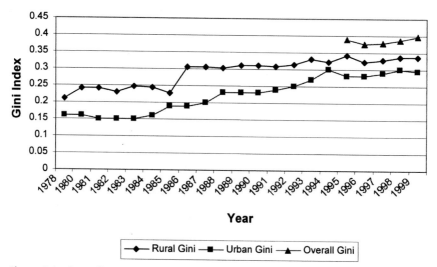

Year

— Rural Gini — Urban Gini — Overall Gini

Figure 9.6   Overall Income Inequality in China (Gini Coefficient), 1978–1999

Note: A Gini coefficient is a measure of relative inequality ranging from 0 (absolute equality) to 1 (absolute inequality). Here we use the data provided by China's State Statistical Bureau, which may have substantially underestimated the degree of inequality. Alternatively, some Chinese scholars estimate that the overall Gini coefficient had reached 0.458 by 2000. See Yang Yiyong and Xin Xiaobo, "Zhongguo dangqian de shouru fenpei geju ji fazhan qushi" [The current situation of income distribution and future trends], in *Shehui lanpishu: Zhongguo shehui xingshi fenxi yu yuce* [Social bluebook: Analyses and forecast of the social situation in China], ed. Ru Xin, Lu Xueyi, and Li Peilin (Beijing: Shehui kexue wenxian chubanshe, 2002), 144.
Source: www.stats.gov.cn/gqgl/gqglwz/200104240017.htm.

General inequality in China can be largely a result of two factors: urban–rural inequality and interprovincial inequality,[36] both of which seem to have widened under greater openness.[37] For one thing, whether or not openness has brought about more job opportunities for unskilled workers, the benefits mainly go to those residing in cities, not to those living in the countryside. Moreover, openness tends to increase the ratio between manufacturing and agricultural wages, a change which is bound to enlarge the urban–rural income gap.[38] As for regional disparities, an overwhelming proportion of China's exports (about 80 percent) originate in eleven coastal provinces where only about 40 percent of China's population live. To begin with, these provinces had been richer than the average; during the past two decades of reform and openness, their growth rates of per capita GDP were generally much higher than those of inland provinces. Khan is right in pointing out that "the export-orientation of China's growth has by and large disproportionately benefited the richest provinces."[39]

In addition, two factors can explain growing inequality within the urban sector. One is rising income gaps between working employees on the one hand, and the employees sent home and people with no job on the other. Since China entered the second phase of reform, economic growth has increasingly become a sort of "jobless growth." This trend is vividly demonstrated in figure 9.7. In the 1980s, every additional percentage of GDP growth brought 0.32 percent increase in employment opportunities. The situation at that time might be called one of job-creating growth. By the mid-1990s, the mode of growth had changed. When GDP grew by an additional percentage point, employment opportunities increased by only 0.14 percent.

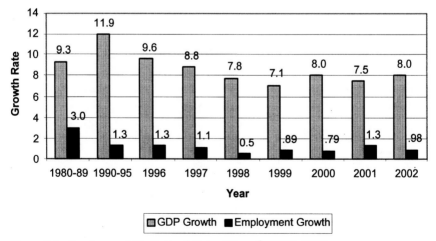

Figure 9.7   Employment Elasticity of Output Growth, 1980–2002

Source: State Statistical Bureau, *China Statistical Yearbook 2003*, CD-Rom (Beijing: China Statistical Press, 2003).

The elasticity of output growth continued to fall throughout the late 1990s. In 2000, GDP grew 8 percent, while employment increased barely 0.8 percent, meaning that every additional percentage of GDP growth brought about only a 0.1 percent increase of employment. As a result, millions of workers have already lost their jobs, and China finds it increasingly more difficult to create job opportunities for the 10 million people who enter the labor market every year.

How might one resolve the paradox that growth based on the expansion of labor-intensive export industries resulted in such rapidly declining growth in employment? One explanation is that during the prereform period and early years of reform, Chinese industries had probably absorbed labor far in excess of what was required. Thus, the declining employment elasticity perhaps reflects an attempt on the part of China's state and collective enterprises to get rid of the enormous underemployment that had built up over the previous decades; otherwise, these enterprises would not be able to respond to global competition. In terms of labor productivity, the reduction of the hidden underemployment appears to be a wise move. It nevertheless increases the number of people whose incomes either disappear or substantially decline.[40] Another possibility is that China's exportables may appear to be labor-intensive in the product mix of the world, but are capital- or skill-intensive in the product mix of China. If that is the case, freer trade may not be able to create sufficient job opportunities for unskilled workers in China, thereby increasing rather than offsetting the rise in wage inequality.[41]

The other factor that explains growing inequality in urban China is increasing return to education. Even before reform, all educational levels already brought significant returns. Market reform and international competition make imperative the adequate rewarding of those with high human capital. Consequently, returns to formal education have greatly increased during the reform era, especially during its second phase.[42]

Of course, the rapid growth of inequality in China has by no means been an inevitable result of the march toward an open market economy. To a large extent, government policies have been responsible for all the above-mentioned factors that contributed to rising inequality. Up to 1996–1997, China's policy environment was pretty much pro-efficiency and anti-equality. The policy of concentrating tax and fiscal incentives as well as investment in China's coastal growth poles, for instance, explains why the benefits of export-led growth did not spread widely to the interior provinces. Policy barriers to rural-urban migration have also aggravated the gaps between urban and rural earnings. Had China chosen to adopt a set of more enlightened policies, the distributional outcome could have been significantly different.[43]

CAUSES OF WORSENING SECONDARY DISTRIBUTION

In theory, even if market reform and openness raise inequality of primary incomes in a country, its government can use the gains generated by market forces to compensate those who are bypassed in normal market operation, while still enhancing aggregate welfare overall. If the compensatory mechanism is well designed and implemented, everyone could be better-off.[44] In practice, however, the government may not be willing and able to deliver adequate compensation packages to those who lose their jobs or face a relative decline in income as a result of such economic changes.[45] Before the late 1990s, capital's threat of exit appeared to have exerted more influence on the Chinese government than did the threat of any rising voice of social forces. Consequently, China did not make much effort to put an adequate compensatory mechanism in place.

Important issues in any discussion of a compensatory mechanism involve two sides of public finance: the revenue side and the expenditure side. In terms of revenue, the key is whether the existing overall tax level (usually expressed as a ratio of tax revenue to GDP) is appropriate. If the government does not have sufficient revenue at its disposal, redistribution is simply out of the question. Even if the tax level is adequate, we still need to determine whether the composition of tax revenue is desirable in terms of its distributional effects. Taxes can be broken into three major categories: income taxes that comprise mainly taxes on personal income and corporate profits; domestic indirect (or consumption) taxes that represent primarily sales tax, turnover tax, value-added tax, and excises; and trade taxes, the bulk of which consist of import duties.[46] Generally speaking, based on the principle of "ability to pay," taxes on income are more progressive than domestic indirect taxes on consumption; this is so because, administratively speaking, it is almost infeasible to implement effectively, on a broad scale, graduated tax rates on consumption.[47] Compared to domestic indirect taxes, trade taxes (also a kind of indirect tax) are more sensitive to external shocks. The proclivity of such taxes to fluctuate in the world market makes them even less desirable. On the expenditure side, two general types of spending can be used to measure the degree of redistribution: social spending (e.g., education and health) and fiscal transfers, both of which are supposed to benefit the poor and thereby reduce inequality. In this section we examine how openness has affected both the revenue and expenditure sides of China's public finance.

Fiscal Revenue

To put China's case in comparative perspective, table 9.1 brings out the salient differences in terms of the level and composition of tax revenue between China and other countries. Most conspicuously, China's overall level of fiscal revenue was extremely low, accounting only for 11.4 percent of GDP, which on average was 20–25 percentage points lower than those of the OECD countries and 6–8 percentage points lower than those of developing countries. In particular, China's revenue from income taxes was very small, a fact which to a large extent explains the low level of overall taxation. Another difference is also worth noting. Under normal circumstances, trade taxation plays a very important role in developing countries. Interestingly, however, the share of trade taxes in China during this period resembled

Table 9.1. China's Level and Composition of Tax Revenue in Comparative Perspective, 1995–1997 (in Percentage of GDP)

	Income Taxes	Trade Taxes	Consumption Taxes	Level of Revenue
China*	2.0	0.6	8.1	11.4
OECD Countries	14.2	0.3	11.1	37.9
America	15.4	0.3	6.7	32.6
Pacific	16.3	0.6	7.8	31.6
Europe	13.7	0.3	12.1	39.4
Developing Countries	5.2	3.5	7.0	18.2
Africa	6.9	5.1	6.5	19.8
Asia	6.2	2.7	7.0	17.4
Middle East	5.0	4.3	6.0	18.1
Western Hemisphere	3.7	2.6	8.0	18.0

Note: Revenue includes income from nontax sources. Revenues from the three major taxes comprised over 90 percent of the total tax revenue of the non-OECD countries, while for the OECD countries they comprised only about 70 percent. The rest was derived from social security taxes. Compared to other regions in the world, "social security taxes were inconsequential in Asia." See Howell H. Zee, "Empirics of Cross-country Tax Revenue Compositions," *World Development* 24, no. 10 (1996): 1662. In China, pension contributions amounted to about 2 percent of GDP in the late 1990s but were not included in the budget.

*The statistics for China are for a slightly different time period: 1994–1998.

Sources: See Ministry of Finance, *Zhongguo caizheng nianjian* [China financial yearbook] (Beijing: Zhongguo caizheng jingji chubanshe, various years); and Vito Tanzi and Howell H. Zee, "Tax Policy for Emerging Markets: Developing Countries," *National Tax Journal* 53, no. 2 (2000): 303–304.

that of the OECD countries rather than developing countries, another factor that contributed to China's overall low level of fiscal revenue.

Figure 9.8 provides disaggregated information on four categories of China's fiscal revenue: corporate income tax (CIT), personal income tax (PIT), domestic indirect tax (DIT), and customs duties.[48] Five observations can be made from figure 9.8. First, China's level of tax revenue as a fraction of GDP suffered a sharp decline between 1985 and 1996, but rebounded somewhat afterward. However, the level of 2002 was still 5 percent below the level of 1985. Second, throughout the period, domestic indirect taxes dominated the list, though their share in GDP dropped a bit. As a matter of fact, the ratio of DIT to GDP returned to the level of 1985 by 2002. Third, the decline in importance of corporate income tax was most drastic, especially prior to 1999, when revenue from this source fell from nearly 8 percent of GDP to barely 1.6 percent. Fourth, the share of customs duties also fell substantially, from 2.3 percent of GDP in 1985 to 0.4 percent of GDP in 1998. Finally, the proportion of personal income tax was almost nonexistent prior to 1993, but began to increase afterward.

It is clear from figure 9.8 that the decline of revenues from corporate income taxes and customs was the main factor contributing to the weakening of the Chinese government's extractive capacity prior to the late 1990s, because together their shares in GDP dropped from more than 10 percent in 1985 to barely 2 percent in

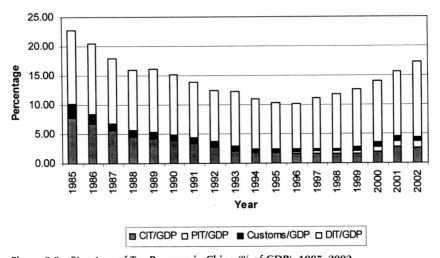

Figure 9.8   Structure of Tax Revenue in China (% of GDP), 1985–2002

Sources: National Taxation Bureau, *Zhongguo shuiwu nianjian* [China taxation yearbook] (Beijing: Zhongguo shuiwu chubanshe, various years).

1998. To what extent was such a decline related to openness? How exactly did openness affect the bases and rates of those taxes? I now try to answer those questions.

The impact of openness on corporate income tax is quite visible. Before 1994, there had been separate laws governing corporate income taxes for domestic and foreign enterprises; under these laws, foreign firms enjoyed very generous tax preferences. In 1994, China undertook a major tax reform that unified tax laws for both types of enterprise. The business tax rate on domestic enterprises was reduced from 55 to 33 percent, which was supposed to be a universal rate. However, legal and illegal tax preferences for foreign investments still existed. Typically, legal preferences included generous tax holidays, reduced tax rates, tax refunds, and various allowances such as depreciation allowances, loss carry-backs and carry-forwards, and other allowable deductions. In addition, in order to attract foreign investment to their administrative jurisdictions, local governments often competed with one another by offering extra preferential tax treatment to foreign investors, thereby violating national laws. Such practice was widespread in China.[49] Available surveys estimated that the effective rates of corporate income tax were around 25–28 percent for domestic firms and 7–14 percent for foreign firms in the mid- to late 1990s.[50] This gap has not narrowed since then.[51] Put differently, on average the tax burden for domestic enterprises was at least twice as heavy as their foreign counterparts. In 2002, the foreign corporate income tax yielded RMB ¥61.6 billion which meant that revenue "lost" from this source alone amounted to around ¥60 billion, far from an inconsequential number.[52]

Turning to the issue of taxes on imports, the relative importance of this source of revenue is normally much more pronounced in developing countries than in industrial countries.[53] China appears to be an exception, however. At first glance, this seems very surprising since China's nominal tariff has been relatively high. Prior to 1992, the unweighted average nominal tariff was 47.2 percent. It fell steadily afterward, dropping to 12 percent in 2002 (see figure 9.9). The nominal tariff was misleading, however, because, as table 9.2 shows, most imports to China were either fully exempt from customs duties (e.g., the imports for processing trade and the import of equipment for technological transformation for foreign-invested firms) or taxed at reduced rates (e.g., those imports given preferential tariff treatment by various levels of government legally or illegally). As late as 2000, only less than 40 percent of China's imports were subject to customs duties in full (see table 9.2). Consequently, the effective tariff (measured by the ratio of imports duties to the total value of imports) was only a small fraction of the nominal tariff and fell progressively in much of the reform era—from a peak of 16.2 percent in 1984 to 2.69 percent in 1998. In 1999 and 2000, the effective tariff recovered a little to around 4 percent, a change which was largely due to a massive crackdown on smuggling in those two years. The falling of both nominal and effective tariffs reflected a powerful tendency toward trade liberalization in China. One of the consequences of this decline in tariffs, however, was a significant loss in potential budgetary revenue.[54] Had the effective tariff remained at the level of 1984, China's revenue from customs duties in 2002 would have been about ¥400 billion rather than the ¥70.4 billion actually obtained.

Although by far contributing very little to total tax revenue, personal income tax

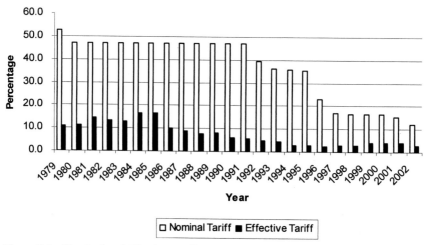

Figure 9.9   Nominal and Effective Tariff in China, 1970–2002 (%)

Source: National Taxation Bureau, *Zhongguo shuiwu nianjian* [China taxation yearbook] (Beijing: Zhongguo shuiwu chubanshe, various years).

Table 9.2. Proportion of Taxed Imports

Year	Imports (billion US$)	Taxed Imports (%)	Imports for Processing Trade (%)	Imports Exempted or Taxed at Reduced Rates (%)	Other Imports (%)
1990	53.4	15.0	40.5	44.5	0
1995	132.1	15.4	44.2	30.7	9.7
1996	138.8	22.2	44.9	26.3	9.6
1997	142.3	23.4	49.3	16.1	11.2
1998	140.2	27.6	48.9	17.3	6.2
1999	165.8	37.8	44.4	14.6	3.2
2000	225.1	38.8	N/A	N/A	N/A

Source: International Taxation Research Council, *Zhongguo jiaru WTO yu shuishou gaige* [China's entry to the WTO and its taxation reform] (Beijing: Zhongguo shuiwu chubanshe, 2000), 78.

also deserves attention. Like many developing countries, China attempted to maintain some degree of nominal progressivity for personal income tax. As figure 9.10 shows, however, the effective rates of personal income tax were regressive rather than progressive for urban residents prior to 2000:[55] tax actually paid as a proportion of total income fell steadily as income rose, meaning that the poor bore a heavier tax burden than their rich counterparts did.[56] Such distribution of tax burdens obviously violated the principle of equity.

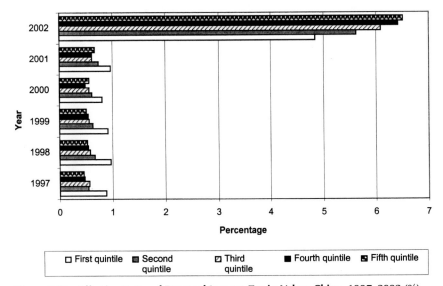

Figure 9.10   Effective Rates of Personal Income Tax in Urban China, 1997–2002 (%)

Source: State Statistical Bureau, *China Statistical Yearbook 2003*, CD-Rom (Beijing: China Statistical Press, 2003).

Widespread tax evasion was the main cause for this anomalous pattern, mainly due to three factors: illegal activities, the informal economy, and poor tax administration. A large portion of the income of some of China's new rich came from such illegal practices as abusing political power via bribing domestic and foreign investors or using insider information in the financial market to make a fortune. Such transactions constituted a major source of base erosion. Taxable incomes in the informal sectors escaped the tax net as well.[57] Often relaxing enforcement in order to pocket bribes from taxpayers, corrupt tax collectors may make the situation even worse.[58]

Yet global integration also contributed to the regressive shift. According to Chinese law, the legal personal exemption was ¥800 per month for Chinese citizens and ¥4,000 for foreigners (including those from Hong Kong, Macau, and Taiwan). Although small in number, foreigners in China typically belonged to the group with the highest income. The ¥4,000 per month amounted to more than ten times the country's per capita income. In order to please foreigners living in China, the Chinese government was not willing to lower the threshold of their exemption. In the period 1994–1998, the revenue from PIT paid by foreigners typically accounted for one-fourth of the total PIT revenue (see table 9.3). Had the personal exemption been the same for both Chinese and foreigners, the government's revenue from PIT would have undoubtedly been much higher.

Clearly, under the pressure of openness, the Chinese government moved its tax structure in a regressive direction up to the mid-1990s. This regression was reflected in the shift from income taxes and trade taxes to domestic indirect taxes. Even income taxes (both personal and corporate) themselves became regressive. This drastic change not only placed the tax burden disproportionately on low- to moderate-wage workers, but also entailed substantial revenue losses that exacerbated fiscal constraints.

Public Spending

If China's system of taxation played no redistributive function, what about its public spending? As fiscal revenue's share in GDP fell between 1978 and 1995, fiscal

Table 9.3. Share of PIT Paid by Foreigners, 1994–1998 (Unit: 1,000 Yuan)

Year	Total PIT	Foreign PIT	Foreign/Total PIT
1994	7,266,882	1,913,149	26.3%
1995	13,149,335	3,249,501	24.7%
1996	19,318,590	4,264,435	22.1%
1997	25,992,578	5,094,256	19.6%
1998	33,864,938	8,427,381	24.9%

Source: National Taxation Bureau, *Shuizhi gaige yilai shuishou tongji ziliao 1994–1998* [Revenue statistics for the period of 1994–1998] (Beijing: Zhongguo shuiwu chubanshe, 2000), 27, 62, 81, 130, 149, 217, 234, 303, 317, 387.

expenditures followed (see figure 9.11). At its lowest point in 1995 and 1996, fiscal expenditures in China accounted for only 11.7 percent of GDP, a much lower level than corresponding figures in most countries, developed or otherwise. The decline of fiscal revenue severely limited the government's ability to serve as an effective redistributor.

With so little at its disposal, the Chinese government simply could not afford the luxury of institutionalizing welfare spending and income-transfer programs. Figure 9.12 provides information about China's social expenditures and transfer payments. The former refers to expenditures on education and health, while the latter covers spending on social safety nets; both of these are supposed to benefit the poor and reduce income inequality.[59] It is noticeable that the GDP shares of the two types of expenditures already were very small in 1986. Such a low level of spending could hardly mitigate the dislocations generated by domestic and international market forces. To make the matter worse, the two categories of public expenditures relative to GDP kept falling afterward and did not stop until 1996 or 1997. The declining proportion of GDP used for redistribution reduced the secondary incomes of lower-income groups more than those of upper-income groups. In terms of the net effects of public expenditures on income distribution, the changing spending patterns of the Chinese government might have aggravated rather than alleviated inequality during this period.[60]

Intergovernmental transfers also shrunk substantially for much of the 1980s and 1990s. During Mao's era, the central government enjoyed considerable control over the distribution of resources across provinces.[61] In the first fifteen years of economic

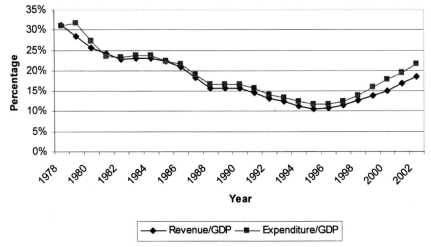

Figure 9.11   Fiscal Revenue and Expenditure in China (% of GDP), 1978–2002

Source: State Statistical Bureau, *China Statistical Yearbook 2003*, CD-Rom (Beijing: China Statistical Press, 2003).

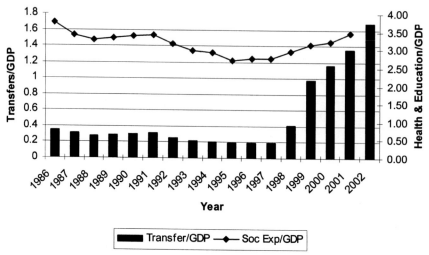

Figure 9.12   Social Expenditure and Transfers (% of GDP), 1986–2002

Source: Ministry of Finance, *Zhongguo caizheng nianjian* [China financial yearbook] (Beijing: Zhongguo caizheng jingji chubanshe, various years).

reform, however, Beijing's ability to allocate intergovernmental transfers was critically enfeebled. Under the fiscal contract system *(chengbaozhi)* that prevailed from 1980 to 1993, all of the provinces, both rich and poor, were compelled to become financially more independent. Most taxes were collected and most expenditures undertaken on a jurisdiction-by-jurisdiction basis.[62] As fiscal surpluses from rich provinces drained off, funds available for the central government to redistribute became increasingly limited.[63] The result was growing fiscal gaps between provinces, a situation which has threatened China's national unity. To arrest this dangerous trend, China overhauled its fiscal system at the beginning of 1994. The new system was called the tax-assignment system *(fenshuizhi)*. One of the manifest goals of the 1994 reform was to restore the central government's ability to redistribute funds so that it could again transfer surpluses from the more developed provinces to the less-developed provinces.

The post-1994 Chinese fiscal flows between the central and provincial governments can be divided into two broad categories: "returned revenue" and "others." The former was designed to compensate each and every province for what it would have to sacrifice to accept the 1994 system. For this purpose, each province's net loss in accepting the new system was calculated. Thereafter, every year each province was entitled to receive a certain amount of central compensation (or "returned revenue") according to a preset formula. Since the mechanism of "returned revenue" was in essence a kind of side payment to ensure that the provinces did not resist the new system, its distribution favored only rich provinces that had done very well under the pre-1994 system.[64] Other types of intergovernmental transfers contained more elements of fiscal equalization.[65]

As figure 9.13 reveals, prior to 1999 the bulk of central transfers took the form of returned revenue, a kind of de facto provincial entitlement about which the central government could exercise little discretional power. If the returned revenue were to be excluded, then the net central transfers were not very significant. Only in more recent years have other transfers begun to swell.

OPPORTUNITIES AND CHALLENGES

This chapter is concerned primarily with the consequences of openness on distribution. A principal conclusion one can draw from sections one to three is that, as the Chinese economy has become increasingly integrated with the world economy, the distribution of primary income has worsened in the country. Although the government's policies, especially its regional policies, are to some extent responsible for having aggravated this trend, the widening inequality of primary incomes is perhaps inevitable anyway. Whatever aggregate gains openness may engender, they are unlikely to be evenly distributed across social strata simply via the operation of the market. Only the government can, through redistribution, correct the rising inequality. The key issue then is whether the government is both *willing* and *able* to extend effective remedies to those who are penalized by structural changes.

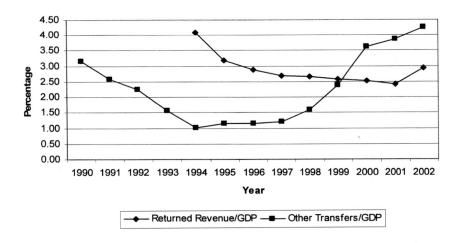

Figure 9.13 Intergovernmental Fiscal Transfers as % of GDP, 1990–2002

Source: Ministry of Finance, *Difang caizheng tongji ziliao* [Local public finance data] (Beijing: Xinhua chuban-she, various years).

The case of China up to the mid-1990s seems to confirm structural power theory. As the theory predicts, economic integration appears to have forced China to restructure its system of public finance. Relative to GDP, customs duties were falling, as were taxes on mobile production factors. Such changes led to two consequences, both of which were detrimental to redistribution in favor of the poor. First, as the importance of trade taxes and income taxes declined, domestic indirect taxation on consumption became dominant, a change which shifted the whole structure of taxation in a regressive direction. Second, overall tax revenues plunged, eventually resulting in the reduction of public spending in general and social expenditures and transfer payments in particular. In the end, the regressive transition in tax structure and the fall in the expenditure-to-GDP ratio impaired the distribution of secondary income.

A closer examination of the data presented in the preceding section, however, may lead to a different conclusion. As figures 9.8–9.13 and table 9.2 reveal, something significant occurred around 1996. Indeed, in September 1995, the Fifth Plenary Session of the CCP Fourteenth Central Committee reversed its biased regional policy of favoring coastal growth, instead giving more support to economic development in central and western areas.[66] This was the first sign that the Chinese government had begun to move away from its previous pro-growth/anti-equality stance. Once the general policy orientation changed, the government could always find instruments to pursue its newly set goals. This possibility was reflected in a number of major adjustments. First, relative to GDP, revenues from both corporate and personal income taxes as well as customs began to rise along with revenues from domestic indirect taxes for the first time since 1985 (see figure 9.8). In particular, the revenue from personal income tax soared—from a negligible ¥8.3 billion in 1994 (the year when a unified personal income tax was introduced) to ¥121.1 billion in 2002, an annual growth rate of 40 percent. Second, after falling incessantly for many years, government revenue as a percentage of GDP began to increase. Between 1996 and 2002, such revenue grew by 7.6 percent, largely recovering ground lost since 1987 (see figure 9.11). Third, as revenue went up, so did expenditures. The difference was that the latter expanded at a much faster pace. Within the seven short years from 1996 to 2002, government expenditures as a percentage of GDP grew by 9.8 percent. By 2002, these outlays reached 21.5 percent, the highest level since 1986 (see figure 9.11). Fourth, social expenditures and transfer payments rose, especially the latter (see figure 9.12). In 1998, the government added a new category of expenditure, "supplementary expenditures on social security," to its budget, an addition of ¥15 billion. The next year saw that outlay more than double (reaching the level of ¥34.4 billion) and the emergence of yet another new category of expenditure, "central funds for social security." The amount of the two outlays came to more than ¥136.2 billion in 2002, or 6.2 percent of total government expenditures for the year.[67] Finally, intergovernmental transfers grew rapidly (figure 9.13), a change which was necessary to reduce regional disparities.

By no means coincidences, these recent changes were the results of deliberate

choices. Evidently, the Chinese government had come to realize the danger of growing inequality by the late 1990s.

In the first phase of reform and openness, everyone gained; it was thus easy to
become obsessed with the neo-liberal doctrine or what some called the "Washington
Consensus."[68] Indeed, from the beginning of the 1980s to the mid-1990s, neither
policymakers nor economists paid much attention to the issue of just distribution
in China. As market-oriented reform and openness deepened, however, they started
to unsettle a growing proportion of the population. In an era of unprecedented prosperity, millions of people were thrown out the workforce or deprived of opportunities to enjoy the benefits of economic growth. Having grown up in an egalitarian
background, many losers of such a zero-sum game had no patience with the new
harsh reality. It was against this background that Chinese society became more volatile, as indicated by the upward spirals of both the incidence of labor disputes and
the number of workers involved (see figure 9.14).[69] Internal official publications and
public opinion surveys also gave voice to those people's frustration and discontent.[70]
By the mid-1990s, the government could clearly see that further restructuring would
make a rising segment of the population more vulnerable. Unless the central leaders
were prepared to shoulder the responsibility of redistributing the gains and risks of
economic liberalization, widespread unemployment and growing inequality could
pose a great threat to social cohesion in China.

Even though China is not an electoral democracy in the Western sense, its government must still respond to changes in societal preferences. After all, this was a regime
that, despite everything, still professes to uphold the socialist principle of equity. To
maintain social stability, the Chinese government had to provide basic social insur-

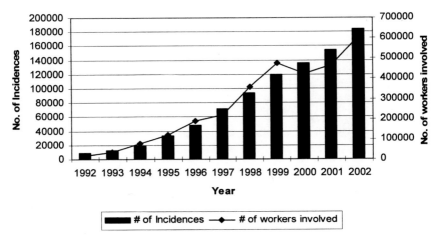

Figure 9.14   Labor Disputes, 1992–2002

Source: State Statistical Bureau, *China Statistical Yearbook 2003,* CD-Rom (Beijing: China Statistical Press,
2003).

ance to the most vulnerable in society. Were it to face increasing inequality with indifference, the system could lose its legitimacy. This explains why taxes have become more progressive, the levels of fiscal revenues and expenditures have risen, and the government has funneled more money into social services and safety net building.

Thus, instead of confirming the prevailing structural power theory, the case of China shows that states are by no means helpless in the face of the forces of globalization. While growing factor mobility may put pressure on national governments to race to the bottom, this does not have to be their only choice. Once societal forces build up countervailing pressures, governments may be forced to raise more taxes from the winners of openness and spend more to build broader safety nets for everyone else. This is not to deny the constraining impact of openness on domestic policy makers' range of choices, but to recognize the transformative capacity of states.[71]

Comparative empirical studies confirm that openness tends to induce the expansion of the public sector rather than its contraction as predicted by structural power theories. In fact, this pattern was initially observed among developed countries.[72] More recently, social scientists have established that the correlation held for developing countries as well.[73] China too is following the pattern. An explanation for such a correlation is that, in countries exposed to a significant amount of external risk, governments have to find ways to mitigate distributive conflicts generated by openness. Unless the governments possess risk-reducing instruments and the requisite extractive capability, the ensuing distributive conflicts may eventually derail the process of opening itself.

In sum, globalization compels governments to make two sets of choices: whether to open their economies and whether to compensate the losers of their open policies (see table 9.4). It is certainly unwise for a country either to go back to protectionism or resign itself too easily to the structural power of capital. With transformative capacity, the government can reinvent its role as the insurer of last resort without undermining the strength of the market as generators of economic growth.[74] Countries that open themselves to the outside world while establishing institutions to ameliorate the adverse effects of opening are more likely to grow and prosper than those where openness simply promotes income inequality, without any possibility for the "losers" to be compensated.[75]

Can China compensate the losers of its open policy? It certainly can if the Chinese government chooses to do so. Of course, compensation is no easy task. Many new transfer programs are financed by debt. It may take some more years for the Chinese

Table 9.4. Four Possible Routes to Globalization

	Openness	Closed Door
With compensation	Growth with equality	Equality but stagnation
Without compensation	Growth with inequality	Stagnation and inequality

government to restore its capacity to affect the distribution of wealth and income in society. However, were the Chinese government to capitulate to the structural power of global capital, and to turn a blind eye to the hardship caused by its policy of liberalization, then the uneven distribution of the gains and costs of greater openness could trigger and exacerbate conflicts between the winners and losers over distribution, and eventually derail China's market reform and imperil its future growth.[76]

NOTES

1. WTO, *International Trade Statistics 2003*, www.wto.org/english/res_e/statis_e/its 2003_e/its03_toc_e.htm; UNCTAD, *World Investment Report 2003*, www.unctad.org/Templates/webflyer.asp?docid = 3785&intItemID = 2412&lang = 1& mode = downloads.

2. In addition to the state, families and nonprofit organizations provide secondary income. These types of transfers are generally minor and negligible in aggregate terms. See Frances Stewart and Albert Berry, "Globalization, Liberalization, and Inequality: Real Causes," *Challenge* 43, no. 1 (2000): 44–92.

3. John Torpey, *The Invention of the Passport: Surveillance, Citizenship, and the State* (New York: Cambridge University Press, 2000).

4. J. Mohan Rao, "Openness, Inequality and Poverty" (background paper prepared for the *Human Development Report, 1999* [New York: UNDP, 1998]).

5. The model was originally developed by two Swedish economists, Eli Heckscher and his student Bertil Ohlin, in the 1920s. Many elaborations of the model were provided by Paul Samuelson after the 1930s and thus the model is sometimes referred to as the Heckscher-Ohlin-Samuelson (HOS) model. For a brief introduction, see Steven M. Suranovic, *International Trade Theory and Policy*, chap. 60: "The Heckscher-Ohlin (Factor Proportions) Model," http://internationalecon.com/v1.0/ch60/60c010.html.

6. Bin Xu, "Globalization and Rising Income Inequality: Implications for China," http://bear.cba.ufl.edu/centers/ciber/workingpapers/xuchina.pdf.

7. Amitava Krishna Dutt and J. Mohan Rao, *Globalization and Its Social Discontents: The Case of India*, Working Paper 16 (Center for Economic Policy Analysis, 2000).

8. Geoffrey Garrett, "The Distributive Consequences of Globalization" (manuscript, Yale University, 2001).

9. Peter H. Lindert and Jeffrey G. Williamson, *Does Globalization Make the World More Unequal?* NBER Working Paper 8228 (2001).

10. Stewart and Berry, "Globalization, Liberalization, and Inequality," 79–81.

11. Stewart and Berry, "Globalization, Liberalization, and Inequality," 53–54.

12. Richard Higgott, "Economics, Politics, and (International) Political Economy: The Need for a Balanced Diet in an Era of Globalization," *New Political Economy* 4, no. 1 (1999): 23–36.

13. Sven Steinmo, "The End of Redistribution? International Pressures and Domestic Policy Choices," *Challenge* 37, no. 6 (1994): 9–18; Sven Steinmo, "The New Political Economy of Taxation: International Pressures and Domestic Policy Choices" (paper, University of Colorado, 1999); Duane Swank, "Funding the Welfare State: Globalization and the Taxation of Business in Advanced Market Economies," *Political Studies* 46, no. 4 (1998): 671–692; Geoffrey Garrett, "Trade, Capital Mobility, and Government Spending around the World"

(paper, Yale University, 1999); J. Mohan Rao, "Globalization and the Fiscal Autonomy of the State" (manuscript, University of Massachusetts–Amherst, 1999).

14. Garrett, "Trade, Capital Mobility, and Government Spending," 5–6.

15. See note 7 above.

16. Ramkishen S. Rajan, "Economic Globalization and Asia: Trade, Finance, and Taxation" (paper prepared as an introduction to a special issue of *ASEAN Economic Bulletin*, January 2001).

17. Using a data set that contains information about 125 countries, Dani Rodrik finds a positive correlation between an economy's exposure to international trade and the size of its government. Moreover, the correlation holds not only in OECD (democratic) countries but also in developing (nondemocratic) countries. See Rodrik, "Why Do More Open Economies Have Bigger Governments?" *Journal of Political Economy*, October 1998, 997–1032. Using different data sets, Geoffrey Garrett confirms this finding in "Globalization and Government Spending around the World (paper, Yale University, July 2000). Both researches suggest that the compensation perspective under globalization is just as accurate in nondemocratic as in democratic countries.

18. Dani Rodrik, "Where Did All the Growth Go? External Shocks, Social Conflict, and Growth Collapses," *Journal of Economic Growth*, December 1999, 358–412. Also see Alberto Alesina and Roberto Perotti, "Income Distribution, Political Instability, and Investment," *European Economic Review*, June 1996, 1202–1229; and Alberto Alesina, Sule Ozler, Nouriel Roubini, and Philip Swagel, "Political Instability and Economic Growth," *Journal of Economic Growth*, June 1996, 189–213.

19. Ethan B. Kapstein, "Winners and Losers in the Global Economy," *International Organization* 54, no. 2 (2000): 359–384; Steinmo, "The End of Redistribution?"; Swank, "Funding the Welfare State"; Garrett, "Trade, Capital Mobility and Government Spending"; Higgott, "Economics, Politics and (International) Political Economy"; Lindert and Williamson, "Does Globalization Make the World More Unequal?"; and Garrett, "The Distributive Consequences of Globalization."

20. This method is problematic because the government embarked on not only external liberalization but also reforms of domestic institutions and policies. Given that the distributional outcomes are affected by many contemporaneous changes, it would seem impossible to attribute the trend in income distribution solely to policy changes affecting external economic relations. Here I do not intend to isolate the effects of external policy changes because of the close relationship between external and domestic policy changes.

21. Theoretically, it is possible for two perfectly open economies neither to trade with each other nor to export/import capital to/from each other if they are identical and have no transportation costs or economies of scale. In the real world, however, no two economies are identical. Thus trade flows and FDI flows have been widely used to gauge the degree of openness.

22. J. Mohan Rao, *Development in the Time of Globalization*, UNDP Working Paper Series, February 1998, 7.

23. World Trade Organization (WTO), *International Trade Statistics 2003*, map 3, www .wto.org/english/res_e/statis_e/its2003_e/world_maps_e.htm. Also see Azizur Rahman Khan, "Globalization, Employment, and Equity: The China Experience" (paper, International Labor Organization, 1996), www.ilo.org/public/english/region/asro/bangkok/paper/glo_chn .htm.

24. Before Deng Xiaoping's famous southern trip in 1992, foreign capital in China, being subject to all sorts of policy restrictions, was not quite footloose and could not easily take the exit option. This may explain why FDI flows were relatively small at the time (see figure 9.1).

25. During this period there were moments when the game looked to be zero-sum. For instance, reports held that in 1988 more than one-third of urban households experienced declines in real income. That was one reason why millions of Chinese took to the streets in the early summer of 1989. See Wang Shaoguang, "Deng Xiaoping's Reform and the Chinese Workers' Participation in the Protest Movement of 1989," in Paul Zarembka, ed., *Research in Political Economy* 13 (1992): 163–197.

26. Fan Ping, "Shichanghua guochengzhong de zhongguo nongcun he nongmin" [Chinese countryside and farmers in the course of marketization], in *Shehui lanpishu: Zhongguo shehui xingshi fenxi yu yuce* [Social bluebook: Analyses and forecast of the social situation in China], ed. Ru Xin et al. (Beijing: Shehui kexue wenxian chubanshe, 2000), 371–387.

27. Lu Li, "Suzhou qianhu nongmin shouru qingkuang de diaocha baogao" [Investigation report on the income of a thousand rural households in Suzhou], http://big5.xinhuanet.com/gate/big5/news.xinhuanet.com/zonghe/2001-10/11/content_75957.htm.

28. There have been countless news reports with regard to falling income for grain producers since the end of the 1990s. That is why the Chinese government has recently given priority to "boosting farmers' income" *(nongmin zengshou).*

29. Azizur Rahman Khan and Carl Riskin, "Income and Inequality in China: Composition, Distribution, and Growth of Household Income, 1988–1995," *China Quarterly* 154 (1998): 221–253.

30. State Statistical Bureau, *China Statistical Abstract 2003* (Beijing: China Statistical Press, 2003), 104.

31. For instance, in the second half of the 1990s, China adopted a host of urban reforms (e.g., pension, medical, housing, unemployment, education, and the like), all of which required residents to make more contributions or higher payments. Whatever their long-term effects may be, such reforms tend to lower people's current disposable income.

32. See Zhu Qingfang, "1996–1997 nian renmin shenghuo zhuangkuang" [People's living conditions in 1996–1997], in *Shehui lanpishu: Zhongguo shehui xingshi fenxi yu yuce 1996-1997* [Social bluebook: Analyses and forecast of the social situation in China, 1996–1997], ed. Jiang Liu et al. (Beijing: Zhongguo shehui kexue chubanshe, 1997), 131.

33. See Jiang Liu et al., "1997–1998 nian zhongguo shehui xingshi fenxi yu yuce zongbaogao" [Summary report on analyses and forecast of the social situation in China], in *Shehui lanpishu: Zhongguo shehui xingshi fenxi yu yuce 1998* [Social bluebook: Analyses and forecast of the social situation in China, 1998], ed. Ru Xin et al. (Beijing: Shehui kexue wenxian chubanshe, 1998), 9.

34. For a thorough discussion of regional disparities in China, see Wang Shaoguang and Hu Angang, *The Political Economy of Uneven Development: The Case of China* (Armonk, NY: Sharpe, 1999).

35. Khan, "Globalization, Employment, and Equity."

36. Shujie Yao, "Economic Growth, Income Inequality, and Poverty in China under Economic Reforms," *Journal of Development Studies* 35, no. 6 (1999): 104–130.

37. Inequalities in rural and urban areas have risen substantially, especially in the past few years. Compared to those of other countries, however, such inequalities in China are not very large.

38. Khan, "Globalization, Employment, and Equity."

39. Khan, "Globalization, Employment, and Equity." Also see Wang and Hu, *Political Economy of Uneven Development*, 155–162, 174–183.

40. Khan, "Globalization, Employment, and Equity."

41. Xu, "Globalization and Rising Income Inequality."

42. Xueguang Zhou, "Economic Transformation and Income Inequality in Urban China: Evidence from Panel Data," *American Journal of Sociology* 105, no. 4 (2000): 1135–1174.

43. Khan and Riskin, "Income and Inequality in China," 253.

44. Isabelle Grunberg, "Double Jeopardy: Globalization, Liberalization, and the Fiscal Squeeze," *World Development* 26, no. 4 (1998): 591–605.

45. Kapstein, "Winners and Losers in the Global Economy," 376–380.

46. Howell H. Zee, "Empirics of Cross-country Tax Revenue Compositions," *World Development* 24, no. 10 (1996): 1659–1671.

47. Tanzi and Zee hold that "in theory consumption can be taxed on the same graduated basis as income, by allowing unlimited deductions from income of savings. However, such a tax is likely to pose tremendous administrative difficulties in most developing countries, as net savings during a tax period eligible for deduction must be tracked and reported to the tax authorities." See Vito Tanzi and Howell H. Zee, "Tax Policy for Emerging Markets: Developing Countries," *National Tax Journal* 53, no. 2 (2000): 306. Two countries that experimented with this tax about forty years ago (India and Sri Lanka) abandoned it soon after its introduction.

48. Before 1980, neither state-owned nor collective-owned enterprises were subject to corporate income taxes. They simply remitted some portion of their profits to the government. China began to experiment with a "tax for profit" *(ligaishui)* idea in some 600 state-owned enterprises in 1980. Beginning from 1983, the reform was gradually extended to all SOEs. Afterward, state- and collective-owned enterprises were required to pay corporate income taxes but were allowed to retain part or all of their after-tax profits. See Xiang Huaicheng and Jiang Weizhuang, eds., *Zhongguo gaige quanshu: Caizheng tizhigaige juan* [Complete book on China reform: Volume on public finance] (Dalian: Dalian chubanshe, 1992), 16–25.

49. Kenny Z. Lin, "Income Taxation and Foreign Direct Investment in China," *International Tax Journal* 25, no. 2 (1999): 78–91.

50. International Taxation Research Council, *Zhongguo jiaru WTO yu shuishou gaige* [China's entry to the WTO and its taxation reform] (Beijing: Zhongguo shuiwu chubanshe, 2000), 36.

51. According to an estimate made in late 2003, the average effective rate of corporate income tax was 25 percent for domestic firms and 13 percent for foreign firms. See *Zhongguo zhengjuan bao* [China Securities Daily], November 25, 2003.

52. The government's total revenue from all types of agricultural taxes only amounted to ¥50 billion in the same year. See State Statistical Bureau, *China Statistical Abstract 2003* (Beijing: China Statistical Press, 2003), 66.

53. Zee, "Empirics of Cross-country Tax Revenue Compositions," 1662.

54. Of course, reduced tariffs may increase real wages by lowering prices on imported goods. However, it is the wealthy who are most likely to benefit from such price changes because the poor rely less on imports.

55. In figure 9.9, the effective rates of personal income tax are derived from two sets of data on urban residents' income: total income and disposable income. China's State Statistical

Bureau defines the latter as "total income minus income tax." The difference between the two, then, should be the amount of income tax. In China, the legal exemption to personal income tax is ¥800 per month. Although the monthly salaries of the bottom quintile are on average lower than ¥800, this group may have to pay tax if their incomes exceed ¥800 in any month (e.g., at the end of year when they receive annual bonuses). Before 2001, even laid-off workers' settlement proceeds were subject to personal income tax in some cities.

56. Rural residents do not have to pay personal income tax. However, nearly all of them are subject to agricultural taxes as well as legal and illegal fees and charges. In many areas, especially in central China, villages often lump together all levies and equally divide the total to each and every household. Consequently, regardless of income level, all households have to assume some kind of poll tax, which is, by definition, regressively distributed. The effective rates of such rural poll taxes are believed to be much higher than those of urban personal income tax. See Xiang Lin and Li Shi, "Shouru fenpei geju de xinbianhua" [Latest trends in income distribution], in *Shehui lanpishu: Zhongguo shehui xingshi fenxi yu yuce* [Social bluebook: Analyses and forecast of the social situation in China], ed. Ru Xin et al. (Beijing: Shehui kexue wenxian chubanshe, 2001), 147.

57. Estimates hold that the size of China's informal sector is equivalent to about 25–30 percent of its GDP. See Huang Weiding, *Zhongguo yinxing jingji* [China's invisible economy] (Beijing: Zhongguo shangye chubanshe, 1996).

58. According to Prime Minister Zhu Rongji, among the Chinese millionaires listed by *Fortune* and *Asia Week*, few have paid personal income tax (personal communication with a Chinese scholar who attended a meeting chaired by Zhu on June 24, 2002).

59. Specifically, transfer payments cover three broad categories of expenditures in the Chinese budget: "expenditures on pensions and social welfare," "supplementary expenditures on social security," and "special funds for social security." The latter two were not institutionalized until 1998.

60. Lixin Colin Xu and Heng-fu Zou, "Explaining the Changes of Income Distribution in China," *China Economic Review* 11 (2000): 149–170.

61. Nicholas R. Lardy, "Regional Growth and Income Distribution in China," in *China's Development Experience in Comparative Perspective*, ed. Robert F. Dernberger (Cambridge, MA: Harvard University Press, 1980), 172–193.

62. Shaoguang Wang, "China's 1994 Fiscal Reform: An Initial Assessment," *Asian Survey*, September 1997, 801–817.

63. For a detailed discussion about the decline of central redistributive capacity, see Wang and Hu, *Political Economy of Uneven Development*, 189–190.

64. For an explanation of how the "returned revenue" for each province was calculated, see Wang, "China's 1994 Fiscal Reform."

65. For a discussion of other types of intergovernmental transfers, see Shaoguang Wang, "For National Unity: The Political Logic of Fiscal Transfer in China," in *Nationalism, Democracy, and National Integration in China*, ed. Leong H. Liew and Shaoguang Wang (London: RoutledgeCurzon, 2004), 221–246.

66. Criticism of the central government's pro-coastal bias emerged as early as 1990. The annual sessions of the National People's Congress provided representatives from interior provinces, especially those from the west, with opportunities to pour out their grievances against Beijing's bias. In 1994, even a report by the State Planning Commission sounded the serious warning that if problems caused by growing regional gaps were not settled properly,

they might one day become a threat to China's social stability and national unity. Facing growing pressure from interior provinces, the central government finally decided to reverse its coastal development strategy in 1995. The new guiding principle was to "create conditions for gradually narrowing regional gaps." This principle was embodied in China's ninth five-year plan (1996–2000), which promised to increase central support to the less developed regions in the central and western parts of the country. For a discussion about the policy shift, see Wang and Hu, *Political Economy of Uneven Development*, 174–183.

67. Ministry of Finance, *Zhongguo caizheng nianjian* [China financial yearbook] (Beijing: Zhongguo caizheng jingji chubanshe, 1999).

68. For a concise explanation of the term "Washington consensus," see www.cid.harvard .edu/cidtrade/issues/washington.html.

69. China has suffered a string of increasingly violent protests in recent years by both workers and peasants who are angry about mass unemployment, illegal levies, and poor working conditions.

70. Wang Shaoguang, Hu Angang, and Ding Yuanzhu, "Jingji fanrong beihou de shehui buwending" [Social instability behind economic prosperity], *Zhanluan yu guanli* [Strategy and Management] 3 (2002): 26–33.

71. Linda Weiss, *The Myth of the Powerless State* (Ithaca, NY: Cornell University Press, 1998), 4–11.

72. David R. Cameron, "The Expansion of the Public Economy: A Comparative Analysis," *American Political Science Review* 72 (1978): 1243–1261; Peter J. Katzenstein, *Small States in World Markets: Industrial Policy in Europe* (Ithaca, NY: Cornell University Press, 1985).

73. Dennis Quinn, "The Correlates of Changes in International Financial Regulation," *American Political Science Review* 91 (1997): 531–552; Rodrik, "Why Do More Open Economies Have Bigger Governments?"; and Garrett, "Distributive Consequences of Globalization."

74. Higgott, "Economics, Politics, and (International) Political Economy," 33.

75. Rodrik, "Why Do More Open Economies Have Bigger Governments?"

76. Wang Shaoguang, "Greater Openness, Distributive Conflicts, and Social Insurance: The Social and Political Implications of China's WTO Membership," *Journal of Contemporary China* 9, no. 25 (2000): 373–405.

IV

CHANGING PUBLIC SPHERE

10

Negotiating the State

The Development of Social Organizations in China

TONY SAICH

One notable feature of the reform program sponsored by the Chinese Communist Party (CCP) has been the expansion of social organizations.[1] With greater social space created by the reforms and with the state unable or unwilling to carry the same wide range of services and functions as before, social organizations with varying degrees of autonomy from the party-state structures have been set up. They have been allowed or have created an increased organizational sphere and social space in which to operate, and to represent social interests, and to convey those interests into the policy-making process. They not only liaise between state and society but also fulfill vital welfare functions that would otherwise go unserved.

Most analyses of the resultant state–society relationship have concentrated on the capacity of party and state organizations to organize and compartmentalize society to frustrate genuine organizational pluralism. The focus has been on top-down control and the binding of organizations into various forms of state patronage. Thus, many analysts have eschewed the idea of an extant civil society in China, although some point to its possible emergence, and instead have provided various tunes on the theme of corporatism to explain state–society relations. This line of analysis seeks to explain how the pluralizing socioeconomic changes induced by market reforms coexist with the continued dominance of the party-state.[2] The opening up of social space can be examined while explaining continued party-state control through indirect mechanisms of coordination and cooptation.

However, exclusive focus on "state-dominant" theories, and even the more "society-informed" concepts of social corporatism or a state-led civil society, risk obscuring the dynamics of change in China and the capacity of the coopted groups to influence the policy-making process or to pursue the interests of their members.[3] First, while the state appears to exert extensive formal control, its capacity to realize this control is increasingly limited. There is a significant gap between rhetoric and practice and between the expressed intent of the party-state authorities, a system that is itself deeply conflicted, and what can actually be enforced for any significant period of time throughout the entire country. Second, such a focus can neglect the benefits the "subordinate" organizations and their members derive from the institutional arrangements. The interrelationships are symbiotic rather than unidirectional. Third, these relationships are symbiotic because social organizations have devised strategies to negotiate with the state a relationship that maximizes their members' interests or that circumvents or deflects state intrusion.

A study of the social organization sector sheds light on these aspects and the complex interplay between the party-state and society.[4] Structures and regulations exist to bind these organizations to state patronage and control their activities. However, social practice reveals a pattern of negotiation that minimizes state penetration and allows such organizations to reconfigure the relationship with the state in more beneficial terms that can allow for policy input or pursuit of members' interests and organizational goals. This chapter reviews the state's strategy for a traditional Leninist reordering of the sector and the strategies of negotiation, evasion, or feigned compliance of the social organizations, and concludes with some comments on the nature of state–society relations in contemporary China.

LENINIST STRATEGIES FOR CONTROL

The social organizations that have been established run across the whole spectrum from the China Family Planning Association, which was set up by the government Family Planning Commission to receive foreign donor funding, to a group such as Friends of Nature that operates as freely as one can in the field of environmental education. Naturally the further one moves along the spectrum of party-state sponsorship toward autonomy, the more vulnerable the group is in terms of administrative interference.

By the end of 2002, there were some 133,357 registered social organizations, defined as community entities composed of a certain social group with common intention, desires, and interests.[5] This is an 18 percent drop from the 1996 high of 184,821 social organizations, of which 1,845 were national-level organizations (1,712 in 1998).[6] This drop was caused by an extensive review of registered organizations in the late 1990s that led many to lose their official registration. In addition, there are 700,000 civilian nonprofit institutions, which are set up by enterprises, social groups, or individuals to provide nonprofit social services.[7] This article is concerned with the smaller group of organizations.

While there is an increasing acceptance of the social organization sector and its further development, senior CCP leaders have made it clear that this is no free-for-all for society to organize itself to articulate its interests. Rather they prefer that the sector be developed within a highly restrictive legislative and organizational framework that ensures CCP and state control. The reasons for this are twofold: the party's Leninist organizational predisposition and the current phase of reforms that will shrink the role of the state in people's lives even further.

Since the 1980s the state has tried to influence key groups in society by binding them into organizations that become dependent on patronage. To head off potential mass opposition, the state will attempt to extend its organization, coordination, and supervision of as much of the population as possible. This is evident in the strategies for control over the social organizations. This move by the state from insulation from society to integration within it can be interpreted as an attempt to prevent a plurality of definitions arising by revising the structure of the regime and the state's relationship to society. In this sense, the state moves to accommodate the increasingly wide range of articulate audiences to thwart or limit the possibility of political–ideological definitions arising. However, it imports varied social interests into the state and, of course, the party. It opens up the party and state to greater influence from society than before and imports fault lines of conflict in society into the state and party.

The natural Leninist tendency to thwart organizational plurality is compounded by the fear of potential for social unrest and the opposition that the reforms have created. There has been a consistent fear that social organizations might become covers for groups engaging in political activities or to represent the interests of disgruntled workers and/or peasants. The phenomenon of Solidarity in Poland remains a very powerful image to many of China's leaders as they grapple with the far-reaching economic reforms and this was reinforced by the fall of Suharto in Indonesia following street demonstrations. Throughout China, a number of underground workers groups have sprung up with names such as the Antihunger League and the Antiunemployment Group. Strikes, go-slows, sit-ins, and rural unrest have become a feature of daily life. Finally, the senior leadership was shocked by the sudden appearance of some 10,000 supporters of the Falun Gong who surrounded the party headquarters in Zhongnanhai and woke up senior leaders for the potential of such faith-based movements to inspire loyalty.[8] This concern and the humiliation that senior leaders felt at being caught by surprise led to the draconian crackdown on the organization, its ban, and the subsequent campaign to discredit the organization. Some senior leaders fear that the vagueness of previous legislation and its lax implementation have allowed suspect groups to register at sporting or cultural events to escape detection and some officially registered groups are said to have linked with dissident and underground religious movements.

Reforms have reduced the intrusive role of the state and have created far greater sponsor social differentiation. With individuals taking greater responsibility for finding their own work and housing, having more individual responsibility for social security and pensions, and becoming consumers in an increasingly marketized economy, they will wish to have a greater political voice, accountability over officialdom, and develop new organizations to fulfill their desires and objectives.

Essentially the CCP is left with a fundamental dilemma. Continued rapid economic growth is deemed vital to party survival but this will entail further layoffs, downsizing of the government bureaucracy, and the shedding of more government functions. This creates the need to expand the social organization sector to take on these functions on behalf of society or the likelihood of social instability and unrest will increase. Pluralism of service delivery is now a fact of life with voluntary organizations supplementing the state in providing basic services and with private institutions in health and education expanding. With many local governments strapped for cash, the nongovernmental organization (NGO) sector is taking on many functions that are being shed. At the same time, however, the party's Leninist predisposition makes it wary, at best, and hostile, at worst, to any organization that functions outside of its direct or indirect control.

Recognition of the necessity of the further development of social organizations received a boost at the Fifteenth Party Congress (1997) and the sector has slowly consolidated since. In his speech to the Fifteenth Party Congress, Jiang Zemin stressed the need to "cultivate and develop" what he termed "social intermediary organizations" as the reforms progressed.[9] Jiang recognized that the key to unlocking the problem of state enterprise reform was the provision of adequate social security coverage, especially for pensions, and restructuring medical and unemployment insurance. The shift of these burdens away from state-run enterprises inevitably requires an expansion of the social organization sector.

The plan for restructuring the State Council that was passed at the First Session of the Ninth Congress (1998) stated that many functions appropriated by government organs be given back to society and handled by new social intermediary organizations. The plan mentioned several times the important role that such organizations could play and Luo Gan, then State Councilor and secretary general of the State Council, complained that the government had taken on too much work that could be handled better by social intermediary organizations. This would allow the government to concentrate better on its core functions.[10]

Subsequently, more ground has been marked out for such organizations to develop. In a major departure from past practice, the current ten-year plan for poverty alleviation explicitly states that NGOs be brought on board to help implement government development projects in poor areas.[11] This trend has been continued under the new leadership of General Secretary Hu Jintao and Premier Wen Jiabao, especially in light of their concern to help those who have not benefited so well from the reforms. In 2004, Premier Wen Jiabao vowed to turn over responsibility for more activities the government should not be engaged in to enterprises, NGOs, and intermediary organizations.[12]

Recognition of the need to expand the sector brought back to the fore the need to tighten regulation.[13] As a result, officials were instructed to push ahead quickly to complete the Regulations on the Registration and Management of Social Organizations, and the State Council approved them in September 1998. The speed took many observers by surprise as severe differences of opinion about the level of control by the state over social organizations had held up the drafting process. The slow progress was also hampered by the fact that noneconomic regulation is not usually accorded high priority in the legislative process.

The regulations provide a clear example of the attempt to incorporate social organizations more closely with existing party-state structures.[14] There are several key features of the legislation that are important for a traditional Leninist reordering of the social organization sector. First, all social organizations must find a professional management unit *(yewu zhuguan danwei)* that will act as the sponsor, and is usually referred to as the sponsoring unit *(guakao danwei)* or "mother-in-law" in Chinese. After finding the sponsor and gaining its approval, the paperwork for the social organization is sent to the Ministry of Civil Affairs or its relevant department (referred to in the regulations as the registration management agency, *dengji guanli jiguan*). This sets up a two-tier registration system where affiliation precedes registration. In comparison with the 1989 provisional regulations, the regulations specified for the first time the role of the sponsoring institution and also raised the requirements, time, and steps necessary for registration.[15] The fact that the 1989 regulations did not outline the details of the duties of the sponsor meant that many social organizations operated in practice with no or minimal interference from the sponsor. The sponsor is expected to examine whether the social organization corresponds to an actual need and will not overlap with other organizations and that its members have the capacity to run the organization. In addition, the sponsor should ensure that the social organization abides by the law and the sponsor is held responsible for the actions of the social organization. Prior to the application to begin preparatory work, the sponsor is responsible for all reviews of the work and it is the responsibility of the sponsor to apply to the relevant department of the Ministry of Civil Affairs for registering the social organization to carry out preparatory work (Articles 9, 10, and 28).

If rejected at any stage, there is no right of appeal and it remains unclear that if a potential sponsor rejects an application, the social organization is free to look for another sponsoring organization. However, in practice, rejection by one organ makes it very difficult to seek approval from another. For example, in the social sciences only the Chinese Academy of Social Sciences may register organizations. However, the academy has been swamped with applicants and does not have the time to review them properly. This leads to insiders having the best chance of registration, while many others will be rejected. Once rejected by the academy it is virtually impossible to find another sponsoring organization. This is what happened to the Chinese Union of Economic Societies that was rejected by the academy for, essentially, reasons of internal academy politics. Each subsequent sponsor it approached rejected it on the grounds that the academy was entrusted to sponsor organizations in the field of social sciences. As a result, the union continued its activities on an informal basis.[16]

This need for a sponsoring organization and its role was the key bone of contention in the drafting of the new regulations and it has remained so since. Reformers proposed eliminating the sponsoring agency and simply requiring registration directly with the Ministry of Civil Affairs. Those who wish to loosen controls have used utilitarian arguments to gain support across the various ministries. They have argued that the sponsorship system forms a burden that costs much time, cannot be maintained properly, and probably would only detect a problem after an organization was found by the police or security authorities to have stepped out of line.[17] They have argued quite simply that the sponsors do not have the capacity to deal with the obligations. This kind of argumentation was persuasive to many ministries and potential sponsor agencies. As a result, an earlier draft that was submitted to the State Council for review abolished the need for the sponsoring organization proposing that social organizations just register with the relevant department of the Ministry of Civil Affairs directly. However, powerful figures such as Luo Gan, were opposed to any relaxation of controls. On seeing the draft, Luo is said to have become very angry and declared that the purpose of the new regulations was to tighten not loosen control over social organizations.[18]

Disagreement has rumbled on and in October 2004 the deputy head of the NGO registration service center under the Ministry of Civil Affairs stated that direct registration would come eventually. This has been a consistent position of the Ministry's in part because of their better understanding of social realities but also because it would strengthen their institutional position. However, they are a relatively weak player and have been consistently overruled by senior party officials in the State Council. The latest example is with the drafting of the Regulations for Registration and Management of Foundations (June 2004). Earlier drafts excluded the need for an intermediary government sponsor but again this was finally rejected.[19]

Secondly, "similar" organizations are not allowed to coexist at the various administrative levels. Thus there cannot be two national calligraphy associations or two national charity federations. This helps control representation to a smaller number of manageable units and has been used to deny registration for some groups. It ensures that the mass organizations such as the All-China Women's Federation and the All-China Federation of Trade Unions enjoy monopoly representation and cannot be challenged by independent groups seeking to represent the interests of women and workers. Conversely, some groups have rejected taking on such a monopoly of representation. For example, Liang Congjie and his Friends of Nature group after waiting ten months on their request for registration received a reply from the National Environment Protection Agency that it could only register if it would take on the responsibility for representing the interests of all the Chinese people sharing environmental concerns. Liang felt this too ambitious a goal and declined. He registered instead as a secondary organization in 1994 with the Academy of Chinese Culture where he is a professor and vice president.[20] It was established as a national level membership group.

Third, social organizations must register with the appropriate civil affairs department from the county level up. This makes it impossible for local groups to enroll members from different areas, thus limiting the potential for the spread of grassroots organizations that could develop national or horizontal representation. Thus, the China Charities Federation, the Ministry of Civil Affairs' own "social organization" for welfare had in 1998 fifty-nine local charity organizations as its institutional members but all are registered separately at the respective governmental levels.[21]

The regulations expressly prohibit national organizations from establishing any kind of regional branch (Article 19). Also, organization names are to reflect the activities and nature of the organization. Names that include China (Zhongguo or Zhonghua) or All-China (Quanguo) can only be approved in accordance with state regulations while under no circumstances can a locally registered social organization use such names (Article 10).

The total intent of this legislation is to mimic the compartmentalization of government departments and limit horizontal linkage. This favors those groups with close government ties and discourages bottom-up initiatives. It keeps people with different opinions on the same issue from setting up "opposing" interest groups. Other aspects of the regulations further hamper bottom-up initiatives or those by the disadvantaged and poorer sectors of society. The need to have substantial assets and the paperwork necessary to register will make it difficult for those groups that lack good connections and a relatively sophisticated organizational apparatus. This preference for large organizations and those close to government is also seen in the Public Welfare Donations Law (September 1999) and the Regulations of Foundations (June 2004).

In addition to the application of the regulations, the state has other means beyond cooptation to attempt control.[22] For groups the state sees as a threat or does not wish to see develop further it has adopted a number of tactics beyond cooptation. The first is outright repression and declaring the group illegal. This has been the case for a number of religious groups and those that appear to have a more political intent. However, groups closed down are not restricted to those engaged in political activities or establishing independent labor organizations. Over the years a number of organizations providing social welfare to groups not officially recognized as having needs have been shut down. For example, in 1993 a discussion club for homosexual men was shut down when its coordinator, Wang Yan, lost his job at the Ministry of Health. He was sacked for allegedly "advocating homosexuality and human rights" and the closure of the discussion group reflects official hostility to the issue of homosexuality in China.[23] Decisions can be idiosyncratic. In 1996, the first home for battered women that had been set up in Shanghai was closed down. One of the prime reasons was that it was improper for an individual to run such an institution rather than the government. The shelter had been set up with funding from a local businessman as an undertaking of his business enterprise. This shows the ambivalence of authorities to the role of both individuals and business in social welfare undertakings.[24] The local government did not take over responsibility for looking after the battered women.

In addition, a Public Security Bureau circular from the beginning of 1997 suggests that a number of administrative measures can be used to stop certain organizations from functioning effectively. The circular proposes three measures: have the sponsoring organization remove its support (this happened to the Women's Hotline in Beijing); pull them up on financial regulations (as with various groups in Shanghai); and identify key members and transfer them to state jobs where they will be too busy to engage in the work of the social organization (this was tried with the leadership of the *Rural Women Knowing All* group).

Finally, the CCP has reactivated the use of party cells within nonparty organizations to try to ensure control and monitoring. In early 1998, an internal circular called for the establishment of party cells in all social organizations and the strengthening of party work in those where a cell already existed. In fact, this circular was only a reminder of party policy. According to the CCP constitution, a cell should be established in all those organizations that have three or more members (Article 29). Where there are not enough members to establish a party cell, individual members are to link to the party cell or group of the sponsoring organization. Even where there is a party cell it is subordinated to the Party Committee of the sponsoring unit and will report to it and receive instructions and direction from it.

STRATEGIES OF NEGOTIATION
AND CIRCUMVENTION

The capacity of social organizations to evade such tight strictures and negotiate more beneficial relations with the state derives from two main factors. The first is the declining state capacity to implement policy consistently. The second is the strategies that the social organizations use either to evade control or to turn the relationship of state sponsorship more to their own advantage.

The state lacks the financial and human resources to implement policy effectively. Government revenue as a percentage of GDP declined to 10.78 percent in 1994 before reviving somewhat to 18 percent in 2002. At the same time "off-budget" revenues have been increasing and form a significant part of local government revenues. Successful resolution lies not only in increasing the tax base of the government, a solution explored by the World Bank and favored by the Chinese central government, or squeezing the rural poor through levies and fees, a strategy favored by many local authorities, but also a rethinking of the kinds of work in which the government should be engaged, its relationship to the local community, and acceptance that many functions previously managed by the local state in the field of social welfare and asset development will have to be taken on by the local communities themselves. In poor and remote communities where marketization has barely begun and where the scope of economic activities will always remain limited, local treasuries have little recourse other than the elimination of services. In general, the decision has been taken to downsize government, and social organizations set up by government departments are seen as a key provider of employment for laid-off government bureaucrats. The financial allocations to these newly formed social organizations will be reduced by one-third each year so that they will be financially independent of the originating government department after three years. Inevitably over time these organizations will develop an identity independent of the state and will become increasingly dependent on society and the business sector for funding.

Even where there is better fiscal buoyancy and a commitment to implement controls, it is questionable how consistently and for how long they can be applied. Human resources are scarce. For example, in the late 1990s the All-China Women's Federation was responsible for some 3,500 social organizations dealing with women's affairs. It seems inconceivable that they have the labor power to discharge their duties responsibly.

One of the most popular strategies for evasion was for a social organization to register as a business under the relevant industrial and commercial bureau. Registration as a business operation required a minimal management structure with a high degree of autonomy. However, the 1998 regulations closed off this method of registration as a commercial entity for social organizations as a commercial entity.[25] While the route of business registration has, in theory, been closed off, the most effective way for social organizations to evade restrictions has not. This method is to register as a "secondary organization." In this case, the organization only needs to secure approval from the agency that has accepted to bring it under its supervision. The organization merely deposits a file at the appropriate administrative level of civil affairs but this organ is not involved in monitoring, or auditing the group and does not require its host agency to submit any reports. Institutions of higher learning are the most popular choice given their generally more open and liberal leaderships. Organizations range from the university's own research centers that can operate more independently of direct Education Ministry scrutiny to centers that provide services to the public at large. An example of the latter is a walk-in legal services clinic for the disadvantaged based in Wuhan. In fact, it was the Hubei Civil Affairs Department that suggested this form of registration to the Center claiming it would "make things easier." Such organizations can simply withdraw into the shell of the university if the atmosphere becomes harsher or less accommodating.[26]

Another method is to register as a subsidiary organization within an essentially dormant social organization. An example of this is a very active family and sexual advice center in Beijing that operates under the moribund China Association of Social Workers. A more political example is that of Chen Ziming and Wang Juntao in the 1980s who were able to weave their way through the system to establish both an influential research institute and newspaper. The Beijing Social and Economic Sciences Institute had a strong political agenda and attained a high degree of financial and intellectual autonomy.[27] Administratively, the Institute was registered to the Talents Exchange Center of the State Science and Technology Commission and had been set up by Chen Ziming's sister in November 1986.[28] To obscure the activities of the institute, Chen and his colleagues then set up a number of subsidiary companies and cultural academic organizations. Activities were often conducted under these other organizations. In March 1988, the institute was able to take over a newspaper, the *Economics Weekly*. This newspaper had been founded in January 1982 and was the official newspaper of the Chinese Union of Economics Societies, representing 418 economic entities with over a million individual members.[29] After the takeover Chen Ziming acted as manager and Wang Juntao as deputy editor in chief. It became one of the most lively pro-reform publications in China.

Other groups do not bother with this burrowing strategy but simply do not register at all but organize an informal group. While technically illegal, there are many "clubs," "salons," and "forums" throughout urban China. In rural China, there has been the revival of traditional philanthropic practices that revolve around clans, kinship, and local place association.[30] Paradoxically, the more complex registration becomes, the more organizations are likely simply not to register. Obviously, it is impossible to know how many organizations are operating illegally but a 1996 report suggests around 20,000. This report cites other surveys from 1994 that suggest that Anhui had over 800 "illegal social organizations" and Hubei over 600, while in June 1995 only 13 of some 100 foundations in Yunnan were properly registered with the People's Bank of China.[31]

Last but not least, because this is still a system where personal relationships overlay the formal structures, some groups have been able to use their connections to register directly with civil affairs departments or have been able to receive the patronage of a sponsoring organization even if the proposed activities do not fit readily within its domain.[32] This is particularly prevalent at the local level and it is difficult to see the Regulations changing customary practice.

Many social organizations have also been effective in negotiating the state to influence the policy-making process or at least to bring key issues to the public domain. Three examples are noted here. The first is that of the China Family Planning Association, an organization set up by the State Family Planning Commission to operate as its NGO, what is referred to as a government-organized NGO (GONGO). The second is that of Friends of Nature, an environmental NGO that operates almost as freely as one can in this field. The third is a group of women activists gathered around the magazine *Rural Women Knowing All (Nongjia nu)*.

The China Family Planning Association has provided significant input into state policy innovation. It provides an interesting example of the extent to which GONGOs function in the traditional Leninist "transmission belt" framework and to what extent, by operating at one remove from government, they can open up social space and provide policy innovation. The association was set up by the State Family Planning Commission to bring in international funding from which the commission was blocked, in part by the hostility of the U.S. Congress, and to be a member of organizations such as the International Planned Parenthood Federation. While it is charged with promoting official family planning policy, the Association has become sensitized through its international contacts and grassroots policy experimentation to the needs of women and the inadequacies of the current methods of policy implementation. The association, particularly its local branches, has run a number of innovative projects on problems to do with sex education for young people, income generation for women, and public health education, and raising women's awareness about their rights. Through its pilot programs, the association has affected the government's approach to family planning and conducted experiments to shift from a target-driven, quota-based system of family planning to one that is more client driven, offering choice of contraception combined with education. This is reflected in the launch by the State Family Planning Commission in 1995 of experimentation in five rural counties with an approach to family planning called Improving Quality of Care. This project and its subsequent expansion have emphasized reorientation toward a reproductive, more client-centered family planning program.[33] In addition, the commission has not always been able to control the association entirely and the latter has begun to develop its own organizational identity and ethos. Attempts by the commission to place its own officials in key posts within the association have been resisted and have not always been successful.

Broadly speaking, those groups working in the field of education and environment have been permitted or have negotiated relatively freer space. Elizabeth Knup has noted with respect to managing environmental problems "it is here that rapid economic development—seen as desirable and essential—conflicts directly with other social needs which it finds difficult to address efficiently on its own."[34] Friends of Nature provides a good example of how effective an organization can be when it is run by an energetic, charismatic individual who has a powerful vision of what they wish to achieve. The fact that this individual is Liang Congjie, grandson of Liang Qichao, and has been a member of the Chinese People's Political Consultative Conference obviously helps.

Liang has been able to use his talents, connections, and political skill to steer Friends of Nature through a number of successes. In particular, his group was involved with the attempts to protect the habitat of the golden monkey that was being hacked away by illegal loggers in Yunnan. This was an issue that caught the attention of young people in Beijing and provided the possibility for Friends of Nature to engage in policy advocacy. Students at the forestry academy in Beijing and at other campuses began to hold candlelight vigils for the monkeys. This greatly worried not only the Beijing municipal authorities but also some central leaders. They were worried that the students' peaceful, candlelit vigils might turn to something more sinister but, at the same time, knew they could hardly break up the actions.[35] Friends of Nature began to mobilize public support for the monkey's cause and its members wrote letters and petitions to central leaders while mobilizing friends in the media to publicize the monkey's plight. The combination of social mobilization, media spotlight, and central leaders' fear of student action caused them to adopt decisions to reinforce the ban on illegal logging. Friends of Nature managed to extract a decision from the local authorities to ban the activities to preserve the golden monkey's habitat.[36]

The group of women activists gathered around the magazine *Rural Women Know-*

ing All has undertaken work ranging from sexual health of rural women, to hotlines for migrant women, to raising concerns about the high levels of suicide among young rural women. The effectiveness of this group comes not only from the social commitment of its members but also because a number of the key figures are senior members of the All-China Women's Federation. The key figure in the group is one of the chief editors of the *China Women's Daily (Zhongguo funu bao)*, the official organ of the federation. This has meant that the group can use the infrastructure and staff of the federation to publish their own journal specifically targeted at rural women and to ensure that important policy issues are taken up in the official newspaper. This means that such issues are immediately in the domain of key policy makers with respect to issues concerning women.

CONCLUSION

The examples given above reveal the increasing complexity of the relationship between state and society under the reforms and defy easy categorization. The problem of definition is compounded by the fact that we are trying to analyze a moving target, a state, and society in transition. We are dealing not only with the dynamics of the interaction and how this has changed over time but also with the changes within the state sector and society. What appears in one place or at one time as a predatory local state may evolve into one of social partnership later. We are also dealing with a country where multiple models of state–society relations may be operating at the same time. It is clear that the local state apparatus in Wenzhou, Zhejiang, with its privatized economy and multiple intermediary organizations operates in quite a different way from a neo-Maoist showcase on the North China plain that stresses collective and state organization. As Baum and Shevchenko have pointed out, there is considerable ideological confusion concerning the analysis of the state in China.[37] One can add that a field of study that was seriously undertheorized and parasitic in terms of the theory used is now seriously overtheorized and has begun to strain the imagination of creative word play.

As the example of social organizations shows, while social space has opened up, the state has continued to retain a great deal of its organizational power and has moved to dominate the space and reorganize the newly emergent organizations. Clearly, from these examples, China is far from creating a civil society as conventionally defined. Analyses that rely on some variant of corporatism capture well the top-down nature of control in the system and how citizens are integrated into vertical structures where elites will represent their perceived interests.

However, such explanations risk both obscuring important elements of change and oversimplifying the complexities of the dynamics and interaction. It can mean that researchers pay less attention to the benefits the subordinate organizations and their members derive. What are the attractions and benefits of participation or at least acquiescence with this process? The discussion of social organizations reveals that they can have considerable impact on the policy-making process, indeed more than if they were to try to create an organization with complete operational autonomy from the party-state. The interrelationships are symbiotic. Even for the more autonomous organizations, it would be foolish not to have strong party-state links. Those with close government links often play a more direct role in policy formulation than their counterparts in many other countries as they do not have to compete in social space with other NGOs for dominance and access to the government's ear on relevant policy issues.

Each social organization in China has negotiated with the state its own niche that derives from a complex interaction of institutional, economic, and individual factors. In some cases, the outcome may be a close "embedded" relationship with the state.[38] In others it may entail formal compliance while operating strategies of evasion and circumnavigation of the state. As the political scientist Kevin O'Brien has suggested, coopted groups become embedded over time in the system and through this process they acquire viability and legitimacy.[39] This study of social organizations suggests that it is not mere expediency that causes new social formations or organizations to tie their fortunes to the existing state structures, especially at the local level, but it is strategically optimal for them. It can enable them to manipulate the official and semiofficial institutions to their own advantage.

The study of social organizations also reveals the tensions inherent in a traditional Leninist party culture under the current development strategy. Many organizations have developed strategies to evade party and state controls and to turn the traditional "transmission belt" function to their own advantage. In addition, with the emphasis on economic development, and the shift in the party's fundamental legitimacy to its capacity to deliver the economic goods, the objectives of party and state are not always synonymous. The party needs to effect its policy intent through both mobilization of party members and organizations at all levels and the implementation and enforcement by state organs. Local governments in pursuit of local developmental goals may take policy options that at best conflict with party policy and at worst run counter to it. The party cannot count on state organs for automatic policy support. A good example is with the privatization of state-owned enterprises that is rife at the local level but is deeply contested at the center. Also, local governments will approve social organizations or other nonstate bodies that contribute to the local economy and well-being. This is irrespective of formal regulatory requirements. With a membership of around 60 million, the party itself is deeply conflicted over fundamental policy issues and visions of the future. This causes a tension between the party's traditional Leninist vanguard role and its other roles as an integrating mechanism and development agency. Last but not least it must be remembered that the party is made up of members who also form a part of the local community. Is the local party secretary who is also a shaman loyal to the party, the locality, his beliefs, or all of them? Does he import his social values into the party and if so to what effect, or are they discreet spheres of activity?[40]

Focusing on vertical integration and lines of administrative control while ignoring the way in which the relationship is negotiated ignores important horizontal relationships in society. As government downsizes further, citizens have greater responsibility for their own welfare, and more functions will be devolved to national and especially local social organizations, people will look more to the local provider of goods than the central party and state directives and regulations. This will become more important as the wealthy business class is given greater freedom over how they choose to dispose of their money.

As the historian Timothy Brook has noted, emphasis on the vertical "minimizes the capabilities and opportunities that people exercise regularly to communicate horizontally and form cooperative bodies."[41] He suggests that we should be more aware of "auto-organization" as a more cooperative principle of social integration at the local level. Certainly many new social organizations and loose groups are not registering with the authorities and local religious and traditional belief groups are flourishing. In the urban areas, native place is the main organizing principle for the migrant communities, many of which have set up their own governing and welfare structures outside of the state.[42]

Social scientists tend to dislike open-ended theories and seek to close down the range of options available for interpretation through a process of imposing order and logic. The notion of negotiating the state tries to do justice to the complexities of social reality in China. In the field of state–society relations, we need to develop explanations that allow for the shifting complexities of the current system and the institutional fluidity, ambiguity, and messiness that operates at all levels in China and that is most pronounced at the local level.

NOTES

I would like to thank Professor Richard Baum and Professor David Apter, for their comments on an earlier draft of this chapter, as well as two anonymous reviewers.

1. A literal translation of the Chinese term *shehui tuanti* is preferred here to the more usual English usage of nongovernmental organization (NGO). This includes both the more autonomous organizations and those set up by state agencies specifically to carry out social welfare functions. While NGO is used by some inside the community, it is clear that the restrictions surrounding their autonomy of action mean that in formal terms they are quite distinct from NGOs in the West. China has followed a number of other Asian countries in adopting restrictive legislation to control and shrink the social space available for such organizations.

2. See Richard Baum and Alexei Shevchenko, "The 'State of the State,'" in Merle Goldman and Roderick MacFarquhar, eds., *The Paradox of Reform of China's Post-Mao Reforms* (Cambridge, MA: Harvard University Press, 1999), 348. For one of the most extensive reviews of the potential for the emergence of civil society that is relevant to this chapter, see Gordon White, Jude Howell, and Shang Xiaoyuan, *In Search of Civil Society: Market Reform and Social Change in Contemporary China* (Oxford: Clarendon, 1996). For one of the most

enthusiastic Chinese accounts of the emergence of civil society, see Deng Zhenglai and Ding Yuejiang, "Building Civil Society in China," in *Zhongguo shehui kexue jikan* [Chinese Social Sciences Quarterly] 1 (1992). For an excellent analysis that uses corporatism, see Jonathan Unger and Anita Chan, "Corporatism in China: A Developmental State in an East Asian Context," in Barrett McCormick and Jonathan Unger, *China after Socialism: In the Footsteps of Eastern Europe or East Asia?* (Armonk, NY: Sharpe, 1996), 95–129.

3. The distinction between state and social corporatism is made in Philippe C. Schmitter, "Still the Century of Corporatism?" in Frederick B. Pike and Thomas Stritch, eds., *The New Corporatism* (Notre Dame, IN: University of Notre Dame Press, 1974). For an initial review of its application to China, see Yijiang Ding, "Corporatism and Civil Society in China: An Overview of the Debate in Recent Years," *China Information,* Spring 1998, 44–67. For the seeming contradiction in terms of a state-led civil society, see B. Michael Frolic, "State-led Civil Society," in Timothy Brook and B. Michael Frolic, eds., *Civil Society in China* (Armonk, NY: Sharpe, 1997).

4. The role of the CCP in analyzing state–society relations provides a complicating factor. Many writers choose the appellation "party-state" to circumvent this problem of analysis. Reforms have led to a more complex relationship, especially at the local level. This issue is returned to in the conclusion.

5. Ministry of Civil Affairs, *Zhongguo minzheng tongji nianjian 2003* [China civil affairs statistical yearbook] (Beijing: China Statistical Press, 2003), 132. Examples include professional associations, academic societies, research associations, and foundations.

6. Ministry of Civil Affairs, *Zhongguo minzheng tongji nianjian 2003*, 159.

7. Deng Guosheng, "New Environment for Development of NGOs in China," in NGO Research Center, ed., *The 500 NGOs in China* (Beijing: United Nations Center for Regional Development, 2002), 26. This category includes private schools, hospitals, community service centers, vocational training centers, research institutes, and recreational facilities. As of 2002 there were 1,268 registered foundations (Ministry of Civil Affairs, p. 160). The State Council adopted new regulations for social organizations on September 25, 1998, and new regulations for foundations came into effect in June 2004.

8. This provides an interesting example, as the Falun Gong was originally registered with the official China Qi Gong Science Research Society. The society decided that it was a Buddhist sect and consequently deregistered the organization in February 1997. Thus it had no linkage to the Ministry of Civil Affairs. Its members mobilized when an article critical of the group was published in Tianjin and when the rumor spread that the group would be declared illegal. Among its members were many senior retired cadres, especially from the military, and many women who believe that the exercise regime of the group will enhance their health.

9. Jiang Zemin, "Hold High the Great Banner of Deng Xiaoping Theory for an All Round Advancement of the Cause of Building Socialism with Chinese Characteristics into the Twenty-first Century," *Beijing Review,* October 6–12, 1997, 10–33. Neither journalistic nor academic reviews of the congress and Jiang's speech have paid attention to his comments on "social intermediary organizations."

10. Luo Gan, "Explanations on Plan for Institutional Restructuring of the State Council Delivered at the First Session of the Ninth People's Congress on 6 March 1998," *Ta Kung Pao,* March 7, 1998, B1–2, translated in FBIS-CHI 98-068, March 9, 1998.

11. State Council, "The Development-Oriented Poverty Reduction Programme for Rural China," Xinhua News Agency, October 15, 2001.

12. *China Daily*, March 13–14, 2004.

13. This formed part of a succession of attempts to reassert party and state control over business, society, and the localities that began after Jiang Zemin's speech entitled "More Talk about Politics" in October 1995. These attempts intensified in late 1996 after the Sixth Plenum of the Fourteenth CCP Central Committee adopted the resolution on the need to build a "socialist spiritual civilization."

14. These regulations retain the essential features of the provisional regulations adopted in 1989 after the student-led demonstrations but are more extensive and imply an attempt to control not only activities but also the number of social organizations. The initial response from foreign journalists and human rights organizations was uniformly critical of the controls these regulations place on the sector. See, for example, Human Rights in China, "Bound and Gagged: Freedom of Association in China Further Curtailed under New Regulations," November 13, 1998; Sophia Woodman, "Less Dressed Up as More? Promoting Non-Profit Organizations by Regulating Away Freedom of Association," *China Perspectives* 22 (1999): 17–27. Although the regulations clearly err on the side of state control, they also mark a significant step forward in terms of official recognition that the sector will play in China's future development. On their indispensability to future development, see the comments of Wei Jianxing, then member of the Standing Committee of the Politburo, to a State Council meeting on the new regulations held in November 1998. "Work Conference on Strengthening the Management of NGOs and Supporting Social Stability," *Xinhua*, Domestic Chinese Service, November 23, 1998.

15. The length of time before a social organization can actually carry out activities has been increased from thirty to ninety days.

16. Retired researcher from the Institute of Marxism-Leninism, Mao Zedong Thought, interview, summer 1996.

17. Senior Ministry of Civil Affairs, interview, October 1996.

18. Interview with senior officials from the Ministry of Civil Affairs involved in the legislative drafting process, September 1997.

19. Ministry of Civil Affairs official, interview, October 2004.

20. Liang Congjie, interview, April 1996.

21. Discussion with federation leaders, April 1998.

22. The state has decided to rely on administrative regulations issued by the State Council rather than a law passed by the National People's Congress. This gives the authorities greater flexibility in implementation and avoids an open-ended discussion of the role of this sector. This point is well made by Woodman, "Less Dressed Up as More?" 18.

23. Interviews with relevant personnel, October 1994.

24. Other reasons cited included unspecified "financial irregularities" and foreign and domestic media attention. Interviews in Shanghai, April 1996, and Human Rights in China, *China*, 19.

25. See also the related regulations "Minban feiqiye danwei dengji guanli zanxing tiaoli" [Provisional regulations on the registration and management of people-run non-enterprise units], in *Renmin ribao* (People's Daily), November 9, 1998.

26. Michaela Raab, *Non-Governmental Social Development Groups in China,* Ford Foundation Report, February 1997, p. 26.

27. The sources for this account are Gu Xin, "The Structural Transformation of the Intellectual Public Sphere in Communist China (1979–1989) (Ph.D. diss., University of Leiden,

1997); Merle Goldman, *Sowing the Seeds of Democracy in China: Political Reform in the Deng Xiaoping Era* (Cambridge, MA: Harvard University Press, 1994); Min Qi, discussions with author, 1995 and 1996.

28. Goldman, *Sowing the Seeds*, 66–77.

29. For the details of the takeover, see Gu Xin, *Structural Transformation*, 129–134.

30. Lily Tsai, "Cadres, Temple and Lineage Institutions, and Governance in Rural China," *China Journal*, July 2002.

31. Qi Hong, *Zhongguo shehui tuanti xianzhuang ji falu tiaozheng kuangjia* [The current situation and legal readjustment and framework for Chinese social organizations] (mimeo, 1996).

32. I have come across numerous examples of this in Beijing and Shanghai.

33. In 1997, four urban districts were added and one more rural county. Current estimates suggest that since 1997 over three hundred counties and districts have been selected as provincial pilots. *The Quality Project. Improving Quality of Care and Client Orientation in Reproductive Health/Family Planning Services in China* (Beijing: Ford Foundation, 1999), 7.

34. Elizabeth Knup, "Environmental NGOs in China: An Overview," *China Environment Series* (n.d.), 10.

35. Party secretaries at the institutions of higher education were instructed to monitor the situation carefully and resolve it swiftly.

36. See also Knup, "Environmental NGOs," 12; Seth Dunn, "Taking a Green Leap Forward," *Amicus Journal*, Winter 1997, 12–14.

37. Baum and Shevchenko, "State of the State," 333–334.

38. For use of the term "embedded," see Peter Evans, *Embedded Autonomy: States and Industrial Transformation* (Princeton, NJ: Princeton University Press, 1995).

39. Kevin J. O'Brien, "Chinese People's Congresses and Legislative Embeddedness," *Comparative Political Studies,* April 1994,101.

40. For an analysis of some of the inherent tensions in a Leninist regime, see Ken Jowitt, *New World Disorder: The Leninist Extinction* (Berkeley: University of California Press, 1992).

41. Timothy Brook, "Auto-Organization in Chinese Society," in Brook and Frolic eds., *Civil Society in China*, 23.

42. Xiang Biao, "How to Create a Visible 'Non-State Space' through Migration and Marketized Traditional Networks: An Account of a Migrant Community in China" (paper delivered to the International Conference on Chinese Rural Labor Force Migration, Beijing, June 1996).

11

The Internet and Civil Society in China

Coevolutionary Dynamics and Digital Formations

GUOBIN YANG

D oes the Internet contribute to China's democratization and civil society development? Answers to this question are typically ambivalent. The short history of the Internet and the lack of sufficient empirical evidence make it hard to spell out an unambiguous case. The ambivalence is also due to the way in which the research question is posed. Historically, technology has changed human societies and it is reasonable to ask what this new technology does to Chinese society today. Yet this is only one side of the coin. Technology is used by members of the society; its diffusion and use depend on social conditions. The conditions of society, in other words, shape technological development.

In this chapter, I ask instead, How do the Internet and civil society in China interact in ways that shape the development of both? To address this question, I will first discuss the developments of the Internet and civil society in China and analyze why the Internet matters for Chinese civil society and vice versa. I argue that Chinese civil society and the Internet energize each other in their coevolutionary development, even as both are constrained by other forces.[1] The Internet facilitates civil society activities by offering new possibilities for citizen participation. Civil society facilitates the development of the Internet by providing the necessary social basis—citizens and citizen groups—for communication and interaction. The Internet and civil society have an interdependent relationship, and yet current literature tends to

303

ignore this relationship and emphasize the unidirectional impact of technology on society.

The interactions between the Internet and civil society take multiple forms. Socially initiated interactions originate in the social world, whereas Internet-originated interactions begin in cyberspace. These interactions have led to two important types of digital formations, namely, virtual public spheres and web-based organizations.[2] The chapter illustrates these interactions and digital formations with empirical examples. The conclusion draws attention to the political challenges facing the coevolution of the Internet and Chinese civil society.

CHINESE CIVIL SOCIETY: INCIPIENT YET DYNAMIC

Civil society is here defined broadly as the intermediate public realm between the state and the private sphere. Citizens and citizen groups participate in organized or unorganized discursive or nondiscursive activities in civil society. This definition will include public sphere, voluntary organizations, and social movements as key components of civil society. Although some scholars have argued that there is no necessary and logical link between civil society and democracy, a robust civil society is often taken as a basis for democratic politics.[3] Many scholars have argued that contemporary Chinese civil society is incipient.[4] I suggest that the incipient nature of Chinese civil society is a favorable condition for the development of the Internet in China. An incipient civil society can be vulnerable but is dynamic. It absorbs new things quickly and is open to innovations. Organizational theory postulates that organizational inertia increases with age.[5] Although civil society does not consist of organizations only, social organizations are a central component.[6] The relative "young" age of Chinese civil society may thus mean that it is more responsive to technological change, especially those technologies that may meet its needs.

The incipient and dynamic character of Chinese civil society is evident at various levels. First, there has been an emerging rights consciousness related to the notion of citizenship rights. Several authors have documented this new trend, showing that while bureaucratic and economic power often encroach on citizen rights, more and more people have begun to use the legal system to defend and protect their rights.[7] This does not mean that China has developed a strong rule of law, but it does indicate that the notion of citizenship has become an increasingly important basis and goal of Chinese civil society development.

Second, there have been significant changes to China's public sphere. Studies of Chinese mass media have consistently revealed a tendency toward the loosening of political control and the parallel trend of commercialization, despite cautionary notes about the limits of political decentralization and the problems of commercialization.[8] Furthermore, as some scholars have argued, public spheres are not only to be found in the media in China, but also in a wide range of social spaces. Two recent volumes show that China's public sphere also resides in living room conversations, McDonald's restaurants, greeting cards, telephone hotlines, discos, and the like.[9] The consumer revolution in contemporary China has the unintended consequence of producing new social spaces for public expression and communication.

Third, social organizations also manifest an incipient yet dynamic character in China. Western and Chinese researchers alike have argued that although the state still maintains strong control, social organizations have not only grown in number but also enjoy more independence than before.[10] Even faced with strong state regulative challenges, social organizations have a lot of room to maneuver. As Tony Saich shows, they have strategies to bypass the government's strict registration policies, such as by registering as a business or as a secondary entity of an existing dormant organization.[11] While social organizations can often negotiate freer space within the system, even the Chinese government has recently called on China's social organizations to fulfill social functions as a "third force."[12]

In short, Chinese civil society is incipient yet dynamic. Its various elements are not well developed but are growing and transforming, providing favorable conditions for the diffusion of the Internet in China.

THE DEVELOPMENT OF THE INTERNET IN CHINA

Current debate on the development of the Internet in China revolves around two themes, political control and political impact. Studies of political control take the Internet as a dependent variable to be explained while works on political impact take the Internet as an independent variable. In their meticulous analysis of the multifarious ways of state control of the Internet and the creative uses of the Internet by dissident groups, Michael S. Chase and James C. Mulvenon argue that "the Internet . . . will probably not bring 'revolutionary' political change to China, but instead will be a key pillar of China's slower, evolutionary path toward increased pluralization and possibly even nascent democratization."[13] Another important study, by Eric Harwit and Duncan Clark, examines political control at the level of physical network and content.[14] They find that both the private sector and the Ministry of Information Industry (MII, the government ministry in charge of information industry) vie for control of the network infrastructure, not necessarily in order to maintain control over content, but to collect revenues and profits. Content control is in the hands of several other government and party organs. Yet for two reasons, content control remains "schizophrenic" and ineffective. First, the concerns of government agencies responsible for content control may conflict with the lucrative interests of MII and the private sector, thus making their job difficult. Second, much of China's Internet content is in private hands and some comes from foreign sources, which exacerbates the difficulty of control. As a result, political control tends to take the form of "killing the chicken to scare the monkeys," such as by occasionally arresting one or two violators.[15] Such a tactic induces self-censorship among users.

While studies of the political control of the Internet show who attempts to control what and how control is maintained and challenged, studies of the political impact of the Internet, though few in number, convey several mixed messages. First, there is some recognition that the diffusion of the Internet will challenge undemocratic state behavior and enhance pluralism.[16] Second, there is evidence that the Internet has important implications for China's public sphere, associational life, and political activism.[17] There are also cautionary tales about the limits of the Internet as a tool for political change. Kathleen Hartford, for example, suggests that "as Internet use and applications expand in China . . . we may well find that its greatest impact lies in intensifying existing social contradictions."[18] Some analysts have warned that the Internet may become a tool for the expansion of Chinese nationalism of both the popular and official types. Todd Munson's analysis of a Chinese tourism website shows how nationalism is "sold" online.[19] C. R. Hughes and Alan R. Kluver have both argued that the Internet may be used to promote nationalism rather than democracy.[20]

Current focus on the political control and impact of the Internet in China has opened key areas for research, yet such a focus has unnecessarily limited the scope of the research questions. Technological diffusion is not only shaped by political and economic factors, nor is the impact of technology confined to the political sphere and state behavior. Broader realms of social life may affect technological diffusion while being mediated by technologies. Social and technological processes may develop along parallel paths with mutual influences. From this perspective, it is crucial to examine how Chinese civil society shapes the development of the Internet, and vice versa.

WHY DOES THE INTERNET MATTER
FOR CHINESE CIVIL SOCIETY?

One way of understanding the significance of the Internet for Chinese civil society is to compare Internet use by civil society with two other areas: e-government and e-commerce. Both have been promoted by the Chinese government, yet they have developed at a rate far slower than, so to speak, China's e-civil society. Commentators have observed the slow development of e-commerce in China even while they are optimistic about its potential size and scope in the future.[21] Statistics published by the China Internet Network Information Center (CNNIC) indicate that although more and more people in China seem to be buying or making payments online, the percentage has remained very small over the years both in absolute and relative terms. In June 1999, 3.2 percent of respondents reported having shopped online, while 21.4 percent reported having used newsgroups and 28 percent having used bulletin boards. The numbers fluctuated, with a curious increase in online shopping up to 14.1 percent in June 2000, while the percentages of respondents who used newsgroups and bulletin boards in June 2000 are 25.4 percent and 21.2 percent respectively. The numbers for all three categories declined after June 2000 and rose again one year later, though still significantly more people reported having used newsgroups and bulletin boards than online shopping or online payment. Table 11.1 shows these numbers from June 1999 to July 2004. E-mail, which has consistently been the most frequently used network service, is added for comparative purposes.

The general pattern is clearly that China's users are more attracted to the social than commercial functions of the Internet. The drop in reported user preferences for newsgroups and bulletin boards in 2001 may have been due to government policies to promote e-commerce and discourage newsgroup and bulletin board activities, but even under conditions of tighter political control, many more people were engaged in online social and political activities than commercial activities.[22]

In January 1999, the Chinese government launched its Government Online project. Its goal is to increase administrative efficiency, reduce costs, and give citizens more access to government information. Within a year, China's gov.cn domain names had increased from 982 to 2,479. By December 2002, China had a total of 7,796 gov.cn domain names, accounting for 4.3 percent of all .cn domain names.[23] Although government websites have been on the increase, how effective they are as a means of providing information and encouraging public participation remains doubtful. Chinese journalists have complained that government websites are often inactive, outdated, or lacking useful information.[24] According to one study, even the website of Qingdao city, one of the top five e-government websites in China, had only about 1,500 hits a day as of December 2000.[25] In contrast, at roughly the same period, China's popular bulletin board *Qiangguo luntan* (Strengthening the Nation

Table 11.1. Most Frequently Used Network Services in China (Multiple Options), June 1999–June 2004 (in Percent)

	E-mail	Newsgroups	BBS	Online Shopping	Online Payment
June 1999	90.9	21.4	28.0	3.2	N/A
December 1999	71.7	17.0	16.3	7.8	1.8
June 2000	87.7	25.4	21.2	14.1	3.7
December 2000	87.7	19.3	16.7	12.5	2.7
June 2001	74.9	10.7	9.0	8.0	1.8
December 2001	92.2	13.4	9.8	7.8	2.1
June 2002	92.9	20.4	18.9	10.3	N/A
December 2002	92.6	21.3	18.9	11.5	N/A
June 2003	91.8	20.7	22.6	11.7	N/A
December 2003	88.4	N/A	18.8	7.3	N/A
June 2004	84.3	N/A	21.3	7.3	N/A

Source: CNNIC survey reports: July 1999, January 2000, July 2000, January 2001, July 2001, January 2002, July 2002, January 2003, July 2003, January 2004, July 2004. See www.cnnic.net.cn.

Forum, or QGLT) had about 100,000 hits and 1,000 posts daily.[26] Even a special- ized bulletin board like *Huaxia zhiqing luntan* (Forum for Chinese Educated Youth), which attracts mainly members of China's "educated youth" generation, had an average of 700 hits daily.[27]

Clearly civil society use of the Internet by far surpasses e-government and e-commerce at this stage. How to explain such disparities? Why could civil society sectors take better advantage of the Internet? In the case of e-government, a main problem lies with the government agencies that run their websites. There is simply too little information there. The slow development of e-commerce involves compli- cated factors, such as the lack of an effective legal framework and security concerns. To understand the relatively high level of Internet use by civil society sectors requires a historical understanding of the conditions of Chinese civil society and some knowledge of the technical features of the Internet.

There are many different descriptions of the technical features of the Internet. Jonathan Bach and David Stark capture them well with their emphasis on the Internet's capacity to "link, search, interact."[28] They explain that the telephone can be used to search for people, link them up so that they can interact, yet this process is only additive. On the Internet this process becomes multiplicative and recombina- tory, where each step—search, link, or interact—forms the basis for other steps. In explicating the political implications of this multiplicative interactive technology, Bach and Stark suggest that Internet use creates a space *for* something to happen as well as a space *within* which something happens, including new social bonds and new forms of organization. It is ideal "for lowering transaction costs, increasing par- ticipation and impact, and streamlining operations."[29]

Of course, the technical features of the Internet do not automatically promote civil society. It may be used by state or nonstate actors to undermine it.[30] Yet the Internet remains a relatively powerful new medium and space for civil society partic- ipation. The term "relatively powerful" is worth emphasizing. Studies of technologi- cal diffusion generally hold that the "relative advantage" of new technologies compared to existing ones is an important facilitating factor in the diffusion of new technologies.[31] New technologies may have relative advantages in the sense that they better meet certain social needs. In China's case, the Internet can better meet peo- ple's needs for personal expression and public participation than conventional media.

A historical perspective may further highlight the contemporary relevance of the Internet. In Maoist China, political participation was strictly guided by the state and political dissent was a risky behavior. In the reform period, mass political campaigns gradually receded from China's political scene while new, individualist modes of political participation appeared.[32] In his study of political participation, Tianjian Shi enumerates twenty-eight political acts used by citizens in Beijing to articulate inter- ests. With the exception of big-character posters, none of these involves public par- ticipation. Most acts, such as "complaints through the bureaucratic hierarchy," involve the airing of personal grievances without the possibility of opening up these grievances for public discussion.[33] A basic conclusion to be drawn from these studies is that while the channels for citizen participation have expanded in the reform era, they are neither adequate nor sufficiently open to the broader citizenry. The Internet offers new possibilities.

WHY IS AN INCIPIENT CIVIL SOCIETY FAVORABLE FOR INTERNET DIFFUSION?

The Internet began to develop in China at a time when a civil society had already been emerging.[34] Since the very beginning, China's emerging civil society has provided favorable conditions for the diffusion of the Internet. First, existing and dormant citizen groups and networks provide a social basis for using the Internet. The interactive nature of the Internet means that for the Internet to be used and popularized, a basic level of online social interactions is necessary. Interactions may take place among total strangers, as is common in chat rooms and bulletin boards. Formal and informal social groups provide networks for online interactions to happen. Examples include professional groups, alumni networks, and other social groups based on some kind of preexisting identities.

Second, the internal dynamics of Chinese civil society also favors the development of the Internet. There are various manifestations of such dynamics, such as the expansion of individual rights and urban public spaces, the proliferation of popular protest, the decentralization of the media, and the expansion of associational life.[35] These dynamics derive from the extraordinary combination and juxtaposition of ambiguities, tensions, contradictions, and hopes in contemporary Chinese life. To take one obvious example: How can we understand all the social problems (such as unemployment, prostitution, and corruption) that have accompanied China's "progress" toward modernity? What to make of modernization in light of these social ills? And how to understand the value of one's personal life if one happens to be a helpless victim of these problems? These are common concerns among the Chinese public, often heard and lamented about in daily conversations. Thus, when the Internet began to spread, users quickly embraced it as a means of expressing and discussing such concerns. Hence the proliferation and popularity of online magazines and bulletin boards. To a certain extent, the government's reinforced measures to regulate the Internet toward the end of 2000 was a response to the widespread online debates about these social problems.[36]

Last, as I noted above, the essence of civil society is citizen participation in public life. Citizens may or may not perceive the Internet as conducive to public participation. Such perceptions influence Internet behavior. A comparative study of public attitudes toward computer-mediated communication in Japan and South Korea shows that although Japan is technologically more developed, people in South Korea are more enthusiastic about the Internet as a tool of communication and information exchange. The stronger interest in Korea seems to derive especially "from the desire for free expression that had been suppressed during the years of dictatorship that ended in 1987."[37] Is there a similar desire for free expression in China? Students made a strong case for this in 1989 with their own actions. Does the passion for free expression still live on today? What is the perception of the Internet as a means of public participation among China's Internet users?

An examination of the posts in the popular BBS *Qianguo luntan* (Strengthening the Nation Forum, or QGLT) helps to answer these questions. QGLT is affiliated with *People's Daily*, the leading official newspaper in China. It practices more censorship than other bulletin boards and is thus a conservative case for analyzing public perceptions of the Internet in China.[38] Even here the message is clear: Internet users generally consider the Internet as a freer and more open space for public participation.[39] Users speak of it as a place for ordinary people to discuss national affairs, communicate feelings, and express opinions (Suisheng yousi guoqiren, 11/03/99),[40] a place for self-discovery and self-expression (Guiyuan, 11/07/99), a space for demanding democratic supervision and independent thinking (Changren, 11/15/99), and a "coffee shop" which "cannot turn away customers, nor dictate what they talk about" (Zuishang bushuo, xinlixiang, 04/08/00). They often compare the democratic potentials of the BBS (Bulletin Board System) forum with the lack of such potentials in conventional media and are excited about the new possibilities of freedom of speech. Thus, the author of one post calls QGLT "a sacred temple where we had our first taste of the sacred rights of freedom of speech" and believes that QGLT "provides an opportunity of expression for grassroots voices that have always been repressed and blocked" (Changren, 01/19/00). The censorship practices in QGLT have incurred repeated criticisms,[41] but by and large users consider the Internet as a means of and space for public participation. This perception influences their likelihood to participate in online communication and interaction.

COEVOLUTIONARY DYNAMICS

Having explained why the Internet and civil society in China energize each other, I now examine their coevolutionary dynamics and consequences. The most important kind of dynamics is Internet–civil society interactions. These interactions take multiple forms, but two broad types may be distinguished. The first may be called socially initiated interactions, where action originates in the social world and then is taken to the Internet, yielding interactions. The second type may be referred to as Internet-originated interactions, in which case action originates on the Internet and then reaches beyond. Reflecting the contemporary conditions of globalization, both types of interactions have a transnational dimension. Thus socially-initiated interactions may originate in the social world outside as well as in China. Similarly, Internet-originated interactions may start from Internet network services both in China and in other parts of the world.

The environmental nongovernmental organization (NGO) Friends of Nature (FoN) provides an example of socially initiated interactions.[42] Friends of Nature was founded in 1994 as China's first environmental NGO. At that time, the Internet was little known in China. By December 1998, however, the number of Internet users in China had reached over 2 million. It was at this time that FoN went online. Half a year later, in June 1999, FoN launched its first website. Since then, it has used its website for many purposes, such as publicizing environmental information and organizing activities. The website hosts a BBS with a series of active forums as well as electronic magazines and newsletters. With these features, the website has become an important space for information and discussion among Chinese environmentalists. Thus when a civil society organization like FoN takes its activities online, it initiates new types of interactions and as a result increases its social influence.

An example of Internet-originated interactions is the U.S.-based Chinese-language website New Threads (Xin yu si). A report in the influential American magazine *Science* describes how a Chinese biochemist uses the Internet to expose corruption in the Chinese academy.[43] In 1994, Shi-min Fang, pen-named Fang Zhouzi, a biochemist based in California, set up a website called New Threads (www.xys.com). Among other things, Fang uses the site to publish reports about plagiarism and other kinds of unethical practices among some natural and social scientists in China. Over the years, these online publications have generated heated responses from China's academic communities. In one case, as a response to a report in New Threads about Chinese biochemists' abuse of their scientific authority, the Chinese Association of Biochemists issued a policy prohibiting its members to appear in commercial advertisements in the name of the association.[44] Reflecting the offline influences of the website, collections of Fang Zhouzi's essays have been published in China and Japan. In 2004, a magazine in Guangzhou named Fang as one of fifty public intellectuals most influential in China.[45]

There are many other examples of Internet-originated interactions. For instance, in May 2000, when news broke out online about the murder of a Beijing University student, China's bulletin board systems were suddenly flooded with protests. In Beijing University, its BBS became a virtual democracy wall for organizing campus demonstrations.[46] Similarly, the beating to death of a young college graduate in Guangzhou in March 2003 provoked widespread online protests and debates about police brutality and legal reform, with intensive online–offline interactions leading to policy change.[47] Indeed, a notable phenomenon in the opening years of the twenty-first century is the growing number of contentious interactions that originate from the Internet. Exactly how these contentious interactions start and influence Chinese society is a topic for future research.

NEW FORMATIONS: VIRTUAL PUBLIC SPHERES AND WEB-BASED ORGANIZATIONS

What has come out of the coevolution of the Internet and civil society? Certainly, a mere ten-year history of the Internet's development in China is too short for producing enduring results. Yet there are some observable outcomes nonetheless. On the one hand, the interactions between the Internet and civil society have influenced civil society development. Budding NGOs like Friends of Nature, for example, find a new organizational tool in the Internet. On the other hand, there have emerged new digital formations such as virtual public spheres and web-based organizations. Due to space limits, I will elaborate on the new formations only.

One main new formation is virtual public spheres. I use the plural "spheres" to indicate the multiplicity and diversity of these Internet spaces. By "virtual," I mean both that the public spheres are Internet-based and that they are fledgling borderline formations. They are not quite "real" public spheres because they are not free from political intervention, yet *virtually real* because they are alive with discussions and debates.

Virtual public spheres are diverse. Among those directly concerned with social issues, several influential types may be identified. One is intellectual websites, consisting of Internet magazines and bulletin boards. In terms of information dissemination and intellectual debates, these websites are where the action is. The second type is literary websites, again consisting of Internet magazines and bulletin boards. They are the institutional base for Internet literature, a lively new phenomenon that has transgressed into China's established institutions of cultural power.[48] The third type is the websites of civil society organizations like Friends of Nature. Again these websites almost always have interactive bulletin boards and thus provide spaces for public discussion. They are more specialized in topics of interest and thus have a smaller user base than the BBS communities run by large portal sites. The final type is the websites of mass media, especially large national newspapers. Because China's mass media are official organs, their websites are under direct official control. Yet just as official mass media have become somewhat more open under the pressure of commercialization, so their websites often not only present large volumes of information but also encourage public participation.[49] One example is the Strengthening the Nation Forum run by *People's Daily*. Table 11.2 sums up the four types of virtual public spheres.

There are no cut-and-dried boundaries between virtual public spheres and some of the loose-knit web-based organizations. In some cases, they are two sides of the same coin. Virtual public spheres both create and depend on some sort of loose community ethos. Web-based organizations provide the social basis for communicative action. Nevertheless, to the extent that web-based organizations constitute a form of digital formation distinct from virtual public spheres, their key feature is the organizational element. Web-based organizations may thus be defined as voluntary associations that form around the use of the Internet. They may originate online or offline, but once born, they typically depend heavily on the Internet for existence while commuting between the online and offline realms.

An example of a web-based organization is Green-Web, an informal environmental association formed around the namesake website. It was born out of interactions on a BBS forum hosted by the popular web portal Netease.com. Since its launching

Table 11.2.   Main Types of Virtual Public Spheres in China

Types	Examples
Intellectual websites	Tianya Club (Tianya Shequ, www.tianyaclub.com); Yannan Shequ, www.yannan.cn)
Literary websites	Banyan Tree (Rong Shu Xia, www.rongshuxia.com); Poem Life (Shi Shenghuo, www.poemlife.com)
Websites of civil society organizations	Friends of Nature (Ziran Zhiyou, www.fon.org.cn); WWF-China (www.wwfchina.org/)
Mass media websites	Strengthening the Nation Forum (Qiangguo Luntan, *People's Daily* online, http://bbs.people.com.cn/bbs/chbrd?to = 14); Green Island (Ludao, *China Youth Daily*, www.cydgn.org)

by a small group of organizers in 1999, Green-Web has become both a website for publicizing environmental information online and an informal NGO that organizes offline activities.[50] Existing in the gray zones of China's fluid political arena, it organizes activities without a formal registered status and operates with minimal financial resources. In February 2002, for example, Green-Web launched an online petition campaign to protect some wetlands in suburban Beijing. The campaign collected hundreds of online signatures, sent petition letters to about ten government agencies, and was reported by the mass media.

The life course of web-based organizations varies. Some are ephemeral; others endure; still others grow, migrate, or undergo transmutation. Because of the short history of the Internet, even the oldest web-based groups are still young. As contributing members of China's fledgling civil society, they also depend on its sustained growth in their future fate.

CONCLUSION

While it is important to understand how politics shapes the Internet, a comprehensive understanding of the evolution of the Internet requires attention to the interactive dynamics of technology and civil society. Conceptualizing the development of the Internet and civil society as a coevolutionary process provides such an analytic approach. Through a discussion of the technical features of the Internet and by comparing e-civil society with e-government and e-commerce in China, I have argued that the Internet matters for Chinese civil society in notable ways. I have also shown that China's incipient civil society—its active or dormant citizen groups, internal dynamics, and need for public participation—has provided favorable conditions for Internet diffusion in China. Finally, I analyzed the coevolutionary dynamics of socially initiated and Internet-originated interactions and described two types of new digital formations—virtual public spheres and web-based organizations. Together, these arguments lead to the conclusion that civil society and the Internet energize each other in today's China.

While this chapter stresses the mutual shaping of the Internet and civil society in China, it by no means ignores political pressures. The history of the Internet and civil society is fraught with political struggles. In the history of the PRC, periods of relative openness were often followed by political contraction. The most recent political assaults occurred in the second half of 2004. In September 2004, Yitahutu (YTHT), a BBS hosted by Beijing University and one of the most influential of its kind in China, was closed down by an administrative order jointly issued by several government agencies. Toward year end, procedures for the annual inspection of registered nongovernmental organizations were tightened.[51] There even appeared articles in the official media warning about the dangers of "public intellectuals" with tones reminiscent of earlier antirightist and antiliberalization campaigns.[52]

Have the incipient civil society and virtual public spheres born out of the interactions of the Internet and civil society gone on a course of disintegration? With visible signs of political contraction at the end of 2004, it is tempting to say yes. Yet the analysis in this article suggests a different vision. The coevolution of the Internet and civil society means that political control of the Internet in China will have to take the form of the control of civil society as well, and vice versa. The simultaneous control of the Internet and civil society will add to the difficulty and complexity of control. The coevolutionary process also means that civil society stirrings will encourage the civic uses of the Internet as much as Internet use will shape civil society. Under these conditions, political control will face the joint challenges of technological and social forces. This scenario may have long-term consequences for democratic struggles in China.

NOTES

An earlier version of this chapter was published in *Asian Survey*, May–June 2003, 405–422. It was updated and substantially revised for this volume. The author thanks Guoli Liu and Lowell Dittmer for inviting him to contribute to this volume and the University of California Press for permission to reprint part of my earlier article in *Asian Survey*.

1. I borrowed the idea of coevolution from Jonathan Bach and David Stark, "Link, Search, Interact: The Co-evolution of NGOs and Interactive Technology," *Theory, Culture & Society* 21, no. 3 (2004): 101–117.

2. Digital formations refer to social forms that emerge around and through the use of information technologies. For a theoretical formulation of the concept, see Robert Latham and Saskia Sassen, "Introduction: Digital Formations: Constructing an Object of Study," in *Digital Formations: IT and New Architectures in the Global Realm*, ed. Robert Latham and Saskia Sassen (Princeton, NJ: Princeton University Press, 2005).

3. On the "neutral" nature of civil society, see Gordon White, Jude Howell, and Shang Xiaoyuan, *In Search of Civil Society* (Oxford: Clarendon, 1996), 5–6.

4. See, for example, Timothy Brook and B. Michael Frolic, eds., *Civil Society in China* (Armonk, NY: Sharpe, 1997); Rebecca R. Moore, "China's Fledgling Civil Society: A Force for Democratization?" *World Policy Journal,* Spring 2001, 56–66.

5. Michael Hannan and John Freeman, "Structural Inertia and Organizational Change," *American Sociological Review,* June 1984, 149–164.

6. Much of the work on Chinese civil society focuses on social organizations. See White, Howell, and Shang, *In Search of Civil Society;* Brook and Frolic, eds., *Civil Society in China;* and Margaret Pearson, *China's New Business Elites* (Berkeley: University of California Press, 1997).

7. One indicator of rising rights consciousness is the growing number of lawsuits filed against violations of property and personal rights. See Minxin Pei, "Rights and Resistance: The Changing Contexts of the Dissident Movement," in *Chinese Society: Change, Conflict and Resistance,* ed. Elizabeth J. Perry and Mark Selden (London: Routledge, 2000), 20–40; Kevin O'Brien, "Rightful Resistance," *World Politics,* October 1996, 31–55; Beverley Hooper, "Consumer Voices: Asserting Rights in Maoist China," *China Information* 14, no. 2 (2000): 92–128. For historical perspectives, see *Changing Meanings of Citizenship in Modern China,* ed. Merle Goldman and Elizabeth J. Perry (Cambridge, MA: Harvard University Press, 2002).

8. See Yuezhi Zhao, *Media, Market, and Democracy in China* (Urbana: University of Illinois Press, 1998); Daniel Lynch, *After the Propaganda State: Media, Politics, and "Thought Work" in Reformed China* (Stanford, CA: Stanford University Press, 1999).

9. Deborah S. Davis, Richard Kraus, Barry Naughton, and Elizabeth Perry, eds., *Urban Spaces in Contemporary China* (Cambridge: Cambridge University Press, 1995); Deborah S. Davis, ed., *The Consumer Revolution in Urban China* (Berkeley: University of California Press, 2000).

10. Scholars have begun to study these social organizations as nongovernmental organizations (NGOs). See Deng Guosheng, "New Environment for Development of NGOs in China," in *500 NGOs in China,* ed. NGO Research Center, Tsinghua University (United Nations Centre for Regional Development and NGO Research Center, Tsinghua University, 2002), 17–29. See also Susan H. Whiting, "The Politics of NGO Development in China," *Voluntas* 2, no. 2 (1991): 16–48; Qiusha Ma, "Defining Chinese Nongovernmental Organizations," *Voluntas* 13, no. 2 (2002): 113–130; Ronald C. Keith, Zhiqiu Lin, and Huang Lie, "The Making of a Chinese NGO: The Research and Intervention Project on Domestic Violence," *Problems of Post-Communism,* November-December 2003, 38–50; and Guobin Yang, "Environmental NGOs and Institutional Dynamics in China," *China Quarterly,* March 2005, 46–66.

11. Tony Saich, "Negotiating the State: The Development of Social Organizations in China," *China Quarterly,* March 2000, 124–141.

12. "Chinese NGOs to Work with Government for Poverty Reduction," *People's Daily,* Beijing, October 28, 2001, http://english.peopledaily.com.cn/200110/28/print20011028 _83359.html.

13. Michael S. Chase and James C. Mulvenon, *You've Got Dissent! Chinese Dissident Use of the Internet and Beijing's Counter-Strategies* (Santa Monica, CA: RAND, 2002), 90.

14. Eric Harwit and Duncan Clark, "Shaping the Internet in China: Evolution of Political Control over Network Infrastructure and Content," *Asian Survey,* May–June 2001, 377–408. See also Jack Linchuan Qiu, "Virtual Censorship in China: Keeping the Gate between the

Cyberspaces," *International Journal of Communications Law and Policy,* Winter 1999–2000, 1–25; Kathleen Hartford, "Cyberspace with Chinese Characteristics," *Current History,* September 2000, 255–262; Nina Hachigian, "China's Cyber-Strategy," *Foreign Affairs,* March–April 2001, 118–133; and Lokman Tsui, "The Panopticon as the Antithesis of a Space of Freedom: Control and Regulation of the Internet in China." *China Information* 17, no. 2 (2003): 65–82.

15. Harwit and Clark, "Shaping the Internet," 395.

16. See Chase and Mulvenon, *You've Got Dissent!* and Geoffrey Taubman, "A Not-So World Wide Web: The Internet, China, and the Challenges to Nondemocratic Rule," *Political Communication,* April 1998, 255–272.

17. Guobin Yang, "The Internet and Civil Society in China: A Preliminary Assessment," *Journal of Contemporary China,* August 2003, 453–475.

18. Kathleen Hartford, "Cyberspace with Chinese Characteristics," 261.

19. Todd Munson, "Selling China: www.cnta.com and Cultural Nationalism," *Journal for Multimedia History* 2, no. 1 (1999), www.albany.edu/jmmh/vol2no1/chinaweb.html.

20. C. R. Hughes, "Nationalism in Chinese Cyberspace," *Cambridge Review of International Affairs,* Spring–Summer 2000, 195–209; Randy Kluver, "New Media and the End of Nationalism: China and the US in a War of Words," *Mots Pluriels,* August 2001, www.arts.uwa.edu.au/MotsPluriels/MP1801ak.html.

21. Ernst Dieter and He Jiacheng, "The Future of E-Commerce in China," *Asia Pacific Issues,* October 2000.

22. The Chinese government announced regulations targeting bulletin boards in November 2000, stipulating that bulletin board services should follow a licensing procedure and that users could be held responsible for what they say online. This may have adversely affected the use of newsgroups and bulletin board systems. For a list of Internet regulations in China, see www.cnnic.net.cn.

23. CNNIC, *Zhongguo hulian wangluo fazhan zhuangkuang tongji baogao* (Statistical report on the conditions of China's Internet development), January 2003, www.cnnic.net.cn/develst/2003-1.

24. "Zhengfu wangzhan heshi huo qilai?" (When will government websites come to life?), www.gov.cn/news/detail.asp?sort_ID=7391 (accessed April 2, 2003).

25. Junhua Zhang, "China's 'Government Online' and Attempts to Gain Technical Legitimacy," *ASIEN,* July 2001, 1–23.

26. The figures are based on data I collected in my online ethnographic research. The 100,000 daily hits are figures for May 2000. The 1,000 daily posts are figures for December 2000.

27. The "educated youth" *(zhiqing)* generation is sometimes known as the Red Guard generation or the Cultural Revolution generation. It refers to the cohort that was sent down to the countryside in the Up to the Mountains and Down to the Villages movement. The movement started in 1968 and was officially called off in 1980. See Liu Xiaomeng, *Zhongguo zhiqing shi: Da chao 1966–1980* [A history of the educated youth in China: High tide 1966–1980] (Beijing: Zhongguo shehui kexue chubanshe, 1998).

28. Bach and Stark, "Link, Search, Interact."

29. Bach and Stark, "Link, Search, Interact."

30. See Greg Walton, "China's Golden Shield: Corporations and the Development of Surveillance Technology in the People's Republic of China," International Centre for Human

Rights and Democratic Development, 2001, www.ichrdd.ca/frame.iphtml?langue = 0 (accessed April 12, 2002).

31. Everett Rogers, *The Diffusion of Innovations*, 4th ed. (New York: Free Press, 1995).

32. Wenfang Tang and William Parish, *Chinese Urban Life under Reform* (Cambridge: Cambridge University Press, 2000).

33. Tianjian Shi, *Political Participation in Beijing* (Cambridge, MA: Harvard University Press, 1997).

34. China was connected to the Internet in 1994, when there were about 10,000 Internet users. By October 1997, Internet users in China had reached 620,000. See CNNIC, "Zhongguo hulian wangluo fazhan zhuangkuang tongji baogao" [Statistical Report on the Conditions of China's Internet Development], October 1997, www.cnnic.net.cn/develst/cnnic199710.html.

35. See essays in Davis, Kraus, Naughton and Perry, eds., *Urban Spaces in Contemporary China*; Davis, ed., *The Consumer Revolution in Urban China*; and Perry and Selden, eds., *Chinese Society: Change, Conflict, and Resistance*.

36. The Chinese government promulgated several Internet regulations in November 2000, including one about bulletin board systems. See www.cnnic.net.cn.

37. Robert J. Fouser, "'Culture,' Computer Literacy, and the Media in Creating Public Attitudes toward CMC in Japan and Korea," in *Culture, Technology, Communication: Towards an Intercultural Global Village*, ed. Charles Ess, (Albany: SUNY Press, 2001), 271.

38. QGLT (http://202.99.23.237/cgi-bbs/ChangeBrd?to = 14) boasted 30,000 registered user names in May 2000 with an average of 1,000 posts daily. As of April 2, 2003, the online community to which QGLT belong has 196,402 registered users. The discussions in QGLT are mostly about current affairs. The forum opens on a limited basis, from 10:00 A.M. to 10:00 P.M. daily, and has computer filters and full-time hosts to monitor posts.

39. This finding is supported by the results of an Internet survey, which shows that compared with newspapers, television, and radio, the Internet is perceived as more conducive to expressing personal views. See Guo Liang and Bu Wei, "Huliangwang shiyong zhuangkuang ji yingxiang de diaocha baogao" [Investigative report on Internet use and its impact], Chinese Academy of Social Sciences and Center for Social Development, April 2001, www.chinace .org/ce/itre (accessed April 2, 2003).

40. "Suisheng yousi guoqiren" is the transliteration of the user name of the person who posted the message. Many of these user names are humorous and expressive. "Suisheng yousi guoqiren" means "a state enterprise employee who, though alive, is like dead." "11/03/99" refers to the date the post appeared in the forum. I will follow the same citation format throughout this chapter. Many of these posts are no longer available online but are part of my personal collection of downloaded files.

41. The following message is only one of many examples of such criticisms: "No one should be domineering and stand above others. People are equal: I hope the administrators and hosts [of QGLT] give serious thought to this issue. . . . We are fed up with reading stuff with the same uniform views. We should be able to read reports of the same event from different angles" (Beidou, 05/16/00).

42. This discussion is based on interviews conducted in July 2002 with the staff of Friends of Nature.

43. Xiong Lei, "Biochemist Wages Online War against Ethical Lapses," *Science*, August 10, 2001, 1039.

44. Fang Zhouzi, "In the Name of 'Science' and 'Patriotism': Academic Corruption in China" (speech delivered at UCSD, November 18, 2001), www.xys.org/xys/netters/Fang Zhouzi/science/yanjiang.txt (accessed April 12, 2002).

45. See *Nanfang renwu zhoukan* (Southern People Weekly), 7 (2004).

46. Guobin Yang, "The Internet and Civil Society in China."

47. Guobin Yang, "Mingling Politics with Play: The Virtual Chinese Public Sphere," *IIAS Newsletter,* March 2004, 7.

48. For a sociological analysis of Internet literature, see Guobin Yang, "Virtual Transgressions into Print Culture: The Rise and Impact of Internet Literature in China" (paper presented at the conference From Woodblocks to the Internet: Chinese Publishing and Print Culture in Transition, Ohio State University, Columbus, Ohio, November 3–7, 2004).

49. Yuezhi Zhao, *Media, Market, and Democracy in China* (Urbana: University of Illinois Press, 1998).

50. For more about this case, see Guobin Yang, "Weaving a Green Web: The Internet and Environmental Activism in China," *China Environment Series* 6 (2004): 89–92.

51. Chinese NGO leader, interview by author, Beijing, December 17, 2004.

52. For example, *Guangming Daily*, China's leading official newspaper targeting an educated audience, published such an article on December 14, 2004. The attacks on "public intellectuals" *(gonggong zhishi fenzi)* reflected a concern with Chinese intellectuals' critical engagement in public affairs in recent years. Such engagement is reminiscent of the culture fever in the late 1980s that influenced the rise of the 1989 student movement.

12

Historical Echoes and Chinese Politics

Can China Leave the Twentieth Century Behind?

JOSEPH FEWSMITH

As the twentieth century wound to a close in China, it was impossible not to be struck by two contradictory thoughts. One was that the echoes of the major political anniversaries of the past century still ring with unnerving clarity, suggesting just how relevant the issues of the late nineteenth and early twentieth centuries remain at the turn of another century. The other was that the social and political changes that are underfoot are so dramatic and fundamental that China really is moving into a new era in which those echoes will finally grow fainter. Which of these impressions becomes the more accurate depends much on the course of the next ten years or so.

There seem to be nothing but anniversaries these days in China. The hundredth anniversary of the Hundred Day reform—the radical reform movement championed by Kang Youwei and Liang Qichao in the closing days of the Qing dynasty—fell in 1998, and Beijing University, which was founded in the course of that movement and became the symbol of political liberalism in modern China, marked its centenary in a grand but contested ceremony. At the same time, 1998 marked the twentieth anniversary of the Third Plenary Session of the Eleventh Central Committee, at which Deng Xiaoping decisively launched China on the course of reform, thus leading everyone to discuss even more fervently the successes and failures of the past two decades.

The following year, 1999, was perhaps even more portentous. It marked the eightieth anniversary of the May Fourth movement, the iconoclastic cultural and nationalistic movement that gave birth simultaneously to liberalism and communism. The fiftieth anniversary of the founding of the People's Republic of China was celebrated with elaborate ceremonies and a well-orchestrated military parade on October 1, 1999. Most sensitive of all, 1999 also marked the tenth anniversary of the Tiananmen demonstrations and their suppression, an event that cuts the reform period neatly in half and has generated continuing controversies about the meaning of reform and the course China should follow in the future.

Finally, the year 2000 marks the hundredth anniversary of the Boxer Rebellion, the xenophobic peasant movement whose magic was believed to protect its adherents from bullets. This anniversary has taken on new saliency as demonstrations and armed outbursts pock the countryside, and as the Falun Gong (Buddhist Law Society) movement, which combines traditional *qigong* exercises with a potent spiritual message, has attracted millions of adherents and most famously mobilized 10,000 people to sit in sudden and silent protest outside Zhongnanhai on April 25, 1999, before the government tried to suppress it (not completely successfully) in a virulent and widespread crackdown that started in July.

These anniversaries resonate with the present because they raise issues of continuing importance: China's relationship with the West (politically, economically, and culturally); the simultaneous desire for wealth and power and social fairness; popular political expression and participation; and the relationship of the present to the past, which is to say the value of the revolution. Moreover, the meanings of these anniversaries remain contested; indeed, it is precisely because they are contested that they continue to have such salience. In fact, one way to try to comprehend the state of Chinese society at the turn of the century is to contrast the way these anniversaries echo today with the way they did just a decade ago. Doing so underscores how very different the China of the 1990s is from the China of the 1980s.

A decade ago, prior to Tiananmen, intellectuals almost universally keyed on the upcoming seventieth anniversary of the May Fourth movement to push the themes of intellectual freedom and democratization further. The West, particularly the United States, was viewed as a model, or at least as a useful embodiment of ideals that could be evoked to propel reform forward. The fortieth anniversary of the founding of the PRC, in contrast, was something few intellectuals were in a mood to celebrate; the phrase from the Confucian *Analects* saying that "at forty-one should not have doubts" *(sishi er buhuo)* could not but be cited with irony. Cosmologist Fang Lizhi wrote off the history of the PRC as "forty years of failure"; others may have demurred from such an extreme judgment, but not by much.[1]

These concerns and doubts reflected the experience of intellectuals and were broadly shared by other sectors of society. Coming out of the Cultural Revolution, intellectuals were obsessed by a desire to understand where the revolution had gone wrong and by a profound wish to prevent anything resembling the Cultural Revolution from ever happening again. Intellectuals placed the blame squarely on leftism.

The enormous excesses of the Chinese revolution—from the socialist transformation of the mid-1950s to the anti-rightist movement of 1957, the Great Leap Forward of 1958–1960, and finally the Cultural Revolution of 1966–1976—were attributed to a leftism that accepted uncritically a (contradictory) mix of Stalinist economic

planning and Maoist mobilization, that rejected the importance of rationality and hence of intellectuals, that emphasized the "class nature" of human beings to the detriment of their humanity, and that turned the nation inward, rejecting the importance of learning from the West. These trends were also encompassed by the term "feudalism," a word of opprobrium that had nothing to do with its meaning for the economic and political history of the West or even its traditional meaning of local self-rule in China, but instead connoted everything negative that had been attributed to Chinese traditional society through the long course of China's revolution, including patriarchalism, authoritarianism, bureaucratism, anti-intellectualism, and fanaticism. As China's revolution had increasingly criticized capitalism, trying desperately in the course of the Cultural Revolution to "cut off the tail of capitalism" and to criticize the bourgeois right, feudalism had flourished. Leftism was thus rooted in feudalism, and the task of intellectuals and reform-minded party people was to expunge these evils and thus set China on a course toward modernity."

Given this basic, if oversimplified, diagnosis of what was wrong with China, it was natural that intellectuals turned to the May Fourth tradition for inspiration and moral sustenance. The May Fourth tradition had always contained contradictory elements: a radical critique of traditional Chinese culture and the demand to learn from the West and to introduce science and democracy were combined with a nationalism that rejected cosmopolitanism in favor of nativism. Chinese Academy of Social Sciences (CASS) Philosophy Institute scholar Li Zehou articulated for his generation of 1980s scholars the need to disentangle the liberal elements of the May Fourth tradition, those that emphasized enlightenment" from those that were caught up in nationalistic efforts to "save the nation." Every time the cultural critique seemed to offer hope of introducing new enlightenment values into Chinese culture, Li argued, it was overwhelmed by nationalism ("national salvation") as China faced one crisis after another.[2] Now, in the 1980s, it was finally time to take up the task of enlightenment and carry it through to fruition.

This enlightenment project dominated intellectual discourse in the 1980s. Whether it was discussions of alienation in socialism,[3] efforts to bring an end to lifelong tenure and create a rational civil service,[4] policy proposals to marketize the Chinese economy,[5] translations of Western thinkers,[6] nascent writings about human rights and democracy,[7] or reconceptualizations of capitalism and socialism to emphasize their similarities, the task was to expunge leftism from Chinese social, economic, and political life. This focus on the dangers of leftism and feudalism assigned a lofty position to the West, particularly the United States. The United States took on an aura of modernity that provided a mirror opposite of the leftism that intellectuals sought to root out. Western culture provided fuel for ongoing critiques of Chinese culture, thus continuing the May Fourth rejection of traditional values, while Western economic and political systems served as foils against which to criticize the planned economy and authoritarian political system of China. If discussions of the United States and other Western countries in the 1980s were superficial, it was because the point was not to understand how those systems actually worked but to provide a fulcrum from which faults in the Chinese system could be criticized. However superficial these discussions may have been, their participants clearly saw themselves as lying within the May Fourth enlightenment tradition and providing a cosmopolitanism that helped support the political relationship being forged with the West as well as reformers within the party.

A decade later, the May Fourth legacy appears badly tattered. The liberal tradition of the May Fourth period has been ignored and suppressed many times since 1919, as Li Zehou points out, because revolution or foreign war seemed more pressing. But never in the seven decades since then had intellectuals themselves come to see the May Fourth tradition as outdated or irrelevant to their concerns. That changed in the 1990s, and the turn away from the enlightenment project of the May Fourth movement marks a major, one is tempted to say fundamental, change in the way many intellectuals view China and its place in the world.

The change in the intellectual atmosphere in China can be dated fairly precisely to the 1992–1993 period. It was in 1992 that Deng Xiaoping made his famous journey to the south of China to reinvigorate his reform program.[8] Deng was highly successful not only in changing the political atmosphere but also in setting off a major upsurge in economic activity (bolstered by a loose monetary policy) and, more important, a critical structural shift in the economy as the private sector finally emerged as a major factor in its own right and as foreign investment expanded greatly.[9] These changes, which have generally received high praise in the Western press, have been greeted by greater skepticism in China because they have challenged vested interests, have created new vested interests, and have been accompanied by a host of social problems: rapidly rising intra- and interregional income inequalities, corruption on a scale that would have been unimaginable in 1989 (when students took to the streets to protest corruption), a massive stripping of state-owned assets as officials have taken advantage of their positions to preside over a large-scale de facto privatization, a large increase in the number of migrant workers looking for employment outside their native areas, increases in crime and other social-order problems, and a growing unemployment problem as hard-pressed state-owned factories finally began to move to reduce the size of their labor forces.

In short, in the eyes of many intellectuals, the *problematique* of China had shifted dramatically from the need to push reform forward by criticizing leftism and feudalism to the need to deal with the effects of reform. For these intellectuals, the left was no longer a problem; it was a spent force that had little, if any, practical effect on China. Marketization was likewise no longer a problem; it had succeeded, perhaps too well. And opening to the outside world, that counterpart to Dengist domestic reforms, had also succeeded. Not only was China opened to the outside world, but it found itself inextricably linked to a new global order that was not necessarily benevolent—as the Asian financial crisis demonstrated forcefully and brutally. Such concerns led many intellectuals to become quite critical of the effects of reform in China and of the global order China was trying to join. This was a wholly different set of concerns from that which had dominated the intellectual agenda in the 1980s.[10]

Ironically, these intellectuals were far more familiar with the West and with the intellectual trends of the West than were those who had dominated intellectual discourse in the 1980s. Many of them had studied extensively in the West before either returning to take up prestigious positions within China or staying in the West in university teaching positions. Indeed, this internationalization of intellectual discourse distinguished the 1990s from the 1980s. In the first decade of reform, Chinese intellectuals generally resided in China and discussed issues with other intellectuals in China; by the 1990s, particularly with the spread of the Internet, the conversation had become truly global, encompassing not only intellectuals in China and those who were studying or working in the West but also non-PRC Chinese intellectuals from Taiwan, Hong Kong, and elsewhere.

What this new, sophisticated, and international group of intellectuals latched onto as they focused on a new set of social problems was a variety of perspectives that are generally referred to as critical methodologies in the West: postmodernism, postcolonialism, deconstructionism, critical legal studies, analytic Marxism, world systems theory, and so forth.[11] Such methodologies were highly critical of capitalism and globalization and were determined to unmask the various power relations that were said to be hidden behind hegemonic rhetoric. Although such critiques are widespread within the U.S. and European academe, they have remarkably little impact on public policy, standing as academic critiques of a dominant capitalist order.[12]

In China, however, their position is quite different and hence highly controversial. First, instead of representing minority critiques of a dominant trend, critical methodologies have arguably become the mainstream of intellectual discourse in China. Second, although advocates of critical methodologies in China argue that they want to transcend such dualities (usually said to be a legacy of Cold War thinking) as East/West, tradition/modernity, and capitalist/socialist, their very focus on these dualities tends to accentuate their importance. For instance, Chinese scholars following in Edward Said's footsteps to unmask the relationship between "Orientalist" rhetoric and the power interests of the United States invariably end up not transcending the East/West duality but emphasizing the need for a nativist response to a Western hegemonic discourse.[13]

Third, it is difficult for followers of critical methodologies to escape from nationalist modes of discourse, and indeed many seek to adopt such rhetoric either because they are concerned with the way they see China being absorbed into an international capitalist order in which it has little say or because they share a sense of frustration with (largely) U.S. rhetoric and policies in the post–Cold War era. In this sense, those who promote critical methodologies ironically adopt a nationalistic attitude that is far from the orientation of those using parallel methodologies in the West. Those opposed to critical methodologies criticize, sometimes in extremely harsh terms, those who adopt them for becoming, in their view, spokespersons for the government, while those who adopt critical methodologies state with equal validity that they are highly critical of the government and its policies.[14]

To point to such harsh polemics is to suggest another feature of the 1990s landscape that is different from that of the 1980s or arguably even earlier. Although there have been some notably harsh polemics throughout the twentieth century, intellectuals in China have generally shared a sense that they were one group. This sense was particularly strong in the 1980s, as intellectuals had endured a common fate during the Cultural Revolution and generally shared a desire to move China as far away from that period as possible. By the 1990s, however, the traditional world of Chinese intellectuals had largely vanished. Some had moved into the government and its think tanks as specialists and technocrats, others had retreated into academia to pursue specialized research, and still others had responded to the rapidly growing commercialization of culture by writing popular literature and the like. Indeed, one of the most interesting intellectual debates of the 1990s, and arguably the only one that was truly indigenous, was about the loss of the "humanistic spirit" *(renwen jingshen)* among intellectuals.[15] It was a debate that reflected the growing marginalization of intellectuals in the face of commercialization. In short, by the end of the 1990s, it was difficult to speak of China's intellectuals as a coherent social stratum or as the conscience of Chinese society, their traditional role.

Critical methodologies, as just mentioned, have an affinity with nationalism, even if they are inherently critical of the government and the course of reform as well. Nationalism is hardly new in China; it has in fact been the leitmotif of twentieth-century China. Chinese intellectuals were just as nationalistic in the 1980s as they were in the 1990s, but in the earlier decade their nationalism took a more cosmopolitan approach, seeking a path to wealth and power through learning from the West.[16] As noted above, this learning from the West simultaneously served the purposes of criticizing leftism and feudalism and promoting reform. As intellectuals have become more critical of reform, they have simultaneously become more critical of the neoclassical economics and political liberalism that have been offered up as models for China's reform. There has been a new desire in the 1990s to forge a uniquely Chinese path to reform, and this desire to explore a native approach to reform that conforms with Chinese culture and tradition necessarily entails an emphasis on asserting Chinese identity.

This assertion of Chinese identity, however, has mingled with other feelings of suspicion directed primarily against the United States that are an outcome of the specific atmosphere that has prevailed in U.S.–Chinese relations since Tiananmen. The sea change in public opinion came in the 1992–1993 period when President Clinton, trying to bridge the gap between his campaign rhetoric and the realities of international relations, extended China's most favored nation status conditionally. This flawed decision, later reversed, was followed by other gaffes that reflected a sensitivity to certain opinion groups in the United States and an insensitivity to opinion in China. Such decisions included the opposition to China's bid to host the summer Olympics in the year 2000 and the forceful inspection of a Chinese ship, the *Yin He,* believed to be transporting chemicals that could be used in the manufacture of chemical weapons to Iran.

One of the most interesting aspects of Chinese intellectuals' response to these and similar incidents is the widespread and deep-seated assumption that the United States was taking such measures in a calculated effort to contain China. Whereas few officials or scholars in the United States could identify a clear-cut "China policy" in the early Clinton administration, much less one that was implemented consistently, Chinese intellectuals could explain in detail how various measures were all clear expressions of a U.S. national interest in keeping China down. This new intellectual focus on interests speaks volumes about the intellectual atmosphere in contemporary China. Intellectuals have been twice disillusioned regarding idealism, first by the Cultural Revolution, which turned into a nightmare, and second by the liberalism of the 1980s, which ended in political disaster. Particularly in the atmosphere of commercialism that has prevailed in recent years, any talk of idealism seems out of place. In some ways, the blunt discussions of national interest are a refreshing change from the ideological stridency of the past, but they reflect not so much realism as it is conceived by Western students of international relations as unvarnished cynicism. Since ideological pretensions have been unmasked in China, so the logic seems to go, it is inconceivable that a nation such as the United States would not be a careful calculator of its national interests.

This "cynical realism" was deeply reflected in Chinese reactions to the war in Kosovo and especially to the tragic bombing of the Chinese embassy in Belgrade. Even before the bombing, there were elaborate scenarios set out to explain how the NATO action in Kosovo reflected U.S. national interests. These generally focused on the shift in NATO's mission statement to reflect an expanded, out-of-area role and explained the conflict in Kosovo as simply a first step in the U.S. plan to dominate the world. Following the bombing incident, the explanations became even more fanciful and far-fetched.[17] Chinese critics were deaf to explanations that suggested that the United States and other nations were in fact concerned with human rights and that the military action with respect to Kosovo largely reflected idealism (whether misguided or not).

Not only has the nature of nationalism changed in China in the course of the 1990s, but its base has also widened substantially. The broadening of nationalist appeals is part and parcel of the decline of elite culture and the consequent flattening out of public discourse. The widening of intellectual discourse started in the 1980s, but it is the commercialization of culture in the 1990s that has reshaped the public arena. The market for Wang Shuo's antiestablishment "hooligan" literature reflected a new populist culture and a new social mood. Wang, who is not college educated, flouted the conventions of Chinese literature and showed no deference to his better-educated colleagues. Another turning point was the popularity of *Yearn-*

ings (Kewang),[18] a soap opera featuring stock characters but written in part by respected writers Zheng Wanlong and Wang Shuo (who were quickly accused of selling out). The show attracted a huge audience and marked a turning point in the commercialization of culture. As Li Xiaoming, the chief scriptwriter, put it, "If you're a television writer, and you know that the majority of your Chinese audience had to save up for years to buy a TV set, then you'd better come to terms with them."[19]

Popular nationalism then emerged on the scene in 1994 with the publication of Wang Shan's book, *Looking at China through a Third Eye*.[20] This was a highly critical look at the state of Chinese society and the impact of the reforms as well as a bold statement of nationalism. Two years later, the better-known *China Can Say No* was published and became an instant best-seller.[21] A whole series of similar books soon appeared, cashing in on the market that *China Can Say No* had pioneered.[22] Indeed, one of the hallmarks of the new era of the 1990s was the way in which official books had to compete more with nonofficial books to influence public opinion. Thus, books such as *Heart-to-Heart Talks with the General Secretary* and *China Should Not Be "Mr. No"* (discussed below) appeared on the market to oppose the upsurge of nationalism.[23] These books were soon followed by others touting the U.S.–Chinese "constructive strategic partnership" as Jiang Zemin and Clinton exchanged summits.

This expansion of the public realm, which was due both to secular changes in Chinese society and to the government's recognition that the sort of heavy-handed ideological campaign it had pursued following Tiananmen was counterproductive, begins to make more explicable the public reaction to the bombing of the Chinese embassy in Belgrade. However, one must also factor in the frustrations that are evident in Chinese society.

POLITICAL IMPLICATIONS OF
SOCIOECONOMIC CHANGE

The very different intellectual atmosphere in China, as well as the fractionalization of intellectuals and their very different relationship with the state, is one of the profound changes that have taken place in state–society relations over recent years. Although these changes have their roots in the early years of reform, they have accelerated in recent years as the marketization, internationalization, and diversification of the Chinese economy have accelerated. Whereas through much of the 1980s most social groups gained from reform, as the 1990s progressed, there were increasingly obvious differences between "winners" and "losers." And as more people joined the ranks of the losers, or at least the relative losers, there were widely felt implications for politics. Put simply, the very different socioeconomic environment that has emerged in recent years not only fuels the tensions that erupt in worker and farmer protests but also generates the critical attitude many intellectuals have adopted in recent years and undermines party discipline as well as the confidence that many party members and social elites have in the future of the party, which in turn stimulates the corruption, illegal transfer of wealth abroad, and cynicism that are themselves so much a part of the problem that China's political elite faces. Management of this complex and rapidly changing sociopolitical environment presents a formidable political challenge, arguably one greater than that faced by Mao or Deng, and inevitably leads to sharply differing political views within the elite.

The single most important change in Chinese society has been the emergence of a class of *nouveaux riches.* In the mid-1980s, there was fevered talk in the Chinese press, which turned out to be exaggerated, of the emergence of "ten thousand yuan households" *(wanyuanhu)*—almost unimaginable in a period when the average rural resident earned only about ¥350 per year. A decade or so later, the reality was that there were at least a million households with annual incomes exceeding ¥1 million. This was an enormous change with profound social, psychological, and political implications. In many ways, of course, this was a long overdue and healthy change seemingly marking the appearance of a middle class, albeit one that was still quite small in terms of China's population, even if one considered only its urban population. Nevertheless, the new middle class, including the much more prosperous *nouveaux riches,* drove the new consumerism of the 1990s, changing the nature and role of culture in Chinese society by commercializing it and diversifying it.

In part, this new middle class marked the internationalization of the Chinese economy; by the mid-1990s, there were some 100,000 joint-venture enterprises employing perhaps 18 million people, and most of them paid salaries that far exceeded those of state-owned enterprises (SOEs). Enterprise managers who formed joint ventures or jumped into the international economy sometimes made very large incomes indeed. The new middle class also marked an important structural change in the Chinese economy as the "knowledge economy" boomed; new high-tech firms sprouted up everywhere. As knowledge became a commodity, some intellectuals, whose incomes had lagged behind in the 1980s, found that their skills were valuable and began enjoying a comfortable lifestyle. Whereas previously their only choice had been to join a university or government research organ, now intellectuals could hang out their own shingles as consultants. Such people developed a stake in the system, and as they did so radicalism waned. Other intellectuals did not do as well, and were profoundly discomforted by the fact that income, not intellectual prowess, had become the measure of success.

The seamy side of this story is that those who did the best in this new economy—and some did very well indeed—had strong political connections. Sometimes they were bureaucrats who had tired of the office routine and jumped into the sea of business but retained their connections to colleagues who could offer all-important approvals or access to scarce resources. Sometimes they were family members of officials still in office. Sometimes they were enterprise heads who used their positions to siphon off large amounts of state-owned assets to private firms that they controlled directly or indirectly. Often they were the offspring of high cadres who used their family connections to amass large sums of money. In other words, corruption—massive corruption—was a major part of the story of income redistribution in the 1990s.

A recent study calls this group the "never-left-out class" *(bu luokong jieji)* because every time Chinese society has entered a new round of adjustment in which resources are reallocated, this group has benefited the most. The same study argues that this group possesses "comprehensive" *(zongtixing)* capital resources, meaning that it is able to mobilize its multidimensional economic and political contacts to monopolize the best opportunities.[24] This is the same group of people that economic journalist He Qinglian described in her 1998 best-seller when she argues that through the marketization of politics, officials or those with close relations with officials have directed millions of dollars' worth of assets into private hands, bringing about a form of "primitive socialist accumulation" that rivals anything Marx and Engels observed about "primitive capitalist accumulation." The result, He argued, has been income inequality surpassing that in either Japan or the United States (keeping in mind that China had a much more equal distribution of income than either of those countries less than a decade ago), the rise of secret societies, and mass resentment. China, she argues, seems to be heading not toward liberal democracy and capitalism but toward a "government and mafia alliance."[25]

The losers in this process are, at least in a relative sense, urban workers, particularly those in smaller cities and towns, who are thrown out of work, furloughed *(xiagang),* not paid for months at a time, or simply made anxious about their prospects. According to official figures, 3.1 percent of the urban workforce—some 5.7 million workers—were registered as unemployed at year end 1998, and an additional 8.9 million workers were furloughed,[26] giving a total unemployment rate of about 8 percent. Unofficial estimates suggest an unemployment rate that is considerably higher.[27] To be a worker in a state-owned enterprise used to be an honored and secure position in society, but today it is relatively less well paid and much less secure, making many workers resentful. There is also an economic impact as workers, worried about their futures, hoard their savings, exerting a deflationary pressure on the economy. Ironically, the "tiger" of savings that economists had long worried would come leaping out of its cage to drive up inflation now cannot even be lured out!

Rural agricultural workers have also lost out, at least in a relative sense. Rural incomes have not increased as quickly in recent years, and local exactions appear not to have abated despite repeated directives from Beijing. Potentially more destabilizing, there remain some 150 million agricultural workers who are grossly underemployed and should shift out of agriculture. But there is no apparent outlet for their services. In the 1980s and 1990s, over 100 million farmers were able to shift out of agriculture by finding jobs in the township and village enterprises (TVEs) that were springing up. By the late 1990s, however, TVEs were undergoing their own readjustment, and many were encountering the same sort of problems that SOEs had previously faced—debts that had been contracted through political relationships and now could not be paid back.[28]

The large numbers of urban and rural people who have been relative losers over the past decade of reform (in contrast to the 1980s when they did relatively well) provide a base of discontent that fuels a constant stream of protest that threatens social order. In a passage worth quoting at length, the authors of the study referred to above write:

> Along with the proliferation of labor disputes, hired workers in many urban and rural enterprises, in an attempt to vent their dissatisfaction with the system, have taken to all sorts of destructive measures, such as burning down factories, sabotaging machinery, and even personal damage to managerial personnel. Such incidents have already become fairly commonplace in the economically developed areas in Southern China. In addition, there are all sorts of focused social movements and actions, such as demonstrations, presentations of petitions and appeals, and labor strikes. Incidences of such petitions and strikes, in which workers in enterprises in large and medium-sized cities raise slogans demanding that their basic livelihood be protected and assured, have become increasingly numerous. Although such information and news is almost never reported in the newspapers—out of consideration for "social stability"—it is already an "open secret."[29]

It is precisely such discontent that provides a potential basis for large-scale social protest and explains why sects—such as the Falun Gong—frighten the leadership so much.

The existence of widespread, if unorganized, discontent explains the leadership's concern with providing jobs. Generating sufficient numbers of jobs in a country in which the workforce grows by more than eight million a year is never easy. Rapid economic growth is critical for creating the necessary jobs: each additional percentage point of growth accounts for about 1.2 million jobs, so growth rates have been at the top of the government agenda. So far, growth has managed to keep the government ahead of the curve—unemployment is up but not unmanageable, and both urban and rural incomes have continued to increase—but the margin for error is not great. Given widespread resentment of corruption and income inequality, the potential for social unrest is real.

The profound socioeconomic changes of recent years offer both hope and concern. On the one hand, the growing wealth of a significant number of mostly urban residents, even if much of that wealth has been acquired in a less than pristine manner, could pave the way for the emergence of a genuine middle class, something that China has never had in its more than 2,000 years of history. Such a development would have profound, and profoundly positive, implications for Chinese culture, society, and politics. At the moment, Chinese society falls well short of such a development, but nevertheless, there is emerging a group of people who have a real stake in the stability of Chinese society, who are outside of (if well connected with) the political system and positioned to make demands on that system, and who may well discover (however belatedly) an interest in law and property rights. Moreover, as Shanghai historian and social critic Xiao Gongqin points out, the diversification that has taken place in Chinese society over recent years means that most problems are localized. Workers and farmers raise demands specific to their own circumstances, and the prospects for societywide social movements are correspondingly reduced.[30] Such optimistic scenarios, however, require a period of continued high-speed economic growth. Unfortunately, the prospects for that are uncertain at best. Should there be a major slowdown in economic growth, to say nothing of a crisis similar to those experienced by many other Asian nations in recent years, the potential for social violence is high.

On the other hand, if this *nouveau riche* group, as the study cited above suggests, squeezes out an emerging middle class and forms the sort of corrupt relationship with the political elite that has long plagued Latin American politics, then the prospects for social and political stability, not to mention democratization, are much less.

There are many indications that China's top leadership is aware of and intensely concerned about these socioeconomic problems and their political implications. The repeated crackdowns on corruption and the efforts to get the military out of business and to stop (or at least significantly slow) smuggling and the illegal remittance of funds abroad reflect this awareness.[31] So too do the ideological campaigns that seem so incomprehensible to Westerners, not to mention many of those forced to take part in them. One of the few tools the party has to fight social and political disintegration is to force party members to study official documents and to write self-examinations in an effort to bolster compliance, but the "three stresses" *(sanjiang)* campaign that Beijing has carried out since early 1999 seems to have created as much resentment among those forced to participate as it has compliance. Campaigns may buy the party some time, but they are not an effective way to build institutions.

POLITICS IN AN ERA OF DOMESTIC CHANGE AND GLOBALIZATION

When one turns to the more specifically political aspects of contemporary China, it is apparent that there are important shifts under way both as generational change forces new adaptations and as the very changed intellectual and socioeconomic environment in which the government operates presents challenges to which the government must learn to respond with greater rapidity and flexibility if it is to survive.

The single greatest change in the political system in recent years has been the passing of the revolutionary generation and the emergence of a new, better-trained, less authoritative generation. Although there remain veteran revolutionaries who continue to constrain the top leadership in various ways, Deng Xiaoping's death in February 1997—which followed the deaths of other senior leaders such as Chen Yun

(April 1995), Li Xiannian (June 1992), and Hu Qiaomu (September 1992)—really brought about the demise of the first generation of Chinese Communist Party (CCP) leadership and of revolutionary legitimacy as well. Deng liked to refer to himself as the core of the second generation of leadership in order to distinguish himself from the discredited leadership and policies of Mao Zedong. But Deng, born in 1904, was merely a decade younger than Mao and had participated in all the great revolutionary struggles, including most significantly the Long March. It was a generation that felt assured both of its right to rule and of its ability to do so. By and large, these claims were accepted by younger people in the party and by society at large.

No such natural legitimacy accrues to Jiang Zemin and his colleagues. In part because neither his nor the party's legitimacy is assured in the way Deng's was, Jiang is intensely conscious of ideology. He understands that both the coherence of the party and the legitimacy of the government depend significantly on articulating a rationale for their continued rule. Reflecting on the challenge he faced, Jiang reportedly once said that Mao Zedong's generation had the theory of revolutionary socialism and Deng Xiaoping's generation had the theory of building socialism with Chinese characteristics, but the third generation (Jiang Zemin's generation) had not yet put its ideological stamp on politics.[32] The absence of such an ideological stamp reflected both the very different state–society relationship Jiang faced and the more particular problem of establishing Jiang's legitimacy vis-à-vis his colleagues. In terms of the party-state's relationship to society, Jiang had (and has) the unenviable task of trying to build an institutionalized, regularized relationship. In a sense, Mao and Deng had the easy jobs: Mao centralized, and Deng decentralized. Neither built viable institutions regulating the central government's relationship either with local levels of government or with the broader society. That task falls to Jiang.

In terms of the narrower political question of establishing his authority vis-à-vis his colleagues, Jiang had the task of replacing leaders of his own generation and older who felt, with some legitimacy, that they were as well qualified as Jiang and thus were reluctant to take orders from him with a younger group who would, he hoped, be more compliant. This was a process that Jiang undertook in several steps, first defeating a challenge from military leader Yang Shangkun in 1992, then elevating protégés at the Central Committee's Fourth Plenum in 1994, and then significantly rejuvenating the Central Committee at the Fifteenth Party Congress in 1997. Yet Jiang has never believed that simply replacing people is sufficient either to ensure his own control or to maintain the party's control over society. The explosion of corruption and smuggling as well as the fusion of party and business, not only in the party but also in the military, was testimony to the erosion of party discipline and the loss of faith not only in any ruling ideology but perhaps in the future of the party as well.[33] That is why Jiang places so much emphasis on ideology and party discipline.

If legitimacy has been Jiang's number one problem, coping with the very rapidly changing socioeconomic conditions outlined above has ranked a close second. There were at least two aspects of this problem. One was that as Chinese society and economy diversified and as the party lost much of its ability to command allegiance, the role of interests became conspicuously greater. Although there continued to be problems with those who objected to reforms on ideological grounds, the influence of the old left—the ideologically more orthodox wing of the party identified with senior ideologue Hu Qiaomu before his death and former propaganda head Deng Liqun—waned after 1992 and nearly evaporated after 1997.[34] Its place, however, was taken by a variety of interests—regional, local, ministerial, and sectoral—that seemed to defend their turf more vigorously and more directly than before. Moreover, a strong sense of nationalism has taken the place on the ideological spectrum once occupied by the old left.

Second, the hard nut of SOE reform, which was inextricably bound up with the increasingly severe problems in the fiscal system, presented an increasing drag on the economy as well as on state resources. Although the size of the state-owned economy shrank from some 75 percent of GNP at the beginning of the reforms to less than 35 percent by 1995, it continues to dominate some sectors of the economy, particularly heavy industry. Because these are important sectors of the economy and because their reform (or lack thereof) has strong implications for the viability of the banking sector, SOE reform is something that simply cannot be avoided. Moreover, half measures have arguably made the situation worse, not better.[35]

Both the interest group nature of contemporary Chinese politics and the severity of sectoral problems in the economy are closely related to China's role in the international economy, particularly to its probable entry into the World Trade Organization (WTO). Exports are essential for shoring up the economy, but entry into the WTO would present formidable competitive challenges to many industries.

The conflicting demands on the political system are reflected both in the composition of the top leadership and in the group of people Jiang has gathered around him to advise on policy. Within the top leadership, there are conservative figures, headed by former premier Li Peng (now head of the National People's Congress), who have extensive ties throughout the government bureaucracy and with party elders. There are also bold reformers, personified by the current premier Zhu Rongji, who understand the need to bring about a rapid and dramatic restructuring of the economy. Within Jiang's own entourage, there is likewise a diversity of people, reflecting Jiang's need to keep in close touch with different constituencies in the party. There are, for instance, conservative officials such as Teng Wensheng, Deng Liqun's protégé, who heads the Policy Research Office of the Central Committee, and Ding Guan'gen, the conservative head of the Propaganda Department, whom Jiang continues to employ despite his being widely disliked within the party, not to mention among intellectuals. At the same time, there are more "liberal" advisers, such as former Shanghai mayor and all-around political mentor Wang Daohan, who has played a critical role in helping Jiang navigate the hidden shoals of elite politics, has shaped much of Jiang's approach to foreign affairs, and has been invaluable as a liaison with the intellectual community. There is also Liu Ji, Jiang's close friend from Shanghai who served as vice president of the Chinese Academy of Social Sciences (CASS) from 1993 to 1997 and has continued to play a very active if much lower profile role since leaving CASS. In between, there are a number of people who have worked to further Jiang's interests bureaucratically. The most important of these is Zeng Qinghong, who served as head of the Central Committee's General Office from 1993 to 1998 and then moved over to head the important Organization Department. Zeng was promoted to alternate member of the Politburo at the Fifteenth Party Congress in 1997 and may well one day emerge as leader of China in his own right.[36]

This effort to pull together, or at least accommodate, divergent views and interests within the party has been reflected in Jiang's political stewardship over the past several years, particularly since he began to come into his own following the Fourth Plenum in late 1994. In general, what Jiang has done has been to steal a page from Deng Xiaoping's book of political strategy by trying to carve out a "middle course" that encompasses a fairly wide spectrum of opinion within the party but nevertheless isolates both ideological hard-liners and "bourgeois liberals."[37]

If one looks back to 1995, one can see the ideologically conservative side of Jiang on display. Coming out of the Fourth Plenum the previous fall, and meeting the challenge raised by the old left in the first of a series of "ten-thousand-character manifestos" *(wanyanshu)*, Jiang stressed ideological orthodoxy by calling for "talking politics" *(jiang zhengzhi)*.[38] This was, perhaps, a natural outcome of the Fourth Plenum, which had taken "party building" as its theme, and of Jiang's overall efforts to secure his own authority in the face of obvious challenges from both the left and the right. By late 1995 and early 1996, one sees Jiang trying to define his program in somewhat more positive terms by giving a series of internal speeches distinguishing Marxism from anti-Marxism in seven areas, including socialist democracy versus Western parliamentary democracy, developing a diverse economy with a predominant public sector versus privatization, and studying what is advanced in the West versus fawning on the West. As such distinctions suggest, Jiang was reaching for a formula that would permit him to move pragmatically beyond the ideological strictures of the old left without leaving him open to the charges of being lax on "bourgeois liberalization" that had toppled his two immediate predecessors, Hu Yaobang and Zhao Ziyang.

The most systematic effort to define a middle course and respond to the criticisms of the left came when Xing Bensi, vice president of the Central Party School, published a long article in the *People's Daily*. Apparently angered by the silence with which the *People's Daily* greeted his speeches—a silence apparently induced by the inability of top leaders to agree on how to respond—Jiang arranged for the publication of Xing's article.

In trying to define what constituted "real" Marxism (and thus refute the old left that positioned itself as the defender of the faith), Xing argued that a lot had changed since the birth of Marx 150 years before. Xing argued that there are parts of Marxism that contain universal truth and are still applicable, parts that need to be supplemented, and parts that are "completely unsuitable for use, which should not be continued or upheld in the present day."[39] Thus, Xing stated, "the criterion for determining the border dividing Marxism and anti-Marxism has to rest on developed Marxism; in present-day China the 'only correct' criterion for distinguishing Marxism and anti-Marxism is the 'theory of socialism' with Chinese characteristics established by Deng Xiaoping," most importantly upholding the "one center [economic construction] and two basic points [the four cardinal principles and emancipating the mind]." Xing thus juxtaposed "Deng Xiaoping theory" against leftist thought and referred explicitly to the first ten-thousand-character manifesto when he criticized those who declared that reform had created a "new bourgeoisie."

At the same time, Xing defined a right that was just as anti-Marxist as the left. Xing cited several manifestations of rightism, including privatization and revisionist interpretations of Chinese history which implied that China had taken the wrong road in pursuing the revolutionary path and that it was now necessary to say "farewell to revolution." This was a reference to a well-known book of the same title by prominent philosopher Li Zehou and leading literary critic Liu Zaifu, both of whom were then living in the United States.[40] The criticism of their book appears to have been a useful bit of political artifice. Although *Farewell to Revolution* does raise uncomfortable legitimacy issues, its primary function in Xing's piece appears to have been to provide a right to complement the left and thus define a middle course for Jiang. It may also have been chosen as a symbol of rightist thinking to warn liberal thinkers to hold their peace as Jiang turned his primary attention to warding off the left.[41]

Another sign of Jiang's effort to distinguish his own political program from those of the left and right was the publication, in late 1996, of *Heart-to-Heart Talks with the General Secretary*. This book brought together fourteen young scholars, mostly based at CASS, to flesh out the contents of the speech Jiang had made on twelve major problems confronting China at the Fifth Plenum the previous year. Part of the intent of the book was to counter the rising tide of nationalism and to point the way to adopting the shareholding system for SOEs, which would be made official the following year at the Fifteenth Party Congress. What was most eye-catching about the volume was the preface and endorsement by Liu Ji, vice president of CASS and close friend of Jiang Zemin. *Heart-to-Heart Talks with the General Secretary* anticipated the publication of a new series of books, called *Contemporary China's Problems* (Dangdai zhongguo wenti), under the sponsorship of Liu Ji that would eventually include more than twenty titles.

Following Deng's death in February 1997, Jiang began to move with remarkable self-confidence. In his eulogy at Deng's funeral, Jiang quoted Deng as saying when he returned to power in the late 1970s that there are two possible attitudes: "One is to act as a bureaucrat, the other is to work."[42] It seemed a risky quotation for Jiang to cite, given his reputation for caution. In retrospect, however, it seems that Jiang was using Deng to make a personal declaration, namely, that he was determined to work, too. Indeed, he did, for by the time of Deng's death, Jiang had the Fifteenth

Party Congress clearly in mind. Within a month of Deng's death, a draft of Jiang's report to the Fifteenth Party Congress, which would make important revisions to the party's understanding of "socialist ownership," was circulated for comment.

Although economic liberals welcomed Jiang's report, ideological conservatives hated it. Rather than again tacking to the left, as he had many times in the past, Jiang went to the Central Party School in late May to give the most important political speech of his career. In a thinly veiled jab at the left, Jiang declared that "there is no way out if we study Marxism in isolation and separate and set it against vivid development in real life." In the unpublicized portion of the speech, Jiang went further, explicitly criticizing the left and laying out his rationale for reform of the ownership structure. Deng had raised the slogan "Guard against the right, but guard primarily against the left" in his 1992 trip to the south, but it had been largely dropped from the official media (except for inclusion in formal party resolutions) following the Fourteenth Party Congress later that year. Now Jiang was reviving it and identifying himself with Deng's reforms. For a leader often criticized as bland, cautious, and technocratic, Jiang was beginning to reveal a boldness previously visible only in his deft maneuvers against political enemies.

The relaxation of the political atmosphere that was associated with the discussions leading up to and following the Fifteenth Party Congress brought about what is sometimes called the "Beijing spring," a period of limited opening up of public discussion that actually started the previous fall. This limited opening can perhaps be traced to the letter that Beijing University economics professor Shang Dewen sent to the Central Committee in August 1997, the first of three such missives. Shang argued that economic reform could not go further without an opening of the political system. In October, a month after the Party Congress, Fang Jue, a reform-minded official in the southeastern province of Fujian, distributed a statement calling for political reform.[43] In December, Hu Jiwei, the crusading former editor in chief of the *People's Daily,* published a series of articles calling for political reform in a major Hong Kong daily.[44] In January, the economics journal *Reform* carried an article advocating political reform written by Li Shenzhi, the highly respected former head of the Institute of American Studies at the CASS, who had been removed in the wake of Tiananmen.[45] In March, the little-known journal *Methods (Fangfa),* carried several articles calling for political reform.[46] And in May, a rapidly edited book titled *Beijing University's Tradition and Modern China* took advantage of the approaching centennial anniversary of Beijing University to emphasize the liberal tradition in China. A preface by Li Shenzhi noted that liberalism is not native to China but that since its introduction into China through Beijing University, liberalism has struck roots and become a part of China's tradition.[47]

The most controversial book of the spring was *Crossed Swords (Jiaofeng).* Written by two journalists at the *People's Daily,* the book starts by tracing the history of the emergence of the Dengist reforms—particularly the opening up of intellectual freedom—against the opposition of Mao's successor, Hua Guofeng. *Crossed Swords* goes on to link this early period of relaxation to the heated debates surrounding

Deng Xiaoping's trip to the south in 1992. Finally, and most controversially, the book details the sharp political debates of 1995–1997. These debates pitted those who wanted to advance reform further against those leftist ideologues who continued to oppose the marketization, and especially the privatization, of the Chinese economy, as well as China's continued integration into the world economy and the progressive abandonment of Marxism. Ignoring certain historical realities— particularly that much of Deng's animus in his 1992 trip was directed against Jiang Zemin, who was then seen as lukewarm at best toward reform—the book portrays Jiang as inheriting and pushing forward the "emancipation of the mind" begun in 1978.[48] Picking up on Jiang's report to the Fifteenth Party Congress and Li Peng's remarks at the same time, the book calls the current opening China's "third emancipation of the mind."

Crossed Swords was even more controversial than other works published during the Beijing spring because it was included in Liu Ji's series, *Contemporary China's Problems,* mentioned above. Despite Liu Ji's close relationship with Jiang Zemin, it seems that the publication of *Crossed Swords* was part of the ongoing conduct of the "court politics" surrounding the party leader, thus reflecting the inevitable conflicts among the diverse group of people Jiang had brought together under his wing. For instance, Wang Renzhi, the former head of the Propaganda Department who was forced to step down following Deng's trip to the south and take up the position of party secretary of CASS, took a very negative view of the publication of *Heart-to-Heart Talks with the General Secretary* and quarreled on more than one occasion with Liu Ji. This may well have influenced Liu's willingness to allow the publication of *Crossed Swords.* Clearly the publication of *Crossed Swords* set off a political maelstrom. Ding Guan'gen, the conservative head of the Propaganda Department, quickly condemned the book. Wang Renzhi was predictably outraged, as was conservative elder Song Ping. On the liberal side, party elder Wan Li had an unusual meeting with the authors in which he defended the book. Nevertheless, leftists, who were angered by the wholesale criticism of them in *Crossed Swords,* organized a meeting in April to criticize the book, to which they invited Communist ideologues from Russia (provoking liberals to mock the event as a gathering of the Communist International). Eventually, the editors of the conservative journal *Zhongliu,* which had published some of the "ten-thousand-character manifestos," took the authors of *Crossed Swords* to court, charging copyright violation. The court eventually dismissed the charges, but not until after some dramatic political theater.[49]

Jiang's limited movement to the right reflected an interesting intersection of domestic and foreign policy. On the domestic front, in view of the very difficult problems facing the economy, Jiang had clearly decided to distance himself from Li Peng's more cautious approach to economic reform and had decided to endorse Zhu Rongji's bold moves to restructure the government, the economy, and the relationship between the two. Major reform measures simply require a more open political atmosphere in China. At the same time, the political relaxation on the domestic front was related to a broad-ranging effort to repair relations with the United States.

The nationalist mood that had welled up in the wake of the *Yin He* incident and particularly following Taiwan president Lee Teng-hui's visit to the United States hampered both domestic reform and the stability of China's international environment, which was seen as essential to continued economic reform and development, which in turn depended on both stable export markets and a large amount of investment from abroad.

Indeed, the evidence strongly suggests that as Jiang was coming into power, his strategy was to ease China's international relations so as to create a better environment for domestic reform and to support a major restructuring of the economy (including making the necessary ideological revisions) while nevertheless sounding certain conservative ideological themes both to shore up support among the conservative wing of the party and to try to reinforce party discipline. Thus, in early 1995, Jiang tried to ease relations across the Taiwan Strait, only to have the policy blow up in his face as Lee Teng-hui traveled to the United States and made highly provocative comments while visiting his alma mater, Cornell University. The crisis that soon unfolded, however, ironically provided a new opportunity to relax international tensions as both the United States and China backed away from the abyss.

Part of this effort consisted of quasi-official initiatives to depict the United States in a more favorable light. That there was a need to do so says much about the public resentment that had built up against the United States in the mid-1990s and about the role that public opinion was beginning to play, even in the formulation of foreign policy.

Perhaps the most important of these initiatives was the publication of *China Should Not Be "Mr. No"* by Shen Jiru, a senior researcher with the CASS Institute of World Economics and Politics. Part of Liu Ji's *Contemporary China's Problems* book series, *China Will Not Be "Mr. No"* joined the long-standing debate about the causes of the collapse of the Soviet Union. Shen argued that it had been the steadfast refusal of the Soviet leaders to cooperate with other countries and open their country up (which earned Soviet foreign minister Andrei Gromyko the nickname of "Mr. No") that had brought about its demise. In opposition to conservatives' argument that it was reform that led to collapse, Shen argued that it was the *lack* of reform that had brought about the failure of socialism in the Soviet Union and Eastern Europe.[50]

Jiang's strategy reflected at least in part the growing recognition in Beijing, particularly in the wake of the Asian financial crisis, that China's fate was bound up with joining the world, not with resisting global trends. Thus, Jiang stated in March 1998, "We have to gain a complete and correct understanding of the issue of economic 'globalization' and properly deal with it. Economic globalization is an objective trend of world economic development, from which none can escape and in which everyone has to participate."[51] It was this recognition that lay behind the exchange of summits between Jiang and President Clinton in October 1997 and June 1998. It also lay behind the far-ranging reforms announced at the Fifteenth Party Congress in September 1997 and the First Session of the Ninth National People's Congress in March 1998 (when a major restructuring of the government was announced), as well as the sweeping efforts made to join the WTO in 1999. Overall, Jiang was remarkably successful in combining this recognition with domestic politics in the first year following Deng's death; he would not be so lucky in 1999.

A POLITICALLY SENSITIVE YEAR

By late 1998, it was already apparent that the last year of the century was shaping up to be one of extraordinary political sensitivity—but no one could have predicted the bizarre twists that would occur. The Asian financial crisis, which had seemed at first to have bypassed China, began to bite as exports became more difficult and foreign investment began to fall. The slowed economy, accompanied by a fall in the consumer index, made the ongoing economic restructuring even more politically sensitive as more than the expected number of workers lost their jobs or could not find employment in the first place. Reports of violence in the countryside suggested the volatile situation there.

It was under these conditions that the Chinese leadership faced the most politically sensitive season in a decade, which would include the fortieth anniversary of the Tibetan revolt (March 10), the eightieth anniversary of the May Fourth movement, the tenth anniversary of Hu Yaobang's death (April 15), the tenth anniversary of Tiananmen (June 4), and, finally, the fiftieth anniversary of the founding of the PRC (October 1). The leadership was clearly already thinking about this series of anniversaries: one of the construction projects that was to be completed before October 1 was a renovation of Tiananmen Square, which somehow required the square to be surrounded by a solid fence for some seven months between December and July, denying the public space to potential demonstrators. Caution was clearly the order of the day as Jiang and others focused on orchestrating a grand birthday party for the PRC.

As carefully as the leadership planned, events would conspire to make 1999 a less than successful year. Neither foreign relations nor the domestic situation fell into place, raising new questions about the ability of the regime to provide a political "soft landing."

Jiang Zemin's November 1998 summit meeting in Japan provided an intimation of what was to come. This trip was intended as the capstone of a successful year of diplomacy. The exchange of summits with the United States and Jiang's trip to Russia just prior to his Japanese sojourn had seemingly repaired or improved all of China's great power relations. The trip to Japan would display Jiang's diplomatic prowess by showing that he could promote good relations on terms favorable to China. But Jiang overreached. Japan had offered a full apology for its history of aggression in Korea to Kim Dae-Jung, and Jiang thought he could extract a similar statement. He also wanted to push Japan on the Taiwan issue, asking that it repeat the "Three No's" that President Clinton had offered during his trip to China. The trip was new foreign minister Tang Jiaxuan's first big test. A diplomat trained as a Japan specialist, Tang might have been expected to orchestrate a smooth visit, but domestic pressures in China made it difficult to pull off. The results were disappointing. Jiang gave his hosts a long lecture on history, and a prepared joint communiqué was left unsigned.[52] Japanese public opinion was alienated by Jiang's seemingly rude behavior, and Jiang returned home not in triumph but to new doubts about his diplomatic skills.

More unexpected, and more serious, than Jiang's diplomatic dustup in Japan was the downturn in U.S.–Chinese relations. The exchange of summits had created a significantly better atmosphere, but this goodwill quickly dissipated as old problems returned and new ones came up. The human rights issue, seemingly tempered by the summit meetings, suddenly returned to plague the relationship as China moved to jail a number of dissidents trying to form a new political party. The arrest and sentencing to long jail terms of Xu Wenli, Wang Youcai, and other China Democratic Party activists in December 1998 was merely the prelude to further arrests and sentencings the following year. Critics quickly charged China with blatant hypocrisy: it signed the U.N. Covenant on Political and Civil Rights in October and then rounded up dissidents in December.

These new outcries came at a time when charges of campaign finance violations involving the United States were once again heating up. Stories of Chinese contributions had first been raised in the winter of 1997–1998 but had died down after the Thompson hearings failed to produce any solid evidence. In May 1999, however, the charges acquired new life as Democratic fund-raiser Johnny Chung finally testified before Congress. According to Chung, Ji Shengde, head of China's military intelligence, had given him $300,000 toward support of President Clinton's presidential campaign—only $35,000 of which was actually passed to the Democrats.[53]

The most explosive charges, however, came from the committee headed by Christopher Cox, which alleged that the Chinese government had systematically stolen the most advanced U.S. nuclear weapons designs. The release of the declassified version of the report in March created a new upsurge of anti-Chinese sentiment, despite the fact that the report was so hedged with suppositions that most weapons experts distrusted its conclusions, or at least the farthest-reaching of its conclusions, doubting that the Chinese had acquired anywhere near as much as the Cox report intimated or that they had put it into production.[54] Chinese American scientist Wen Ho Lee was removed from his job at Los Alamos laboratory, but it was months before he was eventually indicted—on security violations rather than espionage charges.

Against this background, the United States began to bomb Yugoslavia on March 24. Frustrated by its failure to persuade Yugoslav president Slobodan Milosevic to sign a compromise agreement at Ramboulait and by its repeated failure to cow him with threats, NATO embarked on a course of military action intended to force an end to systematic human rights violations in Kosovo. The United States and its

NATO allies clearly saw going through the United Nations as fruitless, whereas the Chinese leadership just as clearly saw the failure to do so as a gross violation of international law. There was certainly much hypocrisy in the position of the Chinese leaders—they consistently ignored Serbian violations of human rights and made no effort to bring about a viable solution in the United Nations—but the willingness of NATO to simply ignore the United Nations raised China's worst fears about U.S. intentions.

It was in this poisonous atmosphere that Premier Zhu Rongji arrived in the United States on April 6 to discuss China's accession to the WTO. With his unique ability to combine humor and intelligence, Zhu almost singlehandedly turned back the wave of anti-Chinese sentiment that had grown up in the preceding months. Making sweeping concessions, Zhu made clear that China wanted to join the WTO and the world. This was a leadership that understood the importance of trade and the inevitability of globalization.

Then, as if to prove that history really does progress without rhyme or reason, mistakes started happening. The first was made by President Clinton. Presented with an opportunity to top off the years he had devoted to improving U.S.–Chinese relations (after notably contributing to their decline during his first two years in office), the president flinched. Once again the trees blinded him to the forest. Trent Lott, in stating his unalloyed opposition to China's entry into the WTO, left no doubt in the president's mind that China policy would be a divisive domestic issue.[55] At the same time, Secretary of the Treasury Robert Rubin, perhaps not adequately briefed on the total package, voiced doubts over the banking and securities portions of the agreement. So the president, perhaps feeling that a yet better deal could be done, sided with the doubters over the advice of his National Security Adviser Sandy Berger and Secretary of State Madeleine Albright.

Zhu returned to Beijing on April 21 to accusations that he had given up too much, but before Zhu had a chance to overcome the naysayers, the domestic atmosphere in China was transformed once again. In spite of having prepared for months for the possibility of demonstrations in the spring, the leadership was caught completely unaware on April 25 when 10,000 members of the Falun Gong—many of them elderly—appeared suddenly and without warning outside of Zhongnanhai, the leadership compound. There were no speeches or protests; the crowd simply sat and meditated, directing their *qi* (inner spirit) at the CCP leadership.

Zhu Rongji, the "passionate premier" as some in Beijing call him, sent people to the gate of Zhongnanhai to ask what was going on. In response, five members of the Falun Gong were deputed to talk to Zhu in Zhongnanhai. What must have been more disturbing than anything said was the rank of the representatives. At least three of the five were reportedly very high-ranking, albeit retired, officials, including one retired major general who had worked in the military intelligence section of the People's Liberation Army's General Staff Department.[56]

Jiang Zemin was clearly disturbed by the demonstration. Sometime after midnight, he reportedly took pen in hand and wrote a letter to his colleagues in the

Politburo Standing Committee. Saying that he could not sleep because of the day's events, he wondered how such a large demonstration could have occurred without any warning from any central department. His concerns could only have been compounded when he received a long letter from Li Qihua, former head of the 301 hospital (the top military hospital that serves the leadership). Li said that Marxism-Leninism could explain many things about the natural world but that there were many things beyond the natural world that it could not explain. The teachings of the Falun Gong filled this void and should not be seen as incompatible with Marxism-Leninism. Jiang Zemin reportedly wrote him a long letter criticizing his views. Li was then visited by two high-ranking officials and subsequently wrote a two-page self-criticism recanting his views.[57]

The subsequent crackdown on the Falun Gong, including arrests, detentions, study sessions, and a wide-ranging propaganda campaign, has evoked new concerns abroad with human rights issues. No doubt the campaign has been, as all such campaigns are, harsher and more ham-handed than necessary, but the government's crackdown draws more on a 2,000-year tradition of political autocracy than it does on Marxism-Leninism or communist dictatorship, just as the Falun Gong itself draws on a long millenarian tradition of combining martial arts with spiritual mysticism. What disturbed Jiang Zemin and other leaders most was the extent of the Falun Gong's organization, its obvious ability to mobilize people quickly, and its deep penetration into the military and security ranks, which potentially diluted the party's ability to control those important pillars of rule.[58] Jiang thus reacted just as China's imperial governments had acted before him; the risk was that the crackdown would further politicize the Falun Gong or similar movements, just as imperial crackdowns had provoked rebellion from the White Lotus, Taiping, and other sects.[59]

Domestic politics and international relations came crashing together dramatically and unexpectedly early on the morning of May 8 (Beijing time) when five laser-guided U.S. bombs slammed into the Chinese embassy in Belgrade, killing three and injuring twenty. The Chinese leadership was stunned and confused. It spent three days in an intense round of meetings, reflecting both the weakness of China's crisis management system and the array of conflicting opinions that existed at high levels. Domestic considerations were the highest priority. The depth of public anger was real and should not be underestimated. Talk of "mistakes" was quickly dismissed by most of the public; not only had the bombs clearly been targeted to hit the building, but also the people believed that U.S. intelligence could not make a mistake of that magnitude. And the event seemed to fit into a pattern of U.S. efforts to hold China down: everything from human rights concerns to the Cox report to U.S. support for Taiwan seemed to reflect hostility toward China. Understanding the need for a public release of anger, the leadership quickly yielded to students determined to march on the U.S. Embassy. The government provided buses to bring the students to the embassy area; directed them to march past the ambassador's residence, the embassy, and the visa section; allowed them to throw stones, bricks, and ink bottles; and then bused them back to their campuses. It was a way of channeling genuine public anger and preventing the alternative, namely, that students would take to the streets outside Zhongnanhai if they perceived the Chinese government as being "weak."

Despite this public show of anger, the Chinese leadership quickly came to two basic conclusions: first, whatever the reason for the bombing, it did not reflect policy at the highest levels of the U.S. government, and second, U.S.–Chinese relations were too important to be sacrificed to the emotions of the moment. Trade and a stable international environment were essential for China's continued economic development, and domestic stability was impossible without economic development.

This basic understanding hardly meant that the Chinese government was unified. Hard-liners quickly spun out scenarios that "proved" that the bombing was deliberate and, more important, that the United States was engaged in a long-term strategy to contain China.[60] The military quickly demanded more money to counter the perceived strategic threat. Even sophisticated and open-minded intellectuals viewed international trends in ominous terms. The focal point for much of this anger and frustration was Zhu Rongji. Conservatives had cautioned against Zhu's going to the United States in the first place (because of the Kosovo situation) and were particularly angered when it was revealed (by the U.S. trade representative office's unilateral posting on the Internet) that he had made sweeping concessions in order to win WTO entry.

Zhu was abused mercilessly by public opinion and criticized within the government. Articles on the Internet as well as student demonstrators labeled him a traitor (*maiguozei*). At the same time, some old cadres were known to mutter that the government's readiness to accept globalization was like Wang Jingwei's willingness to serve as head of Japan's puppet government in occupied China during World War II. Others have called Zhu's compromises in Washington the "new twenty-one demands selling out the country"—a reference to Japan's infamous demands of 1915 that sought to reduce China to a near colony.[61]

By the time the party retreated in late July for its annual conclave at the seaside resort of Beidaihe, Chinese politics had taken on a more conservative tone. Backing away from the limited liberalization of the "Beijing spring," Jiang had directed party cadres to put their thoughts in order through a rectification campaign known as the "three stresses." Then, in response to Falun Gong activities, Jiang ordered the detention or arrest of numerous leaders as well as special study sessions for party members who were also members of the Falun Gong. Still adhering to a middle course, Jiang was nevertheless closer in 1999 to the ideological conservative that he had been in the earlier years of his stewardship than to the more open-minded leader he had seemed in 1997–1998.

Neither Jiang's efforts to bolster his own and the party's authority through study campaigns nor his efforts to prevent social unrest by cracking down on democracy activists suggested a retreat to the old days. Jiang and the party recognize the need to move forward with economic reform, as the Fourth Plenary Session of the Fifteenth Central Committee in September 1999 demonstrated. Nevertheless, the party seems reluctant to endorse the far-reaching measures needed. Following a series of speeches on the reform of state-owned enterprises over the spring and summer, the party endorsed a plan to move economic reform forward by further "corporatization" of SOEs. But further introduction of the shareholding system is not likely to revive the state sector unless hard budget constraints can be enforced. And the intermingling of enterprise party committees with the managerial boards of enterprises—which Jiang called for—seems designed more to make sure the "never-left-out class" never gets left out than to enforce market-conforming behavior.[62] The unstable social and political environment undoubtedly makes the party reluctant to take more decisive measures, while the failure to implement more fundamental reforms, including political reforms, breeds further instability.

CONCLUSION

Since this chapter was originally written, major political changes have occurred: Hu Jintao replaced Jiang Zemin as the head of China, and Wen Jiabao replaced Zhu Rongji as premier of the State Council. Hu replaced Jiang as general secretary of the CCP at the Sixteenth Party Congress in September 2002, took over as president of the PRC at the NPC meeting in March 2003, and finally took control of the Central Military Commission at the Fourth Plenary Session of the Sixteenth Central Commission in the fall of 2004. Even then, Hu was still surrounded by Politburo members and others selected and groomed by Jiang, so the transition from Jiang's third generation of leadership to Hu's fourth generation has been gradual.

Nevertheless there has been a distinct change in rhetorical tone as Hu Jintao (and new premier Wen Jiabao) have begun to confront some of the problems outlined in the pages above. Whereas Jiang Zemin was often an effective promoter of high technology, coastal development, and globalization, Hu Jintao, who spent much of his career in the interior of China (in the poor provinces of Gansu, Guizhou, and Tibet), has struck a more populist note, emphasizing that the party and government should be for (but not "of") the people *(lidang weigong, zhizheng weimin)*. Although there has been little positive change in income disparities (indeed, the gaps in wealth appear to be getting larger), Hu has emphasized social justice issues, has emphasized rule by law (rule of law will have to wait), accountability, and the building institutions (or at least emphasizing institutionalized procedures). These changes in leadership style are still new, so it is perhaps premature to judge their effectiveness; for the moment, they appear to be popular among the general public.

As suggested above, the challenges China faces are formidable. The optimism of the 1980s that reform could easily rectify the problems of the past if only leftism and feudalism could be eradicated has faded. Economic development, diversification, and decentralization have created interests that erode compliance, while ideology has lost the attraction it once had. Nationalism has emerged as the ridgepole supporting the party's claim to rule, but it is also a double-edged sword. Nationalism not only distinguishes and separates China from a world its leadership knows China must join but also presents a powerful, populist critique of the leadership. National-ism is inherently critical of the "never-left-out class" that has gorged itself at public expense for the last decade and more, and it demands that the political system open up to accommodate the true representatives of the people. So far, however, the new leadership has been no more accommodating to these demands than the previous, preferring to articulate their needs *for* them.

The changes in the style and substance of PRC leadership has to do not only with the accumulation of problems in the Jiang Zemin era but also with Hu Jintao's personal history, including his time in China's interior. Hu (and Wen) are part of a new generation that has no personal experience in "old" China (Hu, born in 1942, was only seven years old when the PRC was established). He was thus not educated in China's traditional classics, did not participate in the intellectual and political movements that roiled twentieth-century China, and had no experience living, as Jiang Zemin did, in a cosmopolitan city like Shanghai (although Hu was apparently born in Shanghai, he moved at a young age to Taizhou, Jiangsu Province, not far from Jiang Zemin's hometown of Yangzhou). He was thus too young to experience China before the revolution, but he was also too old to study overseas. By the time Hu graduated from Qinghua University in 1964, the Sino-Soviet split was well under way and whatever chance there might have been for the young engineer to experience life in the Soviet Union was gone. Opportunities to study in the West did not begin to open up until the late 1970s and early 1980s, by which time Hu's career as a party apparatchik was well under way. On a more personal level, Hu's father was a modestly prosperous small businessman, and Hu grew up in a Maoist China that was distinctly anticapitalist. No doubt that to make it in the "new" China, Hu had to study hard and keep his thoughts about his own family back-ground to himself. The result was the highly disciplined, controlled leader we see today. Judging by his public performance in the first two years of office, the young Hu must also have absorbed the idealism of the time; his speeches frequently harken back to the "good" side of the Communist revolution.

This highly intelligent, hard-working engineer rose quickly through party ranks in the post–Cultural Revolution period. Although he has had periods of broader administrative power when he was party secretary of Guizhou (1985–1988) and Tibet (1988–1992), much of his career has been devoted to party work, either run-ning the Communist Youth League (1984–1985) or, after 1992, taking on responsi-bility for party affairs in the Politburo as well as heading the Central Party School (1993–2002). In short, this is somebody who has thought a great deal about manag-ing the CCP in a period of considerable corruption, organizational sclerosis, and ideological confusion, especially as he watched the collapse of socialism in Eastern Europe and the Soviet Union. Although it is still early in Hu's tenure, one conclu-sion that Hu seems to have drawn is that greater discipline is needed, and that has boded ill for China's intellectuals, particularly those on the liberal side of the spectrum. Since Hu has taken over, there has been a campaign against neoliberal economic thinking, a campaign against public intellectuals, a campaign to "maintain the advanced nature of Communist Party members," and arrests of several individuals who have pushed the boundaries of the system.

At the same time, however, the dynamics of socioeconomic change appear to be pushing against these trends of tighter party management. In prosperous areas, particularly along the east coast, the development of the private economy has been rapid, as has been the development of nongovernmental organizations (NGOs). This development does not portend the overthrow of the CCP by the private sector (all studies have concluded that private businesses prefer to work with the party rather than against it) but it does suggest a different pattern of relations between the party and state on the one hand and society on the other. Private entrepreneurs are rapidly joining the party, and the party is trying to penetrate private business (filling in the blank spots, as it is known in China) and NGOs. This policy of cooptation (perhaps even mutual cooptation) suggests a very different model of the party than the one apparently being promoted by Hu Jintao and others in Beijing. Whereas the party organization apparently wants more discipline, local interests want—and are increasingly demanding (however quietly)—a party that will serve their interests.

Although these social and political interests work on a different level than the intellectual concerns with the understanding of history, in fact, they will ultimately drive the interpretation of history. Places like Wenzhou, the celebrated city in southern Zhejiang Province that pioneered the development of the private economy, are clearly proud of their history of chambers of commerce, and their contemporary chambers of commerce are becoming increasingly active. Developments of this nature (and one might mention the concomitant development of religion) suggest a more liberal and pluralist interpretation of history, one that is at odds with the revolutionary narrative being promoted in Beijing.

Although the plethora of anniversaries that greeted the turning of the millennium has passed, there are always new anniversaries and they inevitably become times of reflecting on the development of the Chinese state. As this volume goes to press, the occasion that looms the largest is the sixtieth anniversary of the end of World War II, or as it is known in China, the end of the War of Resistance against Japan. Rather than be healed by the passage of time, the memories have been inflamed by the inability of China and Japan to deal adequately with the history question. The annual visits of Prime Minister Koizumi to the Yasukuni shrine have fanned nationalist fires in China. In the spring of 2005, these sentiments, exacerbated by the approval of another edition of a Japanese textbook that plays down the history of Japanese aggression in Asia and active discussion of expanding the United Nations Security Council to include Japan and other nations, led to thousands of Chinese taking to the streets in the largest demonstrations since Tiananmen. The Chinese government tolerated this demonstration of public sentiment for several weeks before finally cracking down. Thus, the issues of history and nationalism are still very much with us.

Indeed, despite the increasing dependency of China on foreign markets—China's foreign trade dependency now stands at about 70 percent of GDP—there remains a marked ambivalence within the Chinese government about China's integration into the world. The criticism of neo-liberal thinking mentioned above is one aspect of this ambivalence. Hu Jintao has, even more than Jiang Zemin before him, criticized presumed efforts to Westernize and divide China *(xihua fenhua)*. Such criticisms reflect a continuing insecurity, both in political and cultural terms, vis-à-vis the West. These official concerns resonate with those of intellectuals who have adopted so-called critical methodologies. Whether at the official level or at the intellectual level, the arguments that have reverberated through the twentieth century about China's relations with the West continue to find resonance in the contemporary period. The difference is that by the early twenty-first century, despite continuing insecurities and deep-seated socioeconomic difficulties, the Chinese government appears more confident than it did even a few years ago. But whether this confidence proves true or it turns out to be false bravado depends not only on the government's ability to continue to manage China's relations with the outside world but also on confronting questions of history that find their reflections in the role of the CCP in society.

NOTES

1. Fang Lizhi, "China's Despair and China's Hope," *New York Review of Books,* February 2, 1989; reprinted in Fang Lizhi, *Bringing Down the Great Wall* (New York: Knopf, 1991), 250–257.

2. Li Zehou, *Zhongguo xiandai sixiangshi lun* [History of contemporary Chinese thought] (Beijing: Dongfang chubanshe, 1987). Vera Schwarcz's masterful study *The Chinese Enlightenment: Intellectuals and the Legacy of the May Fourth Movement of 1919* (Berkeley: University of California Press, 1986) builds on some of Li's insights.

3. Wang Ruoshui's *Wei rendao zhuyi bianhu* [In defense of humanism] (Beijing: Sanlian chubanshe, 1986) is the classic work in this regard.

4. Yan Jiaqi was one of the first and best-known advocates of a civil service system. See Yan Jiaqi, *Toward a Democratic China: The Intellectual Biography of Yan Jiaqi,* trans. David S. K. Hong and Denis C. Mair (Honolulu: University of Hawaii Press, 1992).

5. Wu Jinglian was probably the best-known early advocate, but there were many others. See Joseph Fewsmith, *Dilemmas of Reform in China: Political Conflict and Economic Debates* (Armonk, NY: Sharpe, 1994).

6. Gan Yang edited a famous series of translations under the general title *Culture: China and the World.* See Chen Fong-ching and Jin Guantao, *From Youthful Manuscripts to River Elegy: The Chinese Popular Cultural Movement and Political Transformation, 1979–1989* (Hong Kong: Chinese University Press, 1997), 159–185.

7. Su Shaozhi was an early and consistent advocate of democratization. See Su Shaozhi, ed., *Marxism in China* (Nottingham, UK: Russell, 1983). See also Su's memoirs, *Shinian*

fengyu: Wengehou de dalu lilunjie [Ten years of storms: The mainland's theoretical circles after the Cultural Revolution] (Taibei: Shibao chuban gongsi, 1996).

8. Suisheng Zhao, "Deng Xiaoping's Southern Tour: Elite Politics in Post-Tiananmen China," *Asian Survey,* August 1993, 739–756.

9. Figures on the size of China's private economy are notoriously hard to pin down, but the official figures give a sense of the explosion of such activity in the wake of Deng's trip to the south. In 1992 there were 139,633 registered private enterprises selling ¥9.1 billion of goods; the following year there were 237,919 private enterprises with sales of ¥68.1 billion. See Li Peilin, ed., *Zhongguo xinshiqi jieji jiceng baogao* [Report on classes and strata in China's new period] (Shenyang: Liaoning renmin chubanshe, 1995), 225.

10. Perhaps the best summation of the changed intellectual atmosphere and concerns of these intellectuals is Wang Hui, "Dangdai Zhongguo de sixiang zhuangkuang yu xiandaixing wenti" [Contemporary Chinese thought and the problem of modernity], *Tianya* (Frontier/ Haikou), September 1997, 133–150.

11. A large number of books and articles have been published from various critical perspectives. See, for instance, Wang Hui and Yu Guoliang, eds., *90 niandai de 'houxue' lunzheng* (Post-ism in the nineties) (Hong Kong: Chinese University Press, 1998); Cui Zhiyuan, *Di'erci sixiang jiefang* (The second thought liberation) (Hong Kong: Oxford University Press, 1997).

12. Gender and race are areas in which such critiques have had a visible impact.

13. See Zhang Kuan, "Wenhua xinzhimin de keneng" [The possibility of cultural neocolonialism], *Tianya,* April 1996.

14. See, for instance, the critical essays contained in Wang and Yu, eds., *90 niandai de "houxue" lunzheng.*

15. Wang Xiaoming, ed., *Renwen jingshen xunsi lu* [Reflections on the humanistic spirit] (Shanghai: Wenhui chubanshe, 1996).

16. Joseph Fewsmith and Stanley Rosen, "The Domestic Context of Chinese Foreign Policy: Does 'Public Opinion' Matter?" in David M. Lampton, *The Making of Chinese Foreign and Security Policy in the Era of Reform: 1978–2000* (Stanford, CA: Stanford University Press, 2001).

17. For instance, Wang Jian, an economist with the State Planning Commission, posted an article on the *Jianchuan zhishi* website on June 2 arguing that the United States bombed the Chinese embassy to keep the war going because it wanted to maintain the value of the U.S. dollar vis-à-vis the euro.

18. Jianying Zha, *China Pop* (New York: Free Press, 1995).

19. Zha, *China Pop,* 38.

20. Luo yi ning ge'er (pseud.), *Disanzhi yanjing kan zhongguo* [Looking at China through a third eye], trans. Wang Shan (Taiyuan: Shanxi, 1994). See also Joseph Fewsmith, "Review of *Disanzhi yanjing kan zhongguo,*" *Journal of Contemporary China,* Fall 1994, 100–104.

21. Song Qiang, Zhang Zangzang, and Qiao Bian, *Zhongguo keyi shuobu* [China can say no] (Beijing: Zhonghua gongshang lianhe chubanshe, 1996).

22. The authors of *China Can Say No* were the first to exploit their own success with a quick sequel called *Zhongguo haishi neng shuo bu* [China can still say no] (Hong Kong: Ming bao, 1996). Imitations quickly followed. See Li Xiguang and Liu Kang, *Yaomo zhongguo de beihou* [Behind the demonization of China] (Beijing: Zhongguo shehui kexue chubanshe, 1996).

23. Weng Jieming et al., eds., *Yu zongshuji tanxin* [Heart-to-heart talks with the general

secretary] (Beijing: Zhongguo shehui kexue chubanshe, 1996); Shen Jiru, *Zhongguo bu dang 'bu xiansheng'* [China should not be "Mr. No"] (Beijing: Jinri Zhongguo chubanshe, 1998).

24. "Zhongguo shehui jiegou zhuanxing de zhongjinqi qushi yu yinhuan" [Trends and hidden shoals in the transformation of China's social structure in the near and mid-term] *Zhanlue yu guanli* (Strategy and Management/Beijing) 5 (1998): 1–17.

25. He Qinglian, *Xiandaihua de xianjing* [Pitfalls of modernization] (Beijing: Jinri Zhongguo chubanshe, 1998). See Liu Binyan and Perry Link, "A Great Leap Backward?" *New York Review of Books,* October 8, 1998, 19–23; Ming Xia, "From Comraderie to the Cash Nexus: Economic Reforms, Social Stratification, and Their Political Consequences in China," *Journal of Contemporary China,* July 1999, 345–358.

26. Ma Hong and Wang Mengkui, eds., *1998–1999 Zhongguo jingji xingshi yu zhanwang* [China's economic situation and outlook, 1998–1999] (Beijing: Zhongguo fazhan chubanshe, 1999), 162.

27. "Zhongguo shehui jiegou zhuanxing de zhongjinqi qushi yu yinhuan." A study by CASS researcher Feng Lanrui which estimated that unemployment in "cities and towns" would peak at around 21.4 percent during the ninth five-year-plan period (1996–2000), meaning that some 153 million people would be jobless. Unfortunately the citation for Feng's study is not given, so the basis for these calculations cannot be checked.

28. Ma and Wang, eds., *1998–1999 Zhongguo jingji xingshi yu zhanwang,* 25–26.

29. "Zhongguo shehui jiegou zhuanxing de zhongjinqi qushi yu yinhuan," 13.

30. Xiao Gongqin, "Zhongguo shehui ge jieji de zhengzhi taishi yu qianjing zhanwang" [The political attitudes of the various strata in China's society, and their prospects for the future], *Zhanlue yu guanli* (Strategy and Management/Beijing) October 1998, 36–43.

31. Joseph Fewsmith, "China in 1998: Tacking to Stay the Course," *Asian Survey,* January–February 1999, 99–113.

32. Joseph Fewsmith, "Jockeying for Position in the Post-Deng Era," *Current History,* September 1995, 252–258.

33. Joseph Fewsmith, "Reaction, Resurgence, and Succession: Chinese Politics since Tiananmen," in *The Politics of China: The Eras of Mao and Deng,* ed. Roderick MacFarquhar, 2nd ed. (Cambridge: Cambridge University Press, 1997), 472–531.

34. The term "old left" generally refers to a group of older CCP cadres who remain wedded to more orthodox understandings of Marxism-Leninism and worry about the impact of trends, such as the growth of private business and new interpretations of ideology, that undermine the traditional social and ideological bases of party rule. In addition to the old left, there are many people with nationalistic or conservative ideas who are not particularly identified with the old left but who constitute a party constituency that is threatened by the changes that are taking place, both domestically and internationally. This pressure must be taken seriously by Jiang Zemin and other top party leaders.

35. Edward Steinfeld, *Forging Reform in China* (New York: Cambridge University Press, 1998), 13–22; Nicholas Lardy, *China's Unfinished Economic Reform* (Washington, DC: Brookings Institution, 1998).

36. This paragraph draws on Gao Xin, *Jiang Zemin de muliao* [Jiang Zemin's counselors] (Hong Kong: Mirror, 1996).

37. On Deng's middle course, see Tang Tsou, "Political Change and Reform: The Middle Course," in *The Cultural Revolution and Post-Mao Reforms,* ed. Tang Tsou (Chicago: University of Chicago Press, 1986), 219–258.

38. The "ten-thousand-character manifestos" referred to a series of conservative ideological statements circulated informally but widely between 1995 and early 1997 that challenged the direction of reform. Although they represented a rear-guard action by the party's more ideologically orthodox wing, they presented a real problem for Jiang at the time. See Shi Liaozi, ed., *Beijing dixia 'wanyanshu'* [Beijing's underground ten thousand character manifestos] (Hong Kong: Mirror, 1997).

39. Xing Bensi, "Jianchi makesi zhuyi bu dongyao" [Uphold Marxism without wavering], *Renmin ribao (People's Daily)*, June 6, 1996, 9.

40. Li Zehou and Liu Zaifu, *Gaobie geming: Huiwang ershi shiji zhongguo* (Farewell to revolution: Reviewing twentieth-century China) (Hong Kong: Cosmos, 1996).

41. Shen Hongpei, "Ershi shijimo gongchan zhuyi dalunzhan" [The great debate over communism at the end of the twentieth century], *Beijing dixia 'wanyanshu,'* 9.

42. Xinhua, February 25, 1997.

43. Fang Jue, "China Needs a New Transformation: Program Proposals of the Democratic Faction," *China Rights Forum,* Spring 1998. This discussion draws on Joseph Fewsmith, "Jiang Zemin Takes Command," *Current History,* September 1998, 250–256.

44. Hu Jiwei, "If the Party Is Correct, Bad Things Can Be Turned into Good Things; If the Party Is Wrong, Good Things Can Be Turned into Bad Things," *Hsin Pao,* December 29, 1997; translated in FBIS-CHI-97-363 (December 30, 1997); Hu Jiwei, "Despotic Dictatorship Lingers On: Notes on Studying the Political Report of the Fifteenth Party Congress," *Hsin Pao,* December 30, 1997; translated in FBIS-CHI-97-364 (January 1, 1998); Hu Jiwei, "Given a Good Central Committee, We Will Have a Good Party; Given a Good Party, We Will Have a Good State: Notes on Studying the Political Report of the 15th Party Congress," *Hsin Pao,* December 31, 1997; translated in FBIS-CHI-97-365 (January 2, 1998).

45. Li Shenzhi, "Cong genbenshang shenhua gaige de sixiang" [Fundamentally deepening thinking about reform], in *Jiefang wenxuan (1978–1998)* (Beijing: Jingji ribao chubanshe, 1998).

46. See *Fangfa* [Methods/Beijing], March 1998, 4–15.

47. Li Shenzhi, "Hongyang beida de ziyou zhuyi chuantong" [Extol the liberal tradition of Beijing University], preface to *Beida chuantong yu jindai Zhongguo* [Beijing University's tradition and modern China], ed. Liu Junning (Beijing: Zhongguo renshi chubanshe, 1998), 1–5.

48. Ling Zhijun and Ma Licheng, *Jiaofeng: Dangdai zhongguo disanci sixiang jiefang shilu* [Crossed swords: The third thought liberation campaign in contemporary China] (Beijing: Jinri Zhongguo chubanshe, 1998).

49. "Zhongliu Loses Lawsuit against 'Jiaofeng,'" *Ming Pao,* April 23, 1999, B15; translated in FBIS-CHI-1999-0423 (April 23, 1999).

50. Shen, *Zhongguo bu dang 'bu xiansheng.'*

51. *Renmin ribao,* March 9, 1998, 1.

52. Jiang Zemin, "Take a Warning from History and Usher in the Future," Xinhua, November 28, 1998; translated in FBIS-CHI-98-333.

53. David Johnson, "Committee Told of Beijing Cash for Democrats," *New York Times,* May 12, 1999, A1; Ann Scott Tyson, "Tale of Deep Pockets and Diplomacy," *Christian Science Monitor,* May 17, 1999, 1. Ji was later reassigned. See Henry Chu and Jim Mann, "Chinese Reassign Intelligence Chief Implicated in Fund Raising Scandal," *Los Angeles Times,* July 3, 1999, A4.

54. Patrick E. Tyler, "Who's Afraid of China?" *New York Times Magazine,* August 1, 1999, 46–49.

55. Paul Blustein and Steven Mufson, "Clinton Urges China Foes Not to Stoke a New Cold War," *Washington Post,* April 8, 1999, A2.

56. Author's interviews; John Pomfret, "China Sect Penetrated Military and Police; Security Infiltration Spurred Crackdown," *Washington Post,* August 7, 1999, A15.

57. Author's interviews; "Resolutely Support the Party Central Committee's Policy Decision, and Forever Listen to and Follow the Party," *Jiefangjun bao,* July 30, 1999; translated in FBIS-CHI-1999-0823 (August 24, 1999); Seth Faison, "Ex-General, Member of Banned Sect, Confesses 'Mistakes,' China Says," *New York Times,* July 31, 1999, A5.

58. John Pomfret, "China Sect Penetrated Military and Police."

59. Daniel L. Overmyer, *Folk Buddhist Religion: Dissenting Sects in Imperial China* (Cambridge, MA: Harvard University Press, 1976).

60. Zhang Wenmu, "Kesuowo zhanzheng yu Zhongguo xinshiji anquan zhanlue" [The Kosovo war and China's security strategy in the new century], *Zhanlue yu guanli,* June 1999, 1–10.

61. Joseph Fewsmith, "The Impact of the Kosovo Conflict on China's Political Leaders and Prospects for WTO Accession," *NBR Briefing,* July 1999.

62. See "Zhongguo gongchandang di shiwuju zhongyang weiyuanhui di sici quanti huiyi gongbao" [Communiqué of the fourth plenary session of the Fifteenth Central Committee of the CCP], Xinhua, September 22, 1999. According to the communiqué, the plenum adopted the "Decision on Issues Related to State-Owned Enterprise Reforms and Development," the text of which was not available at the time this chapter was written. An idea of the content can be gathered from Jiang Zemin's long speech, "Strengthen Confidence, Deepen Reform, Create a New Situation in Development of State-Owned Enterprises," Xinhua, August 12, 1999; translated in FBIS-CHI-1999-0817 (August 18, 1999).

V

VILLAGERS, ELECTIONS, AND WORKERS' POLITICS

13

Village Committee Elections in China

Institutionalist Tactics for Democracy

Tianjian Shi

In November 1987 the Standing Committee of the National People's Congress (NPC) in China adopted the Organic Law of Village Committees (draft). The law stipulated that the chairman, vice chairmen, and members of village committees should be directly elected by the residents of the village. Implementation of the Organic Law began in 1989. Although the Tiananmen incident interrupted the process, the effort survived the criticism of conservatives in the Chinese Communist Party (CCP) and continued.[1]

Initially, outside observers were suspicious of the reform. Some argued that it was merely a propaganda effort to convince villagers that they had a voice and to show the outside world that China was becoming more democratic. Others considered the elections to be a serious effort at reform but believed that the structural constraints built into the Leninist system were so formidable that the exercise could not effect any real change in the local power structure.[2] Even the most optimistic observers argued that any success would be confined to the "experimental villages" directly controlled by the Ministry of Civil Affairs (MCA).[3]

Contrary to this prediction, however, elections have spread beyond experimental villages. In a 1990 nationwide survey 74.6 percent of rural residents reported that village committee elections had been held in their villages and 37.1 percent said the elections were semicompetitive; that is, there were more candidates than seats. Three years later a survey of the same locales revealed that 75.8 percent of respondents reported that their villages had held elections and 51.6 percent of them reported that elections had been semicompetitive.

Even though the CCP still organizes the elections—a breach of international standards of democracy—elections in rural China did create uncertainty for village rulers. Such uncertainty is the essence of democracy. Western journalists report that candidates in many places have even begun to purchase votes, testimony to the ability of the elections to put an entrenched power at risk.[4] In Shandong Province turnover in the 1995 elections reached 30 percent. It indicates that voters ousted between 9,900 and 19,800 incumbent CCP officials from office.[5] In Jilin Province 40 percent of the newly elected village leaders are not CCP members.[6] And a Chinese electoral official told the author privately that villagers in another province had removed 70 percent of the incumbent leaders from office.[7]

The semicompetitive elections in China even induced changes in local governance. Based on a four-county survey, Melanie Manion found that those villages that held competitive elections showed greater congruence between villagers and local cadres on a variety of policy issues than those villages that did not hold competitive elections.[8] These findings led experts from the Carter Center to conclude that elections in Chinese villages "are an important and sincere initiative and, as such, deserve to be taken seriously and supported."[9]

Existing democratization theory can scarcely explain electoral reform in China. Current literature on democratic transitions has focused on three sources of change. The first, advanced by modernization theorists, is socioeconomic development and class structure in society.[10] Besides the well-known criticisms of modernization theory, two other difficulties prevent us from applying it to explain reform in China:[11] (1) the theory expects transition to occur in more developed urban areas rather than in less developed rural areas; (2) according to the theory, increased wealth contributes to democracy by increasing the size of the middle class. Barrington Moore explicitly argues that peasants are major obstacles to a transition to democracy.[12] Contrary to these claims, electoral reforms in China happened in rural areas among peasants.

With more and more not-so-wealthy countries becoming democratic in the 1970s, scholars began to realize that although structural factors shape the prospects for democracy, those factors are never decisive. They found that the strategic choices made by political elites, especially the collaboration between soft-liners and opposition, represent a critical factor in facilitating transitions from authoritarianism.[13] The experiences of the "third wave" of democratization confirm this claim.[14] Unfortunately, the choices of soft-liners within the top level of the government cannot explain electoral reform in China. The most prominent reform leader, Premier Zhao Ziyang, feared losing control over rural reform and therefore opposed introducing elections into Chinese villages.[15] Although Zhao was serious about political reform in urban areas and wanted to introduce elections for intellectuals and workers, his reform plan ignored the peasants.[16] Opposition to the regime, especially among democratic activists and liberal intellectuals, also disputed the rationality of such reform.[17] Many of them believed that attempting to bring electoral reform to rural China was theoretically wrong. They believed not only that such an attempt would be impossible but also that it would help the regime perpetuate its authoritarian rule.[18]

Finally, some scholars noticed that the "resurrection of civil society" served the development of democracy in many ways.[19] In Eastern Europe, autonomous group activities played an important role in undermining communist domination.[20] I am skeptical, however, about the explanatory power of civil society for electoral reform in China. In its original claim, "resurrection of civil society" refers to generalized mobilization triggered by liberalization.[21] But in China there was neither generalized mobilization nor voluntary organized social life.

A more general problem of the current literature on democratic transitions is that the theory is inadequate for explaining incremental institutional changes under the old regime. How is it, then, that such "unthinkable" reform occurred in China? Who promotes reforms in authoritarian societies? What motivates them to do so? Most important, how do relatively weak reformers defeat stronger opponents under authoritarian rule? Thus far, few scholars have tried to answer these questions.

By contrast, Chinese electoral reform provides answers to these important theoretical questions. Like O'Donnell and his colleagues, I believe political leadership to be a crucial factor in facilitating democratic reform.[22] But in findings that differed from theirs, I found that democratically committed midlevel officials rather than top national leaders played the crucial role in bringing endogenous changes to China. During the process of reform, pressure from society is indispensable. In contrast to other societies, the pressure for reform in China came from peasants, not the middle class, and took the form of spontaneous acts, not organized political actions.[23] The accumulation of pressure brought by the peasants appears to have been a gradual process. Thus, at the beginning of the reform, pressure from peasants could scarcely influence the choices of political elites. Once the reform was well under way, however, peasants were gradually mobilized by the reforms themselves to participate in village elections, and their participation, in turn, advanced the reform process.

Most importantly, the key to successful electoral reform lies with the ability of reformers to find an effective way to pursue their goals. Earlier institutionalist studies emphasized how conservatives and local bureaucrats exploited institutional designs within the PRC's governing structure to delay and undermine the implementation of various reforms.[24] What has been neglected is the other side of the coin—that the relatively weak reformers for their part can also use institutional settings, but to overcome conservative opposition. This chapter analyzes how these midlevel government officials maneuvered institutional dynamism to promote reform. In the first section I illustrate the institutional constraints facing the reformers. In the second section I report how these institutional constraints influence the interaction of political actors and shape the strategies of reformers. Next I analyze how Chinese reformers used the implementation process of the Organic Law to defeat powerful opposition. The analyses rely on interviews with reform officials and field observations.

POLITICAL INSTITUTIONS: ACTORS AND RULES

Institutions are humanly devised constraints that structure interaction.[25] They include both formal organizations and informal rules and procedures.[26] In the case at hand the institutional system in which both the electoral reformers and their conservative rivals operated can be outlined in terms of six sets of group actors and five rules of the game. In incremental reform, time is a crucial but usually neglected variable.[27] Dynamic institutional analysis will show how the power relations among the actors and the rules of the game changed as the reforms progressed.

THE ACTORS

Officials in the Ministry of Civil Affairs   MCA

The major protagonists are a group of officials in the Ministry of Civil Affairs who were responsible for implementing the Organic Law. The mastermind of the electoral reform within the MCA was a midlevel official named Wang Zhenyao, a deputy director of the Department of Grassroots Administration in the MCA. Wang grew up in a village and in Mao's era worked as a peasant in Henan Province. This experience taught him that Chinese peasants are capable of making decisions about their own affairs. He also realized that for the peasants to live a better life, it was necessary to change the governing process in rural China.[28]

After Mao's death in 1977 Wang passed the college entrance examination and entered the university. At that time the works of Joseph Gusfield, Reinhard Bendix, S. N. Eisenstadt, Karl Deutsch, Seymour Martin Lipset, and Samuel Huntington were translated into Chinese and published in the PRC. Those works influenced a generation of intellectuals, as many young college students realized that economic development needs to be sustained by certain kinds of political reform. At roughly the same time Chiang Ching-kuo in Taiwan lifted martial law and allowed opposition parties to compete with the Kuomintang (KMT). This development in Taiwan strengthened the belief of young reformers in the possibility of also changing a Leninist party from within. Wang noticed that economic reform in rural China made peasants the first social group to escape from the totalitarian control of the CCP. Unlike many others, he therefore believed that political changes should be easier to effect in rural areas than in urban areas.[29]

Another important factor in the reform efforts also occurred at this time. Deng Xiaoping adopted a policy of retiring revolutionary veterans from various levels of government, which quickly forced many from their leadership positions after the Cultural Revolution. The vacancies were filled in turn by technocrats and college graduates. The changes in the generational and educational composition of the bureaucracy had significant implications for Chinese politics. Unlike the old revolutionary veterans, the technocrats were less likely to be burdened by official ideology and tended to make policy based on a technical rationale. For their part, the college graduates assigned to different levels of the bureaucracy usually brought new ideas they had picked up in their university studies. Thus, after graduation Wang gathered together a group of reformers and joined the government with the goal of promoting political reform in rural China.[30]

The new generation of bureaucrats working in various levels of the government realized that they could not govern according to the old ways. Instead, they turned for guidance to the new ideas that were gaining currency.[31] Although not all younger bureaucrats within the Chinese government were reformers, many did work hard to reform the system from within. Of course, the bureaucratic interests of the ministry and career considerations also motivated Wang and other reformers in the MCA to implement the Organic Law faithfully.[32]

Unfortunately, the MCA is one of the least powerful ministries in the Chinese government.[33] The administrative arm of the MCA in each province, the Bureau of Civil Affairs (BCA, *minzheng ju*), is under dual leadership. The BCAs answer directly to the provincial government, which has exclusive control over promotions, housing allocation, and the welfare of cadres in the BCAs. Their relationship with the MCA is *zhidao guanxi;* that is, they are under the supervision of the MCA only for the bureaucratic function. The MCA is not responsible for their promotions and welfare. Such an arrangement assures that the local BCAs will side with provincial authorities against the MCA in the event of conflict between the two.

National Leaders

The second group of actors consists of the national leaders. They were mixed in their attitudes toward the reform. Although generally a reformer, Premier Zhao Ziyang stood with the conservatives on the issue of village election reform, fearing that such reform would make it impossible for township officials to enforce government policy. To cope with the changes in rural areas, he proposed establishing government offices in villages *(cuigongsuo)* to fill the power vacuum created by the dissolution of the people's communes.[34] Many provincial leaders supported Zhao's proposals.

Peng Zhen, the chairman of the NPC, was strongly opposed to Zhao's proposal[35] and wanted to introduce direct elections of village leaders into rural China.[36] This approach was shaped in part by Peng's commitment to the mass line of the CCP and his personal experiences during the Cultural Revolution. Peng may have supported introducing village elections into rural China to advance bureaucratic interests, but he also genuinely believed that by implementing such reform, one could in fact strengthen the existing political structure of the PRC. As the chairman of the NPC, he wanted to increase its power in the Chinese political process.

Peng worked hard to persuade the Standing Committee of the NPC to support the Organic Law. When the draft law stipulating that members of village committees should be elected by popular vote rather than being appointed by higher authorities was first presented to the Standing Committee of the NPC for review in 1986, most members opposed it and it was defeated. Peng managed to reintroduce the draft law to the Standing Committee and strongly lobbied its members to support it. Thanks to his persistent efforts, the draft finally passed and became law in November 1987, only months before his retirement.

Although Peng's sponsorship was essential to launching reforms that would open up the system, national leaders had little influence over the implementation of the Organic Law. By the time implementation began in 1990, the leading opponent of the reform, Zhao Ziyang, had been purged. Except for one incident after June 4, most national leaders were indifferent to electoral reform.[37]

Local Bureaucrats

A third group consisted of local bureaucrats at the township, county, and provincial levels. Students of Chinese politics sometimes overlook how varied this stratum is and mistakenly analyze it as a single group opposed to reform. In reality, the attitudes of officials at different levels of government can be different. Additionally, attitudes of the same officials about electoral reform may shift over time. In the initial stage most local bureaucrats opposed the reform, fearing it would cause instability in places under their jurisdiction. In the face of the ongoing economic and political reform, some gradually realized that they could no longer rely on the traditional way of governing. Although elections may not have been their preferred choice, many came to see it as the only way to cope with new problems arising in the villages.[38]

Village-Level Cadres

A fourth group of actors consisted of incumbent village-level cadres. Most of them opposed the electoral reforms out of a sense of uncertainty about whether they could hold on to their positions.[39] At a conference on village elections attended by heads of grassroots administration desks of BCAs in 1996, the author asked participants to evaluate attitudes of incumbent village cadres toward reform at the beginning stage of the implementation process.[40] Among the thirty participants, twenty-eight reported that village cadres opposed electoral reform.[41]

Peasants

The fifth group of players were the peasants. The support of Chinese peasants for electoral reform can be traced to the economic reforms begun in the late 1970s. Under the people's communes, peasants had been dependent on village authorities for all aspects of their livelihood. The de facto privatization brought about by the economic reform turned Chinese peasants into resource providers for grassroots administrations.[42] When village authorities asked peasants for money, the peasants began asking in exchange to participate in the decision-making process.[43] The famous peasant rebellion in Renshou County in Sichuan Province in 1993 was the product of such radical changes.[44]

When elections were first introduced into rural China, peasants hardly had any say in the process. Most peasants were suspicious of the government's intentions and few wanted to engage in electoral politics to pursue their goals, preferring to remain spectators rather than participants. Nonetheless, the ongoing reforms gradually redefined the peasants' incentive structure and eventually provided them with resources and power to influence the reform process.[45] When reform transformed elections into a salient institution in rural politics, peasants became important political actors.

Foreign Actors

Students of comparative politics have long understood that international systems can influence domestic politics.[46] Previously, I demonstrated that international systems influenced reform in China through the transmission of democratic values. Foreign actors, including Western foundations, academics, politicians, and journalists, were also directly involved. By providing financial support, advice, and criticism, these actors participated in various stages of the political struggle over the implementation of the Organic Law.

THE RULES

In the case of the electoral reform, many factors and rules of the game shaped the goals, preferences, and strategies of political actors.[47]

First is the official ideology of their nation. The official ideology in China has been hostile to free expression and, more importantly, to popular sovereignty.[48] Such elections as there had been in China in the past were not about letting people choose their rulers. Rather, those elections were designed to mobilize people to carry out predetermined party goals, to socialize them into official norms, and to legitimate the rule of the CCP. Electoral reforms adopted in 1979 enlivened elections for local People's Congresses but did not signal a change in the official ideology, and neither did the village committee election reform of the following decade.[49]

Second, because the structure of authority in China is fragmented, bureaucrats have a lot of room for maneuver in the implementation of policy. As a consequence, policy making is protracted and incremental.[50] For typical policy initiatives, no single decision determines the issue.

Rather, a whole string of mutually reinforcing decisions are required in order to keep any one initiative on track—and the announcement of a decision in the national media tends to cloak this protracted process. A major decision, in brief, does not by itself ensure that the substance of the decision will be implemented. Relatedly, the search for the timing of a particular decision is often misplaced, for the process of making a decision is protracted, as a consensus for it is built.[51]

Third, while outright opposition is dangerous, bureaucrats can engage in covert resistance to policies they do not like. Two frequently used techniques are making requests for special treatment or individual exemptions and formally implementing policies but covertly subverting their intent.

Fourth, since bureaucrats in the administrative arms of the MCA are under dual leadership, they must balance local interests against orders from the central government when implementing policy. Reformers cannot count on their support if local government opposes their policy.

Fifth, there is no adequate means for supervising policy implementation because the organization responsible for implementing policy is also responsible for sanctioning the mistakes of local bureaucrats.

INSTITUTIONAL EFFECTS ON
POLITICAL INTERACTION

Static comparison of the balance of power led officials in the MCA to believe that dramatic reform in China is impossible. To overcome resistance to the reforms, reformers in China embarked on a strategy of deliberately manipulating a crucial but usually neglected variable—time. When I first contacted Wang's colleagues in early 1989, they told me that an "incremental, or Fabian approach" would be the ideal model for China.[52] "According to Huntington," they argued, "the foot-in-the-door approach of concealing aims, separating the reforms from each other, and pushing for only one change at a time" was the only way to bring any meaningful political change to China.[53]

To win over stronger opposition, reformers must abide by the rules of the game shaped by the institutional settings of their society. Institutions influence the interactions of political actors in four ways, as discussed in the following paragraphs.

First, established institutions affect the nature of arguments that are deemed correct in a given political system. "Correct arguments" are those that are convincing to the people they are designed to appeal to yet do not leave themselves open to attack by others.[54] This is true not only in today's China but also in other societies. For example, in Victorian England from 1830 to 1879 centralization and collectivism were alien to the prevailing climate of opinion. Reformers who wanted to increase the power of the government therefore behaved surreptitiously and circuitously. "Where the matter at issue was openly debated they had to be explained away as exceptions, as unusual necessities or even on occasion as subtle applications of the principle of individualism."[55] Study of the behavior of reformers in that era led MacDonagh to conclude that at the time of positive and aggressive individualism,

> if the foundations of the modern state were laid, it happened only because of the immense pressure from beneath of the promoting factors, only because of the great difficulty of measuring particular actions of government and particular statutes against the uncertain yardstick of individualism, and only because a large number of measures slipped through unnoticed.[56]

Reformers in China understood the constraints created by the official ideology. Waving the banner of such Western ideas as liberty and democracy in that political environment would only provoke conservatives and provide them with an opportunity to defeat reform.[57] When he began to reform the socialist economy, Deng Xiaoping felt it was necessary to avoid an ideological confrontation with conservatives in the party.[58] In arguing for political reform, he emphasized the instrumental functions of elections and suggested that such reform was designed for "the development of socialist democracy."[59] I expect that reformers in the MCA, too, will try to avoid ideological debate and will instead emphasize the instrumental functions of elections.

Second, because the MCA does not have direct control over provincial BCAs, reform by decree will not work in China. To persuade local bureaucrats to cooperate with the MCA, reformers need to find ways to change the incentive structure of local bureaucrats. Since the personal and bureaucratic interests of those bureaucrats are usually nonidentical, the MCA may manipulate such differences to persuade local cadres to circumvent the bureaucratic barrier to carry out reform.

Third, the opponents of reform in the Chinese government are stronger than the proponents of reform. But the reformers understood that the "the balance of forces in any conflict is not a fixed equation until *everyone* is involved." Thus, a simplistic calculus of a static balance of power could not provide them with much guidance. Unlike most other people, they were confident that China's peasants would be interested in electoral reform, as long as they could be shown that elections would bring them important tangible benefits. Reformers in the MCA also believed that Chinese peasants were capable of choosing their own leaders by popular vote. Thus, finding a way to reallocate power by managing the scope of conflict is the key to their success.[60] The reformers used two strategies to achieve such a goal: (1) they worked hard to stimulate the political interests of the "uninterested" spectators, that is, ordinary peasants, and recruit them to the implementation process; and (2) they created a situation of path dependency to reduce possible opposition. As the case of village elections shows, the early stages of successful reform were marked by small steps that reveal no coherent strategy or long-term plan. Once the system is opened by top leaders and the reform process begins, each step is so arranged as to appear to be a natural response to unforeseen consequences of the initial reform brought about by previous policy.[61]

And fourth, because no single decision is determinative in the policy process, bargaining and consensus building are required at each step of the way to implementation. Even if reformers managed to push through a comprehensive package, local bureaucrats would still be able to exert their influence to destroy their designs at the implementation stage.[62] Without proper enforcement mechanisms, reformers could rely only on institutional dynamism to win over their opponents. Since institutions themselves are objects of contention in incremental reform, reformers can win political advantage by relying on time to transform structural parameters—that is, by waiting.

The next two sections use the implementation process of the Organic Law to illustrate how Chinese reformers manipulated constraints defined by institutional settings in their society to circumvent much stronger opposition to bringing elections into rural China.

INCREMENTAL POLICY IMPLEMENTATION: STAGE 1

From the start reformers in the MCA clearly eschewed ideological debates. When the implementation process formally began after June 4, 1989, instability in the countryside was one of the regime's major concerns. Realizing that suggestions which helped the regime resolve practical problems could be more readily accepted by political leaders, reformers played on the regime's vulnerability and emphasized the instrumental function of elections. Thus, in each of his public speeches, Wang Zhenyao stressed that introducing elections into rural China could diffuse peasant dissatisfaction and head off local rebellions. In study materials for local election officials, the MCA described elections as a cure for all that ailed the Chinese village and a guarantee of long-term stability.[63] Similar to his predecessors in nineteenth-century England, Wang argued that the reform was an application of socialist principles.[64] Examination of public and internal documents put out by the MCA shows that whenever reformers talked about democracy, they made sure to use the term "socialist democracy."[65]

The cooperation of officials in the provincial BCAs was necessary to overcome provincial opposition to the reform. Although the Organic Law and the 1990 Document 19 required that village elections be held, the BCA officials still looked to provincial leaders for guidance.[66] To induce their cooperation, special incentives had to be created to change the cost-benefit calculations of those officials. To this end, the MCA allocated scarce resources to send officials in BCAs abroad to "study" self-government and observe elections. For officials in Beijing a trip abroad was nothing unusual, but for department heads at the provincial level, let alone for cadres at the prefectural and county levels, the opportunity to visit foreign countries is rare. At several conferences attended by heads of provincial BCAs, leaders of the MCA announced publicly that if elections in the provinces met their standards, the bureau chiefs would have the opportunity to go abroad to study in order to further improve their work. Although we should not overestimate the impact of such visits, the strategy works well in eliciting the cooperation of BCA officials.[67]

Below the provincial level, many prefectural, county, and township leaders—and of course many village officials—opposed competitive elections, fearing the unknown.[68] A careful analysis of the balance of power between proponents and opponents of reform led officials in the MCA to conclude that their only chance at that time was to slip reform through unnoticed.

Because the Organic Law had been passed by the NPC, it was hard for the opponents of reform to argue openly against it. They could, however, claim special hardship in their localities and ask for a delay in holding elections, or they could turn the elections into single-candidate processes that would not threaten their power. Aware of these tactics, reformers in the MCA decided to divide the reform process into two stages. The goal of the first stage was to persuade local officials to organize elections; the second stage sought to improve them.[69] The political logic of such a design was to lock local bureaucrats into elections before the full implications of elections for their own positions became apparent. Underlying this strategy was the reformers' trust in the peasants. They believed that institutional evolution would gradually mobilize peasants to defend their interests. Once peasants learned they could get certain tangible benefits from competitive elections, reformers believed, they would not stand for electoral manipulation. Only then would the type of manipulation tolerated at the early stages of the reform be corrected.[70] As Wang Zhenyao told the author in an interview later on:

> We knew there were strong incentives for local bureaucrats to manipulate elections. But no matter what we did at that time, there was no way for us to prevent such manipulation from occurring. This is not to say that we didn't care about election manipulation. We did care. But we had a more serious problem to deal with at that time. Officials in our provincial bureaus had to deal with the opposition of their provincial governments, especially the opposition of leaders at the prefectural and county governments. If the standard were set too high, there would be open confrontation between officials in the civil affairs system and leaders in prefectural and county government who could always veto the proposed reforms. To reduce opposition, we asked our provincial bureaus to seek support from their provinces to hold elections for village committees but did not worry about the quality of the elections. We were confident that ordinary peasants would be mobilized by the electoral reform to defend their own interests. We therefore instructed our local bureaus to do only two things. The first was to make sure to organize elections and the second was to honor the results of those elections.[71]

Of course, we should not simply accept the claims of reformers at face value. Besides the "art of the possible," an equally plausible explanation of their behavior is that the reformers really wanted to help the CCP consolidate its power and to avert foreign criticism, rather than trying to change the nature of the regime from within.[72] Because the implications of these two explanations for our understanding of Chinese reform are fundamentally different, we need a full assessment of the reformers' intentions. For now, however, we assume that their purpose was to bring competitive elections into rural China and thereby change the political process in grassroots administrations.

As expected by the reformers, when elections were first introduced in the villages, cadres tended to treat them as a formality. Voters did not pay too much attention to them either. In this sense, both cadres and peasants chose their strategies on the basis of incomplete information. But peasants in some of the villages where the cadres were especially corrupt decided to try to defeat them by voting. Local officials usually balked at the results and did not want to honor them. Since this situation occurred in only a small number of villages, local civil affairs bureaus were able to persuade township and county leaders to sacrifice the losers to avoid further trouble. To help them, the MCA sent out cadres to observe the elections. The cadres ignored election manipulation by local cadres but insisted that the election results be honored to preserve the stability of the country.[73]

The news that corrupt officials in certain villages were voted out of office spread through townships and, sometimes, the county and the prefecture. When people in other villages learned that these elections could indeed make a difference, they indicated their intention to express their opinion in the next election. According to officials in the MCA, most villagers did not pay attention to the first round of elections, but some became interested the second time, and by the third time many actively participated.[74]

When more incumbents had been voted out of office, conservative local bureaucrats woke up to the threat and wanted to bring an end to elections. By then, however, elections had won acceptance among the peasants. Once people had tasted democracy, local officials would have a hard time taking away the right to vote. Thus, to manipulate elections, conservative officials could do little more than control the nomination of candidates. When semicompetitive elections became widespread in 1993, electoral manipulation also intensified.

As anticipated by the reformers, institutional dynamism brought about two other changes by that time. One is that some local bureaucrats changed their attitude toward elections. Many county officials realized that elections increased the governability of local government and some of them began to support reform. The other is that peasants now joined in the struggle: realizing that elections had a bearing on their welfare, many began to nominate their own candidates to challenge local bureaucrats. Some of them even lodged complaints with higher authorities about election fraud.[75] These developments drastically changed the balance of power between proponents and opponents of reform.

Based on a nationwide survey, table 13.1 examines the scope and intensity of campaign activities and complaints about election manipulation in the second round of elections, which were held in 1992–1993. More than half of the voters reported having engaged in at least one form of campaign activity. Excluded from the analysis are "easy" campaign acts like attending meetings. Twenty-five percent of villagers engaged in at least one "difficult" campaign activity, usually at the nomination

Table 13.1. Campaign Activities in Rural China

Activities	Percentage	Number[a]
Attending campaign meetings	54.2	724
Nominating candidates	17.0	227
Persuading others to attend campaign meetings	14.9	199
Recommending candidates when asked	12.4	166
Complaining elections are unfair	5.2	69
Persuading others to nominate candidates	4.7	63
Persuading others whom to vote for	2.9	39
Mobilizing others to boycott elections	1.8	24
Persuading others whom not to vote for	1.4	19
N = 1,336		

Source: National Survey on Political Participation and Political Culture (1993).

[a] The N includes only those who claim that their village held semicompetitive elections for people to choose their leaders, not the whole rural population in China.

stage.[76] The table shows that 17.0 percent of voters took the initiative to nominate candidates and 12.4 percent responded to authorities who solicited their opinions on candidate selection.

The enfranchisement of peasants changed the institutional setting facing reformers. Even though there was still no institutionalized enforcement mechanism to guarantee that elections were clean, the MCA could rely on the rural populace to monitor the behavior of local bureaucrats. With more than 5 percent of respondents reporting that they had lodged complaints about election fraud, manipulators now had to fear ordinary citizens.

INCREMENTAL POLICY IMPLEMENTATION: STAGE 2

In 1993 a majority of villages in China held elections for village officials. As more and more village incumbents were voted out of office, elections in many places had begun to jeopardize rather than enhance the power of local CCP organizations. How reformers in the MCA behaved at that time can help us to discern their real intentions. If they wanted to promote democracy, they would continue to push for reform. On the contrary, if they only wanted to help the regime for propaganda purposes, they would stop further reform measures.[77] Careful examination of the reformers' behavior at this juncture reveals that they tried to push additional reforms, in hopes of further changing the CCP from within, rather than stopping the reforms to help local CCP machines consolidate their power.[78]

As growing numbers of elected officials came from outside the party, officials in the MCA began vigorously pushing electoral reform to its second stage. In a change of policy, the MCA no longer tolerated electoral fraud and instead embarked on a campaign to stamp it out. Large numbers of complaints about electoral manipulation enabled the MCA to argue convincingly that such manipulation had begun to hinder the stability of the villages. Such arguments helped them implement four new initiatives to curb election fraud.

In response to reports of violations of the election law, the MCA, first, ordered its local agents to intervene on behalf of peasants. The ministry ordered its local bureaus to enforce exiting rules aggressively, to prevent incumbents from manipulating elections.

Second, the MCA began to lobby provincial People's Congresses to amend existing provisions so as to close up loopholes used by incumbents to manipulate elections. They formally proposed making violations of the electoral law a criminal offense.[79]

Third, they tried to mobilize peasants to monitor election fraud. Students of Chinese politics note that an effective way for political actors to advance their interests is to find an existing government policy favorable to them and press local bureaucrats to implement it. Thus, an effective way to mobilize the peasantry to oversee election fraud was to supply them with ammunition. To this end, the MCA openly published formal documents demanding that election officials curb electoral manipulation.[80]

Finally, the reformers in the MCA began to reform the nomination procedures. During a conference of chief executives of the provincial BCAs, Wang Zhenyao announced that the selection of candidates through consultation should no longer be allowed in village-level elections. He argued:

> The main problem is that the consultation process is too vague and restriction is not strong enough. To reduce the large number of candidates after the initial round of nomination to the rather small number of formal candidates is a very difficult process. . . . How can the formal candidates be selected out of those to be eliminated without a contest of votes? If the consultation process lacks transparency, corrupt behavior would have a chance. Therefore, MCA believed that in the process of determining formal candidates, a preelection is needed. . . . All the proposed candidates should be left to the voters to decide through a vote and those who win the largest number of votes should become formal candidates.[81]

The MCA formally endorsed the method of nomination that combined candidate self-recommendation with villager recommendation.[82]

> Under the political system in which the Communist Party is the ruling party, political organizations should not be allowed to nominate candidates in village-level elections. Only one method, the combination of self-recommendation and villagers' recommendations is the most suitable method. . . . Only when the villagers can judge for themselves which candidate management plan is superior can they improve their ability to select the most capable people as village leaders. . . . If democracy is not practiced in full in the nomination of candidates, if the traditional appointment method is used on

the basis of subjective preferences and if candidate initiative is not stimulated, the election will inevitably be a formality.[83]

To promote the new nomination procedure, the MCA set up model counties. In 1994 it designated Lishu County in Liaoning Province as one such place. In Lishu County candidates are nominated by villagers through nomination ballots *(haixuan)*. Among the nominated, the formal candidates were selected through a primary, rather than by "democratic consultation." The authorities did not intervene at all during the nomination process. Candidates were also encouraged to campaign before election day. A widely circulated document described the Lishu experience as a major breakthrough and called on other provinces to learn from it.[84]

These moves appeared as a natural response to an emerging problem and seemed to be designed to help the authorities preserve stability in the countryside. But they were well-planned measures thought out in advance to achieve long-standing goals.[85] Once the reformers were convinced that developments in rural China had made it almost impossible for conservatives to roll back the electoral reform, they began to enroll foreign participants to acquire resources crucial for implementation of the Organic Law and to further the changes in the balance of power.[86]

To my knowledge, the central government did not allocate funds to the MCA for the purpose of implementing the Organic Law. In the early stages of the reform, money for organizing elections came exclusively from provincial budgets. Beginning in 1993 the MCA sought financial support from foreign foundations for such purposes as organizing conferences for provincial BCA leaders, printing election posters and other materials, and sending BCA officials abroad to observe elections.[87] The Ford Foundation was the first to make a grant to the MCA, followed by the Asian Foundation, the International Republican Institute (IRI), and the United Nations Development Program (UNDP). Without this outside money, many innovative MCA projects could not have been started.

Reformers also played the international card to overwhelm their political enemy. This is hardly new to people in the MCA. In fact, economic reformers in the mid-1980s had used the same strategy.[88] When foreign criticism of human rights in China intensified after 1992, officials in the MCA tried to use such pressure to push reforms. Kelliher found that in debates over village self-government reformers emphasized the possibility of neutralizing outside criticism and improving China's international reputation.[89]

Promoting the elections with foreign audiences helped improve China's international image.[90] But mounting evidence suggests that for the reformers foreign propaganda was less important than was effecting real internal change. MCA officials were candid with foreign journalists and academics about the problems in the election process. During an international conference on village elections sponsored by the Ford Foundation, the MCA sent foreign participants to a village where the election was merely a formality, in hopes of getting their advice on how to resolve the problem in the future.[91] Foreign foundation officers, academics, and journalists encountered no restrictions on what they could see and where they could go to observe elections. Officials of the MCA even encouraged reporters to go to places where the work of implementing the Organic Law was lagging.[92]

As ammunition in internal debates, MCA officials cited the opinions of foreign experts to support their proposals for reform. According to Lorraine Speiss, program officer of the IRI, the MCA took much of her advice for improving procedural arrangements of elections very seriously. Jonathan Hecht, a legal expert who served as program officer of the Ford Foundation in Beijing, played an important role in drafting regulations made by several provincial People's Congresses to implement the Organic Law.

At a conference held in Fujian in 1992, Professor Kevin O'Brien of Ohio State University pointed out that regulations being considered by the provincial People's Congress called for peasants to vote on a family basis. If the provisions were adopted, the principle of one person one vote would be replaced by one family one vote, which would be contrary to democratic principles because it would deprive women and elders of the opportunity to vote differently from the other members of their families.

MCA officials had already tried to persuade Fujian officials to change the provision in question, but local leaders emphasized the difficulty of mobilizing elders and women to vote and refused to cooperate. It was O'Brien's remarks at the conference that turned the discussion around. Reformers in the MCA cited his argument as a warning to local officials that if they did not change the provision, foreigners would label Fujian's elections as false democracy, which would jeopardize China's international image.[93] Provincial leaders were convinced and agreed to amend drafts of the provision before presenting it to the provincial People's Congress for approval. Having successfully persuaded Fujian Province to honor the principle of one person one vote, MCA officials announced at the conference that officials from other provinces should make sure their provisions also specified that the vote belonged to each individual rather than to each family. Because of O'Brien's contribution, the MCA called the article specifying that elections be based on the principle of one person one vote "O'Brien's Law."[94]

Foreign participants were also critical players in the political struggle over the relationship between the party secretary and the chairman of the village committee. Although every Chinese village has a party branch, the major function of which is to supervise the work of the village committee, its leaders are not subject to oversight by ordinary villagers. To resolve this problem, reformers would have to surmount both political and technical obstacles. As reform on this issue would unavoidably undermine party control over villages, any reform proposal would be liable to the charge of being antiparty. The technical difficulty is that it is hard to find a way for nonparty members to have a role in the selection of the party secretary. According to the charter of the CCP, party secretaries can be elected only by party members.

To resolve this problem, reformers in the MCA found that Hequ County in Shanxi Province had developed an experimental double-ballot system. Under this system, peasants were to cast two votes in village elections, one for the chairman of the village committee and the other for the party secretary. Even though the second vote was formally described as a public opinion poll *(minyiceyan)*, party members who received less than 50 percent of the popular vote were disqualified from standing as candidates for village party secretary. Although the arrangement does not provide villagers with the political power to select party secretaries, it does allow them to veto candidates they dislike.[95] Even though the "Hequ experience" was well received by the ministry, no one dared to advocate that it be promoted nationwide.[96]

In a 1995 international conference on village self-government, Professor Jean Oi of Harvard University raised the issue in her keynote speech and called on the MCA to find a way to resolve it. Unless people had some influence in the selection of party secretary, she argued, elections would not be able to change the governing process in Chinese villages. This speech helped to break the barrier. Responding to her criticism, MCA officials asked officials from Shanxi to report the Hequ experience to the conference and suggested that bureau chiefs from other provinces employ the method in their own localities. The events looked like a natural response to foreign criticism aimed at defending China's international image. In fact, it was a well-orchestrated move by officials in the ministry. Even though Professor Oi was not involved in the planning, officials in the MCA had predicted that if she were given a chance to speak, she would raise the issue. They told the author later that a foreigner giving voice to their ideas could neutralize their opponents' criticism.[97]

CONCLUSION

The case study of the implementation process of the Organic Law of Village Committees shows that just as institutional settings can be used by conservatives to resist reform, they can also be used by reformers to promote political change. While a static comparison of the balance of power between conservatives and reformers shows that the opposition of conservatives was formidable, Chinese reformers were able to achieve some success in implementing the Organic Law. Certainly the future of political reform in China is still far from assured, the strategy of reformers in the MCA is fragile, and the process could still be derailed. But the Fabian approach pursued by reformers has succeeded up to now, and the power of their opponents has been diminished.[98] Given the earlier balance of power between proponents and opponents of the reform, the success of the reformers to date would once have seemed unimaginable.

The key to their success lies in their strategic choice to handle Chinese reform incrementally. They divided the implementation process into two phases, so as to confront only one set of opponents at a time. Rather than trying to push for clean, fair, and fully competitive elections at the outset, reformers were willing to settle for manipulated elections in the first stage of the process and strive for improved elections only in the second stage.[99] Because institutions are objects of contention, they may change in ways that allow the forces of reform to gain strength over time. In the case of village elections, endogenous, reform-induced changes brought in new participants and changed the nature of political interaction. As the reforms continued, there were changes in the balance of power between proponents and opponents, in the options available to conservatives to resist reform, and in the opportunities available to reformers to pursue their goals. The enfranchisement of peasants enabled reformers to count on them to curb election manipulation at the second stage of the reform.

The findings of this chapter have important implications for the study of political reform in other societies. Democratically committed midlevel officials may accelerate the wheels of history. While the sponsorship of national leaders was important to get reforms adopted, the success of electoral reform in China should be credited to the efforts of these midlevel officials. In addition, peasants are important forces driving electoral reform in China—a finding that challenges the widely accepted myth that peasants are the obstacles to democracy.

Experience in China also tells us that the winning strategy of political reform can only be formed endogenously. The preferences of reformers at each step of the reform and the strategies designed by them to pursue their goals were shaped by the institutional setting in which they operated, in particular, by the balance of power between proponents and opponents of reform but also by the rules of the game of the society in which they live. To understand reformers in other societies, we need to analyze their behavior in terms of its particular context. To assess a reform design, we need to know both the balance of power between proponents and opponents of reforms and the rules of the game in the particular society. That way we can evaluate whether reformers can take advantage of the rules of the game to alter the balance of power to pursue their goals.

The analysis in this chapter clearly demonstrates that institutional analysis does not mean institutional determinism. Although institutions provide part of the political context in which political actors set goals and strategies, both conservative and reformist actors do not always correctly understand the constraints facing them. Even if they set their goals correctly and find the best strategy to pursue their goals, their opponents may also find critical points at which to protect their interests before it is too late. The intelligence, skill, and sophistication of political actors are key factors in their understanding of institutional constraints, their formulation of preferences, and their design of strategies to pursue their goals. For this reason, politics is an art rather than a set of rules to be applied mechanically.

APPENDIX: SAMPLE DESIGN

The data come from a survey conducted in China from September 1993 to June 1994 in cooperation with the Center for Social Survey of the People's University of China. The sample represents the adult population over eighteen years of age residing in family households at the time of the survey, excluding those living in the Tibetan Autonomous Region. A stratified multistage area sampling procedure with probabilities proportional to size measures (PPS) was employed to select the sample.

The primary sampling units (PSUs) employed in the sample design are counties *(xian)* in rural areas and cities *(shi)* of urban areas. Before selection, counties were stratified by region and geographical characteristics and cities by region and size. A total of forty-nine counties and eighty-five cities were selected as the primary sampling units. The secondary sampling units (SSUs) were townships *(xiang)* and districts *(qu)* or streets *(jiedao)*. The third stage of selection was geared to villages in rural areas and neighborhood committees *(juweihui)* in urban areas: a total of 551 villages and neighborhood committees were selected. Households were used at the fourth stage of sampling. Data analyzed in this chapter include all villages in the sample, as well as neighborhood committees in urban areas with more than 50 percent of residents holding rural household registration.

In the selection of PSUs, the National Population Databook was used as the basic material to construct the sampling frame.[100] The number of family households for each county or city was taken as the measure of size in the PPS selection process. For the successive stages of sampling, population data were obtained either from the Public Security Bureaus of the regions or from the statistical bureaus of local governments. At village and neighborhood committee levels, lists of household registrations *(hukou)* were obtained from police stations in urban areas and village committees in rural areas.

Retired high school teachers were employed as interviewers for most surveys. Although most people in China read and write standard Chinese, people in many provinces in the south speak varying dialects, some of which are difficult for Mandarin speakers to understand. To deal with this problem, professional interviewers from the National General Team for Rural Surveys *(Guojia nongcun diaocha zongdui)* who speak local dialects were hired to interview in seven southern largely dialect-speaking provinces. Interviewers were given formal training before the fieldwork.

Before the interview began, we sent letters to all the sampling spots to check whether there were any changes in addresses. We then removed all invalid addresses from our sampling frame and thereby eliminated the majority of noncontacts. The project scheduled interviews with 3,425 people and 3,287 of the prospective respondents contacted by interviewers answered our questions, for a response rate of 94.5 percent.

NOTES

For generous financial support, I would like to thank the National Science Foundation (SES-88-13023) (NSF-SBR-94-96313), the Henry Luce Foundation, and the Ford Foundation. This chapter benefited from the help of many Chinese friends and colleagues. I wish to thank Andrew Nathan, Barrett McCormick, Kevin O'Brien, Li Lianjiang, and four anonymous readers for their helpful comments on earlier versions of this chapter. I also wish to thank Martin Rivlin and Renan Levine for their assistance.

1. For discussion of the rules and regulations of elections at the provincial level, see Research Group on the System of Village Self-Government in Rural China and the China Research Society of Basic-level Governance, *Study on the Election of Villagers' Committees in Rural China* (Beijing: China Society Publishing House, 1994), 1–4.

2. Barrett L. McCormick, *Political Reform in Post-Mao China: Democracy and Bureaucracy in a Leninist State* (Berkeley: University of California Press, 1990), 29–53; Daniel Kelliher, "The Chinese Debate over Village Self-Government," *China Journal*, January 1997, 84–86.

3. Kevin J. O'Brien, "Implementing Political Reform in China's Villages," *Australian Journal of Chinese Affairs*, July 1994, 49.

4. For reports on vote buying, see Changsheng Lin, *Zhongguo nongcun de zhijie xuanju* [Direct elections in rural China] (Taipei: Committee for Mainland Affairs, 1995), 64–65; Steven Mufson, "China Dabbles in Democracy to Run Villages, Reform Party," *Washington Post*, January 26, 1995, A17; Kathy Chen, "Chinese Villages Get Taste of Democracy," *Wall Street Journal*, May 17, 1995, A14.

5. According to officials in the Ministry of Civil Affairs, voters in Shandong removed more than 30 percent of incumbents from office in the 1995 elections. Most of them were grassroots members of the CCP. Shandong has 110 counties; on average, each county has 15–20 townships and each township has 20–30 administrative villages. Thus 9,900 to 19,800 CCP members in Shandong Province were voted out of office in a single election.

6. Mufson, "China Dabbles in Democracy."

7. Elected official from eastern China, interview by author, July 1996.

8. Based on a four-county survey in rural China, Manion argues that elections made village leaders responsive to both old and newly emerging constituencies, as reflected in significant congruences between village leaders and their selectorates above and the electorate below. See Melanie Manion, "The Electoral Connection in the Chinese Countryside," *American Political Science Review* 90, no. 4 (1996).

9. Carter Center, *Carter Center Delegation Report: Village Elections in China* (Atlanta, GA: Carter Center, 1998), 2.

10. Since Lipset's article, many quantitative studies have confirmed that higher levels of development generate high probability of democracy and stable democracy; see Seymour Martin Lipset, "Some Social Requisites of Democracy: Economic Development and Political Legitimacy," *American Political Science Review* 53, no. 1 (1959); Ross E. Burkhart and Michael S. Lewis-Beck, "Comparative Democracy: The Economic Development Thesis," *American Political Science Review* 88, no. 4 (1994); Adam Przeworski and Fernando Limongi, "Modernization: Theories and Facts," *World Politics*, January 1997.

11. The major criticism is that the theory has the flavor of economic determinism and neglects the short-term political dynamic. See Adam Przeworski, "Some Problems in the Study of the Transition to Democracy," in Guillermo O'Donnell, Philippe Schmitter, and Lawrence Whitehead, eds., *Transitions from Authoritarian Rule: Comparative Perspectives* (Baltimore, MD: Johns Hopkins University Press, 1986).

12. Barrington Moore Jr., *Social Origins of Dictatorship and Democracy: Lord and Peasant in the Making of the Modern World* (Boston, MA: Beacon, 1966), 418.

13. O'Donnell, Schmitter, and Whitehead, eds., *Transitions from Authoritarian Rule*.

14. Samuel P. Huntington, *The Third Wave: Democratization in the Late Twentieth Century* (Norman: University of Oklahoma Press, 1991), 109–163.

15. Zhao favored establishing village administrative offices to replace people's communes; interview by author, August 1996. See also Kevin O'Brien and Lianjiang Li, "The Struggle over Village Elections," in Roderick MacFarquhar and Merle Goldman, eds., *The Paradox of China's Reform* (Cambridge, MA: Harvard University Press, 1999).

16. The reason for Zhao's ignorance of grassroots democracy is complicated. Part of the reason is fear of *luan* (chaos) in rural areas and the loss of governability for local cadres. On several occasions, he expressed the concern that if peasants were allowed to choose their leaders by votes, local cadres would have great difficulty implementing government policy and collecting taxes. Interview by author, Beijing, August 1996. Another reason is that in both Marxist theory and the traditional theory on democratization, peasants are considered obstacles to democracy. In the Marxist intellectual tradition, the peasantry is a class whose disappearance would be its first, last, and only service to the bourgeois revolution and hence to historical progress. Moore also argues, "no bourgeois, no democracy." He treats the peasants as an obstacle to democratization. See Moore, *Social Origins of Dictatorship,* 418 n. 12.

17. Both the reformers and the opposition believed that democratization required changes in the structure of the central government, a free, independent press, and probably a founding election. See Guoguang Wu, "Weishenmme zai nongcun, weishenme shi nongmin: Zhongguo minzhuhua shibai zhongde yige liwai" [Why in the countryside, why are the peasants: An exception of the failure of Chinese democratization], in Mingtong Chen and Yongnian Zheng, eds., *Liangan jicen* [Basic-level elections and political and social change on both sides of the Taiwan Strait] (Taipei: Yuedan, 1997), 428.

18. Both the reformers and the opposition subscribed to social mobilization theory. Interestingly enough, their belief in social mobilization theory, especially the structural requirements for democracy, was reinforced by official ideology inherited from Marxism. Neither thought peasants could help bring democracy to China. Some charged that those who proposed electoral reform in rural China were naive, if not antidemocratic. See Gan Yang, "Gongmin geti weiben, tongyi xianzheng liguo," *Ershiyi shiji* [Twenty-first Century], June 1996.

19. O'Donnell, Schmitter, and Whitehead, *Transitions from Authoritarian Rule,* chap. 5; Larry Diamond, Juan J. Linz, and Seymour Martin Lipset, *Politics in Developing Countries,* 2nd ed. (Boulder, CO: Lynne Rienner, 1995), 27–31.

20. In Eastern Europe the renaissance of autonomous group activity undermined communist domination by puncturing the psychology of fear and passivity, revitalizing social morality, regenerating political efficacy, and reporting the truth about the gross abuses of power. See Christine Sadowski, "Autonomous Groups as Agents of Democratic Change in Communist and Post-Communist Eastern Europe," in Larry Diamond, ed., *Political Culture and Democracy in Developing Countries* (Boulder, CO: Lynne Rienner, 1994).

21. O'Donnell, Schmitter, and Whitehead, *Transitions from Authoritarian Rule,* 48.

22. O'Donnell, Schmitter, and Whitehead, *Transitions from Authoritarian Rule,* chap. 3.

23. O'Donnell, Schmitter, and Whitehead, *Transitions from Authoritarian Rule,* 48.

24. O'Brien, "Implementing Political Reform," 54–56; McCormick, *Political Reform in Post-Mao China,* 131–156; McCormick, "China's Leninist Parliament and Public Sphere: A Comparative Analysis," in Barrett L. McCormick and Jonathan Unger, eds., *China after Socialism* (Armonk, NY: Sharpe, 1996), 37–41; Brantly Womack, "The 1980 County-Level

Elections in China: Experiment in Democratic Modernization," *Asian Survey,* March 1982, 269–270.

25. Douglass C. North, "Epilogue: Economic Performance through Time," in Lee J. Alston, Eggertsson Thrainn, and Douglass C. North, eds., *Empirical Studies in Institutional Change* (New York: Cambridge University Press, 1996), 344.

26. Kathleen Thelen and Sven Steinmo, "Historical Institutionalism in Comparative Politics," in Sven Steinmo, Kathleen Thelen, and Frank Longstreth, eds., *Structuring Politics: Historical Institutionalism in Comparative Analysis* (Cambridge: Cambridge University Press, 1992), 2; G. John Ikenberry, "Conclusion: An Institutional Approach to American Foreign Economic Policy," in G. John Ikenberry, David A. Lake, and Michael Mastanduno, eds., *The State and American Foreign Economic Policy* (Ithaca, NY: Cornell University Press, 1988), 226.

27. North, "Epilogue," 343.

28. Wang worked as a farmer during the Mao era before he passed the college entrance examination and entered college after the Cultural Revolution. During that period he hardly had enough to eat. On one occasion his hunger was so severe that he could hardly move his legs without falling down. Interview by author, Beijing, August 1996.

29. Official in the Rural Development Research Institute, interview by author, Beijing, April 1989.

30. Most of them came from the Rural Development Institute (RDI), a center of economic reform. The RDI was disbanded by the party for its heavy involvement in the democracy movement after June 4. The institute staff members were reassigned to different governmental organizations. Those in charge of implementing the Organic Law were assigned to the MCA.

31. For changes of composition in the Chinese bureaucracy in the 1980s, see Cheng Li and Lynn T. White III, "The Thirteenth Central Committee of the Chinese Communist Party," *Asian Survey* 28, no. 4 (1988); Li and White, "Elite Transformation and Modern Change in Mainland China and Taiwan: Empirical Data and the Theory of Technocracy," *China Quarterly,* March 1990.

32. In the 1950s the MCA was one of the most powerful (if not the most powerful) ministries in China. It controlled not only basic administration but also the police. Many high-ranking officials wanted to restore the ministry to its former power. They believed that organizing elections in rural China would benefit the ministry in its quest for prestige and power. Based on such considerations, they supported the efforts of Wang and his staff. Cadres in the Department of Grassroots Administration, MCA, interview by author, Beijing, July 1996.

33. A good indicator of the status of the ministry is that when Yan Mingfu was demoted by the Central Committee after June 4, he was appointed by the organizational department of the CCP as deputy minister of this body.

34. Changsheng Lin, *Zhongguo nongcun de zhijie xuanju,* 24–25.

35. Since the village committee was codified in the 1982 Chinese constitution, Peng argued, it was improper and illegal to establish government offices in Chinese villages.

36. Li Xueju, *Zhongguo chengxiang jicenzhengquan jianshegongzuo yanjiu* [The study of reconstruction of grassroots administration in rural and urban China] (Beijing: Chinese Society Publishing House, 1994), 72–74. For Peng Zhen's role, see O'Brien and Li, "Struggle over Village Elections."

37. There was one exception to this observation. In the aftermath of the Tiananmen incident, the powerful personnel department of the CCP, in conjunction with provincial leaders,

expressed its opposition to direct village elections. Conservatives within the CCP charged that such elections were "examples of peaceful evolution" and suggested abolishing the plan. At that critical moment two veteran leaders, Peng Zhen and Bo Yibo, rose to challenge those allegations and defend the project. See Changsheng Lin, *Zhongguo nongcun de zhijie xuanju,* 32–33. They summoned Song Ping, director of the personnel department of the CCP, to Peng's home to persuade him to support the implementation of reform. Thanks to their intervention, the project survived an attack from more conservative elements, and elections in rural China were held even as many other reform measures, including economic projects, were suspended. Tyrene White, "Rural Politics in the 1990s: Rebuilding Grassroots Institutions," *Current History* 91, no. 566 (1992): 276; O'Brien, "Implementing Political Reform," 49.

38. With reform already in progress, many bureaucrats realized that elections were the key to better leadership and a guarantee of successful enforcement of party policy under the changing circumstances in China. Although taxes and other collections in a county adjacent to Renshou were much higher than those collected by officials in Renshou, the peasants never rebelled. Further investigation shows that because the MCA designated that county as a model for promoting rural elections, the peasants there actively participated in the decision-making process for public projects. See Yongnian Zheng, "Xiangcunminzhu he zhongguo zhengzhijincheng" [Village democracy and Chinese political process], *Twenty-first Century,* June 1996, 27. Bureaucrats found to their surprise that such participation also enhanced citizens' sense of responsibility, which made the task of governing easier. Ten BCA officials, interview by author, Beijing, July 1996.

39. As correctly pointed out by McCormick, they opposed the reforms because the reforms threatened their personal interests, which could be quite different from those of the regime generally. See McCormick, *Political Reform in Post-Mao China,* 146.

40. The organization responsible for electoral reform in the MCA is the Department of Grassroots Administration *(jiceng zhengquan jianshesi).* The administrative arm of the department is the Desk of Grassroots Administration in provincial BCAs.

41. Interview by author, Weichang, Hebei Province, August 8, 1996.

42. This happened in areas where there were no major collective enterprises. In villages having collective enterprises, the situation was different and remains so.

43. Provincial Civil Affairs Bureaus from Shanxi, Hunan, Jilin, and Henan, interview by author, July 1996. See also Changsheng Lin, *Zhongguo nongcun de zhijie xuanju,* 19–20.

44. Yongnian Zheng, "Xiangcunminzhu he zhongguo zhengzhijincheng," 27.

45. When I visited Hequ and Shenchi counties in Shanxi Province, the heads of the BCA in both counties mentioned that when villages ask peasants for money, the peasants ask in turn to participate in the decision-making process. Author interviews, Hequ and Shenchi counties, Shanxi Province, July 1995.

46. Peter Gourevitch, "The Second Image Reversed: The International Sources of Domestic Politics," *International Organization,* Autumn 1978, 882.

47. For a set of rules to be institutions, knowledge of these rules must be shared by the members of the relevant community or society. Jack Knight, *Institutions and Social Conflict* (New York: Cambridge University Press, 1992), 2.

48. James R. Townsend, *Political Participation in Communist China* (Berkeley: University of California Press, 1969); Lowell Dittmer, "Public and Private Interests and the Participatory Ethic in China," in Victor C. Falkenheim, ed., *Citizens and Groups in Contemporary China* (Ann Arbor: Center for Chinese Studies, University of Michigan, 1987), 18–27.

49. See Andrew Nathan, *Chinese Democracy* (Berkeley: University of California Press, 1985), 193–223. McCormick found that dominant groups in the leadership had rejected crucial aspects of the Western model, such as the relative legal autonomy of civil society and relatively free competition in elections. See McCormick, *Political Reform in Post-Mao China,* 131.

50. Kenneth Lieberthal and Michel Oksenberg, *Policy Making in China: Leaders, Structures, and Process* (Princeton, NJ: Princeton University Press, 1988), 24. For a discussion of policy implementation in China, see David M. Lampton, ed., *Policy Implementation in Post-Mao China* (Berkeley: University of California Press, 1987).

51. Lieberthal and Oksenberg, *Policy Making in China,* 24–25.

52. RDI officials, interview by author, Beijing, January 1989.

53. Huntington says "the most effective method of reform is the combination of a Fabian strategy with blitzkrieg tactics." See Samuel P. Huntington, *Political Order in Changing Societies* (New Haven, CT: Yale University Press, 1968), 346.

54. Many arguments can be right and sensible but not "correct," and the "correct argument" may not necessarily be a sensible one, especially to outsiders. The implications of the arguments made by reformers emerge when considered in the political context of their own society.

55. Oliver MacDonagh, *Early Victorian Government, 1830–1870* (New York: Holmes & Meier, 1977), 8–9.

56. MacDonagh, *Early Victorian Government,* 9.

57. Rather than openly advocate abandoning the socialist system when they started the reform process, reformers in China emphasized the instrumental benefits of reform measures. A good example is the struggle of the late 1970s between the Whatever Faction and the Practice Faction, which led to the demise of Hua Guofeng, the chairman of the Communist Party of China (CCP). Members of the Whatever Faction tried to turn the debate between themselves and veteran leaders represented by Deng Xiaoping into an ideological one. By arguing for compliance with orthodox ideology, they were guaranteed to win. For their part, Deng Xiaoping and his allies, with the strong support of the general populace and powerful figures in the army, tried to shift the debate with the leaders of the Cultural Revolution from an ideological one to an instrumental one. Their slogan—practice is the sole criterion of truth—was designed to effect this shift. Maurice Meisner, *Mao's China and After: A History of the People's Republic,* rev. ed. (New York: Free Press, 1980), 448–465.

58. His famous cat theory was aimed at avoiding ideological debate with his political enemies. After 1989 he openly suggested putting such debate aside and concentrating on economic development to safeguard economic reform.

59. Rural Desk, Department of Grassroots Administration of the Ministry of Civil Affairs, ed., *Textbook for the Study of Village Self-Government* (Beijing: Ministry of Civil Affairs, 1991), 90.

60. E. E. Schattschneider, *The Semi-Sovereign People* (New York: Holt, Rinehart & Winston, 1960), 3–6.

61. Naughton found such a strategy to be the key to the success of the economic reforms in China. See Barry Naughton, *Growing Out of the Plan: Chinese Economic Reform, 1978–1993* (New York: Cambridge University Press, 1996), 309.

62. For strategies used by local bureaucrats to change the essence of policy made by the central authorities, see McCormick, *Political Reform in Post-Mao China,* 145–154; McCor-

mick, "China's Leninist Parliament and the Public Sphere," in McCormick and Unger, eds., *China after Socialism*, 29–53; and O'Brien, "Implementing Political Reform."

63. Research Group on the System of Village Self-Government in Rural China and the China Research Society of Basic-Level Governance, *The Report on Village Representative Assembles in China* (Beijing: China Society Publishing House, 1995), 58.

64. Wang Zhenyao, "Woguo nongcun de lishibiange yu cunminzizhi de biran qushi" [Historical change in Chinese countryside and the necessity of villager self-governance], in Rural Desk, *Textbook*, 41.

65. Kelliher's research on the debate over elections also found that all arguments made by the reformers in the public discussions concentrated on instrumental benefits: elections could bring stability to rural China, help local cadres to enforce government policy, prevent peasants from rebelling, and defend the regime against foreign criticism on human rights violations; see Kelliher, "Chinese Debate over Village Self-Government," 63–86.

66. In provinces where the major leaders supported the reforms, officials at the bureau tended to push hard for rural elections. In provinces where major leaders were indifferent, the attitudes of the officials at the BCA would become critical for the implementation of the Organic Law. In provinces where major leaders were hostile to the Organic Law, the BCA officials could scarcely carry out their mission.

67. Department of Grassroots Administration officials, Ministry of Civil Affairs, interview by author, Beijing, July 1995. As of 1995, the MCA had sent all the leaders from model counties abroad.

68. Not all local officials opposed elections. During the period of people's communes, elections were held in some rural areas. See Xueju Li, "Zhongguo nongcun jicengzuzhi cuimin weiyuanhui" [Basic organization of village committee elections in the Chinese countryside], in Rural Desk, *Textbook*, 249–252.

69. Department of Grassroots Administration officials, interview by author, Ministry of Civil Affairs, Beijing, July 1995.

70. When I contacted the organization responsible for implementing the law in 1989, one official told me this strategy was designed by them to implement the Organic Law. I found this explanation so implausible that I refused to meet their leader, Wang Zhenyao. At that time, I believed they never seriously considered bringing democracy to rural China but only wanted to fool outsiders. Rural Development Research Institute official, interview by author, Beijing, April 1989.

71. Wang Zhenyao, interview by author, Beijing, July 1995.

72. This echoes the argument made by historical institutionalists that preference formation should be treated as endogenous. See Suzanne Berger, introduction to Suzanne Berger, ed., *Organizing Interests in Western Europe* (Cambridge: Cambridge University Press, 1981); Peter Hall, *Governing the Economy: The Politics of State Intervention in Britain and France* (New York: Oxford University Press, 1986); Peter Katzenstein, *Between Power and Plenty: Foreign Economic Policies in Advanced Industrial Societies* (Ithaca, NY: Cornell University Press, 1978); Theda Skocpol, *The State and Social Revolutions* (New York: Cambridge University Press, 1979).

73. MCA officials, interview by author, Beijing, May 1996.

74. Rural Desk officials, Department of Grassroots Administration, MCA, interview by author, Beijing, July 1996.

75. For Western research on appeals of ordinary Chinese to higher authorities, see Tian-

jian Shi, *Political Participation in Beijing* (Cambridge, MA: Harvard University Press, 1997). Kevin O'Brien and Lianjiang Li called such behavior rightful resistance; see "Villagers and Popular Resistance in Contemporary China," *Modern China* 22, no. 1 (1996); O'Brien, "Rightful Resistance," *World Politics,* October 1996. For peasant reports of election manipulation, see Research Group, *Study on the Election of Villagers' Committees,* 104–109; Yihua Bai and Wang Zhenyao, *Zhonghuarenmingongheguo cunminweiyuanhui xuanjugongzuo fanli* [The guiding example of elections for villagers' committees of the People's Republic of China] (Beijing: Social Publishing House, 1996), 160–166.

76. For figures in the United States, see Sidney Verba and Norman Nie, *Participation in America: Political Democracy and Social Equality* (New York: Harper & Row, 1972). For figures in other societies, see Sidney Verba, Norman H. Nie, and Jaeon Kim, *Participation and Political Equality: A Seven Nation Comparison* (Cambridge: Cambridge University Press, 1978).

77. Kelliher worries that if self-government does not produce the right leaders, the right levels of training, taxes, and birth—or if its usefulness outside China as a public relations trinket subsided—then what would the proponents of democracy do? Following their own logic in the published debate, they would abandon democracy and search for something else that works. See Kelliher, "Chinese Debate over Village Self-Government," 35.

78. One may still argue that those elections help the CCP consolidate its power. Even if elections voted a lot of incumbent officials out of office, the thinking goes, if the CCP were clever enough, it could always accept the newly elected officials as members and thus consolidate. If that would happen, reformers would have achieved a silent revolution—transforming the CCP from a Leninist party to a different kind of party—a major political development for the country.

79. Research Group, *Textbook,* 166.

80. Yihua Bai and Wang Zhenyao, *Zhonghuarenmingongheguo cunminweiyuanhui xuanjugongzuo fanli* [Models of village committee elections in the People's Republic of China], 160–162; Research Group, *Textbook,* 105–109.

81. Research Group, *Textbook,* 75, emphasis added.

82. In two conferences I participated in, one in 1995 and the other in 1996, I found that officials of the MCA put their primary effort into persuading officials from different provinces to institutionalize the nomination process. In those provinces where election laws permitted the Communist Party and other political organizations to nominate candidates, they even pressed to amend the law.

83. Research Group, *Textbook,* 74–75.

84. Yihua Bai and Wang Zhenyao, *Zhonghuarenmingongheguo cunminweiyuanhui xuanjugongzuo fanli* [Models of village committee elections in the People's Republic of China], 59, 215–229.

85. In an interview with officials in the MCA in the early 1990s, I asked them why they did not issue a document to curb election manipulation. They told me they had to wait for the right time. MCA officials, interview by author, Beijing, 1993.

86. The reformers believed that achieving limited success would persuade foreign participants to get involved.

87. At that time the MCA had achieved limited success in implementing the Organic Law. They were able to show such foundations that the elections in some places were real and convinced them they would not be throwing away their money if they decided to help.

88. A good example familiar to most students of Chinese politics is the case of reformers in the Ministry of Foreign Trade who used GATT and WTO applications to press for faster reform in many areas and to legitimate China's reformist policies. See William R. Feeney, "China and the Multilateral Economic Institutions," in Samuel S. Kim, ed., *China and the World*, 3rd ed. (Boulder, CO: Westview, 1994), 242.

89. Kelliher, "Chinese Debate over Village Self-Government," 75–78.

90. On their recent trip to China, both Gore and Gingrich cited rural elections as a positive development in China.

91. This happened after an international conference on village elections held in July 1995. Scholars, journalists, and foundation officials visited a village in suburban Tianjin. Because it is a rich village, there was no incentive for peasants to change their leaders. And because there was little chance of defeating incumbents, there was little incentive for anyone in the village to challenge them. After foreign experts observed the elections, officials in the MCA openly sought their advice.

92. Based on field observations as well as on interviews with journalists from Hong Kong, May 1996.

93. Wang Zhenyao, interview by author, Beijing, July 1995. Wang mentioned the case several times, indicating that he thinks that the opinion of a foreign expert holds sway with domestic audiences.

94. Wang Zhenyao, interview by author, Beijing, July 1995.

95. For the Hequ experience, see Lianjiang Li, "The Two-Ballot System in Shanxi: Subjecting Village Party Secretaries to a Popular Vote," *China Journal* (forthcoming).

96. A famous episode involving the Gang of Four further complicated the issue. During the Cultural Revolution in the early 1970s, Jiang Qing proposed nominating a nonparty member as secretary of a party branch in a village. When people reminded her that the nominee was not even a party member, Jiang was reported to have replied that for a party branch at the grassroots level, it did not matter whether the secretary was a member of the party. The story became a well-known political joke after two famous actors made the episode public in a talk show. Any subsequent suggestion to allow nonparty members to select a party secretary brought this incident to mind and was subject to ridicule. The MCA must find a way to overcome this difficulty.

97. The discussion is based on my observations at the international conference about rural self-government in China in 1995, as well as on my interviews with MCA officials in July 1995.

98. Huntington, *Political Order*, 346–362.

99. What is crucial is their deep commitment to democratic values as indicated by their confidence in the ability of peasants in rural China to determine their own fate. The controversial decision to allow dirty, noncompetitive elections at the beginning stage of the process was based on the reformers' confidence that people would understand the importance of the elections and actively participate in them.

100. Ministry of Public Security, *Zhongguo chengxian renko tongji* [Population statistics by city and county of the People's Republic of China] (Beijing: Map Publishing House of China, 1987).

14

Villagers, Elections, and Citizenship in Contemporary China

KEVIN J. O'BRIEN

More than five months had passed, but in December 1995, the oversize characters scrawled on a storefront on Wangjiacun's main street were still legible:
"We're citizens. Give us back our citizenship rights. We're not rural labor power,
even less are we slaves. Former village cadres must confess their corruption." The
village leadership had little doubt who was behind this infuriating graffiti—one of
the twenty complainants who had accused Wangjiacun's Communist Party secretary
and his predecessor of engaging in graft—but felt it was unwise to take any action.
The corrupt cadres were said to be afraid that whitewashing the wall would only add
fuel to the complaint and confirm their guilt. Instead, they would tough it out: they
would refuse to turn over the accounts, stick with their story that the books had
been destroyed in a fire, and wait for the summer rains to weather the charges away.
But in the meantime, the allegations would stand unrebutted, there for all to see
(Lianjiang Li, personal communication, July 1995; author's observation, December
1995).

Claims to citizenship have been a rallying cry for the excluded in many times and
many places. In this one North China village, an enterprising farmer framed his
critique of power in terms of citizenship rights and in so doing hamstrung a group
of hard-nosed cadres.[1] Couching a long-standing grievance in the language of community membership, he made his claim to inclusion unassailable. By reworking
official "rights talk," he had turned a controversial demand for accountability into
a simple plea for respect. Decollectivization had freed him. New political reforms
had promised financial openness. As a citizen, he had a right to inspect the village
accounts, and as a citizen, he had the right not to be treated as a slave.

In Wangjiacun, claims to citizenship have begun to affect how villagers and cadres interact. But this is only one village. Is the language of citizenship alive in the Chinese countryside today? Are Chinese villagers citizens in anything other than the narrowest juridical sense?

In this chapter, I assess the state of political citizenship in rural China. After discussing the often local and rural origins of citizenship and the meaning of the term itself, I review the limited reforms that have taken place in the election of high-ranking state leaders and People's Congress deputies. I then turn to a more promising avenue of inclusion: the villagers committee (VC) elections that began in the late 1980s. Here, we see notable efforts to heighten cadre responsiveness and draw rural residents into the local polity. At the same time, sizable obstacles to inclusion remain, not least because many electoral rules and practices do not enfranchise villagers reliably. The inescapable conclusion that villagers enjoy (at best) a partial citizenship needs to be qualified, however, owing to evidence that some rural people are starting to challenge improper elections using the language of rights. Building on a rules consciousness and a sensitivity to government rhetoric that have existed for centuries, as well as exploiting the spread of participatory ideologies and patterns of rule rooted in notions of equality, rights, and the rule of law, these villagers are advancing their interests within prevailing limits, forcing open blocked channels of participation, and struggling to make still-disputed rights real. In this regard, certain citizenship practices are emerging even before citizenship has appeared as a fully recognized status, and we may be observing the process by which a more complete citizenship comes about.

RURAL CHINA?

At first glance, searching for citizenship in rural China promises to be an excursion into the world of make-believe. Since at least Weber's time, the development of citizenship has been associated with cities—cities mainly in the West (Dagger 1981, 715–716; Turner 1990, 194, 203; Bulmer and Rees 1996, 272; Weber 1998). Moreover, citizenship is often linked with notions such as political equality, civil society, democracy, and national integration (Marshall 1976; Turner 1992; Janoski 1998) that apply badly (if at all) in Chinese villages. Many of the institutions that support citizenship are missing in rural China. Villagers play no meaningful part in choosing national leaders. Country folk are weakly represented in People's Congresses, which have a limited role in making policy and checking executive authority (O'Brien 1990; but for recent changes, see Tanner 1999b; Dowdle, forthcoming).

Still, the subject of citizenship in the Chinese countryside cannot be dismissed with a wave of the hand. Recent studies have shown that the early history of citizenship was often local and parochial as much as it was national and universal. Although citizenship first appeared in the cities of ancient Greece and medieval Europe, it did so in autonomous, relatively small-scale towns (sometimes populated by as few as a thousand people) that were more rural than urban (Riesenberg 1992, xv, 5). Even in England, the origins of citizenship trace to pastoral regions in the fourteenth century rather than to the industrializing cities of the nineteenth century. Long before the Industrial Revolution, certain rural dwellers had translated community autonomy and solidarity into a capacity for association and participation. It was in distant woodlands, not urban areas, where English peasants first appropriated labor laws and interpreted them as conferring citizenship rights (Somers 1993, 594–598; 1994, 83). Citizenship, it would seem, can emerge deep in "the local node of a national legal structure" (Steinberg 1995, 22)—in small communities, where power is unfragmented and manageable size encourages participation and makes it easy to observe one's rulers in action (Dagger 1981).

An insistence on linking citizenship with civil society, democracy, and equality also has a whiff of the ahistorical about it. Charles Tilly (1995, 233) has noted that the authoritarian regimes of Mussolini, Hitler, and Franco all emphasized bonds of citizenship, and Michael Mann (1996) has identified five varieties of citizenship, only one of which is associated with free association, strong legislatures, and liberal democracy.[2] A cursory review of world history also shows that citizenship has long been an organizing principle for regimes riven by class, ethnic, and gender distinctions, and feminist scholars have been quick to point out that the idea of citizenship has always implied exclusion and discrimination as well as inclusion and political equality (Vogel 1991, 61–62; Kerber 1997; Lister 1997).

Since citizenship, cities, democracy, and equality cannot be tied up in one neat bundle, it becomes reasonable to ask whether villagers in contemporary China are becoming citizens. Toiling far from urban centers, living under authoritarian rule, and being subject to institutionalized discrimination do not, in other words, rule out the first stirrings of citizenship. But if citizenship is not invariably associated with a specific location, a regime type, or even equality, what does it entail?

BEING A CITIZEN

In its most general sense, citizenship refers to a privileged legal status. A citizen is a full member of a community (Marshall 1976, 84; Barbalet 1988, 18). As citizens, categorically defined persons perform duties and possess rights, the most basic of which is the right to have rights (Kymlicka and Norman 1995, 310). In nearly all communities, some residents are complete citizens and others fall short. Citizenship thus excludes at the same time that it includes; it draws boundaries and ranks the populace (Riesenberg 1992, xvii; Kerber 1997; Shafir 1998, 24). Some people, such as children, the insane, and criminals, are excluded (at least temporarily) owing to an incapacity to exercise their rights and fulfill their obligations. Others, such as foreigners, refugees, and guest workers, are excluded because they are aliens (Vogel 1991, 62). Citizens are in a privileged position vis-à-vis other community members because they possess rights that noncitizens and incomplete citizens lack.

Citizenship rights have evolved over time and have little fixed content. In today's world, however, citizenship is often understood to have three components (Marshall 1976, 71–72). Civil citizenship involves rights required for personal liberty, such as freedom of speech, the right to make contracts, and the right to a fair trial. Social citizenship entails the right to a decent and secure standard of living, and it conveys education, health, and welfare entitlements, according to a society's standards. Political citizenship, my main concern here, is associated with the right to participate in the exercise of power. It guarantees a person a place in the polity. In modern times, the sine qua non of political citizenship has become the right to elect state leaders—in the executive, in national parliaments, and in local councils.

THE OPPORTUNITY TO PARTICIPATE: ELECTING TOP LEADERS

Ordinary Chinese do not enjoy the right to elect their president or other officials near the apex of power. As early as 1953, Deng Xiaoping announced that because most people were unfamiliar with national policies and the names of state leaders, subjecting top party and government functionaries to a popular vote was impossible (Houn 1955, 205). In the years since Deng spoke, proposals to revise the constitution and allow general elections have occasionally appeared, only to be rejected on grounds that the time was not ripe (Wang Dexiang 1979, 6; Xu Chongde and Pi Chunxie 1982, 58–59). In 1997, President Jiang Zemin once again ruled out national and provincial elections (Tanner 1999b, 248), and a year later Premier Zhu Rongji professed support for democratic elections but pointedly excluded the presidency and premiership. Such an important reform, Zhu said, needed more study, and it was hard to predict when officials of the first rank might begin to be elected (Spaeth 1998).

While villagers (and city dwellers) have no direct means to determine who rules China, they are entitled to have some say over a number of appointments through their deputies in the National People's Congress (NPC) and local congresses. In Mao Zedong's era, this meant little more than a right to hear that one's representative had "voted" for whomever the Party Organization Department had nominated, but since the late 1970s, the process for picking high-ranking members of the executive and judiciary has been revamped. Although the NPC has yet to remove an official on its own accord or reject a nominee placed before it (Yang 1998, 5), competition has been introduced for many positions, and the number of dissenting votes has grown. At the 1995 plenary session, for instance, nearly 37 percent of the NPC's deputies abstained or voted against a party-nominated candidate for vice premier (Tanner and Chen 1998, 41).[3] Local congresses have shown even more mettle when challenging name lists put forward by the party's Organization Department. Among notable instances of assertiveness, provincial assemblies have impeached a vice governor in Hunan, rejected party-sponsored nominees for governor in Guizhou and Zhejiang, and elected a deputy-nominated chief judge over a party-designated candidate in Jiangsu (Xia 1997, 15; 2000, 168–172; Shi 1997, 36).[4]

It is wrong, however, to interpret this newfound feistiness as a sign of significant growth in citizenship rights. People's Congresses have long been negligent in exercising their powers of appointment and recall, and a smattering of newsworthy examples to the contrary does not mean that business as usual has changed. The party still manipulates nominations, and procedures surrounding senior appointments remain "extremely vague and ill-formed" (Dowdle 1997, 104). Legislators, as in the past, are provided scant information about candidates, and campaigning is frowned on. Competition typically entails having one more nominee than the number of positions (e.g., six candidates for five spots), and for top posts (e.g., president, vice president, governor), deputies are usually presented with a single nominee, whom they then vote up or down (Bao Yu'e, Pang Shaotang, and Sun Yezhong 1990, 104; Jacobs 1991, 188, 190–191; Dowdle 1997, 37–41).

Competition at the chief executive rank remains limited even in the lowest reaches of the state hierarchy. In a 1999 election observed by a delegation from the Carter Center, town deputies were presented with five candidates for four deputy magistrate positions but only the incumbents for People's Congress chair and magistrate. To delegation members, it was "very obvious" that once the nominee for a top position was put forward, "all deputies understood the message and refrained from nominating any new candidates" (Carter Center of Emory University 1999, 12). To this day, the selection of nominees mainly reflects the outcome of administrative evaluation, recommendations from the organization department, and the normal workings of the *nomenklatura* system. As a "remedy for occasional defects" (Manion 2000, 775), deputies may veto leaders selected by the party committee one level up, but this power is less an opportunity for choice than an incentive for the party committee to vet its candidates with care.

Ordinary Chinese, of course, have even less say over high-level party positions. Members of the Politburo and its Standing Committee, as well as provincial first secretaries, are all selected at party conclaves with no pretense of mass participation. At the very top, the situation is much as it has been since 1949: there are few constraints on the ruling elite, and formal means of accountability have little weight in a system that is innately elitist and (at times) intentionally unresponsive. Opportunities to participate in the exercise of political power remain closely held. China's top leaders respond to popular opinion as a matter of choice or tactics, not out of obligation or because they fear removal in a democratic election.

ELECTING PEOPLE'S CONGRESSES

The structure of People's Congresses also impedes popular participation. Of special importance to villagers, Chinese electoral laws favor urban over rural districts. Each deputy from the countryside must represent four times as many constituents in county People's Congresses, five times as many in provincial congresses, and eight times as many in the NPC. This discrimination is said to be called for because cities are the nation's political, economic, and cultural centers and because urban leadership is desirable as industrialization proceeds. Equal weighting of urban and rural residents, it is claimed, would produce large majorities of low-quality *(suzhi)* rural deputies, which might diminish the vitality of representative assemblies (Jacobs 1991, 177; Xu Chongde and Pi Chunxie 1982, 64–65). In recent years, some Chinese scholars and deputies have suggested righting this imbalance somewhat (see Bernstein 1995, 14–15), perhaps reducing the disparity to 2 to 1 (see Nathan 1997, 236), but calls to end malapportionment have seldom been heard.

Even advocates of stronger legislatures have doubts about institutionalizing political equality. Despite constitutional provisions guaranteeing equal protection to all Chinese, they feel that undereducated peasants cannot take part in politics and that congresses should be "galaxies of talent" (Tan 1987, 49) stocked with the nation's best and brightest. Such self-proclaimed reformers are hesitant to grant too much power to "backward" country people. Instead, they would replace deputies who cannot read complex legal documents or understand budget proposals with highly qualified officials and professionals. To this end, they would gerrymander election precincts so that cadres and intellectuals would stop "bumping cars" and would be elected in disproportionate numbers (Xu Datong and Li Zhao 1986). These supporters of tinkering with legislative composition argue that the interests of the least educated can be upheld by others, and they have little sympathy for farmer (or worker) deputies who weigh down congresses and dilute the influence of people (like themselves) deemed more able (Chen Yanqing and Xu Anbiao 1990, 11–12; interviewees 1, 2, 3). Although this view is usually expressed in hushed tones and elliptical language, recent election results suggest it has made considerable headway. Should education and professional abilities continue to be valued highly, the underrepresentation of rural people in People's Congresses will only increase (O'Brien and Li 1993–1994).

How legislators are chosen also affects the extent to which villagers are included in the polity. People's Congresses may be symbols of popular sovereignty, but deputies are elected in a popular vote only up to the county level. Above that, members are "produced" *(chansheng)* by deputies who serve in the congress immediately below. Regulations call for a measure of competition, with 20–50 percent more candidates than positions, but by all accounts these "indirect" *(jianjie)* elections are strongly influenced by quotas and party-provided name lists. The selection process is generally secretive, and nominations from the floor are unusual and fare poorly. A lack of campaigning leads to much "blind" voting, and party luminaries are often assigned to represent a region in which they grew up or worked but no longer live (O'Brien 1990, 129, 168; Jacobs 1991, 188–190, 199; Dowdle 1997, 37–39; Tanner 1999a, 119–121).

Proposals to begin direct voting for provincial congresses and the NPC spring up every few years, and since the mid-1990s, NPC research staff have been exploring what would be needed to expand popular elections. But, as one Western researcher observes, "given the undermining of other Leninist states by even modestly competitive legislative electoral reforms, such reforms are unlikely in the immediate future" (Tanner 1999a, 121). To this point, there has been little reason to think that deputies produced via indirect elections would be chosen in a popular vote.

Direct elections to county and township congresses offer greater opportunities for political participation. In the 1980s, the first several rounds of contested county elections took place with much fanfare. Early reports suggested that new provisions requiring more candidates than positions were generally observed and that some nominees put forth by voters had reached the final ballot. At the same time, it was also clear that manipulation of the nomination process was rife, and unapproved nominees were frequently crossed out or replaced. Election officials sometimes offered flattering introductions and a preferred place on the ballot for candidates they favored, and voters had few chances to meet their representatives or find out what they thought (Womack 1982; Nathan 1985, 193–223; McCormick 1990, 130–156; Jacobs 1991, 188, 178–188). Groups of constituents "very rarely" proposed their own nominees, and secret balloting was the exception, especially in rural districts. According to Chinese commentators, many voters simply "went through the motions"; villagers, in particular, often felt elections were "meaningless" (Nie Yulin 1988, 250–251; Jiang Fukun 1989, 10–11; Ji Yu 1990, 254; Kang Fangming 1990, 274, 277–279).

More recently, a team of foreign observers that witnessed a town election expressed concern with ballot secrecy and distribution, voter identification, and limited candidate responsiveness to voters' concerns but was impressed by the large turnout and the eagerness of deputies to criticize the performance of town officials (Carter Center of Emory University 1999, 4). Tianjian Shi's surveys (Shi 1997, 38–39, 110, 177, 179; 1999b) have also shown increased interest in choosing local congress deputies. Although the authorities still work hard to handpick nominees, many voters have apparently decided to take part in imperfect, semicompetitive elections to punish corrupt leaders or promote political change. Private, informal campaigning is on the rise, and better educated, more informed voters are less inclined to boycott elections as a means of showing displeasure with the candidates they are presented (but also see Chen 2000). Instead, they sometimes use elections to get rid of or humiliate leaders they dislike. Insofar as defeat at the polls always causes a loss of face, usually leads to a transfer, and often triggers an investigation, casting a ballot has become a way to exercise a dollop of influence. Small procedural reforms, in sum, have changed voting behavior, and some Chinese have become adept at working a reforming authoritarian system to their advantage. In the cities, this means making the most of limited-choice People's Congress elections. In the countryside, these contests draw less interest, and the most promising avenue of inclusion lies with village-level voting (Choate 1997, 7; Shi 1999b, 1134).

ELECTING VILLAGERS COMMITTEES

That villagers committee elections have attracted much notice in China and abroad
is not surprising. As a breeding ground for citizenship rights, VCs have two decisive
advantages over People's Congresses: they are more autonomous, and they control
things people care about. Legislators may remonstrate for groups or individuals to
whom they feel an attachment (O'Brien 1994a). But congress deputies have few
resources and less power, and they must rely on others to carry out their decisions.

Members of villagers' committees work with fewer constraints. Under the
Organic Law of Villagers Committees (1987, revised 1998), VCs are not part of the
state apparatus; rather, they are "autonomous mass organizations" through which
villagers manage their own affairs, educate themselves, and meet their own needs
(Article 2). VCs are composed of three to seven members, each of whom is elected
for a term of three years. Committees have broad powers and limited but real autonomy from the township governments that sit above them. While committees, for
instance, must "help" townships in their work, they are not subject to top-down
"leadership relations" *(lingdao guanxi),* and townships are prohibited from meddling
in affairs that fall within a VC's purview (Article 4).

Villagers committees also control resources. In eight villages that I visited in
Fujian in 1992, VCs managed on average 15 percent of the yearly income earned
by villagers. Although party secretaries usually dominate enterprise management in
richer areas, even weak VCs own a village's land and usually have "veto power to
decide the general use of village resources—what might be called macro-economic
control" (Oi 1996, 137; see also Oi and Rozelle 2000).

Whether villagers are currently political citizens in more than a formal sense rests
in large part on the quality of VC elections. What rights does the Organic Law
guarantee? Have rural people been enfranchised, and are village elections free and
fair?

The Organic Law details an impressive array of citizenship rights. Notably, all
registered adult villagers are entitled to vote and to stand for office (Article 12). With
the exception of "those deprived of political rights by law," it contains no notion of
being "among the people" or of the class-based identities of the Maoist era. These
provisions repeat standard Chinese eligibility rules, except that in some places,
restrictions have been added that exclude the mentally ill (Elklit 1997, 6).

Special efforts have also been made to protect the rights of women. In the years
after the Organic Law was first passed, balloting on a family basis was common.
This practice often placed a household's vote in the hands of a family patriarch.
More recently, reportedly as a result of foreign prodding, household voting was
banned in Fujian and a number of other provinces (Wang Zhenyao 1998, 246; Shi
1999a, 408). Both the original Organic Law and its 1998 revision also accord
women "appropriate" *(shidang)* representation on VCs (Article 9).

Recent amendments also strengthen voter privacy and freedom of choice. For the
first time, secret voting, semicompetitive elections (i.e., more candidates than the

number of positions), and open counts are required (Article 14). Some provinces have also taken the lead in prohibiting proxy voting, experimenting with absentee ballots, and making primaries mandatory. Since the mid-1990s, the Ministry of Civil Affairs has promoted "sea elections" (open nominations) (Epstein 1996, 409; Shi 1999a, 405–406), and Fujian, a pacesetter in carrying out villagers' autonomy, now requires more than one candidate for each VC post.

Perhaps most important, villagers have been empowered to fight misimplementation of the Organic Law. For many years, civil affairs officials have been receptive to complaints about election irregularities (O'Brien 1996, 44; Li and O'Brien 1999, 139; O'Brien and Li 2000, 482–483), but now voters are expressly authorized to combat dishonest elections ("threats, bribes, forged ballots and other improper methods") by lodging "reports" *(jubao)* with local governments, People's Congresses, and other concerned departments (e.g., civil affairs offices; Article 15). At the same time, the Organic Law clearly states that no organization or individual is allowed to "appoint, designate, remove, or replace" members of a VC (Article 11).

By all accounts, the quality of village elections has improved since the early 1990s, and voter interest is on the rise. In the words of two observers, "local elections appear to be acquiring high salience in the political life of the countryside" (Jennings 1997, 366), and "peasants have shown great enthusiasm for this grassroots political reform" (Wang 1997, 1437). Early on, many villagers had scoffed at their voting rights, and in some places they shunned VC elections (O'Brien 1994b, 51–53; Shi 1999a, 394). But this seems to be changing. According to an official in the Ministry of Civil Affairs, "most villagers did not pay attention to the first round of elections, but some became interested the second time, and by the third time many actively participated" (quoted in Shi 1999a, 402). After seeing that elections could dislodge incompetent, corrupt, and high-handed cadres, some villagers now take them so seriously that a nationwide survey showed that 17 percent of villagers have nominated a VC candidate.[5] There is good reason for them to pay attention—elections have given rural people a way to unseat some horribly unpopular cadres. In balloting between 1995 and 1997, VC turnover in seven provinces ranged from 2 percent to 31 percent, averaging just under 19 percent (Pastor and Tan 2000, 504).[6] In some villages, particularly where economic growth has been disappointing, elections have sidelined a team of village cadres en masse. Freshly installed leaders are said to be younger and more entrepreneurial than the people they replaced (Epstein 1996, 415; Wang 1997, 1437; Howell 1998, 99; interviewees 4, 5, 6). In some locations, write-in campaigns waged by maverick businessmen succeed ("Villagers Spurn Communist," 1999), and as Bruce Dickson (1999, 16) recently found, 15.5 percent of 524 private entrepreneurs surveyed in eight rural counties had been candidates for village chief.

Cadres chosen in popular elections may also be more responsive to their constituents—at least in some regions. Oi and Rozelle (2000, 537) found that "in some villages where there have been elections, there is more open accounting of village spending." Amy Epstein (1996, 413) has argued that elections give villagers more control over how taxes are spent (but also see Bernstein and Lü 2000, 762). A four-county survey designed by political scientists at the University of Michigan and Beijing University showed that cadres in villages with competitive elections were closer to their constituents' positions on the state's role in the economy than cadres in villages that had not held competitive elections (Manion 1996, 741–45). Interviews in the countryside also suggest that where free and fair voting is the norm, village leaders live in a different world than the officials above them. As one VC director explained to Lianjiang Li, "We village cadres depend on the 'ground line' (*dixian*) (that is, villagers' votes); those at higher levels depend on the antenna (*tianxian*) (that is, appointment by higher levels). If we wish to be cadres, we must win the masses' support" (quoted in Li and O'Brien 1999, 140).

LIMITS ON PARTICIPATION

Although VC elections offer villagers entry into the local polity, the inclusion they confer is incomplete. The state has yet to recognize certain citizenship rights, and it has not taken the steps needed to ensure that all the rights it recognizes are honored.

Under the Organic Law, nonresidents cannot take part in village elections (Article 20). This would be of small concern if rural-to-rural migration were not accelerating. In a sprawling, industrial complex in the Tianjin suburbs, I was surprised to hear the party secretary say that the population topped out at 1,100 villagers (interviewee 7). Only later did he mention that the village was also home to more than 2,000 guest workers and their families. The secretary acknowledged that in many places, outsiders were treated like "slaves" *(nuli)* and that it was a struggle to guarantee their labor and welfare rights, let alone to imagine enfranchising them. In a Shandong village that relies on nonresidents to work its gold mine and to perform other backbreaking labor, the exclusion and condescension trained on guest workers were hardly less (interviewee 5).[7]

Women are also underrepresented on VCs. Quotas may exist, but even in provinces that have embraced grassroots elections, few women are nominated to committees, and even fewer serve as VC directors (International Republican Institute 1997, 20). In the twenty-odd villages in which I have done interviews, the VC usually includes one woman, and it is easy to guess her portfolio—the thankless job of enforcing family planning. Male domination may grow further if plans to streamline the government and lighten "peasant burdens" come to fruition. Since the mid-1990s, female representation has begun to drop in some villages as the size of VCs is pared to cut costs (Howell 1998, 99–100).

There are also a number of areas in which election practices and rules are wanting. Practices and institutions that impede political participation include the following:

Election committees. Election steering groups, often led by the village party secretary or a representative of the township, play a murky role in selecting nominees and final candidates (Elklit 1997, 5; Carter Center of Emory University 1997, 10; Howell 1998, 97–98, 101). Sometimes, VC candidates even serve on these committees, despite regulations to the contrary (Carter Center of Emory University 1998, 7; Pastor and Tan 2000, 494). Although the revised Organic Law (Article 13) empowers villagers' assemblies or small groups to "select" (*tuixuan chansheng*) the village steering group, it is unclear how this provision will be implemented and how much control it will provide.

Nomination procedures. VC candidates are chosen in a bewildering number of ways. While formal and informal primaries are becoming more common, procedures for whittling down the number of nominees are far from transparent and leave considerable room for manipulation. Much still goes on behind closed doors, and townships and village party branches have numerous opportunities to prevent unapproved candidates from reaching the final ballot (O'Brien 1994b, 55; Elklit 1997, 8–9; Kelliher 1997, 82; Howell 1998, 97).

Competition. Village elections are short of being fully competitive; in many provinces, only one more candidate than the number of seats is required. This rule makes curbing voter choice a cinch and encourages ruses such as placing an obviously unqualified candidate on the ballot alongside the incumbents or putting up a husband and wife (when only one woman is running and couples are not permitted to serve) (O'Brien and Li 2000, 485; interviewee 7). In some villages, as recently as 1998, no VC races were contested (on limited competition, see Elklit 1997, 6; Howell 1998, 98–99; Chan 1998, 513).[8]

Campaigning. Candidates ordinarily make a brief statement on election day. Spirited speeches brimming with promises appear here and there (Friedman 1998; Pastor and Tan 2000, 496), as does door-to-door campaigning (Elklit 1997, 9; Wang Zhenyao 1998, 248–50; Thurston 1999, 28), but lobbying for votes is not encouraged. Many VC members liken campaigning to self-promotion and regard "pulling votes" *(lapiao)* to be unfair, even corrupt (interviewee 8; Epstein 1996, 410; Chan 1998, 512–13; Thurston 1999, 28). Running against the Communist Party or organizing a new party is, of course, forbidden.

Secret balloting. Before the Organic Law was revised in 1998, comparatively little attention was paid to secret balloting. In some locations, polling booths were provided but not used; in others, voters filled out their ballots in public while milling about and chatting with neighbors (Elklit 1997, 10–11; Chan 1998, 513; Howell 1998, 96; Thurston 1999, 3). Attention to vote privacy may be growing, however. A survey conducted in the provinces of Fujian and Jilin (largely in demonstration areas) showed that nearly 100 percent of the villages had employed a secret ballot (Pastor and Tan 2000, 509). Still, outside democratically advanced locales, it is unclear if the importance of casting a vote privately is fully appreciated by election officials or most voters (Howell 1998, 96; Pastor and Tan 2000, 498, 508).

Proxy voting. Proxy voting is used to boost turnout and protect the rights of the aged, the sick, and those away from home. But as the Carter Center (1998, 5–6, 11–12) and the International Republican Institute (1998, 11) have pointed out, allowing one person to vote for up to three others can compromise voter privacy and freedom of choice. Ann Thurston (1999, 30) discovered that the dominance of a family's senior male was so ingrained in Lishu County, the nationwide model for village elections, "that few women or younger men would even think of casting an independent vote." So far, only Fujian has banned proxy voting, and in some villages, one-fifth or more of the ballots are cast by proxy (Pastor and Tan 2000, 498).

Roving ballot boxes. Roving ballot boxes are used in remote areas and to help the sick and elderly vote. Like proxy voting, this practice attests to a desire to be inclusive but also poses a threat to ballot secrecy and is open to abuse. In some places, mobile boxes are used mainly for the convenience of busy villagers. In one Liaoning village, for example, more than 90 percent of the votes were cast in mobile boxes rather than at polling stations (Pastor and Tan 2000, 497–498). Many election observers advise that proxy voting and roving ballot boxes be replaced by absentee voting to protect the integrity of voting, promote the civic awareness that comes with going to a polling station, and reinforce the principle of voting by and for oneself (International Republican Institute 1997, 26–27; 1998, 11; Carter Center of Emory University 1997, 15).

Certification. Township governments have also been known to annul elections if the "wrong" candidate wins or to dispense with voting and appoint "acting" VC members (Kelliher 1997, 82; Li and O'Brien 1999, 136–139). Sitting cadres may go so far as to bribe township officials to subvert the Organic Law. They may, for instance, coax township officials to cancel or rig an election by offering expensive gifts, hosting lavish banquets, or purposely losing at mah-jongg (interviewees 9, 10). In some counties, semicompetitive village elections have never been held.

VC–party relations. VCs seldom have final say over village political life (Kelliher 1997, 81–85; Howell 1998, 101). In many areas, the influence of the village party branch exceeds that of the VC, and "real power remains in the hands of the party secretary who makes the key economic decisions regarding industry" (Oi 1996, 136). Concurrent membership on villagers committees and party branches is common, as is the convening of joint or consecutive meetings (O'Brien 1994b, 54). The revised Organic Law (Article 3) has further muddied relations between VCs and party branches and increased the temptation to meddle by stipulating that the party branch is a village's "leadership core" *(lingdao hexin).*

Chinese villagers have certain rights, but theirs is a partial, local citizenship. Rural dwellers have few opportunities to participate outside the village, and their inclusion in the wider polity is not well established. While villagers have a foothold in grassroots politics and some resources, their ability to rein in state sovereignty is slight. The inclusion that rural people have been offered is piecemeal and incomplete.

CITIZENSHIP FROM BELOW

If citizenship were solely a status awarded by the state, our story would end here. But citizenship is more than a collection of rights bestowed on passive recipients

(Turner 1992, 2). It is also an outcome of historical processes that emerges as members of the popular classes seek to improve their lot by confronting the powers that be. Citizenship, in other words, arises out of negotiation between representatives of the state and social groups, and all initiative does not lie with the state. In fact, in many places, enlarging the scope of citizenship requires prolonged struggle (Giddens 1982, 165, 171–172), and new rights are acquired only through bottom-up pressure and the painstaking extraction of concessions. Citizenship, in this sense, is less granted than won, less accorded than made.

Understood this way, citizenship is a "way of life growing within" (Marshall 1976, 70) that reflects new aspirations and demands. Its spread depends on changes in people's hearts and minds, and it leads to changes in behavior. As seen in the farmer from Wangjiacun who denounced corruption using the soothing language of community membership, the rise of citizenship signals new identities and a growing fluency in "rights talk." To understand how citizenship develops, it is important to tally up what the central state recognizes and the local state enforces, but tracing changes in claims making and popular consciousness is just as key. In this regard, political citizenship involves adjustments in psychological orientation: in particular, it involves changes in one's awareness of politics, sense of efficacy, and feelings toward government. It implies a willingness to question authority and suggests that people view their relationship with the state as reciprocal. It entails a readiness to enter into conflicts with the powerful and a certain assertiveness in articulating one's interests (Shi 2000).

When the spotlight shifts to how citizenship rights emerge, popular dissatisfaction with incomplete inclusion takes on a new meaning. It becomes a sign that ordinary people are learning to speak the language of power with skill: to make officials prisoners of their own rhetoric by advancing claims in a particularly effective way. Consider the following incidents:

- Two men in Hunan, when facing an illegal snap election, organized their neighbors to plaster seventy-four posters around their village, recommending rejection of handpicked candidates and opposition to "dictatorial elections" (Zhongguo jiceng zhengquan jianshe yanjiuhui 1994, 80).[9]
- Hundreds of Shanxi farmers besieged a county government building, demanding that a VC election be nullified after a cadre seeking reelection escorted a mobile ballot box on its rounds (interviewees 10, 11).
- Residents of two Shanxi villages occupied a township office and refused to end their sit-in unless officials agreed to make their villages "special zones" where free and fair elections would be conducted (Shao Xingliang et al. 1994).
- Nearly a hundred Hebei villagers lodged complaints with the Central Discipline Inspection Commission concerning a township party committee that insisted a village party branch had the right to nominate VC candidates (interviewee 10).
- More than twenty Liaoning complainants, indignant over "minor" technical

infractions, traveled to the county seat, the provincial capital, and finally Beijing, at each stop reciting chapters of the Organic Law while appealing for new elections. (Tian Yuan 1993, 3–4)

In each of these cases, villagers cited specific clauses or the spirit of the Organic Law to back up their charges. By pointing to procedural irregularities that peasants are usually thought to ignore, these strict constructionists turned the gap between rights promised and rights delivered into a political resource. They challenged official misconduct using state-sanctioned symbols and deployed rights claims to protest illegal or undemocratic practices. To protect themselves and increase the likelihood of success, they shrewdly couched their demands in the language of loyal intentions while professing little more than a desire to make the system live up to what it was supposed to be. The regime had promised them a place in the polity, and they expected the system to live up to its billing.

And these are not isolated incidents. Villagers in many locations shower officials with complaints when their electoral rights are abridged. One study reported that two-fifths of the occasions on which rural residents contacted officials concerned elections (Jennings 1997, 366); another survey showed that as many as 5 percent of villagers nationwide have lodged complaints about election fraud (Shi 1999a, 403–404).[10]

Chinese villagers are increasingly identifying, interpreting, and challenging undemocratic elections using the vocabulary of rights (O'Brien 1996; Chan 1998, 519–520; on rights claims outside electoral contexts, see Zweig 2000; McCarthy 2000, 109; Goldman and Perry, forthcoming). Aware that the Organic Law and local regulations have granted them certain protections, they appropriate rights discourses and press to unclog channels of participation. These well-informed, exacting critics exploit the "discursive trappings of democracy" (Howell 1998, 104) to trip up local officials who refuse to acknowledge rights that the central authorities have ostensibly recognized. They often invoke a contractual logic borrowed from their economic life to demand that protections they have been guaranteed are respected. When local cadres dare to manipulate elections, they are quick to step in and charge them with prohibited behavior. Venturing forth in the name of unimpeachable ideals, they say they are simply seeking faithful implementation of the Organic Law.

When villagers come to view state promises as a source of entitlement and inclusion, they are acting like citizens before they are citizens. Certain citizenship practices, in other words, are preceding the appearance of citizenship as a secure, universally recognized status. In fact, practice may be creating status, as local struggles begin in enclaves of tolerance, spread when conditions are auspicious, and evolve into inclusion in the broader polity.

For now, however, the claims villagers put forward mainly demand entry into local politics. Villagers seldom press for wider civil and political rights to association, expression, and unlicensed participation; nor do they often question the legitimacy of existing laws and policies, not to mention the right of unaccountable leaders at higher levels to promulgate laws and policies. Although it is possible that rights-oriented contention may find elite patrons (or generate political entrepreneurs) who organize regionally or even nationally significant pressure groups, no such trend is now apparent. The intervillage organization and national aspirations of most villagers appear to be rather limited. Even the most assertive among them rarely demand provincial or national elections, wisely avoiding an issue that might alienate the allies they need to enforce their claims against local officials (Li and O'Brien 1996, 54–55).

Rural complainants know that they exist at the sufferance of higher levels and that the "rights" they act on are conditional. Unlike some Chinese intellectuals, who employ a different kind of rights discourse, there is little evidence that villagers consider rights to be inherent, natural, or inalienable; nor do most claimants break with the common Chinese practice of viewing rights as granted by the state mainly for societal purposes rather than to protect an individual's autonomous being (Edwards, Henkin, and Nathan 1986). Demanding citizenship is therefore making a claim more to community membership than to negative freedoms vis-à-vis the state. Villagers seldom argue that rights flow from human personhood but rather that the government's right to loyalty depends on ensuring that its officials fulfill their obligations. The duties of those below must be reciprocated by the duties of those above (Wang Gungwu 1991).

Chinese villagers, accordingly, are best thought of as occupying an intermediate position between subjects and citizens. When they use unenforced citizenship rights as a weapon, they are demanding that the representatives of state power treat them equitably, respect their claims, and deliver on promises made by officials at higher levels (O'Brien 1996; Bernstein and Lü 2000, 756–759; Zweig 2000). They are exploiting the spread of participatory ideologies and patterns of rule rooted in notions of equality, rights, and rule of law. By tendering impeccably respectable demands, they have found a persuasive way to agitate for the accountability that the Organic Law calls for and to challenge those who would usurp their electoral rights. Ultimately, their efforts may help make various still-contested rights real. Although villagers are only partial citizens in the local polity, we may be witnessing the beginnings of a more complete citizenship coming about.

SOME HISTORICAL PERSPECTIVE

Although this chapter has highlighted the upsurge in rights-based contention in recent years, rules consciousness and a sensitivity to the power of government discourse are not new in China, or indeed elsewhere. Members of the popular classes have always been adept at taking advantage of government commitments, professed ideals, and legitimating myths (Field 1976; Scott 1990, 101–106). Chinese villagers, in particular, have long seized on official rhetoric—whether framed in terms of Confucianism, class struggle, or citizenship rights—to press claims against malfeasant power holders.

In late imperial China, the Qing government tried "to establish a direct rapport with tenants" (Wiens 1980, 33), and tenants sometimes used official rulings as a pretext to delay or refuse payment of rent. Rural people also objected to taxes when they felt local authorities had ignored proper collection procedures and would back off when faced with popular complaints. Such challenges typically rested on appeals to equity and fairness, focusing on how the tax burden was apportioned, on adjustments for harvest conditions, and on the use of biased measures and conversion ratios. Local officials understood the protesters' logic and, provided that fiscal concerns were not overly pressing, sometimes gave in (Wong 1997, 235–237). Villagers, for their part, often submitted to all sanctioned impositions and used their fidelity to established values to launch attacks in a rhetoric that even unresponsive elites had to acknowledge. In the Laiyang tax revolt of 1910, for example, peasants considered the regular rates to be fair enough and employed them to fend off irregular levies. Like the rural complainants of a later era, their resistance was not only a reactive effort to restore what they had. Beyond demanding the removal of exploitative tax farmers, the Laiyang protesters "also proposed a system to help ensure that corrupt power was not regenerated—namely, the public election of new functionaries to administer reform programs" (Prazniak 1980, 59). This defiance thus transcended run-of-the-mill rules consciousness. As with contemporary villagers who press for free and fair elections, the Laiyang resistance was both loyal and proactive: it was simultaneously a means to advance group interests within existing limits and a way to assert new rights and pry open new channels of participation.

Other elements of today's "rightful resistance" (O'Brien 1996) were also apparent in Republican China, particularly in clashes surrounding taxation. Studies of the Nanjing decade depict a state that was already too fragmented to treat as a unified actor and villagers who did not experience the state as a single entity with a single face. In Patricia Thornton's (1999) telling, provincial leaders, circuit court judges, and the Administrative Yuan regularly received letters of complaint from peasants and "citizen representatives" *(gongmin daibiao)* criticizing official misconduct. But as incidents of tax and rent resistance rose, it was local administrators who bore the brunt of popular ire. "Rural residents seeking redress from fiscal predation of county officials and their minions tended to see central authorities not as culprits or co-conspirators in the fiscal battle being waged against them, but as potential protectors" against their real antagonists—local bureaucratic capitalists (Thornton 1999, 13). Thornton argues that portrayals of the central state in popular sources were more positive and optimistic in the Republican era than they are now. Still, she acknowledges that while Republican taxpayers generally did not perceive the central government to be accountable to the citizenry, "rural residents in the reform era expect more from central authorities in Beijing" (Thornton 1999, 30).[11] Contemporary protesters sometimes find the intercessors they need. State power is divided against itself, and pressure points exist where elite unity crumbles. Resourceful villagers nowadays can often ferret out supporters in various bureaucracies (such as the Ministry of Civil Affairs) who have a stake in seeing their appeals addressed and in upholding the policies they invoke. Villagers may be pessimistic, but they are also sometimes successful in locating advocates to champion their claims.

The Maoist era offers an ambiguous legacy to villagers pursuing citizenship from below. On one hand, rights discourses were not in vogue; late Cultural Revolution–era protests, for instance, were "almost exclusively of a defensive and reactive character. The protesters defied political despotism, but only a few went so far as to demand an expansion of participatory rights" (Heilmann 1996, 34). On the other hand, using the regime's own words as a weapon clearly did not begin in the 1990s. Borrowing slogans from the government arsenal to express heterodox views was a common tactic throughout the Cultural Revolution and the Hundred Flowers movement (Perry 1995; Heilmann 1996). By instilling in the popular consciousness the idea that there is a right to rebel in the name of symbols embraced by those in power, Maoist practices set the stage for the partly institutionalized, partly legitimate resistance we see today. A generation of mass mobilization reinforced existing resistance routines and inspired innovation at the edge of the repertoire of contention. It altered popular expectations and very likely made people more willing to act up when faced with official misconduct (Perry 1995, 34; O'Brien and Li 1999, 377, 384, 391).

It is hardly novel to say that new identities are built on the shoulders of old ones. Contemporary Chinese villagers are the inheritors of a repertoire of contention that has been honed over decades, even centuries. In one sense, our Wangjiacun graffiti artist was using a familiar tactic (writing a wall poster) and seeking a "return" *(huan)* of his rights. In another sense, he was cloaking a daring proactive claim in reactive terms, demanding citizenship rights he had never enjoyed while making it appear he had just been deprived of them.[12]

APPENDIX: INTERVIEWEE LIST

1. City and district People's Congress deputy, May 1990
2. Provincial People's Congress deputy, May 1990
3. Constitutional scholar, May 1990
4. Villagers committee director, August 1992
5. Villagers committee director, August 1994
6. Party secretary and villagers committee director, July 1998
7. Villagers committee director, September 1993
8. Villagers committee members, July 1998
9. Villager, December 1995
10. Ministry of Civil Affairs official, June 1994, January 1997
11. Ministry of Civil Affairs official, June 1994

NOTES

This chapter benefited from the assistance of many Chinese friends and colleagues, most notably my longtime collaborator, Lianjiang Li. Peter Gries, Elizabeth Perry, and Dorothy Solinger also offered helpful comments. For their generous financial support, I would like to thank the Asia Foundation, the Ford Foundation, the Henry Luce Foundation, the Research and Writing Program of the John D. and Catherine T. MacArthur Foundation, and the Research Grants Council of Hong Kong.

1. For more on the village of Wangjiacun and the unfolding of a bitter collective complaint there, see O'Brien and Li (1995).

2. Riesenberg (1992, 176) writes, "Citizenship is today so freighted with notions of individual participation and self-government that we automatically think of it as an intrinsic part of democratic society. In fact, over most of history, considering it as a mechanism of discrimination and reward, it has been compatible with all forms of government." In the Chinese context, Goldman and Perry (forthcoming, 3) have noted that citizenship "is not just another term for democratization."

3. According to one analyst (Dowdle 1997, 105), Vice Premier Jiang Chunyun met opposition because National People's Congress deputies were disappointed with the amount of background information provided. Others have attributed the opposition to Jiang's age, his level of education, and his association with corruption scandals (Pei 1995, 71).

4. In 2001, the Shenyang municipal People's Congress took the uncommon step of rejecting the intermediate court's work report, but it stopped short of demanding that court officials, some of whom were under investigation for graft and ties to organized crime, resign (Chao 2001).

5. The survey data appear in Shi (1999a, 403–404). Other surveys put the number at a still healthy 5 percent (Lianjiang Li, personal communication, September 1999).

6. Shi (1999a, 386) reports that voters ousted 30 percent of incumbent villagers committee (VC) members in the 1995 balloting in Shandong. A Ministry of Civil Affairs official has written that approximately 20 percent of VC chairs are not reelected "in most places" (Wang Zhenyao 1998, 251). These sources do not make it clear if those leaving through ordinary retirement or choosing not to run are included.

7. Whether long-term migrants retain their voting rights varies by location. On the second-class citizenship of urban migrants, see Solinger (1999).

8. In a Muslim village I visited in the Tianjin suburbs in July 1998, primaries were hotly contested, but the final election was uncontested.

9. These posters were written on white paper (a color associated with death and ill fortune). This gesture attracted the attention of county officials, who investigated the charges and ruled that the balloting should be rescheduled and nominations reopened.

10. The figure of 5 percent seems high. In 1994, the Fujian Bureau of Civil Affairs received 562 election-related complaints and deemed 24 elections invalid (International Republican Institute 1997, 27).

11. Kathryn Bernhardt has noted a similarly complex view of the republican state in relation to rents: "In its role as rent dunner, the state was seen as an oppressor, but in its role as the monitor of rents, it was seen as a potential ally" (Bernhardt 1992, 229).

12. Some county officials use the phrase "return *(huan)* power to the people" analogously when promoting village elections, even though the people have never had the power that is being "returned" to them.

REFERENCES

Bao Yu'e, Pang Shaotang, and Sun Yezhong. 1990. "Guanyu Nanjingshi renmin daibiao dahui de diaocha" [Investigation of the Nanjing city People's Congress]. In Zhao Baoxu and Wu Zhilun, eds., *Minzhu zhengzhi yu difang renda* [Democratic politics and local People's Congresses], 87–112. Xi'an: Shaanxi chubanshe.

Barbalet, J. M. 1988. *Citizenship: Rights, Struggle, and Class Inequality.* Minneapolis: University of Minnesota Press.

Bernhardt, Kathryn. 1992. *Rents, Taxes, and Peasant Resistance: The Lower Yangzi Region, 1840–1950.* Stanford, CA: Stanford University Press.

Bernstein, Thomas P. 1995. "Proposals for a National Voice for Agricultural Interests: A Farmers' Association." Paper presented at the conference entitled Rural China: Emerging Issues in Development, Columbia University, March 31–April 1.

Bernstein, Thomas P., and Xiaobo Lü. 2000. "Taxation without Representation: Peasants, the Central and Local States in Reform China." *China Quarterly,* September, 742–763.

Bulmer, Martin, and Anthony M. Rees. 1996. "Conclusion: Citizenship in the Twenty-first Century." In M. Bulmer and A. M. Rees, eds., *Citizenship Today: The Contemporary Relevance of T. H. Marshall,* 269–283. London: UCL Press.

Carter Center of Emory University. 1997. "Carter Center Delegation to Observe Village Elections in China." Atlanta: Carter Center of Emory University

———. 1998. *Carter Center Delegation Report: Village Elections in China.* Atlanta: Carter Center of Emory University

———. 1999. *Carter Center Report on Chinese Elections: Observations on the Township People's Congress Elections, January 5–15.* Atlanta: Carter Center of Emory University

Chan, Sylvia. 1998. "Research Note on Villagers' Committee Elections: Chinese-style Democracy." *Journal of Contemporary China,* November, 507–521.

Chao, Julie. 2001. "Chinese Congresses Refuse to Follow All Party Dictates." *Washington Times,* March 9.

Chen, Jie. 2000. "Subjective Motivations for Mass Political Participation in Urban China." *Social Science Quarterly,* June, 645–662.

Chen Yanqing and Xu Anbiao. 1990. "Lishun renda waibu guanxi tigao renda neizai huoli". [Rationalizing People's Congresses' external relations and heightening their internal vitality]. *Zhongguo faxue* [Chinese Law], November, 11–12.

Choate, Allen C. 1997. "Local Governance in China: An Assessment of villagers' Committees." Working paper 1. San Francisco: Asia Foundation.

Dagger, Richard. 1981. "Metropolis, Memory, and Citizenship." *American Journal of Political Science,* November, 715–737.

Dickson, Bruce J. 1999. "Do Good Businessmen Make Good Citizens? An Emerging Collective Identity among China's Private Entrepreneurs." Paper presented at conference entitled Changing Meanings of Citizenship in China, Harvard University, October 29–31.

Dowdle, Michael W. 1997. "The Constitutional Development and Operations of the National People's Congress." *Columbia Journal of Asian Law,* Spring, 1–125.

———. Forthcoming. "Constructing Citizenship: The NPC as Catalyst for New Norms of Public Political Participation in China." In Merle Goldman and Elizabeth J. Perry, eds., *Changing Views of Citizenship in China.* Cambridge, MA: Harvard University Press.

Edwards, R. Randle, Louis Henkin, and Andrew J. Nathan. 1986. *Human Rights in Contemporary China.* New York: Columbia University Press.

Elklit, Jorgen. 1997. "The Chinese Village Committee Electoral System." *China Information,* Spring, 1–13.

Epstein, Amy B. 1996. "Village Elections in China: Experimenting with Democracy." In U.S. Congress, Joint Economic Committee, *China's Economic Future: Challenges to U.S. Policy.* Washington, DC: Government Printing Office.

Field, Daniel. 1976. *Rebels in the Name of the Tsar.* Boston: Houghton Mifflin.

Friedman, Thomas L. 1998. "It Takes a Village." *New York Times,* March 10.

Giddens, Anthony. 1982. *Profiles and Critiques in Social Theory.* Berkeley: University of California Press.

Goldman, Merle, and Elizabeth J. Perry. Forthcoming. "Political Citizenship in Modern China: Introduction." In M. Goldman and E. J. Perry. eds., *Changing Views of Citizenship in China.* Cambridge, MA: Harvard University Press.

Heilmann, Sebastian. 1996. "Turning Away from the Cultural Revolution." Occasional Paper 28. Center for Pacific Area Studies at Stockholm University.

Houn, Franklin W. 1955. "Communist China's New Constitution." *Western Political Science Quarterly,* June, 199–233.

Howell, Jude. 1998. "Prospects for Village Self-Governance in China." *Journal of Peasant Studies,* April, 86–111.

International Republican Institute. 1997. *Election Observation Report: Fujian, People's Republic of China.* Washington, DC: International Republican Institute.

———. 1998. *Election Observation Report: Sichuan, People's Republic of China.* Washington, DC: International Republican Institute.

Jacobs, J. Bruce. 1991. "Elections in China." *Australian Journal of Chinese Affairs,* January, 171–200.

Janoski, Thomas. 1998. *Citizenship and Civil Society.* New York: Cambridge University Press.

Jennings, M. Kent. 1997. "Political Participation in the Chinese Countryside." *American Political Science Review,* June, 361–372.

Ji Yu. 1990. "Guanyu difang renda daibiao suzhi de diaocha yu yanjiu" [Investigation and research on local People's Congress deputies' quality]. In Zhao Baoxu and Wu Zhilun, eds., *Minzhu zhengzhi yu difang renda* [Democratic politics and local People's Congresses], 242–258. Xi'an: Shaanxi chubanshe.

Jiang Fukun. 1989. "Gaige he wanshan minzhu xuanju zhidu" [Reform and improve the democratic electoral system]. *Lilun neican* [Internal Reference on Theory], September 9, 10–12.

Kang Fangming. 1990. "Guanyu xianxiang zhijie xuanju de jige wenti" [Several issues concerning county and township direct elections]. In Zhao and Wu, eds., *Minzhu zhengzhi yu difang renda,* 272–284.

Kelliher, Daniel. 1997. "The Chinese Debate over Village Self-Government." *China Journal,* January, 63–86.

Kerber, Linda K. 1997. "The Meanings of Citizenship." *Journal of American History,* December, 833–854.

Kymlicka, Will, and Wayne Norman. 1995. "Return of the Citizen: A Survey of Recent Work on Citizenship Theory." In Ronald Beiner, ed., *Theorizing Citizenship,* 283–322. Albany: State University of New York Press.

Li, Lianjiang, and Kevin J. O'Brien. 1996. "Villagers and Popular Resistance in Contemporary China." *Modern China,* January, 28–61.

————. 1999. "The Struggle over Village Elections." In Merle Goldman and Roderick MacFarquhar, eds., *The Paradox of China's Post-Mao Reforms*, 129–144. Cambridge, MA: Harvard University Press.

Lister, Ruth. 1997. *Citizenship: Feminist Perspectives*. New York: New York University Press.

Manion, Melanie. 1996. "The Electoral Connection in the Chinese Countryside." *American Political Science Review*, December, 736–748.

————. 2000. "Chinese Democratization in Perspective: Electorates and Selectorates at the Township Level." *China Quarterly*, September, 764–782.

Mann, Michael. 1996. "Ruling Class Strategies and Citizenship." In Martin Bulmer and Anthony M. Rees, eds., *Citizenship Today: The Contemporary Relevance of T. H. Marshall*, 125–144. London: UCL Press.

Marshall, T. H. 1976. *Class, Citizenship, and Social Development*. Westport, CT: Greenwood.

McCarthy, Susan. 2000. "Ethno-Religious Mobilisation and Citizenship Discourse in the People's Republic of China." *Asian Ethnicity*, September, 107–116.

McCormick, Barrett L. 1990. *Political Reform in Post-Mao China*. Berkeley: University of California Press.

Nathan, Andrew J. 1985. *Chinese Democracy*. Berkeley: University of California Press.

————. 1997. *China's Transition*. New York: Columbia University Press.

Nie Yulin. 1988. *Zhongguo shehuizhuyi minzhu zhidu de fazhan he xiankuang* [The development and current situation of China's socialist democratic system]. Shijiazhuang: Hebei chubanshe.

O'Brien, Kevin J. 1990. *Reform without Liberalization: China's National People's Congress and the Politics of Institutional Change*. New York: Cambridge University Press.

————. 1994a. "Agents and Remonstrators: Role Accumulation by Chinese People's Congress Deputies." *China Quarterly*, June, 359–380.

————. 1994b. "Implementing Political Reform in China's Villages." *Australian Journal of Chinese Affairs*, July, 33–59.

————. 1996. "Rightful Resistance." *World Politics*, October, 31–55.

O'Brien, Kevin J., and Lianjiang Li. 1993–1994. "Chinese Political Reform and the Question of 'Deputy Quality.'" *China Information*, Winter, 20–31.

————. 1995. "The Politics of Lodging Complaints in Rural China." *China Quarterly*, September, 756–783.

————. 1999. "Campaign Nostalgia in the Chinese Countryside." *Asian Survey*, May–June, 375–393.

————. 2000. "Accommodating 'Democracy' in a One-Party State: Introducing Village Elections in China." *China Quarterly*, June, 465–489.

Oi, Jean C. 1996. "Economic Development, Stability, and Democratic Village Self-Governance." In Maurice Brosseau, Suzanne Pepper, and Tsang Shu-ki, eds., *China Review 1996*, 125–144. Hong Kong: Chinese University of Hong Kong Press.

Oi, Jean C., and Scott Rozelle. 2000. "Elections and Power: The Locus of Decision-Making in Chinese Villages." *China Quarterly*, June, 513–539.

Pastor, Robert A., and Qingshan Tan. 2000. "The Meaning of China's Village Elections." *China Quarterly*, June, 490–512.

Pei, Minxin. 1995. "'Creeping Democratization' in China." *Journal of Democracy*, October, 65–79.

Perry, Elizabeth J. 1995. "'To Rebel Is Justified': Maoist Influences on Popular Protest in

Contemporary China." Paper presented at the Colloquium Series of the Program in Agrarian Studies, Yale University, November 17.

Prazniak, Roxann. 1980. "Tax Protest at Laiyang, Shandong 1910." *Modern China*, January, 41–71.

Riesenberg, Peter. 1992. *Citizenship in the Western Tradition*. Chapel Hill: University of North Carolina Press.

Scott, James C. 1990. *Domination and the Arts of Resistance: Hidden Transcripts*. New Haven, CT: Yale University Press.

Shafir, Gershon. 1998. "Introduction: The Evolving Tradition of Citizenship." In *The Citizenship Debates*, 1–28. Minneapolis: University of Minnesota Press.

Shao Xingliang, Cuo Suozhi, Meng Baolin, and Sun Xueliang. 1994. "Yi min wei tian" [Regarding the people as sovereign]. *Xiangzhen luntan* [Township Forum], April, 10–13.

Shi, Tianjian. 1997. *Political Participation in Beijing*. Cambridge, MA: Harvard University Press.

————. 1999a. "Village Committee Elections in China: Institutionalist Tactics for Democracy." *World Politics*, April, 385–412.

————. 1999b. "Voting and Nonvoting in China: Voting Behavior in Plebiscitary and Limited-Choice Elections." *Journal of Politics*, November, 1115–1139.

————. 2000. "Cultural Values and Democracy in the People's Republic of China." *China Quarterly*, June, 540–559.

Solinger, Dorothy J. 1999. *Contesting Citizenship in Urban China: Peasant Migrants, the State, and the Logic of the Market*. Berkeley: University of California Press.

Somers, Margaret R. 1993. "Citizenship and the Place of the Public Sphere: Law, Community, and Political Culture in the Transition to Democracy." *American Sociological Review*, October, 587–620.

————. 1994. "Rights, Relationality, and Membership: Rethinking the Making and Meaning of Citizenship." *Law and Social Inquiry*, Winter, 63–112.

Spaeth, Anthony. 1998. "Village Voices." *Time*, Asia ed. March 30. www.time.com/time/magazine/1998/int/980330/village.html. Accessed April 2001.

Steinberg, Marc W. 1995. "'The Great End of All Government': Working People's Construction of Citizenship Claims in Early Nineteenth-century England and the Matter of Class." *International Review of Social History* 40, supplement 3, 19–50.

Tan, Jian. 1987. "Reform and Strengthen China's Political System." *Chinese Law and Government*, Spring, 44–50.

Tanner, Murray S. 1999a. "The National People's Congress." In Merle Goldman and Roderick MacFarquhar, eds., *The Paradox of China's Post-Mao Reforms*, 100–128. Cambridge, MA: Harvard University Press.

————. 1999b. *The Politics of Lawmaking in China: Institutions, Processes, and Democratic Prospects*. Oxford: Oxford University Press.

Tanner, Murray S., and Chen Ke. 1998. "Breaking the Vicious Cycles: The Emergence of China's National People's Congress." *Problems of Post-Communism*, May–June, 29–47.

Thornton, Patricia. 1999. "Beneath the Banyan Tree: Popular Views of Taxation and the State during the Republican and Reform Eras." *Twentieth-Century China*, November, 1–42.

Thurston, Anne F. 1999. *Muddling toward Democracy: Political Change in Grassroots China*. Washington, DC: U.S. Institute of Peace.

Tian Yuan. 1993. "Zhongguo nongcun jiceng de minzhu zhilu" [The pathway to grassroots democracy in rural China]. *Xiangzhen luntan* [Township forum], June, 3–4.

Tilly, Charles. 1995. "The Emergence of Citizenship in France and Elsewhere." *International Review of Social History* 40, supplement 3: 223–236.

Turner, Bryan S. 1990. "Outline of a Theory of Citizenship." *Sociology*, May, 189–217.

———. 1992. *Citizenship and Social Theory*. London: Sage.

"Villagers Spurn Communist in Chinese Election." 1999. *Atlanta Journal Constitution*, November 22.

Vogel, Ursula. 1991. "Is Citizenship Gender-Specific?" In Ursula Vogel and Michael Moran, eds., *The Frontiers of Citizenship*, 58–85. New York: St. Martin's.

Wang Dexiang. 1979. "Jianquan xuanju zhidu, baozhang renmin dangjia zuozhu" [Perfect the electoral system, guarantee the people as masters]. *Faxue yanjiu* [Legal Research], June, 5–8.

Wang Gungwu. 1991. *The Chineseness of China*. Hong Kong: Oxford University Press.

Wang Xu. 1997. "Mutual Empowerment of State and Peasantry: Grassroots Democracy in Rural China." *World Development*, September, 1431–1442.

Wang Zhenyao. 1998. "Village Committees: The Basis for China's Democratization." In Eduard B. Vermeer, Frank N. Pieke, and Woei Lien Chong. eds., *Cooperative and Collective in China's Rural Development: Between State and Private Interests*. Armonk, NY: Sharpe.

Weber, Max. 1998. "Citizenship in Ancient and Medieval Cities." Gershon Shafir, ed., *The Citizenship Debates*, 43–49. Minneapolis: University of Minnesota Press.

Wiens, Mi Chu. 1980. "Lord and Peasant: The Sixteenth to the Eighteenth Century." *Modern China*, January, 3–39.

Womack, Brantly. 1982. "The 1980 County-Level Elections in China: Experiment in Democratic Modernization." *Asian Survey*, March, 261–277.

Wong, R. Bin. 1997. *China Transformed*. Ithaca, NY: Cornell University Press.

Xia, Ming. 1997. "Informational Efficiency, Organizational Development, and the Institutional Linkages of the Provincial People's Congresses in China." *Journal of Legislative Studies*, Autumn, 10–38.

———. 2000. *The Dual Developmental State: Development Strategy and Institutional Arrangements for China's Transition*. Aldershot, UK: Ashgate.

Xu Chongde, and Pi Chunxie. 1982. *Xuanju zhidu wenda* [Questions and answers on the electoral system]. Beijing: Qunzhong chubanshe.

Xu Datong, and Li Zhao. 1986. "Shilun xuanqu huafen de zuoyong" [Discussing the role of dividing up electoral districts]. *Tianjin shelian xuekan* [Journal of the Tianjin Academy of Social Sciences], October 20–28.

Yang, Dali L. 1998. "Constitutionalism in China? Congressional Oversight and China's Political Future." Paper presented at workshop entitled Cadre Monitoring and Reward: Personnel Management and Policy Implementation in the PRC, University of California, San Diego, June 6–7.

Zhongguo jiceng zhengquan jianshe yanjiuhui [Chinese Basic-Level Political Power Construction Research Society]. 1994. *Zhongguo nongcun cunmin weiyuanhui huanjie xuanju yanjiu baogao* [Research report on the reelection of Chinese rural villagers' committees]. Beijing: Zhongguo shehui chubanshe.

Zweig, David. 2000. "The 'Externalities of Development': Can New Political Institutions Manage Rural Conflict?" In Elizabeth J. Perry and Mark Selden, eds., *Chinese Society: Change, Conflict, and Resistance*, 120–124. New York: Routledge & Kegan Paul.

15

Hegemony and Workers' Politics in China

MARC J. BLECHER

A world to win.

—Karl Marx

Pessimismo dell' intelligenza, ottimismo della volontà.

—Antonio Gramsci

THE PUZZLE

China's workers have lost their world. It was, by and large, a locus of relative privilege within Maoist state socialism: a zone in which they could enjoy stable, secure income; socially provided housing, medical care, and education, guaranteed lifetime employment, a work environment that was far from draconian, and that often involved considerable workers' power, and social and political prestige. Starting in the 1950s Chinese workers benefited from a way of life and a standard of living envied by their fellow proletarians in other poor countries.

The structural reforms begun in 1978 have slowly but inexorably terminated those prerogatives. Employment security has become a thing of the past: Dorothy Solinger concludes that unemployment is incalculable but "massive,"[1] and many laid-off workers find themselves in dire straits.[2] For those fortunate enough to have dodged the ax, wages have not kept pace with those of workers in other sectors or with inflation, and poverty—particularly deep poverty—is skyrocketing.[3] Workers are increasingly conscious of income inequality: in 1997, 44 percent judged disparities to be "relatively large" and another 46 percent "very large."[4] Worse yet, many workers' shrinking wages are often not even being paid. In 1997, over 11 million workers were subject to wage arrears averaging ¥1,900 per worker.[5] Almost 20 percent of those responding to the All-China Federation of Trade Unions (ACFTU) 1997 survey reported experiencing wage arrears, and 46 percent of those said that they were due three months' pay or more.[6] State-supplied housing, medical care, and education have declined in quality and availability, and increased in cost to workers.

All this has left the Chinese working class more and more dispirited. One-third of employed workers responding to the 1997 ACFTU survey thought it "likely" or "very likely" that they too would soon be unemployed, and more than one-fourth anticipated that their firm would soon be bankrupt or subject to merger.[7] Nearly a quarter said that they could no longer bear the present delays and shortfalls in medical expense reimbursement.[8] One-fourth said that their position as "masters of the enterprise" had declined from 1992 to 1997, and that was before some of the profoundest changes in the labor market and enterprise longevity took root.[9]

Many Chinese workers have not taken these changes lying down. The fiercest protests during the maelstrom of 1989 came from members of the working class, some of whom violently attacked security forces.[10] Nor were workers as intimidated as other classes by the crackdown. In the second half of 1989, when a political atmosphere of intense surveillance and repression prevailed, hundreds of strikes broke out in most provinces involving tens of thousands of workers. Four Xian cotton mills were shut down as early as June 6, 1989.[11] During the second half of the year, over 15,000 workers engaged in over 700 incidents of industrial action in state and collective firms throughout the country, protesting management's "failure to guarantee basic living conditions," and that counts only those outbreaks that made it into official reports.[12] The working class thus succeeded in challenging the state even at the moment the state was most intent on intimidating society.[13] As the political situation began to relax after 1992, worker protest intensified. In 1992, official statistics reported more than 540 demonstrations, 480 strikes, and 75 assaults on government offices.[14] In 1993, strike activity in Fujian tripled over the previous year.[15] The Ministry of Labor admitted that in 1994:

> the number of large-scale labor-management disputes exceeded 12,000. In some 2,500 cases, workers besieged plants, set fire to facilities, staged strikes, or detained bosses or leaders. Such events directly threatened the personal safety of party leaders in various factories and mines. In the Jixi Mining Bureau, enterprise leaders did not dare go to the pits for fear that they might be attacked by the workers.[16]

In 1996, the number of protests rose 50 percent over the previous year.[17] By the late 1990s, demonstrations and strikes had become endemic throughout the country.

This pattern of protest is important, and it has begun to receive systematic scholarly analysis.[18] This chapter, by contrast, focuses on the reverse side of the coin.

Workers' protests the since the 1980s, numerous and widely distributed though they may be, have remained spasmodic, spontaneous, and uncoordinated. Strikes and protests have not yet produced significant strike waves and protest movements. The vast majority of Chinese workers, including the unemployed, remain politically passive. In the ACFTU survey of 1997, a year of relative political relaxation (before the onset of the political deep freeze that started in late 1998), 96 percent of respondents said they had not participated in any sort of labor protest at any time during the previous five years.[19] The several dozen Tianjin workers I interviewed between 1995 and 1999 were unanimous in saying that though labor protests in their city were frequent, only a small minority of workers participated in them. Mostly, they averred, the protesters were retired workers whose pensions were not being paid regularly or fully.[20] So far as can be ascertained, local governments have developed a fairly standard and, so far, effective repertoire for dealing with such protests: they conduct an investigation, and, if the protesters' claims seem valid, they find some way of palliating the situation through negotiation followed by promises of remuneration or actual disbursements. Particularly nettlesome ringleaders are sometimes arrested, but in general there are no reprisals against most of the protesters.[21] The Chinese economy and the state's radical restructuring of it—for this is no mere reform—roll on.

Why is China's working class not mounting a coordinated challenge in the face of the fundamental transformations that have so profoundly afflicted so many workers and that threaten so many more who have not yet felt the ax? The question is all the more perplexing in view of the working class's power during the Maoist period—power reflected both in the privileged position it achieved and in the fierceness and frequency with which it expressed and defended its interests when it saw the need and had the opportunity. In terms of the former, workers' incomes and standards of living far exceeded those of farmers starting in the 1950s. Moreover, levels of inequality between workers on the one hand and managers and government officials on the other were extraordinarily low in absolute terms as well as when compared with other countries, a situation that actually continued well into the Dengist period.[22] In the Maoist period, workers' social and political status was very high. It was not uncommon for young people offered the opportunity for university education to choose factory work instead.[23] Cadres often treated workers with respect and kid gloves. For example, during the Great Leap Forward, many officials took smaller food rations than those allotted to workers.[24] Moreover, the Chinese working class's power was also manifest in the aggressive forms of collective action that workers undertook to advance their interests in 1957 and again during the Cultural Revolution.[25] Why then has a class that was so well treated, mighty, confident, and active in the recent past essentially rolled over, or allowed itself to be rolled over, in the past two decades?

There is no shortage of potential explanations: political repression, workers' lack of political resources, a shortage of political opportunities, lack of leadership, political incorporation of would-be leaders and activists, workers' dependence on firms for wages and social services, the fragmentation of the Chinese working class, and the state's skillful use of benefits and other policies and stopgap measures to ameliorate the workers' worst misery. Each of them has some purchase on the problem. This chapter begins to explore a rather different line of explanation—one that has not received much attention in the small literature on Chinese workers' politics under structural reform: that workers have become subject to hegemony of the market and of the state.

HEGEMONY

For Gramsci, hegemony obtains when a politically dominant class has persuaded a politically subordinate class of its own "moral, political and cultural values."[26] At the risk of succumbing to postmodernism's regrettable tendency to take the Marx out of Gramsci, here I will bracket the question of how class relations may be implicated in workers' hegemonic acceptance of the market and the state—specifically, whether and in what ways this hegemony is a matter of class domination, and whether this hegemony has been built by a class or class coalition with inimical interests to those of the Chinese working class. I also want to elide the thorny question of whether the values of the market and the state are in fact inimical to the interests of the working class—an issue that involves serious matters such as comparative referent (i.e., inimical compared to what?) and time frame. In adopting the concept of hegemony, I mean at this point only to assert that the values of the market and of the state that many Chinese workers have come to accept over the past twenty years are associated with institutions that have, over that period, already done serious harm to the working class as a whole and to many individual workers— sometimes in absolute terms compared with the past, sometimes only in relative terms compared with other classes and groups—and that the market and the state threaten to continue to do so into the foreseeable future. China's workers are clearly subordinated to the state, and just as clearly subordinated to other classes and groups in society through the market. Both the state and the market have done measurable net harm, in relative and sometimes even in absolute terms, to much of the Chinese working class. Yet over the past two decades, many (probably most) of China's workers have come to accept the core values of the market and of the state as legitimate. Why and how has this happened, and what are the prospects for this hegemony and for a counterhegemony that would oppose the state and the market?

The values workers have about the market and the state are closely intertwined, of course. The state has ushered in, legitimated, and fostered the market and in turn sought to legitimate and secure itself through the market. For analytical purposes, however, the analysis that follows will treat them as distinct.

The evidence in this chapter comes from interviews I conducted from 1995 to 1999 with several dozen workers. They all hail from Tianjin, a city that has not been at the forefront of industrial "reform" policies such as privatization or globalization compared with the likes of Guangzhou and Shanghai, and whose economic performance has been somewhat ahead of national trends but not extraordinary so.[27] The workers I interviewed are a diverse lot: old, middle-aged and young; male and female; skilled and unskilled; from state, collective, joint-venture and private firms; employed and unemployed; better- and worse-off. Yet despite their heterogeneity, all of them, including even a retired worker and former factory cadre who continues to hold pronounced Maoist sensibilities, evinced a broad acceptance of the values of the market and of the legitimacy of the state.

First, even those who were faring poorly in the new market environment believed nonetheless that competition and market allocation of employment and income were both right and were more effective than the planned economy, even though many had done well under the latter. The following was fairly typical of my interviewees' sensibilities.

> Enterprises' development should not all proceed the same way. I support reform. It is necessary. Competition is right. [This sentiment was surprising coming from a forty-seven-year-old worker whose building materials factory was economically endangered, who was not readily reemployable, and who also had serious complaints.]
>
> Competition is right. But what should we do about the workers in bankrupt enterprises? I think the government should have a policy to guarantee the workers' basic livelihood. There are lots of things about which I am dissatisfied. I go to work every day and make contributions to the factory, but my wages are so low. My wife goes out to work, and together the two of us try to support our family. But we barely have enough to eat and can't save anything. Our life is pretty tight. The factory leaders ought to have some sympathy for the workers, but they're not like that.[28]

One sea change for workers brought about by marketization occurred when, starting in the middle to late 1980s, their wages and livelihoods became dependent on the economic health of their particular enterprise rather than on the state more broadly. As enterprises became more fully independent economically, for the first time workers in prosperous firms experienced high wages, better employment security, and more ample benefits than those in firms in more dire straits. For workers, the economic health of their enterprise was often a matter of the luck of the draw. If they happened to find themselves in a sector that was faring badly, or in a plant with particularly incompetent management, they would lose out, often seriously, compared with their more fortunate fellows. Prima facie, this new economic structure provided an objective material basis for a sense of injustice among workers on the losing end. Yet few of my informants had developed such sentiments. When I raised the issue in interviews, most of my interlocutors developed a puzzled, faraway look indicating that they had not thought about their circumstances quite that way before. It was difficult to get them to understand the changed situation to which I was inviting their reaction, even though they lived it on a daily basis. That itself is evidence of market hegemony. When I succeeded in doing so, which was not always possible (an indication of the depth of this particular aspect of market hegemony), the following responses were typical.

Yes, it's unfair that some people lose out simply because their enterprises are doing badly. I did feel this. But I didn't express it. Partly this is because I saw that enterprises all over Tianjin were suffering. Mine wasn't the worst.[29]

The change [from all workers being treated the same to some doing better and some doing worse because of the condition of their factories] happened in 1995. Yes, now that I think of it, this was a big change, and it was hard for workers to accept. Yes, of course it's unfair. But if you don't accept it, you still have to accept it [*ni bu jieshou, ye dei jieshou*]. There's no way around it [*mei banfa*].[30]

The last two sentences reflect an important aspect of hegemony: the view that a situation is natural and inevitable—in Gramsci's terms, it becomes common sense. My interviewees clearly evinced this sensibility.

Others grounded their acceptance of the situation in the logic of the market:

Workers' dependence on the uneven economic fate of their factories started for me in 1988. It's fair that factories that can sell their products should do better than those that cannot. But no, I suppose it's not fair that the workers should have to suffer because of these differences.[31]

Once they began to think about the new enterprise-based inequalities among them, whom or what did workers hold responsible? Many drew a blank.

In the 1970s all workers were paid around the same. Now the differences are pretty large. I feel this is unfair. Some people earn too much money, and some earn too little. They are all workers, so why should the differences be so great? So ordinary people don't understand why the differences should be so great. I can't say whose responsibility this is. There are lots of ways of understanding this. . . . I don't know why workers who do a good job have to be laid off. . . . Maybe it's that the country is too large and overpopulated—I can't figure it out. There definitely are lots of unreasonable things going on. Ordinary people can't say clearly what's happening.[32]

Yes, of course it's unfair that I worked for a factory that was doing poorly while others did not. I have a classmate who today has ¥100,000,000.
[Question:] Who has responsibility for this?
I don't blame the government. I just blame the situation *(xianxiang)*. But what can you do? Things are still better today than they were before the reforms started. Even those worse off than me would say so.[33]

As these accounts make clear, these workers had a great deal of trouble determining who or what was responsible for the change. Significantly, they interpreted my questions about responsibility in terms only of possible ameliorative efforts, not cause. This exchange is typical:

> It's not fair that the workers should have to suffer because of these differences.
> [Question:] Who is responsible for this suffering?
> The union is useless in this regard.
> [Question:] Is the government responsible?
> Yes, the government is responsible for assuring a livelihood for workers.[34]

Like many of my interlocutors, this bright, experienced thirty-year-old man simply did not grasp the question about who or what might have brought about the situation in which his livelihood had come to depend on the economic fortunes of his enterprise, or that the state and its policies of structural reform might have done so.

Most workers conceptualized the issue of their dependence on their firms' economic condition not in terms of its underlying roots, but rather by focusing directly on the causes of their firms' particular economic condition. Where it was poor, they tended to blame a number of factors, but usually not the state. Some chalked up their declining situation to fate or bad luck.

> Many workers just feel that they have a bad fate *[mingyün]*, that they went through the wrong door *[zou cuomen]*; if they had joined another industry when they first started work, things would be all right.[35]

Often they blamed their managers rather than the state.

> The main responsibility for the factory's problems is the factory. The government's policy is to let everyone get rich. Whoever is capable will have food to eat. The government doesn't want to see factories do poorly, and doesn't want workers to lack for food. But some [factory] leaders' methods are mistaken. If you're a worker, what can you do? China's workers don't fear exhaustion, but only want to have work to do, to have hope. They don't fear being really tired; they are just afraid that their factory will not do well.[36]

> Some workers in my plant did express their dissatisfaction about the factory's economic problems. Mainly it was people whose livelihoods were hurt most by the layoffs, and whose personalities were such that they would speak out. They sought out the plant leadership [to complain]. No one sought out the government. I didn't feel that the government has responsibility for solving this, since there are enterprises all over the city in this situation. Moreover, the reason for the problem wasn't the government, but the enterprise leadership, which wasn't too smart.[37]

> Even those who are doing poorly after being laid off do not hold the government responsible for their welfare. They hold their enterprises responsible, and they think that the government's responsibility is limited only to making sure that enterprises live

up to policies. You can't hold the government responsible; there are so many laid-off workers, and the government can't support them all. Workers generally know this.[38]

In the past our leadership helped other districts build small factories. We gave them our technology free of charge. Now these factories' costs are lower than ours, because they have fewer people and because their business methods are very flexible. Whoever sells their products gets a commission; but our leaders never do this. Our leaders are numb-skulls (*naozi bijiao jianghua*); they don't think flexibly. So now our products don't have buyers.[39]

脑子比较僵化

Some did blame local government officials, though.

Yes, of course it's unfair that my wages are lower and I have to endure wage arrears just because I happen to work in a plant that is not doing well. Does the state have responsi-bility? The state's policies are good. It's the implementation that is no good. Sometimes middle-level officials mess things up. . . . Some people just turn bad after becoming officials.[40]

I still think Deng is good. It's just that many of the people below him are not so good; they are just out for themselves.
[Question:] But isn't such behavior an inevitable result of the market, which Deng brought in?
Yes, it's a contradiction.[41]

Yet holding local officials responsible is a different matter from blaming the state. As several of these accounts state explicitly, generally my interviewees did not blame the state for their problems or even expect the state to solve their problems, whatever the cause may be. One exception may be older workers—those who came of age in the heyday of the centrally planned economy oriented to rapid, heavy industrializa-tion.

Many older workers—especially those who worked in the 1960s and 1970s—do hold the state responsible for their livelihood. But many others do not.[42]

This last assertion, uttered by a thoughtful, analytically minded, and rather criti-cal retired worker-cum-shopfloor cadre with decidedly Maoist commitments, was borne out by my interviews. To reiterate what one older woman worker who has seen her family income plummet because of her layoff said:

I didn't feel that the government has responsibility for solving this, since there are enter-prises all over the city in this situation. . . . The reason for the problem wasn't the government.[43]

Workers' behavioral responses to the crises they face also evince the hegemony of the market. Many adopted market-based coping strategies.

Yes, of course it's unfair that some workers lose out just because their factories are doing badly. But most workers think that the way to deal with the inequality is to try to make more money for themselves. . . . At first, most workers were afraid of being laid off. But then after it happened most found out that it wasn't so bad; that they could make do in various ways. Many are better off now. . . . Most workers in my old plant found some way to make a living. You have to eat, after all. Some go into petty business, some find jobs on the labor market.[44]

All the laid-off workers in my plant found other work making about what they made before or more.[45]

Others said that workers' dependence on their ailing firms increased labor incentives.

If the plant does badly, people know they won't have work to do. So everyone works hard. When there's a lot of work in the plant, people go all out.[46]

A common response was for workers to develop all manner of advice for turning their firms around, and often to proffer it to their management.

Our factory has two labs, both of which have lots of administrators and experiment personnel; but they have nothing to do. No new products come out of there. We feel that the bosses should make them go do some other work, or at least put them all together so the other building can be vacated and used for a factory or rented out. Our factory has a great location, and the rent could pay some of our workers' salaries. . . . We workers complain to our factory manager about this all the time. We just talk to him when we bump into him in the plant. We can speak very frankly. We tell him to close down one of the labs, because the people who are supposed to be doing research there just sit around and play cards. But he won't do it. He likes to have two laboratories around. We workers shouldn't have to pay for this. But the manager runs the factory like a patriarch.[47]

Some workers put their entrepreneurial ideas for their firms into action.

When things are going badly for the factory, everyone thinks of a way to help out—through friends and relatives—to get business for the factory. The plant also encourages people to help the factory to market its products. It gives out bonuses according to how much workers helped out with marketing.[48]

Many aspects of the thinking adumbrated in these accounts—the difficulty workers having conceptualizing a causal or even an ameliorative role for the state, and the way they focus their complaints and even their market-oriented responses on their enterprises rather than on themselves as individuals—reflect the continuing power of work unit collectivism in workers' worldviews. We shall return to this question in the conclusion.

Finally, workers' views about protest reflect their hegemonic acceptance of the economic, political, and existential realities in which they find themselves.

There are so many workers who are doing poorly that there is nothing the government can do about it. There is no point in protesting.

I have heard that some workers create disturbances. But there's no use in doing so. The workers in our factory have not done so. Every worker is trying to think of a way to make money, to change their position. If you create a disturbance, you can't make much money.[49]

We older workers would not make trouble. If we have opinions, we raise them to the higher levels, and after it investigates the government will take some measures to address the problem.[50]

We were owed six months' accumulated wage arrears—not six months straight, but six months altogether. Workers were unhappy about this, and some protested to the management—not to the government. But everyone knew that the factory didn't have money, so what's the point? I was too embarrassed to raise opinions about this.[51]

Here is further evidence of work unit–based thinking: these workers focused their protest on their enterprise, not the government that owned it. And the energy and expectations brought to the protests by the minority who engaged in them were low, since they knew their enterprise's coffers and its capacity to help them were low.

Protest is understood, probably correctly, as behavior engaged in by people who are desperate and who have no other recourse through the market or through normal channels.[52]

The people who protest down at city hall are old workers who are not receiving their pensions and have no other way out.[53]

In some factories retired workers have not received their pension benefits or their medical expenses cannot be reimbursed. Some of these people create disturbances. No one from my factory has done so.[54]

At first my fellow workers were afraid of being laid off, but in general they didn't make trouble. Those with special problems did protest to the management, and generally they were just kept on in the plant. For most workers, though, after they were laid off they found they could do other things, so it was okay.[55]

One said:

Very few workers go down to government offices to make trouble. Those who do generally are either retired workers who are not getting their pensions, or else workers with special problems such as illness, injury, or some special problem in their family's livelihood. There are several hundred thousand laid-off workers in Tianjin now, but only a few tens of thousands engage in this sort of thing; it's a tiny percentage.[56]

In other words, protest is an extraordinary response to workers' problems; ordinary responses revolve around the market or appeals through channels. And hegemony is, of course, a way of defining the ordinary.

Moreover, even when political conflict, including contentious politics, does break out, it can reflect and even reinforce hegemony. David Laitin conceptualizes hegemony in terms of the creation of a dominant political cleavage agreed on by all combatants, including those who stand to lose from battles drawn along such a line:

> [Hegemony] involves a concept of culture "not as values which are upheld but, rather, as 'points of concern' which are debated."[57]

> A successful hegemony, then, doesn't yield "order"; rather, it yields a set of conflicts that automatically and common-sensically stand at the top of the political agenda.[58]

Chinese workers' protests reflect the hegemony of the market and of the state against which they are protesting. The most common slogans reported at protests demand food, not social change. Even the kind of food demanded can evince workers' acceptance of inequality: in one case, they chanted: "We don't demand fish, meat, and eggs—we only demand a mouthful of rice."[59] At their most political, workers' demands are more often focused on the behavior of and revenge against individuals, not on the policies and structures that underlie that behavior. "What do we workers hope for? We hope there will be another Cultural Revolution and all those corrupt cadres will be killed."[60] These workers do not associate themselves with the truly radical demands of the Cultural Revolution for economic democracy and equality or for draconian restrictions on markets. Their demands are, rather, well within the hegemony of the state, which itself has been dishing out capital punishment for a handful of notorious cases of corruption.

THE SOURCES OF HEGEMONY

How did the thinking of most Chinese workers, even the most immiserated and politically active ones, become subjected to the hegemony of the market and the state? To give some order to this inquiry, I will divide the discussion into categories of market and state hegemony, and, within those, to explanations rooted in general factors common to many markets and states, and to those specific to China.

MARKET HEGEMONY

General Factors

Markets have well-known structural features that contribute to their acceptance by those who are nonetheless dominated within them. They atomize those they subject, offering the prospect of individual solutions, which in turn undermines the potential for forming collective solidarities that could challenge the market. This certainly is happening in China. The workers I interviewed who had any strategy for coping with the difficulties imposed on them by the market tended to think that their best approach was an individual one: to work harder, to seek out a new job, to get more education. (Such individual market-based strategies were more common than the collectivist, unit-oriented market-based ones discussed above.) Such an approach is, one can hypothesize, more likely to appear in a city like Tianjin (not to mention Beijing, Guangzhou, or Shanghai), where the economy offers some realistic prospects along these lines, than in China's more economically decimated rust belts in parts of Manchuria or the west. Markets also fragment classes, which makes broad class-based coalitions more difficult to fashion.[61] In younger and middle-aged Chinese workers' dismissive reports of protests as mainly a pastime for immiserated retirees, and in middle-aged and older workers' plaintive accounts of how easy it is for younger workers to find jobs if they are laid off—which are echoed confidently by the younger workers—the obstacles to a broad working-class movement come into clear focus.

Markets also divert away from politics the energies of lively, smart people with leadership potential. The most dynamic workers I interviewed were, not surprisingly, those who were managing nicely in China's new economy, by achieving and maintaining good positions in their firms or through private entrepreneurship. Factory cadres are often those best able and most inclined to capitalize on the new market opportunities that appear daily in China.[62] Conversely, among my interviewees, those in the direst straits tended to be the dimmest bulbs and the most depressed spirits—decidedly not the sorts capable of fashioning a localized protest, not to mention a social movement.

Markets also create experiences that mitigate against opposition to them. Where and when they work well, they create a pool of consumer goods that, while not lifting all ships, can have an energizing effect.[63] They can convince even those who are sinking that the palpable tide may eventually lift them. Among the workers I interviewed, many who were suffering nonetheless had the general economic development of the past two decades in mind when they averred that reform was still a good thing, and that there could be no return to the Maoist period, no matter how fondly some of them recalled the stability, camaraderie, high public-spiritedness, and clean government of those days (which many did). They saw the "success" of the market in the prosperity and rapid growth that is so palpable all around them even if it is out of their reach. Some expected that they would benefit by way of enhanced opportunities for spouses or children; others thought growth was robust enough to hold out a reasonable hope of something coming their way, such as a foreign buyer for their enterprise.

China-Specific Factors

Many Chinese workers brought high hopes and spirits to the triumph of the revolution in 1949 and to the Cultural Revolution of the 1960s.[64] And many still hold fond (if selective) memories both about the past and about its relevance to solving some of today's problems, for example, the workers who want to deal Cultural Revolution–style with their corrupt managers and local officials.[65] By and large, though, the Cultural Revolution did not fulfill their hopes, and even those who still think it a noble experiment generally regard it as a failure because of its overwrought politicization, its perversions of class-based political struggle, and its social and economic havoc. This view still helps fuel the hegemony of both the market and the Dengist state, producing both a palpable sense that, in a phrase favored by Margaret Thatcher, there is no alternative to the reforms, as well as some favorable comparisons of the present with the worst of the past to balance the more positive memories of days gone by.[66]

Likewise, national (and nationalistic) comparisons, made only more apposite by the coincidence of Dengism with the age of rapid globalization of information technology that have brought glittering images of prosperity abroad before the eyes even of China's poorest, have helped foster support for market-based development in China. The fact that Japan, South Korea, and Taiwan have prospered so well under capitalism—never mind that they in fact adopted a heavily statist variant—was specifically used by the Dengist leadership to mobilize support for its reforms in the early 1980s. And the fact that China is doing so well compared with Russia and much of Eastern Europe and Central Asia is, for many workers, the proof of the market pudding.

The hegemony of the market over even those suffering from it in China should come as no surprise, since market-oriented values and social networks showed extraordinary resilience throughout the Maoist period. Despite the vehemence with which the state attacked them, especially after 1956, markets repeatedly and irrepressibly sprang back to life even in Mao's day. In the wake of the disasters of the Great Leap Forward, many villagers returned land to those, including many class enemies, who owned it before collectivization, sometimes having preserved exact knowledge of the old boundary markers and holdings. Although many of those who quickly became active merchants and entrepreneurs in the early 1960s were criticized for speculation and other capitalistic activities in the Cultural Revolution, the suffering and repression heaped on them did not discourage them from going right back into business in the early 1980s. The market was a potent and durable institution that proved capable of withstanding everything the Maoist state could throw at it for three decades. This resilience may help explain, however undialectically, why Chinese workers laid low by the market can nonetheless see it at least as inevitable.

STATE HEGEMONY

General Factors

Nicos Poulantzas has explicated the complex ways that the capitalist state acquires hegemony out of the structural separation of the economic and the political, and, accordingly, the state's relative autonomy from the bourgeoisie.[67] In China, the state has drawn strength and longevity from the fact that it has persuaded many workers that it is no longer responsible for their specific economic situations or even capable of doing much to ameliorate their problems. As we have seen above, insofar as they blame anyone or anything, the workers I interviewed generally tended to attribute their problems to their firms' management or to local leaders rather than to the state as an institution. Many also apprehended China's high level of unemployment as a problem that overtaxes the state rather than as one caused by it.

Yet the state's autonomy from the economy is only relative, in two senses. First, while the workers I interviewed do not regard the state as responsible for their specific vicissitudes, they do give it credit for the overall prosperity and growth that China has achieved since 1978. That is, the unevenness and inconsistency in workers' conception of the autonomy of the state works in its favor. They also view the state generally as offering a modicum of protection from the worst effects of the market, through the layoff allowances, unemployment benefits, and subsidies to the poor that it routinely, if unevenly, dispenses directly or that it funds indirectly through enterprises, as well as the special allotments it arranges to mollify protesting workers.

China-Specific Factors

The Chinese state has worked to reinforce the structural bases for its hegemony with a drumbeat of ideological interpellation. Hegemony operates most profoundly, of course, at the level not so much of what people think as of the categories in which they think. The press induces China's workers to think in terms of relatively harmless categories. In one very common example, a *Workers Daily* story on state enterprise reform tried to appear objective by presenting survey data. But all the questions were framed in terms of the specific characteristics of enterprises.

> When asked to choose whether they preferred to work in state-owned, private, joint venture, or stock companies, 58 percent chose state-owned. . . . They were then asked whether they would approve if their factory were doing pretty well and were made to take over a money-losing plant. 55 percent said they would approve, 30 percent disapproved, and 15 percent said they would have to look at the situation to decide.[68]

Such a story induces workers to think about their problems in terms of the ownership forms or the economic fortunes of their firms and not in terms of the market or of state policies themselves. Another typical story directed at workers blamed their plight in part on the unwillingness of enterprises to provide training, which directs workers' thinking to human capital rather than to capital or to the capitalistic state.[69]

Likewise, the state works hard to persuade workers that their problems come not from the state but from the market and their own failure to adapt to it. This same survey "found" that workers thought the second leading cause of enterprises' (and therefore, workers') problems, after "poor leadership," was "poor conditions in the market."[70] The state also continues to hector workers about how they ought to accept market-based logic in their own lives. For example, *Workers Daily* published a reader's debate over a story it had published about a model worker named Ren Jianye, who turned down a cash prize that accompanied his honor. One of Ren's critics argued:

> For him not to accept it reflects a spirit of not asking for anything. But it has bad side effects. Not to accept it plays into the spirit of eating out of the same pot, in which some people rest easy on the fruits of others' work, in which some people work more but don't get more, all of which depresses the labor activism of many people. If people like Ren are paid more, this protects the people who work and contribute more, which in turn disturbs the people who waste their days.[71]

Here we begin to see a more insidious rhetorical approach that divides the working class. For another example, the *Workers Daily* depicted young workers as lazy "good for nothings" *(mei chuxi),* lacking pride in their work and unwilling to upgrade their skills. In a fascinating twist, it blamed other mass media for promoting an ethic of high living.[72] Many other accounts blame (male) urban workers' problems on rural migrants and women, who are frequently urged to return from whence they came. In an extraordinary and perverted combination of subtlety and cheek, the *Workers Daily* has even tried to divide employed from unemployed workers. For example, it published another "debate" in which one reader argued that while unemployment may be unfair to the unemployed, efforts to prevent unemployment for some, especially those for whom there is no work, would be unfair to the unemployed![73]

The state makes at least two other kinds of ideological appeals to the working class. First, it argues that the current situation facing workers coincides with modern international norms. For example, Britain's workfare program was cited favorably in support of a plan to deny benefits to workers who do not join training schemes.[74] Likewise, the 1995 Labor Law is justified on the grounds that it is similar to legislation of other industrial countries.[75] Second, as noted above, it has argued that there is no alternative either to the reforms or to the problems that they have brought in tow for workers. "At some stages of development, unemployment represents and is a necessary stage for social progress," a *Workers Daily* reader wrote in its pages.[76]

Aside from ideological appeals, a number of political factors have helped the state develop and maintain its hegemony over the working class. Its bold and decisive reversal of the overbearing political radicalism of the Cultural Revolution remains important, especially to those who lived through it. The state's willingness to respond positively or at least not aggressively in the face of many local protests both mollifies flashpoints and helps persuade other workers that it can play a positive role for them. Likewise, the state's willingness to open up limited space for grumbling and even criticism—some of it, as above, published in the official press—helps workers blow off steam and is meant to persuade them that the state is not an utterly implacable enemy.[77] Finally, the fanfare with which the state publicly attacks corruption may actually help place it in common cause with workers angry at their shady bosses and complicit local officials. Workers I interviewed seemed to believe that corruption was systemic, and thus largely beyond the capacity of the state to ameliorate. That position can, paradoxically, contribute to state hegemony insofar as it helps relieve the state of significant responsibility for eliminating corruption in workers' eyes. As in their views of the market, they did not hold the state responsible for creating the political economy that lies at the root of corruption.

CONCLUSION

The Chinese working class—those who work in industrial settings for a wage, or who have done so for most of their working lives until they were laid off or terminated—are an extremely diverse lot that is, moreover, in rapid flux. China's workers are responding to their lived experiences in a wide variety of ways. Many are participating in various forms of collective action. Cai emphasizes the structural opportunities for protest provided by workers' and local leaders' knowledge that workers can appeal to local leaders' superiors for relief which, if granted, would undermine the local leaders. He also stresses the importance to successful collective action of effective grassroots leadership.[78] Feng traces the roots of worker protest to subsistence crises, thereby echoing a major theme in the peasant moral economy literature pioneered by James Scott.[79] Hurst and O'Brien focus on the special circumstances that impel pensioners to protest and provide the resources and opportunities for them to do so.[80] Lee, taking issue with Burawoy and Lukács's analysis of the soporific effect of poststate socialist market transition, argues that in China the legacies of state socialist egalitarianism and Maoist-era radicalism provide ideological bases, linguistic discourses, and repertoires for proletarian protest.[81]

Balancing all this ferment is a set of countervailing forces identified in various literatures that dampen working class collective action. Scott has argued that in general workers are more subject to the ideological hegemony of the state than peasants, because they are more easily saturated with the state's discursive and symbolic messages.[82] Burawoy and Lukács focus on the atomizing effects of the market transition, which holds out the prospect of individual rather than collective solutions to workers' problems. They also highlight the way the transition undermines state socialist shop floor regimes, associated with the shortage economy, that reinforced worker solidarity.[83] Cai mentions the obstacles to the emergence of grassroots protest leadership, the problems workers have coordinating collective action across enterprises, and the state's skill in phasing in layoffs so as to disperse the shock over time.[84] To all this can be added, of course, the repressive apparatus of the state and its denial of any space in civil society for working-class self-organization—a not wholly convincing argument, since, as we have seen, many workers engaged in bold forms of collective action in the second half of 1989, when the state was at its most repressive.

The analysis presented here can be grouped with this second set of factors. It partakes in a general way of Scott's argument about workers' susceptibility to ideological hegemony, but expands it by emphasizing the hegemony of the market as well as the state. It has quite a bit in common with Burawoy and Lukács's argument about Hungary, though it does not focus on the shop floor and it emphasizes that Dengist-era market and state hegemony is rooted as much in a dark as in a radiant view of the past.[85]

The argument of this chapter is not meant to minimize, much less refute, scholarship that focuses on and emphasizes the importance and potential of worker protest. Such collective action is all too real, and, particularly in a crisis, it could develop into a far more potent force than it has proven to be to date. The point of this chapter, though, is to attempt to explicate one set of factors that appear to be arrayed against such a development. They are not insurmountable by any means.

These findings about the forces of hegemony over Tianjin workers and their effects in producing general working-class political passivity can be squared, at least in a preliminary and hypothetical way, with scholarship that focuses on protest. Tianjin is no economic avatar, but it is doing a good deal better than the hardluck towns in which Lee and Hurst were able to do their impressive fieldwork. The subsistence crises identified as key by Feng did not obtain in my sample of Tianjin workers. There are such workers in Tianjin, but far fewer in relative and probably even absolute terms than can be found in the hard-hit Liaoning or Shanxi rust belts. Likewise, my sample did not include pensioners deprived of their benefits, though they too exist, of course, in Tianjin; and, as Hurst and O'Brien would predict, the old-timers protest there as well.[86]

How durable is the hegemony of the market and of the state over the thinking of the working class? One issue raised above is the continuing power of work unit collectivism over the thinking of many workers. To be sure, the material bases of work unit life are eroding: workers are being laid off, housing markets are rising, many enterprises are no longer paying social benefits (and some benefits are beginning, haltingly and incompletely, to be provided by city governments), and labor markets are developing. Over time, then, the capacity of work unit collectivism to shape workers' weltanschauungen may well erode.[87] Even if it does, though, the hegemony of the market and the state may find new defenses and forms. Collectivistic forms of market hegemony, especially those that fail, can readily metamorphose into individualistic ones. As for state hegemony, work units are only one of many possible institutions that can legitimate the state or insulate it from society; others include the rule of law, new forms of intermediate organizations, and the market itself.[88]

The stunning rapidity with which hegemony of the market and the Dengist state have emerged since 1978 could affect that hegemony's future either way. On the one hand, it might suggest that working-class thinking is capricious, responding primarily to the immediately preceding crisis (in this case, of the Maoist period) and/or to the positive aspects of the macroeconomic and political changes of the Dengist period. If this is so, then the hegemony of the market and the state might be fragile, particularly in the event of a serious and sustained economic crisis. On the other hand, the fact that many of the core political and economic values of the Maoist period were tossed aside so quickly might suggest that they had not really taken root. In this case, market and state hegemony would appear more durable.

For Gramsci, hegemony and counterhegemony are built by political movements, a project requiring extraordinary patience, skill, and determination, as well as a civil society in which to grow. So long as the People's Republic continues to survive as China's state in anything like its present form, there seems almost no likelihood that a robust working-class political movement capable of building a counterhegemony against the market or the state could emerge. And if the state falls, the ensuing political situation would, in all likelihood, be confused and unstable enough to provide a poor environment for a durable, vigorous antimarket social movement of the kind that, for example, the Italian Communist Party aspired to be, and in some ways was, from the 1950s through the 1980s.

As a Marxist, Gramsci also knew that economic crisis could undermine hegemony and create opportunities for the development of counterhegemony. The state's hegemony is built on its ability to guarantee and claim credit for China's stunning economic expansion since 1978. Were that economic growth to end in a serious, sustained economic crisis, workers might respond with outbursts that could threaten the survival of the People's Republic of China. But even in that scenario, it is difficult to see how the hegemony of the market would be undermined. In the last days of the Soviet Union, striking coal miners saw the market as their salvation from the grips of a corrupt state and a political economy that had failed them.[89] While the comparison with China is inexact, since Chinese workers are already living in—and many are suffering under—an established market system, the tendency under capitalism for economic crises to find expression primarily as political crises can be observed in a wide variety of countries and contexts. In China as elsewhere, a deep economic crisis would be far more likely to incubate a movement against the state—an overt, palpable target—than against the market itself. The latter is far more diffuse, amorphous, and invisible an object of political struggle. Mobilization against the market also requires a robust left in command of considerable political resources, something not at all likely in the context of a China that has been moving against its own left and which, in the scenario being adumbrated here, would just have thrown out its Communist Party. That the party had presided over a systematic transition to capitalism would probably make little difference even to immiserated workers; they would, at a moment of crisis, be more likely to blame it for being too left than too right. In short, even if state hegemony were to fail, market hegemony would probably survive and might even be strengthened, at least in the short or medium run.

For a latter-day Gramsci interested in elaborating a working class political movement, then, China today provides good cause for the "pessimism of the intellect" professed by the master, and a sore test of the "optimism of the will" he strove so nobly to affirm.

NOTES

My thanks to the many colleagues who commented on earlier versions of this chapter, including Kevin O'Brien, Dorothy Solinger, and all the participants in the Cornell University East Asia Program China Colloquium, especially Sherman Cochran, Mark Selden, Vivienne Shue, and Sidney Tarrow, which invited me to produce and present the first draft.

1. Dorothy Solinger, "Why We Cannot Count the Unemployed," *China Quarterly*, September 2001, 671.

2. Dorothy Solinger, "Labor Market Reform and the Plight of the Laid-Off Proletariat," *China Quarterly*, June 2002, 304–326.

3. Azizur Rahman Khan and Carl Riskin, *Inequality and Poverty in China in the Age of Globalization* (Oxford: Oxford University Press, 2001), 35–40, 70–75. Khan and Riskin are unable to disaggregate their data by occupation. Since their urban samples include only registered urban residents and not migrants, though, it seems reasonable to conclude that the urban poor must consist primarily of industrial workers.

4. Quanguo zonggonghui zhengce yanjiushi [All-China Federation of Trade Unions Policy Research Office], ed., *1997 Zhongguo zhigong zhuangkuang diaocha* [Survey of the status of Chinese staff and workers in 1997] (Beijing: Xifan chubanshe, 1999), 1240. Hereafter cited as ZZZD.

5. Quanguo zonggonghui zhengce yanjiushi, *Zhongguo gonghui tongji nianjian* [Chinese trade unions statistics yearbook] (Beijing: Zhongguo tongji chubanshe, 1999), 147.

6. ZZZD, 1239.

7. ZZZD, 1247.

8. ZZZD, 1243.

9. ZZZD, 1250.

10. It is probably no coincidence that, after weeks of indecision, the crackdown came hard on the heels of the first stirrings of the self-mobilization of labor. Nor is there anything accidental about the fact that working-class protesters met with much harsher repression than did students, intellectuals, and other members of the urban middle classes. As the popular protests climaxed, in Beijing an audacious young man named Wang Weilin, who did not appear to be a worker, made history by stepping, briefcase in hand, in front of a line of tanks traveling down Changan Avenue. The tanks stopped. But in Shanghai, when workers with the same bold spirit placed themselves in front of a train, up to twenty were run over. Three of the infuriated workers who attacked the train driver for his brutality were executed. After the crackdown, student and intellectual dissidents were hunted down in nationwide dragnets, hauled before kangaroo courts, and sentenced to jail. But dozens of workers were summarily executed by a state that, in doing so, demonstrated that it feared the power of the working class more than any other. "China has differentiated between intellectuals and workers in its handling of the aftermath of Tiananmen. At least 40 workers were reported executed, while young student leaders have received prison sentences ranging from two to six years." "China Vowed to Have No More Trials of Dissidents," UPI, March 19, 1991. Reprinted in *China News Digest*, March 21, 1991.

11. Foreign Broadcast Information Service (FBIS), June 16, 1989.

12. FBIS, July 19, 1991.

13. In the fall of 1990, furloughed workers began to be recalled to their factories even though there was no work for them to do. According to a Beijing Labor Bureau official, "We're paying to keep them in the factory. They can sweep the floor or attend classes to occupy their time. Just don't let them idle at home for fear that they would become emotionally unstable" (*China News Digest*, March 21, 1991). In the summer of 1996, two longtime members of the Communist Party—an intellectual and a worker, both leaders of their respective work units—confided to me that "the government doesn't seriously fear the students; it most fears the workers." Interview by author, July 9, 1996.

14. FBIS, March 10, 1993.

15. FBIS, March 31, 1994.

16. *Dangdai* [The Present Age], May 15, 1994.

17. FBIS, July 22, 1997.

18. See Cai Yong Shun, "The Resistance of Chinese Laid-Off Workers in the Reform Period," *China Quarterly* 170 (June 2002): 327–344; William Hurst and Kevin J. O'Brien, "China's Contentious Pensioners," *China Quarterly* 170 (June 2002): 345–356. See also Feng Chen, "Subsistence Crises, Managerial Corruption, and Labour Protests in China," *China Journal*, July 2000, 41–63; Ching Kwan Lee, "From the Specter of Mao to the Spirit of the Law: Labor Insurgency in China," *Theory and Society*, 2002. See also Antoine Kernan and Jean-Louis Rocca, "Social Responses to Unemployment and the 'New Urban Poor': Case Study in Shenyang City and Liaoning Province," *China Perspectives*, January–February 2000, 35–51; Ching Kwan Lee, "The 'Revenge of History': Collective Memories and Labor Protests in Northeastern China," *Ethnography* 1, no. 2 (2000): 217–237; Ching Kwan Lee, "Pathways of Labor Insurgency," in Elizabeth J. Perry and Mark Selden, eds., *Chinese Society: Change, Conflict, and Resistance* (London: Routledge, 2000), 41–61.

19. ZZZD, 1244.

20. See also Hurst and O'Brien, "China's Contentious Pensioners."

21. For a textured discussion of the state's response to worker protest, see Lee, "Pathways of Labor Insurgency."

22. Wenfang Tang and William Parish, *Chinese Urban Life under Reform* (Cambridge: Cambridge University Press, 2000), 5, 90.

23. Interview by author, Hong Kong, 1975.

24. Interview by author, Tianjin, 1997.

25. Elizabeth Perry, "Shanghai's Strike Wave of 1957," *China Quarterly*, March 1994; Elizabeth Perry and Li Xun, *Proletarian Power: Shanghai in the Cultural Revolution* (Boulder, CO: Westview, 1997).

26. James Joll, *Antonio Gramsci* (London: Penguin, 1977), 129.

27. From 1991 to 1999, gross value of industrial output in Tianjin grew 14.2 percent per year, compared with 10.9 percent nationally. It is more difficult to find consistent time-series data on household income over this period, but the following may provide a rough guide. In 1999, urban "real income" *(shiji shouru)* in Tianjin was ¥7,671, which was 368 percent higher than the average urban "cash income" *(xianjin shouru)* of ¥2,087 in 1991. Comparable national figures are ¥5,889 and ¥1,996, a 295 percent increase. Tianjin's average urban real income in 1999 was significantly below that of Shanghai (¥10,989), Guangdong (¥9,206 [not Guangzhou, which would be higher]), and Beijing (¥9,239). *Zhongguo tongji nianjian 2000*

[Statistical yearbook of China] (Beijing: China Statistics Press, 2000), 319; *Zhongguo tongji nianjian* 1992 (Beijing: China Statistics Press, 1992), 288.

28. Interview by author, May 28, 1999.

29. Interview by author, June 10, 1999.

30. Interview by author, June 7, 1999.

31. Interview by author, May 25, 1999 (2).

32. Interview by author, May 28, 1999.

33. Interview by author, May 29, 1999.

34. Interview by author, May 25, 1999 (2). Tellingly, even here he let the state off the hook. "But what can the government do? There are so many workers who are doing poorly that there is nothing the government can do about it." We return to the question of the state and hegemony below.

35. Interview by author, May 25, 1999.

36. Interview by author, May 25, 1999 (2).

37. Interview by author, June 10, 1999.

38. Interview by author, June 7, 1999.

39. Interview by author, May 25, 1999 (2).

40. Interview by author, May 28, 1999.

41. Interview by author, May 25, 1999 (2).

42. Interview by author, May 25, 1999.

43. Interview by author, June 10,1999.

44. Interview by author, June 7, 1999.

45. Interview by author, June 8, 1999 (2).

46. Interview by author, May 28, 1999.

47. Interview by author, May 25, 1999 (2).

48. Interview by author, May 28, 1999.

49. Interview by author, May 25, 1999 (2).

50. Interview by author, May 28, 1999.

51. Interview by author, June 7, 1999.

52. Aside from the interview accounts below, this point is also made in Feng Chen, "Subsistence Crises."

53. Interview by author, May 25, 1999 (2).

54. Interview by author, May 28, 1999.

55. Interview by author, June 8, 1999 (2). See also Hurst and O'Brien, "China's Contentious Pensioners."

56. Interview by author, June 7, 1999.

57. David Laitin, *Hegemony and Culture: Politics and Religious Change among the Yoruba* (Chicago: University of Chicago Press, 1986), 29.

58. Laitin, *Hegemony and Culture*, 107.

59. Feng, "Subsistence Crises," 51.

60. Feng, "Subsistence Crises," 51.

61. Elizabeth Perry has argued that in twentieth-century China class fragmentation has facilitated mobilization by subgroups or strata of the working class. That may be true, but it may also help account for the working class's ultimate failure to become hegemonic. See Perry, *Shanghai on Strike: The Politics of Chinese Labor* (Stanford, CA: Stanford University Press, 1993); Perry, "Shanghai's Strike Wave of 1957"; Perry and Li, *Proletarian Power*.

62. Perhaps the model developed by Cai Yongshun, in which laid-off factory cadres become leaders or coordinators of collective action, is more the exception than the rule—though of course in politics such exceptions are often precisely what make history when history is made. See Cai, "Resistance of Chinese Laid-off Workers."

63. Herbert Marcuse, *One-Dimensional Man* (Boston: Beacon, 1964).

64. See Stephen Andors, *China's Industrial Revolution* (New York: Pantheon, 1977); Perry and Li, *Proletarian Power*.

65. In another example, in March 1997 an angry "mob of workers waited at the factory gate. They loaded [their factory manager] Huang onto the back of a flatbed truck and forced him into the painful and demeaning 'airplane position'—bent at the waist, arms straight out at the sides. Then they marched 10 kilometres through the rain to downtown Nanchong [Sichuan] and paraded him through the streets. 'It was just like the Cultural Revolution,' says a Nanchong journalist who was forbidden to run the story." Matt Forney, "We Want to Eat," *Far Eastern Economic Review*, June 26, 1997.

66. Feng ("Subsistence Crises," 44) also mentions workers' sense that there is no alternative to the structural reforms.

67. Nicos Poulantzas, *Political Power and Social Classes* (London: Verso, 1973).

68. "Zhigong poqie qiwang jiakuai guoqi gaige budai gaohao guoyou qiye qicheng zhigong chongman xinxin" [Seventy percent of workers urgently hope for the acceleration of state-owned enterprise reform to lead to incremental improvements in state-owned enterprises], *Gongren ribao* [Workers Daily], January 14, 1997.

69. Zhou Ningguang, "Qinggong, jiangong, wei nar chuan?" [Young workers, lightweight workers, where should they sail?] *Gongren ribao*, June 20, 1996.

70. "Zhigong poqie qiwang."

71. *Gongren ribao*, January 18, 1996.

72. Ningguang, "Qinggong, jiangong, wei nar chuan."

73. "Jiuye nan zai nar?" (Where are the difficulties in employment?), *Gongren ribao*, July 10, 1997.

74. "Weishemma yao jianli laodong yübei zhidu?" (Why should a labor preparation system be established?), *Guangming ribao* [Enlightened Daily], July 16, 1997.

75. Trade union officials, interview by author, Kunming, December 4, 1995.

76. To the paper's credit it also printed a riposte from another reader on the question of history.

These days the newspapers and television are always saying that the reason workers are unemployed is that they don't have enough skills and enough ability to make a living. I say that a phenomenon cannot be separated from its historical conditions. For many decades, our country advocated "if you have a line of work, you should love it and become good at it." Well, I am an automobile worker. I don't want to boast, but my skills are first-rate, and in the past I was named a good worker. Now suddenly they say that if you only have one skill you can't be counted as a good worker. You have to learn lots of skills to ward off the danger of unemployment, they say. So, should I regard my work as my rice bowl, or as a way to lose my rice bowl? If a society doesn't acknowledge history, if it doesn't encourage honest workers, if it fails to acknowledge that unemployed workers gave their all to contribute to today's flourishing society, if it just tells them curtly to drop out, to get laid off, is this fair? Can this convince us in our hearts? ("Jiuye nan zai nar?")

Why *Workers Daily* chooses to print this sort of complaint is unknown. Surely it encourages down-and-out workers to read the paper, where they are exposed to its generally, if sometimes subtle, pro-reform drumbeat.

77. "Jiuye nan zai nar?"

78. Cai, "Resistance of Chinese Laid-off Workers."

79. Feng, "Subsistence Crises"; James C. Scott, *The Moral Economy of the Peasant: Rebellion and Subsistence in Southeast Asia* (New Haven, CT: Yale University Press, 1976).

80. Hurst and O'Brien, "China's Contentious Pensioners."

81. "From the Specter"; Michael Burawoy and János Lukács, *The Radiant Past: Ideology and Reality in Hungary's Road to Capitalism* (Chicago: University of Chicago Press, 1992).

82. James Scott, "Hegemony and the Peasantry," *Politics and Society* 7, no. 3 (1977): 267–296.

83. Burawoy and Lukács, *Radiant Past*.

84. Cai, "Resistance of Chinese Laid-off Workers."

85. In future work I expect to do so. My preliminary hypothesis is that the kinds of "hegemonic" shop floor practices identified by Burawoy as characteristic of Fordist capitalism also prevail in reform era state enterprises in Tianjin, with the attendant hegemonic effects discussed by Burawoy in his pioneering scholarship on the Fordist-era workplace. See Michael Burawoy, *Manufacturing Consent* (Chicago: University of Chicago Press, 1979); Burawoy, *The Politics of Production* (London: Verso, 1985).

86. Personal communication from a source who must remain anonymous.

87. See also Lü Xiaobo and Elizabeth J. Perry, *Danwei: The Changing Chinese Workplace in Historical and Comparative Perspectives* (Armonk, NY: Sharpe, 1997).

88. Lee emphasizes the centrality and implications of the "rule of law" in the state's present approach to the working class. See "From the Specter." Wang Yi argues that the state is emphasizing law to insulate itself from protest by the losers from the structural reforms; see Wang Yi, "From Status to Contract?" in Chaohua Wang, ed., *One China, Many Paths* (London: Verso, 2003).

89. Stephen Crowley, *Hot Coal, Cold Steel: Russian and Ukrainian Workers from the End of the Soviet Union to the Post-communist Transformations* (Ann Arbor: University of Michigan Press, 1997).

VI

EMERGING PROBLEMS:
THE SHADOW SIDE
OF REFORM

16

A Broken Compact

Women's Health in the Reform Era

Veronica Pearson

According to the World Bank (2004) Chinese men have a 16.5 percent chance of dying between the ages of sixteen and sixty. For women it is a 10.4 chance. Life expectancy for women in China is about three years longer than it is for men; seventy-two years as opposed to sixty-nine years (World Health Organization 2004). It may seem rather contrary, then, to go on and argue that women are more vulnerable than men in a number of health areas in China. However, put in another context the figures are not so positive.

China is still two years short of the expected five-year difference in life expectancy in those countries where men and women have equal access to health and survival resources. A WHO/World Bank collaborative study (Murray, Lopez, and Jamison 1994) found that the years of life lived with a disability were 15 percent lower for men in China than for women. According to a survey conducted by the World Bank (2004) there are 115 counties whose mortality rate for men is higher than that of China in comparison with 100 countries whose mortality rate for women is higher than that of China. What are the potential explanations for this? Without suggesting that it accounts for all differences, it is very clear that there are a number of social, economic, and policy factors that impinge on women in different and frequently more negative ways than men. Of particular interest are the one child population policy, the continuing discriminatory practices and attitudes toward women based on traditional culture and present circumstances, and the consequences of economic policies pursued in the reform era (i.e., from 1978). The end result of this is a suicide profile that is considerably worse for women than for men.

431

POPULATION POLICY AND ITS EFFECT
ON WOMEN'S WELL-BEING

China has only 7 percent of the world's arable land on which it has to support 21 percent of the population (Peng 1994). When the People's Republic of China was founded in 1949 it had a population of 540 million. In January 2005 it reached 1.3 billion, making China the most populous nation on earth. Of this population 36 percent was classified as urban and 64 percent as rural in 2003 (UNICEF 2004). In the eyes of the government, population growth has led to a sharp reduction in arable land and overexploitation of resources. It has aggravated environmental pollution (Banister 1998) and posed severe difficulties in education, employment, medical care, housing, education, and social welfare. It has to be accepted that the problem is genuine and severe. The debate is over viable solutions.

The response of the government has been to implement a population control policy of a rigor never attempted elsewhere, allowing it to claim that 300 million births were prevented between 1982 and 2002. China's population policy was implemented via administrative procedures and local regulations and was not based in law until 2001 when its first Law on Population Control and Family Planning was promulgated (Winckler 2002). The current basic aims, first articulated in 1994 (Peng 1994) are as follows:

1. To promote late marriage and later, fewer (but healthier) babies with prevention of birth and genetic defects.
2. To advocate the practice of "one couple, one child."
3. To persuade rural couples with difficulties (their first child is a girl or has a disability) who wish for a second child to have a proper spacing (4–6 years between children).
4. To let the governments of autonomous regions or provinces inhabited by the national minorities lay down their family planning requirements in accordance with local conditions. Usually the rule is to permit couples to have two or three children.

The implementation of the law will be left to the individual provinces and funding will have to be found by local governments. This is often the way with legislation in China but it means that the central government has little leverage over the provinces and municipalities who feel free to ignore their responsibilities unless the central government provides funding. Legislation in China can be more a statement of what the government would like to happen than what is likely to be enforced. Since the law was promulgated several provinces have taken advantage of the greater flexibility it permits to announce new categories of people who are allowed to have a second child. For instance, Anhui Province now has thirteen categories including divorcee couples who only had one child in their previous marriages, and coal miner's families in recognition of the dangerous nature of their occupation (Lee 2002).

The history of the population policy is available elsewhere (Banister 1987) and will not be discussed in detail here. Suffice it to say that by 1979 the government was becoming worried by the growth in population and announced a new policy whereby women were to be encouraged to have only one child. This was to be achieved through a series of rewards and sanctions. Thus only children whose parents had signed a pledge to have no more were given priority in kindergarten places, medical services, extra grain rations, and so on. Initially, a second child was supposed not to attract any penalties but this soon changed and the effective policy became that any couple having more than one child was to be fined, suffer a reduced grain ration, not be allocated any additional housing space for the new baby and be charged full fees for the child's medical care and education (Banister 1987). The intended consequence of this was that the total fertility rate dropped from 4.17 births in 1974 to 1.8 births in 1996. The birth rate went from 24.2 to 17 per 1,000 over the same period (Peng 1994; Banister 1998). What about the unintended consequences?

Unintended Consequences

The one child policy is the most unpopular policy the government has implemented in the past thirty years. In urban areas, although unwelcome, the policy has been easier to enforce. Administrative control is stronger through the *danwei* (work unit) system, the rewards are more tangible, people are better educated and can be more easily persuaded of the benefits for themselves and the country of restricting population growth. One baby, a healthier baby properly educated and cared for, made sense in an urban context. Thus in the urban areas with approximately 36 percent of the population, the policy was reasonably successful. Indeed, in Shanghai it has been so successful that newspapers have reported the failure of the city government's attempts to encourage citizens to have two children, including canceling the payment of subsidies to childless couples (*South China Morning Post,* September 21, 2004). Officials are concerned about the graying of the population and want more children to increase economic output.

It was in the rural areas, with about 64 percent of the population, that the population control policy really needed to work. However, it has been ferociously resisted for several reasons. First, traditional preference for sons continues to be very strong, despite fifty-five years of Communist Party propaganda against the remnants of feudal thought. Traditionally, women in China have been severely discriminated against: daughters were pieces of brick as opposed to sons who were pieces of jade. Sons, because of the tradition of patrilocal residence and shared households, look after their parents in old age. Daughters marry out and belong to their husband's families. Thus couples with no sons look forward to a destitute old age, a very real fear given the government's inability to introduce a functioning social security and pension system in rural areas due to the cost (Liu 2004; Woo, Kwok, Sze, and Yuan 2002; Wong 1998). Second, a son is needed to carry on the family name, still an important priority in a society where filial piety continues to be influential; another remnant of feudal thinking that the government has not managed to eradicate. Third, although women perform many of the heaviest farming chores, men are still believed necessary for farming work. Fourth, farming in China is still labor intensive and there are many jobs that even very young hands can perform. Thus, as far as the peasants are concerned, having several children makes economic sense. As the old saying goes, the greater the number of children, the wealthier the family. At the very least, if they were permitted only one child, they wanted it to be a boy.

Compulsion

How has the population program affected women? Although the government has always denied that the population control program was coercive, it is abundantly clear that the cadres at provincial and grassroots levels routinely used force. This was hardly surprising. Their job performance was measured on the success of the one child policy in their area. If babies in excess of those permitted by the state plan were born, the cadres were punished (through fines for each excess birth, severe criticism, and possible demotion). If they were within their target they were given a bonus. Thus the government maintained that participation in the policy was voluntary while ensuring that local officials were under very severe pressure to guarantee compliance. The government then denied knowledge of any irregularities that might occur, as well as responsibility for the actions of overenthusiastic local officials. Although the extent is difficult to determine, women have been subjected to compulsory abortion and sterilization (Aird 1990; Banister 1987; Mosher 1983). Wu, Viisainen, Wang, and Hemminki (2003) demonstrate that many perinatal deaths that are registered as stillbirths are actually abortions.

In addition, particularly at the height of the campaign in the early and mid-1990s, resources to carry out such operations became overloaded. For instance, between January 1983 and August the same year 10 million sterilizations were carried out. Between September 1982 and the end of 1983, 21 million people were contraceptively sterilized, including 16.4 million women and 4.2 million men (Banister 1987). It can be seen from this last figure that women were targeted for the operation four times as frequently as men, despite the fact that tubal ligation is a more complicated procedure than vasectomy, as well as being more expensive. This difference has been maintained. According to the State Family Planning Commission women account for 89 percent of all sterilizations. Interuterine devices account for 46 percent of all contraception, sterilization accounts for 38 percent. Pills, injections, and condoms complete the remaining 8 percent (Winckler 2002; Crossette 2003). Women may be targeted because matters to do with childbirth are more closely associated with women, because women are easier to intimidate, and because men are more concerned with their loss of virility. In the mid-1980s officials became worried about the number of botched operations endangering women's lives, due to the pressure on available medical resources and the lack of sufficient skilled personnel (Banister 1987).

Missing Girls

However, the most significant result has been the number of "missing" girls. The normal sex ratio at birth is 100 girls to approximately 105–106 boys. Throughout the 1960s and 1970s this was the case in China. But in 1981 it was 108.5, in 1986 it was 110.9, and in 1989 it was 113.8 (Zeng, Tu, Gao, Xu, Li, and Li 1993). This last figure is based on the 10 percent tabulations of the 1990 census. Originally the government tried to argue that this was no more than a "slight imbalance" (*Beijing Review*, January 3, 1993, 19). However, in demographic terms these figures are grossly skewed and it is most unlikely that they could be naturally occurring. When the 2000 census figure of 117 was published the government had publicly to face that this could only be the result of human interference and that it posed a major threat to social stability with so many "bare branches" (men who cannot find wives) and their capacity to create mayhem (Hudson and den Boer 2004). The imbalance is greater in the rural areas, 119.3, than the urban areas, 113.2 (Hudson and den Boer 2004). In a speech given at Beijing's Foreign Affairs University on December 30, 2004, Gu Xiulian, chairwoman of the All-China Women's Federation and vice chairwoman of the National People's Congress said:

> During the years since China embraced the one child policy as a principal national policy, we have only paid attention to ways to dispense with the second child but we ignored who was given up. Now state leaders have realized the critical nature of the imbalance. (*South China Morning Post*, December 31, 2004, A12)

In addition, national figures iron out local variations as well as variations according to parity (birth number). Aird (1990) quotes sources from Anhui and Gansu of county-level ratios of 139 and commune/township levels of 175. Zeng and colleagues (1993) demonstrate that as parity increases so does the sex ratio until, at fourth order births and above, it reaches 131.7. Greenhalgh, Zhu, and Li (1994) give ratios of 133 for first-order births, 172 for second-order births and 1,100 for third-order and higher births for the three villages that they studied over a period of six years. Wu and colleagues (2003) in their study of rural townships found an over all ratio of 151. Similar figures are given in Liu (2004). Early neonatal mortality was twice as high for females than males and increased dramatically with parity, being six times higher for second births than for first. Hudson and den Boer (2004) estimate that between 1985 and 1995, 10.68 million females went missing from China's birth population and that every year since then has added a further million plus. So where have they all gone?

Those Who Are Alive: Underreporting and Abandonment

The answer to this question is the subject of heated debate and considerable speculation. The alternatives are that daughters are not being officially registered so that
parents can try again for a boy. Thus they may give the girl up (or sell her) for an
informal adoption, register her later as an immigrant to the village, or bribe a local
official to ignore her existence. In their study of abandoned babies, Johnson, Huang,
and Wang (1998) found that the typical profile was of a healthy newborn girl with
older sisters and no brothers. Parents routinely told the researchers that they did not
want to abandon their daughter but considering they had no son the birth planning
regulations left them "no choice." Girls are subjected to sex selective abortion and
infanticide. The latter was common in China before 1949 but was partially eradicated under Communist rule until the introduction of the one child policy. A girl
may be abandoned, either to be carried away by the elements or wild animals (e.g.,
on a hillside) or in the hope that someone will find her (e.g., in a public toilet). At
a later age girl children may be subject to neglect. Ren (1993) has shown that in
Shaanxi girl toddlers' chances of surviving childhood are significantly less than boys'.
He attributes this to the allocation of scarce survival resources and inferior health
care. Banister (1998) points out that the leading cause of death in toddlers in urban
areas and developed areas of the countryside was "external causes," meaning accidents and injuries, so it is possible that adult carers watch over boys more carefully
than girls.

Those Who Are Not Alive: Infanticide and Sex Selective Abortion

The government denies that infanticide has a major role to play, pointing out that
both the Marriage Law (Article 21, 2002) and the Law on Maternal and Infant
Health Care (1994) stipulate that drowning and other forms of harm to babies are
forbidden. But this is a largely disingenuous stance, a public washing of hands. Since
the early 1990s infanticide, which was always a very blunt instrument, has been
displaced (if not entirely eradicated) by sex-selective abortion. China initially
imported and then began manufacturing ultrasound machines capable of detecting
a baby's sex. According to the minister of health, every county in China is now
equipped with such machines, operated by skilled technicians (Zeng et al. 1993).
There were reports in the early 2000s that technicians had set up shop in shopping
malls for the added convenience of their customers. Government regulations banned
the use of such machines for identifying the sex of babies (Zeng et al. 1993), a position that was reiterated and strengthened in the 1994 Law on Maternal and Infant
Health Care (Pearson 1995a). The new Law on Population Control and Family
Planning criminalizes the practice with imprisonment as a punishment. But in Hainan, where the sex ratios are the most skewed of any province and criminalization
was introduced in October 2004, no one was arrested in the following four months
(Parry 2005). It will also be a very difficult case to prove, for there are many legiti-

mate reasons for a woman to request a scan that also happen to reveal the baby's sex. A commonly understood code between patient and scan operator of a broad smile and a nod for a boy and a frown and a shake of the head for a girl, with not a word being spoken, makes it virtually impossible to garner enough evidence to take a person to court. Cost is no deterrent either. Although not cheap (perhaps about one month's wages) a scan is affordable, particularly for an enterprise as important to the family as ensuring a precious son.

The Army of Bachelors

The consequences for those who have been denied life are obvious, but even those who are alive and unreported suffer. They grow up knowing that they are a burden to their families with no extra grain rations, no medical insurance, difficulties in school placement (thus exacerbating the problem of the undereducation of girls, particularly in the rural areas), and so on. There are also problems from the government's point of view because it becomes impossible to plan services because the population estimates are inaccurate. In the long term one of the most serious consequences from the government's point of view is the growing army of bachelors who cannot and will not be able to find wives and are therefore likely to pose a threat to public order. The 2000 census suggests that there are 41 million surplus men about half of whom are in the age group 15 to 34. The men most likely to lose in the marriage stakes are those who are poor and uneducated. Women migrate from these areas to seek marriage in wealthier parts of the country or to look for work in the manufacturing centers in the south of China and on the eastern seaboard (Gilmartin and Tan 2002). Hudson and den Boer (2004) make a powerful case for the capacity of these men to foment unrest, as they have demonstrated in the past in similar circumstances in China and may well do it again. They have no investment in a family, no investment in China's growing prosperity, see no hope in their future, and have no exposure to the calming influence of marriage and children. In short, they have very little to lose. Whether women should be viewed as a palliative for male aggression (or in some cases, as we shall see, an alternative outlet) is a moot point.

Of course, China is not the only country with the problem of "missing girls." Amartya Sen (1989, 1992) was among the first to point out that South Asia, West Asia, China, and parts of Africa shared the problem. At that time he estimated that at least 100 million women were missing in parts of the developing world. Klasen and Wink (2002) calculate that between 65 million and 110 million are missing in those regions based on 1995 data. While the situation in Bangladesh and Pakistan has improved, India has the highest share followed by China and both because of sex-selective abortion.

Abduction and Sale of Women and Girls

Even in 1993 (figures based on the 1990 census data) there was a significant imbalance in the number of unmarried women and unmarried men ages 20–24 in the rural population—100 to 162 (Gilmartin and Tan 2002). The missing girls phenomenon is not the only reason why women of marriageable age are in such short supply in rural areas. Young women leave the villages to find work elsewhere (e.g., as nannies in large cities or manufacturing workers in the special economic zones in Guangdong) or as marriage migrants to wealthier areas, opportunities that are not available to young men (Gilmartin and Tan 2002). This has given rise to the phenomena of abduction of women, girls, and female babies for sale since the end of the 1980s. Numerous government crackdowns have failed to stamp the practice out. *China Daily* (March 19, 1993) reported that in the previous two years 40,000 abducted women had been located and returned to their families, which begs the question of how many have never been found. Zhang (1994, quoted in Gilmartin and Tan 2002) reports that women abducted to be sold as brides made up 14.7 percent of his survey sample of 18,000 female marriage migrants. Bueber (1993) cites an example from the hospital where she worked.

Ms. Yang is a 23-year-old woman with a five-year history of schizoaffective disorder. Three years ago, she was abducted from a railway station by a soldier who took her to a remote mountainous village in a distant province and sold her to a peasant farmer for 4,000 yuan (a significant sum of money in Chinese terms). Ms. Yang lived with this "husband" for a year and a half and bore him a child but when her mental state became unmanageable he sold her to a 45-year-old man in another village who often beat her and forced her to have sex with him. Communication with the outside world from this isolated village was impossible and all the villagers co-operated with her "husband" to prevent her from escaping. Ms. Yang finally managed to run away when an acting troupe passed through the village. She dressed up as one of the actresses and escaped when the troupe left the village. When she reached a police station she was agitated but able to enlist the policemen's aid. She was returned to her hometown. (Bueber 1993, 313)

Traffickers have expanded their activities to countries bordering China. Watkin (2000) reports on the abduction and smuggling of Vietnamese women into China. In China there is a saying "marry a chicken, follow a chicken." In other words, once a woman is married she has no choice but to stay with her husband and his family, whatever the circumstances. For at least some abducted women this means that once they have borne a child, they accept that their fate is sealed and cease to be prisoners and become permanent residents in their new communities (Gilmartin and Tan 2002). She receives little support from those around whose sympathies lie with the family that spent a large portion of its life savings to buy her and who perceive her, therefore, as belonging to her husband in much the same way as a fertile piece of land. Abduction carries the death penalty in China, while purchase attracts a three-year prison sentence but local sympathy for the purchasers means that cases are almost never taken to court.

There is also a lively trade in baby girls. Although boys get a better price, few families would be willing to part with a healthy baby boy. Selling female babies and children in times of hardship and famine has a history in dynastic China but was supposed to be eradicated under the Communists. Babies are usually from poor rural villages and are sold to middlemen who sell them at vast profit to childless couples in richer areas, or those who want to extend their family. The babies are usually those born excess to the official plan being second or higher parity daughters. Those involved argue that selling them is better than infanticide or abandonment. One case that received considerable publicity (Ma 2003) involved sixty-four baby girls who were provided to middlemen via doctors, nurses, and midwives from the local county hospital, including the head of the Department of Gynecology who set the system up. Babies sold for between US$6 and US$25 but were traded in distant provinces for US$375. Many of those involved, probably genuinely, claimed that they did not know that baby trading, abandonment, and infanticide are illegal. Officials lay the blame at the door of legal ignorance and "remnants of feudal thought" (i.e., son preference). Rarely, at least in public, do they acknowledge the connection to the government's one child policy.

Maternity and Child Health Services

It can, of course, be argued that the one child policy has brought benefits to women's overall health; relief from early and continuous childbearing with all its attendant dangers would be an obvious example. In addition to this, the government has come to realize that implementing population control is much easier if women have easy access to a network of maternity and child health clinics and services (Hillier and Jewel 1983; Winckler 2002). These then serve two purposes. They permit the government to have more efficient and easier control over women's fertility, while also bringing genuine benefits to women. Between 1980 and 1992 there was a 205.7 percent increase in the number of maternal and child care clinics; a 180 percent increase in health personnel working in these clinics; and a 156 percent increase in maternal and child care hospitals (*Beijing Review*, October 24, 1994). Keeping a check on women's fertility and gynecological health is not difficult in urban areas because of the already existing network of health care. It is in the rural areas that the government has been focusing its efforts.

There are large disparities in health service indices between rural and urban areas. The World Bank (1992) cites a survey carried out by the Ministry of Public Health (with the assistance of UNICEF and UNFPA) of 300 of the poorest counties in China. They found that only one-third of women in the survey received antenatal or postpartum care and only 36 percent of deliveries met basic standards of hygiene. Maternal mortality averaged 202 per 100,000 in the surveyed counties, more than twice the national average of 95 per 100,000. Two-thirds of maternal deaths occurred at home or en route to medical facilities and 4.5 percent of those who died had not seen a health worker in the twenty-four hours before their death. Postpartum hemorrhage and infections accounted for 55 percent of maternal deaths. According to statistics published by the World Bank (2004) and UNICEF (2004) the situation overall has improved somewhat, although figures were not available for the poorest counties. The national maternal mortality rate had dropped to 56 per 100,000 live births by 2000, and between 1995 and 2003, 90 percent of pregnant women were seen at least once for an antenatal checkup by trained medical personnel (doctor, nurse, or midwife).

Given these figures, it would not be surprising if women welcomed improvement in the maternity care available to them, even at the cost of fertility control. This is confirmed by a study of three villages in Shaanxi Province by Greenhalgh and colleagues (1994). They found that a combination of strategies had been implemented with some success. Increased funds had been made available for all aspects of implementation, including incentives for cadres and couples. A birth planning association run by the Communist Party had been established to concentrate on education and propaganda regarding birth control. Gynecological checkups were mandatory twice a year. These latter were "sold" as a means to improve woman's health which, indeed, they had done, for instance, by detecting ovarian and cervical cancer at an early stage. However, they were also used to detect "out of plan" babies, whereupon abortion was strongly recommended. Greenhalgh and colleagues (1994) make the point that it was the routinization of these new strategies combined with incentives (like state pensions for couples with two daughters) that seemed to make them acceptable. Rather than being subject to unpredictable and aggressive birth control campaigns, gynecological checkups, contraception control, sterilization, and even abortions had become a predictable part of the annual cycle. As Winckler (2002) points out, while the Law on Population Control and Family Planning stresses citizens' rights, it is the right to receive services, not to refuse them. Likewise, the phrase "population policy" implies both the state regulating reproductive behavior and providing reproductive health services.

WOMEN AND MENTAL HEALTH

A significantly greater number of women than men are diagnosed with depression in China (Pearson 1995b), a pattern that is observed in the Western world. There are also a significantly greater number of women diagnosed with schizophrenia, a pattern that is most emphatically different from that observed in Western countries and that reflects genuine differences rather than underreporting or problems in case finding (Phillips, Yang, Li, and Li 2004). However, two issues are of particular interest. The first concerns marriage and domestic violence because as yet it is infrequently dealt with in the international literature and the second is female suicide and attempted suicide because the profile is so different from the rest of the world.

Domestic Violence

Domestic violence has a deleterious effect on a woman's mental and physical health (Romito, Turan, and De Marchi 2005; Campbell 2002). There is no reason to suppose that women in China are any different in this respect, although research has yet to be carried out. There is a common saying in Chinese that marriage is a woman's career. The "success" of a marriage and children's behavior and achievements, or lack of it, tends to be laid at the woman's door, particularly when the outcomes are negative. Rightly or wrongly, most women's sense of achievement and well-being is intricately connected to marriage and children in a way that is not so obviously the case for men. For a number of reasons, marriage in China can be a threat to women's physical and mental well-being.

In rural areas over 90 percent of wives are habitually beaten (*Beijing Review*, November 15, 1993, 18). A survey based on the Chinese Health and Family Status Survey with a nationally representative sample of 3,806 respondents, found that 34 percent of women had experienced being hit by their partner, as had 18 percent of the men (15 percent of which was classified as mutual hitting) (Parish, Wang, Laumann, Pan, and Luo 2004). Women reported being hit more severely than men. Men were more inclined to report that they had hit their partners than women were to report that they had been hit, suggesting that women thought that it was something shameful and best hidden, while men considered it more normal. Statistical associations were found between women being hit and the low socioeconomic status of the male partner, patriarchal attitudes, when either partner uses alcohol, and when the woman contributes only a small percentage of the household income. Health outcomes for women included increased rates of mental distress, having unwanted sex, being made to perform unacceptable sex acts, and having recent genitourinary symptoms. Another survey of domestic violence with 3,543 respondents (Liu and Pearson 2005) found that 72 percent had been beaten as children and that these were more likely to become perpetrators of violence (males) and objects of violence (females). The respondents were asked to rank the causes of domestic violence and put patriarchal attitudes at the top of their list (unequal status between men and women where men are expected to discipline their wives) followed by alcohol, gambling, and extramarital affairs, and the low education and financial status of the couple.

Official explanations of the phenomenon tend to blame remnants of feudal thought (which may well be true) and the breakdown of socialist morality, a consequence of the Cultural Revolution. There seems to be a reluctance to analyze current Chinese society for explanations, such as social and economic dependence of wives on their husbands and the difficulties involved in seeking redress (Honig and Hershatter 1988; Liu and Chan 1999). Gilmartin and Tan (2002) have a detailed discussion of the migration of women from poor rural areas to *zhao ge hao duxiang* (find a better husband) thus fleeing rural poverty. They estimate, using various reports based on the 1990 census data, that by the early 1990s the number of female marriage migrants had reached over 17 million and have been increasing ever since. Marriage migrants in the late 1980s and early 1990s comprised over 28 percent of female migrants. Women who marry under these circumstances are going to be considered outsiders, be isolated in their new communities, and lack their own network of family and friends who could be sources of support and mediators in marital and in-law family disputes. They are likely to be looked down on by their new families who will only have agreed to the marriage because they are in the lower financial strata of their own village and therefore not able to compete in the local marriage market. No local woman would want to marry into a poor family if they could possibly do better for themselves and anyway the family could not afford the bride price. While it is hard to state definitive figures, the bride price for an immigrant bride is likely to be one-tenth that of a local woman in some areas. It is not a recipe for quality marriages or personal contentment.

SUICIDE AND ATTEMPTED SUICIDE

At the time of writing the most accurate suicide figures for China are contained in Phillips, Li, and Zhang (2002). China is unusual in having rates for completed suicide that are higher among women than among men. The national rate for women is 32.1 per 100,000 and for males it is 20 per 100,000. Suicide is the leading cause of death for women in the age group 15–34. However, what is particularly noteworthy are the extremely elevated rates in the rural areas, where 93 percent of all suicides occur. Among rural women aged 15–34 the rate is 37.8 and among men 22.8. This contrasts with the corresponding urban rates of 10.8 and 9.5. The rate of suicide deaths among rural women in this age group is 7.3 times higher than all deaths related to medical complications during pregnancy, childbirth, and puerperium. Taking into account all age-groups, suicide is the fourth most important cause of death for rural women and the eighth for rural men and urban women. It ranks fourteenth for urban men. Youth, female gender, and rural residence are a potentially lethal combination.

It is a common view in Western psychiatry that suicide goes hand in hand with mental illness, usually depression and schizophrenia, in almost all cases. This is not a view shared by psychiatrists in China (Pearson, Phillips, He, and Ji 2002). Nor is it supported by the evidence. In a national psychological autopsy study it was found that 63 percent of those who had killed themselves had a diagnosable mental illness (Phillips, Yang, Wang, Ji, and Zhou 2002). The authors concluded that the most likely explanation was that many suicides were impulsive acts by people who did not have a mental illness. Their logistical regression model suggested that of importance were acute stress triggered by severe negative life events in the two days prior to the death. Usually these were intense interpersonal conflicts: severe marital disputes (9 percent), conflict with parents (2 percent), conflicts with children (2 percent), acute loss of face or embarrassment (1.3 percent), being beaten by spouse (1 percent). The most common means of dying was poisoning with organophosphate compounds or rat poison, both freely available in rural households. Given the lethality of the method, the impulsivity of the act and the unavailability of medical services in many villages it is likely that women die who may not have had the intention to do so, or may have been revived if they had lived in a different location. A detailed account of an individual's death is given in Pearson and Liu (2002).

A psychological autopsy study of attempted suicide among young rural women in China demonstrated an even clearer link between suicidal behavior and family difficulties (Pearson, Phillips, He, and Ji 2002). Only 37.4 percent showed any signs of formal psychiatric disturbance and their suicidal behavior (usually poisoning) was characterized by extreme impulsivity. Respondents were asked to identify life events that they had experienced out of a list of sixty-six. The five most frequently cited were an unhappy marriage (64.5 percent), followed by financial problems (42.5 percent), being beaten by spouse (38.3 percent), conflict with mother-in-law (32 percent), and other family problems (27 percent). Contraceptive treatment (21.28 percent) came in at number 9. The young women, the accompanying family member, and the investigator were all asked to name what they thought was the main cause of the suicidal behavior. Family problems were cited in approximately 60 percent of cases by all three. Nothing else came close.

Conclusions can be tentative based on the available evidence, but the picture that has emerged is of marriages contracted for practical and strategic reasons to advance the status of the woman and her family, where liking and respect (never mind affection) are not given high priority. Typically these marriages are conflicted and characterized by a high level of verbal and physical violence that, to some extent, is routinized by custom and practice. Pressure, particularly in the villages, is placed on a young woman to produce a son and she is blamed (knowledge of genetics not withstanding) if a son fails to materialize. A young bride has little status in her new family until she has produced a son and not a great deal more after that. Attempts to make her voice heard can involve extreme actions that are life threatening, albeit there may be no real desire to end her own life. In Western thought suicide attempts are often designated as cries for help. In China, they might be better seen as an angry and frustrated demand to be heard.

THE CONSEQUENCES OF THE REFORM ERA

The liberation and equality of women was one of the primary planks of the Communist Party's manifesto when it came to power in 1949. In the early days much progress was made, underpinned by legislation like the Marriage Law of 1950 and a new constitution that guaranteed equal rights for women. For as long as the government and the Communist Party practiced centralized control, they were able to ensure that women's treatment was more equitable. Places at university, jobs, and so on were allocated by the authorities. However, with the decision of the government in 1978 to introduce aspects of the market into agriculture and eventually industry and all other aspects of economic life, the structures enforcing women's equality were undermined and women became much more vulnerable to being laid off, or simply not hired (World Bank 1992). As managers became responsible for generating profit and for making decisions regarding hiring and firing, the old attitudes toward women reemerged. Managers were reluctant to hire them because of maternity leave and energy split between work and running a home. One effect is that women are increasingly not covered by health insurance that is usually provided through the workplace. Henderson, Shuigao, Akin, Zhiming, and colleagues (1995) found that at state-run enterprises women were significantly less likely than men to have health insurance, possibly because there is a larger proportion of women in peripheral or temporary jobs that do not offer the usual employment benefits.

Evidence for how this affects women's access to health care comes from research carried out by the author in two psychiatric hospitals in China (Pearson 1995b,c). In the long-stay hospital, twice as many men as women had their fees paid by health insurance (19.4 percent as against 10 percent). More women than men were charity cases or had to have their fees paid by their families. Evidence from the acute hospital fleshes out this picture. At this hospital, many treatments were offered in addition to the basic "bed, board, and medication" arrangement and were billed separately. These treatments included laser therapy, music therapy, acupuncture, psychotherapy, occupational therapy, behavior therapy, and ECT. Only in the last two was there no significant difference between men and women, suggesting that they were being offered on the basis of need rather than the ability to pay. The overall difference in the cost of treatment between men and women was significant at the <00 level. This suggests that either men had more health insurance or that families were willing to pay inflated costs for men but not for women. Interestingly, in the long-term hospital where the monthly costs were all-inclusive, no difference in treatment available to men and women was noticed. Phillips, Xiong, and Zhao (1990) found that length of stay in the psychiatric hospitals in their study was most significantly related to whether the hospital costs were being met by the family or by health insurance. Neither diagnosis nor severity of the condition was as important. Presumably this is because women less frequently have health insurance, are less often admitted to a hospital, stay for a shorter time when they are, and may receive less treatment during their stay than men.

The Special Economic Zones

As part of the economic reform the government gave permission to set up special economic zones (SEZs) to encourage investment from overseas, most often in manufacturing. Many of these SEZs are found along the eastern seaboard of Guangdong and Fujian, where there are ties of language and kinship with the Chinese communities of Hong Kong and Taiwan. SEZs are permitted much more freedom from central control and have local regulations that encourage a market economy environment. The Guangdong Statistical Bureau, based on the 2000 population census, estimated that there were 10 million migrant workers in Guangdong, of whom at least 60 percent were women. In the Shenzhen SEZ in 2003, 70 percent of the 5.5 million migrant workers were women. These women tend to be between the ages of 18 and 23 and unmarried (*China Labour Bulletin,* 2004).

The garment, textile, footwear, toys, and electronics factories that typify the SEZs in Guangdong prefer to hire young female migrant workers because they are less likely to become pregnant, more willing to work long hours for low pay, have nimble fingers, are easy to intimidate, and do not demand their statutory rights. Because jobs in this area are in high demand, employers can squeeze wages and provide fewer benefits by frequently flouting the Chinese labor laws. Many of the migrant workers have not registered as temporary workers and so are technically illegally employed and so not entitled to social welfare benefits or labor protection (Jacka 1992; Wong 1994; Wong and Lee 1994). International companies favor setting up their factories here because of cheap labor but also because they can escape the labor protection and industrial safety laws in their own countries (Chan 1994). Thousands of female migrant workers suffer from debilitating or deadly diseases caused by working in factories laden with chemical fumes. Toxic fumes from benzene and chromium are particularly prevalent in the small factories that produce textiles, shoes, and toys (*China Labour Bulletin,* 2004).

Flagrant abuse of safety regulation has led to a number of very serious fires, most notably that which occurred in Zhili handicraft factory owned by a Hong Kong businessman (*South China Morning Post,* November 20, 1993; *China Labour Bulletin,* 2004). Over eighty people were killed and around sixty injured. Most of them were young women from Hunan and Sichuan. The fire was the result of an electrical fault but the deaths occurred because doors and windows were locked (to discourage workers from stealing, said the managers) and there were no fire escapes. It was alleged that bribes had been paid to the local Fire Department to overlook breaches of industrial safety regulations.

CONCLUSION

A number of circumstances have combined in the reform era to put women at a more disadvantageous position now than at any time since 1949. Some of them reflect age-old prejudice and others are the result of economic reform, but the two join in a synthesis to threaten women's continuing search for equality. It is possible to identify some of these factors being played out in the health arena. The one child policy has meant that women have lost control over their own bodies in relation to their reproductive function. They are subject to abortions and sterilizations that have on occasion stretched the health services beyond that with which they can safely cope. At the same time the pursuit of this objective by the government has also meant a gain for women in the provision of better maternal and child care services, particularly in the rural areas.

In turn the one child policy has led to a skewed birthrate and a concomitant shortage of women of marriageable age. Rather than raising women's status, this has increased the level of abduction and sale of women (into marriage or prostitution) and female children to the extent that the government has recognized it as a serious problem. The rates of suicide and attempted suicide among young women have attracted international concern because they are so high. Indeed, there is almost an epidemic of suicide among young rural women of newly married age. What is currently known about causes suggests that they are related to family problems and difficulties that doubtless include issues to do with failure to bear a son and the fact that many marriages are based on economic advancement rather than mutual liking and respect.

The devolution of economic and social control to local areas and enterprises has allowed a reversion to centuries-old habits of discrimination against women. There is evidence that women are being hired as temporary workers rather than formal workers. This makes them easier to dismiss and removes them from the safety net of health insurance. In turn, that means they may receive less treatment for similar health problems than do men. Factories in the economic boomtowns in the SEZs prefer to hire women from the backward rural provinces as temporary workers because they can pay them less, with less likelihood of complaint. Industrial safety and fire regulations in these SEZs are frequently ignored, subjecting women to increased hazards from industrial accidents and fires.

The emancipation and equality of women was a main platform of the Communist government when it came to power in 1949. Through the Chinese constitution and the Marriage Law it set about trying to change a pattern of relationships between the sexes that had existed for a thousand years and more. For as long as it pursued policies that were highly centralized and aimed at enforcing an equality of poverty, it was able to ensure that women received relatively fair treatment. As more and more authority and decision-making power have devolved to the grass roots, women's improved status has been increasingly challenged. In addition, women have carried the brunt of the physical, social, and psychological consequences of one of the largest pieces of social engineering ever attempted by any government anywhere. These factors have fed back into health issues, often a sensitive indicator of disadvantage in any society. Chinese women, especially those in rural areas, could be forgiven for wondering if the government and Communist Party have broken the compact with them that formed such a significant foundation for the New China.

REFERENCES

Aird, J. S. 1990. *Slaughter of the Innocents: Coercive Birth Control in China.* Washington, DC: AEI Press.

Banister, J. 1998. "Population, Public Health, and the Environment in China." *China Quarterly* 156: 986–1015.

———. 1987. *China's Changing Population.* Stanford, CA: Stanford University Press.

Bueber, M. 1993. "Letter from China." *Archives of Psychiatric Nursing* 7, no. 5: 311–316.

Campbell, M. 2002. "Health Consequences of Intimate Partner Violence." *Lancet* 359: 1331–1336.

Chan, A. 1994. "Behind the 'Made in China' Label." *China Now* 150: 25–27.

China Labour Bulletin. 2004. "Dagongmei: Female Migrant Workers." www.chinalabour .org.hk/iso/news_item.adp?news_id = 5282. Accessed January 24 2005.

Crossette, B. 2003. "Behind the Great Wall: China's Population Policies." *Conscience* 23, no. 4: 12.

Gilmartin, C., and L. Tan. 2002. "Fleeing Poverty: Rural Women, Expanding Marriage Markets, and Strategies for Social Mobility in Contemporary China." In E. N. L. Chow, ed., *Transforming Gender and Development in East Asia*, 203–216. New York: Routledge.

Greenhalgh, S., C. Z. Zhu, and N. Li. 1994. "Restraining Population Growth in Three Chinese Villages, 1988–1993." *Population and Development Review* 20, no. 2: 365–393.

Henderson, G., J. Shuigao, L. Akin, L. Zhiming, W. Jianmin, M. Haijiang, H. Yunan, Z. Xiping, C. Ying, and G. Keyou. 1995. "Distribution of Medical Insurance in China." *Social Science and Medicine* 41, no. 8: 1119–1130.

Hillier, S., and J. A. Jewell. 1983. *Health Care and Traditional Medicine in China, 1800– 1982*. London: Routledge & Kegan Paul.

Honig, E., and G. Hershatter. 1988. *Personal Voices: Chinese Women in the 1980s*. Stanford, CA: Stanford University Press.

Hudson, V. M., and A. den Boer. 2004. *Bare Branches: Security Implications of Asia's Surplus Male Population*. Cambridge, MA: MIT Press.

Jacka, T. 1992. "The Public/Private Dichotomy and the Gender Division of Rural Labor." In A. Watson, ed., *Economic and Social Change in China*, 117–143. New York: Routledge.

Johnson, K., B. H. Huang, and L. Y. Wang. 1998. "Infant Abandonment and Adoption in China." *Population and Development Review* 24, no. 3: 469–510.

Klasen, S., and C. Wink. 2002. "A Turning Point in Gender Bias in Mortality? An Update on the Number of Missing Women." *Population and Development Review* 28, no. 2: 285–312.

Lee, E. 2002. "One Child Policy Should Not Be Relaxed Too Fast, Warns Official." *South China Morning Post*, December 28, 2002.

Liu, M., and C. Chan. 1999. "Enduring Violence and Staying in Marriage: Stories of Battered Women in Rural China." *Violence against Women* 5, no. 12: 1469–1492.

Liu, M., and V. Pearson. 2005. "Domestic Violence." In E. Davis, ed., *Encyclopaedia of Chinese Culture*. London: Routledge.

Liu, S. S. 2004. "Where Have All the Young Girls Gone?" *China Rights Forum* 4: 50–55.

Ma, G. H. 2003. "China: The Baby Girl Trade." *Women's Feature Service*, November 17.

Mosher, S. 1983. *Broken Earth: The Rural Chinese*. New York: Free Press.

Murray, C. J. L., A. D. Lopez, and D. T. Jamison. 1994. "The Global Burden of Disease in 1990: A Summary of Results, Sensitivity Analysis, and Future Directions." *Bulletin of the World Health Organization* 72, no. 3: 495–509.

Parish, W. L., T. F. Wang, E. O. Laumann, S. M. Pan, and Y. Luo. 2004. "Intimate Partner Violence in China: National Prevalence, Risk Factors, and Associated Health Problems." *International Family Planning Perspectives* 30, no. 4: 174–182.

Parry, S. 2005. "Born to Be Wild." *South China Morning Post*, January 1, 2005.

Pearson, V. 1995a. "In Search of Quality: Population Policy and Eugenics in China." *British Journal of Psychiatry* 167: 1–4.

———. 1995b. "Goods on Which One Loses; Women and Mental Health in China." *Social Science and Medicine* 48, no. 8: 1159–1173.

————. 1995c. *Mental Health Care in China: State Policies, Professional Services, and Family Responsibilities*. London: Gaskell/American Psychiatric Press.

Pearson, V., and M. Liu. 2002. "Ling's Death: An Ethnography of a Chinese Woman's Suicide." *Suicide and Life Threatening Behavior* 32, no. 4: 348–358.

Pearson, V., M. R. Phillips, F. S. He, and H. Y. Ji. 2002. "Attempted Suicide among Young Rural Women in the People's Republic of China: Possibilities for Prevention." *Suicide and Life Threatening Behavior* 32, no. 4: 359–369.

Peng, P. 1994. "China's Experience in Population Matters: An Official Statement." *Population and Development Review* 20: 448–491.

Phillips, M. R., X. Y. Li, and Y. P. Zhang. 2002. "Suicide Rates in China, 1995–1999." *Lancet* 359, no. 9309: 835–840.

Phillips, M. R., W. Xiong, and Z. A. Zhao. 1990. *Issues Related to the Use of Assessment Instruments for Negative and Positive Symptoms*. Hubei: Science and Technology Press.

Phillips, M. R., G. H. Yang, S. R. Li, and Y. Li. 2004. "Suicide and the Unique Prevalence Pattern of Schizophrenia in Mainland China: A Retrospective Observational Study." *Lancet* 364, no. 9439: 1062–1069.

Phillips, M. R., G. H. Yang, Y. P. Zhang, L. J. Wang, H. Y. Ji, and M. J. Zhou. 2002. "Risk Factors for Suicide in China: A National Case Control Psychological Autopsy Study." *Lancet* 360: 1728–1736.

Ren, S. K. H. 1993. "Infant and Child Survival in Shaanxi, China." *Social Science and Medicine* 38, no. 4: 609–621.

Romito, P., J. M. Turan, and M. De Marchi. 2005. "The Impact of Current and Past Interpersonal Violence on Women's Mental Health." *Social Science and Medicine* 60, no. 8: 1717–1727.

Sen, A. 1992. "Missing Women." *British Medical Journal* 304: 586–587.

————. 1989. "Women's Survival as a Development Problem." *Bulletin of the American Academy of Arts and Sciences* 43: 14–29.

UNICEF. 2004. *The State of the World's Children 2005*. Oxford: Oxford University Press.

Watkin, H. 2000. "People Trafficking Ring Exposed." *South China Morning Post*, June 25, 2000.

Winkler, E. A. 2002. "Chinese Reproductive Policy at the Turn of the Millennium: Dynamic Stability." *Population and Development Review* 28, no. 3: 379–418.

Wong, L. 1994. "China's Urban Migrants: The Public Policy Challenge." *Pacific Affairs* 67, no. 3: 335–355.

————. 1998. *Marginalization and Social Welfare in China*. London: Routledge.

Wong, L., and G. Lee. 1994. "Welfare in a Stratified Society: Shenzhen's Social Policy Challenge." Paper given at the workshop on the Pearl River Delta, December 10, City University of Hong Kong.

Woo, J., T. Kwok, F. K. H. Sze, and H. J. Yuan. 2002. "Aging in China: Health and Social Consequences and Responses." *International Journal of Epidemiology* 31, no. 4: 772–775.

World Bank. 2004. *World Development Indicators 2004*. Washington, DC: World Bank.

————. 1992. *China: Strategies for Reducing Poverty in the 1990s*. Washington, DC: World Bank.

World Health Organization 2004. *China: Health Indicators 2002*. www3.who.int./whosis/country/indicators.cfm?country = countryCHN&language = english. Accessed January 24 2005.

Wu, Z. C., K. Viisainen, Y. Wang, and E. Hemminki. 2003. "Perinatal Mortality in Rural China: Retrospective Cohort Study." *British Medical Journal* 327, no. 7427: 1319.

Zeng, Y., P. Tu, B. C. Gao, Y. Xu, B. H. Li, and Y. P. Li. 1993. "Causes and Implications of the Recent Increase in the Reported Sex Ratio at Birth in China." *Population and Development Review* 19, no. 2: 283–302.

17

New Trends in China's Corruption

Change amid Continuity

TING GONG

Marked by the Fifteenth Congress of the Community Party in 1997, China entered a "third wave" of economic restructuring, following the first wave that began in 1978 and the second one inspired by Deng Xiaoping's southern tour in 1992. The current economic reform is no longer "feeling stones when crossing the river." It instead has unequivocal goals and specific focuses.[1] Aimed at "creating a socialist market economic system by 2010,"[2] the focus of China's reform has shifted from providing profit incentives and expanding local autonomy to implementing a wide range of macroeconomic restructuring and institutional innovations.[3] Reform has broadened its scope to include ownership diversification in the existing enterprise system and macroeconomic adjustments in price system, financial market, labor market, information management, housing and social security, and many other areas.

Deepened marketization has added momentum to China's economic growth. However, it has been accompanied by a surge of corruption in various areas. Contrary to the conventional wisdom, new and different, if not more, corruption has occurred in recent years despite the gradual shrinking of nonmarket elements in the economy. The intensification of corruption in the reform era has drawn a great deal of scholarly attention.[4] However, the relationship between corruption and reform has always been a contending issue. Some point to the existence of "socialist corruption" as a chronic problem, using as evidence the similarities between China and the former Soviet Union in political structures and corruption patterns. For example, Jowitt suggests that in communist countries corruption testifies to the absence of either market or bureaucratic impersonalism.[5] Harris lists six structural characteristics, such as hierarchy, oligarchy, closeness, all-embracing ideology, and socialist planning, that render communist systems particularly susceptible to corruption.[6] Oi agrees that communist systems are inclined to foster behavior that most would call corrupt, because of the structure of the state and the economy.[7] Many others, having noticed the recent changes taking place in the communist countries, pay more attention to the vulnerability to corruption of transitional societies, especially those undergoing capitalist transitions. Meaney considers the hybrid or "two-track" economy of plan and market the major cause of corruption in the reform context because it is not a "true market," but a "plethora of networks protected by cadres and bureaucrats."[8] Ostergaard and Peterson present strong evidence of "official speculation" in connection with China's dual-track price system where government officials buy cheap and sell dear in the cracks between the state-set prices and market ones.[9]

These explanations, while holding true for the pre- and immediate postreform periods, demonstrate limitations as China's reform moves more rapidly toward a market economy. As the bulk of prices are now decided by the market, how much room for arbitrage is still left? Is corruption diminishing as the dual-track economy fades away? If not, what forms of corruption have become more visible in recent years and why? To what extent are they related to the development of reform? Or, more generally, what is the relationship between corruption and market? Would increased economic marketization reduce corruption? In order to answer these questions, this chapter examines some new trends in China's corruption. It looks at how and why certain forms of corruption have become prevalent. The discussion centers on the relationship between market and corruption but also examines the social and political impact of corruption on China's future.

FROM CASH CORRUPTION TO CAPITAL CORRUPTION

Under an economic system dominated by public ownership like the one China had in its prereform and immediate postreform periods, state assets are under the tight control of the government and the chance for transferring public property into private ownership remains minimal. Corruption mainly takes the form of extravagant consumption of public funds or embezzlement of cash, which this chapter refers to as "cash corruption." While taking possession of public funds is difficult, corrupt government officials consume them to satisfy their avarice. The popular saying "eating bravely and taking carefully" *(dadandechi, xiaoxindena)* well describes the situation that taking into one's own pocket several hundreds of thousands of yuan may cause trouble, whereas consuming an equal amount may not be a major problem.[10] Cash corruption reached its peak in the mid-1990s as public funds were consumed for personal pleasure and special perks of government officials. In addition to sumptuous repasts, public money was spent on various kinds of entertainment including dancing, bowling, sauna bathing, and spa vacations. Sightseeing activities were organized in the name of business trips and study tours abroad. Luxurious vehicles, fancy office furniture, and sometimes housing were purchased with public funds as perks for individual officials. As estimated by the National Statistical Bureau, about two-thirds of the revenues of the big and medium-size restaurants in the country came from lavish banquets with public funds each year; at least ¥100 billion was spent annually on banqueting, an amount three times the state's educational spending. It was also reported that 68 percent of the revenues of the nation's big sauna bathing services came from public funds. An investigation in Shanghai revealed that 70 percent of expenses at the city's thirty-one bowling centers were paid with business checks rather than personal money.[11]

Cash corruption pleases corrupt officials by providing them with sensual enjoyment but does not satisfy their avarice for wealth since they could only spend, rather than possess, public funds. After all, the ultimate goal of predatory officials is to accumulate personal wealth.

As the scope of reform broadens, especially in the process of reforming SOEs (state-owned enterprises), however, opportunities become available for unsanctioned transfers of state assets into the private hands of government officials in charge of them, a process this chapter refers to as "capital corruption." Different from cash corruption, capital corruption is aimed at seizing production capital which will bring in more money, rather than merely spending money as cash corruption does. Capital corruption is a more rapacious form of encroachment on state property than cash corruption. It also requires more sophisticated tactics as illustrated below.

Illicit Transfers of State Assets in Ownership Diversification

As the Fifteenth Party Congress removed ideological barriers to ownership diversification, the government has taken new initiatives to reform SOEs in order to alleviate the government's chronic financial burdens. Among the new measures was an approach known as "keep the large, free the small" *(zhuada fangxiao)*. It means that the state retains the ownership and control of large SOEs in strategically important sectors while allowing smaller SOEs to explore various ownership options such as shareholding, merger, acquisition, divestiture, and bankruptcy.

Capital corruption surges in the process of transforming the bulk of SOEs into shareholding companies where corrupt officials use different methods to get more individual shares or increase the capital value of the shares they control. As noted, a large part of the shareholding companies converted from SOEs had government appointed officials as managers, at least in the early stage of restructuring. Consequently, government officials directly in charge of corporation reforms often become large shareholders at little cost as the government allows the company's stock to be sold to its managers at its face value.[12] The tactics employed to chip away at state assets include (1) lowering the value of the state assets or boosting that of the private capital during an asset assessment process; (2) setting higher dividend rates for individual shares than state shares; and (3) split individual shares only, not those owned by the state, so as to gradually increase the proportion of shares in individual hands. Despite different methods, the result is the same: more money flows into private hands than the state treasury. This type of capital corruption takes advantage of loopholes in asset assessment processes as capital assessment is new to China where property alienation was virtually nonexistent for more than thirty years. By 1998 there had been only some 13,000 certified asset assessors working for about 3,300 agencies nationwide.[13] Many uncertified agencies and personnel participated in asset assessment but they made mistakes. Even certified assessors often failed to adhere to correct principles and procedures. The National Audit Bureau recently discovered that four major asset management companies mishandled ¥70 billion worth of state assets in the four years since 1999, of which ¥6.7 billion were sold to foreign banks at inappropriately low prices.[14] Worse yet, many of the state asset assessors were bribed to make their assessment in favor of private interests. According to an investigation of the Central Disciplinary Inspection Commission, in Shen Zhen city the assets of an SOE worth ¥80 million were deliberately underestimated as ¥40 million. In other cases, land leases worth billions of yuan were priced for ¥10 million only.[15]

The second and third methods are also widely used to privatize state property when SOEs are converted into shareholding corporations. For example, a Wuhan shareholding company set a 11.5–13.7 percent dividend rate for state shares, 17–17.5 percent for collective shares, and 20 percent for shares held by its employees at each dividend distribution for more than five years.[16] While this is often done in the name of tying the interest of workers to the development of the company and providing them with more incentives to work hard, what actually happens is that the officials in charge of the company usually get many more individual shares (often called management shares) than everybody else.[17]

Capital corruption sometimes takes more subtle forms. Establishing shadow companies is one of them. A shadow company is a private enterprise that produces the same or similar product as a state-owned one. Many shadow companies originated from public funds and are controlled by retired government officials or offspring of officials. They siphon off and launder state property by (1) taking over profitable projects and product orders of the SOE; (2) channeling state-owned production materials and equipment into their production; and (3) using the trademark and the network of the SOE to sell their products. In other words, while they are private business entities, they have easy access to profitable projects and production orders provided by the government due to their connections with the latter. They have advantages over their competitors as they are never short of valuable inputs and convenient outlets for their products. A shadow company is like a parasite on a state-owned enterprise; as the former grows richer and stronger, the latter is driven closer to bankruptcy, as shown by the following case. In Guangzhou, the deputy manager of a state-owned printing company introduced more than 80 percent of the company's customers to his son's company, a private one doing the same business. While the son (and certainly the father) made a lot of money, the state-owned suffered great loss and became debt ridden.[18]

Rise of Cadre Entrepreneurs

Since the advent of reform, an increasing number of party and government cadres have entered the marketplace, taking key positions in many so-called administrative enterprises. While some quit their official jobs, more are holding concurrent positions in the government and in a business. The Chinese euphemism refers to these people as "red-hat businessmen" *(hongding shangren)* to reflect their double identity as a government cadre and a businessperson. This dual identity allows cadre entrepreneurs to maneuver in both public and private realms, acting as representatives of state and collective units in the free market and, at the same time, as representatives of business firms in the state's market.

The rise of cadre entrepreneurs results from the government's policy to encourage administrative agencies to create earnings *(chuangshou)* for themselves so as to reduce the central government's budgetary responsibility. These earnings go into off-budget funds which remain at the institution's disposal. This policy has inspired a proliferation of subsidiary companies *(zigongsi)*, auxiliary enterprises *(fuzhuqiye)*, and service companies *(sanchan)* affiliated with government agencies and these affiliates are either controlled by incumbent officials or retired ones. Although the central government has repeatedly launched screening and consolidation campaigns to crack down on illicit, speculative activities of administrative companies, many red-hat businesses have survived and continued to make profit in the nexus of public and private sectors. Some local governments continue to encourage their officials to take part in business activities. Some provincial governments even stipulated that government employees can keep their original jobs, continue to receive the basic salaries and fringe benefits, and be qualified for promotion in the first three years after they join a private company.[19]

The fading distinction between cadres (the public, political domain) and businessmen (the private, economic domain) leads to the making of a new, powerful, and well-connected business elite. This elite group is intimately connected with government institutions while conducting business activities in the marketplace that is not well bound by administrative ethics. In the battle for profit, cadre entrepreneurs are much better positioned to win, as they have secured access to important resources such as capital and information. Through many years of government services, they have nurtured not only working relationships but also various personal connections, the valuable assets for doing business in China. In her close scrutiny of China's *guanxi* phenomenon, Mayfair Yang distinguishes four forms of capital—symbolic capital, office capital, political capital, and gift capital—which are able to yield more than their own value in social exchanges, when manipulated appropriately.[20] As she correctly points out, the distribution of capital is not systematized or universalized in China. Cadre entrepreneurs can easily obtain all four types of capital.

Backed up with personal connections and with capital in hands, cadre entrepreneurs are able to make more money and may do so in different ways. One is to create a market monopoly. Companies affiliated with government agencies usually do not have much difficulty selling their products or services. Here is just an example. The party secretary of a city's party committee accepted the offer to become the chair of the board of trustees of an automobile corporation. After the news was released, the cars manufactured by the corporation quickly became the best-seller and soon took over the auto market in that city.[21] Second, cadre entrepreneurs are usually able to get more funding for their business activities through administrative channels. They may find excuses to obtain extra funds from the government but the profit generated by these funds is at their disposal. For instance, when a local Communist League committee was going to build an entertainment center for children, it made up excuses and obtained ¥400,000 extra funds from the city government. With the money, a six-story building, instead of the originally planned four-story one, was built. The committee then rented out one floor for office use and opened a retail store on another floor. The income from both sources was taken by the committee itself.[22] Third, administrative companies may impose higher/extra charges or service fees. It has happened that some government relief agencies bought relief goods at lower prices with relief funds and then sold them to disaster areas at much higher prices. Another example is equally illustrative. As government agencies, municipal construction inspection commissions cannot charge fees for their inspections. In order to get around this regulation, however, the inspection commission of a city established a construction inspection company and entrusted it with the task of inspection. The company, as an economic entity, charged an incredibly high inspection fee at 6 percent of the total investment of each project inspected. Though the fee was charged in the name of the inspection company, a big part of it went into the pocket of the officials of the commission. Finally, cadre entrepreneurs may simply extort money when other moneymaking methods fail to work. The officials of a county planning committee, for example, forced all the enterprises that were seeking official approval for their projects to pay high "evaluation fees" to it when submitting their applications. Small private businesses are usually victims of extortion and often have to resort to bribery in order to stay in business. Two small companies in Guangdong had to spend more than ¥600,000 on gifts and banquets in order to seek approval of loans by government officials.[23]

The above are just a few examples of profiteering activities of cadre entrepreneurs. These cases testify to a critical nonmarket factor in China's economic marketization: using government power and connections to do business is highly profitable and it can have money made in a much quicker and effective manner than using market mechanisms. Government power also serves to restrict avenues of mobility for new entrants, as it is difficult for ordinary businesspeople to compete with cadres or former cadres backed up with official connections. This is why "doing business with power" (yi quan jing shang) has become a shortcut to wealth in China.

Land Corruption

Land is the most important state capital in China. In the late 1980s, the government abandoned the traditional practice of administrative allocation of land and began to yield use rights of land to individuals and collectives. The market transfer of land use rights is also allowed. This has resulted in the formation of a new land management structure that consists of three major markets: the primary market where the government owns and leases out land; the second-level market for developers to compete and develop real properties on the leased land; and the third-level market where the completed real properties are traded. The reform of land management has led to rapid development in real estate industries. Shanghai alone, for example, built more than 1,000 skyscrapers in the 1990s and expected to have some 500 more in the following ten years.[24] The use right of land has become a hot commodity and its price is often driven up many times higher in a few market transactions.

Market allocation of land resources through public leasing has increased the efficiency of land use. By including private businesses in public finance, land leasing helps ease up the government's financial burden. However, it has also brought about numerous opportunities for corruption. Public power and private interest often get intertwined to encroach on state assets in transactions of land use rights. Local officials who possess the de facto power to decide whether, how, to whom, and at what price to lease land are often bribed, while many of them engage in aggressive "rent-seeking" activities. Experts estimate that in some areas more than 20 percent of the money spent on property development actually went into bribery and other dishonest practices.[25]

Corruption becomes possible because land leasing in China is often subject to price negotiations, or *xieyi zhuanrang* (negotiated transfers), despite the central government's general call for "public bidding" in land transfers. It was reported that only about 5 percent of the 300,000 hectares of land that was leased out nationwide in 2000 went through a bidding process; the rest was done through negotiations. "Negotiated transfers" often take place in an opaque rather than transparent process; nor are they subject to effective regulation. Illicit deals between public power and private interest are made in these negotiated transfers, causing huge losses in state revenue. Government officials may arbitrarily lower the price of land leasing, for instance. Or they may utilize their net of *guanxi* (connections) to help relatives or friends get favorable bank loans to complete land deals. In 2002 the average cost of land leasing in Guangdong was only ¥107 per square meter, while the price of real property developed on the leased land reached as high as ¥4,000 per square meter.[26] Corruption may take place in bidding processes as well, since local officials can disclose critical information to the party in their favor or set preferential bidding procedures for that party. Cheng Kejie, former chairman of Guangxi Autonomous Regional Government, is the highest-ranking government official convicted for land corruption so far. To please his mistress, Cheng provided a close friend of hers with a land lease of 85 mou at ¥550,000 per mou, ¥30,000,000 lower than the normal price.[27] He also made arrangements for this friend to obtain loans totaling ¥188 million plus several profitable construction projects. In return, Cheng and his mistress received ¥17.3 million and HK$8.04 million in bribes from this friend.[28] In addition to Cheng, some other high-ranking officials (at the provincial and ministerial level) also fell from land corruption, including governor of Yunan Province Li

Jiating, governor of Guizou Province Liu Fangren, party secretary of Hebei Province Cheng Weigao, minister of land and resources Tian Fengshan, chief justice of Liaoning Province Tian Fengqi, and deputy governor of Anhui Province Wang Huaizhong. These cases provide effective footnotes on the rampancy of land corruption.

Rent-seeking activities in land transfer have caused huge losses in state assets. As the Ministry of Land and Resources estimates, illegal land transfer incurs an annual loss of at least several million yuan in state revenue in small cities while the loss could be billions a year in big cities.[29] The nationwide total loss incurred in land leasing is as high as ¥20 billion a year.[30] Land corruption is also responsible for the suffering of farmers because corrupt officials always try to get as much land from farmers at as low prices as possible. The statistics of the Ministry of Land and Resources show that farmland requisitioned for nonagricultural purposes has been on the rise since 1999, with the area of land lost in 2002 doubling the figure for 2001.[31] This is confirmed by the World Bank's country brief that arable land in China shrank by 4.3 percent in 2003 alone.[32] Large-scale land enclosure, coupled by avaricious profiteering activities, has detrimental impact on farmers. As a report in *People's Daily* points out, "on one side of a land deal, local authorities reap hefty assignment charges, and developers profit amid current property boom. On the other side, however, farmers whose land is acquired usually get meager compensation."[33] It is not surprising to see a surge of protests by villagers against undercompensated land requisitioning in recent years. A study conducted by the Institute of Rural Development at the Chinese Academy of Social Sciences gathered 130 cases of rural protests in the early part of 2004 and found that 87 of them were related to land disputes.[34]

FROM INDIVIDUAL CORRUPTION
TO COLLECTIVE CORRUPTION

Corruption is known as a clandestine exchange due to its illegal nature, and corrupt activities tend to engage the least possible number of people.[35] Corruption as individual behavior thus takes place when a financial officer embezzles public funds for personal use, when a school principal arranges "backdoor" admissions for his relatives or friends, or when a government official accepts bribes from his subordinates in exchange for favorable treatment. Either these practices are conducted by a single person who seeks personal gain in an individual manner or they occur between two parties where a patron (usually an official) grants a client preferential treatment in exchange for goods or services.

As China's reform spreads to new economic areas, corruption is growing in complicity and sophistication. One of the new patterns emerging in recent years is the collectivization of corrupt activities or what I call collective corruption: government officials collude with each other or with people outside the government when engaging in corruption. In many cases, corruption is a collective undertaking rather than an individual action, with collaboration serving as an effective vehicle for individual gains. Corruption is no longer an isolated behavior corrupt in and of itself, but a network of interactions involving exchanges and tradeoffs among a group of corrupt people who seek to maximize individual interests and minimize potential risks. Examples of collective corruption include organized smuggling, collective embezzlement, receiving bribes by a group of officials, and group consumption such as lavish banquets, extravagant office equipment, and public-funded sightseeing trips.

The nature of the collectivization of corruption is similar to what Wheeler and Rothman point out about the organization of white-collar crime, "The organization . . . is for white-collar criminal what the gun or knife is for the common criminal—a tool to obtain money from victims."[36] Nevertheless, some distinction should be established between collective corruption and organized crime, a concept that Western criminological literature has studied rather extensively. While both are characterized by the coordinated activity of a group of actors, organized crime is conducted by "self-perpetuating, structured, and discipline associations of individuals, or groups."[37] These crime groups continue to exist outside of a particular criminal undertaking. They are believed to comprise the following major attributes: a financial base, a hierarchical structure, a clear division of labor, strict discipline, and continuity in operation.[38] In contrast, participants in collective corruption work like ad hoc teams who come together for specific ventures and form opportunistic partnerships. Collaboration in collective corruption thus takes place on an as-needed basis to enable the participants to fulfill their individual goals. Once a venture is completed, the partnership created for the venture may dissolve. Moreover, in collective corruption, government officials are active and principal money seekers, not just "associates" of the law breakers who seduce them into wrongdoing (although some do). In the realm of organized crime, the participation of public officials is seen as being passive as they are *corrupted* by organized criminals.[39]

Collective corruption also differs from organizational corruption, a group behavior that aims at monetary or material gains of an institution.[40] In organizational corruption, the collective interest of a small group or an organization (e.g., an enterprise or a government unit) constitutes at least the immediate goal of corrupt activities and individuals benefit only when institutional gains trickle down. This happens when an institution breaks regulations in the interests of its employees or corporate executives overstep law to seek profits for their companies. In a sense, organizational corruption resembles corporate crime—illicit practices conducted by business firms such as false advertising claims, marketing of unsafe products, pollution of the environment, and falsification of records to hide illegal activities.[41] Despite important differences, organizational corruption and corporate crime share a key feature: it is an organization, not a particular individual, that stands to benefit. Thus the best way to distinguish collective corruption from organizational corruption is similar to what some scholars have used to distinguish organizational crime from occupational crime: to see whether it is an individual gain by means of organization or an organization profits regardless of individual advantage.[42]

Collective corruption takes place under at least one of the following conditions: (1) when concerned value or anticipated benefit from corruption is high; (2) when the technical difficulty of corruption requires greater cooperation among accomplices; and (3) when the stake is high so that divided responsibilities among collaborators may reduce risks. Corruption as a collective operation may also make it difficult to distinguish principal offenders from accessories so the former may escape from heavier punishment.

Corruption has become increasingly risky in recent years, though gains from corruption may have multiplied. The central government drastically intensified its anticorruption campaigns, with the number of rules and regulations against corruption increasing by a quantum leap in the past decade.[43] Since 1996 the government has asked all the cadres at or above the division level *(chu ji)* to report their income from all sources. The interim provisions for the leading Chinese Communist Party (CCP) cadres to engage in government honestly, issued in 1997, is a summation of many anticorruption regulations. Moreover, as a response to the public skepticism about its commitment to tackling corruption of its own cadres, the party leadership has publicized a number of major cases concerning high-ranking party and government officials. In the year 2000 alone twenty senior cadres at the provincial level were convicted and punished.[44]

The need for protection grows together with the risk of being caught for such a high-stake enterprise as corruption. Collective corruption becomes prevalent because in many cases support and protection from the "above" is necessary. By engaging one's supervisor or the supervisor's supervisor in collaboration, a corrupt official may create a safety network against detection. In a bribery case, for instance, if the bribed shares his gifts, either material or monetary, with his boss, thereby making the latter a bribe taker as well, the chance for him to be caught may diminish since the boss, compelled by the need for self-protection, will spare no efforts to protect him. This is exactly what happened in Taian, a city of Shandong Province, where almost all the leading cadres in the city government were found guilty of bribery and corruption. The case started with an unemployed person named Wang. He got to know and then bribed the city's police chief, Yan, in order to obtain licenses for his smuggled cars. Yan shared bribes with his boss, Li, the chief of the Public Security Bureau. Li further bribed Kong, the vice mayor in charge of the city's legal affairs to seek protection. Bribes finally reached the city's deputy party chief and chief. Hu, the party chief and a young and once promising leading party official, accepted more than ¥600,000 worth of bribes alone in this case and was sentenced to death.[45]

Collective corruption has occurred on a massive scale in recent years, often implicating a large group of people inside and outside the government who, through various exchanges, collude with each other to make corrupt transactions possible. This is evident in the notorious Zhanjiang smuggling case which involved more than 150 government officials in total, ranging from the city's party secretary, the customs house, the local state tax bureau, the frontier defense subbureau, the commodity inspection department, and even the city's antismuggling office itself. In an even bigger smuggling case, the scandal of the Yuanhua Company in Xiamen, more than 500 people were involved.[46] Even highly furtive corrupt behavior such as embezzlement displays a tendency to collusion. A big collective embezzlement incident in Jianyang city of Sichuan Province, for instance, implicated about thirty city government officials, including the party chief, mayor, three of the seven deputy mayors, and eight of the eleven standing members of the city's party committee. These corrupt officials embezzled money through an economic entity affiliated with the Office of the City Party Committee. Ridiculously, all the important positions of this profit-making company were occupied by key government officials. The director of the Office of the City Party Committee served as the chairman of the board of trustees. The position of the chief manager was taken by a former deputy party secretary. Two deputy directors of the office of the party committee held the purse strings of the company by making themselves its accountants. They used their power and connections to make profits for the company and then divided the economic gains among themselves.[47]

Collective corruption usually involves bigger sums of money than individual corruption, ranging from hundreds of millions to hundreds of billions. Here exists a vicious circle: the involvement of more people requires a bigger sum to be divided, so each can get a "fair" share; the big sum, in turn, makes it necessary to engage more people because the difficulty of a corrupt activity tends to increase as its anticipated economic outcome gets bigger. As Rose-Ackerman points out, "Initially, payoffs to superiors may be a means of buying their silence, but if payments are institutionalized, they become a condition of employment, organized by superiors for their own gains."[48] Such interactions may also occur between officials with no formal hierarchical connections.[49] As anticipated economic outcomes become more tempting, more people will be willing to participate so that taking collective action will not be difficult. This results in what Rose-Ackerman calls "an upward spiral of corruption," meaning that the corruption of some officials encourages additional officials to get involved until all but a few impeccably honest ones are corrupt.[50]

FROM DOMESTIC CORRUPTION TO TRANSNATIONAL CORRUPTION

China's corruption is becoming increasingly transnational, as many corrupt activities are collaborative operations of domestic government officials with overseas individuals or organizations. The causes for the rise of transnational corruption are manifold, but one thing is for sure: as China's economy becomes more and more open toward the outside world, there are more opportunities for corruption through international collaboration.

China's economy has undoubtedly been integrated with the world economy. In the early years of the reform, trade plans coexisted with exchange controls and border measures mainly in the form of tariffs. The restrictiveness of the trade regime was also enhanced by extensive nontariff barriers. Over time, however, tariffs have been brought down steadily and nontariff barriers have also been reduced. Against the backdrop of reform, China rose to the world's third largest trading country in 2004. Its growth in foreign trade has averaged 15 percent annually since 1978, with more than $1 billion of foreign direct investment (FDI) flowing into the country each week.[51] An even larger market beckons foreign investment as China acceded to the World Trade Organization in 2001. In the first twelve months after the WTO entry, China's direct investment from abroad exceeded $50 billion for the first time, making it the world's leading destination for foreign investment.[52] It is not just FDI that is booming. China's exports and imports increase at a frantic rate as well. The World Bank estimates that China's exports now represent a quarter of China's GDP, five times the level of 1978.[53] At the same time, the government has encouraged companies to seek opportunities abroad. Chinese companies, flush with cash and in command of the low-cost manufacturing factories, are doing foreign investing. Direct investment overseas by China rose 27 percent to $3.62 billion in 2004 from a year earlier. About 69 percent of the investment, or $2.51 billion, was spent acquiring equity in overseas companies.[54]

All this testifies to China's close interactions with the world economy. While there is no question that the country has greatly benefited from its open-door policy, the expansion of international contact has also brought corrupt activities across borders. Corruption in China has become increasingly transnational in scope and by nature, as shown in the surge of smuggling and transnational money laundry.

Smuggling

Smuggling, referring to illegal import or export of goods, is nothing new to China. However, as overseas business connections expand, smuggling has experienced quantitative and qualitative changes and become an important profiteering enterprise in recent years. In 2000 the then-premier, Zhu Rongji, stated that smuggling might have cost China several hundred billion yuan each year.[55] Recent smuggling demonstrates some new characteristics in addition to its increased magnitude. First, smugglers have significantly expanded the scope of their activities. In the past, smuggling mainly concentrated on scarce consumer goods such as cigarettes and home electronics and smuggling operations were usually kept on a small scale. According to an official report, the five chief items of smuggling trade in the early 1990s were sugar, fibers, vegetable oil, cigarettes, and chemicals, which accounted for about 60 percent of all the seized smuggled goods.[56] In recent years, however, smugglers seem to have become much more avaricious and showed great interest in big items— producer goods and raw materials. It was reported, for instance, in Zhanjiang city of Guangdong Province, a place once referred to as "smugglers paradise," the value of three major smuggled goods (steel, petroleum, and automobiles) exceeded ¥10 billion in a period of just two years. From 1997 to July 1998, 753,800 metric tons of finished oil products, equal to one-tenth of the total volume of petrol and diesel oil imported into the country, were smuggled into China through that city.[57]

The increased scale of smuggling activities leads to the second characteristic of recent smuggling: transferring big items requires organized operations and often leads to close collaboration between smuggling agents and local government institutions. The aforementioned Zhanjiang case shocked the country not just by its big quantity of smuggled goods, but also by the large number of party officials, law enforcement officers, and government personnel involved. In the Zhanjiang customs house alone, more than 100 officials were implicated and each of them, on average, took ¥500,000 worth of bribes. The city's party secretary, deputy mayor, the director of Customs, the head of the Border Security Bureau, and many other key government officials were all involved. They provided protection for the city's three major criminal rings headed respectively by a "king of petroleum smuggling," a "king of vehicle smuggling," and a "king of customs clearance."[58]

Finally, the collaboration of smugglers with foreign companies or overseas Chinese businesses gets extensive. The Yuanhua scandal, which smuggled over ¥53 billion worth of scarce goods and production materials and evaded some ¥30 billion taxes, was first revealed in its deals with a U.S.-based shipping company to smuggle vegetable oil. This American company used its five ships to transport hundreds of thousands of tons of vegetable oil to Xiamen, where Yuanhua was based. Yuanhua also developed close connections with some Hong Kong businesses. The chief operator of the Yuanhua scandal, Lai Cangxing, originally a farmer in China, began his business in Hong Kong as a mainland immigrant. Though his Hong Kong business was not successful, this overseas experience earned him the label of "Hong Kong businessman," as well as many personal connections in Hong Kong, both of which proved to be very useful in his later smuggling adventures in Xiamen. Through bribery and other networking tactics, Lai soon became a good friend of many government officials in Xiamen after he returned from Hong Kong. His smuggling operations were assisted by several hundreds of officials including a vice minister of Public Security in Beijing, two deputy mayors of Xiamen, and the director of the city's Customs.[59]

Transnational Money Laundering

Although money laundering is one of the most common transnational crimes in the world, prereform China, a closed society, was not susceptible to it. As China's economy gets inextricably intertwined with the outside world, transnational money laundry is booming in the backdrop of intensified corruption. Nowadays, the increased economic integration, the globalization of financial transactions, and technological advancement also allow money, "clean" or "dirty," to flow in and out of a country with greater ease. As a result, each year sizable amounts of dirty money move across China's borders. It was reported that China's illegal capital flight reached $20 billion in 2002.[60] China has been identified as one of the world's top five countries of origins for money laundering, together with the United States, Russia, Italy, and Germany.[61]

Money laundering, defined as "the process by which criminals or criminal organizations seek to disguise the illicit nature of their proceeds by introducing them into the stream of legitimate commerce and finance," is intimately connected with corruption.[62] This is because corrupt public officials are usually anxious to conceal or squander their ill-gotten gains from bribery, embezzlement, extortion, financial fraud, or other forms of illicit activities. After going through a money laundering process, they can wash off, or at lease minimize, the taint of corruption.

Dirty money may be laundered in different ways. One is to deposit money into underground banks which then remit the money to an overseas account designated by launderers. Underground banks, known as "underground money houses" *(dixia qianzhuang)* have long existed in China, especially in the southern provinces such as Guangdong and Fujian. They have been used to evade exchange control restrictions and expensive foreign transaction fees. In recent years, money laundering has become a flourishing business for these "money houses," which launder about ¥200 billion a year.[63] Among the funds handled by these underground financial organizations, more than half are illegal gains from graft, smuggling, and drug trafficking, while the rest are deposited by private companies or foreign corporations to evade taxes.[64] The aforementioned Yuanhua Company used several underground banks in Jinjiang and Shishi areas of Fujian Province to launder its gains from smuggling totaling ¥12 billion. The money was first deposited into the underground banks in yuan. The banks then instructed their Hong Kong branches to pay Yuanhua's Hong Kong office the same amount minus service charges in Hong Kong dollar. Yuanhua got the money back in a foreign currency and free from domestic financial regulations.

Money launderers sometimes bypass domestic underground banks to send money directly across the borders, as long as they have overseas connections of their own. They may deposit money into foreign banks that are registered under the name of a front company, a family member, or a close friend. Some offshore financing centers have helped China's corrupt businesses and government officials channel out a lot of illegal money in recent years.[65] Corrupt officials may also send money to the so-called window companies that many Chinese companies set up in Hong Kong. While most window companies are legal, some of them operate in a gray area and often speculate in Hong Kong stocks and real estate.[66] Hong Kong has found favor in the eyes of money launderers due to its privileged position as a special administrative region under the "one country, two systems" policy and as an international financial center. Each year huge sums of money, recorded as foreign direct investment from the mainland in official booking, flow into Hong Kong through these companies or in other ways, while no one considers Hong Kong a magnet for foreign investment. A big proportion of the money then leaves for somewhere else or simply goes back to China after acquiring a Hong Kong identity. In the year 2000 alone, while $64.3 billion flowed into Hong Kong, about 62.9 billion described as outward FDI left the city over the same period.[67] However and wherever money is moved, the purpose of money launderers is to legalize their dirty money and allow it to establish a new identity so as to be brought back into the legitimate financial system. Money laundering thus enables corrupt officials to enjoy the fruits of corruption without jeopardizing the sources of their gains.

CONCLUSION

Although the origin of corruption as a theoretical notion can be traced back to the founding fathers of Western political thought such as Thucydides, Plato, and Aristotle, the forms and characteristics of corruption have changed over time and differed across societies.[68] Changing political and economic environments give rise to new patterns of corruption. As the preceding discussion shows, more opportunities for corruption have become available and therefore led to some new trends in corruption in recent years as China broadens its market-driven reform. Capital corruption, instead of illegal cash consumption, has prevailed as corrupt officials snatch state assets to amass personal fortunes. This is to a large extent due to the fact that the effective regulation of capital market has failed to keep pace with the rapid development of market in such areas as land leasing, ownership diversification, and financial transactions. The surge of collective corruption further proves that corrupt officials may change their strategy under new economic conditions in order to get more direct and effective access to money. The international attribute of corruption has also become obvious, paralleling the rapid pace of China's economic globalization. All this indicates that sources and forms of corruption are not only complex but also changing. In contrast to the conventional wisdom that increased economic marketization may reduce corruption, free market is not a panacea.

This chapter thus argues that despite the gradual marketization of the economy, corruption continues to pose many, if not more, problems for China. The deepening of the market reform in recent years has not reduced corruption as much as altering its forms and characteristics. In the early reform period corrupt officials simply took advantage of the discrepancy between the plan and the market and used administrative means to profiteer, whereas today's corruption often results from direct economic activities of government officials. The reasons can be found in two ongoing parallel processes of China's reform—power decentralization and economic marketization. The market-driven reform, seen as a cure for overcentralization and a release of initiatives and incentives for growth, has reshuffled economic power among different levels of the government, but it does not significantly change the nature and magnitude of power exercised by government officials. Power may have changed hands from the upper levels to lower ones as a result of decentralization, but the same decentralization process has placed local economies at arm's length of local officials, who can now easily shove their oar in economic operations. Vivienne Shue is right in pointing out that the greatest beneficiaries of the decentralization in the context of marketization have been party-state authorities at the middle and lower-middle levels of the system.[69] They have got more freedom to maneuver beyond as well as within the state apparatus, while at the same time being exposed to more and immediate money-making opportunities.

This said, the point being made here is not that there is anything wrong with the reform, but that corruption is a kind of human behavior which responds to political and economic changes. The surge of corruption in China should not be attributed to too much reform; rather, as Jean Oi correctly points out, it is a result of the incompleteness of the reform.[70] For example, while many market mechanisms are being introduced, the failure in establishing necessary rules and regulations over the market has left economic marketization vulnerable to power abuse. In addition, while people, including many former government officials, are encouraged to make money in business activities, an environment for fair competition does not exist as yet due to very uneven distribution of resources. Finally, public supervision over government officials has remained weak in China as a result of the lagged political reform and underdeveloped legal institutions.

Corruption is not going to fade away as China's economic marketization continues. Without political reform, a market economy cannot effectively contain corruption. The continued surge of corruption has had an inverse impact on China's marketization and modernization efforts as it results in an economic loss of approximately 13–16 percent of GDP every year, as conservatively estimated.[71] It also threatens social stability, the very environment China needs for economic development. Rampant corruption has caused not only public cynicism and disillusionment, but also street protests or even riots where people found it unbearable.[72] The leadership cannot afford to see its public image being tarnished by corruption, but it remains equally challenging whether and how to carry out political reform without causing political trouble for the government itself.

NOTES

1. Yang Jirui et al., *Tiaozhan xinshiji: Zhongguo disanlun dagaige* [Challenging the new century: China's third round of reform] (Chengdu: Sichuan chubanshe, 1998), 9.

2. See the ninth five-year plan of the National Economic and Social Development and the 2010 long-term goals outlines of the People's Republic of China.

3. The World Bank, *China: Macro Economic Stability in a Decentralized Economy* (Washington, DC: World Bank 1995).

4. See, for example, Ting Gong, *The Politics of Corruption in Contemporary China* (Westport, CT: Praeger, 1994); Michael Johnston and Yufan Hao, "China's Surge of Corruption," *Journal of Democracy* 6, no. 4 (1995): 80–94; Hilton Root, "Corruption in China: Has It Become Systemic?" *Asian Survey* 36, no. 8 (1996): 741–757; Julia Kwong, *The Political Economy of Corruption in China* (New York: Sharpe, 1997); Lu Xiaobo, *Cadre and Corruption: The Organizational Involution of the Chinese Communist Party* (Stanford, CA: Stanford University Press, (2000); Andrew Wedeman, "Great Disorder: The Paradox of Endemic Corrup-

tion and Rapid Growth in Contemporary China," *China Review* 4, no. 2 (2004): 599–617; Yan Sun, *Corruption and Market in Contemporary China* (Ithaca, NY: Cornell University Press 2004).

5. Kenneth Jowitt, *New World Disorder: The Leninist Extinction* (Berkeley: University of California Press, 1992).

6. Peter Harris, "Socialist Graft: The Soviet Union and the People's Republic of China: A Preliminary Survey," *Corruption and Reform* 1, no. 1 (1986): 13–32.

7. Jean C. Oi, *State and Peasant in Contemporary China: The Political Economy of Village Government* (Berkeley: University of California Press 1989).

8. Constance Squires Meaney, "Market Reform in a Leninist System: Some Trends in the Distribution of Power, Status, and Money in the Urban China," *Studies in Comparative Communism* 22, no. 2–3 (1989): 210.

9. Clemens S. Ostergaard and Christina Peterson, "Official Profiteering and the Tiananmen Square Demonstrations in China," *Corruption and Reform* 6, no. 1 (1991): 87–107.

10. In 1998 a deputy bureau chief in Tainjin was sentenced to death with a two-year reprieve for spending ¥530,000 public funds on eating and entertaining during a fourteen-month period. This is believed to be only the first case of harsh punishment for extravagancy. *Mingbao*, November 1, 1998.

11. Huang Weiding, *Shiluo de zhunyan* [The lost dignity] (Beijing: Zuojia chubanshe, 1998), 208.

12. The face value of a stock is low because it is based on the original purchase prices of the company's capital assets (minus depreciation) instead of the market prices. Value-added factors are also excluded. X. L. Ding, "Who Gets What, Who, How? When Chinese State-Owned Enterprises Become Shareholding Companies," *Problems of Post-Communism* 46, no. 3 (1999): 35.

13. *Liaowang* [Outlook] 17 (1998).

14. *Huanqiu* [Globe] 5 (2005), www.xinhuanet.com/globe/globe.htm.

15. *Zhongguo jiancha* [Supervision in China], March 2004.

16. He Qinglian, *Xiandaihua de xianjing* [Pitfalls of modernization] (Beijing: Jinrizhongguo chubanshe, 1998), 109.

17. Huang Weiding, *Shiluo de zhunyan*, 251.

18. Huang Weiding, *Shiluo de zhunyan*, 161.

19. Yang Guangfei, "Difang hezuo zhuyi zhongde quanli yuewei" [The power abuse in the local corporatism], *The Twenty-first Century* 6 (2004).

20. Mayfair Mei-hui Yang, *Gifts, Favors, and Banquets: The Art of Social Relationships in China* (Ithaca, NY: Cornell University 1994), 199–200.

21. Yang Guangfei, "Difang hezuo zhuyi zhongde quanli yuewei."

22. Interview by author, Shanghai, 1997.

23. *Liaowang* [Outlook] 36 (1989).

24. Joshua Cooper Ramo, "The Shanghai Bubble," *Foreign Policy*, Summer 1998, 64.

25. Rousseau Chen, "The Trouble with All This New Money," *Shanghai Star*, May, 23 2002.

26. *Beijing wangbao*, January 3, 2003.

27. 1 mou is equal to 0.164 acre.

28. Ling Fei, *Xiayige shishui?* [Who is next?] (Beijing: Dazhong chubanshe, 2001).

29. Chen Jian, *Liushi de zhongguo* [Loss of Chinese property], (Beijing: Zhongguo chengshi chubanshe, 1998), 48.

30. *Beijing wanbao*, January 3, 2003.

31. Ministry of Land and Resources, *Guotu ziyuan diaoyan* [An investigation of national assets] (Beijing: Zhongguo dadi chubanshe, 2003).

32. www.worldbank.org.cn/English/content/China04-04.pdf

33. *People's Daily*, August 7, 2004.

34. Zhao Ling, "Significant Shift in Focus of Peasants' Right Activism," *Southern Weekend*, September 3, 2004. Translated by Manfred Elfstrom.

35. Yves Meny, "'Fin De Siecle' Corruption: Change, Crisis, and Shifting Values," *International Social Science Journal* 48 (1996): 309–320.

36. Stanton Wheeler and Mitchell Lewis Rothman, "The Organization as Weapon in White Collar Crime," *Michigan Law Review* 80, no. 7 (1982): 1406.

37. Howard Abadinsky, *Organized Crime* (Chicago: Nelson-Hall, 1985).

38. Patricia Rawlinson, "Russian Organized Crime: A Brief History," in Phil Williams, ed., *Russian Organized Crime: The New Threat* (Portland: Frank Cass, 1997), 32.

39. For a description of the orthodox view of the role of public officials in organized crime, see Donald Liddick, *An Empirical, Theoretical, and Historical Overview of Organized Crime* (Lewiston, NY: Mellen, 1999), 40–41.

40. See Kwong, *Political Economy*, 69–73; Xiaobo Lu, "Booty Socialism, Bureau-preneurs, and the State in Transition: Organizational Corruption in China," *Comparative Politics* 32, no. 3 (2000): 273–294.

41. Corporate crime is different from corruption, as it is seldom straightly connected with public power and is not conducted in a way that whittles away the state's assets and resources to enrich certain groups or individuals. Corporate crime tends to directly victimize consumers while collective corruption is intended to steal public resources and milk the state treasury. Corporate crime takes place within and is largely confined to the private economic domain. Collective corruption, on the other hand, denotes abuses of political power and transactions between power (public domain) and wealth (private domain).

42. James W. Coleman, "Toward an Integrated Theory of White Collar Crime," *American Journal of Sociology* 93, no. 2 (1987): 406–439.

43. Knowing that the festering corruption within will eventually destroy itself, the party leaders have warned on numerous occasions that the struggle against corruption is "a matter of life and death for the party and the state. . . . If we don't do anything about it, we are risking our future." See, for example, *People's Daily*, September 1, 1993.

44. For an analysis of major cases, see Ting Gong, "More Than Mere Words, Less Than Hard Law: A Rhetorical Analysis of China's Anti-Corruption Policy," *Public Administration Quarterly* 27 (2003): 159–187; Andrew Wedeman, "The Intensification of Corruption in China," *China Quarterly* 180 (2004): 895–921.

45. Anjiang Yide and Chuan Jin, *Taian fantan fengbao* [Anti-corruption storm in Taian] (Beijing: Xinhua chubanshe, 1996).

46. "PRC Authorities to Conclude Xiamen Corruption Case," *Mingbao*, May 14, 2000, FBIS-CHI-2000-0515, May 17, 2000.

47. Li Xuehui and Li Xueqin, *Zhongguo: Jingti shizhong fubai xianxiang* [China: Careful about ten corruption phenomena] (Tianjin: Nankai University Press 1999).

48. Susan Rose-Ackerman, *Corruption and Government: Causes, Consequences, and Reform* (Cambridge: Cambridge University Press 1999), 83.

49. Olivert Cadot, "Corruption as a Gamble," *Journal of Public Economics* 33 (1987):

223–244; Harendra Kanti, "The Genesis and Spread of Economic Corruption: A Micro-theoretical Interpretation," *World Development* 17 (1989): 503–511.

50. Rose-Ackerman, *Corruption and Government,* 124.

51. "Survey: Behind the Mask," *Economist,* March 20, 2004, 4.

52. Nicholas Lardy, "Sweet and Sour Deal," *Foreign Policy* 129 (2002): 20.

53. CBS News Online, January 13, 2005.

54. *Wall Street Journal,* February 8, 2005, 16.

55. Hai Yun, *Xiamen yuanhua an* [The Xiaman Yuanhua case] (Beijing: Zhongguo xinwen chubanshe 2001), 1.

56. *People's Daily,* May 11, 1995.

57. Jiao H, "Zhanjiang zuosian" [Zhanjiang smuggling case], *Falu yu shenghuo* [Law and life] 8 (1999): 20–23.

58. Jiao H, "Zhanjiang zuosian."

59. "PRC Authorities to Conclude Xiamen Corruption Case," *Mingbao,* May 14, 2000, FBIS-CHI-2000-0515, May 17, 2000.

60. David Lague, "China's Money Laundry," *Far Eastern Economic Review* 164, no. 24 (2001): 56–58.

61. J. Walker, "Modeling Global Money Laundering Flows," http://members.ozemail.com.au.

62. Kris Hinterseer, *Criminal Finance: The Political Economy of Money Laundering in a Comparative Legal Context* (Norwell, MA: Kluwer Law International, 2002), 11.

63. N. Liu, "Crackdown on Money Laundering," *Economic Review* 3 (2000): 78.

64. *Beijing qingnianbao,* August 5, 2003.

65. *Taipei Times,* August 10, 2004.

66. Sony Yang, "Money Laundering in China: A Policy Analysis," *Journal of Contemporary Criminal Justice* 18, no. 4 (2002): 370–380.

67. Lague, "China's Money Laundry," 56.

68. Arnold Heidenheimer, Michael Jonston, and Victor T. LeVine, *Political Corruption* (New Brunswick, NJ: Transaction, 1989).

69. Vivienne Shue, "State Power and Social Organization in China," in J. Migdal, A. Kohli, and V. Shue, eds., *State Power and Social Forces: Domination and Transformation in the Third World* (New York: Cambridge University Press, 1994), 65–88.

70. Oi, *State and Peasant.*

71. Hu Angang, "Public Exposure of Economic Losses Resulting from Corruption," www.iwep.org.cn/wec/english/articles/2002_04/2002-4huangang.pdf.

72. Feng Chen, "Subsistence Crises, Managerial Corruption, and Labor Protests in China," *China Journal* 163 (2000): 41–63.

18

Market Visions

The Interplay of Ideas and Institutions in Chinese Financial Restructuring

EDWARD S. STEINFELD

I n studies of transitional systems, negative economic outcomes are often associated with "partial" or "stalled" reform—a reform that signifies an institutional departure from standard market operation. Such departures are often traced to sociopolitical contestation or political preferences. Focusing on China's intertwined financial and enterprise reforms, this chapter challenges that approach on two fronts. First, it argues that institutional change and resultant economic outcomes are driven less by contestation than by societally held assumptions regarding the nature of economic causation in market contexts. The analytical lenses that actors employ to understand their environment shape expectations about how markets function, influence the manner by which economic problems are diagnosed, and profoundly affect the ultimate institutional evolution of the system. Second, such lenses are necessitated by substantial uncertainties at the theoretical level regarding market function—uncertainties that make characterizations of economic behavior as "irrational" highly problematic.

In December 2003, the Chinese government announced a US$45 billion recapitalization of two of the nation's four main banks. This followed a US$32.6 billion bailout of the four main banks in 1998 and a US$157 billion carve out of nonperforming loans (NPLs) in 1999. Yet, for all this effort, levels of NPLs remain staggeringly high and distressingly opaque. In 1997, the government officially estimated NPLs at 24 percent of total outstanding loans.[1] By the time of the 2003 recapitalization, NPLs at the four major state banks were still officially estimated at 16.9 percent

471

of total outstanding loans, and that was after a third of all NPLs had been removed from the bank balance sheets in the 1999 carve out (Baglole 2004). Independent analysts today paint an even grimmer picture, routinely estimating NPLs at 40 percent, or higher, of total outstanding loans (F. Hu 2004; Ma and Fung 2002). Unfortunately, the most recent data offer little cause for optimism. New loan extensions in 2003 surged 20 percent over the previous year, thus diluting NPL ratios by adding dubious new loan assets to bank balance sheets, a portion of which assets themselves are likely to become nonperforming in the future (F. Hu 2004; Holland and Lague 2004). China today faces a major problem of capital misallocation, one that has deepened in recent years despite considerable governmental attention and a series of highly publicized ameliorative measures.

Why has this situation persisted? Why do China's financial reforms seem gripped by institutional paralysis, and how can such paralysis be explained in the context of other more successful reforms—price liberalization, the rise of a vibrant private sector, and a substantial downsizing of state-owned industry? What accounts for the dichotomous nature of China's institutional transformation overall?

In answering the above, I will challenge explanations that treat stalled institutional reform as a departure from economic rationality—a departure from an essentially unitary model of market function that must be explained by an alternative noneconomic logic, be it political, social, or ideological.[2] The argument is that partial, stalled institutional transformation stems from the manner in which decision makers and other economic actors conceptualize and understand markets. More specifically, outcomes are driven in large part by assumptions that actors make about cause and effect under market conditions. Such assumptions influence expectations about what *should* obtain empirically in the real world, and the extent to which what actually does obtain is understood as constituting a problem requiring redress.

These widely shared, often tacit common understandings serve as frameworks for ordering highly complex, highly uncertain environments, the very sort of environments characteristic of modern economic affairs. They are, in effect, societally shared lenses for constructing reality in the face of tremendous uncertainty (Hall 1989). As will be illustrated in the Chinese case, these shared ways of understanding the world—by grouping together discordant and even contradictory assumptions—at times lack internal consistency (Swidler 2001). Nonetheless, they lead to routinized behavioral responses (Swidler 2001) that persist even as their ineffectuality becomes increasingly apparent to outsiders employing different frameworks, different principles of causality (Dobbin 1994). Although these frameworks may not be determinative (indeed, they often allow for considerable debate within societies), they provide a common language for discussing problems and a circumscribed palette of options from which various solutions can be drawn and debated (Swidler 2001). They are, in effect, societal constructions of reality that provide a common discourse in which different opinions, ideas, and options can be discussed.

The argument presented here constitutes a distillation of interview data collected over the past decade in China. During a seven-month research visit in 1994, a six-month visit in 1999, a three-month visit in 2000, and numerous shorter stays between 1993 and 2003, I conducted over 250 formal interviews and even more informal conversations with central policy architects, central and local administrative officials, bankers, asset managers, and enterprise managers and staff. Though the initial aim of these interviews was to understand the diverse interests surrounding financial reform—and hence, respondents were chosen to cover the broadest array of interests possible—I was struck, over time, by the similar ways in which these highly diverse respondents framed the problems of reform and their potential solutions. Interviews intended to illustrate the policy impact of competing interests inadvertently uncovered something entirely different—shared societal understandings that profoundly guide behavior.[3]

CHINA'S CONTEMPORARY POLITICAL ECONOMY

Twenty-five years into the reform era, China's political economy today embodies an amalgam of dichotomous outcomes—which seem to indicate, in some cases, extraordinary market transition and, in others, extraordinary institutional derailment. In the past decade, there has been dramatic private sector growth, substantial state sector downsizing, and aggressive governmental efforts to promote market liberalization through World Trade Organization (WTO) accession. At the same time, however, there has been deepening insolvency in the national banking system, a rapid accumulation of contingent liabilities on the government's budget (unfunded liabilities to depositors in the state banking system, and unfunded liabilities to participants in the state pension system), ineffectual financial sector bailouts, and a continued governmental effort to support large industrial conglomerates, many of which have been failing commercially (Yusuf, Nabeshima, and Perkins 2004; Woo 1999; Steinfeld 1998).[4]

At the dawn of reform in the late 1970s, virtually no private enterprise existed in China's state-dominated economy. Twenty years later, private industry was not only the fastest growing portion of the economy, but in static terms it already accounted for approximately 33 percent of GDP (Gregory, Tenev, and Wagle 2000). Between 1993 and 1999, the share of China's total industrial labor force employed in private firms quintupled, a figure underscoring the private sector's status as the major vehicle for job creation in the contemporary Chinese economy (Broadman 2001).

In a manner consistent with Chinese reform generally, the government's stance vis-à-vis the private sector by the 1990s entailed a combination of incremental measures to stimulate sectoral growth and relative silence regarding the sector's legal legitimacy. Only when positive outcomes were achieved did the government scramble to accord legitimization and formalization. Private industry in 1999 was officially recognized by the Chinese constitution as an important—and, by definition, legitimate—part of the national economy. Two years later, Communist Party general secretary Jiang Zemin formally welcomed entrepreneurs—capitalists, in effect—into the ranks of the vanguard party (Xinhua News Service 2001).

The rise of the private sector has coincided with an equally impressive drawdown of state industry, particularly with respect to smaller-scale state firms. This is consistent with the *fang xiao* ("relinquishing the small)" side of the government's dual enterprise reform strategy since 1994 of *zhua da fang xiao* ("grasping the large and relinquishing the small"). From 1993 to 1999, China's state industrial sector shrank from over 100,000 to approximately 61,000 firms (State Statistical Bureau 2000). *Zhua da fang xiao* encouraged state divestiture from smaller, primarily loss-making SOEs (state-owned enterprises) and a refocusing of governmental resources on a smaller population of core firms. In 1995, 72 percent of China's approximately 59,000 locally controlled SMEs (small and medium-size state enterprises) were estimated to be loss making (Tenev and Zhang 2002). Five years later, 82 percent of the total population of SMEs had been officially termed "transformed," whether through public listing, liquidation, merger, sale, or a variety of other measures. Meanwhile, all of this occurred in the context of extraordinary year-on-year growth in national income.

On the other side of the ledger, however, a series of more alarming outcomes emerged. As indicated earlier, NPLs in China's bank-dominated financial system have soared in both absolute terms and, by many estimates, as a percentage of GDP. Today, the government's official estimate that NPLs in the four major state banks amount to 26 percent of GDP (F. Hu 2004; Ma and Fung 2002) constitutes an open acknowledgment of the insolvency, at least in technical terms, of the nation's banking system. Independent researchers at the Bank for International Settlements, however, have recently estimated the ratio of NPLs to GDP at 35 percent, and the ratio of NPLs to outstanding loans at 42 percent (Ma and Fung 2002). While much of China's real economy has marketized, the efficiency of financial intermediation has seemingly declined rather than increased. By late 1993, leading Chinese economists like Wu Jinglian were quite publicly warning that China's most urgent economic problem was misuse of capital (Restall 2003).

Throughout the reform era, China's financial sector has been dominated by state banks, entities that still account for approximately 70 percent of all intermediated capital in China. Since the 1980s, household savings have poured into these banks, but the funds have been directed toward activities—loans to large-scale state industrial firms—that have yielded decidedly low returns. What results, of course, are distressed loan assets—NPLs.

The underlying pattern is fairly clear. Despite significant liberalization, Chinese banks still lend primarily to state firms (World Bank 1999a; Lardy 1998; Beijing University CCER 1999), and particularly to the larger *guojia dui* ("national team") firms (Nolan 2001) deemed part of the *zhua da* ("grasping the large") side of the government's *zhua da fang xiao* strategy. Even after decades of reform (and the major winnowing of smaller loss makers noted previously), such firms have consistently proven unable to meet their financial obligations. Particularly in the first half of the 1990s, as the economy boomed and banks pumped in loans, SOEs blundered into a variety of asset-destroying activities, most notably breakneck capacity expansion and ill-advised real estate speculation (Zhu 1996; Woo 1999; Steinfeld 1998). By middecade, as inflationary upsurge gave way to deflationary downturn, these activities yielded returns insufficient to cover the cost of capital, and NPLs soared. With the renewed lending surge in 2003—and related indications of inflation, real estate speculation, and overcapacity in heavy industry—concerns are deepening that the pattern of ill-advised lending to large-scale industrial incumbents has returned. Whether due to governmental direction or the bankers' own faith in traditional industrial borrowers, the problematic nexus between large state-owned industrial firms and large state-owned banks in China remains unbroken.

In this context, unfunded liabilities related to China's pension system have also soared. Estimates of the present value of this implicit governmental debt—the portion of the pension obligation not covered by future enterprise contributions and payroll deductions—are highly uncertain, but range anywhere from 45 to 95 percent of GDP (Bottelier 2001). In a fashion analogous to state banks, SOEs in past years behaved as if these liabilities were ultimately guaranteed by the state and thus severely underfunded them. Today, even as the narrowly defined system of the present lapses into insolvency, China's modernization process continues to march onward, bringing with it an increasing flow of workers from traditional agriculture into urban wage employment and, with that, rising pressure on the government for even broader pension provision in the future (Hussain 2000).

Unfortunately, whether as an alternative channel for financial intermediation nationally or as a vehicle for resolving the specific problem of pension liabilities, China's growing stock markets offer little cause for hope. China's two exchanges, in Shanghai and Shenzhen, respectively, if taken as a single whole, constitute the world's eighth largest in terms of total market capitalization (Green 2003). Yet, only a third of the market's shares are permitted to trade, whereas the rest remain controlled by organs of the state (Green 2003). Listed on this market are high-profile public corporations—many of which fall into the category of *guojia dui* SOEs— whose shares trade internationally and whose business activities extend well into the global economy, but whose ownership remains state dominated. Moreover, given that the government values the market's nontradable shares at exactly the same price as that commanded by the minority of shares that do trade, we should view the total market capitalization figures skeptically. The market's low float (the small percentage of tradable to nontradable shares) pushes up prices, which would surely fall, and indeed have fallen, whenever the float is increased. Just as the nexus between large firms and financial institutions has proven impervious to reform, so too has the sense that, in China, financial institutions serve not to allocate capital impartially to all potential recipients, but rather to fund a privileged group of core industrial producers. The real question is why.

STANDARD EXPLANATIONS: "MARKET FORCES VERSUS DISTORTIONS"

For many observers, the above trends signify partial reform, a situation in which market forces (those that have led to GDP growth and industrial restructuring) are understood as contending with governmentally induced nonmarket "distortions" (those that have led to the capital misallocation and asset destruction associated with China's financial system) (Lardy 1998; Shirk 1993). From this perspective the market is treated as a well-understood unitary entity (the heavily dashed pathway in figure 18.1). Ideal institutional change, then, is conceptualized as movement along a path of economic rationality from the inefficient plan to the well-understood unitary market. Departures from the optimal path (the lighter pathways in figure 18.1) are taken as departures from economic rationality, and hence are understood as stemming from an alternative, noneconomic logic (Hirschman 1963; Bates 1981).

The "market forces versus distortions" framework shapes a number of related perspectives. One variant, emphasizing concerns over social stability and political legitimacy, argues that the Chinese government, even at the expense of massive long-term problems of capital misallocation, shields SOEs and banks from market forces to avoid near-term problems of social unrest. When push comes to shove, the government tempers the kind of market forces that would shut down major firms, drive up urban unemployment, and possibly ignite social upheaval (Lin 2004).

Although not entirely inaccurate, this perspective fails to explain the degree of

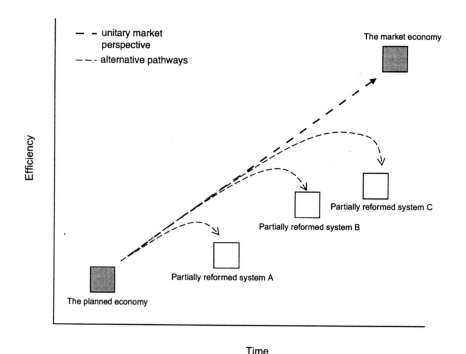

Figure 18.1   Postsocialist Transition and Divergences from Economic Rationality: Alternative Political Rationalities

societal dislocation that actually *has* occurred in recent years—a dislocation that has been actively initiated by the government. Urban joblessness in China has steadily moved upward since the mid 1990s (Giles, Park, and Cai 2003), a trend in large part related to the government's *zhua da fang xiao* policy. Utilizing independent surveys, economist Hu Angang has estimated that the national unemployment rate rose from 4.3 percent in 1995 to roughly 6.2 percent in 1998, a period that coincides with the state's policy of severing its support for smaller SOEs (Hu 1999). Current estimates place the figure at 7 percent (*Zhongguo nanfang zhoumo* 2002). In 1999, Hu estimated the actual unemployment rate within urban industry at approximately 10 percent, though that figure does not include the highly prevalent phenomena of "furloughing" and "unemployment on the job" (workers who remain officially employed but receive a small fraction of their salary and benefits). Between 1997 and 1998, the total number of on-the-job workers in China decreased by 23.3 million, or roughly 16 percent (Hu 1999).

In contrast to its position during the first decade of reform, the Chinese government by the mid-1990s was willing to induce unemployment *even* in the absence of a functioning social safety net. During the 1996–1997 unemployment spike, only a third of China's industrial workers were covered by unemployment insurance; and a scarcity of funds meant that only around 40 percent of the officially registered unemployed could collect the benefits to which they were entitled (Hu 1999).

A second variant of the nonmarket distortions argument points toward issues of political contestation and interest articulation. The idea here is that certain reforms—those involving heavy industry and banking—are habitually deferred in order to protect the interests of politically powerful social groups (Shirk 1993; World Bank 1995). The argument, therefore, would be that SOEs are—and have always been—propped up to protect loyal party insiders, be they managers, state bureaucrats, or others. Banks, in turn, serve as convenient financing mechanisms, since liabilities can be spread out across a powerless, voiceless population of household depositors. What ostensibly results is a patronage system bearing tremendous long-term cost to the nation's macroeconomy, but great short-term benefit to political authorities and their loyal supporters.

Again, there are virtues to this argument. The Chinese reform process, like such processes anywhere, has at every stage produced winners and losers. Moreover, Chinese political leaders, like leaders anywhere, undoubtedly seek to maintain public support for policies, even as those policies dynamically—and unpredictably—affect various constellations of winners and losers.

Nonetheless, it is one thing to observe that reform measures produce winners and losers, but another thing to argue (Shirk 1993; Shleifer and Treisman 2000) that those constellations of interest actually *drive* policy. What is so interesting in the Chinese case is that, although it has been relatively easy in hindsight to identify winners and losers at each stage of reform, it has proven exceedingly difficult to predict which interests will best be served by the next stage. Put somewhat differently, Chinese political leaders have proven willing to pursue measures pernicious to the interests of precisely those groups that would have been considered prime candidates for insider protection.

Through the course of the 1990s, one privileged group after another suffered unexpected hurt at the hands of central reformers. First, urban SOE workers, for decades promised lifetime employment and benefits, began to face joblessness on a grand scale (Hu 1999; Solinger 1999, Giles et al. 2003). Second, as part of the effort to shield China from Asia's financial contagion, the central government summarily deprived local party bosses of control over state bank branches, the prime vehicle by which local officials had previously dispensed investment to favored interests while passing risks upward through the national banking system (Lou et al. 1998; Xie 1996). Local authorities took another hit with the *zhua da fang xiao* policy, as the center, on a grand scale, withdrew funding for locally supervised SMEs, and thus forced local governments either to accept financial responsibility for such firms, or otherwise cede ownership to other stakeholders (Gregory et al. 2000; Tenev and Zhang 2002). Third, bureaucrats in the industrial line ministries—the commanders of the "commanding heights" of yore—witnessed in the late 1990s the elimination of their ministries through Premier Zhu Rongji's governmental restructuring program, the transfer of the firms they had once controlled to state asset management organs, and the exposure of their former industrial charges—through the premier's extraordinary WTO accession bid—to head-to-head global competition (interviews with current and former ministerial officials, Beijing 1999 and 2000). By all accounts, the WTO accession agreement was roundly opposed by traditional industrial bureaucrats. Tellingly, in the midst of all this change, China's head of state, Jiang Zemin, moved not so much to mollify traditional insiders but to coopt outsiders, private entrepreneurs, by inviting them into the party (Dickson 2003). Interests may count in Chinese politics, but policy makers have proven surprisingly willing to act against the very interests that once would have been deemed inviolable.

Finally, there is the argument, well represented in the literature, that the Chinese government—or any government, for that matter—distorts markets simply to maximize control (Huang 2003; Fang 2001; Shleifer and Vishny 1998). That governments seek control is, in a certain sense, irrefutable. What is so interesting about control, however, are the myriad forms it may take and the fluidity with which it may transform over time.

During China's command era, the government enjoyed vast direct control over the economic system and society more broadly. Through the direct manipulation of prices, political authorities shaped the composition and flow of material goods, the movement of capital, and the disposition of the population throughout the entire country (Lin, Cai, and Li 1996). What the unfolding of the reform era signifies is that, although control may be an aspect and ambition of governance, it is but one of many. In a pattern that has obtained from the early 1980s through the present, Chinese policy makers have repeatedly chosen to trade direct and (from their perspective) well-understood forms of control (ownership over producers and control over prices) for alternative mechanisms of indirect control that were poorly understood and difficult to manage.

Why has this occurred? Presumably, economic growth, national strength, and political legitimation were also goals of the leadership, and direct control increasingly came to be viewed as an obstacle to their attainment. Although reforms have been incremental and halting, authorities have, at every turn, ultimately chosen to move further down the path of decontrol. Consequently, we may attribute any given outcome in the Chinese system to governmental ambitions for control. However, it has proven exceedingly difficult to predict which forms of control the government will defend and which it will cede. Given our knowledge about how reform has actually played out, the safest bet at any given moment would have been to guess (against better judgment) that the government would yield rather than uphold its direct control.

Control, though obviously crucial, is but one goal of many. Attributions of particular economic outcomes, generally negative ones, to political ambitions for control are simplistic at best and empirically inaccurate at worst. Surprising to most observers of the Chinese scene is that we have yet to discern a figurative Rubicon across which Chinese reformers are unwilling to tread. We may assert that China today protects a limited number of SOEs and resists financial liberalization because the government seeks control, but why should we believe that the particular combination of free markets and state intervention obtaining today represent a final endpoint, an ultimate degree of decontrol beyond which the government will not budge? Why particularly should we do so when, over the past two decades, at each point when it seemed certain the government would halt reforms to preserve control, the government has moved (or muddled) forward?

AN ALTERNATIVE APPROACH

The arguments described above employed a framework in which an empirical outcome—in the Chinese case, capital misallocation—is measured against a presumed market standard. The problem, however, is that in reality the standard—even at the abstract, theoretical level—has long been subject to dispute, confusion, and differences of opinion.

Within the Western tradition, there exist at least two broad visions of the market, conceptions that, while standing in considerable analytical tension, together suffuse key economic institutions. The first of these formulations, what might be termed the "market as selection perspective," understands the market primarily as a mechanism for allocating resources. The firm is viewed as a particular deployment of resources at a given historical moment, a deployment that exists at the behest of—and remains subordinate to—the overall process of market allocation. Through the continual process of reallocation, firms rise and fall, with older, more conservative incumbents repeatedly yielding to innovative, entrepreneurial upstarts. Indeed, it is precisely this process of "creative destruction" that drives innovation and growth (Schumpeter 1968; Hayek 1960; Kornai 2000, 13–14; Christensen 1997). Ensuring the sustenance of a given incumbent is not the market's aim. Rather, its role is to achieve growth and asset expansion across the entire economy through a continual winnowing of winners from losers, a continual redeployment of assets from older to newer organizational forms.

From the market as selection perspective, misallocation of the type experienced in China can (and frequently does) occur under market conditions. The reason, however, has less to do with exogenously induced distortions than with conditions inherent in markets themselves—the complex agency relationships and information asymmetries associated with modern production organizations (Berle and Means 1968; March and Simon 1958; Alchian and Demsetz 1972; Stiglitz 1982). To the extent that modern firms intersect with myriad agency relationships—whether between dispersed owners and managers within the firm's boundaries or creditors and debtors across those boundaries—monitoring of those actually controlling assets becomes difficult, incentives get skewed, and asset-destroying activities arise (Stiglitz and Weiss 1981).

A second intellectual strain, one that may be termed "market as salvation," posits an entirely different set of assumptions and causal mechanisms. In this view, the firm, with its given constellation of assets, precedes the market and in some sense enjoys a privileged position over the market (Amsden 2001). In particular, the modern firm—the large production organization—is envisioned not only as a repository of vast tacit knowledge and innovative capacity, but also as the key nexus for extended supplier networks and local economies (Chandler 1990; Chandler and Hikino 1997; Amsden 2001). As such, the large firm is accorded intrinsic value separable from the market's selection process. Innovation and development are understood as driven not through the rise of upstarts, but rather through the evolution and sustenance of established incumbents (Schumpeter 1976).[5] The firm, particularly the modern industrial conglomerate, becomes the linchpin for the market, rather than vice versa.

Similarly, the market becomes a treatment applied to the preexisting producer, the idea being that markets, through the mechanisms of private property and competition, create incentives at the microlevel (whether for the individual or the complex organization) for the maximization of productivity (Smith 1985). The producer, assumed to have inherent organizational value and latent commercial potential, realizes its potential through exposure to the incentives of the market. This perspective appeared in much of the literature advocating rapid privatization in the early phase of Russia's postsocialist transition (Boycko, Shleifer, and Vishny 1995; World Bank 1995). To the extent that markets are permitted to function, we should, in this view, witness increasing efficiency, increasing specialization, and better performance for all producers.

Market as selection suggests that firm-level incentives are inseparable from, and indeed can be understood only as emanating from, the system-wide process of "creative destruction." Market as salvation alternatively suggests that market incentives, by encouraging firms to maximize efficiency, obviate (or at least reduce the likelihood of) such destruction. In this latter view, if selection begins spontaneously to operate—if losers start to appear, particularly on a grand scale—then something is assumed to have interfered with the market, be it politicization, insufficient liberalization, or excessive regulation. Economic distress is associated not with market failure, but rather with government failure (Shleifer and Vishny 1998).

As illustrated by figure 18.2, differing assumptions about fundamental market function lead to differing assessments of what outcomes actually constitute economic rationality. Such assessments, though, underpin the observer's determination of the degree to which a particular economic outcome represents a problem requiring policy redress, and the observer's expectation that a particular kind of policy will lead to a viable solution.

As argued earlier, these assumptions are often tacit, widely shared across a given society and quite entrenched. In China today, virtually all citizens believe in the market, but the question is what kind of market they actually believe in. The Chinese approach, again in a manner often found in other market systems, tends to be dichotomous. For situations in which agency relationships tend to be absent or at a minimum—for firms with concentrated and generally local ownership, relatively few employees, virtually no employees with governmentally provided social welfare entitlements, and few formal credit relationships—the Chinese government, particularly the center, has long adopted a market as selection perspective.[6] For at least two decades now, considerable churning (enterprise entry and exit) has been tolerated on the peripheries of the economy, which, perhaps not surprisingly, have also constituted the highest growth portions of the system (Naughton 1996; Qian and Xu

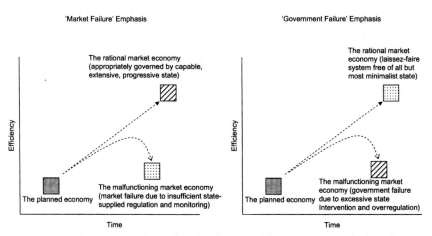

Figure 18.2   Alternative Notions of Rational Postsocialist Transition: Which Path to Rationality? Which Market Endpoint?

1993). In the 1980s and early 1990s, much of this entry and churning occurred among *xiangzhen qiye* ("township and village" enterprises), smaller rural industrial firms formally owned by local governments (Oi 1992, 1999). In recent years, as the popularity of *xiangzhen qiye* has waned, the pattern has shifted over to the emergent private sector (Gregory et al. 2000).

Alternatively, for situations in which agency relationships are complex and extensive—cases involving large firms with dispersed ownership, ownership extending out to the entire national population, large workforces that enjoy substantial government entitlements, key positions within broad supply chains, and extensive credit relationships—policy makers adopt a more distinctly market as salvation orientation. In their treatment of such firms, they place far greater emphasis on the inherent value of the organization, the need to tap its inherent commercial capacity, and its overall centrality as driver of national growth (Nolan 1996, 2001). When such firms run into trouble, the conclusion is generally that something unrelated to the market has occurred, something that requires not the dissolution of the firm but rather a policy treatment and more often than not, a policy treatment ostensibly exposing the firm to the market.

The view, though appearing idiosyncratic in today's context, is actually comparable to attitudes prevalent in the United States and much of the rest of the industrialized world through at least the 1960s (Nolan 2001).[7] It is easy to forget that the mainstream emphasis in the United States on smaller, entrepreneurial start-ups—as opposed to traditional large corporations—as drivers of innovation and growth dates back only a decade.

ILLUSTRATIONS FROM THE CHINESE CASE

What evidence exists for a particular Chinese market vision? First, it should be noted that in using terms such as "Chinese vision" or "American understanding," I am asserting neither that entire national populations march lockstep in line with rigid ideologies, nor even that debate within any given country is suppressed. As Fewsmith (2001) argues, rich open debate occurs in China over appropriate economic strategy. Rather, the point is that in many national contexts, certain widely held worldviews—subtle assumptions about cause and effect—frequently pervade all sides of given debates, shape the terms of debate, and often permeate discourse at both the elite and grassroots levels. In China, the overall market conception appears through at least two channels: (1) the phraseology that is used within discussions over reform and (2) the analytical devices that elite and grassroots actors employ to explain particular economic outcomes.

Several examples will perhaps suffice to illustrate the point. The first involves China's initial attempt at financial reform in the early 1980s, and the way in which the results of that are interpreted even today. In 1984, the government, through its policy of *bo gai dai* ("transforming subsidies into loans"), shifted its mode of financing

SOEs from direct budgetary subsidies to interest-bearing loans from state banks (Yi 1994; Xie 1996). The presumption and expectation was that the change in financing method (from "free" subsidies—essentially equity financing—to interest-bearing credits) would create managerial incentives for market-oriented (commercially successful) behavior. Under the policy, however, SOE performance failed to improve, and firms simply ended up amassing vast levels of debt that they had no ability to service.

From the market as selection perspective, this outcome could be considered a success. After all, by attaching a nominal price to capital and thus suggesting an expectation of minimal returns, the policy provided a means of signaling (through shifting enterprise asset–liability ratios and other financial indicators) which firms were showing returns and which were not. The information on which selection could operate was thus established. Presumably, the failure of a firm to meet its financial obligations should have served as a signal that resources should be allocated away from that firm. It would then be up to policy makers to act on these signals.

Yet, approaching from a market as salvation orientation, Chinese policy makers did not interpret *bo gai dai* as successful, and they were anything but willing to follow it up with measures to close failing SOEs. Instead, rising levels of SOE debt, and concomitantly NPLs in state banks, were treated not as indicators of the commercial nonviability of the debtors, but rather as indicators of the inadequacy of the *bo gai dai* policy itself. Hence, large debtors have not been shut down, but instead, time and again, the government has set out on new searches for better policy solutions, ones that can truly *gao huo* ("rejuvenate") the firm and make it market oriented. The response makes sense only to the extent that we believe that the firm somehow precedes the market, embodies some inherent, albeit latent, commercial capacity, and requires only the right treatment to unleash its competitiveness.

These assumptions about cause and effect have pervaded China's twenty-year history of *qiye gaige* (enterprise reform). Historically, the term *qiye gaige* has been used with respect to large producers, and has (even for the most diametrically opposed parties to the debate) involved a quest for treatments to revive firms (Wu 1993). More conservative elements may have argued that the right way was to provide better incentives for managers or reduce social burdens upon the firm as a whole. Moderates may have called for better governance (Zhou 1999a), ownership clarification and the imposition of a *xiandai qiye zhidu* (modern enterprise system). Radicals may have even called for outright ownership transfer, depoliticization, and privatization *(siyouhua* or *minyinghua)*. Yet, for all these disparate views, the debate has revolved around a common assumption that, with the right treatment, the expected outcome across the entire population of firms should be better enterprise performance, not enterprise collapse.

Interestingly, some observers, writing from outside the Chinese context, employ the same assumptions. An entire literature written on SOE reform revolves around the idea that these firms—whether through the maintenance of state ownership or privatization—are somehow reformable, somehow capable of being transformed into commercial competitors (Ramamurti and Vernon 1991; Boycko et al. 1995). The idea, furthermore, is that microlevel reforms will transform the macroenvironment.

A second example involves the Chinese government's contemporary response to the NPL problem. The previous policy of *bo gai dai* involved a switch from equity to debt financing. Ironically, the contemporary response to the travails of *bo gai dai* involves a reversal from debt back to equity. Beginning in 1999, the central government introduced its policy of *zhai zhuan gu* (converting debts to stock shares), debt–equity swaps between state banks, indebted SOEs, and newly created state asset management companies (AMCs) (Zhou 1999a; Beijing University CCER 1999b). The details of the policy are complex and somewhat convoluted, but the basic idea is that state banks sell off their distressed assets (NPLs to SOEs) at par to AMCs. The AMCs pay for those assets by issuing bonds that are turned over to the banks and that pay an annual coupon of 2.25 percent. The assets (again, debt obligations on the part of SOEs) are then converted by the AMCs into equity stakes, again at par, in the debtor firms (Ma and Fung 2002; Langlois 2000; Steinfeld 2000; Bottelier 2001). The AMC switches from being the firm's creditor to the firm's owner. The immediate result is that AMCs, through their bond issues, take on financial obligations to state banks, and those AMCs at the same time become major shareholders in large industrial firms. Presumably, then, AMCs will be able to reap significant returns from their enterprise assets, and these returns will be passed onward to the state banks. Ideally, the financial system will return to solvency as a result, and state banks will be able to meet their obligations to the ultimate creditors in this whole daisy chain—household depositors.

The policy makes sense only under a particular set of market as salvation assumptions. First, there is the belief that state firms default because they are simply burdened by too much debt. As Chinese managers, banking officials and policy makers frequently assert, SOEs are undercapitalized—their balance sheet has too much debt relative to equity (Zhou 1999a). Once relieved of unceasing debt payments and provided some breathing space, these firms will—with a certain amount of restructuring and upgrading—prove capable of realizing good returns for their AMC owners.

Second, there is the notion that the book value of the distressed asset, in this case an industrial firm, represents some sort of intrinsic meaning, a value that somehow comes prior to—and can be understood as separable from—the value placed on it by buyers in the market. Under that assumption, it made sense for policy designers to have AMCs purchase the distressed assets from banks at absolutely no discount. The related idea is that ultimately outside buyers in the market will come to understand the intrinsic value of the asset (represented by book value) and pay accordingly by purchasing restructured firms from the AMC. The AMCs, then, will have achieved full recovery on their distressed assets, the proceeds will be filtered up through the state banking system, and all the commitments made initially to depositors will be honored at no additional cost to the government, the banks, or the population at large.

Third, continuing the logical flow, the overall notion that divergences between the book and market value of an asset are essentially fleeting temporal situations, representing neither serious capital misallocation nor any real destruction of assets. So, for situations in which banks or AMCs have high-priced assets on their books, but no outsiders are willing to purchase those assets at that price, the assumption is not that the book value needs to be reduced or that the asset somehow has become permanently degraded (a conclusion that would require somebody paying the difference between book value and market value). Rather, the view is that the market will ultimately catch up, ultimately understand that the assets in their current disposition have value, and ultimately pay the assessed book price. Of course, market as selection would dismiss each of these assumptions, instead arguing that enterprise default indicates low returns and nonviability, regardless of whether financing comes in the form of debt or equity; that assets do not have inherent value separable from that attached to them by potential purchasers in the market; and that long-term divergences between the book and market value suggest real destruction of assets and real capital misallocation, thus necessitating the painful absorption of write-off costs.

Unfortunately, though perhaps not surprisingly, the results of the debt–equity swap program to date have been poor. In 1999, approximately one-third of the Chinese banking system's US$500 billion in distressed loan assets were transferred over to AMCs. Since then, the AMCs are estimated to have disposed of only 35 percent of the assets on their books, and the cash recovery rate in those disposals is estimated at only 17.3 percent of the assets' book value (Holland and Lague 2004). AMCs have held only two international debt auctions since 1999, the most recent being in December 2003. That auction sold less than 10 percent of the US$2.7 billion in assets that were up for offer. The bottom line is that the loan disposal has been lagging and the cash recovery rate low, thus putting liquidity pressures on the AMCs and leaving hundreds of billions of distressed assets sitting in inventory on their books (Ma and Fung 2002).

A final example involves the Chinese government's recently aborted effort to use state assets sales—sales of minority positions in publicly listed SOEs—to recapitalize the nation's severely underfunded pension system (Naughton 2002). When Chinese state firms list on stock exchanges, they issue three types of shares (Green 2003; Tenev and Zhang 2002): tradable shares (available for general purchase by the public), legal person shares (nontradable shares held by domestic enterprises, utilities, banks, and other institutions), and state shares (nontradable shares held by central and local governments). That each type accounts for approximately one-third of the total on China's two stock markets effectively means, as noted earlier, that only a third of the shares on the market are available for public purchase. In this context, the government announced in June 2001 that it would off-load some of its state shares (thus raising the float in the market) and then redirect the proceeds from those sales to other public uses—pension fund recapitalization (Hong Kong Trade Development Council 2001).

The logic is quite similar to the AMC debt–equity swaps noted earlier. Insiders would make a determination about which assets (SOEs) had value, and then a scheme would be introduced by which the general public could purchase a claim on the future revenue streams of those assets (though no real claim over control, since only minority stakes were being offered). In the 1999 debt–equity swap program, the sale of future revenue streams through public listing would come only late in the game—presumably after some time was spent under AMC tutelage—and the proceeds would go to the banking system. In the 2001 state asset sell-down plan, the claims would be sold immediately and the proceeds go to a nationally pooled pension fund (Wang 2001). Although the ultimate denouement of the AMC situation has yet to be seen, that of the state asset off-loading program was reached quite rapidly. Within three months of its inception, the program was summarily canceled, as the government faced collapsing share prices and considerable popular outcry.

From the market as selection perspective, it is easy to understand what happened. Insiders did what insiders always do: they overestimated the value of the assets in their possession (interviews, senior Chinese policy architects, Beijing 2000). Outsiders, in turn, did what outsiders always do: they discounted because of concerns about asset quality, large asset inventories, and problematic control rights. What insiders felt constituted a terrific opportunity for the public to tap into future revenue streams was apparently—and understandably—perceived by the public as a dubious effort by the state to unload its contingent liabilities on them. The market, from this perspective, worked, for it confirmed that state assets have little intrinsic value. State assets sales, from this view, cannot resolve China's banking and pension problems, because the problems stem from the low and steadily degrading quality of state assets themselves.

Chinese officials, employing market as salvation assumptions, provide an entirely different take. In their view, there are at least two certainties: first, a certain number of firms within the total SOE population are viable and, second, the people best situated to judge exactly which ones are viable are official insiders (interviews, senior Chinese policy architects, ministerial officials 1999, 2000, 2003). Should outsiders in the market fail to agree with this judgment, as they apparently did in the autumn of 2001, the problem stems not from the quality of the assets but rather from the inadequate knowledge of purchasers or structural irregularities in the market. Hence, potential investors are described as excessively skittish, and the market as excessively volatile or immature. The problem is with the market, not the assets.

Such explanations have been posited not just by Chinese officials, but also by ostensibly impartial experts from the global policy community. On numerous occasions, outsiders either endorsed the logic beyond the state asset off-loading plan or attributed the program's failure to excessively narrow capital markets, inadequate market transparency and regulation, and excessively speculative investors. Their point, in other words, seems to be that if only more channels were provided for the off-loading of state assets (e.g., through bond markets or expanded, more liquid stock markets), and if only regulators could ensure better information flows to investors, all the pent-up money seeking good investment opportunities in China would flock to the state asset sell-downs. Even better, such sell-downs, by shifting the ownership structure of the firms involved and bringing in more private investors, would improve governance and rejuvenate performance (James 2001; Zhou 2002; Pitsilis, von Emloh, and Wang 2002). Moreover, all of this could be achieved without any painful paying down of all the previous years of capital misallocation—a misallocation signified, ironically, by the very existence of so many state firms and the very size of the nation's banking and pension problems.

CONCLUSION

Despite an impressive record of growth, the Chinese economy in recent years has exhibited substantial and persistent problems of capital misallocation. Such problems have been underscored by repeated governmental efforts at bank recapitalization and persistently high levels of NPLs in the system. Inextricably linked with these phenomena have been poor growth outcomes and high levels of volatility in China's securities markets, and disappointing performance outcomes among Chinese AMCs.

In this chapter, in explaining these interlinked financial outcomes within the specific context of China, I have sought to make three broader points. First, institutional change and related economic outcomes are deeply impacted by societally shared assumptions about market function, assumptions that may differ across societies and historical periods. In the Chinese case, a particular interpretation of how markets function has coincided with a period of intense faith in the ameliorative power of markets more generally. Second, assumptions about market function, though subject to change and evolution over the long term, often prove sticky in the near term. Thus, they lead actors consistently to diagnose problems in particular ways and adopt routinized solutions, even as those solutions—at least to outsiders— appear increasingly ineffectual. In the Chinese case, these routinized solutions have led to repeated bailouts of commercially nonviable banks and enterprises.

Finally, and most importantly in terms of the argument's ramifications beyond China, that assumptions count should not be taken to mean that economic actors, through idiosyncratic thinking, somehow misconstrue an objectively correct, theoretically indisputable model of market function. Rather, assumptions can and do play such a prominent role in guiding interpretation and behavior precisely because tremendous uncertainty exists—including at the theoretical level—regarding the fundamental operation of markets. In the world of ideas, just as in the world of practice, competing and fundamentally irreconcilable frameworks for conceptualizing market function abound, intermingle, and coexist. That they do so should make us suspicious both of claims of the existence of a unitary economic rationale and scholarly analyses depicting institutional outcomes as departures from that rationale.

NOTES

1. Dai Xianglong, then governor of China's central bank, publicly stated in 1997 that 24 percent of outstanding loans in the banking system were nonperforming and 5–6 percent were unrecoverable (*Guoji jinrong xiaoxi bao* 1998).

2. By "market function," I mean the mechanisms and processes through which the market operates to achieve some sort of economic outcome. Conceptions regarding market functions, therefore, often relate to both the processes by which the market operates and the outcome that the market ultimately achieves.

3. Research in 1994 was conducted in my capacity as an affiliate of the Institute of Economics, Chinese Academy of Social Sciences, Beijing. Interviews during that period—focusing primarily on issues of heavy industrial restructuring and enterprise financing—were conducted in Beijing, Shanghai, Liaoning, Jiangsu, and Anhui. Research in 1999 and 2000 was conducted in my capacity as a visiting scholar at the China Center for Economic Research, Beijing University. The eighty-two formal interviews in that period—focusing primarily on the problem of NPL resolution, debt–equity swaps, and asset management company (AMC) operation—were conducted in Beijing, Chongqing, Fujian, Shenzhen, and Guangdong. The aim of the interviews was initially to grasp the operation of the policy-making and policy-implementation process for a major national program, the effort in the wake of the Asian financial crisis to tackle China's domestic problem of distressed bank assets through debt–equity swaps. Hence interviews tended to be semistructured and open-ended, with questions requiring the respondent to narrowly describe his or her daily involvement in the policy program. Opinions regarding the overall advisability of the program were not directly solicited. However, respondents were asked to explain how the program at their level of interaction works, what performance outcomes at the firm level were likely to obtain, and on what terms success should be understood and measured. As noted, respondents ranged from senior officials at the national headquarters of banks and AMCs, to banking and AMC officials at the municipal level, current and former managers of firms participating in debt resolution programs, and lower-level employees in those firms.

4. Debate exists in the literature regarding the actual financial performance of Chinese SOEs (state-owned enterprises). A more positive assessment of SOE performance generally can be found in Lo (1999), and a more optimistic perspective on China's large enterprise groups can be found in Keister (1998, 2000).

5. Note the differences between Schumpeter's 1942 perspective and his 1911 views cited earlier.

6. Along similar lines, Walder (1995) argues that the center has imposed hard budgets on local governments and firms owned by those governments.

7. Well into the 1980s and early 1990s, the emphasis on Japan's model of big corporations (and cooperative strategies between government and firm) persisted in the United States. For example, see Vogel (1979) and Thurow (1992).

REFERENCES

Alchian, A., and H. Demsetz. 1972. "Production, Information Costs, and Economic Organization." *American Economic Review* 62, no. 5: 777–795.

Amsden, A. 2001. *The Rise of the Rest*. New York: Oxford University Press.

Baglole, J. 2004. "China's Bank Bailouts May Not Be Enough." *Wall Street Journal Europe*, January 14.

Bates, R. 1981. *Markets and States in Tropical Africa*. Berkeley: University of California Press.

Beijing University China Center for Economic Research (CCER). Macroeconomics Group. 1999a. *Hong-guan zhengci tiaozheng yu jianchi shichang quxiang* [Macro-policy adjustment and maintaining market orientation]. Beijing: Beijing University Press.

Beijing University China Center for Economic Research (CCER). 1999b. "Dangdai zhai zhuan gu mianling de zhuyao wenti" [Major issues in contemporary debt-equity swap]. *Jingji shehui tizhi bijiao* [Comparative Economic Systems] 6: 18–28.

Berger, S., and R. Dore, eds. 1996. *National Diversity and Global Capitalism*. Ithaca, NY: Cornell University Press.

Berle, A., and G. Means. 1968. *The Modern Corporation and Private Property*. New York: Harcourt, Brace & World.

Bottelier, P. 2001. "China's Domestic Debts." Paper presented at the Conference on Financial Sector Reform in China, Harvard University, Cambridge, September 11–13.

Boycko, M., A. Shleifer, and R. Vishny. 1995. *Privatizing Russia*. Cambridge: MIT Press.

Broadman, H. 2001. "The Businesses of the Chinese State." *World Economy* 24, no. 7: 849–875.

Carruthers, B., and T. Halliday. 1998. *Rescuing Business*. Oxford: Oxford University Press.

Chandler, A. 1990. *Scale and Scope*. Cambridge, MA: Harvard University Press.

Chandler, A., and T. Hikino. 1997. "The Large Industrial Enterprise and the Dynamics of Modern Economic Growth." In A. Chandler, F. Amatori, and T. Hikino, eds., *Big Business and the Wealth of Nations*, 24–57. Cambridge: Cambridge University Press.

Christensen, C. 1997. *The Innovator's Dilemma*. Cambridge, MA: Harvard Business School Press.

Claessens, C., et al., eds. 2001. *Resolution of Financial Distress: An International Perspective on the Design of Bankruptcy*. Washington, DC: World Bank.

Dickson, B. 2003. *Red Capitalists in China*. New York: Cambridge University Press.

Dobbin, F. 1994. *Forging Industrial Policy*. New York: Cambridge University Press.

Fang, X. 2001. "Reconstructing the Micro-Foundation of China's Financial Sector." Paper presented at the Conference on Financial Sector Reform in China, Harvard University, Cambridge, September 11–13.

Fewsmith, J. 1999. "China and the WTO: The Politics behind the Agreement." *NBR Analysis* 10, no. 5.

———. 2001. *China since Tiananmen*. New York: Cambridge University Press.

Fukuyama, F. 1995. *Trust: The Social Virtues and the Creation of Prosperity*. New York: Free Press.

Giles, J., A. Park, and F. Cai. 2003. "How Has Economic Restructuring Affected China's Urban Workers?" Paper submitted to the *Journal of Economic Behavior and Organizations*.

Green, S. 2003. *China's Stockmarket: A Guide to Progress, Players, and Prospects*. London: Economist.

Gregory, N., S. Tenev, and D. Wagle. 2000. *China's Emerging Private Enterprises: Prospects for the New Century*. Washington, DC: World Bank.

Guoji jinrong xiaoxi bao [International Financial News] 1998. January 9.

Hall, P., ed. 1989. *The Political Power of Economic Ideas*. Princeton, NJ: Princeton University Press.

Hall, P., and D. Soskice, eds. 2001. *Varieties of Capitalism*. New York: Oxford University Press.

Hart, O. 2000. *Different Approaches to Bankruptcy.* Working Paper 7921. Cambridge, MA: National Bureau of Economic Research.

Havrylyshyn, O., and D. McGettigan. 1999. *Privatization in Transition Countries.* Working Paper WP/99/6. Washington, DC: International Monetary Fund.

Hayek, F. 1960. *The Constitution of Liberty.* London: Routledge.

Hirschman, A. 1963. *Journeys toward Progress.* Garden City, NY: Doubleday.

Holland, T., and D. Lague. 2004. "Wasteful Transfusion." *Far Eastern Economic Review,* January 22.

Hong Kong Trade Development Council. 2001. "State Council Unveiled Rules for Sale of State Shares." www.tdctrade.com/econforum/citi/010603.htm.

Hu, A. 1999. "Kuaru xinshiji de zui da tiaozhan: Wo guo jinru gaoshiye jieduan" [The greatest challenge of the new century: China enters the stage of high unemployment]. Beijing: Chinese Academy of Sciences/Tsinghua University Joint Center for Chinese Studies.

Hu, F. 2004. "Restarting China's Bank Reforms." *Asian Wall Street Journal,* January 13.

Huang, Y. 2003. *Selling China.* New York: Cambridge University Press.

Hussain, A. 2000. *Social Welfare in China in the Context of Three Transitions.* Working Paper 66. Center for Research on Economic Development and Policy Reform, Stanford University.

Jackson, T. 1986. *The Logic and Limits of Bankruptcy Law.* Cambridge, MA: Harvard University Press.

James, E. 2001. *How Can China Solve Its Old Age Security Problem?* Working Paper 15/01. Moncalieri, Italy: Center for Research on Pensions and Welfare Policies.

Keister, L. 1998. "Engineering Growth: Business Group Structure and Firm Performance in China's Transition Economy." *American Journal of Sociology* 104, no. 2: 404–440.

———. 2000. *Chinese Business Groups: The Structure and Impact of Interfirm Relations during Economic Development.* New York: Oxford University Press.

Kindleberger, C. 1996. *Manias, Panics, and Crashes: A History of Financial Crises.* New York: Wiley.

Kornai, J. 2000. "Ten Years after the Road to a Free Economy." Paper presented at the World Bank Annual Bank Conference on Development Economics, Washington, DC, April 18–20.

Langlois, J. 2000. "Taxing China's Banks into Oblivion." *Wall Street Journal,* October 12.

La Porta, R., F. Lopez-de-Silanes, A. Shleifer, A., and R. Vishny. 1998. "Law and Finance." *Journal of Political Economy* 106, no. 6: 1113–1155.

Lardy, N. 1998. *China's Unfinished Economic Revolution.* Washington, DC: Brookings Institution.

———. 2000. "When Will China's Financial System Meet China's Needs?" Paper presented at the Conference on Policy Reform in China, Stanford University, November 18–20, 1999. Revised February 2000.

Lin, J. 2004. *Lessons of China's Transition from a Planned Economy to a Market Economy.* Working Paper E2004001. China Center for Economic Research, Peking University.

Lin, J., F. Cai, and Z. Li. 1990. *The China Miracle.* Hong Kong: Chinese University Press.

Lo, D. 1997. *Market and Institutional Regulation in Chinese Industrialization, 1978–1994.* New York: Macmillan.

———. 1999. "Re-appraising the Performance of China's State-Owned Industrial Enterprises, 1980–1996." *Cambridge Journal of Economics* 23, no. 6: 693–718.

Locke, R. 1995. *Remaking the Italian Economy.* Ithaca, NY: Cornell University Press.

Lou, J., et al. 1998. *Zhongguo guoyou zhuanye yinhang shangyehua gaige* [Commercialization reform of China's state-owned specialized banks]. Beijing: China Financial Publishing House.

Ma, G., and B. Fung. 2002. *China's Asset Management Corporations.* Working Paper 115. Basel: Bank for International Settlement.

March, J., and H. Simon. 1958. *Organizations.* New York: Wiley.

Naughton, B. 1996. *Growing Out of the Plan.* Cambridge: Cambridge University Press.

———. 2002. "Selling Down the State Share." *China Leadership Monitor,* no. 1, pt. 2.

Naughton, B., ed. 1997. *The China Circle.* Washington, DC: Brookings Institution.

Nolan, P. 1996. "Large Firms and Industrial Reform in Former Planned Economies: The Case of China." *Cambridge Journal of Economics* 20, no. 1: 1–29.

———. 2001. *China and the Global Business Revolution.* London: Palgrave.

North, D. 1990. *Institutions, Institutional Change, and Economic Performance.* New York: Cambridge University Press.

Oi, J. 1992. "Fiscal Reform and the Economic Foundations of Local State Corporatism." *World Politics* 45, no. 1: 99–126.

———. 1999. *Rural China Takes Off.* Berkeley: University of California Press.

Perkins, D. 1994. "Completing China's Move to the Market." *Journal of Economic Perspectives* 8, no. 2: 21–46.

Pitsilis, E., D. von Emloh, and Y. Wang. 2002. "Filling China's Pension Gap." *McKinsey Quarterly* 2.

Putnam, R. 1993. *Making Democracy Work.* Princeton, NJ: Princeton University Press.

Qian, Y., and C. Xu. 1993. "Why China's Economic Reforms Differ." *Economics of Transition* 1, no. 2: 137–170.

Ramamurti, R., and R. Vernon, eds. 1991. *Privatization and Control of State-Owned Enterprises.* Washington, DC: World Bank.

Restall, H. 2003. "Forget Overheating, Stop China's Waste of Capital." *Asian Wall Street Journal,* December 19.

Roland, G. 2000. *Transition and Economics.* Cambridge: MIT Press.

Schumpeter, J. [1911] 1968. *The Theory of Economic Development: An Inquiry into Profits, Capital, Credit, Interest, and Business Cycles.* Cambridge, MA: Harvard University Press.

———. [1942] 1976. *Capitalism, Socialism, and Democracy.* New York: Harper & Row.

Shirk, S. 1993. *The Political Logic of Economic Reform in China.* Berkeley: University of California Press.

Shleifer, A., and D. Treisman. 2000. *Without a Map.* Cambridge: MIT Press.

Shleifer, A., and R. Vishny. 1998. *The Grabbing Hand: Government Pathologies and Their Cures.* Cambridge, MA: Harvard University Press.

Smith, A. [1776] 1985. *An Inquiry into the Nature and Causes of the Wealth of Nations.* New York: Random House.

Solinger, D. 1999. *Contesting Citizenship in Urban China.* Berkeley: University of California Press.

State Statistical Bureau. 2000. *China Statistical Yearbook 2000.* Beijing: China Statistical Publishing House.

Steinfeld, E. 1998. *Forging Reform in China.* New York: Cambridge University Press.

————. 2000. "Free Lunch or Last Supper." *China Business Review*, July–August, 22–27.

————. 2001. "Chinese Enterprise Development and the Challenge of Global Integration." Paper prepared for the East Asia Prospects Study, World Bank, Washington, DC.

Stiglitz, J. 1982. "Ownership, Control, and Efficient Markets." In K. Boyer and W. Shepherd, eds., *Economic Regulation: Essays in Honor of James R. Nelson*. Ann Arbor: University of Michigan Press.

————. 1999. "Whither Reform?" Paper presented at the World Bank Annual Bank Conference on Development Economics, Washington, DC, April 28–30.

Stiglitz, J., and A. Weiss. 1981. "Credit Rationing in Markets with Imperfect Information." *American Economic Review* 71, no. 3: 393–410.

Swidler, A. 2001. *Talk of Love: How Culture Matters*. Chicago: University of Chicago Press.

Tenev, S., and C. Zhang. 2002. *Corporate Governance and Enterprise Reform in China*. Washington, DC: World Bank.

Thurow, L. 1992. *Head to Head*. New York: Morrow.

Vogel, E. 1979. *Japan as Number One*. Cambridge, MA: Harvard University Press.

Wade, R. 1990. *Governing the Market*. Princeton, NJ: Princeton University Press.

Walder, A. 1995. "Local Governments as Industrial Firms: An Organizational Analysis of China's Transitional Economy." *American Journal of Sociology* 101, no. 2: 263–301.

Wang, X. 2001. "China's Pension System Reform and Capital Market Development." Paper presented at the Conference on Financial Sector Reform in China, Harvard University, Cambridge, September 11–13.

Weber, M. 1958. *The Protestant Ethic and the Spirit of Capitalism*. New York: Scribner's.

Woo, W. 1999. "The Real Reasons for China's Growth." *China Journal*, January 14, 115–137.

World Bank. 1995. *Bureaucrats in Business*. Oxford: Oxford University Press.

————. 1999. *China: Weathering the Storm and Learning the Lessons*. Washington, DC: World Bank.

Wu, J. 1993. *Dazhongxing qiye gaige* [Large and medium-size enterprise reform]. Tianjin: Tianjin Renmin Chubanshe.

————. 1999. *Dangdai zhongguo jingji gaige* [Contemporary Chinese economic reform]. Shanghai: Yuandong.

Xie, P. 1996. *Zhongguo jinrong zhidu de xuanze* [Choice of China's financial system]. Shanghai: Shanghai Yuandong.

Xinhua News Service. 2001. "Jiang Zemin's Speech Marking 80th CPC Founding Anniversary." July 1.

Yi, G. 1994. *Money, Banking, and Financial Markets in China*. Boulder, CO: Westview.

Yusuf, S., K. Nabeshima, and D. Perkins. 2004. *Under New Ownership: Privatizing China's State-Owned Enterprises*. Washington, DC: World Bank.

Zhongguo nanfang zhoumo. 2002. "Zhongguo shiji shiyelu yi da jingjiexian" [China's real unemployment rate has reached the warning point], June 13.

Zhou, X. 1999a. "Guanyu zhai zhuan gu de jige wenti" [Several issues of debt-equity swap]. *Jingji shehui tizhi bijiao* [Comparative Economic Systems] 6: 1–9.

————. 2002. *China's Social Security Reforms: The Institutional Arrangements*. Working Paper. Beijing University, China Center for Economic Research.

Zhou, X. ed. 1999b. *Chongjian yu zaisheng*. Beijing: China Financial Press.

Zhu, R. 1996. "Guoyou qiye shenghua gaige ke burong huan" [No time shall be lost in further reforming state-owned enterprises]. Speech presented at the fourth session of the Eighth National People's Congress. *Renmin ribao* [People's daily], overseas ed., March 11.

Conclusion

China's Reform Deepening

Lowell Dittmer

China's "reform and opening" *(gaige kaifang)* policy, introduced by Deng Xiaoping and his followers at the Third Plenum of the Eleventh Party Congress in December 1978, has been one of the most brilliant success stories in the history of the industrial revolution, even in East Asia, where Japan and the "small tigers" have set impressive growth records of their own. In 1978, the country was one of the poorest in the world. From that year until 2002, the Chinese economy grew at an average 9.3 percent per annum, nearly quadrupling the nation's GDP in two decades. China's "opening to the outside world" was even more impressive. In 1978, China was one of the most isolated countries in the world, with a total foreign trade of only about US$20 billion. By 2003, the amount of goods passing through Chinese ports had increased almost tenfold, making China the world's third biggest trading nation, while the number of tourists had leaped to more than 10 million. China had also overtaken the United States as the world's leading host of foreign direct investment (FDI), creating a vibrant "foreign-invested sector" whose exports amount to about half the nation's total. The Chinese urban middle class, comprising slightly less than 10 percent of the country, has seen its disposable income rise sharply from roughly ¥340 (US$41) in 1978 to nearly ¥6,300 (US$761) in 2000. Chinese Internet users have mushroomed from fewer than 1,000 in 1997 to over 100 million in 2005, second only to the United States, and China now has more than 300 million cell phone users.

Although there are many reasons for this stunning economic breakthrough—including the unleashed entrepreneurial talents of the Chinese people (long repressed in a largely quixotic campaign to radicalize Chinese culture)—the political elite appropriated credit in the name of the enlightened policies promulgated by the Communist party-state. And, in view of the comprehensive powers of that state and

493

the timing of economic expansion following enabling policy changes by the leader-ship, such an interpretation, however self-serving, is in my view quite persuasive in this instance. Despite retaining the chain of ideological and structural continuity to the Maoist period, the reforms launched since 1978 have been so comprehensive they have been likened to a second revolution.[1] Many of the erstwhile socialist cor-nerstones, such as centralized planning and the collective ownership of private prop-erty, have been reconsidered and abandoned.

What were the key reform policies introduced by the party-state to replace the verities it had so boldly discarded? Much like the 1949 revolution to which it has been likened, China's reform did not occur suddenly but in a series of steps, as in the old metaphor "crossing the river by feeling for stones." And as elsewhere in the political world, these changes were adopted partly in response to urgent domestic political–economic expediency, partly in response to international pressure, and only partly in fulfillment of the leadership's visionary design of their nation's future.

The most momentous paradigm shift was unquestionably the change from "con-tinuous revolution" to "reform," usually dated from the Third Plenum of the Elev-enth Party Congress in December 1978. The era of reform and opening to the outside world has introduced at least three new parameters of change, which have lasted to the present day.

First, in contrast to Mao's "politics in command," economic development was given a much higher priority ranking on the nation's political agenda. In order to endow it with full legitimacy, this new priority ranking was given ideological expres-sion in a number of doctrinal reformulations: the forces of production (i.e., those contributing directly to increased productivity) were conceived to be more impor-tant at this stage of history than the relations of production (notably class and class struggle, involving fights over redistribution). This stage of history was not only socialism (as opposed to communism), but the primary stage of socialism, when many admitted vestiges of capitalism, such as the market economy, unequal income distribution, and other social inequities, might continue to exist—and this early stage could be expected to last a hundred years or longer. The market was at first accepted as a provisory expedient supplementing the plan, then finally embraced as a socialist market economy in 1992. Private property was ideologically accepted more slowly, but ultimately won legitimacy in a constitutional revision adopted by the Ninth National People's Congress (NPC) in March 1999. Foreign policy was also affected, as the reform regime discovered that a climactic world war between capital-ism and socialism was no longer inevitable and that the PRC could hence stop exporting revolution and foster relations of "peace and development" with other countries.[2]

Second, reform was characterized by greater emphasis on institutionalization and social stability. Whereas institutionalization was viewed with disdain and mistrust by the first generation of revolutionaries, who launched one mass campaign after another leading up to the Great Proletarian Cultural Revolution, the greatest upheaval of all, the reformers viewed the social disruptiveness and outbreaks of violence and vandalism unleashed by campaigns with more misgivings. Turbulent class struggles were disavowed, intellectuals and children of "black" class categories became honorable members of the working class, and the public posting of big-character posters was constitutionally prohibited. Although the Deng Xiaoping leadership continued to launch mass campaigns in the early 1980s (e.g., the drives against "bourgeois liberalization" or "ill winds"), these typically lasted only a few months before being brought to an early end. After one unwelcome by-product of this campaign culture, the series of mass-initiated movements in the mid-1980s culminating in the 1989 Tiananmen protest, was brought to a sanguinary end, the regime avoided mass movements altogether, preferring more sedate mass celebrations (such as the well-regimented parades on national holidays). "Stability supersedes all" *[wending ya dao yiqie],* as Deng put it. Elite gatherings have likewise become much more carefully regulated, now meeting on a regular schedule with elaborately prearranged consensus on an agenda leaving room for few surprises. Such discipline has been imposed on the public appearances and speeches of top leaders that "protocol evidence" of factional splits has become difficult to find.

Third, there has been a steady deradicalization and rationalization of political power, particularly at the core of the dictatorship, the party center (i.e., the Central Committee and its Politburo). This may be attributed to at least two processes: One is through the division of power, either within the center itself, as in the assignment of greater responsibility to the NPC or other bodies still controlled by the center but formally detached from it; or through the decentralization/devolution of power to regional and local levels. Once power has been divided, it is difficult for leadership to act arbitrarily or radically, as procedures for preliminary circulation of policy drafts among wider and wider circles of elites become institutionalized. To further limit elite power, China's revolutionary veterans were retired between the Twelfth and Sixteenth Party Congresses (1982–2002) and the old system of lifetime tenure superseded by term limits and age limits. Second is increasing elite constraint via a process of meritocratic self-screening. This takes place by progressively raising the formal educational credentials for vertical mobility, the assumption being that a highly trained and credentialed elite is likely, ceteris paribus, to act with greater political predictability than a band of professional revolutionaries. Previously cadres were recruited and promoted based on two criteria, "red" (activism) and "expert"— now, increasingly, only one. Both of these innovations represent a trend about which the officialdom has clearly been quite ambivalent, but this process of what we might call authoritarian self-limitation, once in training, has proved difficult to reverse.

Although the PRC leadership has consistently read from the same reform playbook since 1978, there have been at least two acts in the play, which correspond, not entirely coincidentally, with major leadership transitions. The first began in the early 1980s, with the rise of Deng Xiaoping and his yeomen, pushing aside the neo-Maoist leadership of Hua Guofeng and the "small Gang of Four" and setting forth their own agenda. The second period began with the Tiananmen protest movement and its violent suppression in June 1989 and took coherent form during the political reevaluation undertaken in its wake, culminating in Deng Xiaoping's spring 1992 "voyage to the south" and formalized at the Fourteenth Party Congress: reform must continue, the leaders decided, but not as before—a tune-up would be necessary. Though less contentiously than the first, Maoist succession, this second period also began with a leadership transition, resulting in the rise of Jiang Zemin and his followers, sometimes called the "Shanghai gang."

Whereas our chief concern here is with this more recent period of "deep" reform, because the problems encountered during early reform to some extent set the agenda for deep reform (just as reform itself represented a reaction to Cultural Revolution radicalism), a preliminary survey of the first decade of reform may be useful. Reform began in the countryside, with the introduction of the household responsibility system whereby land was returned to individual peasant families for them to cultivate as they deemed fitting and profitable, selling their above-quota crops on spontaneously generated free markets, and in 1984 reform moved into the cities with the devolution of power to local authorities to retain profits and run factories and other economic establishments with much greater autonomy, all of which resulted in the marketization of (at least) retail prices. The results in the countryside were strikingly successful in boosting agricultural output while at once raising peasant incomes substantially for the first time since the early 1960s.[3] The shift to urban industrial reform after 1984 raised more complicated issues, but also increased production impressively, particularly in the myriad township and village enterprises (TVEs) that benefited from the shift from heavy to light industry. Yet, as the 1989 Tiananmen confrontation attests, there were also problems.

The main ones include the following. First, the "emancipation of the mind" that the leadership initially sanctioned in response to the ideological straitjacket imposed during the Cultural Revolution resulted in an intellectual market prone to follow exciting new ideas (e.g., the concept of political alienation that wafted in from Eastern European neo-Marxist thinkers), quickly and monolithically, resulting in a demand surge that threatened to flood the system. Moreover, in this high point of Sino-American strategic cooperation against Soviet "social imperialism," many of these ideas came from the West, a far more liberal (and, to orthodox Chinese Marxists, libertine) culture, culminating in such media fantasies as the 1988 *River Elegy* documentary that attributed China's historical lag mainly to its walling off all foreign influences. This surge mentality was so threatening because new ideas were immediately translated into action implications, giving rise to mass youth protest movements, to which officialdom could not immediately respond with the demanded reforms. Embarrassed and threatened by these movements, the leadership typically cracked down on the protesters.[4]

Second, the contraction of central planning and unleashing of economic control over the economy to autonomous agricultural and industrial actors also resulted in a primitive commodity and capital market without effective central fiscal controls, resulting in a vicious boom and bust cycle consisting of overinvestment binges followed by the imposition of tight money policy resulting in "hard landings" of unemployment and drastically reduced output. Moreover, there was a tendency for this boom–bust cycle to correlate with and to reinforce the above-mentioned intellectual opening and-closing [fang shou] and its attendant mass movement cycles.

Third, as marketization occurred in the context of shortage (an almost inevitable artifact of central planning), it stimulated inflation. To alleviate the plight of the majority of urban people still living on fixed incomes, the leadership introduced a multitrack pricing system whereby prices still under jurisdiction of the plan would be held constant while market prices could fluctuate with market supply and demand. Thus the same commodity might have different prices depending on the market in which it was sold. Unfortunately, as Ting Gong makes clear, this "dual-track price system" created the possibility of corruption, as cadres with access to the commodities distributed under the plan could buy large quantities of these commodities to "arbitrage" in free markets for much higher prices. Marketization thus coincided not only with inflation but with increasing corruption [guan dao].

Fourth, although the reform leadership initially seemed politically homogeneous, several informal elite cleavages manifested themselves in the course of navigating the clips and shoals of reform, looming menacingly as the issue of Deng's retirement arose in the late 1980s. One cleavage was policy based, splitting "radical reformers" bent on speedy and comprehensive reform from the "moderate reformers" or "conservatives" who mistrusted the market and sought to preserve ideological fundamentals and the party's hold on power. A second cleavage, coinciding to some extent with the first, split the first-generation revolutionary veterans, many of whom had been pushed into nominal retirement, from the younger generation now holding a majority within the Politburo. Their majority was, however, formal but not actual, for their seniors continued to wield veto-proof informal influence. Deng Xiaoping mediated between these two coalitions. These splits were useful in helping structure the policy-making conversation. But as polarization grew in the late 1980s, elite disagreements rigidified, aggravating the investment and movement cycles punctuating social equilibrium.

All of these problems came to a head in the large and spontaneous protest movement that arose in Beijing in April-May 1989 and quickly spread to many other Chinese cities. Inflation (and attendant corruption) peaked in the summer of 1988; thus further reforms were suspended while the regime threw the brakes on the economy, in the context of which intellectual debate intensified, followed as usual by student mass activism. This movement, according to most observers, posed no threat of violent overthrow of the regime, nor did it (as alleged by Central Committee documents at the time) really throw the capital into "chaos," for the protesters created their own miniature government to maintain order. Yet its peaceful and reasonable facade made it all the more difficult to repress, and it came (in the eyes of the authorities) to comprise the greatest threat to legitimacy the regime had faced since the Cultural Revolution. The leadership felt vindicated in its outlook by the fall of fraternal Eastern European regimes within months to similar such popular uprisings. As prologue to the self-dissolution of international communism as a "pole" in the global Cold War, the Tiananmen "incident" stimulated a closed but sober and thorough rethinking of China's reform experience. The leadership agreed not to reverse but to "deepen" reform. The policies unveiled in the following decade were to reveal in detail what this entailed.

To eliminate the 1980s oscillation between opening and closing and the attendant cycle of mass movements followed by governmental crackdowns, the regime undertook several measures. First, elite factionalism was largely suppressed, as Cheng and White relate in greater detail; this would be a more disciplined, centralized regime, led by a unified political elite. The split between radical reform and moderate groupings was effaced by two factors: First, of course, Zhao Ziyang and the reform grouping he led were largely purged from the leadership. Second, by adopting the "socialist market economy" as an explicit model and therewith completing economic marketization and privatization, and by opening the economy to international markets to an unprecedented extent, the radical reform agenda was essentially coopted. Thereafter, as Dittmer and Wu note, economic policy was no longer a political football in factional disputes, but formulated more strictly according to economic criteria. In place of the intellectual opening and closing of the 1980s that had stimulated cyclical student movements came a more consistent repression of open dissent, shifting however from the spectacularly violent repressive tactics of June 1989 (which incited an international backlash) to a more discreet regimen of detentions and involuntary emigration.

These countercyclical policies were reinforced by a series of measures designed to ensure social stability. Vertical discipline was enforced by a major augmentation of the military budget, maintaining a series of double-digit budgetary increases throughout the 1990s, along with a similar bolstering of the internal security apparatus. Along with the suppression of intellectual dissidence, academic salaries were boosted substantially and selected policy intellectuals were granted consultative relationships with the policy-making elite. Higher education also expanded vigorously after the Fifteenth Party Congress, resulting in a threefold increase in college students from 1998 to 2002 (giving China the world's second largest college student population after the United States). As the chapters by Dickson and Saich tell us in much richer detail, the regime also launched a series of drives designed to bring the nongovernmental organizations (NGOs) that had spread like wildfire in the 1980s under the organizational control of the party. The Western "bourgeois" ill wind that had exerted such an undermining influence throughout the 1980s was to some extent countered by the regime's campaign against "peaceful evolution," which blamed not only Tiananmen but the collapse of European communism on an insidiously successful American campaign to promote internal decay. But the longer-term solution, as Joseph Fewsmith relates in his grand overview of political and intellectual trends, was a new focus on the cultivation of Chinese patriotism or nationalism, in the context of which many of the cultural icons once smashed in the Cultural Revolution (such as Confucius, or patriotic dynastic officials like Zeng Guofan) were disinterred and restored to positions of honor. Although *Farewell to Revolution*, a book published abroad by exiled dissidents, was of course repudiated, the Jiang Zemin regime had to a considerable extent shifted what Baogang Guo calls the regime's "legitimacy of origin" from revolution to tradition.[5] Invocation of the Confucian virtues of harmony, forbearance, and respect for authority were more conducive to stability than continuing revolution and class struggle. International politics conspired to reinforce China's turning away from the West, which had applied sanctions and seemed bent on isolating and containing China in its appalled reaction to the Tiananmen crackdown.

Fundamental to the new order was a clear separation of politics from the economy; while reform could resume apace in the economic arena, politics would henceforth be sequestered from international cultural trends, economic vicissitudes, and social movements. A new social contract was forged at the beginning of the 1990s, in which the regime agreed to withdraw from the economy, giving market forces full sway, in return for which the people (including erstwhile party or government officials) could plunge into commerce *[xia hai]* but were then expected to stay out of politics. Marketization of retail prices was completed in the early 1990s and privatization, despite ideological controversy, was thrust boldly forward in the 1997–1998 reforms. The urban housing sector was privatized, the military industrial sector was privatized, and under the slogan "grasp the big, drop the small," small and medium-size state-owned enterprises (SOEs) were privatized or allowed to be bought out or merged or in the worst case go bankrupt, leaving the state in control of only the largest, strategically vital SOEs (the "commanding heights"). Meanwhile, notwithstanding official rhetoric, democratization was essentially frozen in place. Fortunately the Organic Law permitting "quasi-competitive" village council elections antedated Tiananmen (draft in 1986, finalized in 1998), and it was indeed implemented, creating competitive elections in about a third of China's 2,000-odd counties, according to Tianjian Shi and Kevin O'Brien. But subsequent efforts to expand from the village to the township or to China's urban districts have so far been blocked. Instead, people were encouraged to work hard and get rich, and by 2004 some 30 percent of China's entrepreneurs had joined the party (according to Dickson), a process sanctioned by Jiang Zemin's heralded contribution to the ideological canon, the "three represents," which announced that the CCP no longer represented just the workers and peasants but the advanced productive forces (i.e., the emerging urban middle classes), advanced culture (i.e., China's educated elites), and the interests of the broad masses. This meant class structure was no longer subject to political manipulation (as in Maoist class struggle) but left to the market. And under the "dual hegemony" (i.e., state and market) described by Marc Blecher with regard to the urban proletariat (but applicable to other classes as well), the market became the new faceless master that set wages and working conditions without realistic political recourse. Although the leadership now backed away from "Party-government separation" *[dang zheng fenkai]* as a meaningless distinction without a difference, the attempt to separate Party from enterprise management *[dang qi fenkai]* has continued, Randall Peerenboom assures us, running the SOEs by market principles while transferring regulatory functions to the government. The central leadership, though thus relieved of much economic responsibility by the market, has so much at stake in continuing productivity that its own agenda has become preoccupied with fostering favorable market conditions, as in the 1993–1994 financial reforms that reorganized the state banking sector, revalued the currency, and strengthened the state's fiscal capacity by reorganizing the tax structure.

What emerged from this set of reforms has in many ways been a great success. The economy resumed GDP growth at a very convincing pace following Deng's southern voyage, and although inflation revived along with growth, the 1994 financial reforms enabled the government to take more effective remedial measures, achieving a "soft landing" in 1995–1997, yet without falling victim to the Asian financial crisis that afflicted China's neighbors. Although the business cycle continued, shorn of its elite factional dimension or its intercalation with the (now extinct) mass movement cycle, it became politically innocuous. The academy now reinforced the regime's turn to nationalism with a focus on postmodernism, postcolonialism, political realism, and other analytical approaches far more critical of the West. Although it is perhaps too soon to declare a victor in the ongoing struggle between Internet users and the state apparatus built to police it, one plausible interpretation is that the former may "win" in the long run but that their discourse has become prevalently supportive and "patriotic." Meanwhile the separation of politics from economics has meant that nationalism can successfully coexist with an accelerated opening to the outside world, as foreign trade, foreign direct investment, and tourism have expanded explosively, culminating in China's successful entry into the World Trade Organization at the turn of the millennium.

Will China's rise continue under "deepened" reform, or will it ultimately fall? While this is an oversimplified way of posing the question (perhaps both are true), the scholarship collected here supports the general impression that China will continue to rise for some time, though the current rate of growth cannot be sustained indefinitely. As Steinfeld has noted, the central elite has maintained its focus on national development with unwavering consistency, resisting the protests of the export sector (in 1994) to revalue the currency, resisting popular pressure to reflate the economy (in 1986 or 1989), resisting capture by the exposed agricultural sector or the industrial ministries in order to gain WTO accession in 2001. Although the government has clearly been interested in retaining political control, it has repeatedly demonstrated a willingness to cede control when that seemed useful to enhance production.

Which is not to say China's "rise" will be unproblematic. The financial sector has serious problems even after its reorganization in 1993–1994, continuing to lend almost exclusively to the SOEs, many of which are insufficiently profitable to repay them, giving rise to a high proportion of nonperforming loans (NPLs). One question is why this sector has thus far proved so stubbornly resistant to reform. The answer, according to Steinfeld, seems to consist of a combination of ideological attachments to the "commanding heights," which China hopes to forge into an internationally competitive "Fortune 500," and a concern for the welfare of the industrial workforce. As the banks continue to feed money into a sector that produces excess capacity in a number of industries, giving rise not only to an export boom but to domestic price deflation. While Japan has had somewhat analogous problems with its financial sector, it seems unlikely that China is floating a bubble in danger of bursting, leading to protracted stagnation. Although some bank funding has indeed been diverted into the real estate sector where it has resulted in short-term bubbles, much of this funding is simply a defrayal of welfare and unemployment costs by a different name. The introduction of asset management corporations has proved to be a melioration rather than a cure; perhaps the best hope of forcing the banking sector into greater financial accountability is China's opening to Western banks, now scheduled for 2007 (after negotiating a two-year delay with the WTO).

A second difficulty with deep reform concerns the returning problem of class. The new, market-based class structure has, according to Shaogang Wang, resulted in much greater inequality, intraregional as well as interregional (but especially the latter), which intensified in the 1990s, despite implementation of a highly successful poverty reduction program. According to Veronica Pearson, inequality is also gender based, overriding a revolutionary tradition that women hold up "half the sky," as footloose young women have great hand dexterity useful for detail work in factories and are eminently exploitable at very low wage rates (although women also reportedly make up nearly 20 percent of China's new entrepreneurs).[6] The emerging new class structure is remarkably symmetrical with those in established capitalist democracies, with upwardly mobile strata consisting of well-educated entrepreneurs, professionals, and intellectuals while the classic proletariat of workers and peasants appears to have fallen through the cracks; ironically, the military and security personnel in charge of enforcing class harmony are (according to Dittmer and Hurst) among the economic losers.

This is not a problem in terms of the emergence of a middle class, long deemed a necessary foundation for modern industrial democracy. The problem is with the emergence of a "lower" and an "upper" class. At the lower end are strata (mostly those without family connections or education) and whole regions (mostly in the underdeveloped West and the northeastern rust belt) that consider themselves unjustly deprived. Whereas relative deprivation has occasioned surprisingly little protest, it is a source of growing strain, contributing to rising rates of crime, drug abuse and prostitution, and a vast influx of underemployed migrant workers into the cities, not to mention dismay over this betrayal of socialist ideals.

At the other end of the scale, the rise of an industrial bourgeoisie of independent means might seem to provide a natural new class base for the CCP (particularly at local levels), but it also presents at least two problems. First, the origins of this new upper class is riddled with selected beneficiaries of the recent privatization of state assets, a process that has proceeded with little transparency and is sometimes tainted by corruption, as Ting Gong documents. The emerging nexus between political and economic elites discredits the whole "get rich through labor" social contract, arousing the resentment of those left out of the deal. Second, the newly rich constitute a source of potential rivalry to the party-state, and the regime's plan to lure this emerging elite into the party may have become inhibited by the old Maoist nightmare that the party could be coopted by the bourgeoisie. While the percentage of entrepreneurs in the party has continued to grow, Dickson notes, these are no longer independent entrepreneurs but former bureaucrats in the growing pool of privatized SOEs. Since the Sixteenth Party Congress, the new leadership of Hu Jintao and Wen Jiabao has devoted more symbolic attention to the problem of those left behind by reform. It is still too soon to tell whether remedial efforts will go beyond populist rhetoric. The emergence of conspicuous beneficiaries of reform, though certainly annoying to the party's old and new left, is a serious problem only to the extent that they are perceived to be corrupt or unentitled, in which case the regime's efforts to strengthen the legal system and crack down on corruption will be closely monitored.

While the scholarship collected here broadly concurs with the popular conception of "China rising," there is no clear consensus on where, once arisen, it wants to go. One formulation favored at the turn of the millennium was that of "peaceful rising" *[heping jueqi]* or "peaceful development" *[heping fazhan]* to the status of a "responsible great power." Clearly China seems intent on reclaiming the central position in East Asia suggested by its name and historical legacy. But what does this mean with regard to domestic politics: what kind of national identity does China want to have? Clearly it wants to be a modern industrial nation-state, with a standard of living at least at a *xiao kang* (moderately comfortable) level, no doubt eventually approximating those of its developed Asian neighbors (already tantalizingly within reach in Shanghai and Beijing). Is democracy in the cards? This question, very important to Western observers familiar with the implications of democratic peace theory, is perhaps less salient in present-day China than the attainment of economic development. Less surprising than the CCP leadership's lack of interest is the fact that the urban middle classes have shown so little interest in seeing democracy spread. But as Tianjian Shi points out, democracy in China made its first gains in the relatively backward countryside among the peasantry, defying Western precedent and social scientific prediction. Whereas China under reform has been urbanizing rapidly after a long period of politically imposed mobility constraints, it is still around 60 percent rural, and any demographically representative democratization would subordinate the eastern urban areas to the most economically and culturally backward regions. As for the peasants, already practicing democracy (however limited), their interest is focused on retaining and if possible improving it rather than seeing it spread to the cities. Can nationwide democratization occur on such a tenuous social base? Perhaps it will have to wait until population migratory trends can assure the urban middle classes of maintaining their currently predominant political position.

For those familiar with the political experience of Eastern Europe since the end of the Cold War, the advent of civil society seems a useful if not necessary prelude to democracy. But the PRC leadership, also familiar with developments in Poland

and other former fraternal socialist republics, has been understandably wary. One of the social developments that has been taking place in the course of China's reform is that a society once rigidly structured by a cross-cutting framework of work units and neighborhood committees in the cities and communes, brigades and teams in the countryside is becoming much more mobile. The regime has permitted this to happen, most recently by loosening the household registration *[hukou]* system that previously tied rural people to their places of residence, thereby creating an industrially useful mobile labor market. At the same time, the government has reserved the option of rescinding this license whenever expedient; thus the migrant labor shantytowns constructed, largely along provincial lines, in major eastern cities, are subject to dismantlement and their populations subject to removal if local authorities claim the land for (say) redevelopment. But despite this official ambivalence qua flexibility, the dominant population migratory trend, now probably unstoppable, has been from rural villages to the cities.[7]

Meanwhile the rural communal structure has been dismantled and the urban work unit structure seriously weakened by labor mobility, leaving society increasingly unstructured. From the regime perspective, any breakdown of horizontal structure is dangerous, making the population susceptible to the sort of mass movements deemed most destabilizing and disruptive—June 4, the Cultural Revolution. One of the redeeming features of the movement to establish voluntary nongovernmental organizations (NGOs) that swept China in the 1980s, creating some 20,000 informal (illegal) organizations, was that it created a new cross-cutting social structure; a second is that the NGOs (many of which had international connections) offered an alternative source of funding for China's flagging social welfare and health networks. Might a socialist civil society offer a way to fulfill Zhu Rongji's 1998 pledge, "small government, great society"? Their biggest drawback, from the regime's perspective, is that NGOs threaten to run out of control, in some cases allegedly lending tacit support to protests against local authorities (most vividly exemplified by the 1999 Falun Gong protest in Beijing). This has precipitated numerous central drives for registration and control. Yet as Saich makes clear, some of these organizations have been quite skilled at informally expanding the latitude left to them to set their own agendas even after formal incorporation. So the answer to the question of the future of civil society is likely to be a formal "no," still however leaving some room open for informal expedients.

Certainly also relevant to democratization is the spread of liberty. The advent of the market has clearly broadened the range of freedom for the Chinese citizenry, at least in the economic realm. But any generalization of market freedom would require at least two additional supports: legal support for some concept of individual rights, and expanded access to objective information about relevant public events. With regard to the former, Peerenboom sees a path-dependent process leading in time to a "thin" rule of law, partly in response to popular demand, partly in convergence with Western legal procedures imported to protect the growing influx of foreign industry and commerce. With regard to freedom of information we naturally turn to the mass media, which proliferated during the reform era in every technolog-ically conceivable form, including one of the world's most rapidly growing internet and telecom markets, as Guobin Yang informs us. Envisaged during the Maoist era as a pipeline through which the leadership could monitor the scattered notions of the masses and synthesize them into more coherent elite directives to guide them, the fiscal crisis of the state in the early reform years prompted the government to download financial responsibility for the media to local authorities, and the media are now largely self-financed through advertising. Will editorial autonomy follow financial autarky? The PRC has never imposed prepublication censorship, but at the same time tends very quickly to blame the media for any untoward political repercussions that can plausibly be attributed to the messenger. This has resulted in one of the most vigilantly controlled media sectors in the world (Reporters Sans Frontieres rates China last of all countries listed in press freedom), and fiscal devolu-tion has been accompanied by construction of an increasingly sophisticated moni-toring apparatus. Particularly suspect are those media able to send as well as receive messages (e.g., Internet, fax, and text messaging). Thus far, control efforts seem to have remained quite effective. Ownership has had no perceptible impact on editorial or reportorial independence, in part because the media sector remains in legal limbo, still without a press law. The international media and software suppliers, eager to participate in the world's largest ad market, have thus far been willing to comply with governmental restrictions on content as well. If the media are eventually able to carve out a realm of political immunity for objective reportage, this seems likely to begin in those walks of life most dependent on accurate information and least threatening to the authorities, such as popular entertainment or financial markets.

The identity of the Chinese state is an increasingly intriguing one as its Marxist–Leninist bona fides fade from view one after the other in the context of moderniza-tion and globalization. What is after all still identifiably communist, or socialist, about China? The former ideological hallmarks, first central planning, then social-ization of the means of production, have given way to free markets, private property, social stratification. To improve its economic prospects within the WTO framework Beijing has been trying to persuade its leading trade partners to accept it as a market economy. It would seem that the last thing still distinguishing China as "commu-nist" is that it is still ruled exclusively by the Communist Party, which continues to embrace Marxist–Leninist ideology (however contortedly reconstrued). Even this has come into question among some of China's bolder intellectuals, who have sug-gested changing the party's name. But even in this unlikely instance, the state is likely to remain for the foreseeable future a strong one, in the pattern of its imperial predecessor, or such conspicuously successful neighboring developmental dictator-ships as South Korea, Taiwan, or Singapore. This means continued reliance on a strong military and security apparatus, a legal system that will remain asymmetrical even as it becomes stronger and more comprehensive, and a muscular industrial pol-icy even amid marketization and privatization. As Peerenboom points out, though the state has shifted from planning to regulation, the next step to deregulation is not a realistic option in view of China's still underdeveloped markets, and the absence of a civil society limits efforts to rely on local voluntarism or political experimentation. The leadership complains that premature democratization is apt to precipitate "chaos" *[luan]*. The problem for democracy advocates is that this has been historically true, as an objective review of recent Chinese history will attest. But the problem for the authorities is that by depriving the masses of all opportunities for democratic practice, it decreases the likelihood that they will ever learn how to exercise civil democracy.

Forecasting the future is an exercise for soothsayers and prophets rather than social scientists, but there are at least three reasons to suppose that in the long run, despite current prospects that are hardly encouraging, if economic modernization continues, China will follow its East Asian neighbors in the development of some form of representative democracy. First, the constitutional structure of the state is formally democratic, and as Nathan points out, there is a long tradition of constitutional engineering in China, dating back to the first republic, for current parliamentarians to build upon.[8] The processes of institutionalization and rationalization we have identified with the reform era throughout both early and "deepened" periods are both conducive to an incremental broadening of the decision-making arena, growth of representative institutions, further division and delegation of power, and other trends favorable to democratization. Second, the growth of freedom in the marketplace is likely to accustom both business people and consumers to expect the same freedom in other aspects of their lives, including eventually the political. Already a highly competitive political market has emerged, in which exchange plays a major (if often corrupting) role.[9] Third, as Kevin O'Brien has pointed out, the Chinese people, from Zhao Ziyang to the "stainless steel mouse," in both rural and urban venues, have long been characterized by extraordinary civil courage, willing to stand on principle and criticize unjust authority in the face of hopeless odds against ever-prevailing and very likely political retribution.

NOTES

1. Harry Harding, *China's Second Revolution: Reform after Mao* (Washington, DC: Brookings Institution, 1987).

2. See Guoli Liu, ed., *Chinese Foreign Policy in Transition* (New York: de Gruyter, 2004).

3. "In 1984, the income gap [between urban and rural incomes] dropped to 1:6, an historic, never-repeated law." Zhao Manhua, "The Income Gap in China," *World Bank Group Transition Newsetter*, February–March 2001.

4. This gave rise to the popular saying, Once there is an opening, it becomes lively; once it becomes lively, it becomes chaotic; once it becomes chaotic, there is a crackdown; once they crack down, it becomes dead *[yi fang jiu huo, yi huo jiu luan, yi luan jiu guan, yi guan jiu si]*.

5. Li Zehou and Liu Zaifu, *Gaobie geming: Huiwang ershi shiji Zhongguo* [Farewell to revolution: Reviewing twentieth century China] (Hong Kong: Cosmos, 1996).

6. *Christian Science Monitor*, August 16, 2005.

7. After graphic designer Sun Zhigang died in custody in June 2003 following his detention as a vagrant, the government rescinded the administrative decree that authorized "detaining and sending back vagrants and beggars in the cities."

8. In addition to his chapter in this volume, see Andrew J. Nathan, *Peking Politics, 1918– 1923: Factionalism and the Failure of Constitutionalism* (Berkeley: University of California Press, 1976).

9. See Yi-min Lin, *Between Politics and Markets: Firms, Competition, and Institutional Change in Post-Mao China* (Cambridge: Cambridge University Press, 2001).

Index

About the Contributors

Marc J. Blecher is professor of politics and East Asian Studies at Oberlin College. His recent books include *China against the Tides* and *Tethered Deer: Government and Economy in a Chinese County* (coauthored with Vivienne Shue).

Bruce J. Dickson is associate professor of political science and international affairs and director of the Sigur Center for Asian Studies at George Washington University. He is the author of *Democratization in China and Taiwan: The Adaptability of Leninist Parties*; and *Red Capitalists in China: The Party, Private Entrepreneurs, and Prospects for Political Change*.

Lowell Dittmer is professor of political science at the University of California–Berkeley and editor of *Asian Survey*. He has written or edited *Sino-Soviet Normalization and Its International Implications*; *China's Quest for National Identity* (with Samuel Kim); *China under Reform, Liu Shaoqi and the Chinese Cultural Revolution* (rev. ed.); and many other analyses of Chinese domestic and foreign policy. His most recent book (with Haruhiro Fukui and Peter N. S. Lee) is *Informal Politics in East Asia*.

Joseph Fewsmith is professor of international relations and director of the East Asian Interdisciplinary Studies Program at Boston University. His most recent books are *China since Tiananmen*; and *Elite Politics in Contemporary China*.

Ting Gong is professor of political science at Ramapo College of New Jersey. She is the author of *The Politics of Corruption in Contemporary China: An Analysis of Policy Outcomes*.

Baogang Guo is assistant professor of political science at Dalton State College and research associate at China Research Center at Kennesaw, Georgia. He is the associate editor of the *Journal of Chinese Political Science*.

William Hurst is a Ph. D. candidate in political science at the University of California–Berkeley. He has published articles in *China Quarterly* and *Issues and Studies*.

Cheng Li is professor of government at Hamilton College. He is the author of *China's Leaders: The New Generation* and *Rediscovering China*.

Guoli Liu is associate professor of political science at the College of Charleston. He is the editor of *Chinese Foreign Policy in Transition*, coeditor (with Weixing Chen) of *New Directions in Chinese Politics for the New Millennium*, and author of *States and Markets: Comparing Japan and Russia*.

Andrew J. Nathan is the Class of 1919 Professor of Political Science at Columbia University. He is the author of numerous books, including *Chinese Democracy* and *China's Transition*.

Kevin J. O'Brien is professor of political science at the University of California–Berkeley. He is the author of *Reform without Liberalization: China's National People's Congress and the Politics of Institutional Change*.

Veronica Pearson is professor in the Department of Social Work and Social Administration, the University of Hong Kong. She is author of *Mental Health Care in China: State Policies, Professional Services, and Family Responsibilities*, and editor of *Women in Hong Kong*.

Randall Peerenboom is professor of law at the University of California–Los Angeles. His books include *China's Long March toward Rule of Law*; *Doing Business in China*; and *Lawyers in China: Obstacles to Independence and the Defense of Rights*.

Yingyi Qian is professor of economics at University of California–Berkeley. He is coeditor of the *Economics of Transition*.

Tony Saich is professor of international affairs at Harvard University. He is the author of *Governance and Politics of China* (2nd ed.) and editor of *The Rise of Power of the Chinese Communist Party: Documents and Analysis*.

Tianjian Shi is associate professor of political science at Duke University. He is the author of *Political Participation in Beijing*.

Edward S. Steinfeld is associate professor of political science at the Massachusetts Institute of Technology. He is the author of *Forging Reform in China: The Fate of State-Owned Industry*.

Shaoguang Wang is professor of political science in the Department of Government and Public Administration, the Chinese University of Hong Kong. His recent publications include *The Political Economy of Uneven Development: The Case of China*; *The Chinese Economy in Crisis: State Capacity and Tax Reform*; and *Nationalism, Democracy, and National Integration in China*. He is the chief editor of *The China Review*.

Lynn White is professor at the Woodrow Wilson School of Public and International Affairs, Princeton University. His most recent works include *Policies of Chaos: The Organizational Causes of Violence in China's Cultural Revolution*; *Unstately Power*, vol. 1; *Local Causes of China's Economic Reform*, vol. 2; and *Local Causes of China's Intellectual, Legal, and Governmental Reforms*.

Yu-Shan Wu is professor of political science at the National Taiwan University. He is the author of *Comparative Economic Transformations: Mainland China, Hungary, the Soviet Union, and Taiwan*.

Guobin Yang is assistant professor of sociology at the University of Hawaii–Manoa. He has published articles in *China Quarterly, Asian Survey*, and the *Journal of Contemporary China*.